# AMERICA'S
# HISTORIC SITES

VOLUME 2

Iowa—NEW YORK

457-912

*from* **The Editors of Salem Press**

*Managing Editor*
**Tracy Irons-Georges**

SALEM PRESS, INC.

Pasadena, California          Hackensack, New Jersey

*Editor in Chief:* Dawn P. Dawson
*Managing Editor:* Tracy Irons-Georges     *Acquisitions Editor:* Mark Rehn
*Research Supervisor:* Jeffry Jensen     *Photo Editor:* Philip Bader
*Research Assistant:* Jeff Stephens     *Layout:* Ross E. Castellano
*Production Editor:* Joyce I. Buchea     *Design and Graphics:* James Hutson

Maps in this volume are adapted from Cartesia's MapArt™ Geopolitical Deluxe v2.0 (1998)

**Library of Congress Cataloging-in-Publication Data**

America's historic sites / the Editors of Salem Press; managing editor, Tracy Irons-Georges.
    p. cm.
   Vol. 1-3.
   Includes bibiographical references and index.
    ISBN 0-89356-122-3 (set : alk. paper) —ISBN 0-89356-123-1 (vol. 1 : alk. paper) — ISBN 0-89356-124-X (vol. 2 : alk. paper) — ISBN 0-89356-147-9 (vol. 3 : alk. paper)
    1. Historic sites—United States—Encyclopedias. 2. United States—History, Local—Encyclopedias. I. Irons-Georges, Tracy. II. Editors of Salem Press.

E159 .A45 2000
973'.03—dc21

00-056337

First Printing

# Contents

# America's
# Historic Sites

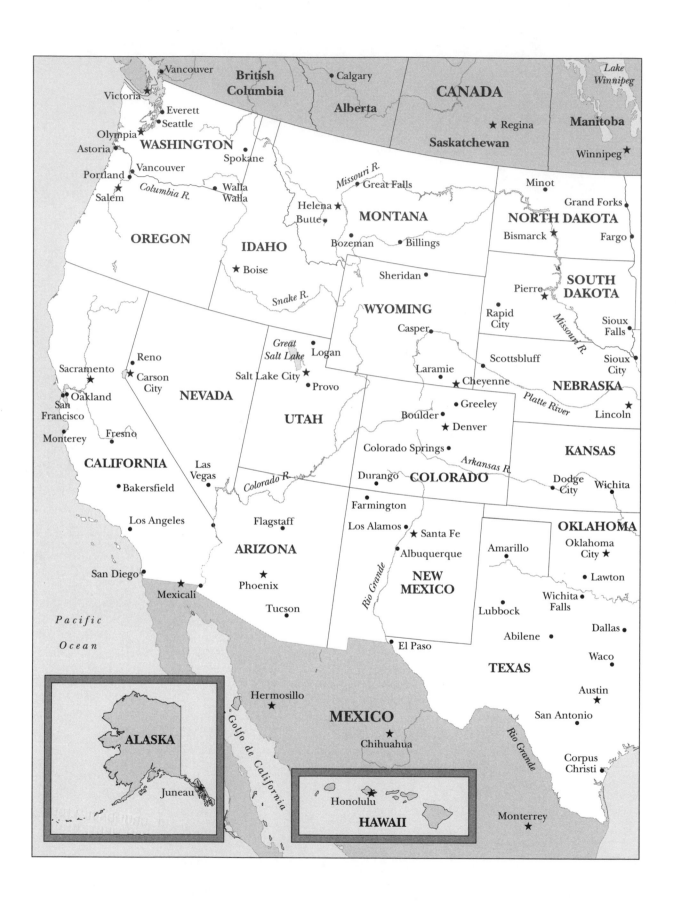

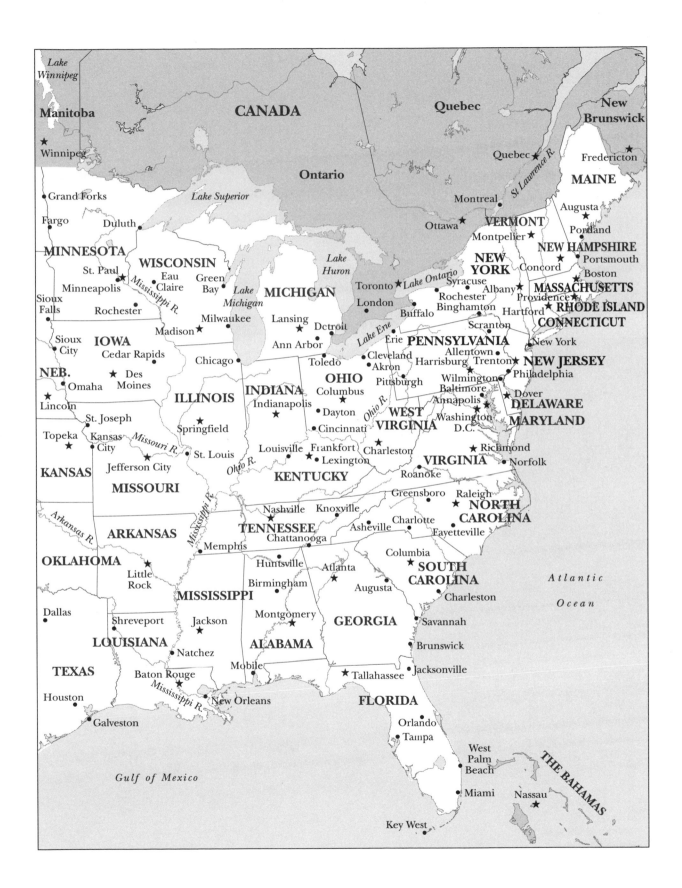

# Iowa

*Des Moines.* (PhotoDisc)

# History of Iowa

Defined by the Mississippi River on the east and the Missouri River on the west, Iowa is a rolling stretch of lush, green prairie with rich, black soil and ample rainfall for growing crops. The fertility of the earth and the lack of trees make for excellent farmland, and as a result, Iowa has been and remains a state focused on agriculture.

### Early History
The Paleo-Indians, nomadic hunters and gatherers, lived in the Iowa region more than ten thousand years ago. They were followed by other nomadic Indians and the mound builders. The Ioway, who controlled most of Iowa in the seventeenth century, left their name to the state and to one of its rivers but gave up all claim to land in the state in 1838, settling in Kansas and Nebraska. About seventeen different tribes are believed to have lived in what became Iowa.

In 1673, Father Jacques Marquette and explorer-mapmaker Louis Jolliet entered the Mississippi River from the Wisconsin River and gazed on Iowa, the "land across the river." They went ashore on June 25, finding members of the Illini tribe, who probably actually lived on the east side of the Mississippi. In 1682 France claimed all the lands along the Mississippi River, and in 1803, in the Louisiana Purchase, the United States bought the land from France. The following year, William Clark and Meriwether Lewis traveled up the Missouri River searching for a waterway that would take them to the Pacific Ocean.

In 1812, Iowa became part of the Territory of Missouri. Eight years later, Missouri became a state, and in 1834, the Territory of Michigan was expanded to include Iowa. In 1838 the Territory of Iowa was created.

### The Indians
The U.S. government pushed the Sauk and the Mesquaki (Fox) Indians out of western Illinois and into Iowa, where the Sioux already lived. In 1832, Chief Black Hawk, a respected Sauk leader, sought to reclaim his tribe's land on the Illinois side of the Mississippi River. For three months, in what is known as the Black Hawk War, the Illinois militia pursued Black Hawk, chasing him to the mouth of the Bad Axe River in Wisconsin, where he gave up. In a treaty signed on September 21, 1832, the Mesquaki and Sauk were required to relinquish a strip of land along the Mississippi River and vacate the land by June 1, 1833. Large numbers of white settlers began to move into Iowa, pushing the Indians farther west or into Missouri. In 1842, the Sauk and Mesquaki signed a treaty agreeing to leave Iowa by May, 1845. By 1851 the Sioux had also been forced to give up all land in Iowa. In 1856, a few Mesquaki negotiated with the governor of Iowa to buy back a portion of their former land in modern-day Tama County, eventually buying back about 3,200 acres.

### White Settlement and Statehood
In 1838, 23,000 people settled on land in the newly established Territory of Iowa, buying the land for

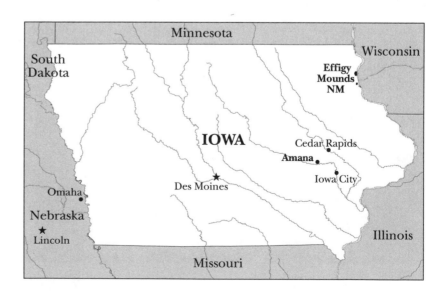

$1.25 an acre. The first settlers were primarily of northern European ancestry. Many were families who had lived in eastern states such as New York, Pennsylvania, or Ohio, and many were originally from Germany. The 1840 census showed Iowa to have a population of 43,000, exclusive of American Indians. By 1846 the population of Iowa had reached 96,088. Iowa became the twenty-ninth state of the Union in 1846.

### Industry, Education, and Religion

In the early 1850's, railroad companies sprung up in Iowa. The Chicago, Iowa, and Nebraska line became the first railroad to cross the state, in 1867. Soon tracks crisscrossed Iowa, providing year-round transportation to markets and giving birth to new industries such as an oat-processing plant that would come to be known as Quaker Oats.

Early settlers soon established township elementary schools, but high schools were not common until after 1900. State officials created the University of Iowa in 1855 to provide traditional and professional education, Iowa State College of Science and Technology (later Iowa State University) in 1858 for agricultural and technical training, and Iowa State Teachers' College (later University of Northern Iowa) in 1876 for teacher training. Many religious groups, including Congregationalists, Roman Catholics, and Methodists, which had come to the state beginning in the 1830's, founded private colleges.

Although major religious denominations usually set up churches across the state, smaller religious groups tended to settle in specific areas. The Quakers settled in West Branch and Springdale, the Reorganized Church of the Latter-day Saints (a Mormon offshoot) in Lamoni, and the Mennonites in Johnson and Washington Counties. From 1855 to 1865, a group of German Pietists established the seven cities of Amana in Iowa County. The residents of the Amana Colonies practiced communal living for about eighty years. The Amana name lives on in refrigerators, air conditioners, and microwaves, although the colonies sold the business in 1937.

### The Civil War

The biggest change the Civil War brought in Iowa was to create a one-party state. At the beginning of Iowa's statehood, the state was largely Democratic, although it contained some Whigs. However, many Iowans opposed slavery, and Iowa would later become an important station in the Underground Railroad. The identification of the Democratic Party with a proslavery stance, among other issues, caused many Iowans to turn to the new Republican Party. By the mid-1850's, the state was solidly Republican and would stay that way through the first half of the twentieth century.

After the outbreak of the war, Iowans quickly responded to President Abraham Lincoln's call for troops. During the course of the war, the state sent 70,000 soldiers, of whom 13,001 died and 8,500 were seriously wounded. Iowans fought at Wilson's Creek to keep Missouri in the Union, accompanied Ulysses S. Grant to Vicksburg, and participated in William Tecumseh Sherman's March to the Sea.

### Immigration

The population of Iowa grew from 674,913 in 1860 to 1,194,020 in 1870. The state encouraged immigration from northern Europe and attracted many Germans, Swedes, Norwegians, Danes, and Hollanders, as well as people from the British Isles. Many of these immigrant groups created rural neighborhoods with distinct ethnic identities and churches. The coal mines in central and southern Iowa, which promised immediate employment and required few skills, drew people from Italy and Wales and large numbers of former slaves, who formed camps near the mines.

### Farming and Economic Growth

By the 1870's, Iowa had become blanketed by small towns and family farms, connected by railroads. Farmers were raising cattle and hogs and increasingly corn instead of wheat. Scientific research led to the introduction in the early 1900's of soybeans, which eventually became second only to corn in terms of acreage and value. During World War I, farmers prospered, but after the war ended and farm subsidies were eliminated, farmers began to experience difficulties in paying off the money they had borrowed during boom times. A group of farmers formed the Farm Holiday Association, which attempted to withhold farm products from the market in order to force prices up, but the association's efforts had little impact.

Native Iowan Henry A. Wallace became secretary of agriculture under President Franklin D.

Roosevelt in 1933. He believed that farmers would prosper if production was restricted and farmers were compensated for withholding land from production, and he incorporated these ideas into the Agricultural Adjustment Act of 1933, part of the New Deal. In 1926, Wallace and a partner founded what became Pioneer Seed Company, the first commercial company to produce hybrid seed corn, which led to increased yields and a more uniform plant that made mechanization of the harvest much easier. By 1944, nearly all corn planted in Iowa came from hybrid seed.

Farmers prospered when World War II and the Korean War boosted corn prices and again in the 1970's, when land prices rose and many farmers borrowed money to expand their operations. In the 1980's, however, land prices crashed, and many farmers lost their farms, initiating a trend away from family farms and toward farming corporations. In 1985 the Iowa legislature introduced legislation designed to help troubled farmers deal with creditors and keep their farms. In the 1990's, the family farm was challenged on another front as large-scale hog-producing corporations moved into the state, driving down hog prices and forcing small hog producers out of business.

Although agriculture dominates Iowa's economy, the state has also supported business and manufacturing operations, some of which are farm related. Major concerns include farm implement producer John Deere, the washing machine and appliance company Maytag, Winnebago motor homes, the Sheaffer Pen Company, and Iowa Beef Processors. In 1991 Iowa legalized riverboat gambling, creating a somewhat controversial source of revenue.

### Middle America

Iowa is largely rural, an assemblage of small towns and family farms. In 1994 the state's population reached 2.8 million, and the population of its largest city, Des Moines, was 193,422. During the 1970's and 1980's, and to a lesser extent in the 1990's, the state became the focus of national attention early in each presidential election year during the Iowa caucuses. These early tests of presidential strength provided boosts to some candidates, including Jimmy Carter in 1976 and George Bush in 1980. Although the state is not a microcosm of the nation, its reputation as Middle America—a stable place

where family values dominate—lends weight to its preferences. As more and more farm corporations are formed and the number of family farms decreases, the nature of Iowa, its character and makeup, which reflect this rural dominance, may undergo a transformation.       —*Rowena Wildin*

# Amana Colonies

**Date:** Founded in 1855
**Relevant issues:** Cultural history, religion, social reform
**Significance:** The Amana Colonies are the longest-surviving utopian community in the United States. They consist of Amana, Middle Amana, South Amana, High Amana, East Amana, West Amana, and Homestead. The Amana Colonies are a National Historic Landmark.
**Location:** Eighteen miles southwest of Cedar Rapids, in Iowa County
**Site Office:**
The Amana Colonies Convention and Visitors Bureau
39-38th Avenue, Suite 100
Amana, IA 52203
ph.: (800) 579-2294
Web site: www.amanacolonies.com

The Amana Colonies are the most successful of the several utopian communities founded in the United States during the nineteenth century. The Amana Colonies, originally known as the Community of True Inspiration, are the only nineteenth century utopian community still in existence. The Inspirationalists, as the community members were known, faced persecution in their native Germany in the eighteenth century for their rejection of traditional Lutheran religious doctrines. Eventually the Inspirationalists settled in Iowa, erecting seven villages laid out on 26,000 acres. The architecture is simple and functional, with each village having a linear arrangement. The Amana Colonies were reorganized in 1932 under the Amana Society, and they were listed as a National Historic Landmark in 1976.

### History of the Community of True Inspiration

The history of the Amana Colonies began in 1714 in southwestern Germany. Johann Friedrich Rock

*A gift shop in Amana Colonies.* (Iowa Tourism)

munity of True Inspiration, although there have been no *Werkzeuges* since 1883.

The followers of Gruber and Rock preached their message throughout Germany, Switzerland, Holland, and other European countries. Because the followers of Rock and Gruber did not believe in baptism, desired their own school system, and refused to bear arms for Prussia, they faced persecution in their homeland. Despite the public castigation, the number of followers began to multiply. At times they sought refuge by renting large estates in Ronneburg in the province of Hessen, since that province possessed the most liberal government in eighteenth century Germany. However, the Inspirationalists faced persecution there as well. French troops and Russians constantly plundered their property.

The plundering took its toll, as did the deaths of the original leaders. Gruber died in 1728 and Rock in 1749, causing a decline in membership around the mid-eighteenth century. By the beginning of the nineteenth century only a few large congregations remained. Gottlieb Schneuner, a contemporary writer, suggested that there were other factors that contributed to the society's decline. The preaching styles of the current elders, the fact that persecution had ended, and the general upheaval in Europe at the time that impaired communication networks all negatively affected the number of followers. The decline continued until 1817, when Michael Krausert became *Werkzeuge*. Krausert was a journeyman tailor from Strasbourg who, seeking inspiration, found the writings of Rock. According to tradition, a revival ensued after the Lord spoke to Krausert and he started preaching the doctrines of the Inspirationalists. A few months after Krausert's conversion, Christian Metz, a carpenter, and Barbara Heinemann, a servant maid, also received the "gift of Inspiration" and became *Werkzeuges*. This revival threatened the established authority, and once again the Inspirationalists faced persecution. There was also internal conflict,

and Eberhard Ludwig Gruber began attracting followers to their nontraditional doctrines and broke from the Lutheran Church. Rock and Gruber believed that God revealed himself through intermediaries, either prophets or inspired persons. Gruber was a member of the Lutheran clergy and Rock the son of a Lutheran clergyman. Both men were disenchanted by the direction of the Lutheran Church when they started to meditate together. Gruber and Rock believed that divine guidance came through certain individuals endowed with a "miraculous gift of Inspiration." Through these *Werkzeuges*, as these individuals were called, the Lord spoke directly to his followers. *Werkzeuges* were considered passive instruments in the hands of the Lord. This doctrine is still known as the Com-as the elders were hostile to Krausert, and he soon left the community. Metz and Heinemann then assumed leadership of the community, reorganizing the followers of what was now known as the New Community.

Heinemann became a powerful influence in the community, although she had started as only an uneducated servant. She sought out the community after seeing visions; the community hesitated before allowing her in their circle. She learned to read with the Bible as her textbook. Still, Heinemann, because she was an outsider, was at one point banished from the community for marrying someone from outside the community. Twenty-six years later, she was again summoned by the Lord, and she stayed with the community until her death in 1883. During the time when Heinemann was absent, Christian Metz, a native of the community, was endowed with the "gift of Inspiration" and became the spiritual leader upon the group's relocation to Iowa. A man of commanding presence and pietism, Metz was greatly revered within the community along with Heinemann.

Still facing milder forms of persecution, the members had two alternatives: return to Lutheranism or leave the country. Once again, the community flocked to Hessen. Metz founded a colony here at the cloister of Marienborn. Three other estates were soon used as refuges, and it was the proximity of the groups that dictated the need for communal living. The Inspirationalists prospered until war broke out in Europe, bringing about a need for men to serve in the army. In addition, landlords increased rents to raise money for war. These conditions were exacerbated by a drought. During this time it was revealed to Christian Metz that he would lead them to a land where they could live in peace and liberty. In 1842 the Inspirationalists set sail for the New World.

### The Community of True Inspiration in the New World

Arriving in New York, the group journeyed to Albany and then to Buffalo. The Inspirationalists purchased five thousand acres of land from the Seneca Indians and established four colonies in America and two in Canada. These colonies became known as the Ebenezer Society. In 1843, although it was not originally part of its religious doctrine, the Ebenezer Society adopted a provisional constitution in which the members agreed to organize as a communitarian society to signify their unification in a new land. The constitution provided that all the clothing and household goods should be held in common, while the prosperous members were to cover all expenses, receiving a proportionate share of the whole as security. This constitution would be virtually the same one adopted at Amana less than two decades later. At the time of the constitution's establishment, the Inspirationalist community was decidedly not communal. The intention of the community was to live simply as a Christian congregation. Originally, members were to pay into a fund; each person would receive a share of the land proportional to his or her contribution. Soon it was evident that the economic disparity between members prohibited some from purchasing land. Sheer necessity dictated that the Inspirationalists form a communal society.

Eight hundred members moved to America, most from the artisan and peasant classes. The Seneca Indians were at first hostile to them, and the group had to acquire assistance from the U.S. government to expel them. The society prospered, but the acreage was not large enough to support its growing numbers. The society's mills and factories had gained a reputation in the outside world, and by 1854 the society realized the necessity of relocating. Christian Metz led a committee of four elders west to Kansas, but they did not achieve their goal of finding suitable land. A new committee was then formed that purchased an eighteen thousand-acre tract in Iowa.

### The Amana Colonies

The colony began a ten-year removal, ultimately increasing the size of its holdings to twenty-six thousand acres. Amana, or Bleibe Treu (German for "remain faithful"), was the first village erected in 1855. West Amana, South Amana, High Amana, East Amana, and Middle Amana followed. Homestead was purchased for its link to the railroad in 1861, a cause of concern because of outside influences. Twelve hundred persons relocated to Iowa and settled in these towns that were designed much like German villages, with forty to one hundred houses arranged in a linear pattern and few streets extending off the main road. Barns and sheds occupied one end of town and factories the other, with orchards and gardens throughout. Of the town's twenty-six thousand acres, five hundred were occupied by factories and villages, one hundred by gardens and orchards, ten thousand by timberland, seven thousand by cultivated fields, and four thousand by grazing land. Hotels became a necessity after curious travelers began to visit the Amana Colonies in the mid-nineteenth century.

In 1859, the Community of True Inspiration was incorporated under Iowa law as the Amana Society, adopting a constitution similar to that of the Ebenezer Society. The declared purpose of the society was to serve God "according to His law and His requirements in our own consciences, and thus to work out the salvation of our souls, through the redeeming grace of Jesus Christ, in self-denial, in the obedience to our faith and in the demonstration of our faithfulness in the inward and outward service of our community." The Inspirationalists formed the Amana Society to preside over all secular and sacred functions of the Colonies. This elective body of thirteen elders was the high court of appeal for all disputes and constituted the Great Council of the Brethren—the high governing authority in spiritual affairs. Each village was governed by a board of seven to nineteen elders who supervised the work in the village according to the mandates of the Great Council and the Board of Trustees.

The Inspirationalists' belief in humility and functionalism is evident in the structures that they erected. Many were built between 1850 and 1880, and most continue to be used today. The buildings are very similar in style: two stories in height, sturdy, rectangular, with gabled roofs, and made of brick, clapboard, or sandstone. Decoration is minimal except for porches or wooden hoods over doorways, simple brick hoodmoulds, and sills on the windows, all painted white. Most of the houses retain their original gardens, and many have wooden trellises attached to the walls.

Needing water to power their woolen mills, the Inspirationalists dug their own six-mile-long canal that gave them access to the Iowa River. Each village was self-supporting, having its own farm department, bakery, slaughterhouse, ice house, store, blacksmith shop, wagonmaker shop, harness shop, and other necessities for a rural farm economy. There was a degree of specialization in some of the villages: Amana, Homestead, and Middle Amana each had a pharmacy, and Middle Amana

had a printing office. Food for the communities was prepared in large, communal kitchens, and each village had a church building. The church was the focal point of each village, located in the center of town. Women and men sat on opposite sides during the church ceremonies, which today are still conducted in German. Masses have retained their original form since 1714, with no musical accompaniment and communion services held every two years. As many as eleven church services a week were held until 1961.

The community kitchens were probably the largest buildings in the villages. The rooms accommodated thirty to fifty people at a time, and bakeries were often located next door. Agricultural buildings were clustered at the ends of the villages. These buildings were framed, clapboarded, shingled, and painted white. Outside each village was the village cemetery, protected by pine trees. Members were buried in the order of their death. Each family was assigned a living quarters, where they could keep such personal property as they were permitted to acquire with their small allowances. All the men and women worked for the society, either in farming or in smaller industries.

Men's clothing was made by the village tailor; historians describe the clothing as "plain." Women made their own dresses in dark blue, black, or what is known as Amana calico. The waist and skirt were sewn together in a wide band, with the skirt very full. Women wore a small black cap and a shawl to cover the body. The only headdress was a sunbonnet in summer and a wool hood in the winter. Marriages had to be blessed by the *Werkzeuge*.

In their industrial and agricultural organization, the Amana Colonists took advantage of mechanization and most modern scientific methods in the nineteenth and twentieth centuries. The Board of Trustees had ultimate power over the agricultural work. A field boss reported to the board. The agricultural products were mostly ryes, barley, oats, corn, potatoes, and onions. The Inspirationalists raised livestock and dairy products not for the market but only for consumption by the community. Despite their willingness to use technology, the Inspirationalists used oxen for heavy hauling well into the twentieth century. Perhaps the best known of the Amana products was the woolens. At the beginning of the twentieth century, the Inspirationalists had 3,000 sheep producing wool, and

4,500 yards of calico were printed every day. The woolen mills were the only industry that actively employed women.

### The Amana Society and the Amana Colonies Today

Fulfilling the needs of the community was the primary objective of the Amana Society. By 1932 the Inspirationalists realized that the increasingly modern world demanded a reorganization of their communal way of life. Secular and sacred affairs were segregated as the communal kitchens, bakeries, and washhouses were abandoned and the Inspirationalists organized the Amana Society as a joint stock company. Each member received stock entitling him or her to one vote, as well as shares proportional to the member's length of service. Families received free medical and dental care for their families as long as they continued to work for the society.

Today the Amana Society manages Iowa's largest farm and private forest, in addition to its businesses. Each village has numerous restored restaurants and shops selling traditional German crafts and food. Some of these are the Amana Furniture Shop, Amana Woolen Mill, Amana Meat Shops, Amana Stone Hearth Bakery, Amana General Store, and Amana General Store Appliances. The majority of these businesses are located in the original buildings, though they have been modified for their current uses. Three nineteenth century buildings in Amana house the Museum of Amana History, while the Community Church Museum and the Communal Agriculture Museum are in Homestead and South Amana, respectively.

—*Kathleen Kadlec*

### For Further Information:

Neubauer, Allyn, ed. *The Amana Colonies: Featuring Seven Historic Villages.* Amana, Iowa: Amana Society, 1999.

Schroer, Blanche E. *Amana Colonies.* National Historic Landmark Form. Washington, D.C.: U.S. Department of the Interior, 1976.

Shambaugh, Bertha M. *Amana: The Community of True Inspiration.* Iowa City: State Historical Society of Iowa, 1908.

Strohman, James. *Amana Colonies Guide to Dining, Lodging, and Tourism.* Ames: Iowa State University Press, 1997.

# Effigy Mounds National Monument

**Date:** Established on October 25, 1949
**Relevant issues:** American Indian history
**Significance:** The monument was founded to preserve and protect a representative example of prehistoric American Indian moundbuilding culture and the wildlife and scenic wildness around the area. While moundbuilding was widespread throughout the eastern half of North America, only in the upper Mississippi Valley was a culture established that specialized in mounds built in the shape of living creatures such as eagles, falcons, bison, deer, turtles, lizards, and especially bears.
**Location:** In eastern Iowa, along the Mississippi River; Three miles north of Marquette, on Highway 76
**Site Office:**
Effigy Mounds National Monument
151 Highway 76
Harpers Ferry, IA 52146-7519
ph.: (319) 873-3491
Web site: www.nps.gov/efmo/

Effigy Mounds National Monument, established by presidential proclamation in 1949, preserves 191 examples of ceremonial and burial earthen mounds built by a variety of prehistoric Indians, as well as a large collection of related artifacts. The monument contains 1,481 acres that include forests, tall grass prairies, wetlands, and rivers. The site contains a number of linear and conical mounds. Still, the monument is best known for the twenty-nine mounds built in the shape of living creatures such as eagles, falcons, bison, deer, turtles, lizards, and especially bears, called Effigy Mounds. Moundbuilding culture was rich and varied, and this historic site provides a good introduction to the histories of the moundbuilding peoples.

Early European settlers and later nineteenth century archaeologists did not agree on the origin of the mounds and the people who built them. A variety of myths grew up in an attempt to explain the mounds, and some of these myths were used to help justify unjust policies toward Indians by the United States in the nineteenth and early twentieth centuries. Careful study of the mounds during the twentieth century has helped to clarify who built the mounds and why. Still, much about the culture of the people who built the mounds, and complete knowledge about how the mounds were used, remains debatable. Since its founding, the park has embarked on a mission of conserving the mounds and the surrounding landscape, making hiking trails and educational programs available year-round.

**Moundbuilding Culture**

The mounds at Effigy Mounds National Monument date back over one thousand years and are part of a larger moundbuilding culture that originated in the Upper Mississippi Valley and the eastern half of North America during what is known as the Woodland Period. This era lasted from 1000 B.C.E. until 1200 C.E. Mounds were built throughout the Woodland Period, but the type of mounds and their uses would change throughout that period. During the Early Woodland Period (1000 B.C.E.-300 B.C.E.), conical mounds (round-shaped) were constructed and mostly used for burial purposes. During the Middle Woodland Period (300 B.C.E.-400 C.E.), more complicated mounds were built. Larger conical and linear (cigar-shaped) structures, as well as mounds that combined conical and linear shapes, were formed. Some of those continued to be used for burial, while others took on ceremonial uses. A few mounds excavated at Effigy Mounds National Monument are from that period.

It was during that time that a civilization known as the Hopewell occupied much of the Upper Mississippi Valley. Between 400 C.E. and 1200 C.E., or the Late Woodland Period, a new culture of moundbuilders constructed conical, linear, compound, and, for the first time, effigy-shaped mounds that resembled a wide variety of living creatures. It appears that very few effigy mounds were used for burials, and the few that were held the remains of what probably were some of the most important religious and civic leaders of the group. Archaeologists believe it more than likely that instead of being burial mounds, the effigy mounds had symbolic or ceremonial purposes. Those mounds may have been symbols of the moundbuilders' clans, monuments or totems to animal spirits, or territorial markers.

Archaeologists speculate that the builders first cleared a large area and then made an outline of their proposed shape to help guide their work. They then began the process of forming the mound. Individuals or small groups of people used sticks and reed baskets to dig and then transport baskets of rich soil and yellow clay from the surrounding areas and riverbanks. It probably took hundreds of trips to form the mound into the right shape and height. Evidence of fires set on the mounds at the head, flank, or heart of the animal likeness has been found. These fires were probably used at some point for specific ceremonies. Conical mounds are typically two to ten feet high and twenty feet in diameter. Linear mounds range from two to four feet high and six to eight feet across. Some have been found to reach one hundred feet across. A typical effigy mound is three to four feet high, twenty feet wide, and seventy-five feet long. The Great Bear Effigy Mound at the monument is 137 feet long and 70 feet wide at the shoulder.

Excavations of the park over the years have led archaeologists to conclude that Indians of the Oneota culture probably supplanted the Effigy Mounds people between the fourteenth and fifteenth centuries. Other tribes living near the monument that may have lived in the area after the Effigy Mound people include the Ioway, for which the state of Iowa is named. During the seventeenth century, when European explorers and traders began to explore and look for animal skins and trade in the area that is now within the monument, Indian occupation of the area ended.

**Early Archaeology of the Effigy Mounds**

Louis Jolliet and Father Jacques Marquette were the first white men to reach the northeast region of Iowa while exploring the Wisconsin and Mississippi rivers in 1673. Nevertheless, it was other explorers, fur traders, and finally western settlers who recognized the mounds as things built by human hands. The first written account by a European of the effigy mounds in northeast Iowa was in fur trader Jonathan Carver's *Travels Through the Interior Parts of North-America in the Years 1766, 1767, and 1768* (1778). In the early accounts, some wondered if an ancient civilization had constructed the great earthworks. Much speculation about the creators of the mounds and their function took place, but it was not until the mid-nineteenth century that the first systematic research of the effigy mounds in northeastern Iowa took place. In 1881 Theodore H. Lewis and Alfred J. Hill surveyed the mound groups of the Mississippi River Valley. The Lewis-Hill surveys produced first-rate maps of a large number of mound groups, many of which were within the present-day monument. Still, the maps reveal that hundreds of mounds that were initially surveyed were gone by the time the monument was established in 1949.

After those initial surveys, several years passed without much scientific study of the mounds. At the end of the nineteenth century, Ellison Orr (1857-1951), who grew up in the region, became interested in the mounds. He spent much of his life documenting them with maps and surveys and collecting artifacts at the mounds. As a lay archaeologist, he gained a national reputation for his early work on the mounds. During the Great Depression, the Federal Emergency Relief Administration (FERA) sponsored an important archaeological survey of the mound sites in northeastern Iowa, and Orr was appointed the head surveyor. That survey led to a presidential proclamation in 1949 establishing the National Monument on one thousand acres. More acreage was added in 1951 and 1961 to help preserve additional mounds.

## Myth of the Moundbuilders

Unable to recognize the earthen mounds as products of the ancestors of the native peoples living in the Upper Mississippi Valley—because it was believed that the contemporary native peoples lacked an advanced culture and were incapable of such construction—European explorers, westbound settlers, and early archaeologists developed a mythical explanation for the origins of the mounds. A whole mythology, and even a religion, developed that focused on a "lost civilization" of giants who had once lived in North America but had been destroyed by contemporary native peoples. Others argued that native peoples from Mexico and Central America like the Toltecs had built the mound structures. In short, the legends contended that the mounds had to have been created by some group—almost any group would do—other than the American Indians currently occupying the lands where the mounds stood.

For about a century, the myth was advanced and often used by a variety of nonnative peoples to justify removal of, and unfair policies toward, those American Indians who occupied lands coveted by non-Indian people. Those non-Indians justified violent removal by arguing that the same native peoples under attack had been in earlier generations the destroyers of the advanced civilization that was believed to have constructed the mounds. Finally, in the 1880's, many in the scientific community began to debunk those myths. The best known of these scientists was Major J. W. Powell, founder of the Smithsonian Institution's Bureau of American Ethnology. Cyrus Thomas, in a seven hundred-page volume, showed overwhelming evidence that the mounds were indeed the creations of known American Indian nations or their ancestors, not some "lost civilization."

## Places to Visit

A visit to the monument will probably begin with a stop at the visitors' center. A museum within the center provides an overview of the prehistory and history of the region. It also contains artifacts found during the years when the mounds at the monument were being excavated. Examples of the maps and surveys conducted over the years also can be seen in the museum. A section of the museum concerns the ongoing efforts for mound conservation. A significant part of the monument's mission remains conservation of the earthwork structures. Since the nineteenth century, when many of the original surveys of mounds were conducted, more than 80 percent of the known mounds have been destroyed through logging, agriculture, and other types of development. A fifteen-minute video outlining the history and culture of the moundbuilding civilization provides a good background for further exploration of the monument. The visitors' center is open year-round from 8:00 A.M. to 4:30 P.M. except for New Year's Day, Martin Luther King, Jr., Day, Presidents' Day, Veterans Day, Thanksgiving, and Christmas Day.

Besides the mounds, the 1,481 acres of the monument contain many of the plants and animals that are typical of the Upper Mississippi region. The best way to see the monument is by taking either a ranger-guided tour (available May to September) or a self-guided walk of the many trails. The Yellow River divides the monument into two units, North and South. A 3.5-mile hike in the North Unit to Hanging Rock (named for a rock formation that at one time jutted out over the edge of a bluff and was blasted to make way for the railroad) takes you by several effigy mounds including the Little Bear Mound and the Great Bear Mound. Also of interest in the North Unit is Fire Point, believed to be a favorite spot of the Woodlands people for fires, possibly for ceremonial purposes. To explore the South Unit, a four-mile hike leads through hardwood forest and restored tall grass prairie to the Marching Bear Group Effigy. This series of mounds is composed of ten bear and three bird effigy mounds. It is one of the largest effigy mounds remaining in the region. Picnicking and camping are not allowed in the monument, but picnic and camp sites are available nearby on Highway 76. Motels and restaurants can be found in the nearby towns.

Effigy Mounds National Monument is just one of the places to see when visiting the area. Eight miles south of the monument, visitors can find Pikes Peak State Park. Just eight miles north of the park are Yellow River State Forest and Wyalusing State Park. Prehistoric Indian mounds are also preserved at those parks, as well as at other places throughout southern Wisconsin and northeastern Iowa. Across the river at Prairie du Chien, Wisconsin, is the Villa Louis State Historic Site. Prairie du Chien was an important point of exploration and settlement for early European settlers in the Upper Mississippi Valley.    —*Neva Jean Specht*

**For Further Information:**

Alex, Lynne Marie. *Exploring Iowa's Past: A Guide to Prehistoric Archaeology.* Iowa City: University of Iowa Press, 1980. Examines various sites and artifacts from the archaeological record.

Clark, Mallam R. *Iowa Effigy Mounds Manifesation: An Interpretive Model.* Iowa City: Office of the State Archaeologist, University of Iowa Press, n.d. More technical information on the construction of the Effigy Mounds.

Effigy Mounds National Monument and the Office of the State Archaeolgist. *Prehistoric Cultures of Iowa: A Brief Study.* Iowa City: University of Iowa Press, 1995. A booklet containing reprints which outline the development of prehistoric cultures of Iowa.

Mainfort, Robert C., and Lynne P. Syllivan, eds. *Ancient Earthern Enclosures of the Eastern Woodlands.* Gainesville: University Press of Florida, 1998. Edited volume that explores topically several ancient sites in North America.

O'Bright, Jill York. *The Perpetual March: An Administrative History of the Effigy Mounds National Monument.* Omaha, Nebr.: National Park Service, Midwest Regional Office, 1989. Examines the history of the historic site and the way the site has changed.

Silverburg, Robert. *The Mound Builders.* Athens: Ohio University Press, 1986. This work is an abridged edition of *Mound Builders of Ancient America: The Archaeology of a Myth* (Greenwich, Conn.: New York Graphic Society, 1968). It explores the creation and debunking of the legends that evolved concerning the construction of the mounds.

# Other Historic Sites

## Blood Run Site

*Location:* Sioux Falls, Lyon County

*Relevant issues:* American Indian history

*Statement of significance:* Blood Run Site is the only known mound group attributable to the Oneota culture, which is ancestral to many midwestern Native American groups. The archaeological complex consists of the remains of a village that once included more than 158 visible conical burial mounds and an effigy earthwork. Limited archaeological data indicate Native American occupation of this site in the early 1700's extending back perhaps as far as 1300 C.E.

## Floyd Monument

*Location:* Sioux City, Woodbury County

*Relevant issues:* Western expansion

*Statement of significance:* This one hundred-foot obelisk commemorates the burial of Sergeant Floyd, the only member of the Lewis and Clark Expedition to lose his life during the expedition.

## Fort Des Moines Provisional Army Officer Training School

*Location:* Des Moines, Polk County

*Relevant issues:* African American history, military history, World War I

*Statement of significance:* Here, on June 17, 1917, one thousand black college men and two hundred noncommissioned officers from the Twenty-fourth and Twenty-fifth Infantry and the Ninth and Tenth Cavalry Regiments were sworn into the Provisional Army Officer Training School; on October 15, 639 men graduated from the course and received their commissions. Black units led by the officers trained here were assembled in France as the Ninety-second Division; this gallant division, composed entirely of African American troops, received many citations and awards for meritorious and distinguished conduct in combat against the Imperial German Army on the approaches to Metz in the Lorraine.

## Hepburn House

*Location:* Clarinda, Page County

*Relevant issues:* Political history

*Statement of significance:* From about 1867 to 1916, this was the residence of William P. Hepburn (1833-1916), the congressman who introduced the Hepburn Act (1906), giving the federal government the power to set railroad rates, a precedent in federal regulation of private industry.

## Hoover Birthplace

*Location:* West Branch, Cedar County

*Relevant issues:* Political history

*Statement of significance:* This was the birthplace of Herbert Hoover (1874-1964), the thirty-first president of the United States (1929-1933). This two-room frame cottage in West Branch was his home in 1884.

## Toolesboro Mound Group

*Location:* Toolesboro, Louisa County

*Relevant issues:* American Indian history

*Statement of significance:* First excavated in 1875, this is the best-preserved Hopewell site in Iowa, representing an extension of the "classic" Hopewellian mortuary practices of the Illinois River Valley.

## Weaver House

*Location:* Bloomfield, Davis County

*Relevant issues:* Political history

*Statement of significance:* From about 1865 to 1890, this was the home of James B. Weaver (1833-1912), Populist candidate for president and antimonopolist. Weaver was a proponent of the graduated income tax and principal sponsor of free coinage of silver.

# Kansas

*Statues of cattle drivers erected near Caldwell, at the Oklahoma border, recall the days when great herds moved between Abilene and Texas on the Chisholm Trail.* (Kansas Department of Commerce & Housing, Travel and Tourism Division)

# History of Kansas

Within Kansas, slightly northwest of Lebanon, is the geographical center of the forty-eight contiguous states. The Spanish explorer Francisco Vásquez de Coronado first ventured into the area in 1541 seeking gold. Native Americans had occupied the region since prehistoric times, possibly as early as 14,000 B.C.E. The Pawnee, Osage, Wichita, and Kansa Indians lived there during the early Spanish exploration. They were mostly hunters and farmers living along the Kansas River.

Later members of some seminomadic tribes, mainly the Kiowa, Cheyenne, Arapaho, and Comanche, also dwelled in the area. After 1830, however, the federal government forcibly moved many Native Americans from eastern tribes into the territory it had acquired through the Louisiana Purchase of 1803. Among the tribes whose members were relocated were the Cherokee, Miami, Potawatomi, Ottawa, Creek, Chickasaw, Choctaw, Delaware, and Shawnee. In all, about thirty tribes were assigned to Kansas for relocation.

**French and American Settlement**

The French moved into the area after the Spanish had been defeated by the Pawnee Indians in Nebraska. In the early 1700's, the French, attracted by the fur trade, built a trading post and military outpost, Fort Cavagnial, near present-day Leavenworth.

With the Louisiana Purchase, American exploration began. Meriwether Lewis and William Clark set out to explore the newly acquired area, which included all but a small part of southwestern Kansas bought in 1850 from Texas.

These explorers were followed in 1806 by Zebulon Pike, who made an east-west journey across the territory. As the eastern United States began to be developed, the federal government was under pressure to claim Native American lands for development. Relocating American Indians to the West provided the government with a convenient solution to a difficult problem. The Native Americans who were relocated are usually referred to as the emigrant tribes.

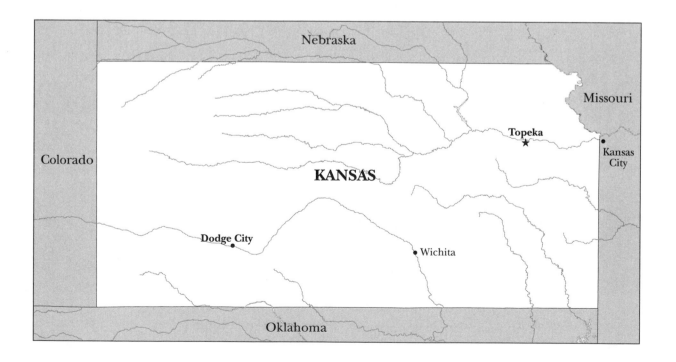

Between 1827 and 1853, Kansas was inhabited mostly by Indians. Some thirty-four thousand Indians from over thirty tribes and only fifteen hundred white inhabitants, mostly missionaries and the personnel that maintained the government forts constructed at Leavenworth, Fort Scott, and Fort Riley, lived there.

### The Kansas-Nebraska Act of 1854
So great was the incursion of European settlers to the area after 1854 that the Native Americans who lived there, both original dwellers and the emigrant tribes, were removed from the state and settled elsewhere. In 1854 Kansas was created as a territory in the western part of what had previously been called the Missouri Territory. The early borders of the rectangular-shaped territory were much as they are today. Kansas is bounded by Missouri on the east and Colorado on the west. To the north, the boundary is Nebraska, and the southern border is Oklahoma. The only natural boundary is in the northeast, where the Missouri River constitutes part of the state line.

Soon after Kansas gained territorial status, the Kansas-Nebraska Act of 1854, which replaced the Missouri Compromise, opened the territory to settlement. Under the terms of this act, citizens of a territory decided whether it would be slave or free, whereas under the Missouri Compromise, an artificial balance between slave and free states was imposed.

Opinions were strongly divided about which choice Kansas should make. Its neighboring state, Missouri, had slaves. Nebraska opted to be free, but proslavery sentiment was strong in Kansas. When the issue came to a vote, hundreds of land-hungry people who had come to Kansas stuffed the ballot boxes.

Kansas was plunged into controversy between the proslavery and antislavery forces. Abolitionists were recruited to come to Kansas from New England and make it a free state. Abolitionist John Brown led the Pottawatomie Massacre in May of 1856. In 1863 an angry proslavery mob, led by William Clarke Quantrill, attacked Lawrence, Kansas, killing around 150 of its citizens.

### Moving Toward Statehood
With the proslavery and antislavery forces fighting against each other, both sides drew up constitutions, neither of them acceptable to the United States Congress. Finally, in 1859, the antislavery Wyandotte Constitution was approved. This cleared the way for Kansas to achieve statehood on January 29, 1861, just as many southern states were seceding from the Union. Kansas was the thirty-fourth state admitted to the Union.

### The Homestead Act of 1862
Following passage of the Homestead Act of 1862, Kansas grew rapidly. Under the terms of this act, upon the payment of a ten-dollar filing fee, heads of family or anyone over twenty-one years old could receive 160 acres of government land, which they would own if they lived on it for five years and improved the property. This opportunity was a magnet that drew thousands of easterners to Kansas.

The railroads that served the area received large land grants, chunks of which they sold to the early settlers. The Union Pacific Railroad began operating in Kansas in 1857, the Atchison and Topeka Railroad was chartered in 1859, and the Missouri, Kansas, and Texas line soon followed. Eventually twelve railroads operated on more than six thousand miles of track in Kansas.

### The Kansas Economy
Because of the nature of its founding, Kansas was originally a rural state concentrating heavily on agriculture. During the Civil War, it sided with the North, and many of its citizens joined the Union army. Shortly after the war, cow towns began to develop in Kansas. These were towns that had railway connections, notably Abilene, Dodge City, Ellsworth, and Wichita.

Texas at this time had no railroad service, so until the mid-1880's, when rail service became available, Texan cattle ranchers drove their herds across Oklahoma to the railroad towns of Kansas, from which they were shipped to other destinations.

Eastern Kansas was settled early, but soon other settlers moved into the central and western regions, as far as Great Bend near the Colorado border. A diverse population developed as Europeans from Russia, Germany, Bohemia, France, England, and Italy came to the state, which also had a sizable African American population, being one of the free states that attracted freed slaves following the Civil War in what was called the "Exoduster movement."

Kansas, with a growing season of about 150 days in its northern reaches and more than 200 days in the southeast, is hospitable to agriculture. The rainfall ranges from sixteen inches annually in the west to more than forty inches in the east, although droughts are a frequent problem. In the early to mid-1930's, the dust bowls of Kansas and Oklahoma put many farmers out of business.

The state constructed more than twenty large reservoirs to control flooding, provide drinking water, and afford irrigation to farmers. Also, early Russian immigrants into Kansas brought with them a drought-resistant strain of wheat, Turkey Red, which is grown extensively in the state.

Although Kansas was originally rural, it increasingly moved toward manufacturing, commerce, and service occupations, causing a population shift to urban areas. Of its more than six hundred incorporated cites, fifty have populations exceeding five thousand. Nevertheless, more than two-thirds of the total 1990 population of about 2.5 million lived in urban areas.

Besides its agricultural and cattle industries, Kansas has a thriving aircraft industry centered in Wichita, where both private planes and commercial aircraft are produced by such companies as Boeing and Cessna. One of the nation's leading mental hospitals, the Menninger Neuropsychiatric Clinic, is located in Topeka. Kansas also has impressive oil reserves, as well as natural gas, coal, lead, salt, and zinc.

### Kansas Conservatism

Kansas has traditionally been a conservative state, largely a Republican stronghold, although it has strong Populist leanings as well and has elected Populists as governors and representatives. It gave a moderate, Nancy Landon Kassebaum, three terms in the United States Senate.

In 1880 the state adopted prohibition and essentially remained a dry state. In 1899, Kansan Carry Nation single-handedly undertook the enforcement of Kansas's prohibition law by destroying saloons with her renowned axe.

### Kansas Economy in the 1900's

The economy of Kansas had a significant resurgence during World War I, when the price of wheat escalated, bringing considerable money into the state's economy. The economy grew until the 1930's, when a drought that continued for several years devastated wheat farming.

The financial woes of the 1930's did not end until World War II again stimulated the economy and brought considerable industry into the state. The road building in the state during and after World War II resulted in one of the best road systems in the country. Kansas is served by 125 public and 250 private airports that provide excellent commercial air transport and encourage private ownership of airplanes.

—*R. Baird Shuman*

# Brown v. Board of Education National Historic Site

**Date:** Case decided on May 17, 1954; established as a National Historic Site on October 26, 1992

**Relevant issues:** African American history, education, legal history, political history, social reform

**Significance:** This site commemorates one of the most significant and far-reaching decisions by the United States Supreme Court in the twentieth century. It marks a major turning point in the constitutional and social issues related to segregation.

**Location:** Topeka is located about fifty-five miles west of Kansas City, on Interstate 70

**Site Office:**
*Brown v. Board of Education* National Historic Site
Suite 220, Main Post Office
424 South Kansas Avenue
Topeka, KS 66603-3441
ph.: (785) 354-4273
fax: (785) 354-7213
Web site: www.nps.gov/brvb/

The case of *Brown et al. v. Board of Education, Topeka, Kansas* represents a milestone in the struggle for civil rights. On May 17, 1954, the United States Supreme Court, in a unanimous decision, held that separate educational facilities were inherently unequal and as such deprived the plaintiffs in the case of equal protection of the laws

*Monroe Elementary School in Topeka, the site of the integration controversy that led to the landmark case* Brown v. Board of Education. (National Park Service, *Brown v. Board of Education* National Historic Site)

as guaranteed by the Fourteenth Amendment to the United States Constitution. This decision provided the foundation for a series of changes that in the years to come would eliminate segregation in public schools. To commemorate this landmark decision, the U.S. Congress on October 26, 1992, passed Public Law 102-525, which established a National Historic Site in Topeka, Kansas.

**Before the U.S. District Court: Unresolved Issues**
On February 28, 1951, a group of thirteen African American parents with school-age children, all of whom had been refused admission to neighborhood schools because of the color of their skin, initiated an action against the Board of Education of Topeka in the U.S. District Court for the District of Kansas. Linda Carol Brown, a student at the all-black Monroe Elementary School, sought admission to the all-white Sumner Elementary School, which was located only a few blocks away from the Brown home. When her father, Oliver Brown, the lead plaintiff, attempted to enroll his daughter in Sumner Elementary School, he was turned down. Brown argued that it was both unfair and unsafe for his eight-year-old daughter to have to cross both a railroad yard and Kansas Avenue, a major thoroughfare in Topeka, and then take a bus ride to an all-black school some twenty blocks away.

The plaintiffs sought to prevent enforcement of an 1879 Kansas law that allowed, but did not require, that cities with a population of more than fifteen thousand maintain segregated elementary schools. The plaintiffs claimed that the Kansas law deprived them of equal protection of the laws as guaranteed by the Fourteenth Amendment (1868). They were represented by several African American attorneys from Topeka and two staff attorneys from the Legal Defense Fund of the National Association for the Advancement of of Colored People (NAACP) in New York.

The defendants—the Topeka Board of Education; Dr. Kenneth McFarland, superintendent of the Topeka schools; and Frank Wilson, principal of Sumner Elementary School in Topeka—justified the existence of segregated elementary schools on the basis of the Kansas statute. Trial was set for June 25, 1951.

While the defendants presented arguments in support of the constitutionality of the Kansas statute, the plaintiffs introduced extensive testimony from expert witnesses from the fields of education and the behavioral sciences. All of them agreed that segregation, even if legal, amounted to a denial of equal educational opportunity.

In the unanimous opinion of the three-judge district court, the black schools and the white schools in Topeka were substantially equal in terms of facilities, quality of teachers, curricula, and transportation. The district court felt bound by the legal precedent established by the 1896 U.S. Supreme Court decision in the case of *Plessy v. Ferguson*. In that instance the Court had upheld a Louisiana statute that required separate but equal accommodations for African American and for white railroad passengers.

Although the district court had little choice but to deny the plaintiffs' petition, it attached a significant "finding of fact" to its opinion that agreed with much of the expert witness testimony introduced by the plaintiffs. This finding noted that segregation had a detrimental effect on African American children because it suggested that they were inferior. This suggestion of inferiority, the court noted, hampered the educational development of these children and hence denied them the benefits they would receive while attending racially integrated schools.

In the course of the next phase—an appeal to the U.S. Supreme Court—*Brown v. Board of Education* served as the lead case in a group of four other segregation-related cases: *Briggs v. Elliott, Clarendon County, South Carolina; Davis v. County School Board of Prince Edward County, Virginia; Gebhart v. Belton, Delaware;* and *Bolling v. Sharpe, District of Columbia.* In spite of substantial differences among the cases, the Court held that the common legal issue merited joint consideration. On September 5, 1953, the board of education in Topeka agreed on what amounted to a declaration of intent to end segregation in the Topeka schools, without committing itself to a specific date.

## Before the U.S. Supreme Court

On December 9, 1952, *Brown et al. v. Board of Education* was argued before the Court. The makeup of the Court had changed since the date when the case was first heard. Chief Justice Fred M. Vinson, who had not been inclined toward changing the existing segregation laws, had died in 1953, and President Dwight D. Eisenhower quickly appointed Earl Warren to succeed him as chief justice.

Basically, the plaintiffs argued that segregated public schools were not equal by their very nature and could not be made equal. Hence, they deprived students of the equal protection of the laws guaranteed under the Fourteenth Amendment. The defendants based their argument on the decision in *Plessy v. Ferguson*, which, in spite of its original connection to transportation, had been used in the past to apply also to the field of education. In the unanimous decision of the U.S. Supreme Court delivered by Chief Justice Earl Warren on May 17, 1954, the Court rejected the doctrine of "separate but equal" and focused instead on the role of education in the life of the nation. Stating that separate educational facilities were inherently unequal, the Court concluded that they denied persons equal protection of the laws. In a relatively brief opinion, often referred to as *Brown I*, the Court further held that segregation in and by itself created a feeling of inferiority in African American children. Therefore, segregated educational facilities had a tendency to slow down their educational and mental development. That sense of inferiority was made all the more serious since it had the weight of the law behind it.

Focusing less on historical and legal precedent, the Court based its finding to a large measure on evidence from the social sciences. In the famous footnote 11, which was to become the focus of a great deal of criticism, the Court relied on evidence from a variety of sociological and psychological works, among them a study by Kenneth B. Clark, *Effects of Prejudice and Discrimination on Personality Development* (1950), and the massive study by the Swedish economist Gunnar Myrdal, *An American Dilemma: The Negro Problem and Modern Democracy* (1944).

Because the Court treated the matter as a class action suit, its findings would pertain not only to the plaintiffs in the specific cases but also to other individuals in similar situations. However, the Court was silent on the crucial question of how and when its findings were to be implemented. In the months following the decision, several hundred school districts in a number of states moved toward integration. However, a number of southern states showed little or no willingness to cooperate with the Court, seeking to delay implementation by pointing to, among other things, the huge logistical difficulties posed by desegregation.

## The Challenge of Implementation: *Brown II*

Aware of southern opposition to the decisions in *Brown I* and of the complexities involved in implementing it, the Court proceeded with great caution. While the NAACP, under the forceful leadership of Thurgood Marshall, pressed for an early end to segregation, suggesting at one point that the process be completed by September, 1956, many southern states favored a far more gradual implementation.

After several delays and postponements, on May 31, 1955, the chief justice delivered a decree, sometimes referred to as *Brown II*. Clearly seeking to find an acceptable middle ground between upholding the changes it had ordered in *Brown I* and issuing a peremptory decree, the Court directed the lower courts to require the defendants to comply with the Court's decision. To facilitate the implementation process and, in particular, to determine whether extra time was needed, the lower courts could consider a host of logistical and administrative issues faced by the various school districts. At the same time, the Court abandoned the class action character of *Brown I* and agreed that it should apply only to the five localities involved in the original suit.

In an effort to mollify *Brown*'s opponents, the Court also avoided setting specific time limits for implementation. Instead, the Court settled on a phrase introduced by Justice Felix Frankfurter that suggested that implementation must be pursued "with all deliberate speed." Given the widespread hostility to *Brown II*, even the NAACP accepted the absence of a deadline, hoping that it would keep opposition under control.

Opposition to *Brown II* was, in fact, considerable. In 1957, 101 U.S. senators and congressmen signed a "Southern Manifesto" challenging the authority of the Court and pledging themselves to reversing the *Brown* decision altogether. Several southern senators, among them Senate Majority Leader Lyndon B. Johnson, a Democrat from Texas, refused to sign the manifesto.

In the years that followed, implementation of *Brown II* proceeded at a very slow pace. Critics pointed out, in reference to the Court's formula of "all deliberate speed," that there was too much de-liberation and far too little speed. Until the passage of the Civil Rights Act of 1964, the U.S. Department of Justice played only a minor role in advancing desegregation in public education.

## Visiting the Site

The headquarters of the site, located on the second floor of the Main Post Office in downtown Topeka, is open to visitors Monday through Friday from 8:00 A.M. to 5:00 P.M. It is closed on federal holidays. The site features audiovisual programs, literature, exhibits, and a modest library. The National Park Service, in cooperation with the Brown Foundation for Educational Equity, Excellence and Research, offers a variety of tours and off-site interpretive programs. The permanent location of the *Brown v. Board of Education* National Historic Site at the renovated Monroe Elementary School will feature additional exhibits and expanded library facilities. The new site is scheduled to open by October, 2003.

—*Helmut J. Schmeller*

## For Further Information:

Kluger, Richard. *Simple Justice: The History of "Brown v. Board of Education" and Black America's Struggle for Equality.* New York: Vintage Books, 1977. Highly acclaimed scholarly and comprehensive treatment of the topic. Indispensable.

Schwartz, Bernard, with Stephen Lesher. *Inside the Warren Court, 1953-1969.* Garden City, N.Y.: Doubleday, 1983. Lively and very readable account of the major decisions and the personalities of the Warren Court.

Whitman, Mark, ed. *Irony of Desegregation Law, 1955-1995: Essays and Documents.* Princeton, N.J.: Princeton University Press, 1998. Traces the development of segregation-related case law beginning with *Brown II*. Very useful.

_____. *Removing a Badge of Slavery: The Record of "Brown v. Board of Education."* Princeton, N.J.: Markus Wiener, 1993. A compilation of edited versions of the most important documents of the case. Useful introductory essays.

Wilkinson, J. Harvie, III. *From Brown to Bakke: The Supreme Court and School Integration, 1954-1978.* New York: Oxford University Press, 1979. An excellent scholarly work.

Wilson, Paul E. *A Time to Lose: Representing Kansas in "Brown v. Board of Education."* Lawrence: University Press of Kansas, 1995. A very readable account by the Assistant Attorney General of Kansas who argued the state's case before the Supreme Court. Includes photographs.

Wolters, Raymond. *The Burden of Brown: Thirty Years of School Desegregation.* Knoxville: University of Tennessee Press, 1984. Focuses on the specific changes in the school districts where desegregation originated. Helpful statistical tables.

# Dodge City

**Date:** Founded in 1865 as Buffalo City; changed to Dodge City in 1872 with the coming of the Atchison, Topeka, and Santa Fe Railroad

**Relevant issues:** Business and industry, cultural history, western expansion

**Significance:** This cattle boomtown of the American West is remembered today primarily for its lawlessness, but it was an important cattle trading center until 1885.

**Location:** Southwestern central Kansas, approximately five miles from Fort Dodge; the seat of Ford County

**Site Office:**
Dodge City Convention and Visitors' Bureau
P.O. Box 1474
Dodge City, KS 67801
ph.: (316) 225-8186
Web site: www.dodgecity.org

A Wild West boomtown if ever there was one, Dodge City has become an indelible part of the mythos of the American West. The city that inspired the phrase "time to get out of Dodge" is located on the Arkansas River in southwestern central Kansas, approximately five miles from Fort Dodge, the U.S. Army post from which the city took its name. Dubbed the "Cow Capital of the World," Dodge City's heyday as one of the most important—and notorious—outposts along the cattle trail from Texas to the northern states lasted a mere thirteen years, from the city's founding in 1872 to the passage of legislation in 1885 that forbade the driving of Texas cattle through the state of Kansas.

Dodge City is still the seat of government in Ford County, but the ways of the residents have changed with the times. Numerous buildings and sites of his-torical importance have been carefully preserved or restored, and all are readily accessible to visitors intent on learning more about the "Queen of Cowtowns" and its role in the building of the American frontier.

**Early History**
Responding to the needs of settlers putting down roots throughout the West, the U.S. Army had begun in the early 1800's to build a series of forts across the country wherever there was a need to protect settlers from hazards such as roaming thieves or Native Americans hostile to the westward expansion of the United States. In 1865 Major General Grenville M. Dodge established Fort Dodge on the banks of the Arkansas River in order to protect the commerce of settlers following the Santa Fe Trail along the Arkansas River to the west. American settlers began to use the Santa Fe Trail in 1821, but the ford across the the river had been used by Spanish conquistador Francisco Vásquez de Coronado as early as 1541 during his search for the Seven Cities of Cíbola.

Where there were soldiers, there was a market, and soon after the establishment of Fort Dodge, a small tent city appeared five miles upriver to sell liquor and other amenities not usually provided by the government to the soldiers stationed at the fort. This camp, which is all it was, was originally named Buffalo City as it soon became an important center for the slaughter of buffalo, which were valued for their hides.

Buffalo City's status changed rapidly with the coming of the Atchison, Topeka, and Santa Fe Railroad in 1872. Fueled by a direct line to the outside world, the tiny camp changed its name to Dodge City and soon became the largest cattle market in the world. It also became famous for its vices, and it is this side of the city's history that has endured the most.

The cowboy of legend was born on the prairies of Texas shortly after the U.S. Civil War. Prior to the war, Texas had been the primary producer of livestock in the newly settled West. Several hundred thousand head of Spanish cattle originally transplanted to the state during its days as a province of Mexico multiplied rapidly in the temperate climate of Texas, and the state's thin prairie grass, called "buffalo grass," provided a perfect diet to sustain the herds.

## After the Civil War

The coming of the Civil War in 1861 put a temporary halt to the Texans' steady but profitable business. Access to northern markets was cut off and the southern economy was in steep decline. Cattle continued to multiply despite the fact that sales dropped precipitously, and many a rancher found himself stuck with thousands of head but virtually no market in which to sell them. Ranchers who should have been wealthy were known as "cattle poor" and did their best to make do with small sales until the war was over.

The end of the war, in 1865, not only put an end to the ranchers' frustrations but also made them wealthier than they had ever been before. The years of slow sales and constant breeding had swollen the state's herds to an estimated three to six million head of cattle, and in 1865 preparations were made to drive hundreds of thousands of cattle northward as soon as possible. The cattle were herded to the northeastern portion of the state, and the first major drive began in the summer of 1866.

Fully 270,000 head of cattle were driven northward that summer, beginning a way of life that would eventually become one of the cornerstones of U.S. history. Cowboys were hired to herd the cattle off the open ranges and into fenced-off ranches to be branded with the distinctive logo of their new owners before being driven north. The Texas longhorn cattle of the day bore little resemblance to the domesticated cows of today, for they were much larger and more sleek and possessed fearsome horns that sometimes reached six feet from tip to tip. They were also public property, free for the taking to whoever rounded them up first.

Initially, cattle were driven north to the railroad stations of Missouri to be sold to dealers who would then transfer them onto cattle cars for shipment to the major markets of the North and East. Trails taken to the stations varied widely, as the practice of driving cattle north was a new one and the terrain, for the purposes of moving thousands of cattle, was relatively unknown.

## The Great Cattle Trails

Trails soon developed along the route. Given such names as the Chisholm Trail and the Southern Texas Trail, these preferred routes were all characterized by plentiful grasses, relatively flat land, and something approaching safety, although cattle driving was never a safe occupation. The Texas longhorns were not like the placid cows of modern ranching, and stampedes were common. Hostile Native Americans regularly attacked cattle drovers, and wandering thieves and highwaymen, leftovers from the guerrilla units that operated on both sides during the Civil War, levied stupendously high fees—akin to protection money—upon any drover unlucky enough to cross their paths. It was nearly impossible to avoid these brigands, as herds of several thousand cattle were notoriously difficult to hide.

Problems with easterly routes through the Ozark Mountains, which brought cattle to train stations in Missouri in battered and bruised condition, necessitated the development of a route that would take cattle straight north from Texas into Kansas. In 1867 construction began on the Kansas Pacific Railroad, destined to stretch westward across Kansas from its starting point at Kansas City. At this point, the era of the cowtown began.

## "Cowtowns"

The first of the new cowtowns was Abilene, Kansas. Situated approximately 165 miles southwest of Kansas City, Abilene was a sleepy town of few inhabitants before the railroad came. Shortly thereafter, it became the first of the "wickedest little cities in America."

In 1867, its first year as a cattle market, 36,000 head were shipped from Abilene. By 1868, this figure had climbed to 75,000 head, and by 1869 the number had leapt to 160,000. By 1870 the new business was in full swing, with more than 300,000 head being transported from Abilene.

In 1871, 600,000 cattle were driven to Abilene to be sold. The bubble on the boom market had burst, however, and fully half of the massive herd had to be driven west for the winter, unsold, in order to graze. The harshness of the winter of 1871-1872 killed thousands of cattle, and the business went into a slump. This was by no means the end of the cattle business, however, but rather a warning to overzealous Texas ranchers too eager to flood the market at any cost. The business rebounded by 1872, but Abilene's prestige did not, and new cowtowns grew up to take its place.

The next new cowtown was Ellsworth, Kansas, located forty miles farther west along the Kansas

Pacific route. It, too, became a "wicked little city," as did newcomers Newton and Wichita, both situated along the new Atchison, Topeka, and Santa Fe Railroad line, which claimed an ever-larger share of the business due to its more southerly location.

## The Railroads and Dodge City

Eventually the Atchison, Topeka, and Santa Fe came to Dodge City, and Dodge quickly grew into the most famous of the cowtowns and the largest cattle market in the world. When the railroad arrived in 1872, only 2,000 cattle were driven to Dodge, although the buffalo hide industry took advantage of the railroad, and business boomed for a few more years until the buffalo had nearly been exterminated. In 1876, 322,000 head of cattle were driven to Dodge and nearby Ellis, with the vast majority going to Dodge. From 1876 to 1885 the number of cattle shipped from Dodge City each year fluctuated from a low of approximately 60,000 to a high of about 300,000, while some cattle were simply penned in Dodge temporarily on their way to markets in Nebraska, the Dakotas, Montana, and Wyoming. All told, more than seven million cattle were marketed at Dodge during the 1870's and 1880's. Everybody came to Dodge.

Dodge was distinguished from its cowtown forebears primarily by the nature of its people. While earlier cowtowns had mostly been tiny villages prior to the coming of the railroad, Dodge, when it was still known as Buffalo City, already had been well known for its vices for several years. While the other cowtowns had indeed become "wicked cities," the nature of their wickedness was transitional, because everybody knew that the railroad would someday push farther south and that the boomtown atmosphere would pass soon enough. The coming of the railroad may have enhanced Dodge City's less-than-perfect image, but it did not create it.

## Rapid Growth

Dodge went from tent city to real city in a matter of weeks. The main street, called Front Street, was built on either side of the railroad tracks. Consisting primarily of one-story frame buildings, Front Street was obviously built in haste: few of the buildings were situated squarely on their owner's property, and many proprietors were forced to buy expensive easements. Cattle pens for holding newly arrived longhorns were built in the flatlands surrounding the city. The city in its heyday never had more than twelve hundred full-time residents, although the population during the busy season was usually several times as many, and in the beginning the nearest law enforcement was in Hays City, seventy-five miles away.

The only legitimate business in Dodge was cattle, and even it had its share of ruffians and shysters. Big-money hustlers from the North turned wheeling and dealing into a fine art, and the lack of credible law enforcement allowed questionable transactions to flourish. The cattle business did, however, provide the money that supported the city's other economic activities, which consisted primarily of drinking, gambling, and prostitution. Dance halls, brothels, and saloons formed the bulk of commercial buildings in the city, and with thousands of dollars trading hands in Dodge on a daily basis, the business of vice boomed, attracting almost as many ne'er-do-wells and assorted criminals as the cattle business did cowboys. It was said that only in Dodge could a man break all ten of the commandments in one day, die with his boots on, and be buried in the famous Boot Hill Cemetery.

## Center of Booze and Vice

In 1876, the year in which Dodge became the undisputed leader in the cattle trade, nineteen establishments were licensed to sell liquor in the city, or one tavern for every sixty-one permanent residents. While this number of taverns may have been acceptable during the summer season, when the city was filled with transient cowboys and cattle dealers, it was absurdly high during the slow periods when the establishments had to depend upon the full-time residents for business. These slow periods resulted in fierce competition among the liquor-selling establishments, often forcing them to drastically reduce their prices. This cheap liquor also attracted an unsavory element to Dodge.

The only liquor-selling establishment in Dodge that could claim any amount of respectability was the Long Branch Saloon, named after a famous resort on the Atlantic Coast. Prosperous cattle dealers, buffalo hunters, and railroad tycoons were the standard clientele of the Long Branch Saloon, which, like most of the city's other taverns, was located on Front Street. Other notable, if not as posh, saloons included the Junction Saloon, Muller and Straeter's Old House Saloon, Varieties Dance Hall, Beatty and Kelly's Alhambra Saloon, Gambling Hall and Restaurant, A. B. Webster's Alamo, the Opera House Saloon, and the Green Front.

Most of these establishments were not simply taverns but also dance halls offering entertainment in addition to liquor. They were also purveyors of prostitution. Prostitutes were the most effective way for the saloons to attract trail-weary cowboys, who usually had seen no women for months.

Prostitution and dancing were about the only lines of work open to women in Dodge City. Women who came to Dodge to be entertainers often wound up doubling as prostitutes, and vice versa. The most famous of these Dodge City women was Fannie Keenan, known as the Queen of the Fairy Belles. Keenan was the most popular of the dance hall women, and it was rumored that she had been a grand opera singer prior to making the trip to Dodge.

Keenan had acquired her legendary status not only through her performing but also through her good works in a town where good works were rare. She regularly played the role of nurse to sick or wounded cowboys who had nobody else to turn to and was known to buy tickets home for unfortunate strangers who lost their money through gambling. Keenan was killed in 1878 by a visiting Texan named James W. "Spike" Kennedy following an altercation between Kennedy and then-mayor of the city, James H. "Dog" Kelley, owner of the Alhambra Saloon.

Gambling was Dodge City's other major activity, and one that made a great deal of money for the owners of the gambling houses. Gambling was con-

*The Dodge City Peace Commission in 1882, including Bat Masterson (back row, far right) and Wyatt Earp (front row, second from left). (AP/Wide World Photos)*

sidered somewhat more respectable than drinking or prostitution. Even legendary lawman Bat Masterson, who served as sheriff of Ford County from 1877 to 1879, said gambling "was not only the principal and best-paying industry of the town, but was also reckoned among the most respectable." Professional gamblers were held in high esteem in Dodge City, and opportunities to win large sums of money from just-paid visiting cowboys eager for some excitement were readily available. Gambling was practiced in virtually every saloon in the town, and the laxity of law enforcement practically invited pickup poker games to be played anywhere and everywhere.

The intensity supplied by the visiting cowboys and cattle dealers combined with the sheer lawlessness of the town resulted in the early deaths of a large number of people. As the town grew and death became more frequent, bodies came to be buried on Boot Hill, near the bank of the Arkansas

River. Although existing records regarding the death rate in Dodge City are, at best, sketchy and incomplete, it is known that at least twenty-five people were killed in 1872, when Dodge had a population of about five hundred. This is a murder rate of five for every hundred residents. Today, a murder rate of thirty for every hundred thousand residents is considered high, even in the most crime-ridden cities.

## Boot Hill

Boot Hill got its name from the fact that most of the people interred in it were buried with their boots on. There was no marble on the plains to use for headstones, and wood to make caskets had to be shipped in from elsewhere at great expense. Furthermore, because so many of those killed were just passing through and had no friends or relatives to see to a proper burial, most of the dead were buried just as they were found. If they were wrapped in a saddle blanket, their burial arrangements were considered luxurious.

Despite its long-lasting fame, Boot Hill was used for burial for only about six years. In 1879 the city's leaders decided to build a new schoolhouse on Boot Hill, proving that the city was not all bad, so the bodies were moved to a potter's field next to the new Prairie Grove Cemetery northeast of the city. Because graves on Boot Hill were dug haphazardly and were so poorly marked, if at all, it is possible that some bodies remain there today.

## Famous Visitors

Dodge City's notoriety both as an important center of commerce and as an outpost of rampant vice attracted a steady stream of famous people during its heyday. Some of the notable visitors included General George Armstrong Custer, General William Tecumseh Sherman, General Nelson A. Miles, General Philip Sheridan, Senator John J. Ingalls, and Kansas governor Thomas Carney, although Carney did not visit until after he was out of office. Even President Rutherford B. Hayes stopped in Dodge, but he refused to leave his presidential train car during the brief stop, apparently not wishing for it to be known that he had voluntarily consorted with the citizens of such a place as Dodge.

Several of the West's most legendary lawmen devoted portions of their careers to trying to clean up Dodge. Their efforts were, for the most part, unsuccessful, but without their presence, the carnage likely would have been even worse. Bat Masterson originally came to Dodge City in 1873 as an Indian scout and buffalo hunter. In 1875 he moved on to Sweetwater, Texas, where in 1876 he killed a man and a dance-hall hostess in an argument, then returned to Dodge City. It was at this time that he became Ford County sheriff. In 1879 he was elevated to the position of U.S. deputy marshal. Probably only in Dodge could a man with Masterson's record become a lawman. Wyatt Earp, who was destined to play a major role in western history as a participant in the gunfight at OK Corral in Tombstone, Arizona, in 1881, was also a Dodge City lawman, serving as a police officer from 1876 to 1877 and as assistant marshal in 1878-1879. Gunfighter John "Doc" Holliday, who fought alongside Earp at the OK Corral, ran a dental office in Dodge in 1878-1879, when he and Earp first met.

## Decline

Dodge City's salad days could not last forever, and the beginning of the end came in 1885 when the governor of Kansas issued a proclamation forbidding all "through" Texas cattle—that is, cattle driven directly from southern Texas without a winter stopover—to enter the state of Kansas. The reason for this legislation was the splenic fever, commonly called the "Spanish fever," a malady long known to the cowboys but accepted as part of doing business. The fever was brought north from Texas by ticks attached to the big longhorns. At the time, no one realized the ticks were the means of transmission, but it was known that Texas longhorns, who were immune to the disease, somehow spread it to local cattle upon their arrival. During Dodge City's boom, many people had come to the area to establish ranches in the fertile prairies of Ford County and raise cattle indigenous to Kansas. Their cattle were susceptible to the fever, and when, in 1884, the splenic fever spread among the stockyards of Kansas City, St. Louis, and Chicago, Kansas ranchers demanded that their government put a stop to the cattle drives. The last cattle drive from Texas to Dodge City took place in 1885, although the city remained an important shipping point for local ranchers for many years afterward.

With the slow death of the city's economic mainstay, the rest of the economy also suffered. The state of Kansas had passed a dry law forbidding alcholic beverages as early as 1880, but the law had been completely ignored in Dodge until the city passed its own dry law in 1887. Even with the new law, the last liquor-selling establishment in Dodge did not close until 1903. The sale of cigarettes, cigars, tobacco, opium, and narcotics was outlawed in 1896. Dodge continued to be an important horse market after the cattle days, and the city, as a whole, remained economically viable and did not become a ghost town, as had so many of the earlier boom towns.

Today the Boot Hill Museum houses many of the relics of Dodge City's colorful past, including a re-creation of Front Street, most of which burned in 1885. The visitors' center is housed in a replica of the original Great Western Hotel. The original Fort Dodge Jail, which stood at the military post during the heyday, has been moved to the city. The 1878 Hardesty House still stands as a typical example of the homes lived in by prosperous cattle dealers. Several original structures from Fort Dodge can also be seen at the Kansas Soldiers' Home five miles east of Dodge City. Parts of the old Santa Fe Trail, founded in 1821, can still be seen in the prairie west of Dodge City.                 —*John A. Flink*

**For Further Information:**

Ford County Historical Society. *Dodge City and Ford County, Kansas, 1870-1920: Pioneer Histories and Stories.* Dodge City, Kans.: Author, 1996.

Rich, Everett, ed. *The History of Kansas: Selected Commentaries on Past Times.* Lawrence: University of Kansas Press, 1960. A collection of essays and reflections on the history of Kansas, some written by modern historians, others culled from the writings of people who actually lived during the era. The essay entitled "Cattle Trails of the Prairies," by Charles M. Harger, is particularly illuminating.

Vestal, Stanley. *Queen of Cowtowns: Dodge City, the Wickedest Little City in America, 1872 to 1886.* New York: Harper, 1952. Undoubtedly the most comprehensive overview of the pivotal years of Dodge City's history. The book is long on fanciful recollection but is replete with hard facts supplied by Vestal, a Rhodes Scholar and western historian from the University of Oklahoma.

Whittemore, Margaret. *Historic Kansas: A Centenary Sketchbook.* Manhattan, Kans.: Plint Hills, 1974. Contains brief chapters on several aspects of the state's history, showcasing Dodge in context with the rest of Kansas history.

# Other Historic Sites

## Council Grove Historic District

*Location:* Council Grove, Morris County

*Relevant issues:* Western expansion

*Statement of significance:* With its water, abundant grass, and timber, Council Grove was a natural stopping place on the Santa Fe Trail. It is named for the occasion of an 1825 treaty negotiation between the federal government and the Osage Indians which guaranteed the Santa Fe caravans safe passage through Osage territory.

## El Cuartelejo

*Location:* Scott City, Scott County

*Relevant issues:* American Indian history

*Statement of significance:* This pueblo ruin is attributed to a group of Picuria Indians who left the Southwest because of friction with the Spanish. El Cuartelejo is a state park.

## Fort Larned

*Location:* Larned, Pawnee County

*Relevant issues:* Western expansion

*Statement of significance:* One of the best-preserved mid-nineteenth century western military posts, this was among the more important forts along the Santa Fe Trail in the 1860's and early 1870's.

## Fort Leavenworth

*Location:* Leavenworth, Leavenworth County

*Relevant issues:* Military history, western expansion

*Statement of significance:* Established in 1827 to protect caravans on the Santa Fe Trail, the fort played a major role in several wars and became the temporary capital of the new territory of Kansas in 1854.

## Haskell Institute

*Location:* Lawrence, Douglas County

*Relevant issues:* American Indian history, education

*Statement of significance:* Founded in 1884, this was one of the first large off-reservation boarding schools for Indian students established by the federal government. It served students from the southern Plains and upper Midwest; in 1965, it became Haskell Indian Junior College.

## Hollenberg (Cottonwood) Pony Express Station

*Location:* Hanover, Washington County

*Relevant issues:* Business and industry, western expansion

*Statement of significance:* The only surviving un-moved and unaltered Pony Express station, this was the most westerly such station in Kansas throughout the duration of that service (1860-1861). It also served as a relay station for the Overland Mail.

## Lecompton Constitution Hall

*Location:* Lecompton, Douglas County

*Relevant issues:* Political history

*Statement of significance:* Passage of the Kansas-Nebraska Act of 1854 precipitated a bloody struggle for dominance by proslavery and antislavery factions in Kansas, as well as a fierce constitutional debate. The Lecompton Constitution of 1856, a proslavery document drafted in Lecompton, the territorial capital of Kansas and also the headquarters of proslavery elements in the territory, was supported by President James Buchanan but rejected by Congress and served to inflame the growing sectional dispute which was shortly to burst into Civil War. This simple white frame building is the only remaining structure associated with the drafting of Kansas's first constitution.

## Marais des Cygnes Massacre Site

*Location:* Trading Post, Linn County

*Relevant issues:* Disasters and tragedies, political history

*Statement of significance:* On May 19, 1858, a band of thirty proslavery sympathizers crossed into Kansas from Missouri, captured eleven men in the vicinity of Trading Post, and shot them in a nearby ravine known today as the site of the Marais des Cygnes Massacre. The murderous episode touched off a national outcry which lent its force to the defeat of the proslavery Lecompton Constitution; John Brown and his men constructed a fortification near the massacre site.

## Medicine Lodge Peace Treaty Site

*Location:* Medicine Lodge, Barber County

*Relevant issues:* American Indian history, political history

*Statement of significance:* Here, near the confluence of Medicine Lodge and Elm Creeks, members of a Peace Commission created by Congress met with about five thousand Kiowa, Comanche, Plains Apache, Arapaho, and Southern Cheyenne Indians in October, 1867. Under the terms of the Medicine Lodge Treaty, the first to include provisions aimed at "civilizing" the Indian, Plains Indians were to give up nomadic ways and relinquish claims to ancestral lands, in return for federal economic and educational help.

## Nation House

*Location:* Medicine Lodge, Barber County

*Relevant issues:* Social reform

*Statement of significance:* From 1889 to 1902, this was the residence of Carry Nation (1846-1911), the temperance leader who became the foremost symbol of a reinvigorated prohibition movement at the turn of the twentieth century.

## Nicodemus Historic District

*Location:* Nicodemus, Graham County

*Relevant issues:* African American history

*Statement of significance:* Established on homestead land and named after a legendary slave, the town of Nicodemus was officially founded on September 17, 1877. It is the only remaining town of those established by blacks of the "Exoduster" movement, which was organized mainly through the efforts of Benjamin "Pap" Singleton, who was responsible for founding eleven colonies in Kansas between 1873 and 1880.

## Shawnee Mission

*Location:* Fairway, Johnson County

*Relevant issues:* American Indian history, education, political history

*Statement of significance:* From 1839 to 1862, Indian children of many nearby tribes were taught English, manual arts, and agriculture at the school established in 1830 by the Reverend Thomas Johnson. Also, the first territorial governor of Kansas had his executive offices here in 1854, and the first territorial legislature met here in 1855.

## Spring Hill Ranch

*Location:* Strong City, Chase County

*Relevant issues:* Business and industry

*Statement of significance:* The Spring Hill Ranch represents the transition from the open range to the enclosed holdings of the large cattle companies in the 1880's. The enclosure and consolidation of ranches during the late nineteenth century were accompanied by the improvement of range cattle through purebred breeding programs and, in the Flint Hills region of Kansas, a distinctive practice of fattening southwestern cattle on bluestem pastures during the summer before shipping them to market in the fall. The enclosed ranches helped transform the expanding cattle industry from a primitive frontier activity into a modern industry. The ranch headquarters and intact ranch lands illustrate an important chapter in the history of the southern plains of the United States.

## Tobias-Thompson Complex

*Location:* Geneseo, Rice County

*Relevant issues:* American Indian history

*Statement of significance:* The complex is composed of a cluster of eight village sites along the Little Arkansas River, all of which relate to the Little River Focus of the Great Bend Aspect dating from 1500 to 1700. These sites have been related to a historic culture, the Wichita Tribe, and may have been among the villages visited by Francisco Vásquez de Coronado in Quivira in 1542.

## Warkentin Farm

*Location:* Halstead, Harvey County

*Relevant issues:* European settlement, science and technology

*Statement of significance:* Bernard Warkentin (1847-1908) was a significant figure in the history of American immigration for promoting German-Russian Mennonite settlement in the Central Great Plains region of the United States, and in the history of agriculture for introducing and improving Central European wheat varieties that revolutionized American grain production. Warkentin owned this property from 1874 until his death; the house he built in 1884 still stands, along with other farm buildings and some plots used in his wheat hybridization experiments.

# Kentucky

*Louisville.* (PhotoDisc)

# History of Kentucky

Kentucky, popularly known as the Bluegrass State, was the first state west of the Appalachian Mountains populated by settlers from the original thirteen English colonies. From its earliest days it served as a gateway from east to west and as a border state between the North and South. For most of its history an agricultural and mining state, during the second half of the twentieth century Kentucky began a rapid transformation into a modern industrial economy.

### Early History and Settlement

Evidence suggests that Native Americans first entered the area of modern Kentucky as long as fifteen thousand years ago and were primarily hunters and gatherers. Later, agriculture and trade were established leading to a period around 450 B.C.E. known as the Adena culture, when burial mounds were constructed in the northern Kentucky area. Around 1000 C.E. two distinct Native American cultures developed in the area, the Mississippian in the west and the Fort Ancient in the east; the two groups had many similarities, including the cultivation of beans and corn from the south and the use of agricultural implements including the hoe. The first European explorers found the Cherokee, Delaware, Iroquois, and Shawnee Indian tribes in the territory, although the central portion was not permanently settled by any of these groups. Instead, it seems to have been used as a common hunting ground by all of them. It may also have been reserved for a battlefield for their disputes.

During the mid-1700's English settlers from the colonies on the East Coast, in particular from Virginia, began to push over the mountains into the area known as Kentucky. The word itself is derived from an Indian word which most likely means "land of tomorrow." Among these English explorers and settlers was Dr. Thomas Walker, who charted the Cumberland Gap, the entryway to Kentucky, and was the first European to build a permanent shelter in the area.

Another and more famous traveler was Daniel Boone, who explored the area first in 1767 and again in 1769. In his second journey, Boone reached as far as the central plateau of the state, soon known as "bluegrass country" for its distinctive vegetation. Boone's initial attempt at settlement in 1773 was a failure, but the following year James Harrod and colonists from Pennsylvania established Harrodstown. Boone returned the year after, and Fort Boonesborough was established in 1775. In 1776 the state of Virginia formally claimed the entire territory, giving it the name of the County of Kentucky.

### Revolution and Statehood

Native Americans were bewildered and angered by the various treaties they had made with the settlers. The Native Americans felt that these treaties had robbed them of the use of the lands which had been common to all for generations; ownership, in the European sense of the word, was an alien concept to the American Indians. As a result, many tribes throughout the area beyond the mountains allied themselves with the British during the American Revolution, and their attacks on Kentucky threatened the entire American settlement. In response, pioneer George Rogers Clark launched an offensive against the British and Native American strongholds north of the Ohio River. In a campaign that pitted small forces against one another in extremely difficult terrain in the middle of winter, Clark won a crucial victory when he forced the besieged British to surrender the frontier fort of Vincennes in 1779. However, Kentucky remained under threat from British and Native American attack until the Battle of Blue Licks in 1782, which has been called "the last battle of the Revolution."

Shortly after the Revolution ended in American independence, Kentuckians began agitating for their own independence, with the creation of a state separate from Virginia. During the 1780's, ten separate conventions were held, which gradually drafted the provisions that eventually established Kentucky as a state in its own right. On June 1, 1792, Kentucky was admitted to the Union as the fifteenth state, with Frankfort as its capital. It was

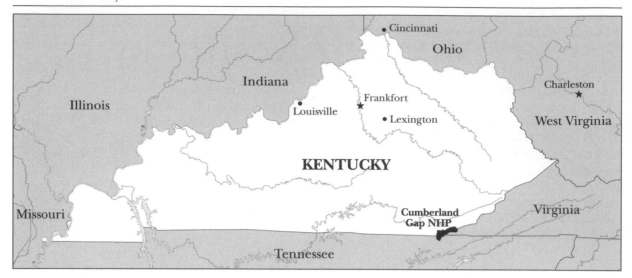

the first state of the new United States established west of the Allegheny Mountains.

During the years that followed, Kentucky encouraged one struggle, the War of 1812 against England, and sought to avoid a second, the American Civil War. Kentucky's most famous statesman of the years before the Civil War, Henry Clay, played a key role in both efforts. As a War Hawk congressman in the early 1800's, Clay advocated a conflict with Great Britain that he and others hoped could lead to the United States acquiring Canada. Later, as a U.S. senator, Clay helped craft the Missouri Compromise of 1820 and the Compromise of 1850, which delayed, if they did not prevent, war between the states over slavery.

### The Civil War and Early Modern Times

As a border state, Kentucky shared qualities of both the North and the South. The majority of its residents were small farmers who owned few or no slaves, and they were inclined to neutrality in the Civil War. There were a number of slaveholders in the broad central portion of the state, and while their sympathies were with the South, they also sought to remain aloof from the struggle. The northern part of the state shared in the developing commerce of the Ohio Valley, and crops of tobacco and cotton were often shipped south down the Mississippi to New Orleans; thus all parts of the state feared that war would disrupt this commerce. Along the eastern, more mountainous portions of the state, where slaves were few, pro-Union senti-

ment was strongest. Perhaps the fact that most dramatically illustrated the state's precariously balanced position was the fact that both Abraham Lincoln, president of the Union, and Jefferson Davis, president of the Confederacy, were born in Kentucky within a year of one another.

As the controversy over slavery grew more intense and the nation drifted toward war, Kentucky hoped to find yet one more compromise to avert struggle. When the Civil War finally erupted in 1861, Kentucky declared its official neutrality and was promptly invaded by both the Confederacy and the Union, which seized strategic points in the state. Some seventy thousand Kentuckians served with the Union forces; approximately thirty thousand rallied to the Confederacy. After a powerful Confederate thrust north was turned back in the summer of 1862, Kentucky was kept firmly in Union hands for the duration of the war.

Following the Civil War, Kentucky continued to develop its agriculture, most notably the tobacco industry. In addition, the state expanded its reputation for outstanding horse breeding and racing; the first Kentucky Derby was held in Louisville in 1875. Whiskey, especially bourbon, had been produced in the state since the 1820's and became world famous for its quality. The expansion of the railroads into the eastern, more mountainous portions of the state opened new coal fields for exploitation, often through the destructive process of strip mining, which left a barren wasteland behind. Life for coal miners and their families was hard and often dangerous.

The Great Depression, which began in 1929, coupled with years of drought and then flood, caused enormous damage to Kentucky's economy. By 1940 Kentucky ranked last in the nation for per capita income. President Franklin Roosevelt's New Deal and then the economic energy unleashed by World War II brought a measure of recovery to the state, including even parts of the Appalachian Mountains. However, poverty remained an endemic problem, especially in Appalachia, even through President Lyndon Johnson's Great Society programs of the mid-1960's.

### The Modern Era

After World War II, northern Kentucky in particular experienced an economic boom, with growth in manufacturing companies, which supplied industries in fields such as chemicals, automotives, office supplies, electric appliances, and wood products. In addition, the state took the lead in fields such as health care, with Humana, a Kentucky-formed company and one of the largest health care corporations in the United States, having established its headquarters in Louisville. State government actively sought to recruit industry, especially "light industry" which can fit into the Kentucky environment with minimal impact on natural resources. Such concerns are important, as horse breeding and tourism are major parts of Kentucky's overall economic picture and depend on precisely these natural resources for their continued viability.

Kentucky also took its place in the developing automobile industry in the Southeast. Under Democratic governor Martha Layne Collins, the state recruited a $3.5 billion investment by Japanese automaker Toyota in Kentucky, which, by the early 1990's, was employing more than twenty thousand workers. The success of Toyota in Kentucky was one of the reasons that other international automobile makers chose to locate in the area, most notably BMW in South Carolina in 1993 and Mercedes-Benz in Alabama in 1994. In addition to the automobile manufacturing plants themselves, the companies also attracted large numbers of suppliers for the parts needed in the production of the finished vehicle.

*—Michael Witkoski*

# Cumberland Gap

**Date:** Surveyed in 1750; named a National Historical Park on June 11, 1940

**Relevant issues:** American Indian history, business and industry, Civil War, colonial America, European settlement, western expansion

**Significance:** Gateway in Cumberland Mountains through which hundreds of thousands of settlers moved on their way west in the late eighteenth and early nineteenth centuries. In the Civil War, the gap was an important strategic site for both sides.

**Location:** Near the Kentucky and Tennessee border between Harrogate and Middlesborough off U.S. 25E; one and a half hours from Knoxville, Tennessee

**Site Office:**

Cumberland Gap National Historical Park
U.S. 25E South
P.O. Box 1848
Middlesborough, KY 40965
Ph.: (606) 248-2817
fax: (978) 248-7276
Web site: www.nps.gov/cuga/

Located at the intersection of Kentucky, Tennessee, and Virginia, Cumberland Gap, a narrow five hundred-foot-deep notch in the Cumberland Mountains that forms part of the Appalachian range, was the site of the famous Wilderness Road Trail. The geologic origins of the gap go back to the Paleozoic period and its 200 million years of erosion. Early explorers include Thomas Walker in 1750 and Daniel Boone in the 1770's. The road followed the path of migrating animals and was used by the Native Americans (the Shawnee name for the trail was Warrior's Path), as well. It is estimated that perhaps 200,000 to 300,000 men, women, and children made their way through the gap along the Wilderness Road on their way west. Many of them settled in Kentucky.

### Early History

In the 1740's, the Loyal Land Company was formed in Virginia with the aim of exploring and exploiting the resources beyond the Cumberland Mountains. Dr. Thomas Walker was hired by the company to survey nearly one million acres of land granted to the company. With five others, Walker traveled west through the Cumberland Gap in 1750. He carefully recorded his findings and followed the course of the Cumberland River. A primitive log cabin was built in what is now Knox County near the small city of Barbourville. It was Walker who gave the notch in the mountains its present name after the infamous duke of Cumberland, known as "the butcher of Culloden."

In 1769, Daniel Boone led a party of six through the gap exploring, hunting, and trapping. The Transylvania Company engaged Boone by 1775 to use thirty axmen to clear and mark what would be called "Boone's Trace" that ran through the Cumberland Gap to Fort Boone on the Kentucky River. By the end of the American Revolution, twelve thousand people had gone through the gap to the west. The historian and surveyor John Filson's 1784 book *The Discovery, Settlement, and Present State of Kentucky*, printed along with the first map to concentrate on the state, promoted settlement by promising a rich land "flowing with milk and honey." The peak years for the gap came following the Revolution. By June, 1792, Kentucky entered the Union as the fifteenth state. The first governor of Kentucky, Isaac Shelby, raised money to improve the unpaved trail to allow wagon passage. By 1800, over 200,000 settlers had traveled along the Wilderness Road across the Cumberland Gap.

**The Civil War**

The outbreak of the Civil War in 1861 saw the border state of Kentucky deeply divided. Official state policy was one of neutrality. Kentuckians volunteered in large numbers to serve on both sides during the war. Later in the year, a Confederate state government was formed with Bowling Green as its capital. The Cumberland Gap took on significant strategic importance as a potential route for both Union and Confederate troops. The gap provided Union forces with the quickest way to attack the rail lines connecting the West and Virginia. Confederate forces then occupied Cumberland Gap. Thirty miles away at Barbourville, Camp Andy Jackson, filled largely with Union sympathizers from eastern Tennessee, was opened. By September, a Confederate force under the command of General Felix Zollicoffer marched from the gap into Kentucky. Subsequently, after the Battle at Camp Wildcat near London, the Confederate forces withdrew

back to the gap. The Confederates stationed a garrison at Cumberland Gap and began to fortify their position. Union forces cautiously scouted the Confederate defenses.

In 1862, Union forces sought ways to outflank the strong fortifications at Cumberland Gap. With a mixed contingent of infantry, cavalry, and even artillery, Union troops had successfully outflanked the Confederates. On June 17, the Union forces found that the gap had been evacuated. Thus, the much-prized Cumberland Gap and its fortifications had been taken without any losses. President Abraham Lincoln wired his congratulations to the Union commander Major General George W. Morgan. The road from the gap to central Kentucky was repaired. An army engineer was dispatched to improve the Union defenses. New batteries were erected and ten thousand troops stationed at the gap and along the approaches from Virginia and Tennessee. The much-delayed plan for a Union advance into eastern Tennessee failed to materialize as Confederate troops advanced into Kentucky. As the main Confederate force pushed on to Lexington, cutting off the Union forces defending the Cumberland Gap, a two-month siege forced the defenders to abandon their position. What could not be hauled away in the retreat was destroyed by the Union army. Guns defending the gap were spiked, ammunition destroyed, and the road leading to the fortifications mined. Yet the Confederate invasion of Kentucky was turned aside at the Battle of Perryville on October 8, 1862. The Confederates withdrew back down the Wilderness Road and across the gap into Tennessee.

The following year, Union troops returned to the Cumberland Gap. Confederate defenses were weaker than before, following their earlier destruction at the hands of Morgan's Union soldiers. Confederate forces numbered about twenty-five hundred men. Union forces moved to encircle the gap by September, 1863. Believing their position untenable, the Confederate forces surrendered without firing a shot. The Cumberland Gap was once again in Union hands. In early 1864, General Ulysses S. Grant arrived to inspect the gap and its defenses. Following his inspection, Grant remarked that with two brigades he could have held off Napoleon's entire army. While the gap and the wilderness roads were important strategic positions in the Civil War for both sides, neither was fully able to

*Civil War cannons still stand in Cumberland Gap National Historical Park on the Kentucky-Virginia border.* (AP/Wide World Photos)

use the gateway to full advantage. Confederate plans to invade and occupy Kentucky had failed. Union plans to cross the gap and operate against important railway lines and capture eastern Tennessee were not realized.

### The Cumberland Gap After the Civil War

After the Civil War, the next significant development near the Cumberland Gap was a period of economic boom fueled by much speculation. Alexander Alan Arthur from Scotland became convinced of the economic potential of the immediate area at the base of the gap. He received money from European investors to develop the iron, coal, and timber resources. Over 100,000 acres were purchased, and the town of Middlesborough was laid out by the 1890's. Railways were built that opened the region further to the outside. A railroad tunnel was bored beneath the gap in the late 1880's. The venture was a failure. Iron deposits turned out to be less than expected, and the Panic of 1893 saw the flight of investment out of Middlesborough. On the Tennessee side, a plush seven hundred-room resort hotel known as the Four Seasons was built in 1892. However, occupancy remained low. The hotel was torn down and sold as salvage by 1893. The economic boom was over. Only coal continued to provide a source of revenue.

Noted for it ruggedness, the old road across the gap had fallen into a sad state. Local county leaders from Kentucky, Virginia, and Tennessee made an appeal to the federal government in Washington, D.C., for help. By 1907, engineers from the Federal Office of Public Roads began a survey of the gap. Later that year work began on building a paved road across the Cumberland Gap. The road was completed by October, 1908. By 1926, following a period of road-building activity in Kentucky, "Dixie Highway" (U.S. Federal Highway 25) was paved from the Cumberland Gap to the Ohio River. Highway 25 became the alternate route between Asheville, North Carolina, and Corbin, Kentucky. The arrival of the automobile and paved roads gave rise to tourists traveling between the North and South. The old Wilderness Road had new life as tourist-related business opened along the route. Since that time, Highway 25E (Cumberland Gap Parkway) has been expanded to four lanes on the Kentucky side, with twin tunnels built beneath the gap.

### The Founding of the Park

As roads began to open up the Cumberland Gap, efforts began to gain recognition of the historical importance of the site by making it a national park. An association was created in 1937 to promote the idea. Three years later, President Franklin D. Roosevelt signed a law that provided for the creation of the Cumberland Gap National Historical Park. Some 20,305 acres were purchased for the new park by the state governments of Kentucky, Virginia, and Tennessee. It took fifteen years to purchase all the necessary land for the park. Finally, on September 14, 1955, the Cumberland Gap National Historical Park was established formally. Vice President Richard M. Nixon attended the official dedication ceremonies on July 3, 1959. A visitors' center was also opened a little later. It is estimated that the park attracts one million visitors each year. With the replacement of roads with tunnels on 25E, efforts are under way to restore a portion of the Wilderness Road to its late eighteenth and early nineteenth century character.

### Places to Visit

In the immediate vicinity of the park is the Abraham Lincoln Museum at Lincoln Memorial University. Kentucky's Pine Mountain State Park is also nearby in Pineville, Kentucky. The Wilderness Road State Park in nearby Virginia has beautiful scenery and an 1870's mansion house. The historic town of Cumberland Gap, Tennessee, is located near the park with shops and a small village atmosphere. Bicycles, canoes, and tube rentals are available from private outfitters. The town of Middlesborough is located on the Kentucky side of the gap. Some buildings of historic interest can be viewed, such as St. Mary's Episcopal Church. A P-38 restoration museum at the Middlesborough airport can be visited.

Cumberland Gap National Historical Park is open to visitors year-round. Peak visitation occurs in July and in the fall when the park is filled with the color of autumn leaves. The park has a visitors' center with a bookstore and Appalachian crafts, picnic areas, a museum, campsite, and fifty-five miles of hiking trails. The Pinnacle Overlook, at 2,440 feet, provides a view of three states (Kentucky, Virginia, and Tennessee). Hensley Settlement offers a restored early pioneer community. Visitors can also hike to the 3,500-foot-high White Rocks above the valley. The park can accommodate tents, trailers, and recreational vehicles. However, other accommodations are available in the nearby area.

—*Van Michael Leslie*

### For Further Information:

Burns, David M. *Gateway: Dr. Thomas Walker and the Opening of Kentucky.* Bell County, Ky.: Bell County Historical Society, 2000. Much useful information on the early history of the gap and Walker's role in opening the trail west. With photographs by Adam Jones.

Channing, Steven A. *Kentucky: A History.* New York: W. W. Norton, 1977. A general history written on the occasion of Kentucky's bicentennial.

Harrison, Lowell H. *The Civil War in Kentucky.* Lexington: University of Kentucky Press, 1975. Best single treatment of the war in Kentucky.

Harrison, Lowell H., and James Klotter. *New History of Kentucky.* Lexington: University of Kentucky Press, 1997. Recent study of the history of the state.

Kinkaid, Robert L. *The Wilderness Road.* Middlesborough, Ky.: Bobbs-Merrill, 1973. Offers a popular history of the road with much information on the history of the Cumberland Gap.

# Other Historic Sites

### Beard Boyhood Home

*Location:* Covington, Kenton County
*Relevant issues:* Cultural history, literary history
*Statement of significance:* This was the boyhood home of Daniel C. Beard (1850-1941), American author, illustrator, and key figure in the movement that led to the founding of the Boy Scouts of America in 1910. "Uncle Dan" served as a Na-

tional Scout Commissioner from 1910 until his death.

## Burks' Distillery

*Location:* Loretto, Marion County

*Relevant issues:* Business and industry

*Statement of significance:* The oldest Kentucky distillery site still in use, Burks' Distillery's origins extend back to 1805. Representing the growth of distilling as a major industry in Kentucky after the Pinckney Treaty (1795) gave U.S. citizens the right to unhampered passage down the Mississippi to New Orleans, it also marks the development of bourbon into a distinctive liquor marketed worldwide.

## Churchill Downs

*Location:* Louisville, Jefferson County

*Relevant issues:* Sports

*Statement of significance:* Modeled after Epsom Downs in England, this track was laid out in 1874 by Colonel Meriwether Lewis Clark, a prominent Louisville horse breeder, in an attempt to stimulate the thoroughbred industry. Since 1875, it has been the home of the Kentucky Derby, the internationally renowned race of three-year-old thoroughbred horses, the first phase of the Triple Crown.

## Clay Home

*Location:* Lexington, Fayette County

*Relevant issues:* Political history

*Statement of significance:* From 1811 until 1852, this two-story brick mansion was the residence of Henry Clay (1777-1852), the distinguished pre-Civil War political leader, statesman, and presidential candidate. Clay served as a U.S. senator, Speaker of the House, and secretary of state. The house was reconstructed after Clay's death on the original plan.

## Fort Boonesborough Site

*Location:* Richmond, Madison County

*Relevant issues:* European settlement, Revolutionary War, western expansion

*Statement of significance:* Fort Boonesborough served as the primary defensive sanctuary, communication center, and political seat for hundreds of settlers who entered Kentucky in the 1770's to 1790's. Boonesborough was one of the earliest attempts at European American settlement in Kentucky. The role of this western frontier settlement in the American Revolution was pivotal in securing and holding the trans-Appalachian area for future American settlement. The site of Fort Boonesborough is of national significance with regard to western expansion of the American frontier, for its association with Daniel Boone, and for its research potential to provide information on the lifeways of early settlers of Kentucky and the Appalachian frontier.

## Jacobs Hall, Kentucky School for the Deaf

*Location:* Danville, Boyle County

*Relevant issues:* Education, social reform

*Statement of significance:* Established in 1823, the Kentucky School for the Deaf was the first publicly supported institution for the education of the deaf in the country. Jacobs Hall, a four-story brick structure completed in 1857, is the oldest surviving building at the school.

## Keeneland Race Course

*Location:* Lexington, Fayette County

*Relevant issues:* Sports

*Statement of significance:* Completed in 1936, this is the most conspicuous manifestation of horse raising and racing in Lexington, the heart of Kentucky "bluegrass" country. It is the site of the Phoenix Handicap, the oldest stakes race in the United States, and the Blue Grass Stakes; it is also preeminent for its annual horse sales. The track was begun in 1916 by Jack Keene, an extraordinary figure in American racing.

## Locust Grove

*Location:* Louisville, Jefferson County

*Relevant issues:* Revolutionary War

*Statement of significance:* This two-story brick house was the residence of George Rogers Clark (1752-1818), who lived here with his sister and her husband as a semi-invalid from 1809 until his death in 1818. Clark was the hero of the Western theater of the American Revolution, achieving fame for his conquest of the trans-Ohio frontier at such places as Vincennes, Indiana, and Kaskaskia and Cahokia, Illinois.

## McDowell House

*Location:* Danville, Boyle County

*Relevant issues:* Health and medicine

*Statement of significance:* Here, in the two-story frame house that served as both home and office, Dr. Ephraim McDowell (1771-1830) performed the first successful ovariotomy. In December, 1809, McDowell was called to treat Jane Todd Crawford of Greensberg, Kentucky, whom he diagnosed as suffering from an ovarian tumor. After warning his patient of the risks involved, McDowell asked her to make the journey to his office (Crawford traveled the distance on horseback), where, assisted by his nephew James, McDowell excised the tumor. The complete recovery of his patient did much to dispel the misconception among both physicians and laymen that exposing the inner wall of the abdomen invariably produced fatal infection and eventually led to the development of a new area of surgical practice.

## Middle Creek Battlefield

*Location:* Prestonsburg, Floyd County

*Relevant issues:* Civil War, military history

*Statement of significance:* Control of Kentucky, the ninth most populous state at the time of the Civil War, was very important to President Abraham Lincoln, who had been born there and appreciated its strategic value. The eastern Kentucky campaign that resulted in this battle was part of the overall Union strategy to keep Kentucky within the fold. At the Battle of Middle Creek (January 10, 1862), Union forces led by Colonel James A. Garfield met and defeated Rebel forces under the command of Brigadier General Humphrey Marshall, thus securing eastern Tennessee. The battle was an important early victory for the Union and brought hope to a disheartened Northern population.

## Perryville Battlefield

*Location:* Perryville, Boyle County

*Relevant issues:* Civil War, military history

*Statement of significance:* This is the site of the battle in October, 1862, which climaxed the major Confederate invasion of Kentucky and, in conjunction with the Battles of Antietam, Iuka, Corinth, and Newtonia, broke the back of a Confederate offensive along a one thousand-mile front.

## Pine Mountain Settlement School

*Location:* Bledsoe, Harlan County

*Relevant issues:* Cultural history, education, women's history

*Statement of significance:* The construction of Big Log House in 1913, the first building of the Pine Mountain Settlement School, launched one of the most important efforts to adopt the urban settlement house to a rural community. Katherine Pettit and Ethel de Long, the founders of this school, were moved by the limitations of the one-room schools, the primitive dwellings, and the harsh lives of women living in the region. While offering instruction in traditional subjects to resident students, the school included such classes as furniture making, home nursing, weaving, and stockraising in the curriculum; also, the preservation of ballads, folk songs, and dances served to instill a knowledge and appreciation of mountain heritage.

## Shakertown at Pleasant Hill Historic District

*Location:* Shakertown and vicinity, Mercer County

*Relevant issues:* Religion

*Statement of significance:* The Shakertown at Pleasant Hill, among the most successful of nineteenth century religious communitarian settlements, was founded in 1805. The community plan was laid out in 1808, and from 1809 to 1860 the village grew to its maximum size and prosperity. By 1820, some five hundred Shakers lived here on three thousand acres of land. The community was dissolved in 1910.

## Taylor House

*Location:* Louisville, Jefferson County

*Relevant issues:* Political history

*Statement of significance:* From about 1790 to 1808, this two-and-a-half-story brick house was Zachary Taylor's boyhood home, as well as the scene of his marriage in 1810. Taylor (1784-1850) returned here often during his military career and briefly again before his short term as the twelfth president of the United States (1849-1850).

## Wendover

*Location:* Hyden, Leslie County

*Relevant issues:* Health and medicine

*Statement of significance:* Established in 1925 by Mary

Breckinridge (1881?-1965), this marked the first effort to professionalize midwifery in the United States. Up until the 1930's, an American woman was more likely to die in childbirth than from any other disease except tuberculosis; the mortality rate was especially high in rural areas. Breckinridge and her nurses provided quality prenatal and maternity care. Their skill and devotion to the cause of improving the health of mountain people has had a great impact in a formerly isolated and rural area.

## Young Birthplace and Boyhood Home
*Location:* Lincoln Ridge, Shelby County

*Relevant issues:* African American history, social reform

*Statement of significance:* This simple two-story frame house, on the campus of the school where his father served on the faculty, was the birthplace and boyhood home of Whitney Moore Young, Jr. (1921-1971), civil rights spokesman, adviser to three presidents, and influential ambassador to major corporate leaders for the cause of racial equality. Young, the executive director of the National Urban League from 1961 to 1971, drew unprecedented support for the league's social and economic programs, working for an equality beyond civil rights causes.

# Louisiana

*The State Capitol Building in Baton Rouge.* (Louisiana Office of Tourism)

# History of Louisiana

Much of Louisiana lies in the Mississippi Alluvial Plain, flat lands that stretch from each side of the Mississippi River. As the river moves south to the Gulf of Mexico, the elevation of the land becomes progressively lower, and most of it is damp and swampy. Far western and northwestern Louisiana is part of the West Gulf Coastal Plain. In the northern area of this region, the land is hilly, and it becomes prairie further south. On the eastern side, near Mississippi, lies the East Gulf Coastal Plain, which is similar to the territory in the west. These three regions correspond roughly to the historical and cultural divisions of Louisiana. The swampy south central and southwestern areas have corresponded to French Roman Catholic Louisiana. The western region and the eastern region have been home to mostly Protestant, English-speaking people.

### Early History
During prehistoric times, Louisiana was populated by people who lived in highly organized farming societies. These societies are often known as the Mound Builders, after the great ceremonial earth mounds they constructed. The Mound Builders may be divided into the people of the Hopewell culture, who flourished from about the first century until about 800 C.E., and the people of the Mississippian culture, who were present from about 800 C.E. until about 1500.

When the Europeans arrived, Louisiana was inhabited by Native Americans of three language groups. Those of the Caddoan language group lived in the northwestern area. Those who spoke Muskogean languages lived in east central Louisiana near the Mississippi River. Speakers of the Tunican languages generally lived near the coast of the Gulf of Mexico. Louisiana's Native American population declined as a result of warfare, diseases introduced by the Europeans, and intermarriages with Americans of European and African descent. Some, such as the majority of the Choctaw nation, were forced westward into Indian Territory in modern Oklahoma by the U.S. government in the 1830's. Contemporary Louisiana is home to communities of the Chitimacha, Houma, Tunica-Biloxi, Coushatta, and Choctaw.

### European Exploration and Colonization
The Spanish and the French were the first Europeans to explore the territory of the lower Mississippi River. In 1542 a Spanish expedition led by Hernando de Soto crossed through Louisiana. At the end of the 1600's, the French explorer René-Robert Cavelier, Sieur de La Salle, journeyed down the Mississippi River to its mouth and claimed all of the land drained by the Mississippi in the name of France. La Salle named this huge expanse of territory Louisiana, in honor of King Louis XIV of France.

In 1718 the French explorer Jean Baptiste Le Moyne, Sieur de Bienville, founded a settlement at a strategic location near the mouth of the Mississippi on the shores of the lake that the French had named Lake Pontchartrain. Bienville named his settlement Nouvelle-Orléans (New Orleans) in honor of the regent of France, the duke of Orleans. In 1722 New Orleans would become the capital of Louisiana.

The Acadians, or Cajuns, one of Louisiana's best-known population groups, arrived in the region between 1763 and 1788. These were French-speaking people from the former French colony of Acadia in Canada expelled by British troops in the French and Indian Wars (1754-1763). The Acadians settled in the swampy areas of southwestern Louisiana and on the Mississippi just north of New Orleans. Isolation enabled them to keep the French language. Although the use of French largely disappeared in other parts of Louisiana after World War I, it would continue to be spoken in the Acadian region.

The British conquest of Canada also greatly reduced the strategic value of Louisiana for France. In order to entice the Spanish into entering the war against Britain, France transferred ownership of Louisiana to Spain in 1762. The following year, France and Spain lost the war. The Louisiana territories east of the Mississippi River became the property of Britain, and Spain was allowed to keep

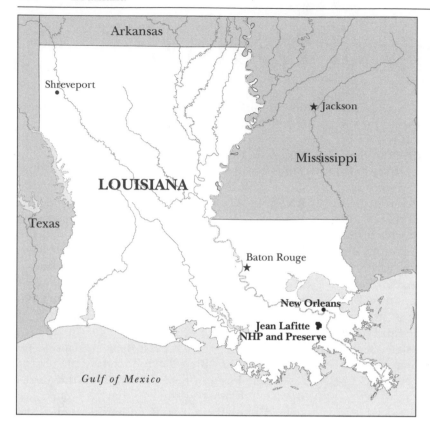

1812 the Territory of Orleans entered the United States as the state of Louisiana.

English-speaking settlers from other areas of the United States moved into Louisiana in large numbers. Most white Louisianians, both French-speaking and English-speaking, were small farmers. The most prosperous crops, however, were cotton and sugarcane. Both of these were plantation crops, which required intensive labor. As a result, slavery became a prominent part of the economic and social life of the state, especially in the southwestern bayou country, where the sugarcane flourished. Slave markets also became important to the economy of New Orleans.

One of the unique racial characteristics of Louisiana was the existence of a large group of free people of mixed race, known as the *gens de couleur libres*, or free people of color. Free people of color were sometimes quite prosperous and even owned slaves. According to historian John Hope Franklin, 3,000 of the 10,689 free people of color in New Orleans were slaveowners.

the lands west of the Mississippi, including New Orleans. Many of the French Louisianians had been born in America—Creoles—but they retained a devotion to France. The French Creoles revolted against Spanish rule, but Spanish troops quickly put down the rebellion. Spain, under the influence of French ruler Napoleon Bonaparte, returned the Louisiana territories to France in 1800. Bonaparte then sold the colony to the United States in 1803 in order to fund his own wars.

### The American Period

The year after the United States purchased the huge Louisiana Territory, which extended the length of the Mississippi River, the United States split the region into the Territory of Louisiana and the Territory of Orleans. The Territory of Orleans became modern Louisiana. In 1810 American settlers in Spanish West Florida declared their independence from Spain and asked to join the United States. The American governor of Louisiana, William C. C. Claiborne, incorporated West Florida, as far as the Pearl River, into Orleans Territory. In

### Civil War and Reconstruction

By the 1850's, the southern states, which were dependent on agriculture and slavery, were losing control of the U.S. Congress and presidency to the industrialized North. Many southerners believed that the southern way of life, including the institution of slavery, could only be preserved by seceding from the United States. In 1861, after the election of President Abraham Lincoln, southern states began declaring their independence. Louisiana withdrew from the Union on April 12, 1861. One year later, though, the U.S. Navy captured New Orleans and soon afterward captured Baton Rouge.

Louisiana still had a large number of people of mixed race after the Civil War, and many of them were well educated. They made up the core of Louisiana's black political leadership during Reconstruction (1866-1877), when about one-third of the state's governmental leaders were black. In 1872 Louisiana's P. B. S. Pinchback became the first black governor in the United States.

After the withdrawal of Union troops, whites in the state reacted against Reconstruction violently. Taking control of the government, whites systematically excluded African Americans from many areas of public life. Legal segregation and the prevention of voting and political organization by African Americans continued until the 1960's, when Louisiana became a focal point of the Civil Rights movement.

### The Legacy of Huey Long

Louisiana continued to be a rural and agricultural state after the Civil War. During the 1920's, prices of agricultural goods, especially cotton, dropped. The charismatic politician Huey Long rose to power by championing the interests of workers and small farmers. One of Long's chief targets was Standard Oil Company, which had begun operating in Louisiana after the discovery of oil and gas deposits in the early twentieth century. Brilliant and ruthless, Long became governor in 1928. In 1930 he was elected U.S. senator, but he waited until 1932 to take his seat in the Senate, placing a handpicked successor in the governor's position.

By the time Long was assassinated in 1935, he had almost total control over the Louisiana government. He helped to improve the lives of many Louisianians, but he also raised the level of corruption in state government. The Long political machine continued to operate under Huey's brother Earl Long through the 1950's, and the good and bad legacies of Huey Long would long remain with Louisiana politics.

### Social and Economic Change

Although historically Louisiana has been a rural and agricultural state, the period after World War II saw substantial movement to cities. By 1990, 68 percent of Louisiana's people lived in urban areas. Sugarcane and rice farming continued to be economically important, but these agricultural activities became heavily mechanized and use only a small amount of human labor, mostly at planting and harvest times. Oil mining became increasingly important in the late twentieth century, and among the states Louisiana is second only to Texas in oil production.

Louisiana has one of the largest African American populations in the United States. About one out of every three Louisianians was African American in 1997. Despite the state's history of slavery and racial segregation, black Louisianians have made substantial progress toward political equality. During the 1990's, the state legislature was 16 percent black, and by 1992 there were two black Louisianians in the U.S. House of Representatives. One of these representatives, Cleo Fields, made it into the runoffs for governor in 1996. Despite these advances, incomes and living conditions of African Americans in Louisiana lagged far behind those of whites. It also appeared that racism was still prevalent. David Duke, a former leader of the Ku Klux Klan, won a majority of white votes in the 1991 election for governor. Duke was defeated only because black voters turned out in record numbers.

—*Carl L. Bankston III*

# The French Quarter, New Orleans

**Date:** New Orleans founded in 1718

**Relevant issues:** Art and architecture, cultural history, European settlement, western expansion

**Significance:** A sixty-six-square-block area of the city of New Orleans, comprising both residential and commercial buildings that are among the oldest continuously occupied structures in the United States, many of them excellent examples of French and Spanish provincial and colonial architecture. The French Quarter is the home of many historic sites and landmarks, including the St. Louis Cathedral, the Cabildo and Presbytere, Jackson Square, the French Market, the former U.S. Mint, and the Ursuline Convent.

**Location:** Rampart Street (northwest boundary) to the Mississippi River (southeast boundary); Canal Street (southwest boundary); to Esplanade Avenue (northeast boundary); in New Orleans, Louisiana, eighty miles northwest of the mouth of the Mississippi River

**Site Office:**
New Orleans Metropolitan Convention and Visitors Bureau
1520 Sugar Bowl Drive
New Orleans, LA 70112
ph.: (800) 672-6124; (504) 566-5003
Web site: www.nawlins.com

The French Quarter of New Orleans, Louisiana, is like no other place in the United States. New Orleans is known as the "city that care forgot"; the quarter is very much a place that time forgot. Also known as the Vieux Carré (old square), the quarter is rich in historic structures, many of which are at least one hundred fifty years old and some of which are nearly two hundred years old. The buildings' age and their styles—primarily developed by the early French and Spanish colonists—give the quarter a European atmosphere. Added to that is the influence of other cultures, particularly that of African Americans, making the quarter a truly cosmopolitan area, a center of historical and architectural treasures, unusual shops, fine restaurants, great music, and an ongoing series of festivals, the most famous of which is Mardi Gras.

### Early History
In the late 1600's, French King Louis XIV was looking for a way to consolidate his gains in North America and to flank the English colonies on the eastern seaboard and limit their ability to expand westward. French settlers and cultures already were well established in eastern Canada. The king's representatives made their way westward through the Great Lakes and down the Mississippi River. In 1682 René-Robert Cavelier, Sieur de La Salle, led an expedition in search of the river's mouth. What he found was a constantly expanding and moving delta, with the river splitting into dozens of channels and changing its course through a seemingly endless expanse of semisubmerged canebrakes and muck. La Salle placed a plaque near the mouth of the river, claiming the land for France and naming it Louisiane, in honor of the king. Then La Salle and his party sailed back to France.

At Versailles La Salle had no trouble convincing the king and his court that the territory was valuable. They were convinced that it would expand French influence in the New World and serve as a buffer against the colonies of other European empires. They also probably did not picture the land very clearly; they likely envisioned a clear river harbor like those in France, not an insect-infested swampland. Even if they had had an accurate idea of the territory, however, they still may have found it desirable: They believed that if France did not claim it, a rival power would.

The king sent La Salle back to the area, but with the highly inaccurate maps that existed, La Salle's party landed several hundred miles to the west of the mouth of the river. When La Salle attempted to go overland to find the river, he was killed by his own men.

### First Settlements
It was not until 1699 that a young Quebecois, Pierre Le Moyne, Sieur d'Iberville, led the next party down the river. His mission was to build a small fort, which he eventually did, near the site of present-day Biloxi, Mississippi. About one hundred men were garrisoned at the outpost. Iberville's twenty-one-year-old brother, Jean Baptiste Le Moyne, Sieur de Bienville, became commander of the fort the next year. Iberville had left the fort and traveled to Havana, where he died of yellow fever in 1706. Bienville, who was extremely resilient, managed to avoid the disease that was to become the scourge of the future city of New Orleans and stayed to make his mark on the history of the city.

After a short period, the fort was moved to a site near what is now Mobile, Alabama. Although the French government sent livestock, tools, and young women, and although a few French Canadians arrived by river, the colony struggled. By this time France was at war with England, and the country's treasury was too strained to aid the settlers.

French influence in the area was bolstered, oddly enough, by a Scottish gambler named John Law. Law arrived in Paris in the first years of the eighteenth century. He had a knack for winning money and for public relations. In 1717 he began to sell stock in a company that he claimed would exploit the riches of the territory of Louisiana. His Compagnie d'Occident (Company of the West, later Company of Indies) attracted investors from all over France. After three years, it became apparent that Louisiana offered few riches, at least not in the short term. The investors lost their capital, and Law had to flee France. This incident became known as the Mississippi Bubble. By then, however, the infrastructure of the tiny settlement of New Orleans was in place.

There were no compelling reasons for French colonists to go to Louisiana. Unlike their colonial competitors, the English, the French did not allow religious dissenters to settle in their colonies. The French colonies did not hold veins of gold and silver, as did the land of their Spanish competitors, nor was France overcrowded like Holland. The new colony had to be held, however, so the king's agents swept the streets of the homeless, the diseased, and unguarded children and shipped them to the muddy wilderness.

### Selection of New Orleans's Site

In 1718, Bienville, by order of the Company of the Indies, chose a permanent site for the struggling colony. The prospects were not good, as nearly all the land along the lower Mississippi was below sea level, but he chose a crescent-shaped bend where an ancient Indian portage led to a four-mile-long bayou, Bayou St. John, which flowed into Lake Pontchartrain. The site also provided a point from which to monitor the river traffic. Bienville's party of slaves, convict laborers, and a few trained carpenters set about clearing the canebrakes and cypress trees. To this day, when deep excavations are made in the French Quarter, the huge trunks of those cypresses cleared by Bienville's men are found.

By this time, Louis XIV was dead, and the new king was his great-grandson, the child-king Louis XV. The young king's regent was Philippe, the duke of Orleans. The settlement was named La Nouvelle Orleans in his honor.

### Laying out of New Orleans

At the same time, the French engineer-in-chief, Le Blond de la Tour, designed the street plan in a classic grid style and directed his assistant, Adrien de Pauger, to start laying out the streets. The streets were given names associated with the royal fam-

*A street in the French Quarter, with St. Louis Cathedral at the end.* (American Stock Photography)

ily—Bourbon, Royal, St. Louis, Burgundy, Toulouse, and Dumaine. The quarter's basic street plan has not changed since then.

The first buildings were log houses, which were either swallowed by mud or blown over by the frequent hurricanes. These problems led to the development of an architectural style in which a simple frame cottage was raised above the ground on brick pilings. The river frequently overflowed its banks, so the settlers began building levees.

By the 1720's New Orleans had one hundred bark huts, a small church, warehouses, and a house for Bienville. The original St. Louis Cathedral was destroyed by a hurricane in 1722 and rebuilt shortly thereafter. The second cathedral was destroyed by fire in 1788; its successor was completed in 1794. That structure is still standing, although it underwent numerous alterations in 1849-1850, and has been declared a minor basilica by the Vatican. Mass is still spoken in Latin there on special occasions, and the colorful frescoes on the interior tell the story of French King Louis IX, who was canonized as St. Louis. The cathedral is the centerpiece of the French Quarter and probably the most photographed structure in the city.

## French Administration

In the 1730's the French government took over management of the settlement from the Company of the Indies. New Orleans was now attracting different types of settlers. Together the government and the company had convinced a few rich French men and women to go to the city, and Catholic religious orders sent contingents there. The appearance of New Orleans evolved as well. Builders began using a construction method that combined cypress timber, stone, and mud adobe. This type of construction can be seen today in structures like Jean Lafitte's blacksmith shop. The government also granted more and more planters property along the river both above and below New Orleans. Planters believed that whites could not survive hard physical labor in a hot, humid climate, so they began bringing in black slaves from Africa.

By the 1750's some New Orleans residents were living in luxury, but most of the settlement was still struggling. In 1762 France rid itself of the troubled settlement; Louis XV ceded New Orleans to his first cousin, King Charles III of Spain, in a secret treaty. News of the transfer did not reach New Orleans for four years. When the Spanish colonial governor, Don Antonio d'Ulloa, arrived in 1766, some of the French residents took up arms in rebellion. The rebellion was quashed by the arrival of Spanish troops under the command of Don Alexander O'Reilly.

## Spanish Influences

Though they ruled the French Quarter for only three decades, the Spanish had a great effect on the area's architecture, if not its culture. As the older French buildings deteriorated, they were replaced by structures in the Spanish tradition, with arched windows and doorways, tile roofs, and courtyards. The Spanish also made lavish use of wrought-iron grillwork, still visible on many of the galleries, balconies, archways, and door handles of the French Quarter. The Spanish also painted many of their buildings in pastel colors and often included a service floor between the first and second stories of their structures.

Spanish rule was authoritarian, and the colony was not officially allowed to trade with any country but Spain. Colonial officials were easily corrupted, however, and soon English ships plied the river and anchored opposite the city. Their cargoes of fancy foods, luxury dry goods, and other delicacies were coveted by the Spaniards. When Spain took the side of the American colonists during the American Revolution, a few Americans were granted trading privileges. It was the beginning of a rich history of trade, illegal and legal, which fueled the growth of the city, developed its cosmopolitan atmosphere, and made it one of the largest ports in the United States.

In March, 1788, on Good Friday, candles left unattended started a fire that raged through the French Quarter, destroying most of its buildings, including the second St. Louis Cathedral. Another fire, six years later, again nearly wiped out the city. There was now very little left of the French colony, and the citizens struggled to rebuild the quarter, with the cathedral as the center. The Cabildo, built in 1795 with financing by prominent businessman Don Andres Almonester y Roxas on the upriver side of the church, was the capital house for the Spanish colonial governing council. Almonester also funded the reconstruction of the cathedral.

## American Intrusion

By the end of the eighteenth century, many Americans, including rough frontiersmen from the interior and merchants in sailing ships, were coming to the city, bringing goods from the fledgling United States, in exchange for much-needed hard currency. The Spanish and French used the American goods to build docks, sidewalks, and houses.

In 1800, Napoleon Bonaparte negotiated the return of the Louisiana Territory to France. Thomas Jefferson, elected U.S. president that year, was distressed by the idea of Napoleon controlling so much territory in North America, so Jefferson sent emissaries to buy at least a portion of it for the United States. They ended up buying the entire territory, for fifteen million dollars, in 1803. New Orleans was incorporated as a city in 1805, and Louisiana became a state in 1812.

The quarter's French and Spanish residents, known as Creoles, somewhat resented the Americans. Yet the quarter and the rest of New Orleans thrived under U.S. ownership, and the Americans could not help but be charmed by the city, with its stately cathedral and government buildings as well as European-style homes, the Ursuline Convent, and a variety of shops, docks, and warehouses. Trade flourished in cotton, lumber, liquor, finished goods, and slaves. The once-quiet levee became a beehive of commerce; steamboats plied the river, bringing passengers and merchandise from faraway places such as St. Louis and Ohio; and the population grew. The French Market, originally built by the Spanish in 1791, along what is now Decatur Street next to the levee, became an open-air center of commerce where vegetables, arms, and people could be bought and sold only blocks from the cathedral. The city was growing, but it was not out of danger.

### The Battle of New Orleans

In January, 1815, after a treaty had already been signed ending the War of 1812, a fleet of British warships anchored in the river downstream from the city, which the British intended to seize. Andrew Jackson had been placed in command of a small garrison based in old Spanish barracks in the French Quarter. Jackson had made an uneasy alliance with the French pirate Jean Lafitte, who had masqueraded as a legitimate businessman with a blacksmith shop at Bourbon and St. Philip Streets for years, and the pirate brought cannon from his ships to the battlefield. It was probably the good defensive position of Jackson's troops and the withering fire from Lafitte's cannon that saved the quarter from yet another change in ownership.

### Under American Rule

With the city secure, and with the influx of American spirit, capital, and entrepreneurship, the French Quarter soon became a center of growth. Jackson's leadership was commemorated in an equestrian statue, which became the centerpiece of Jackson Square, in front of the cathedral.

The city grew beyond the French Quarter and became a commercial center, with many banks and mercantile exchanges being established. Yet the quarter remained the center of commercial activity throughout the 1830's, the golden age of building in New Orleans. Sites outside the quarter were more suitable for large businesses, and through the next decades, other portions of New Orleans developed commercially while the quarter took on a more residential character. It was during this period that the Pontalba Buildings, commissioned by Micaela Almonester de Pontalba, daughter of Don Andres Almonester y Roxas, were completed. They were built on the north and south sides of what would become Jackson Square, facing perpendicular to the cathedral. They were occupied in 1850 with shops and offices on the ground floors and luxury apartments on the second and third stories.

With the outbreak of the U.S. Civil War, Louisiana joined the Confederacy. Union troops captured New Orleans, quickly and bloodlessly, early in 1862, and occupied it for the remainder of the war. Union general Benjamin F. Butler was appointed military governor of New Orleans, and his autocratic rule made him unpopular with citizens in the French Quarter as well as other parts of the city. The residents of New Orleans nicknamed him "the beast." One of the marks he left on the quarter was the statement he ordered carved into the base of the Andrew Jackson statue in Jackson Square: "The union must and shall be preserved."

### Post-Civil War Recovery

Economic recovery after the war was slow, but the French Quarter retained its unique character and remained a center of entertainment, as it had been before the war. The quarter's public ballrooms were popular places for white men to meet and flirt with women of color, often of mixed Creole and African descent, and for socializing in general. The city's European heritage also led to interest in classical theater and music. The Grand Opera House, built in 1859 at Bourbon and Toulouse Streets, was the site of many first-rate performances, but like many entertainment houses it was often closed in the summer because of the heat. It burned in 1909, and many theaters were susceptible to the same fate. The city's real reputation in the area of entertainment was spawned outdoors. Blacks, Creoles, and others would congregate in the public squares for music, gambling, and other diversions.

## New Orleans Jazz

New Orleans's most famous product, jazz, developed throughout the city, but with important contributions from the French Quarter. River steamboats, gambling houses, bars, and brothels in the quarter were perfect venues for the musical form, named with a word derived from the West Indian Mandingo tribe's word jasi, meaning "to act out of the ordinary." Many jazz progenitors worked in Storyville, the city's red-light district, just to the north of the French Quarter, but the music they played came from the spirited outdoor parties of the quarter. The quarter became a place where musicians who played the music could work steadily, a tradition that persists today. Among the many testaments to the importance of jazz in New Orleans and the French Quarter are the numerous music clubs along Bourbon Street in the quarter, the city's annual Jazz and Heritage Festival, and the park named for great jazzman Louis Armstrong, along Rampart Street. Armstrong was born in New Orleans in 1900.

Visitors to the French Quarter today will find a wealth of historic sites. St. Louis Cathedral, particularly beautiful at night, is still the centerpiece of the area, and no building in the quarter rises higher than the cathedral's central spire. The cathedral is flanked by the Cabildo, site of the transfer of Louisiana to the United States after the Louisiana Purchase, and the Presbytere, built to house clergy but never used for that purpose; it was used as a courthouse instead. The Cabildo and Presbytere are both part of the the Louisiana State Museum. In front of the cathedral at Jackson Square, Andrew Jackson, mounted on his horse, tips his hat to passersby. The Pontalba Buildings still flank the square. Other attractions around the quarter include the Old U.S. Mint, the Ursuline Convent, the French Market, and numerous historic homes, such as the Beauregard-Keyes House, home in the nineteenth century to Confederate general Pierre G. T. Beauregard and in the twentieth century to novelist Frances Parkinson Keyes. Other prominent writers, such as playwright Tennessee Williams, have lived in the quarter as well.

The French Quarter in the late twentieth century is a monument to times past. It is a testament to human ingenuity in overcoming hostile land, disease, and natural disasters with grace, elegance, and respect for the past.

It is the main magnet for tourism, which has become the second largest industry in New Orleans, next to the port, and still exemplifies openness, ease of living, and a gracious European style not available in other U.S. cities. Its survival against the odds has made it the center of the "city that care forgot."

—*Thomas B. Ford*

### For Further Information:

Cable, Mary. *Lost New Orleans.* Boston: Houghton Mifflin, 1980. An excellent examination of New Orleans and its origins. Although it mentions many buildings and places that are no longer in existence, it is a fine description of the early history of the city.

Lynn, Stuart M. *New Orleans.* New York: American Legacy Press, 1977. A pictorial work, with extensive captioning, that gives a sense of the feeling and look of the French Quarter.

Villiers du Terrage, Marc de. *A History of the Foundation of New Orleans, 1712-1722.* Ville Platte, La.: Provincial Press, 1999. Ths work is reprinted from the *Louisiana Historical Quarterly* 3, no. 2 (April, 1920).

# Jean Lafitte National Historical Park and Preserve

**Date:** Established in 1978

**Relevant issues:** African American history, American Indian history, art and architecture, Civil War, cultural history, European settlement, military history, western expansion

**Significance:** The park preserves significant examples of the natural and cultural resources of Louisiana's Mississippi Delta region and teaches visitors the influence of environment and history on a unique region and its equally unique blend of cultures.

**Location:** In southern Louisiana, the park has seven physically separate sites: the Acadian Cultural Center in Lafayette, the Prairie Acadian Cultural Center in Eunice, and the Wetlands Acadian Cultural Center in Thibodaux interpreting the Acadian cultures of the area; the Chitimacha Reservation and Museum near

Charenton in the Atchafalaya basin paying tribute to the Chitimacha tribe that thrived in the region long before the Europeans arrived; the Barataria Preserve in Marrero on the west bank of the Mississippi capturing the natural and cultural history of the uplands, swamps, and marshlands of the region; the Chalmette Battlefield and National Cemetery, six miles southeast of New Orleans, the site of the 1815 Battle of New Orleans and the final resting place for American soldiers; and the French Market of the historic French Quarter of New Orleans providing an overview of that city's history and of the Mississippi Delta region's diverse cultures.

**Site Office:**

Jean Lafitte National Historical Park and Preserve Headquarters
365 Canal Street
Suite 2400
New Orleans, LA 70130-1142
ph.: (504) 589-3882, ext. 100 or 102
fax: (504) 589-3851
Web site: www.nps.gov/jela/
e-mail: JELA_Superintendent@nps.gov

The importance of the sites preserved or paid tribute to in the Jean Lafitte National Historical Park and Preserve (named for the pirate who was so instrumental in this region's history) extends back to the pre-European days of the Chitimacha; to the period of the French and Spanish in southern Louisiana; to the rise of the slave trade; to New Orleans as a naval, military, and market center; to the Louisiana Purchase, the War of 1812, the Civil War, and the long ecological battle to preserve the unique flora, fauna, and terrain of the Louisiana swamps and marshlands from the inroads of the Gulf of Mexico. These sites also celebrate the Acadian, Cajun, Native American, and African American cultures.

### Acadian Culture

When immigrants from western France were forced from Acadie (now Nova Scotia, Canada) during "The Grand Derangement" (1765 to 1785), some fled to south Louisiana and settled in the rural Mississippi Delta region. By the turn of the nineteenth century, over three thousand Acadians had settled in Louisiana. Three of the Jean Lafitte Park Centers commemorate this Acadian culture. The Acadian Cultural Center in Lafayette demonstrates Acadian cultural resources and provides ways to interact with and understand traditional and contemporary Acadian culture, including the forty-minute film *The Cajun Way: Echoes of Acadia*. This facility's extensive exhibits and artifacts tell the story of today's Cajuns—their origins and history, language, music, architecture, and culture—through their recreational and farm implements, clothing, furnishings, religious items, and cuisine.

In turn, the exhibits of the Wetlands Acadian Cultural Center, along Bayou Lafourche near Thibodaux, the heart of this wetlands area, bring to life the rich combinations of cultures found in the swamps, marshes, and coastal waters of southeastern Louisiana and the realities of water-based lifeways (fishing, hunting, and trapping). This center features talks about the region, music programs (including Cajun jam sessions), and a variety of videos and films about the history, culture, ecology, and wildlife (both human and animal). The center has an art gallery displaying local arts and crafts, a two hundred-seat theater for productions by the Thibodaux Playhouse and for other programs about Acadian culture, and a craft room for demonstrating boat building, duck carving, net making, and other local crafts.

When the Acadians expanded westward beyond the Atchafalaya basin onto the prairies of southwest Louisiana, they evolved a new lifestyle suited to cattle raising and rice farming. The Prairie Acadian Cultural Center employs live demonstrations, video and film presentations, exhibits, and artifacts to capture how the lush grasslands transformed the Acadian heritage. Workshops demonstrate local crafts, spinning and weaving, and the musical techniques of the region, including musical instrument making, and even an Acadian kitchen where local food specialties are prepared. The center also features *The Rendezvous des Cajuns*, a two-hour live Saturday night radio broadcast of Cajun and zydeco music, stories, anecdotes, recipes, and local humor, in Cajun French, performed at the restored fifty-year-old Liberty Theatre in downtown Eunice.

### Chitimacha Culture

The tiny Chitimacha Reservation, bounded by cane fields and Atchafalaya basin swampland and dominated by a casino, boasts an interpretive cen-

*Visitors learn about Jean Lafitte National Park.* (Louisiana Office of Tourism)

ter and two craft shops with traditional handiwork—highly prized basketwork, tribal weapons, pipes, beads, and jewelry.

**Barataria Preserve**
Approximately twenty thousand acres of hardwood forest, cypress swamp, and freshwater marsh, with eight miles of hard-surfaced hiking trails (including 2.5 miles of boardwalk) and over twenty miles of waterways, nine miles of which is accessible only by canoe, constitute the Barataria Preserve, subtropical delta land in constant flux. Plants include live oaks and other hardwoods on the elevated natural levee, forest palmettos on the levee backslope, giant blue iris and bald cypress amid the standing water of the lowest portion of the levee, and marsh grasses in the flat eastern expanses.

The visitors' center highlights Barataria's natural history, ecosystems, culture, and ways of life with dioramas, photographs, maps, wildlife displays, and a twenty-five-minute film, *Jambalaya: A Delta Almanac*. Its raised walkways make accessible a representative section of the delta's environment—natural levee forests, bayous, swamps, and marshes filled with nutria, alligators, fox, armadillos, swamp rabbits and swamp deer, owls, hawks, eagles, herons, egrets, migratory birds, and a wide variety of frogs, turtles, snakes, lizards, and seasonal insects such as spectacular butterflies and orb-weaving spiders.

Though teeming with wildlife, this seeming wilderness contains signs of prehistoric human settlement (two thousand-year-old Native American village sites along the bayous), colonial farming (the 1779 Spanish government's Isleño settlements—Canary Islanders—along the banks of Bayou des Families), plantation agriculture (sugarcane), logging (cypress), commercial trapping, fishing, hunting (still ongoing—by permit—as the numerous "camps" or hunting cabins testify), and oil and gas exploration (in the 1930's); down one canal the city of New Orleans is visible in the distance. Guided nature walks and canoe treks (some by moonlight) are available.

## Chalmette Battlefield

The Chalmette Battlefield and National Cemetery is on the St. Bernard Highway in Chalmette, on the east bank of the Mississippi River. It marks the site of Andrew Jackson's surprising victory in the Battle of New Orleans on January 8, 1815—the last battle in the War of 1812 and the last battle ever fought between England and the United States. This decisive victory over the British was the greatest American land victory of the War of 1812.

The victory was unanticipated because the British had already burned the White House and Capitol in Washington, D.C., and subsequently sent ten thousand battle-tested soldiers into the fray under thirty-six-year-old British major general Sir Edward M. Pakenham. Pakenham had orders to capture New Orleans and control the mouth of the Mississippi River in order to seriously hamper the American economy and westward expansion. The Americans had only five thousand militia and volunteer soldiers (including a contingent of pirate Jean Lafitte's Baratarians), but forty-seven-year-old Major General Andrew Jackson took the battle to the enemy. On December 23, with Pakenham's troops within nine miles of the city, Jackson led a fierce night attack that caught the British off guard. Cherokees fought alongside American troops against their traditional enemies, the Creeks, who were British allies. The Americans withdrew behind a canal bank on a narrow strip of dry land between the Mississippi River and an impassable cypress swamp. In this advantageous position, with stubbled sugarcane fields providing devastatingly open fields of fire, Jackson's men stood behind a shoulder-high mud rampart on the canal bank thick enough to withstand cannon shot. When they could not dislodge the American troops, the British were forced to attack head-on into withering fire.

The major fighting was over in thirty minutes and the entire Battle of New Orleans in less than two hours; two thousand British and thirteen Americans were killed. This victory not only enhanced American patriotism and pride but also preserved America's claim to the Louisiana Purchase, a claim confirmed by immediate migration and settlement along the Mississippi River. The victory made Jackson a national hero and paved the way for his election as president.

Modern facilities include a tour road, a monument, a visitors' center, the Malus-Beauregard House (c. 1833), and the adjacent national cemetery. The 1.5-mile tour of the battlefield begins at the visitors' center with exhibits and an audiovisual program explaining the battle's significance and continues with six stops at important features of the battlefield, including a thirty-two-pounder naval gun put into play by the Battalion of Louisiana Free Men of Color. The Chalmette Monument, laid out on the twenty-fifth anniversary of the battle, was not completed until 1908. The Malus-Beauregard House, a country residence built eighteen years after the battle, is a fine example of French-Louisiana architecture. The Chalmette National Cemetery was established in May, 1864, as a burial ground for Union soldiers who died in Louisiana during the Civil War, but it later served as a burial site for veterans of the Spanish-American War, World Wars I and II, and the Vietnam War.

The park features regular talks about the Battle of New Orleans and, on the second Saturday of each month, living history demonstrations; it commemorates the Battle of New Orleans during the second weekend of January, with British and American living history encampments set up on the battlefield.

## The French Quarter

The exhibits, performances, demonstrations, and walking tours of the French Quarter Visitors' Center provide a political and cultural historical overview of Louisiana's Mississippi Delta region and of the French Quarter or Vieux Carré (old square) of New Orleans. Now a National Historic District, the quarter was established shortly after the French founded New Orleans in 1718. The regular walking tours explore delta cultures, the architecture of the garden district and the French Quarter, and the music and history of New Orleans (from its beginnings as a small French outpost in an unhealthy wilderness area to today's ethnic and cultural diversity).

## Amtrak Educational Programs

The National Park Service, Jean Lafitte National Historical Park and Preserve, National Park Foundation, and Eastern National combined with Amtrak (National Railroad Passenger Corporation) to provide on-board educational programs for passengers traveling on trains through the southeastern United States. The Trails and Rails Program is offered during the summer months on board the *Sunset Limited* between New Orleans and Houston, Texas, the *City of New Orleans* between New Orleans and Jackson, Mississippi, and the *Crescent* between New Orleans and Atlanta. National Park Service rangers and volunteers provide information and occasional special programs on the significant natural and cultural sites, history, environment, and cultural diversity along each route.

—*Gina Macdonald*

**For Further Information:**

"A Cajun Christmas." *Southern Living* 33 (December, 1998): 64. Tours of park areas.

"Carry Me Back to 1815." *Southern Living* 31 (January, 1996): 12. Tours of park areas.

Greene, Jerome A. *Historic Resource Study: Chalmette Unit, Jean Lafitte National Historical Park and Preserve.* Denver: U.S. Department of the Interior, 1985. Fortifications and military installations.

"On the Watery Trail of Jean Lafitte." *Southern Living* 25 (February, 1990): 28. Tours of park areas.

Roush, J. Fred. *Chalmette National Historical Park, Louisiana.* U.S. National Park Service Histori-cal Handbook Series 29. 1958. Reprint. Washington, D.C.: U.S. Government Printing Office, 1982. Park history, significance, and offerings.

Swanson, Betsy. *Terre Haute de Barataria: An Historic Upland on an Old River Distributary Overtaken by Forest in the Barataria Unit of the Jean Lafitte National Historical Park and Preserve.* Harahan, La.: Jefferson Parish Historical Commission, 1991. A valuable historical overview of the natural history, archaeology, and founding of the park; with a comprehensive bibliography, including archival collections.

"Touring the Streets of New Orleans." *Southern Living* 21 (October, 1986): 32-34. Tours of park areas.

U.S. Department of the Interior. National Park Service. *Barataria Preserve Unit: Jean Lafitte National Historical Park and Preserve, Louisiana.* Denver: U.S. Department of the Interior, 1996. Explores wetland ecology and environment.

Young, David. "A Tour Through Bayou Barataria: Jean LaFitte National Park." *National Parks* 58 (July/August 1984): 16-19. A walking guide.

# Other Historic Sites

## Cable House

*Location:* New Orleans, Orleans County

*Relevant issues:* Literary history

*Statement of significance:* From 1874 to 1884, this modest house was the residence of George Washington Cable (1844-1925), voice of the Louisiana Creoles. Cable made major contributions to American regional literature with his tales of New Orleans life; his work made the term "Creole" better known and understood.

## Chopin House

*Location:* Cloutierville, Natchitoches County

*Relevant issues:* Literary history, women's history

*Statement of significance:* From 1880 to 1883, this was the home of Katherine O'Flaherty Chopin (1850-1904), novelist and short-story writer. Louisiana Bayou folk culture provided the backdrop for many of Kate Chopin's most noted works, among them the controversial novel *The Awakening* (1899) and *Bayou Folk* (1894), a col-lection of short stories. It was Chopin's experiences in Cloutierville that led her to record the history, folklore, and lifestyles of the people of the Cane River area.

## Delta Queen

*Location:* New Orleans, Orleans County

*Relevant issues:* Naval history

*Statement of significance:* One of only two sternwheel passenger boats operating under steam and the sole remaining Western Rivers overnight passenger boat, *Delta Queen* was built to operate on the Sacramento River in California. In World War II, it served as a yard ferryboat on San Francisco Bay for the U.S. Navy. After the war, it made a hazardous voyage under tow from California, through the Panama Canal, to the Mississippi, where it was reconditioned for work on the Western Rivers system. Today, *Delta Queen* carries passengers on overnight cruises over nearly the entire Western Rivers system and serves as a reminder of the time when steamboats carried the people and supplies that opened the West.

## Fort Jackson
*Location:* Triumph, Plaquemines County
*Relevant issues:* Civil War, military history
*Statement of significance:* Constructed from 1822 to 1832 to help guard the Mississippi River approaches to New Orleans, the fort saw no military action until the Civil War, when along with Fort St. Philip on the opposite bank it formed part of the most important link in the defense of New Orleans. After a six-day bombardment ending April 24, 1862, these forts were passed by the Union navy under Flag-Officer David G. Farragut; New Orleans surrendered, depriving the Confederacy of an important port and opening up the river initially for Union forces from New Orleans to Vicksburg.

## Fort Jesup
*Location:* Many, Sabine County
*Relevant issues:* Military history, political history
*Statement of significance:* This was the most southwesterly military outpost in the United States from its establishment in 1822 until the Mexican War. In March, 1845, Texas was offered admission to the Union and General Zachary Taylor's "Army of Observation," stationed at Fort Jesup, was ordered to hold its troops ready to march into Texas. After Texas joined the Union, Taylor was ordered to move into the new state. The site is now Fort Jesup State Monument.

## Fort St. Philip
*Location:* Triumph, Plaquemines County
*Relevant issues:* Civil War, military history
*Statement of significance:* Located on the east bank of the Mississippi River across from the later Fort Jackson, this fort was built by the French in 1746 and rebuilt by the Spanish in 1791. Like Fort Jackson, Fort St. Philip surrendered to Union forces after its bombardment and passage by Flag-Officer David G. Farragut's squadron in April, 1862.

## Louisiana State Capitol
*Location:* Capitol Drive, Baton Rouge, East Baton Rouge County

*Relevant issues:* Art and architecture, political history
*Statement of significance:* Dedicated in May, 1932, the capitol is a thirty-four-story, 450-foot skyscraper ornamented inside and out with features depicting the activities and ideals of the state. Built at the direction of Governor Huey Long (1893-1935), it was meant to mark the end of the "old order," a physical symbol to the people of Louisiana that their state had entered the modern era.

## Natchitoches Historic District
*Location:* Natchitoches, Natchitoches County
*Relevant issues:* European settlement
*Statement of significance:* Established by the French in 1714, Natchitoches was a trading center on the Red River and an important link in pack train trails. The historic district has a mixture of architecture from the eighteenth, nineteenth, and early twentieth centuries.

## New Orleans Cotton Exchange Building
*Location:* New Orleans, Orleans County
*Relevant issues:* Business and industry
*Statement of significance:* Since 1921, this eight-story steel-framed stone building has been the headquarters of the New Orleans Cotton Exchange. Organized in 1871, the exchange was the principal spot market of the world and a leading futures market, outranked only by Liverpool and New York, well into the 1920's. The success of the exchange was due in large part to its first superintendent and longtime secretary, Henry G. Hester, the "Father of Cotton Statistics," whose work reduced investment risk.

## Poverty Point
*Location:* Delhi, West Carroll County
*Relevant issues:* American Indian history
*Statement of significance:* The largest and most complex ceremonial earthworks of its kind yet found in North America, the site is dominated by the huge Poverty Point Mound, which is 640 feet by 710 feet in base dimension and rises to a height of nearly 70 feet.

## White House
*Location:* Thibodaux, Lafourche County
*Relevant issues:* Legal history
*Statement of significance:* This one-and-a-half-story

frame house was birthplace, childhood home, and estate of Edward Douglass White (1845-1921), associate justice of the Supreme Court and chief justice of the United States (1894-1921). His greatest impact resulted from his "rule of reason" for the enforcement of the Sherman Antitrust Act.

## Yucca Plantation

*Location:* Melrose, Natchitoches County
*Relevant issues:* African American history, art and architecture

*Statement of significance:* Established in the late eighteenth century by Marie Therese Coin-Coin, a former slave who became a wealthy businesswoman, the grounds of Yucca Plantation (now known as Melrose Plantation) contain what may well be the oldest buildings of African design built by blacks, for the use of blacks, in the country. The African House, a unique, nearly square structure with an umbrella-like roof which extends some ten feet beyond the exterior walls on all four sides, may be of direct African derivation.

# Maine

*The State Capitol Building in Augusta.* (Maine Office of Tourism)

# History of Maine

Maine, the largest of the six New England states, is filled with natural wonder and beauty. It has more than five thousand lakes and ponds, woodlands cover almost 90 percent of the state, and 2,500 miles of its Atlantic coastline twist from New Hampshire to Canada. The harsh, brutal winters have always made living there difficult, and the state remains relatively sparsely populated.

As far as it is known, the first Native Americans to settle in the area were members of the Abenaki (people of the dawnland) tribe. They, and the tribes that followed them, were hunters and gatherers, living on fish, deer, moose, beavers, and bears. Like many Native Americans of New England, they lived in wigwams and were generally peaceful—until European settlers began to come.

### Early Exploration and Settlement

Viking leader Leif Eriksson and other Norse sailors most likely explored part of Maine during their travels in 1000. John Cabot, sent by King Henry VII of England, claimed Maine as territory for England around 1497. In 1524 explorer Giovanni da Verrazano claimed Maine for France. In 1605 British captain George Weymouth landed in Maine, kidnapped five Abenaki men, and took them back to England. Upon meeting the American Indians and hearing stories of the land, King James I agreed to sponsor a settlement there, sending Sir Ferdinando Gorges and Sir John Popham to lead the expedition. In 1607 the British explorers reached the coast where the Kennebec River meets the ocean. There they began the Popham Colony, where they built the *Virginia*—the first English ship built in North America. Success was short-lived, however, as a typically bitter Maine winter, combined with attacks from the Abenakis, drove the entire colony back to England in 1608.

Soon, however, both English and French explorers returned and claimed different parts of the state for their kings. The English fought with the Native Americans often. Englishman John Winter founded one of Maine's first shipyards around 1637, and Maine was on its way to becoming a major shipbuilding center. The ships built in Maine supplied fish, fur, lumber, and masts to England's navy. The empty ships returning brought more settlers, and as settlers moved inland, farming gained importance. As in most of New England, native corn was Maine's primary crop. Primarily because of the harsh winters, Maine did not grow as quickly as the other New England colonies. The small population and weak government motivated the colonists there to merge with Massachusetts in 1658, and they remained part of it for nearly 150 years.

### Two Wars

In 1754 tension over the colonies between France, which ruled Canada, and England broke into the French and Indian War. Thousands of Maine settlers fought against the French. The French and Indians were eventually defeated, and many of the warring tribes fled to Canada. The victory was costly, however, and it left Great Britain deeply in debt. When the war ended in 1763, Maine was doing well. The colony had twenty-five thousand settlers and nearly fifty towns. Each year, Maine shipped millions of pounds of fish and lumber to cities in Europe. Like the other colonies, Maine started resenting Britain's meddling. Britain, trying to relieve its war debt, continually raised the taxes of the colonists.

In 1774 a group of men from York, Maine, burned English tea to protest the high taxes in what would be called the York Tea Party. In 1775 the Revolutionary War began in Massachusetts. On June 12 of that year, the first sea battle of the war occurred off Maine, when colonists from Machias rowed out and attacked an English ship. Soon after that the English retaliated, and the city of Falmouth (later Portland) was bombarded and burned. By the time the colonists won the war, about one thousand residents of Maine had given their lives.

After the war, the Massachusetts government sold Maine land to new settlers for less than a dollar an acre. Maine's population increased significantly, and by 1785 Maine started lobbying for statehood. The new and growing country had

came the capital. By then, potatoes were replacing corn as the most profitable crop, and lumbering became the state's largest industry. The city of Bath became the leading shipbuilding city in the country.

Maine was admitted to the Union as a free state, as it had a history of supporting people of African descent: When Bowdoin College opened in Brunswick in 1802, it was the first U.S. college to admit black students. John Russwurm, the college's first black graduate, cofounded *Freedom's Journal,* the country's first black-run newspaper, in 1827.

Antislavery Maine governor Hannibal Hamlin became President Abraham Lincoln's vice president in 1861. The Civil War erupted that year, and many Mainers heeded the call to arms. In the election of 1864, Lincoln was in political trouble, and he quietly allowed moderate southern Democrat Andrew Johnson to replace Hamlin as his vice president to ensure his reelection. By the time the Civil War ended in 1865, about 7,500 Maine soldiers had been killed fighting.

other problems, however. In 1812 the United States again went to war with Great Britain. Britain, at that time at war with France, would attack and capture American ships and conscript Americans into service. Maine's growing dominance as a shipbuilder played a major role in the American success, and after the war, it pushed even harder for statehood.

## Statehood

In 1820, in an effort to diffuse the hotly contested issue of slavery in America, it was proposed that Missouri be admitted as a slave state if Maine were admitted as a free state, thus keeping a balance of proslavery and antislavery states. Known as the Missouri Compromise, this agreement is credited with postponing civil war. Maine then separated from Massachusetts and became the twenty-third state, and the last New England state accepted into the Union. Portland served as the state capital until 1832, when the more centrally located Augusta be-

## Industrial Revolution

In the 1850's the Industrial Revolution began to influence American cities, and Maine came to operate textile and leather factories. Like the rest of New England, Maine was successful at building factories, and thousands of French Canadians crossed the border to find jobs. Many Irish came to Maine to escape the horrible potato famine that began in the 1840's. In 1894 the Arrostock Railroad was completed, and trains began to move the wealth of Maine potatoes to the markets of other American cities. During this time Maine became one of the country's great potato-growing areas.

## Economic Decline

In the 1900's tourists discovered Maine: its mystique, unspoiled beauty, and lack of crowded cities. The upsurge in tourists helped Maine's economy as the state's other industries began to falter. The development of iron steamships damaged Maine's wooden-ship building industry, and the traditional activities of lumbering, fishing, and farming did not provide enough jobs for everyone.

There was a small break in economic decline when World War I began in 1914. Many Mainers did not wait for the United States to enter the war and joined Canada's armed forces to fight the Germans. The United States entered the war in 1917, and thirty-five thousand Mainers joined the U.S. forces. Maine's shipbuilding industry sprang back to life, and farmers and fisherman saw a significant increase in price for their harvests. After the war ended, however, times were difficult in Maine. When the country entered World War II in 1941, Maine again sprang back to life. In the 1950's and 1960's, Air Force bases were built, which employed many locals, but unemployment remained higher in Maine than in the rest of the nation.

### Modern Maine

In 1954 Edmund Muskie became the first modern Democrat elected governor in the traditionally Republican state. In 1957 he was the first Maine Democrat elected to the Senate. The popular senator went on to run unsuccessfully for the vice presidency in 1968 and the presidential nomination of the Democratic Party in 1972.

In 1972 Maine's Native Americans filed a lawsuit against the United States, claiming their lands had been wrongly seized and showing a 1794 treaty as proof. In 1980 the federal government paid the tribes $81.5 million for their land. It was the largest such settlement ever awarded to Native Americans.

In the 1980's the state's economy became strong again, particularly in the largest city, Portland, although industry declined to the point that service industries represented 70 percent of the state's economy. Maine lobster is often referred to as the best in the country, and the state produces 22 million pounds of it each year. Maine also produces 98 percent of the nation's blueberries.

The state is relatively underpopulated, with only about one million residents. In the northern part of the state, there are few developed cities. In the 1990's less than 1 percent of the population was Native American, and most Mainers are descendants of emigrants from Great Britain, France, and Canada.
                                          —*Kevin M. Mitchell*

# Fort Kent and Madawaska

**Date:** Madawaska settled in June, 1785; Fort Kent built in 1839

**Relevant issues:** Business and industry, European settlement, military history, political history

**Significance:** The town of Fort Kent grew up around the fort of the same name. The fort was built in 1839 as a means of securing the northern U.S. border, which at the time was subject to dispute. The fort has been restored as a historic museum. Madawaska was the site of settlement in the late eighteenth and early nineteenth centuries by French speakers who had been expelled from their former colony of Acadia in Canada. Madawaska is still populated by many people of Acadian descent and has several sites commemorating the early settlers.

**Location:** Fort Kent lies at the junction of the St. John and Fish Rivers in Aroostook County in northern Maine, at the northern terminus of U.S. Route 1 and fifty-six miles north-northwest of Presque Isle; Madawaska, the northernmost town in Maine, is on the St. John River twenty miles northeast of Fort Kent

**Site Offices:**

Fort Kent State Historical Site
Blockhouse Road and West Main Street
Fort Kent, ME 04743
ph.: (207) 834-3866

Fort Kent Historic Site
c/o Department of Conservation
1235 Central Drive
Presque Isle, ME 04769
ph.: (207) 764-2041

Madawaska Historical Society
P.O. Box 258
Madawaska, ME 04756

Fort Kent, in the "big country" of Aroostook County in northern Maine, contributed in a symbolic and tangible way to the establishment of the northeastern boundary between the United States and Canada. It was one of several forts that were built in an attempt to secure the northern U.S. border. Three expeditions were responsible for these forts: the U.S. Army, from 1828 to 1845; the Maine land agents' "civil posses," from 1834 to 1841; and the Maine militia, between February and May of 1839. It was a civil posse that established Fort Kent, but all three forces occupied the garrison at one time or another.

### Early History

Before the boundary conflicts in the nineteenth century, the area around Fort Kent—particularly the Madawaska Territory in the St. John River valley—was notable for its population of exiles from Acadia. The Acadians had emigrated from France in the early seventeenth century to settle in an area that includes present-day Nova Scotia, New Brunswick, and Prince Edward Island, as well as parts of Quebec and Maine. Acadia—geographically isolated from other French Canadian settlements—was subject to repeated upheavals as the French and British vied for supremacy over the eastern maritime region.

After yet another round of conflicts, control of Acadia passed from the French to the British through the Treaty of Utrecht in 1713. For a quarter of a century, the French-speaking Catholics were not seriously affected by British control. The Acadians repeatedly refused to take a blanket oath of allegiance to England's monarchs—an oath that might require them to fight the French—but even so, the repercussions of this intransigence were minimal. As the Acadian population grew, however, so did the anxiety of the British. Nova Scotia governor Charles Lawrence determined that the Acadian opposition was insidious and had to be removed. He wished to repopulate the peninsula with pro-British New Englanders. Lawrence succeeded in exiling an estimated ten thousand Acadians through multiple expulsions, beginning in 1755; some fled before being forcibly removed.

The actual removal of the Acadians from their lands was swift and brutal, as the population was ordered to board ships immediately. Many of the displaced Acadians headed for the New England colonies, especially nearby Massachusetts, where they were accommodated, but with little enthusiasm.

The Acadians often did not settle permanently at their destination points; some of the exiles tried to return to Acadia, and others, such as the settlers in the Madawaska Territory along the St. John River, did not arrive there until thirty years after the initial exile.

### Resettlement of the Acadians

They first tried settling in other parts of New Brunswick, which had been separated from Nova Scotia in 1784, but encroachment by New Englanders after the American Revolution displaced the Acadians once again. Finally, the governor of Quebec provided for two hundred acres per family on land one and a half miles below the mouth of the Madawaska River, near the present St. David's Church. The first Acadians arrived there in June, 1785. In that remote location they built a colony of log houses, where they were able to live with little interference from either the British or the Americans; the settlers more frequently encountered the British, however, for whom the St. John River was an important waterway.

The French-speaking settlers also migrated farther downstream, to a small American settlement that had been established in 1817 along the St. John River, near the eventual site of Fort Kent. The first Acadian to move there was Jose Nadeau, who settled in 1829 at the confluence of the Fish and St. John Rivers. The Acadians throughout the valley were mostly farmers and remained largely isolated, both physically and culturally, from the settlements that were being established in western Maine by New Englanders. By the time Maine achieved statehood in 1820, the Acadians were well established in Madawaska. Occasional commercial disputes between the United States and Great Britain over the Aroostook Valley's valuable fur, lumber, and minerals were negotiated to the satisfaction of both parties without inconvenience to the area's residents.

### Exploitation of the Land

In fact, the major concerns really were about access to the land and its commercial benefits, not necessarily ownership of the territory. A sort of commercial tolerance developed as fur trappers and lumbermen were allowed to cross from New Brunswick into Maine, and vice versa. Increasingly, however, timber was cut from private lands along the

Aroostook River and its tributaries and sent down the St. John River to British subjects who shipped it to England. Canadian shipbuilders also had an eye on Maine's lumber supply. By 1838 Maine and New Brunswick were contending ever more seriously for absolute control of the lucrative spruce, cedar, and white pine forests in the Aroostook Valley. The lumber trade was so active in the area that as late as 1840 shingles occasionally served as currency in parts of the Aroostook.

The residents along the St. John River had carried on with their lives, remaining more or less unaffected by the quibblings about the border that had begun in 1783, when the treaty ending the American Revolution had been signed. Serious friction occurred in 1827, when settlers on the St. John near Madawaska were arrested by New Brunswick authorities after celebrating the American Independence Day. Furthermore, since 1825 Maine and Massachusetts land agents had been investigating New Brunswick's timber depredations, and in September, 1827, it was determined that arbitration was required. Treaty conventions led to the selection of King William I of the Netherlands to arbitrate the boundary dispute. Available facts about the local terrain were so scanty that in his 1831 decision the king could offer only a vague resolution to the territorial dispute.

The era of the boundary dispute had seen the rise of various local militia companies and small, ad hoc fortifications, but by the end of the 1830's, hostilities intensified to the point of war. The stage was set in the winter of 1838-1839, when the governments of the United States, Great Britain, Maine, and New Brunswick amassed thousands of troops in the disputed border areas. The Aroostook War officially began on February 20, 1839, when Maine legislated that a militia should join the civil posse in the area. The U.S. Congress prepared for a major military effort, approving the dispatch of fifty thousand troops and a budget of ten million dollars. Thanks to the intervention of U.S. General Winfield Scott and British negotiator Sir John Harvey, the Aroostook War remained a bloodless one. Forces reached a truce only weeks later, on March 21, 1839, and the soldiers departed the area.

### Joint Occupancy

Under the terms of joint occupancy, New Brunswick was to hold the Madawaska settlement, while Maine would control the Aroostook River. Madawaska in particular remained disputed, because it was ambiguous whether New Brunswick was to control just the north bank of the river or both sides. Maine took the initiative in defending what it considered its rightful territory on the south bank of the St. John River and insisted to President Martin Van Buren that the federal government step in and remove the foreign invaders. Maine also had the backing of Massachusetts, which had formerly owned Maine and was still a major property holder in the state.

On March 27, 1839, Charles Jarvis, provisional land agent for Maine, ordered Captain Alvin Nye and twenty-three civil posse and militia volunteers to an island at the confluence of the St. John and Fish Rivers. His intention was to erect a boom to stop the British from transporting timber from the south on the Fish River, and to protect that facility with a blockhouse. Nye was not to cross the adjoining St. John River, however, as this would be an obvious encroachment on New Brunswick. Ironically, the Aroostook War was ending just as Jarvis was planning these bold maneuvers. On March 23, 1839, the Maine legislature withdrew the state's militia from the area, and word reached Jarvis six days later. Though his men were recalled, Jarvis deemed the establishment of jurisdiction to be vital to Maine's interests.

By April 23 the boom was in place, and construction of the blockhouse was under way. One correspondent referred to the project, perhaps facetiously, as "Fort Jarvis." The boom—from the island south to the mainland—stopped six hundred to eight hundred tons of timber. Rumors of construction of a British blockhouse stepped up the building of the fort in late summer of 1839. Captain Stover Rines, who replaced Nye, and thirty-five members of the civil posse had to build the fort before winter set in, and they continued with the blockhouse, cookhouse, and other service structures.

The new fort was remote from the rest of Maine—there were no serviceable land connections—but New Brunswick saw the fort not as an outpost but as an intrusion near vital transportation routes. Even as the British protested this new garrison, however, they were busy beefing up their own defenses. In reality, the fort was little threat: Lack of funds precluded a cannon, and supplies were scarce. The force there soon was reduced to twenty-five men, and eventually to eighteen.

As negotiations stalled in the national capitals, the contentious local face-off continued through 1840. In November of that year, the valley's Americans attempted to vote in the presidential election, and a New Brunswick official from Madawaska interfered. The ensuing personal insults and affronts led to more troops being sent to the area.

Despite the continuing hostilities, the atmosphere at Fort Kent was more farmlike than siegelike. No stockade was built to surround the heavy timber blockhouse, and surrounding the blockhouse, cookhouse, stables, and other buildings were two hundred acres of cultivated land and livestock. The blockhouse itself was an anomaly: The square cedar-log building was an anachronistic structure. Its bulky, rough-hewn timbers and second-story overhang topped by a hip roof harked back to fortification design of the pre-Revolutionary period.

### Adoption of the Name "Fort Kent"

The Fish River post became known as Fort Kent only in 1841, named in honor of Maine's new governor, Edward Kent. On August 14, 1841, U.S. forces relieved the civil posse at Fort Kent, and a month later, Captain Lucien B. Webster arrived to take charge. He continued to use Fort Kent's upper story and attic as living quarters, and the lower story remained a guardhouse and clothing depot. He did commission the building of an additional officers' quarters, which was completed the next spring.

The British had responded to Maine's bold maneuver by setting up their own stronghold twenty miles from Fort Kent. Tensions in the area eased with the arrival of the more professional federal troops. The British military rightly considered them to be less volatile than the local regiments. In fact, the U.S. and British officers fraternized frequently, to the point that the Americans requisitioned additional rations so they could properly entertain their peers from across the border. While at Fort Kent, the federal troops improved the facili-

*Daniel Webster negotiated the Webster-Ashburton Treaty, which resolved the border dispute between Maine and Canada.* (Library of Congress)

ties there. In addition to completing a new officers' quarters, they outfitted the blockhouse with new floors and built a hospital, log huts for the company's laundresses, and a school for the few children at the post.

New leaders of both the United States and Great Britain were more inclined toward diplomacy than toward war. The two powers set out to resolve a number of long-standing mutual disagreements, including the issue of the Maine–New Brunswick border. Great Britain sent Alexander Baring, Lord Ashburton, to represent its interests, while Secretary of State Daniel Webster was to negotiate for the United States.

Webster approached the whole affair with compromise in mind, prepared to relinquish some of the land claimed by Maine in favor of strategic concessions elsewhere along the border. Lord Ashburton had every reason to be conciliatory, too, and even pro-American. He had spent some time as a young man in New York, handling the American aspect of his father's banking business, and he was married to the daughter of a Pennsylvania senator. His business interests in the United States continued.

Important to New Brunswick and the British was the maintenance of an adequate defense and commercial corridor that would follow the St. John River around Maine from the Atlantic coast to Montreal; this presupposed control of the northern and western parts of the disputed area. In exchange for a boundary that would allow such control, Ashburton was prepared to ensure the free transport of U.S. lumber products on the St. John River.

**Settlement of the Land Dispute**
After much negotiation, including resolving doubts about contentious maps and surveys that had been made in 1783 and earlier in the nineteenth century, the Treaty of Washington—also known as the Webster-Ashburton Treaty—was signed on August 9, 1842. The U.S. Senate ratified the treaty on August 20 by a vote of thirty-nine to nine, and the United States and Great Britain proclaimed the boundary's settlement on November 10, 1842.

In the Fort Kent-Madawaska area, the St. John River ultimately was determined as the border between Maine and New Brunswick, and families with members on both sides of the river were split between the two nations. There were occasional infractions and arrests as the new boundary took effect. Residents on the American side remained concerned about the British and requested maintenance of federal troops at Fort Kent. The United States prepared to withdraw its men in September, 1843, partly because Fort Kent simply was too difficult to service; there still was no suitable road from the south to the St. John River valley. Maine passed a resolution calling for the continued presence of federal troops, though, and the government briefly complied, keeping a reduced force there through 1844.

Generally, the treaty resolved amicably the hostilities between Maine and New Brunswick, and Fort Kent's brief role in defending U.S. interests

at the border came to a close. By 1858 all the property had been sold for private residential use. The town of Fort Kent was incorporated in 1869. The fort returned to the public realm in 1891, when Maine—in what likely was the first publicly funded preservation attempt in that state—authorized three hundred dollars to purchase the fort for restoration.

**Modern Preservation Efforts**
Today the blockhouse—near the center of town and mostly restored to its original form—serves as a state-run museum of local history, including exhibits of antiques related to river transportation and lumbering. Further information that relates to the fort's immediate history explores the era when the northeastern boundary of the United States and Canada was anything but certain.

In Madawaska, where the Acadian dialect can still be heard, the early settlers are commemorated by a number of sites. The Madawaska Historical Society has preserved a one-room schoolhouse used by the Acadians, as well as a nineteenth century homestead. An Acadian cross marks the immigrants' point of entry to Madawaska.

—*Randall J. Van Vynckt*

**For Further Information:**
Callahan, James Morton. *American Foreign Policy in Canadian Relations.* New York: Macmillan, 1937. Offers a scholarly account of the entire border crisis, including an excellent chapter on the Webster-Ashburton Treaty.

Clark, Charles E., James S. Leamon, and Karen Bowden, eds. *Maine in the Early Republic: From Revolution to Statehood.* Hanover, N.H.: University Press of New England, 1988. Covers the Acadian settlements.

Corey, Albert B. *The Crisis of 1830-1842 in Canadian-American Relations.* New Haven, Conn.: Yale University Press, 1941. Narrows the discussion about the two countries to the period of their most trying conflicts, including the Maine-New Brunswick crisis that was resolved by the Webster-Ashburton Treaty.

Griffiths, Naomi. *The Acadians: Creation of a People.* Toronto: McGraw-Hill Ryerson, 1973. A more immediate, detailed account about the original settlements of the Acadians in North America leading into an extensive discussion of the deportations of the eighteenth century. For its small size, this book offers an excellent range and depth of insights into the motivations of the Acadians and those who governed them.

Louder, Dean R., and Eric Waddell, eds. *French America: Mobility, Identity, and Minority Experience Across the Continent.* Translated by Franklin Philip. Baton Rouge: Louisiana State University Press, 1993. Adapted from the collection *Du continent perdu à l'archipel retrouvé: Le Québec et l'Amérique française* (Quebec: Presses de l'Université Laval, 1983). Puts the Northeast Acadians in the context of the larger Acadian migrations that included Europe and Louisiana.

McDonald, Sheila. "The War After the War." *Maine Historical Society Quarterly* 29, nos. 3-4 (1990). Provides a remarkably detailed look at the whole system of defenses during the boundary dispute with the British and at the minutiae of how Fort Kent came to exist.

McInnis, Edgar W. *The Unguarded Frontier: A History of American-Canadian Relations.* New York: Russell & Russell, 1970. Further explores the border issues as a prime determinant in relations between the United States and Canada.

Scott, Geraldine Tidd. "Fortifications on Maine's Northeast Boundary, 1828-1845." *Maine Historical Society Quarterly* 29, nos. 3-4 (1990). A detailed look at the system of defenses during the boundary dispute with the British and at how Fort Kent came to exist.

# Kennebunkport

**Date:** Settled by 1629

**Relevant issues:** American Indian history, business and industry, colonial America, political history

**Significance:** Kennebunkport was one of the earliest European settlements in North America. In its four hundred-year history it has been important as a battlefield for skirmishes between Europeans and American Indians, as a fishing and trading center, and as a summer resort area.

**Location:** Seventy miles north of Boston in southern coastal Maine, at the mouth of the Kennebunk River

**Site Office:**
Kennebunkport Historical Society
P.O. Box 1173
Kennebunkport, ME 04046-1173
ph.: (207) 967-2751
fax: (207) 967-1205
Web site: www.kporthistory.org
e-mail: kporths@gwi.net

Kennebunkport was first used by Europeans and Indians alike as a summer fishing area, but it eventually gained prominence as a center for shipbuilding and fishing. These industries produced great wealth, and the Kennebunkport historic district features many grand homes from the eighteenth and nineteenth centuries. Later, the town became a popular resort area and a colony for artists and writers. During the presidency of George Bush (1989-1993), the town attracted new attention as the Bush family's summer residence.

### The Founding of the Town

The area in which Kennebunkport now lies was heavily forested and a rich site for fishing in the sixteenth century. Although about forty thousand Pequots, Abenakis, and others lived there, Martin Pring, a British explorer on the Kennebunk River in 1603, found evidence of Native American fires but no permanent settlements and no people. The British established small summer fishing camps along the coast and alternately enjoyed the hospitality of the Native Americans and quarreled with them, while the French also made settlements and managed to remain on good terms with the Indians. The French were driven away by 1613, and the British and the Native Americans continued to compete for the land.

In 1614 Captain John Smith came to Maine to trade and survey. Seeing a school of porpoises while he was standing on a cape, he named the land Cape Porpoise. In 1620, when the Pilgrims were given a charter to lands that included Maine, Cape Porpoise was a thriving spot for fishing and trading, but only in the summertime; men would sail to Cape Porpoise during warm months and return to England for the winter. The settlement soon became a permanent town.

### Growth and Development

After Cape Porpoise and its neighbors tried unsuccessfully for a few years to govern and protect themselves, the Commonwealth of Massachusetts as-

*Kennebunkport.* (Jeff Greenberg/Maine Office of Tourism)

sumed control of Maine in 1652. For the next hundred years, however, the area suffered greatly from a series of battles with the French and the Indians. Many people died on all sides from war, brutality, and disease. After the town was nearly wiped out in a battle with Indians, it was reorganized in 1719 with the new name Arundel.

After the Revolutionary War, Arundel became an important center for fishing and shipbuilding, and the port was important for the lumber industry. Fortunes were made, and shipbuilders, merchants, and sea captains were able to build large homes, many of which still stand. Maine was granted statehood in 1820, and Arundel officially changed its name to Kennebunkport in 1821, hoping to attract more notice because the Kennebunk River was already well known as an important shipping route.

### A Change in Fortunes

By the end of the nineteenth century, the need for shipbuilders had decreased dramatically because of the spread of railroads and industrialization. Kennebunkport took on a new status as a summer resort area for wealthy New Englanders who were attracted to the beautiful coastal scenery, the ocean breezes, and the lovely homes already there.

In the early part of the twentieth century, Kennebunkport was discovered by artists and writers. Booth Tarkington, author of two Pulitzer Prize-winning novels, did his writing on his schooner *Regina*, floating just off the coast. Kenneth Roberts, another resident, wrote a series of historical novels about the area that are set during the Revolutionary War.

Although it has many beautiful mansions built for wealthy residents, Kennebunkport was a quiet and little-noticed town for most of the twentieth century. When one of the summer residents, George Bush, was elected president of the United States in 1988, Kennebunkport became famous again as the Bush family's summer residence.

### Places to Visit

Kennebunkport still has many visual reminders of its history and former prosperity. Its post office bears a sign proudly proclaiming that Kennebunkport is "the only town in the world so named."

Several old houses stand in the town's historic district, including the Captain Lord Mansion, begun in 1812, with a distinctive octagonal cupola and widow's walk, and the Nott House, a Greek Revival house from the early eighteenth century.

The Kennebunkport Historical Society, which has its headquarters in the 1899 School House, offers exhibits of history and art, and also makes available guided and self-guided walking tours of important architectural landmarks. The Clark Shipwright's Office, formerly a shipyard office on the Kennebunk River, contains a museum of maritime history. The buildings are generally open mid-June through mid-October, Tuesdays through Saturdays.　　　　　　　　—*Cynthia A. Bily*

**For Further Information:**

Bearse, Ray. *Maine: A Guide to the Vacation State.* 2d ed. Boston: Houghton Mifflin, 1969. Arranged alphabetically, with generous passages on local history. Kennebunkport section identifies several historical sites.

Bradbury, Charles. *History of Kennebunkport: From Its First Discovery by Bartholomew Gosnold, May 14, 1602, to A.D. 1837.* 1837. Reprint. Kennebunk, Maine: Durrell, 1984. This narrative is largely compiled from quotations in original documents.

Butler, Joyce. *Kennebunkport Scrapbook.* 2 vols. Kennebunk, Maine: Rosemary House Press, 1989, 1998. Collections of photographs and documents.

Muse, Vance. *The Smithsonian Guide to Historic America: Northern New England.* New York: Stewart, Tabori & Chang, 1989. Travel guide focusing on historical attractions, with many color photographs and maps.

Rich, Louise Dickinson. *The Coast of Maine: An Informal History.* New York: Thomas Y. Crowell, 1956. Well-researched history narrated in a highly readable, conversational tone.

Roberts, Kenneth Lewis. *Arundel: A Chronicle of the Province of Maine and of the Secret Expedition Led by Benedict Arnold Against Quebec.* 1933. Reprint. Camden, Maine: Down East Books, 1995. Highly regarded historical novel of Kennebunkport during the American Revolution.

Scott, Connie Porter. *The Old Photographs Series: Kennebunkport.* Augusta, Maine: Alan Sutton, 1994. Over two hundred well-annotated photographs dating from the 1830's through the 1950's.

# Old York Gaol

**Date:** Built in 1719
**Relevant issues:** Colonial America
**Significance:** The gaol (jail) is one of the oldest buildings, and probably the oldest British government building, still standing in the United States. It offers a vivid exhibition of the vast difference between the criminal justice systems of colonial America and modern times.
**Location:** Sixty miles north of Boston in York, on the Maine coast.
**Site Office:**
Old York Historical Society
P.O. Box 312
York, ME 03909-0312
ph.: (207) 363-4974
Web site: www.yorknet.org

The story of the Old York Gaol begins with the Pilgrims, who arrived in what is now New England in 1620 and settled along the Atlantic coast. In 1624 they established the town of Agamenticus, which grew quickly. It became the second formal chartered city in Maine in 1642 and was renamed Gorgeana for Sir Ferdinando Gorges, the governor-general of New England. In 1652 it was reorganized once again, this time as a town of the British Commonwealth of Massachusetts. The town was renamed for the last time, becoming "York" after the county in England.

York was chosen as the location for the King's Prison for the District of Maine in 1653. Until that time, court cases were decided swiftly and punishments, which might include fines, servitude, or the stocks, were administered immediately. From then on, certain lawbreakers and debtors would be sentenced to spend time in prison. A small prison was built in the 1660's, with one dungeon and no heat.

**The Present Building**
The present building was built in 1719, when the original jail had fallen into disrepair. With stone walls nearly three feet thick, it was built to be secure and to last. Additions over the next half century included a chimney and fireplace, a cellar, a wooden addition with a kitchen and large room, and a second story. Through much of the eighteenth century the stone structure was referred to as the Gaol, and the wooden addition as the Gaol House.

*The Old Gaol Museum in York, the oldest municipal building in the United States.* (Maine Office of Tourism)

Historical Society raised money to repair the building, and the Old Gaol was opened as a museum on the Fourth of July, 1900. The Old Gaol has been administered by the Historical Society ever since, with funds for maintenance provided by an endowment established by Elizabeth Perkins, who set about in the early 1900's to preserve as much of historic York as she could. She recognized the value of the Old York Gaol, thought to be the oldest surviving government building in the United States.

The jail had one underground dungeon and two jail cells; it held both felons and debtors. The dungeon had no toilet, and none of the rooms had adequate ventilation. There was a "yard," or outside secured area, and prisoners who could afford to post a bond were allowed to go outside during part of the day. Most prisoners, however, could not afford to pay. At the end of the eighteenth century, a new law required that felons and debtors must be housed separately, but there was not enough room at York for this arrangement. In 1806 more expansions and improvements were made, bringing the building to its present form. The newly remodeled building held prisoners for more than fifty years.

### The Old Gaol Retired and Restored
By 1860 the stone part of the jail was no longer used to hold prisoners, and the wooden addition was also gradually phased out. A resourceful deputy jailer offered paying customers tours of the old dungeons as early as the 1860's, and in the 1880's a local merchant rented the building to use as a warehouse. In the 1890's the Todd family rented the jail and lived in it, and the building also served as a schoolhouse for a time.

Finally, in 1898, the editor and author William Dean Howells, a summer resident of York, suggested that the building be restored. The Old York

### Visiting the Old York Gaol
The Old York Gaol is part of a complex in York Village administered by the Old York Historical Society. Visitors to the Gaol are encouraged to meet the "jailer's wife," a costumed guide, and to visit the old dungeons and cells. The pillory in front of the jail is a popular prop for photographs.

Other sites near the Old York Gaol include the Old School House, built in 1745; the John Hancock Warehouse, dating from the eighteenth century; and the mid-nineteenth century George Marshall Store. York features several old homes, some privately owned but two open to visitors. The Emerson-Wilcox House, built in 1742, showcases Maine decorative arts. The Elizabeth Perkins House was built in 1732 and contains Perkins's personal collection of Colonial Revival furnishings.

Jefferd's Tavern, built in 1750, is the visitor center and exhibition hall for the Historical Society complex. The sites are open to visitors six days a week (closed Mondays) from June through Columbus Day, with more limited hours during the spring. —*Cynthia A. Bily*

### For Further Information:
Baker, Madge. *Woven Together in York County, Maine: A History 1865-1990.* Shapleigh, Maine: Wilson's Printers, 1999. Well-researched work by a local historian.

Beard, Frank A. *Maine's Historic Places: Properties on the National Register of Historic Places.* Camden, Maine: Down East Books, 1982. Descriptions of important historic buildings in Maine, with illustrations and maps.

Ernst, George. *New England Miniature: A History of York, Maine.* Freeport, Maine: Bond Wheelwright, 1961. Reprint. Salem, Mass.: Higginson Book Company, 1993. A history of York from its settlement in the 1630's through the 1950's. Includes generous quotations from early documents.

Hunt, Kenneth. "Maine's Old-Time York." *Colonial Homes* 22, no. 3 (June 1996): 54-58. Illustrated overview of York, focusing on historic homes but also including the Gaol and other public buildings.

Muse, Vance. *The Smithsonian Guide to Historic America: Northern New England.* New York: Stewart, Tabori & Chang, 1989. Travel guide focusing on historical sites, with many color photographs and maps.

Rich, Louise Dickinson. *The Coast of Maine: An Informal History.* New York: Thomas Y. Crowell, 1956. Well-researched history narrated in a highly readable, conversational tone.

Sullivan, James. *The History of the District of Maine.* 1795. Reprint. Bowie, Md.: Heritage Books, 1994. Facsimile edition of an eighteenth century history of Colonial Maine.

# Other Historic Sites

## Blaine House

*Location:* Augusta, Kennebec County

*Relevant issues:* Political history

*Statement of significance:* From 1862 until his death, this substantial two-story frame and clapboard house was the residence of James G. Blaine (1830-1893), Speaker of the House of Representatives, twice a senator, twice secretary of state, and an unsuccessful presidential candidate in 1884. He helped establish the Pan-American Union in 1890.

## Bowdoin

*Location:* Castine, Hancock County

*Relevant issues:* Naval history

*Statement of significance:* Built in 1921 specifically for Arctic exploration, the auxiliary schooner *Bowdoin* was the brainchild of Admiral Donald Baxter MacMillan, an Arctic explorer, aviator, author, anthropologist, and philanthropist who made twenty-six of his twenty-nine voyages to the Arctic on *Bowdoin*. It is one of a handful of historic Arctic vessels left in the world and exemplifies the rugged conditions and the hardy navigators who braved the frozen north to unlock its secrets. Much of the information and knowledge of the Arctic, Labrador, and Greenland that exists to date was gathered aboard *Bowdoin*. During World War II, *Bowdoin* and MacMillan were commissioned by the U.S. Navy to serve on the important Greenland Patrol. When the schooner was retired from Arctic service in 1954, MacMillan sailed *Bowdoin* south to commence a career as a museum vessel.

## Cushnoc Archaeological Site

*Location:* Augusta, Kennebec County

*Relevant issues:* European settlement

*Statement of significance:* This site contains the remains of Cushnoc, a Plymouth Colony trading post, one of the most important English outposts along the mid-seventeenth century Acadian frontier. No exact dates for Cushnoc's construction or abandonment are documented, though evidence suggests Plymouth Colony merchants established the outpost soon after obtaining a patent to land there in 1628 and may have used this site until the establishment during the 1660's of another outpost a few miles downstream. Fort Western, built by British troops in 1754 during the Seven Years' War, is nearby.

## Dow House

*Location:* Portland, Cumberland County

*Relevant issues:* Political history, social reform

*Statement of significance:* For sixty-seven years, this well-preserved two-and-a-half-story house was the residence of Neal Dow (1804-1897), called the "Napoleon of Temperance." A leading nineteenth century proponent of Prohibition, Dow was a candidate for the presidency in 1880 on the Prohibition Party ticket.

## Fort Halifax

*Location:* Winslow, Kennebec County
*Relevant issues:* European settlement, military history
*Statement of significance:* A defensive outpost during the French and Indian War, the fort was built for protection against Indian raids. The sole remaining structure is the oldest extant example of a log blockhouse (1754) in the country.

## Fort Western

*Location:* Augusta, Kennebec County
*Relevant issues:* Colonial America, European settlement, military history, Revolutionary War
*Statement of significance:* Constructed in 1754 by the British, the fort is a little-altered example of an eighteenth century log fur trading post. In September, 1775, it served as the starting point and principal supply base for Colonial Benedict Arnold's march on Quebec.

## Gilman Summer House

*Location:* Northeast Harbor, Hancock County
*Relevant issues:* Education
*Statement of significance:* From the late 1880's until his death, this three-story shingled house was the residence of Daniel Coit Gilman (1831-1908), American educator. As the first president of The Johns Hopkins University (1875-1902), Gilman made graduate education a recognized university responsibility.

## Homer Studio

*Location:* Scarborough, Cumberland County
*Relevant issues:* Art and architecture
*Statement of significance:* From 1884 until his death, this converted carriage house was the studio of Winslow Homer (1836-1910), an artist noted for his Civil War scenes, landscapes, genre works, and particularly his powerful paintings of the sea.

## Jewett House

*Location:* South Berwick, York County
*Relevant issues:* Literary history, women's history
*Statement of significance:* This was the home of Sarah Orne Jewett (1849-1909), who lived and wrote in this house for most of her life. She wrote over twenty novels and collections of short stories that remain quintessential in their description of the lives and landscapes of rural Maine in the late nineteenth century. In addition to being valued for the historical perspectives it contains, Jewett's writing is of interest to scholars of women's literature who have explored the matriarchal and mythic qualities of her work.

## Lewis R. French

*Location:* Rockland, Knox County
*Relevant issues:* Naval history
*Statement of significance:* Built in 1871, this is the oldest surviving sailing vessel built in Maine, the center for wooden-ship building in the United States after the Civil War. *Lewis R. French* worked mostly as a coasting schooner, carrying a variety of cargoes both as a sailing and later as a motor vessel; currently, it is a Maine windjammer, its schooner rig restored.

## Lightship No. 112 "Nantucket"

*Location:* South Portland, Cumberland County
*Relevant issues:* Naval history
*Statement of significance:* The 1936 Lightship No. 112, known by its last official designation, *Nantucket*, outlasted all other lightships assigned to that station, having marked it for thirty-nine years. The nation's most significant lightship station for transatlantic voyages, *Nantucket*, established in 1854, marked the limits of the dangerous Nantucket Shoals and the eastern end of the Ambrose shipping canal into New York harbor. It was the last lightship seen by vessels departing the United States as well as the first beacon seen entering the country.

## Longfellow House

*Location:* Portland, Cumberland County
*Relevant issues:* Literary history
*Statement of significance:* From 1807 to 1822, when he entered Bowdoin College, this was the home of Henry Wadsworth Longfellow (1807-1882), poet. Longfellow composed several of his best-known poems in this house, which he continued to regard as his home until his second marriage in 1843.

## Pemaquid Archaeological Site

*Location:* New Harbor, Lincoln County

*Relevant issues:* American Indian history, European settlement

*Statement of significance:* Pemaquid contains the remains of a large English town occupied throughout the early period of contact on the Maine Coast along the frontier separating French Acadia from New England. European settlement of the area dates to around 1628, when New England colonists erected their first houses at the site; these first English colonists fished, farmed, and traded food and manufactured goods for furs with their Indian neighbors. As the first and most important early center for intercultural relations between Indian people and English settlers in Maine, the large amounts of artifacts and other materials preserved in Pemaquid's fieldstone foundations, cellar-holes, chimney-bases, hearths, and other features have yielded much valuable information associated with this time period.

## Reed House

*Location:* Portland, Cumberland County

*Relevant issues:* Political history

*Statement of significance:* From 1888 until his death, this was the residence of Thomas B. Reed (1839-1902), the powerful Republican Speaker of the House of Representatives. In 1890, "Czar Reed" reformed House procedures with the introduction of the "Reed Rules."

## Robinson House

*Location:* Gardiner, Kennebec County

*Relevant issues:* Literary history

*Statement of significance:* From his infancy to the mid-1890's, this two-story white clapboard house was the home of Edwin Arlington Robinson, a Pulitzer Prize-winning poet who wrote much of his poetry here.

## Sabbathday Lake Shaker Village

*Location:* Sabbathday Lake and vicinity, Cumberland County

*Relevant issues:* Religion

*Statement of significance:* Founded in 1793, this was one of the last of the Shaker communities. A representative collection of Shaker implements and furniture is housed in the buildings.

## Stowe House

*Location:* Brunswick, Cumberland County

*Relevant issues:* Literary history

*Statement of significance:* From 1850 to 1852, this two-and-a-half-story frame house was the residence of Harriet Beecher Stowe, author of a widely influential indictment of slavery. Her book *Uncle Tom's Cabin: Or, Life Among the Lowly* (1852) was written here in 1851.

# Maryland

*Baltimore.* (PhotoDisc)

# History of Maryland

In many ways, Maryland is a microcosm of much of the United States, combining elements from the north, south, east, and west. Physically located in the middle of the English colonies, it was the center state of the new nation and thus the logical site for a capital, which is located in the District of Columbia. After the Revolution, Maryland led efforts to develop the nation westward; it remained in the Union during the Civil War but sent soldiers to both the North and the South during that conflict. After World War II, the state managed to preserve its historic traditions and environmental legacy while advancing into the future.

**Early History and Settlement**

It is uncertain when Native Americans first entered the area now known as Maryland, but tribes of the Iroquoian and Algonquian peoples were certainly present several hundred years prior to European arrival. The major Iroquoian tribe was the Susquehannock, sometimes known as Conestoga, who came south from the Pennsylvania area. The Algonquians included the Choptank, Portobago, and Wicomico, names which still survive on the map of Maryland. The major Algonquian tribes were the Piscataway on the western shore (the mainland) of the Chesapeake Bay and the Nanticoke on the eastern shore (the peninsula between the Chesapeake Bay and the Atlantic coast). Both Iroquoian and Algonquian Indians lived and farmed in permanent settlements.

The Algonquian tribes welcomed the English settlers, but the Susquehannock proved hostile, although their attacks were aimed as much against Native American allies of the English as against the English themselves. In any event, the colonists successfully defended themselves and in 1652 concluded a peace with the Susquehannock, which included the American Indians' departure from Maryland. Between the 1690's and the mid-1700's, first the Piscataway and then the other Native Americans also moved away from the area.

The Spanish were the first Europeans to explore the area, but the English were the first permanent settlers. English colonists from Virginia under councilman William Claiborne established a trading post on Kent Island in Chesapeake Bay in 1631. The following year, King Charles I granted George Calvert, Baron Baltimore, land north of the Potomac River, which included Maryland. It was on this land that Calvert's son Cecilius, known as Lord Baltimore, established a colony in 1634. Led by Leonard Calvert, half brother of Cecilius, the colonists included many Roman Catholics, among them two priests. At this time Roman Catholics were forbidden by British law from voting or holding office. In part, Maryland was founded with the tacit understanding that it would be a refuge for English Catholics. In fact, the name of the colony, while officially honoring Queen Henrietta Maria of England, was often interpreted as referring to the Virgin Mary. In 1649 the colony adopted an "Act Concerning Religion," the first act of religious toleration in the colonies. Soon afterward, a group of Puritans arrived from Virginia.

In the meantime, Maryland settlers under Leonard Calvert disputed Virginia's claims to Kent Island. In 1654 Virginian Claiborne led the Puritans in a revolt that exiled Calvert, an action recognized by the English Commonwealth that had overthrown and executed Charles I. However, in 1658 Calvert and proprietary government were restored to Maryland. In 1692 Maryland became a royal colony, and the Church of England was declared the established, or official, church. In 1718 Roman Catholics were denied the right to vote.

By far the most important influence on Maryland's history has been the Chesapeake Bay, the largest inlet on the East Coast. The bay is nearly two hundred miles long from north to south and as wide as twenty-five miles and is important for commercial fishing, oystering, and crabbing. At the head of the bay is Baltimore, one of the major American ports since its founding in 1729 and Maryland's largest city.

**Revolution and Growth**

Marylanders joined with other colonists in their distaste for the high taxes imposed by Britain, and in 1774 a group of patriots boarded the *Peggy Stew-*

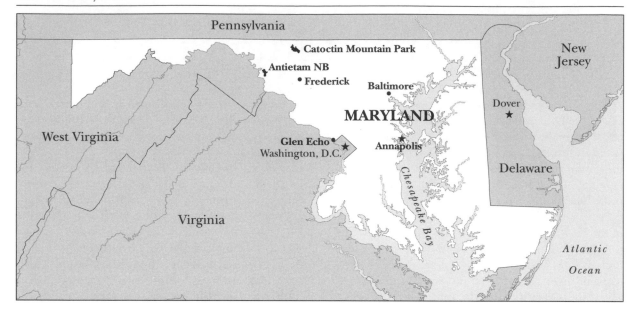

*art* in Annapolis Harbor and destroyed more than two thousand pounds of its cargo of tea. During the Revolution, when the British threatened the capital of Philadelphia, the Continental Congress moved to Baltimore, then to Annapolis. Maryland troops were among the best in the Continental Army, and their straight ranks and orderly battle lines earned Maryland the nickname "The Old Line State" from General George Washington.

In 1791 Maryland and Virginia ceded land to the United States to create the District of Columbia as the site of the new national capital. Construction of the White House began in 1793 and of the Capitol in 1794. In 1800 Congress moved to the new capital city from Philadelphia. During the War of 1812, British forces seized Washington, D.C, and burned the White House but were unable to force their way past Fort McHenry to capture Baltimore. It was while watching this bombardment from Baltimore harbor that Francis Scott Key composed the poem "The Star-Spangled Banner," which later became the national anthem of the United States.

In its key central position, Maryland took a leading role in the growth of the new nation, especially in its westward advancement. The Cumberland Road, also known as the National Pike, was a prime avenue for settlers heading into the interior of the continent; by 1818 it reached the Ohio River. Maryland was also active in the construction of canals,

essential for transport of cargo during that period. Two vital waterways, the Chesapeake and Delaware and the Chesapeake and Ohio, connected the bay to those two rivers. The state also took the forefront in exploiting the new technology of the steam railroad, with the Baltimore and Ohio (B&O) starting operations in 1830 as the first American railroad to carry both passengers and freight.

### Civil War

Slavery was legal in Maryland, and when the Civil War came there was considerable sentiment in the state for it to join others in the South in seceding from the Union. However, in 1861 the Maryland legislature rejected a bill of secession; still, many of the state's residents left to fight with the Confederate army, and many others were sympathizers. During the first months of the war mobs attacked Union troops as they marched through Baltimore. However, these disturbances were suppressed, and soon a ring of Union forts was erected to protect Washington, D.C., from Confederate attack.

A number of battles were fought in Maryland during the Civil War, the largest being that of Antietam, fought in 1862. Antietam was the single bloodiest day of battle of the war, with more than twenty-three thousand casualties. It was a narrow Union victory, but enough for President Abraham Lincoln to feel justified in announcing the Emancipation Proclamation, which freed the slaves in the

Confederacy and transformed the nature of the war to a crusade for liberty. During the summer of 1863, Confederate general Robert E. Lee's Army of Northern Virginia passed through the state on its way to the Battle of Gettysburg. In 1864 Confederate forces under General Jubal Early threatened Washington, D.C., but were driven back at the last moment by federal reinforcements.

### Post-Civil War Progress

Agriculture had been dominant in Maryland prior to the Civil War, with the major crop of tobacco being shipped through the port of Baltimore. However, after the war the state's economy shifted toward manufacturing. Baltimore remained a key shipbuilding and weaponry production center; in the twentieth century the city would make rockets and missiles for the U.S. military. Both shipbuilding and weapons manufacture were spurred by government purchases during the two world wars.

Education in the state received an infusion of resources during the second half of the nineteenth century, especially with donations from philanthropists such as Johns Hopkins, who provided the financial backing to create the prestigious university that bears his name. Later, in the 1960's, federal funds were allocated for the National Institutes of Health at Bethesda and the Goddard Space Flight Center.

### Toward the Future

As the twentieth century advanced, Maryland's agriculture remained important, with the chief crops being tobacco, corn, hay, and soybeans. Manufacturing continued to expand, primarily in shipbuilding, transportation equipment, and modern technology such as electronics. Fishing in the renewed Chesapeake Bay provided much of the seafood sold nationally. However, it was commerce which led Maryland's revitalization, especially in its largest city.

Throughout most of Maryland's history, trade and commerce focused on Baltimore, which underwent a striking revival starting in the 1950's. Under Kurt Schmoke, the first African American elected mayor of the city, Baltimore completed an ambitious reconstruction of its inner harbor, with its centerpiece being the USS *Constellation*, the first warship commissioned by the U.S. Navy, in 1797. In 1992 the Baltimore Orioles opened their new stadium, Camden Yards, widely hailed as one of the best-designed and most attractive of modern baseball parks.

Perhaps Maryland's most visible success is its reclaiming of Chesapeake Bay and its adoption of a policy of smart growth to combat urban sprawl. After decades of environmental neglect, including drainage of agriculture chemicals, unregulated dumping of waste, and overfishing, the bay was seriously endangered. Governor Marvin Mandel established a Chesapeake Bay Interagency Planning Committee, and a widespread Save the Bay organization was created—two parts of a comprehensive effort that linked grassroots activists, government, and the private sector in addressing the problem. Spurred by the growing success of this effort, an association of environmental and citizen groups known as the Thousand Friends of Maryland began to campaign for strategic planning and "smart growth" to control urban sprawl, save Maryland's traditional farmlands, and preserve its small towns and their unique character. Supported by Governor Parris Glendening, who made smart growth an issue in his reelection campaign, the Maryland smart growth program became a national trendsetter for the twenty-first century.

—*Michael Witkoski*

# Annapolis

**Date:** Town founded in 1694; U.S. Naval Academy established in 1845

**Relevant issues:** Colonial America, military history

**Significance:** Annapolis was the capital of colonial Maryland. The downtown area is a registered National Historic Landmark District; the most notable landmark is the State House, the oldest state capitol in the United States. Annapolis also is the site of the U.S. Naval Academy.

**Location:** Anne Arundel County, at the mouth of the Severn River, at the point at which it empties into the Chesapeake Bay; thirty-five miles east of Washington, D.C., off Route 50

**Site Office:**
Historic Annapolis Foundation
18 Pinkney Street
Annapolis, MD 21401

ph.: (800) 603-4020; (410) 267-7619
fax: (410) 267-6189
Web site: www.annapolis.org

Situated at the mouth of the Severn River, where it empties into the Chesapeake Bay, Annapolis has been the capital of Maryland—first as a colony, then as a state—since 1694, and it boasts the oldest state capitol still in use in the country. With its eighteen miles of scenic shoreline and beautifully preserved colonial buildings, Annapolis is also famous for the U.S. Naval Academy, which has been part of the Annapolis landscape since 1845.

### Early History
Few would guess that present-day Annapolis, peaceful, quaint, and capital of a small, progressive-minded state, had its origins in violent religious conflicts carried over from the Old World. Cecilius Calvert, the second Lord Baltimore, was a Catholic who desired to carry out his dead father's wish—to establish a haven of religious toleration in the New World, since he despaired of ever realizing such a haven at home. Charles I, king of England, was himself a Catholic and sympathetic to the young Lord Baltimore's aspiration. In 1632, the king granted him a charter to establish a colony in an area ceded from the colony of Virginia, which Lord Baltimore promptly named in gratitude Terra Mariae (after Charles I's wife), or Maryland. The first boatload of one hundred fifty colonists arrived shortly afterward—ironically, few of them Catholics. The majority of them, Puritans and Anglicans, soon sowed the seeds of religious bigotry and discord. In 1649, a law, progressive for that day and age, was enacted by the Maryland legislature that guaranteed religious toleration to all Christian creeds. This only encouraged more Puritans to emigrate from heavily Anglican Virginia to Maryland.

A group of Puritans, disdaining to settle in the only city in Maryland, St. Mary's, because of its Anglican majority, opted instead for land on the Severn River (where the future U.S. Naval Academy would be established). They would become the first European settlers in the area that would one day become Annapolis. Naming their new settlement Providence, they proceeded to defy the governor, Thomas Stone, who had generously granted them their land, by refusing to take an oath of allegiance to the proprietor of Maryland, the Catholic Calvert family. When they also defied Governor Stone's ultimatum, a contingent of Maryland militia under Stone's command confronted the aggressive Puritan force, who in short order killed over twenty of Stone's men and captured the governor himself, in what would come to be known as the Severn, in March, 1655.

### Religious Conflicts in England
The Puritans had been encouraged in their bellicosity by happenings in England, where the Roman Catholic monarchy was violently overthrown in 1649 by Puritans, who established a religious dictatorship under the helm of Oliver Cromwell. Cromwell revoked Lord Baltimore's charter, ending his ownership of Maryland, to the glee of the colony's Puritans. However, when opposition to Cromwell slowly swelled and he stood in need of allies, he restored the charter, enabling Lord Baltimore once again to reassert his authority over the wayward colonists.

Even with the overthrow of the dictatorship and the restoration of yet another monarch, the Anglican Charles II, religious dissension simmered and finally exploded when Charles II's son James, a Catholic, became king in 1685. He was himself overthrown in 1688 in a peaceful revolution, bringing Protestant monarchs, William and Mary, to the English throne. One year later, in 1689, Protestant Marylanders overthrew the government of the Catholic Calverts. At this point the real history of Annapolis begins.

Until then, Annapolis was a sleepy hamlet called Anne Arundel Towne, situated just outside the Puritan settlement of Providence. Because most of the Catholic population of St. Mary's now harbored antigovernment sentiments, the Maryland legislature voted in favor of changing the capital to the town of Anne Arundel. The change occurred in 1694. Three years later, the legislature voted to change the name of the town to Annapolis, or "City of Anne," after Princess Anne, the sister of Queen Mary, who would herself become queen of England in 1702.

### Early Years as State Capital
Despite the strong religious motivation in moving the capital, religious dissension in Annapolis soon took a back seat to more worldly issues. For the first fifty years of its history as capital of Maryland,

Annapolis was a rough frontier town, with pigs freely roaming the unpaved streets and garbage strewn wherever it happened to fall. Francis Nicholson, the governor of Maryland in the 1690's, had designed the new capital city himself and awarded contracts for a church, state capitol building, and school. Major streets were to radiate from the two circles in the city center, one containing the church and the other the state capitol. This neat arrangement was violated time and again, however, by the helter-skelter arrangement of the buildings and private residences. Nicholson left the state in 1698 and subsequently became governor of Virginia and the founder of Williamsburg.

Annapolis grew slowly. When the State House was struck by lightning and burned to the ground in 1704, all the land deeds literally went up in smoke, halting new housing construction until the disorder could be straightened out. With the years, the raw town grew and gentrified. Unlike the planters in Virginia to the south, Maryland plantation owners gravitated to city life in the fall and winter months. Prosperity, derived from tobacco and wheat exports and the slave trade, enabled them to begin building the Georgian homes for which Annapolis is now famous and to throw lavish entertainments.

**Development of the Port**

Annapolis was becoming the most important port on the mid-Atlantic seaboard. Moreover, every year the Maryland assembly gathered in the State House and the courts began their sessions, creating the need for hotels, shops, and taverns and supplementing the town's prosperity. By the mid-1700's, Annapolis entered its golden age, which lasted from approximately 1755 to 1775. Leading families such as the Pacas, the Prices, the Scotts, and the Ridouts engaged architects for their splendid homes and were patrons of the town theater and horse racing and founders of the Jockey, Tuesday, Homony, Forensic, and South River Clubs. Prior to the Revolutionary War, George Washington traveled at least eighteen times to the lively city on Maryland's eastern shore, no mean undertaking in the eighteenth century for someone who lived over fifty miles away, at Mount Vernon in Virginia (his travel would have been along the riverways, by boat). Washington would bring his family to enjoy Raceweek in September and was a member of the Homony Club, which had been founded to "promote innocent mirth and ingenious humor." King George I in 1715 restored the charter of the Catholic Calvert family, who once again became proprietors of the province of Maryland. This time no discord or rebellion ensued, in part because the citizens were too busy making money.

The peaceful climate would soon end, however; by the early 1770's, revolutionary

*Cadets lining up at the U.S. Naval Academy, which opened in Annapolis in 1845.* (Middleton Evans/Maryland Office of Tourism)

fervor ran high in Annapolis. In 1774, just prior to the outbreak of hostilities between Great Britain and the colonies, a crowd of Annapolitans burned the ship *Peggy Stewart* because its owner, a native of the city, had paid the tea tax. Two years later, three Annapolis men—William Paca, Samuel Chase, and Charles Carroll—signed the Declaration of Independence.

## The Revolutionary War

War, when it arrived, did not touch Annapolis directly. Famous men, such as Generals Marquis de Lafayette, Comte de Rochambeau, Baron de Kalb, and George Washington, spent time in the city during those dramatic years, either to provision or assemble their forces. Far more stirring were the events following the conclusion of peace. The Treaty of Paris ending the conflict in 1783 was ratified in the Maryland State House by the Continental Congress. On December 23 of that year, George Washington resigned as commander in chief of the Continental Army in the State House, an event that artist John Trumbull sentimentally commemorated in a painting now hanging in the U.S. Capitol. For a period of ten months, from November, 1783, to August, 1784, Annapolis served as the de facto capital of the thirteen independent states. Annapolis also witnessed a convention of representatives from five states in 1786, gathered to determine how to strengthen the central government. Before adjourning, the delegates voted to meet again in Philadelphia the next year, setting the stage for the historic constitutional convention.

## Nineteenth Century Decline

By 1800, if not before, Annapolis had begun a slow decline into provincial obscurity. The city lacked Baltimore's deep water harbor; consequently, Annapolis's port facilities grew increasingly inadequate and shipping declined. Furthermore, its location, away from western markets and hemmed in on three sides by waterways, limited its growth and discouraged the building of canals and, later, of railroads. There was even talk in the Maryland State Assembly of removing the capital to Baltimore. Agricultural spokesmen, distrusting "big city" Baltimore, successfully exerted pressure on the assembly to retain the capital in rural Anne Arundel County.

## The War of 1812

Times grew dangerous again when the fledgling United States went to war with Great Britain in 1812. Although Admiral George Cockburn sailed with a sizable fleet of fifty ships into the Chesapeake Bay, the vessels did not touch down in the insignificant harbor of Annapolis. Instead, they decided to move on to more tempting ground—Washington, D.C.—which Cockburn's forces burned to the ground. Annapolis did score more than a footnote in this drama. A native son and graduate of St. John's College in Annapolis, Francis Scott Key, was moved to compose "The Star-Spangled Banner" as he watched Fort McHenry being bombarded by the British. Prior to that attack, Major William Barney in Annapolis had observed the British fleet sailing past the city from his vantage point in the State House (on the highest hill in the city). He was able to relay to the commander of Fort McHenry the number of British ships, and as a result, the Americans were prepared, the British were trounced, and a national anthem was born.

When the war ended in 1814, Annapolis returned to its sleepy isolation. Not until 1840 would a railroad line come to the city, and this would remain the only one until 1887. Improvements in the hygiene and comfort of the town were made as well: for instance, sidewalks were paved in brick in the 1820's. It was in that decade that the Maryland Assembly began lobbying Congress to establish a naval academy in Annapolis. This project had been in the docket for years. Old Fort Severn, an army base, was decaying and useless. However, it was difficult to persuade congressmen to fund an institution that they feared would turn out "trifling or effeminate" men and, worse, men who upon graduation would become dissatisfied and possibly dangerous in times of peace.

In the early 1840's, President James K. Polk finally appointed the historian George Bancroft secretary of the navy. Unwavering in his belief in a professional navy, he declined to lobby Congress to support a naval academy, fearing long-winded hearings. Instead, he overrode Congress during a recess and turned directly to the War Department. With no use for the decaying fort on the Severn River, the army gladly ceded it to the navy on August 15, 1845. It took two months to prepare the school to open as a naval academy. Situated just outside the city limits on a campus of three hundred acres, it would in time help lift the veil of obscurity from the beautiful colonial town.

**The Civil War**

At a time when sectional differences were flaring up between North and South, there was little doubt that the city of Annapolis, like the rest of the state, was clearly pro-Southern. The only exceptions were the mayor of Annapolis and the editor and publisher of the Annapolis *Gazette*. However, this was not enough to save the city from Union occupation throughout the Civil War years. Those cadets at the naval academy whose loyalties were with the South returned to Dixie; the rest were transferred from Annapolis to Newport, Rhode Island, the home of the academy for the rest of the war. The academy grounds and buildings at Annapolis served as a Union hospital.

President Abraham Lincoln's Emancipation Proclamation did not affect the status of slaves in Union or technically "loyal" states, such as Maryland. However, knowing which way the wind was blowing, the Maryland legislature voted to free all slaves in the state on November 1, 1864, nearly two years after the Proclamation. This liberated from bondage nearly five hundred slaves in Annapolis, although real freedom would take another century.

Annapolis dwellers yearned for an end to the occupation and a return to normalcy. When Southern forces finally accepted surrender, Annapolitans submitted to the return of the old order. The U.S. Naval Academy reestablished itself in the city, which would also witness a steady growth of prosperity, an expansion of state and local government, and the beginnings of a historic preservation movement.

**Twentieth Century Development**

The expansion of state government was reflected in the doubling of the size of the State House in the early twentieth century, followed in the late 1930's by a row of new state office buildings that would continue to expand until well after World War II (including one of the least favorite, a state income tax building, in 1967). With over half of all employed residents working for either state or local government by 1976, the mainstay of the city's economy no longer was centered on fishing and ag-

riculture. The need for ever greater expansion of government, usually requiring the demolition of old buildings for the erection of modern ones, fueled an incipient historic preservation movement in the city as early as the late nineteenth century. The Local Improvement Society, led by Annapolis native Frank Mayer, decried the modernization of the State House and began raising the consciousness of the city's inhabitants to the priceless historic character of their buildings. In 1925, the Company for the Preservation of Colonial Annapolis was established.

In 1940, when Henry Ford tried to acquire the Hammond-Harwood House, one of the finest colonial homes in America (which he planned to dismantle and reassemble in Michigan), another Annapolis group, the Hammond-Harwood Association, came together to thwart him and succeeded. Historic Annapolis, Incorporated, founded in 1952, became more successful than any other preservation group in Annapolis. This group labored intensively on behalf of the preservation of downtown Annapolis, which in 1966, thanks to their efforts, became registered as a National Historic Landmark District. Annapolis now ranks with Williamsburg, Virginia, as the most authentic colonial urban area in the nation. This active preservation group has proved time and again the economic value of saving historic buildings from destruction. The downtown area of Annapolis, which for decades had been slipping further into shabby decline (the growth of state and local government deprived the city of a tax base), has led in the revitalization of the area and the burgeoning of small businesses.

**Historic Buildings**

There are numerous buildings of notable historic interest, including the U.S. Naval Academy, with which the city has become increasingly identified. Not until Theodore Roosevelt became president did the academy witness major expansion, which necessitated razing some buildings of historic interest. In their place were established new classrooms, Bancroft Hall (a dormitory), a chapel, and other buildings centered on a quadrangle. The campus houses a museum displaying naval mementos going back to 1812, a collection of sailing ship models from 1650 to 1850, and many other historic artifacts.

Within the city limits lie a rich array of historic buildings, the most prominent of which is the State House, which boasts the largest wooden dome in the country. On view within the State House are the Old Senate Chamber, with eight pieces of original furniture dating from the period 1783 to 1784; the Old Senate Committee Room, with exhibits on Washington's original resignation from the Continental Army; and the Constitution Room, with paintings depicting Maryland's history. The Old Treasury Building, on the grounds of the State House, was constructed in 1737 and is now the tour office of Historic Annapolis, Incorporated.

St. Anne's Church, on Church Circle, was built in the 1780's and lovingly restored after a fire burned it to the ground in 1858. On display in the church is a silver communion service that was the gift of King William III, husband of Queen Mary. In the church burial ground, the oldest grave (containing the remains of Amos Garrett, the first mayor of Annapolis) dates from 1727; this cemetery also contains the grave of the last colonial governor of Annapolis (Sir Robert Eden).

In Annapolis's dock area stands the birthplace of Charles Carroll, signer of the Declaration of Independence and one of the wealthiest men of his day. This house is only one of several outstanding examples of eighteenth century colonial architecture in Annapolis. On Prince George's Street, for instance, there is the Paca House, whose namesake was another signer of the Declaration of Independence. Consisting of thirty-seven rooms situated on a two-acre formal garden, the house was considered the most elegant home in colonial Annapolis. It was saved from demolition after World War II by preservationists, who in the 1960's and 1970's extensively restored it to its original splendor.

Rivaling the Paca House in historic importance are the Hammond-Harwood House on Maryland Avenue, designed by famed Annapolis architect William Buckland in the 1770's, and the Chase-Lloyd House across the street, the interior of which was completed by Buckland. Maryland's first public school, King William's School, established in 1694, was transformed into St. John's College in 1696. George Washington's two nephews graduated from this school, as did Francis Scott Key. From 1937 to the present day, St. John's has adopted the Great Books program of liberal education, which eliminates specializations; professors are called tutors and often teach outside their fields. A famous landmark on the campus is the four hundred-year-old Liberty Tree, which witnessed earnest discussions of independence from Great Britain and a return visit of General Lafayette in 1824.                      —*Sina Dubovoy*

**For Further Information:**

Anderson, Elizabeth B. *Annapolis: A Walk Through History.* Centreville, Md.: Tidewater, 1984. For a solid, readable, and illustrated discussion of Annapolis history and a tour of its most important historic landmarks, this is still one of the best accounts available.

Calnek, W. A. *History of the County of Annapolis.* Edited and completed by A. W. Savary. Bowie, Md.: Heritage, 1999. According to the subtitle of this book, it includes *Old Port Royal and Acadia, with Memoirs of Its Representatives in the Provincial Parliament, and Biographical and Genealogiical Sketches of Its Early English Settlers and Their Families.*

Miller, Roger. *Annapolis: A Portrait.* Baltimore: Image, 1987. Similar to Anderson's work above, although less solid.

Papenfuse, Edward C. *In Pursuit of Profit: The Annapolis Merchants in the Era of the American Revolution, 1763-1805.* Baltimore: The Johns Hopkins University Press, 1975. Specialized, but highly informative and readable.

Warren, Mame. *Then Again—: Annapolis, 1900-1965.* Annapolis, Md.: Time Exposures, 1990. Specialized, but highly informative and readable.

# Antietam

**Date:** Battle fought on September 17, 1862; established as a National Battlefield on August 30, 1890

**Relevant issues:** Civil War, military history

**Significance:** The bloodiest one-day battle of the Civil War took place in the fields and woods between the town of Sharpsburg, Maryland, and Antietam Creek. The Battle of Antietam (called the Battle of Sharpsburg by the Confederacy) resulted in more than twenty-three thousand casualties.

**Location:** Northeastern Maryland, near the West

Virginia border, near the intersection of Maryland Routes 34 and 65

**Site Office:**

Antietam National Battlefield and Cemetery
National Park Service
Box 158
Sharpsburg, MD 21782
ph.: (301) 432-5124
Web site: www.nps.gov/anti/

At the start of the Civil War, the acreage between Antietam Creek and the town of Sharpsburg consisted of farm fields and woods. Several farmhouses dotted the landscape, and a Dunker church stood about one mile north of town. At the commencement of hostilities between the North and South, Maryland had declared itself neutral. It was a slave state that had remained loyal to the Union by refusing to secede from the United States as other Southern slave states had done. Maryland's neutrality was violated in September, 1862, when forty thousand Confederate troops commanded by General Robert E. Lee marched north from Virginia across the Maryland border. As Lee's Army of Northern Virginia marched north, the Army of the Potomac, eighty-seven thousand federal troops under the command of General George B. McClellan, moved from Washington, D.C., into Maryland to check the Confederate advance. The two armies engaged in the woods and fields east of Sharpsburg in one of the major battles of the Civil War. The site of that fierce battle is preserved as the Antietam National Battlefield and Cemetery.

### Lee's Maryland Campaign

In early September of 1862, President Jefferson Davis of the Confederacy and General Lee, encouraged by several recent stunning victories against Northern troops on Virginia soil, launched a bold plan to invade the North. Lee's goal would be to march through Maryland into Pennsylvania and capture the city of Harrisburg, an important railroad link between the large eastern cities and Chicago. Davis and Lee assumed that a large rebel force on Northern soil would cause the United States citizenry to panic and pressure the federal government to recognize the Confederacy's independence and end the war. When Lee began his march into Maryland, however, President Abraham Lincoln assumed that Lee's goal was to invade Washington, D.C. He urgently ordered General McClellan to position his large army between the capital and Lee's troops. As Lee approached Maryland he divided his troops, sending almost half his men under Major General Thomas "Stonewall" Jackson to capture a lightly guarded federal arms arsenal at Harpers Ferry, Virginia.

On September 13, McClellan became aware of Lee's plan. In a field near Frederick, Maryland, a Union corporal had found three cigars wrapped in a piece of paper containing Lee's orders. McClellan quickly pushed his men westward toward Lee. On September 14, Yankee and rebel troops skirmished at three passes in South Mountain. The next day, Lee, sensing a major confrontation, moved his men to ground that would be easy to defend—the crest of a three-mile ridge just east of Sharpsburg. In front of Lee's army was Antietam Creek, and McClellan began to form his lines east of the creek facing Lee's army.

### The Battle of Antietam

Had McClellan attacked Lee on September 15, he might have crushed Lee's army. Lee had barely twenty thousand men—the rest were at Harpers Ferry—facing McClellan's army of eighty-seven thousand. In earlier campaigns, however, McClellan had shown himself to be a cautious general who consistently overestimated the strength of his enemy's army. He spent two days positioning his troops before attacking, a delay that allowed the bulk of Stonewall Jackson's army to depart from Harpers Ferry, which the rebels had captured, and join Lee at Sharpsburg.

On the morning of September 17, McClellan gave the order to attack. Before dawn, a Union artillery barrage commenced on Lee's left flank, posted at the Dunker church north of Sharpsburg and anchored by Jackson. At first light, Union infantry under the command of Major General Joseph Hooker advanced on Jackson's men, pushing them backward and almost turning the flank. Lee sent Jackson reinforcements, and his line held. A fierce battle between Hooker's and Jackson's forces developed in a cornfield. The five-foot-tall cornstalks were cut down by musket and cannon shot, and thousands of soldiers fell.

At around 9:30 A.M., McClellan attacked the center of the Confederate line. Rebel troops there under the command of Colonel John B. Gordon had positioned themselves in a sunken road, and they opened fire on Yankee infantry charging across an open field, inflicting heavy casualties. For four hours, waves of Yankee troops attacked the sunken road but were repulsed by determined rebels. Finally, men from a New York regiment moved to some higher ground where they could shoot down at the Confederates holding the sunken road. Rebel soldiers began falling in great numbers, and the sunken road—later called Bloody Lane—filled with dead bodies. Finally, the Confederates retreated, but McClellan failed to press the attack.

Just after Yankee troops attacked Lee's center, Union regiments under the command of Major General Ambrose Burnside attacked the Confederate right flank. There, fewer than five hundred Georgia infantrymen were dug in on a ridge overlooking a stone bridge that crossed Antietam Creek. Four times Burnside's men assaulted the bridge, but the Georgians held them off. Finally, after three hours of furious fighting, Burnside's troops crossed the bridge and routed the rebels, sending them on a hasty retreat toward the town of Sharpsburg. Burnside requested reinforcements to press the attack, but the cautious McClellan held back.

Lee's army was near destruction. Jackson was barely holding out on the Confederate left flank. Lee's center had broken, and Burnside had smashed the rebel right flank. McClellan, however, remained cautious and refused to send his reserves into the battle. At around 1:00 P.M., McClellan ceased his attack to re-form his lines. For almost two hours, Lee's men had a reprieve from the fierce Yankee assaults.

At around 3:00 P.M. the federals renewed the attack. Within an hour, however, Lee received desperately needed reinforcements. Three thousand Confederate infantry—a division under the command of Lieutenant General A. P. Hill that had been left behind to hold Harpers Ferry—arrived at Sharpsburg after a rapid seventeen-mile march. Hill's troops attacked Burnside immediately, checking the federal advance on Lee's right. The rebels drove Burnside's Yankees back to the bridge that they had taken a few hours earlier, and the Yankee troops established a defensive position.

*Antietam Battlefield.* (Middleton Evans/Maryland Office of Tourism)

McClellan, fearing that he was outnumbered, called off the attack. The battle died down as dusk fell.

The casualties were staggering. September 17, 1862, was the bloodiest day of the Civil War. Federal casualties—defined as killed, wounded, captured, or missing in action—amounted to 12,410 men. The Confederates lost 10,700, more than a quarter of Lee's army. Eight thousand men had been killed or wounded in the early-morning battle in the cornfield. Another six thousand fell in and around the sunken road. Whole regiments had been obliterated. In several minutes of fierce fighting, the Twelfth Massachusetts Regiment lost 224 of 334 men. As the sun set on the Antietam battlefield, thousands of men lay wounded and dead in the fields and woods outside Sharpsburg. Houses in the town that had not been hit by stray shells were turned into makeshift field hospitals, where overtaxed surgeons worked to save the wounded.

Citizens of both the North and the South were aghast at the slaughter at Antietam Creek. A battle with similar casualties had never before been fought on American soil. Two weeks after the battle, the photographer Mathew Brady opened an exhibition titled "The Dead of Antietam" at his New York gallery. One reviewer commented that Brady, via his gripping battlefield photographs, had virtually laid the dead "in our door-yards and along [our] streets."

### The Battle's Aftermath

On September 18, Lee, ever eager for a battle, reluctantly ordered a retreat. His army had suffered too many casualties to fight another day. He moved southward, back into Virginia. When Lee retreated, McClellan claimed a victory. He had stopped Lee's invasion of the North.

President Lincoln, however, did not view the Battle of Antietam as a total victory. He had wanted McClellan to destroy Lee's army. He had urged McClellan to block Lee's retreat; Lincoln did not want to give Lee the opportunity to regroup and fight again. Two weeks after the battle, Lincoln pressed McClellan to move against Lee's depleted army, now encamped in Virginia, but McClellan claimed that his army's horses were too tired. A month later, Lincoln relieved McClellan of command of the Army of the Potomac, and McClellan retired to his home in New Jersey. Lee continued to fight for another two and a half years.

Though he was not completely satisfied with the outcome at Antietam, Lincoln used the battle politically. Since the beginning of the war, abolitionists in Congress had urged Lincoln to emancipate the slaves in the states that had seceded from the Union. Lincoln had been reluctant to free the slaves because he had consistently asserted that the war between North and South was a conflict over secession, not over slavery. By the summer of 1862, however, Lincoln had come to realize the necessity of freeing the slaves, but he wanted to wait for a Northern victory on the battlefield before taking any action. Before the Battle of Antietam, Lincoln had prayed that McClellan's army would stop Lee's invasion of the North. Lincoln had told members of his cabinet that he would view a Union victory as a sign from God that the slaves should be freed.

On September 22, five days after the great battle at Antietam Creek, Lincoln issued a Preliminary Emancipation Proclamation, announcing that he would free all slaves in the states in rebellion on January 1, 1863, if those states did not return to the Union. No Southern state rejoined the Union, and on January 1 Lincoln issued the Emancipation Proclamation.

### Visiting Antietam National Battlefield

The National Park Service administers the Antietam National Battlefield, which is open to visitors daily except on Thanksgiving, Christmas, and New Year's Day. Signs on Maryland Route 65 direct motorists to the visitors' center, which houses a small museum containing photographs, uniforms, weapons, flags, and other relics from the battle. An audiovisual program shown at the visitors' center provides an overview of the battle.

From the visitors' center, tourists can take an auto or bicycle tour of the Antietam battlefield over a paved road. Markers are set at key points—the Dunker Church (a replica of the original, which was destroyed by a storm in 1921), the cornfield, Bloody Lane, and Burnside's Bridge. The tour takes about two hours.

The area around Antietam battlefield remains relatively undeveloped. Woods and farm fields still dominate the landscape east of Sharpsburg, giving visitors the illusion that they have stepped back into the mid-nineteenth century when the bloodiest one-day battle of the Civil War took place.

—*James Tackach*

**For Further Information:**

Long, E. B. *The Civil War Day by Day: An Almanac.* Garden City, N.Y.: Doubleday, 1971. A detailed guide of military operations during the Civil War.

McPherson, James M. *Battle Cry of Freedom: The Civil War Era.* New York: Oxford University Press, 1983. An excellent single-volume study of the Civil War.

Oates, Stephen B. *The Whirlwind of War: Voices of the Storm, 1861-1865.* New York: HarperCollins, 1998. Oates uses first-person narrators—Lincoln, Lee, Davis, and others—to tell the story of the Civil War.

Sears, Stephen. *Landscape Turned Red: The Battle of Antietam.* New York: Warner Books, 1983. A detailed book-length analysis of the battle.

Ward, Geoffrey C., Ric Burns, and Ken Burns. *The Civil War.* Alfred A. Knopf, 1990. This illustrated history of the Civil War complements Ken Burns's award-winning documentary film.

# Camp David

**Date:** Created in 1942

**Relevant issues:** Cultural history, political history, Vietnam War, World War II

**Significance:** A presidential retreat that offers relaxation and refuge from the demands of Washington, D.C., Camp David has given American presidents since Franklin Delano Roosevelt the opportunity to think, reflect, and make decisions away from the White House during times of stress and responsibility.

**Location:** In the Catoctin Mountains; Camp David is not open or accessible to the public, but the eastern hardwood forest of Catoctin Mountain Park is a U.S. National Park with camping, picnicking, fishing, miles of hiking trails, and scenic mountain views.

**Site Office:**

Superintendent
Catoctin Mountain Park
6602 Foxville Road
Thurmont, MD 21788-1598
ph.: (301) 663-9330, 663-9388

A site for presidential weekends away from the pressures of the White House, Camp David has amusements and recreational facilities including a bowling alley, bridle paths for horseback riding, a golf course, a heated pool, a helicopter pad, movie screens and projectors, a skeet range, a staff pool, and a tennis court. Nearly two dozen wooden cabins can accommodate the president, his family, White House staff, cabinet officers, and, sometimes, international heads of state. Some presidents have used Camp David almost exclusively for recreation; others have crafted international agreements with foreign dignitaries at the mountain retreat.

**A Fabulous Fiction Made Real**

President Franklin Delano Roosevelt (FDR) chose the site and the name for the retreat in 1942. He called it "Shangri-La," after the mythical community described in James Hilton's 1933 novel *Lost Horizon.* President Dwight D. Eisenhower's grandson, David Eisenhower, in the foreword he wrote to W. Dale Nelson's *The President Is at Camp David* (1995), explains this choice of names.

Why should a president have a retreat like Camp David? In theory, the American presidency is a democratic office charged primarily with tending to the welfare and happiness of the citizens who elect the president. For a long time, though, the president has been much more than that; since the 1930s, Americans have reluctantly but inevitably accepted responsibilities for world peace and progress, and the presidency has been the institution responsible for coordinating American action toward that end. So it is today, and so it became at some indefinable moment at about the time *Lost Horizon* was published in 1933.

Hilton's novel clearly foretells the catastrophe of World War II. It describes the mission of the mythical community of Shangri-La in undertaking to spare mankind's cultural treasures from the plague of barbarism about to descend. In the story, Hugh Conway, a British diplomat, is anointed by the High Lama of Shangri-La to assume charge of the community and its mission. Conway declines at first and leaves Shangri-La, sensing that the task would be beyond him. The book ends just as Conway resolves to try after all and begins his arduous journey back.

It is not a stretch to conceive of FDR during 1941–42 as seeing parallels between Conway's mis-

*President John F. Kennedy (left) and former President Dwight D. Eisenhower discuss the Cuban Missile Crisis as they walk along a path at Camp David in 1961.* (AP/Wide World Photos)

president. The site in the Catoctin Mountains was chosen on April 22, 1942, but the pressures of World War II upon the president quickly made the mountain retreat a working extension of the Oval Office. Winston Churchill, the British prime minister, conferred with FDR at the camp when it was called Shangri-La over the details of the Allied invasion of Normandy. They also managed to make time to fish together in nearby Hunting Creek.

FDR's confinement to a wheelchair due to polio made it necessary to equip "the Bear's Den," as the main presidential cabin was called, with special features. A nine-foot-high wall was erected around the camp, and Marines were stationed to guard the camp's perimeter. Seclusion was, and is, essential to the camp's charm. It is off limits to the press, permits few visitors, and is vigilantly guarded. FDR spent more than twenty weekends at Shangri-La from 1942 to 1944. Eleanor Roosevelt was a less frequent visitor to the camp than other First Ladies who followed her. It is likely that her relationship with FDR had cooled after Mrs. Roosevelt discovered FDR's affair with his social secretary, Lucy Mercer.

The dress code at the presidential camp was the opposite of what it was at the White House: casual clothes, no suits, no ties. A staff of nearly one hundred (including the Secret Service) occupied the twenty unheated cabins near the president's lodge. Few cabins had running water, and fewer had hot water. Cabin occupants washed outside in metal troughs, some twenty-five chilly yards from the cabins where they slept. In "the Bear's Den" building, fireplaces were added to the four bedrooms, since nights at 1,800 feet of elevation can be quite chilly, even in summer.

The camp could not easily be seen from the air because the natural wood buildings blended into the dense forest. Still, the Secret Service managed to restrict air traffic over the camp, as it did over the White House. FDR's successor, Harry S Truman, was not impressed by the rustic seclusion of

sion and his own; that as president of the United States it was his duty to mobilize America to serve as a bastion against the assault of fascism and twentieth-century totalitarianism. Conceivably, like Conway, he felt that he would need a camp, a "paradise" where he could be fortified to face the decisions he knew were necessary to defend America and the future of civilization. The cold war challenged his successors in the same way.

For a long time his doctors had advised Roosevelt to leave the swampy heat of Washington, D.C., whenever possible, particularly during the sweltering summers. Roosevelt's asthma made higher elevations and cooler mountain air desirable for the

Shangri-La. Thirty men went to work felling trees, and they created a clearing that would later be Dwight D. Eisenhower's golf course. In nearly eight years as president, Truman visited the camp only nine times. He did have the buildings winterized for year-round use. When uncertainty about the camp's fate followed Roosevelt's death, it was Truman who decided that it was to remain a presidential retreat. The slender wooden gate that guarded the camp during FDR's day was replaced during the Reagan administration by a reinforced metal fence at the camp's entrance, guarded by a contingent of Marines.

### Golf and Cold War Diplomacy

After Truman, President Dwight D. Eisenhower renamed Shangri-La "Camp David" after his father and grandson. Periodic efforts were made over the next several decades to restore the original name that FDR had given the camp, but the image of the retreat had become fixed in the public's mind as Camp David, and the name had international recognition as well. The White House of Bill Clinton reported that suggestions to restore the earlier name were no longer made during Clinton's tenure as president.

Because Eisenhower had campaigned on an austerity platform, the president initially objected to the camp as an unnecessary luxury. Mamie Eisenhower insisted on further modernization if the president were to keep the camp as a retreat. A small, three-hole golf course was installed, one that Eisenhower enjoyed but President Gerald R. Ford would later complain about as too small.

Eisenhower, recovering from a heart attack in 1955, met with his cabinet at Camp David. He was the first president to introduce helicopter travel between Washington, D.C., and Camp David. An underground bomb shelter was added to the camp to serve as a sort of presidential command post in the event of nuclear war. Soviet Premier Nikita Khrushchev was a guest at Camp David in 1960, a meeting that came to be known as "the spirit of Camp David." The two world leaders shared a fondness for Western films, and the talks between them represented a temporary thaw in the Cold War relations between Moscow and Washington, D.C.

President John F. Kennedy met with former president Eisenhower at Camp David in 1961 after the failure of a United States-organized force to invade Cuba at the Bay of Pigs. Although a pony ring was built for Caroline Kennedy's pony at Camp David, the Kennedys visited the camp less than two dozen times. Kennedy's successor, Lyndon Baines Johnson (LBJ), visited Camp David twenty-nine times over the five and one-half years of his presidency. Often the domestic turmoil surrounding the Vietnam War drove LBJ to the mountain retreat, where mental peace eluded a president who presided over a very unpopular war.

Johnson's successor, Richard Nixon, went to Camp David to draft presidential speeches on Vietnam, as persistent a problem for him as it had been for LBJ. Important decisions about the American economy were made at the camp by Nixon and his aides. After Vice President Spiro Agnew resigned office amid a bribery scandal, Nixon, at Camp David, chose Gerald R. Ford as vice president. In June, 1973, Soviet Premier Leonid Brezhnev visited Camp David for talks on nuclear weapons. By 1973 Nixon had made 149 visits to Camp David, entertained eleven foreign visitors, and made Camp David more central to his presidency than any other president. The Nixon administration's frenetic efforts to cover up its role in the break-in at the Democratic National Committee in the Washington Watergate building led Nixon and his aides to retreat to Camp David to strategize, but the scandal ultimately compelled Nixon to resign from office.

President Gerald R. Ford permitted television crews to film parts of Camp David and to interview him there. His successor, Jimmy Carter, invited Egyptian president Anwar el-Sadat and Israeli prime minister Menachem Begin to Camp David. The thirteen days of meetings at this Middle Eastern summit resulted in a major international agreement, known as the Camp David Accords. The Camp David Accords led to a peace treaty between Israel and Egypt on March 26, 1979. Both Begin and Sadat were awarded the Nobel Peace Prize for their efforts at Camp David.

Carter's successor, Ronald Reagan, visited the camp a total of 187 times, more than any other president. Reagan used the camp primarily as a personal haven for himself and his wife, Nancy, and seldom invited foreign visitors, although British prime minister Margaret Thatcher visited twice. Horseback riding was a favorite pastime for the Reagans. By 1986 the maintenance and operations budget for Camp David had grown to $1.6 million annually. A chapel, at the cost of $1 million, was added in 1991. George Bush, Reagan's successor, met with Defense Secretary Dick Cheney at Camp David to decide to dispatch military forces to repel Iraq's invasion of Kuwait in 1991. William Jefferson Clinton, Bush's successor, did not use Camp David with the frequency of other presidents.

**An Imperial Presidency or a Necessary Retreat?**
Camp David, in its distance from the nation's capital, has permitted American presidents to both make history and escape history. It has provided a locale for important international and domestic conferences that have had far-reaching effects. Perhaps as important, it has given the occupant of the White House a physical alternative to the fenced-in urban dwelling the president regularly inhabits.

Rather than being an extravagant expression of the president's imperial powers, as Dwight D. Eisenhower initially thought, Camp David has offered most of its presidents a measure of tranquillity and a temporary haven from the rigors of what may be the most demanding job on earth.

—*Roberta Schreyer*

**For Further Information:**
"Catoctin Mountain Park." www.atevo.com/guides/parks/item/0,3653,38,00.html. A guide to the Catoctin Mountain Park near Camp David, a U.S. National Park open to the public. Good description of park facilities and recreational activities. See also the National Park Service site at www.nps.gov/cato/.

home.rose.net/~dingdong/CDHistory/. A general history of the camp, the presidential activities there, and Camp David's role in international diplomacy. A Web site written by the Department of the Navy. A good resource.

Nelson, Dale W. *The President Is at Camp David.* Syracuse, N.Y.: Syracuse University Press, 1995. An excellent history of the camp and the personalities who have given it national importance. A very readable account.

Parker, Thomas. *The Road to Camp David.* New York: Peter Lang, 1989. A history of the Middle Eastern dispute, the 1967 Arab-Israeli War, and the solutions arrived at in the Camp David Accords.

Quandt, William B. *Camp David Peacemaking and Politics.* Washington, D.C.: Brookings Institution, 1986. Written by an expert in foreign affairs, this is a detailed study of Jimmy Carter's role at Camp David in brokering a peace for the Middle East.

Telhami, Shibley. *Power and Leadership in International Bargaining: The Path to the Camp David Accords.* New York: Columbia University Press, 1990. Extensive analysis of the camp's famous international agreement.

# Clara Barton National Historic Site

**Date:** Home occupied by Barton in 1897; made a National Historic Site in 1975

**Relevant issues:** Civil War, military history, social reform, women's history

**Significance:** This house in Glen Echo, home to nurse Clara Barton (1821-1912) and her American Red Cross, is the first National Historic Site dedicated to a woman's life and public record of achievement.

**Location:** Glen Echo, by way of the Capitol Beltway and the Clara Barton Parkway; the site is administered by the George Washington Memorial Parkway

**Site Office:**
Clara Barton National Historic Site
5801 Oxford Road
Glen Echo, MD 20812
ph: (301) 492-6245
Web site: www.nps.gov/clba/

This National Historic Site was established in 1974 to commemorate Clara Barton's dedication to public service. Within it are preserved the beginnings of the history of the American Red Cross and the last home of its founder, Clara Barton. Barton spent the last fifteen years of her life in this Glen Echo home, usually busily occupied with the affairs of the American Red Cross. The National Park Service has restored eleven of the Glen Echo house's thirty rooms; including the Red Cross offices, Barton's parlors, and her bedroom. Visitors to the site receive a guided tour through the three levels of the home to witness how completely interwoven Clara Barton's life was with her humanitarian commitments.

## Barton Merges Private and Public Life

Barton's home at Glen Echo was the result of a charitable donation by two brothers, Edwin and Edward Baltzley, who planned to develop an intellectual and cultural community in Glen Echo. The Bartleys hoped that attracting a resident as famous and admired as Clara Barton would validate their project. In 1890, Barton was also searching for a new headquarters and supplies warehouse for the Red Cross. In a characteristic act that testifies to how inseparable Barton's life was from her work, the site was deeded to her as a private individual, but it was publicly announced as a property owned by the American Red Cross. Built in 1891, the Glen Echo house was initially a storehouse for Red Cross supplies, and in 1897 it was remodeled to serve both as official headquarters for the American Red Cross and as the home of the organization's founder. Located just outside Washington, D.C., the thirty-room house speaks volumes to visitors about the Red Cross and the tireless zeal of Clara Barton on behalf of humanitarian causes. Through-

out her life, Barton was happiest when she was busily responding to urgent human needs caused by war and by natural disasters.

One biographer, Elizabeth Brown Pryor, has analyzed Barton's personal motivation for public service: "In reality her whole life had been spent in a search for the public acclaim that served as a salve for the indifference of her family." She seems to have suffered, Pryor adds, from "a sad lack of self-esteem and a need to project an image of perfection," dying her hair well into her eighties and lowering her age when asked it. Barton's autobiographical memoir, *The Story of My Childhood* (1907), portrayed her actions and achievements in as idealized a manner as possible. In her memoir, Barton sometimes falsified facts in order to make herself the center of attention. Clearly her self-doubts and her need to overcome the struggles of her youth against an indifferent and often hostile mother played a powerful role in her efforts to compensate for the inadequacies of her upbringing.

Added to her painful family history as she grew

*Clara Barton (second from left) on the porch of her home in Glen Echo in 1904, the day after she resigned as president of the American Red Cross.* (US National Park Service, Clara Barton NHS)

up were the rigid social assumptions about women and their appropriate behaviors in the decades leading up to and just after the Civil War. Barton was probably correct in her view of herself as a social outsider, torn between a social imperative toward conformity and her urgent emotional and psychological tendencies toward rebellion. The traumatic results of this inner division occurred when she was not a battlefield nurse or agent of the American Red Cross. Periods of inactivity or passivity usually culminated in severe bouts of depression or in periods of nervous breakdown.

## Nineteenth Century Attitudes Toward Women

Clara Barton's pattern of emotional difficulties was not unusual for women in the nineteenth century. Energetic and ambitious women were prescribed the Weir-Mitchell rest cure when they were diagnosed with hysteria, neurasthenia, or nervous depression. According to this "cure," intellectual activity of any sort was forbidden and rest, seclusion, and inactivity were prescribed to restore the natural balance in a woman's well-being. Women, however, often understood their symptoms differently than the male medical establishment.

For many women in Barton's time, the conflict between their worldly public aspirations and their need for recognition were diametrically opposed to the prevailing Victorian and American ideal of domestic life and wifely devotion, often called "The Angel in the House" ideal after a popular British poem celebrating female virtues. As late as the 1920's, the British novelist Virginia Woolf wrote of the constricting power of the Angel in the House mentality that was directly opposed to a woman having a mind of her own. Woolf wrote that she strangled the Angel herself, in order to have freedom to think, to create, and to write. Certainly internalization of the domestic ideal harmed and inhibited female expression in some women. The Angel in the House metaphor embodied repression of female energies by cultural sanctions.

Driven by her own demons of personal and professional ambition, Clara Barton, rather than become the angel in the house as some man's wife and the mother to his children, chose to become the Angel of the Battlefield. During the Civil War, as a single woman not trained as a nurse, Barton worked tirelessly to bring medicine and supplies to the front lines of combat.

## A Life of Vital Activity

Even the barest outline of Clara Barton's life is full of crises and incidents. She was born December 25, 1821, in Oxford, Massachusetts, and christened Clarissa Harlowe Barton after a melodramatic heroine in Samuel Richardson's 1747-1748 novel *Clarissa*. She was educated in the Liberal Institute at Clinton, New York, from 1850 to 1851, and in 1852 in Bordentown, New Jersey, she began a free school that enrolled over six hundred pupils. The townsmen, unwilling to permit a woman to head so large a school, subsequently appointed a male principal, and Barton decided to resign rather than face demotion. Barton was an early advocate of equal treatment for the sexes, and her actions were as defiant as her words. She once told a school board, "I may sometimes be willing to teach for nothing, but if paid at all, I shall never do a man's work for less than a man's pay." On another occasion, she appeared in a classroom with a horsewhip to command the attention of unruly students.

She sought advancement as the only single woman employed at the Patent Office in Washington, D.C., from 1854 to 1857 and again in 1860, where she often endured the ridicule and derisive comments of her male coworkers about her lack of womanly modesty in choosing to work. At the outbreak of the Civil War, she organized supplies and medicine for the soldiers wounded at the first Battle of Bull Run. "If I can't be a soldier, I'll help soldiers," she said. Not content with sending supplies to the battlefield, Barton decided to join the effort as a nurse. Both sides of the conflict lacked nurses; soldiers' wounds were often made lethal by infection and neglect. Some died of thirst while waiting for transport to hospitals. Barton's father, a military captain, encouraged his daughter to follow her conscience. In the Second Battle of Bull Run, she found three thousand wounded soldiers lying on straw, many without food, awaiting amputations or operations. Her timely aid and distribution of supplies during this crisis earned her the tribute of the title the Angel of the Battlefield. At war's end in 1865, President Abraham Lincoln made Barton responsible for the Bureau of Records to aid in the search of missing soldiers.

After the war Barton worked for the extension of suffrage, or voting rights, to women, and for the empowerment of the newly freed blacks. She spoke at the American Equal Rights Association and at rallies with Frederick Douglass, the former slave who spent his life as a powerful orator on behalf of the rights of women and African Americans championing equality. In 1869-1870, she went to Europe for a rest, where the Franco-Prussian War erupted, and Barton found herself again in the midst of a relief effort for war victims. While in Geneva, she met the founder of the International Committee of the Red Cross. This organization was created by the Geneva Convention of 1864 and produced a treaty aimed at the humane treatment of the wounded, prisoners of war, and civilians during wartime conditions. The Geneva agreement had been inspired by a memoir of wartime events written by Jean-Henri Dunant, *Un souvenir de Solferino* (1862; *A Memory of Solferino*, 1939). Dunant dedicated his life to seeing that European nations ratified the Geneva Convention, and he received the first Nobel Peace Prize in 1901.

In America, Clara Barton personally petitioned the administration of President Rutherford B. Hayes to approve the Geneva Convention. Hayes was succeeded by President James A. Garfield, but the process of ratification was deferred several months by the assassination of Garfield in 1881. The new president, Chester A. Arthur, supported the Red Cross, and on March 16, 1882, the United States Senate formally ratified the Geneva treaty. Barton's "singular perseverance and her powers of persuasion," in the words of a biographer, founded a monument to her industry—the American Red Cross.

At age seventy-seven, Barton led the relief workers to the Spanish-American War in Cuba for civilian aid and to relieve the wounded. Under her leadership, the constitution of the Red Cross was amended to provide relief during peacetime for famines, floods, earthquakes, cyclones, and pestilence. Barton served as president of the Red Cross until 1904, when complaints about her authoritarian management style forced her to resign, as did lack of support for her leadership from President Theodore Roosevelt. Barton died at her Glen Echo home on April 12, 1912. Her death at age ninety occurred after two bouts of double pneumonia she suffered that year.

The Clara Barton National Historic Site is open daily from 10:00 A.M. to 5:00 P.M. The house is shown by guided tours only, which start on the hour. Admission is free, and visitors should allow thirty to forty-five minutes for the house tour.

—*Roberta Schreyer*

**For Further Information:**

Burton, David H. *Clara Barton: In the Service of Humanity.* Westport, Conn.: Greenwood Press, 1995. Covers Barton's life and career thoroughly.

Mann, Peggy. *Clara Barton: Battlefield Nurse.* New York: Coward-McCann, 1969. Barton is considered exemplary material for writers of juvenile biography. This is part of the Famous Women series for grade-school readers. A good effort at dramatized telling of the highlights of Barton's life.

Oates, Stephen B. *A Woman of Valor: Clara Barton and the Civil War.* New York: Macmillan Press, 1994. A good discussion of Barton's role on Civil War battlefields. Heavy emphasis on Civil War military history.

Pryor, Elizabeth Brown. *Clara Barton: Professional Angel.* Philadelphia: University of Pennsylvania Press, 1987. A comprehensive biography interested in Barton's psychology based on her letters and diaries.

U.S. Department of the Interior. *Clara Barton National Historic Site.* Washington, D.C.: U.S. Government Printing Office, 1981. Available for purchase by writing to the Government Printing Office, this richly illustrated handbook to the National Historic Site offers one of the best and most succinct biographies of Clara Barton and a capsule history of the major events of her time. A chapter by biographer Elizabeth Brown Pryor is also included, as well as summary descriptions of other historic sites of related interest.

www.civilwarhome.com/images/barton.jpg. Offers summaries of events in Barton's life and questions and answers for student readers to evaluate.

# Fort McHenry

**Date:** Authorized as a National Park on March 3, 1925

**Relevant issues:** Military history

**Significance:** A pentagon-shaped fortress completed in the early nineteenth century, Fort

McHenry is famed for its defense of Baltimore during the War of 1812, when a fleet of British ships attacked and were repulsed by a much weaker and smaller force. The battle inspired Francis Scott Key to write "The Star-Spangled Banner," the U.S. national anthem. Since 1933, Fort McHenry has been operated by the National Park Service. In 1939, Congress declared Fort McHenry a National Historic Shrine, the only one in the country.

**Location:** On Whetstone Point, the tip of a peninsula that juts between branches of the Patapsco River, a few miles from Baltimore's Inner Harbor

**Site Office:**

Fort McHenry National Monument and Historic Shrine
Baltimore, MD 21230-5393
ph.: (401) 962-4290
Web site: www.nps.gov/fomc/

Fort McHenry's history predates the War of 1812, during which it experienced its shining moment with the defeat of the British, a battle that inspired "The Star-Spangled Banner." Because of that event, U.S. Congress in 1939 designated it a National Monument and Historic Shrine, the only official historic shrine in the country.

Few realize that Fort McHenry would have faded into oblivion after its brief glory in the War of 1812 had it not been for its role in two other American wars. From 1861 to 1865, during the Civil War, Fort McHenry served as a detention center for prisoners of war and political prisoners, all of whom had been arrested without charge and denied the right to an attorney. After the Civil War, Fort McHenry's days as an active military installation were numbered; in 1914, it became a city park and recreation center. Yet, it would experience one more unusual twist of fate that would contribute to its historical significance: the establishment in 1917 of General Hospital No. 2, the largest in the country during World War I. The most severely wounded doughboys were treated at the three thousand-bed facility, where revolutionary surgical operations were performed. Although the hospital closed its doors in 1923, its prominence during the war revived historical interest in the site. In 1925, it became a national park; the National Park Service has operated the site since 1933.

### Early History

The land on which Fort McHenry stands is a peninsula, jutting out from between branches of the Patapsco River. Europeans settled on the peninsula as early as 1661; the area was named "Whetstone" by the man who bought the land in 1702. When rich deposits of iron ore were discovered on Whetstone Peninsula twenty years later, it would become the property of an English iron-refining company as a source of raw material. Not until the Revolutionary War broke out did the citizens of Baltimore think of building a fort there. When a British ship sailed into the Chesapeake Bay one day, wholesale alarm seized hold of Baltimoreans, and they raised money by subscription for the erection on Whetstone Point of what came to be known as Fort Whetstone.

Baltimore remained unscathed throughout the Revolutionary War, and the eighteen-gun earthen battery was never used. The defenses were abandoned after the war, but not for long. In 1793, tensions escalated between revolutionary France and Great Britain. The United States, which continued to carry on trade with both countries, decided to erect fortifications to protect shipping. In that year, Congress passed appropriations for new defenses on Whetstone Peninsula; a succession of French military engineers (America was a haven for educated and well-trained French aristocratic exiles) worked out the plans, and the result in the early nineteenth century was a sizable fort in the shape of a pentagon. Each of the five points was visible to the other points and was fortified. The man who helped bring about the fort and wring the necessary appropriations from a stingy Congress was Secretary of War James McHenry, a resident of Baltimore. An Irish immigrant, McHenry fought on the side of George Washington and the colonies when war broke out, and afterward he rose high in both the state and federal governments. Fort Whetstone was renamed Fort McHenry in his honor.

### The War of 1812

The fort was completed during a period of mounting tension between Great Britain and the United States, which was mainly the result of British impressment of American sailors into the Royal Navy and British confiscation of neutral American ships. To Americans, it appeared that England was trying to fold the United States back into the British Empire. The British government and press had only contempt for the U.S. Congress's declaration of war against Great Britain on June 18, 1812. The United States was woefully unprepared to fight a war with the largest navy on earth.

Word of the declaration of war spurred many Baltimore ship owners to outfit privateers to prey on British shipping. Subsequent fears of British retaliation against the city, in addition to the more general fears of British invasion, made Fort McHenry the object of feverish preparations. The defense of Baltimore, put under the military command of General Sam Smith, was supervised by a local committee of public supply. The militia inside Fort McHenry were put under the command of Major George Armistead, and a trained engineer was engaged to oversee the strengthening of the fortifications. Meanwhile, a call went out for volunteers to man the fort. By the time the British attacked Fort McHenry in September, 1814, one thousand men garrisoned it. This was a citizen army, composed primarily of local residents and Maryland militiamen.

The British fleet had arrived rather late following the declaration of war because of its preoccupation with defeating Napoleon Bonaparte in Europe. By the spring of 1813, only ten warships, commanded by Rear Admiral Sir George Cockburn, had arrived at the Chesapeake Bay. Still, the British plundered and burned the coast, and Baltimoreans feared that their city would be next. When Napoleon finally was defeated the following spring, British troops were free to face the American enemy. Fifty British ships, manned with six thousand battle-hardened veterans, arrived in the late spring of 1814 in the Chesapeake Bay, successfully fought off American troops at the Battle of Bladensburg in Maryland, and with the help of Cockburn's forces, destroyed Washington, D.C. Such easy victories were expected by the British. The governor general of Canada vowed to postpone a victory celebration until Baltimore was captured.

Sixteen British ships sailed within sight of Fort McHenry on September 13, 1814. Nothing seemed to go right for the beleaguered American force shut up in Fort McHenry: The cannon mounted on the ramparts turned out to have inadequate range, unable to hit the British attackers. Meanwhile, British ships bombarded the fort for twenty-five hours, lobbing more than one thousand shells against the hapless men trapped inside. Ultimately what gave Americans their victory was the heavy rainfall, which foiled a British attempt to land and seize the fort, as well as the blocking of the entrance to Baltimore's harbor by sunken American merchant vessels. Finally, when two British vessels approached the fort and came within the range of its cannon, they came under ferocious fire and fled with heavy casualties.

Casualties at Fort McHenry had been surprisingly light—four killed and twenty-four wounded out of a thousand men—despite the inability of Fort McHenry to defend itself adequately. One of the casualties was the only African American among the recruits, twenty-one-year-old escaped slave William Williams. Some months earlier, he had fled his Maryland owner and enlisted in the defense of Baltimore. Normally a slave had no right to enlist, but the recruitment officer asked no questions. Mortally wounded during the bombardment, Williams died two months later.

### Francis Scott Key

A week before the British attack on Baltimore, Francis Scott Key, a prominent Maryland lawyer with a successful practice in Georgetown, was on a prisoner exchange boat headed for the British fleet on Chesapeake Bay. A deeply religious man, Key had adamantly opposed Congress's declaration of war, but once his country was invaded, there was no doubt about his loyalty. He was headed to the fleet to arrange the parole of his good friend, Dr. Edward Beanes, who was being held prisoner by the British. With Key was Colonel John K. Skinner, the U.S. government's agent for arranging prisoner exchanges.

When the small prisoner exchange boat with the white flag discharged its passengers on one of the British warships, they were met by courteous British officers. They agreed to free Beanes to the custody of Key and Skinner but would not allow them to leave, for fear they would spread word of the imminent attack against Fort McHenry. The bombardment began as they were placed back on their prisoner exchange boat. As the story goes, a British sailor had told Key that night to take one last look at the flag flying from Fort McHenry, because by morning, it would be gone. Key was a witness to the terrible battering of Fort McHenry's

*Francis Scott Key, who composed "The Star-Spangled Banner" after having witnessed the battle at Fort McHenry in 1814.* (Library of Congress)

walls that evening. Nonetheless at "the dawn's early light," the Americans were astounded to see the rent flag still waving and even more shocked when the British gave up their attack as hopeless.

It is unclear whether or not any of the Americans, including Key, realized that the flag they were looking at (now in the Smithsonian Institution) was the largest in the world, especially commissioned for Fort McHenry. The dimensions of the flag were truly staggering: more than thirty feet wide by forty-two feet long; the stripes alone were two feet wide. General Smith and Major Armistead had ordered not one but two flags from Mary Young Pickersgill, a Baltimore widow who specialized in sewing flags for private merchant ships. With the help of her thirteen-year-old daughter, Pickersgill set to work not as she usually did in her upstairs bedroom, which proved too tiny, but in a nearby brewery house. The larger flag cost more than four hundred dollars; ironically, the cloth was of English wool. Both the larger and the smaller

flag were designed to be seen easily by British forces, even at a great distance. It is conjectured that the smaller flag flew the first night; the larger "Star-Spangled Banner" on the following morning.

## "The Star-Spangled Banner"

It is known what effect the sight of the flag had on Francis Scott Key, whose poem about the experience would eventually become the lyrics of America's national anthem. A friend published his untitled verses, and a songwriter set them to a popular melody of English origin, "To Anacreon in Heaven." The new song was titled "The Star-Spangled Banner." It was not officially adopted as the national anthem until 1931. Key went on to fame but not fortune; he died in Baltimore in 1843, well loved and remembered.

Fort McHenry underwent a slow decline after its days of glory in September, 1814, although there were efforts in the 1830's to improve its fortifications and expand them. The fort, however, had outlived its usefulness as a strategic defense bastion. During the Mexican War from 1846 to 1848, Fort McHenry was used as a training base for recruits. Robert E. Lee, an army officer, spent time there. Nevertheless, the fort seemed headed for oblivion.

## The Civil War

The outbreak of the Civil War in 1861 brought Fort McHenry back into prominence. It was used as a prison for those who sided against the federal government, and in Baltimore there were many. Unlike fifty years earlier, the guns of Fort McHenry were now turned away from the bay and aimed toward the city, which was put under military occupation early in the war. Ironically, the grandson of Francis Scott Key (also a lawyer) was imprisoned there, as was the grandson of Major George Armistead (caught with a Confederate flag in his possession). What changed Fort McHenry's reputation from a citadel of American liberty to the "Baltimore Bastille" was the incarceration of political prisoners without charge and without legal counsel. Hundreds of prominent rebels and rebel sympathizers were thrown into Fort McHenry's dark, dank cells.

President Abraham Lincoln was widely denounced for rescinding the writ of *habeas corpus* within the Washington-Baltimore-Philadelphia area, an action he regarded as critical to the capital's defense. Chief Justice Roger B. Taney (onetime law partner of Francis Scott Key) harshly criticized Lincoln for overstepping his authority; only Congress had the right to suspend this constitutional right. (Lincoln had ordered its suspension when Congress was not in session, citing a national emergency.) Lincoln's response to Taney's widely publicized condemnation was to condemn the rebels, who were willing to destroy the constitution itself, not just one constitutional right.

Those incarcerated at Fort McHenry in these years were usually freed if they took an oath of allegiance to the Union. While in prison, they were able to receive visitors, parcels, and food. Fort McHenry accommodated thousands of prisoners of war as well; more than seven thousand were housed within its walls after the battle of Gettysburg. These POWs were held in Fort McHenry only temporarily before being transferred to other prisons.

### After the Civil War

With the end of the Civil War, Fort McHenry returned to a peaceful but purposeless existence. Its primary function seemed to be as a parade ground. When the Spanish-American War broke out in 1898, Fort McHenry once again became a training camp for recruits. By 1912, Fort McHenry had no active soldiers on duty; two years later, Congress approved its transformation into a city park. It might have lost most of its historical character had it not been for the outbreak of World War I.

When the United States became involved in that conflagration in 1917, Fort McHenry was transformed into a hospital. Over the next year, one hundred temporary buildings were erected on its grounds to receive the wounded from Europe. General Hospital No. 2, as Fort McHenry was called, became the largest military hospital in the United States. The two hundred doctors and three hundred nurses worked around the clock to care for the twenty thousand men who made their way to Fort McHenry from 1917 to 1923. Fort McHenry

in that time became a bastion of hope. New surgical techniques were performed there, including reconstructive plastic surgery and revolutionary neurological operations that restored the use of damaged limbs.

The hospital was closed in 1923, and the temporary buildings were carefully dismantled in 1925, although a few of them were left standing as memorials. Maryland Congressman J. Charles Linthicum lobbied to save Fort McHenry as a historic site and turn it into a national park run by the army, rather than having it revert to a city recreation area. His bill passed, and in 1925 Fort McHenry officially became a national park. The army proceeded to clean up the fort, plant trees and shrubs, and make an attempt to restore it. Funds, however, were insufficient, and restoration proceeded slowly, at times imperceptibly. Finally, in 1933, the park was transferred to the National Park Service, and in 1939 Congress declared Fort McHenry a Historic Shrine. Not until after World War II were ambitious plans carried out to restore Fort McHenry to its original, nineteenth century appearance and to educate the public about its significance in American history.    —*Sina Dubovoy*

**For Further Information:**

Lord, Walter. *The Dawn's Early Light.* New York: W. W. Norton, 1972. The standard account of the War of 1812 and the attack on Fort McHenry. This is a highly readable, gripping account of that dramatic time.

Rukert, Norman G. *Fort McHenry: Home of the Brave.* Baltimore: Bodine, 1983. A detailed, richly illustrated history of this historic landmark.

Sheads, Scott S. *Fort McHenry.* Baltimore: Nautical & Aviation Publishing Company of America, 1995. A history of Fort McHenry itself and of the National Monument.

# Frederick

**Date:** Established in 1745

**Relevant issues:** Civil War, colonial America

**Significance:** Frederick was named the capital of Frederick County in 1748; its downtown area was designated a National Historic Landmark District in 1973. Monacacy Battlefield is found three miles outside the city limits.

**Location:** North-central Maryland, forty-five miles from Washington, D.C., on U.S. Interstate 270, and from Baltimore on U.S. Interstate 70

**Site Office:**
Historical Society of Frederick County
24 East Church Street
Frederick, MD 21701
ph.: (301) 663-1188
fax: (301) 663-0526
Web site: www.fwp.net/hsfc

If Annapolis is a showcase of excellently pre-served eighteenth century upper-class mansions, then nearby Frederick is renowned for its down-to-earth, middle-class nineteenth century architecture. As the capital of Maryland, Annapolis was a magnet for nearby gentry in the two decades prior to the Revolutionary War. These wealthy planters built themselves luxurious town homes with spacious gardens. At the same time, Frederick, the county seat for Frederick County, was a magnet primarily for German immigrants from nearby Pennsylvania. As late as the first third of the nineteenth century, German was spoken as much as English in the streets and surrounding farms of Frederick. The first Frederick newspaper in 1786 had both English and German editions. When General Edward Braddock's forces stopped in Frederick during the French and Indian War in 1755 for provisions, the aristocratic British officer was dismayed that the inhabitants of the town, who were far from starving, nonetheless had few wagons or luxuries of any kind to spare his troops. The slaveholding family was rare, and a large proportion of the blacks in Frederick County were free. Consequently, during the Civil War, the city of Frederick was strongly pro-Union, in contrast to genteel pro-Confederate Annapolis.

Because city leaders after the Civil War intended to preserve Frederick's pleasant, small-town character, industry and manufacturing were discouraged and development was sporadic. While this led after World War I to an exodus of youth and the city's slow growth—the population was only fourteen thousand in 1914—most of the city's architectural heritage remained intact. After World War II, there emerged a strong grassroots movement to preserve the downtown district as an official historic area. In 1970, the Maryland Assembly passed an Enabling Act permitting cities to designate such areas. This was followed three years later by the downtown area's being placed on the National Register of Historic Places.

**Early History**
The origins of Frederick, or as it was known until the 1820's, Fredericktown, are well documented. The area was thinly populated by Europeans prior to the town's founding in 1745. German farmers, attracted to the low price of land, made their way from Pennsylvania, and other German immigrants came directly from the old country via the port of Annapolis. These thrifty, hardworking men and women quickly tackled the Maryland wilderness in the 1730's, erecting log houses, barns, and log churches. They leased their land at first from the English, with whom the German settlers had had little contact prior to their arrival in America. The average tract was two hundred acres, and the lease was payable after three years. These were irresistible lures for the steady stream of German settlers and also for the English-speaking settlers from nearby Montgomery County. There were also Indians in the area surrounding Frederick. Prior to the outbreak of the French and Indian War in 1755, there was no record of open conflict between European and native Americans.

In 1744 an American-born lawyer, Daniel Dulany, bought a seven thousand-acre tract of land called "Tasker's Chance" from Benjamin Tasker. Aware of the attractiveness of the area to settlers, Dulany quickly designed a town, with streets running east-west and north-south at right angles, and began selling lots. He called the town Fredericktown, but to this day there is only conjecture surrounding the name, which may have derived from the first name of the last (and sixth) Lord Baltimore, the English Catholic founding family of Maryland. Three years after the town officially was founded in 1745, the Maryland Assembly in nearby Annapolis created Frederick County; as the sole city in the county at the time, Fredericktown became the de facto county seat. By 1755, only ten years after its founding, the city boasted at least two hundred homes, owned mostly by Germans, and two churches.

**German Influences**
The pervasiveness of German culture was noted by

*The Evangelical Lutheran Church, part of the "Clustered Spires" of Frederick.* (The Historical Society of Frederick County)

road would come early to Frederick, in 1831, and until then, local canals and toll roads conveyed produce to distant markets in Philadelphia, Baltimore, and Washington, D.C. Streets in eighteenth century Frederick were unpaved; there was no street lighting and no sewers or system of drainage. Dead animals rotted in the streets, and the water often was unsafe, leading to periodic cholera outbreaks, typical for cities in that era. Frederick did boast some fine buildings, such as the elegant Court House—erected soon after the city became a county seat in 1748—churches, and private homes.

### Anti-British Feeling in Frederick

Because the majority of Frederick residents in the colonial period (and for at least half a century after independence) were non-English, there was little loyalty among inhabitants for the British Crown. British authority was identified with arbitrariness and taxes. In the spring of 1755, the townsmen were incensed that General Edward Braddock, heading a regiment of fourteen hundred men bound for Fort Duquesne in Pennsylvania, requisitioned all the wagons in and about the city, and worse, ordered town residents to feed and house his troops for the duration of his army's stay.

all outsiders. These settlers introduced the custom of dyeing eggs for Easter; they also introduced their own foods, dress, and style of architecture (with unusually thick walls, even in that era of heavy walls). They were known for using animal fertilizer on their farm land, and they disdained raising tobacco (which exhausted the soil) in favor of grains and corn. They did not own slaves, although some of the English settlers did.

From the beginning, Frederick was a prosperous town. The agricultural area was rich, the rail-

One interesting footnote to this experience was that the young colonel George Washington joined up with Braddock's forces in Frederick. For nearly two centuries, the house in which Washington stayed during his Frederick sojourn stood intact, until it was torn down in the twentieth century to make way for "development."

After the French and Indian War, when the British Parliament sought ways of paying the exorbitant costs of that conflict, Fredericktonians were outraged at the new taxes imposed upon all the colonies. The Stamp Act of 1765 was the last straw. It occasioned widespread rioting until its repeal in 1766. In Frederick, the stamp distributor had been burned in effigy; even more noteworthy was the repudiation of the Stamp Act by twelve justices of the Frederick Court, the first official action against British authority in the colonies.

## The Revolutionary War

The American Revolution brought many notables to Frederick, including George Washington and the Marquis de Lafayette. While battles raged outside the Frederick area, the city was little affected. Revolutionary sentiment was universal in the city—a barracks went up to house prisoners of war, many of whom were Germans from the state of Hesse who had hired themselves out to the British army as mercenaries, a common practice in those days. With little loyalty to the British side, many of these prisoners opted to work for area farmers, the majority of whom were German, and many of them also deserted, a serious problem for the British as the war dragged on.

After the Revolutionary War ended, and despite the problems occasioned by a weak and ineffective central government, Frederick flourished. There were by then over two thousand inhabitants. Agriculture carried out by a free and efficient German American farming community yielded bumper crops of grains and fruits in season. The town had gristmills to grind the grain into flour as well as iron furnaces, forges, and hundreds of liquor stills. In 1784, a German immigrant, Johann Friedrich Amelung, arrived in Frederick County and set up Bremen Glass Works a few miles outside of town. He brought with him from the old country one hundred glassmakers and eventually hired several hundred more. They lived in a German village setting on his 2,100-acre tract, a baronial estate by Old World standards. Eventually he went out of business, and the Amelung works disappeared.

The town had by then a distinguished physician, Dr. John Tyler (the first town doctor had arrived in 1769), whose fame as an oculist spread even to Europe. He went down in medical history as the first doctor to perform successful cataract surgery in the United States. Frederick also had its first newspaper, the *Maryland Chronicle or the Universal Advertiser*, which for decades contained only national or international news. Because Frederick was such a small city, everyone knew what was happening locally. By 1850, competition arose with big city papers, and Frederick newspapers began to shift to local news.

Frederick was the scene of much coming and going of troops during the War of 1812, which actually touched all Marylanders directly when a British fleet sailed up the Chesapeake Bay in September, 1814, and bombarded the port of Baltimore. There were tremendous celebrations in Frederick after the defeat of the mighty British Navy at Fort McHenry. After the war, Frederick prospered again and made civic improvements—adding street lighting, pavement, and a water system. Cholera decimated the town in 1832, with smaller outbreaks occurring periodically afterward, alternating with diphtheria. Not until 1886 was a Public Health Department formed, which held men and women accountable for hygiene and waste disposal.

## The Civil War

The small city did not escape the sectional conflicts that led to the Civil War. The number of slaves in the city by then had increased to the point where 10 percent of the inhabitants were blacks in bondage. Nonetheless, the male voters of Frederick County were in the majority opposed to secession; however, because of the existence of slavery in the state, especially the southern counties, abolitionists everywhere in Maryland were a tiny and despised minority. There were no votes for Abraham Lincoln in 1860, and states' rights advocates in the Maryland assembly decried his election as president. Anti-Lincoln sentiment was never as vehement in Frederick as in Baltimore, where the president-elect's life was endangered by a mob when his train traveled through the city to Washington, D.C.

While Frederick escaped the fighting in other wars, this would not be the case during the Civil War. By the end of 1861, the small city of a few thousand inhabitants (which shrank during the war years) was occupied by a huge Union force of fifteen thousand. Frederick would be battered by both sides during the war: canals and railroads would be destroyed, crops burned or otherwise damaged, and the city held ransom by Confederate general Jubal T. Early and looted more than once.

Two bloody battles took place outside Frederick, at Antietam Creek in 1862 and at the Monocacy

River in 1864. While the Battle of Antietam was a dubious Union success, it nonetheless drew President Lincoln to Frederick on October 1, 1862, to view the battlefield and to visit the wounded, over twenty thousand of them, crowded into twenty makeshift city hospitals. This memorable visit is commemorated on a plaque affixed to the house where Lincoln lived during his brief stay in Frederick. Two years later, when the Southern cause was all but lost, General Jubal T. Early's forces ravaged the city and attacked Union forces protecting the road to Washington, D.C., in a last-ditch attempt to relieve the pressure on General Robert E. Lee in Richmond. While the brief, bloody encounter on the Monacacy River barely merits a footnote in Civil War histories, General Early's stay was long remembered by Fredericktonians because of the $200,000 ransom he demanded and received from them in return for sparing their town from destruction by fire.

Visitors to Frederick gravitate to the Barbara Fritchie Home, reconstructed as it appeared in 1862, when Thomas J. "Stonewall" Jackson's force occupied the city briefly. Union sentiment was strong in Frederick, and few welcomed the Confederates. According to legend, ninety-five-year-old Fritchie brazenly displayed a Union flag outside her home, knowing that Stonewall Jackson's troops would be marching by on their way out of the city. When a shot rang out and tore a hole through the flag, she leaned out of her window and challenged the troops to shoot her, rather than their country's flag. According to John Greenleaf Whittier's poem memorializing the incident, Jackson lowered his eyes in shame at her words and ordered his troops to cease their fire. Several months later, Barbara Fritchie died of old age.

## Post-Civil War Recovery

There was jubilation in the city when the war ended, so great was the desire to return to normal life. The town quickly rebuilt itself, repairing damaged roads, telegraph wires, and railroad tracks and replanting crops. The industrial growth of America passed Frederick by, however, largely because city leaders were afraid that industrialization and unhindered growth would lead to a deterioration in the city's quality of life. Much of historical Frederick—the churches, private homes, the Court House—was preserved, but the town's growth was hindered. Interestingly, the city remained prosperous, with agriculture still the dominant element of its economy. While agriculture suffered in many parts of the country in the late nineteenth century, Frederick farmers had switched from grain farming to much more lucrative and secure dairy farming, and they suffered no adversity. The city, however, would not be spared the ill effects of the Great Depression. The lack of business and industry meant that recovery from the economic disaster took longer there than in other parts of Maryland, and the town did not recover until the onset of World War II.

During the war and until the 1970's, Fort Detrick in Frederick became a major center of biological weapons manufacturing; after the war, new industries arrived in the city, and growth finally led to a population explosion. Frederick became the second-largest city in Maryland in 1990, with a population of forty thousand (overtaken recently by the city of Rockville).

## Historic Buildings

Today one can enter the small city of Frederick and visit the Court House and the same five churches that John Greenleaf Whittier visited in the 1860's. Court House Square boasts not only the old Court House but also the house on 119 Record Street that Lincoln visited in October, 1862. At 103 Council Street stands the building where Lafayette resided when he returned in 1824 to visit the town. Away from the square one comes upon the Roger Brooke Taney House/Francis Scott Key Museum, housed in the original building completed in 1799. This was for many years the home and office of Supreme Court Justice Taney (of Dred Scott fame), who practiced law in Frederick; for a few years, his partner was Francis Scott Key, who wrote the words to "The Star-Spangled Banner." On display are items that belonged both to the Taney and Key families.

On West Patrick Street downtown stands the Barbara Fritchie House and Museum. Her home had been demolished in 1867, five years after her death, but was restored to its original appearance in the 1920's. She is buried, along with Key and nearly one thousand Confederate dead from the Battles of Antietam and Monacacy, at Mount Olivet Cemetery, in the southern end of Frederick. Antietam Battlefield, like Gettysburg in nearby

Pennsylvania, is a national landmark and lies approximately forty miles outside of the Frederick city limits. The Monacacy Battlefield is a few miles outside the city.                    —*Sina Dubovoy*

**For Further Information:**

Ashbury, John W. *And All Our Yesterdays: A Chronicle of Frederick County, Maryland.* Frederick, Md.: Diversions, 1997. A history of Frederick with a chronology.

Huffman, Amy Lee. *In and out of Frederick Town: Colonial Occupations.* Frederick, Md.: Reed, 1985. A book with a narrower focus than Whitmore and Cannon's below, but just as interesting and well illustrated.

Whitmore, Nancy F., and Timothy L. Cannon. *Frederick: A Pictorial History.* Norfolk, Va.: Donning, 1981. The best book on Frederick. A fascinating read, it is loaded with rare photographs (including many of buildings long since demolished) and interesting anecdotes about the city from its foundation to the late 1970's.

# Other Historic Sites

## Baltimore and Ohio Transportation Museum and Mount Clare Station

*Location:* Baltimore, Baltimore County

*Relevant issues:* Business and industry, science and technology

*Statement of significance:* At the Mount Clare Station, regular passenger rail service in the United States was inaugurated in 1830. The nation's first telegraph message passed through the station in 1844. The Roundhouse contains the historical collections of the Baltimore and Ohio Railroad.

## Carson House

*Location:* Silver Spring, Montgomery County

*Relevant issues:* Health and medicine, science and technology, social reform

*Statement of significance:* From 1956 to 1964, this was the home of Rachel Louise Carson (1907-1964), biologist, naturalist, writer, and poet. Carson was already famous when she wrote *Silent Spring* (1962), a book many consider to have changed the way Americans think about their natural environment and which is responsible for beginning the modern environmental movement. *Silent Spring* drew popular attention to the poisoning of the earth and the endangerment of public safety by the indiscriminate use of modern chemical pesticides and herbicides.

## Chambers Farm

*Location:* Westminster, Carroll County

*Relevant issues:* Political history

*Statement of significance:* This was the home of Whittaker Chambers (1901-1961), an ex-Communist whose revelations about his past espionage activities with Alger Hiss, a former State Department official, had major political repercussions after World War II. Here Chambers turned over the Pumpkin Papers implicating Hiss and later wrote *Witness* (1952), his best-selling autobiography.

## Chestertown Historic District

*Location:* Bounded by the Chester River, Cannon St., Maple Ave., and Cross St., Chestertown, Kent County

*Relevant issues:* Business and industry

*Statement of significance:* This district flourished between 1750 and 1790 as the chief tobacco- and wheat-shipping port on the eastern shore of Maryland. Wealthy merchants and planters constructed the elaborate brick Georgian townhouses found in the district.

## Constellation

*Location:* Pier 1, Pratt Street, Baltimore, Baltimore County

*Relevant issues:* Military history, naval history

*Web site:* www.constellation.org

*Statement of significance:* Among the longest commissioned vessels in the U.S. Navy, *Constellation* was the first American ship to engage and defeat an enemy vessel.

## Edna E. Lockwood

*Location:* St. Michaels, Talbot County

*Relevant issues:* Business and industry, naval history

*Statement of significance: Edna E. Lockwood* is the last Chesapeake Bay bugeye to retain its sailing rig and working appearance, and it is the only unaltered representative of the fleet which once harvested the Chesapeake oyster fishery. Its maritime architectural significance is vested in its multi-log hull, one of the largest in existence; this unusual log or "chunk" style of shipbuilding was practiced nowhere else in the world. *Edna E. Lockwood* was built in 1889 by master boat builder John B. Harrison, probably at Chicken Point, for Daniel W. Haddaway of Tilghman Island. It dredged every oyster season from 1889 to 1967.

## Fort Frederick

*Location:* Big Pool, Washington County

*Relevant issues:* European settlement, military history, Revolutionary War

*Statement of significance:* This is the southern colonies' largest and best preserved architectural example of an eighteenth century frontier fort erected for frontier defense against Indians. It sheltered some seven hundred people during the 1763 Pontiac War, and from 1777 to 1783, it served as a prisoner-of-war camp for captured British and German soldiers during the War for Independence.

## Gaithersburg Latitude Observatory

*Location:* Gaithersburg, Montgomery County

*Relevant issues:* Science and technology

*Statement of significance:* This observatory is one of six observatories located in the United States, Russia, Japan, and Italy which are associated with an important and long-lived program of international scientific cooperation. The International Polar Motion Service, established in 1899 by the International Geodetic Association, was a cooperative effort among scientists from around the world to study the earth's wobble on its rotational axis. Gaithersburg Latitude Observatory was established in 1899.

## Greenbelt Historic District

*Location:* Greenbelt, Prince George's County

*Relevant issues:* Cultural history

*Statement of significance:* The development of Greenbelt from 1935 to 1946 represents the first government-sponsored planned community in the United States built on "garden city" principles and embodies the regional planning principles and architectural ideals of the mid-1930's. Three "greenbelt towns" were built by Franklin D. Roosevelt's New Deal government along garden city lines to respond to the Depression and a housing crisis in American cities. Greenbelt, the first and largest of the three towns, was an attempt to build a large-scale, scientifically planned suburban community that would decentralize the population of Washington, D.C.

## Kennedy Farm

*Location:* Samples Manor, Washington County

*Relevant issues:* Civil War, political history

*Statement of significance:* This farm appears substantially as it did when John Brown (1800-1859), abolitionist leader, planned and led his 1859 raid on the Harpers Ferry armory and arsenal from here.

## Lightship No. 116 "Chesapeake"

*Location:* Baltimore, Baltimore County

*Relevant issues:* Naval history

*Statement of significance:* The 1930 Lightship No. 116, now known by its former designation, *Chesapeake,* is the best-preserved example of a generation of lightships designed to be powered by diesel-electric plants. Known as the 113-Foot Class, these were the last lightships built by the U.S. Lighthouse Service before it was absorbed into the U.S. Coast Guard. In addition to serving the Fenwick, Chesapeake, and Delaware stations, No. 116 served as an examination vessel off Cape Cod and helped protect the important port of Boston during World War II. Owned by the National Park Service, No. 116 is on a twenty-five-year loan to the city of Baltimore and is operated as a floating exhibit.

## Mencken House

*Location:* Baltimore, Baltimore County

*Relevant issues:* Literary history

*Statement of significance:* This typical three-story Baltimore row house was the home of journalist-editor H. L. Mencken (1880-1956), distinguished essayist and caustic critic of American society, from his childhood until his death in 1956.

## Monocacy Battlefield

*Location:* Frederick, Frederick County

*Relevant issues:* Civil War, military history

*Statement of significance:* Confederates under General Jubal T. Early repulsed Union troops commanded by General Lew Wallace here in July, 1864. Wallace's troops delayed Early's forces, though, giving the Union Army time to prepare a defense of Washington, D.C., saving it from Confederate capture.

## Peale's Baltimore Museum

*Location:* Baltimore, Baltimore County

*Relevant issues:* Cultural history

*Statement of significance:* This was the first building in the United States designed and erected exclusively for museum use. It now houses exhibits covering the history of Baltimore.

## Phoenix Shot Tower

*Location:* Baltimore, Baltimore County

*Relevant issues:* Business and industry

*Statement of significance:* This is one of a very few shot towers left in the United States. Shot was manufactured by dropping molten lead from this fourteen-story tower through a sievelike device into a vat of cold water. Some one million bags of shot were produced yearly in this way. It was the tallest structure in the United States until work was resumed on the Washington Monument in the District of Columbia after the Civil War.

## Poe House

*Location:* Baltimore, Baltimore County

*Relevant issues:* Literary history

*Statement of significance:* Edgar Allan Poe (1809-1849) occupied this house (1833-1835) at a time when his short stories were beginning to attract favorable critical attention.

## Riversdale Mansion

*Location:* 4811 Riverdale Road, Riverdale, Prince George's County

*Relevant issues:* Art and architecture, education

*Web site:* www.inform.umd.edu/UMS+State/MD_Resources/counties/PG/PG300/mncppc/riversdale.html

*Statement of significance:* Dating from the beginning of the nineteenth century, Riversdale is one of the last of Maryland's great five-part Palladian mansions. Of stuccoed brick, it was built for Belgium émigré Henri Joseph Stier and was for a time the repository of the Stier family's collection of Old World master paintings, the most outstanding collection of its type in the country at the time. Riversdale is also significant for its association with Charles Benedict Calvert, Stier's grandson. Calvert helped establish the Maryland Agricultural College on part of the extensive Riversdale acreage and was instrumental in the establishment of the federal-level Bureau of Agriculture, now the U.S. Department of Agriculture. Riversdale, now restored, is open to the public as a historic house museum.

## Rowland House

*Location:* Baltimore, Baltimore County

*Relevant issues:* Education, science and technology

*Statement of significance:* This was the home of Henry Augustus Rowland (1848-1901), America's best-known and most accomplished nineteenth century physicist. Rowland's most important contribution was in the area of electromagnetism, most particularly in the area of spectrum analysis. He also shaped the Johns Hopkins Physics Department into a model which spread to the other universities across the country.

## Saint Mary's City Historic District

*Location:* St. Mary's City, St. Mary's County

*Relevant issues:* European settlement

*Statement of significance:* This was the capital of the Maryland Colony until 1695 and the third permanent English settlement in America. Foundations of some sixty buildings remain for archaeological study.

## Sheppard and Enoch Pratt Hospital and Gate House

*Location:* Towson, Baltimore County

*Relevant issues:* Health and medicine

*Statement of significance:* This is a leading private institution for the treatment of the mentally ill. The hospital buildings, dramatic Norman Revival structures, mark an important stage in psychiatric planning because they provide for separation of patients according to the nature of their illnesses.

## Sion Hill

*Location:* Havre de Grace, Harford County
*Relevant issues:* Naval history
*Statement of significance:* Situated on a gentle hill with a panoramic view of Havre de Grace and the point at which the Susquehanna broadens to form the Chesapeake, this brick mansion was the seat of the seafaring Rodgers family, the most notable of American naval families. Their generations-long careers cover the world and affect virtually every aspect of American naval history from the presidency of Thomas Jefferson to the New Deal.

## Star-Spangled Banner Flag House

*Location:* Baltimore, Baltimore County
*Relevant issues:* Cultural history, military history
*Statement of significance:* The flag that flew over Fort McHenry during the British attack in 1814 was made here and inspired Francis Scott Key's "The Star-Spangled Banner."

## Thomas Point Shoal Light Station

*Location:* Annapolis, Anne Arundel County
*Relevant issues:* Naval history
*Statement of significance:* Thomas Point Shoal Light Station is the last unaltered screwpile, cottage-type lighthouse on its original foundation in the United States. Screwpile foundation technology greatly improved the aids to navigation system in that it allowed lighthouses to be built in offshore locations that previously could be marked only by buoys or expensive lightships. As many as one hundred spiderlike screwpile lighthouses were built throughout the Carolina sounds, the Chesapeake Bay, and Delaware Bay; along the Gulf of Mexico; and even at Maumee Bay on Lake Erie in Ohio. Replacing an onshore station in 1875, the Thomas Point Shoal Light Station continues to serve as an active aid to navigation maintained by the U.S. Coast Guard.

## Torsk

*Location:* Baltimore, Baltimore County
*Relevant issues:* Military history, naval history, World War II
*Statement of significance:* A World War II Tench class submarine that sank two Japanese coastal defense ships on August 14, 1945, *Torsk* is credited with firing the last two torpedoes and sinking the last combatant ships of the war. After the war, *Torsk*'s operations as a training vessel helped it establish a world record of 11,884 dives.

## Welch House

*Location:* Baltimore, Baltimore County
*Relevant issues:* Health and medicine
*Statement of significance:* This was the home (1891-1908) of the distinguished Johns Hopkins professor William Henry Welch (1850-1934), who transformed American medical research and teaching and became known as the dean of American medical science.

## William B. Tennison

*Location:* Solomons, Calvert County
*Relevant issues:* Business and industry, naval history
*Web site:* www.nps.gov/history/maritime/nhl/tennison.htm
*Statement of significance:* Built in 1899 by master carpenter Frank Laird near Oriole, Maryland, *William B. Tennison* is the last bugeye oyster buy-boat on Chesapeake Bay. It represents one of the first bugeyes to be converted to power and one of the few log-hulled vessels left in the world. *William B. Tennison* was a part of the sailing oyster dredge fleet of the Chesapeake; the bugeye type dredged more oysters than any other vessel type in the world. As the oyster harvest on the Chesapeake began to wane, the smaller, easier-to-handle, and cheaper-to-build skipjack became popular, replacing the bugeye. Buy-boats bought the catch off these skipjacks; in the off season, the buy-boats were used to haul produce, lumber, and even livestock to markets in Baltimore, Norfolk, Richmond, and Washington, D.C.

# Massachusetts

*A windmill on Cape Cod.* (PhotoDisc)

# History of Massachusetts

Massachusetts was one of the original thirteen colonies, and its capital, Boston, is considered the cradle of the American Revolution. The state was home to some of the greatest American leaders. Its reputation for excellent education is due to its many great universities and colleges, including the world-famous Harvard and Massachusetts Institute of Technology (MIT). Geographically, the state forms a narrow rectangle. Relatively small, it is forty-fifth in area among the states, yet thirteenth in state population.

### Native American History

The Algonquians were a large family of tribes, related by language and customs, who lived throughout the northeastern United States. Several of these tribes made their homes in the fertile farming and hunting grounds of the area. The Nauset lived on Cape Cod, while the Wampanoag, the Massachusetts (for whom the state is named), and the Patuxet fished and hunted along the coast. Women played a central role in Algonquian society. They owned the tribe's land, which they cleared and farmed communally. When a young man married, he left home to become a member of his bride's family.

### Early Exploration and the Pilgrims

In 1602 English navigator Bartholomew Gosnold visited Massachusetts Bay and named it Cape Cod. Two years later explorer Samuel de Champlain explored the coast, followed by Captain John Smith in 1614.

In September of 1620, an English merchant ship called the *Mayflower* set sail from the port of Southhampton with 102 passengers bound for the Americas. Of these passengers, 41 were Separatists, members of a renegade congregation that had broken away from the Church of England. These people considered themselves religious pilgrims. Before the pilgrims and the others left England, the group leaders wrote and signed a document that became the foundation of American democracy,

the Mayflower Compact. It decreed a representative government.

Despite legend, the ship did not land at Plymouth Rock, but rather at the tip of Cape Cod, the site of modern Provincetown. After a little exploring, Plymouth proved a better place to found a village. After the harsh winter of 1621, however, half the settlers were dead. Spring came, and the pilgrims met a Patuxet Indian named Squanto. Years earlier he had been captured by slave traders and sold in Spain. After escaping to England and becoming fluent in English, he made his way back to his homeland, only to find his tribe wiped out by disease. Squanto taught the pilgrims how to farm and served as an interpreter, making treaties with other tribes. After the first harvest in October, 1621, for three days the pilgrims hosted about ninety Native Americans in a feast. It became the first Thanksgiving, a tradition that would long be celebrated in the United States.

The colony began to prosper, and every year brought more colonists seeking religious freedom. In 1630 John Winthrop, with a charter for "The Governor and Company of the Massachusetts Bay in New England," landed at Salem with more than one thousand colonists. Winthrop and his followers did not want to separate from the church, but they believed it needed to be purified from within and thus were called Puritans. The Puritans felt the law must be strictly obeyed if the community were to be strong. A set of wooden stocks stood in the center of many towns, and wrongdoers were put in them for crimes as small as swearing.

### The Witch Trials

Ironically, while Winthrop and his followers left England to seek religious freedom, they had little tolerance of others' religious philosophies. In the 1660's Puritan authorities hanged several Quakers as heretics. By 1692 this intolerance, mixed with superstition, turned into one of the New World's most shameful chapters, the Salem witch trials. Tituba, a West Indian slave woman, told locals tales of African magic. When some of the girls began to

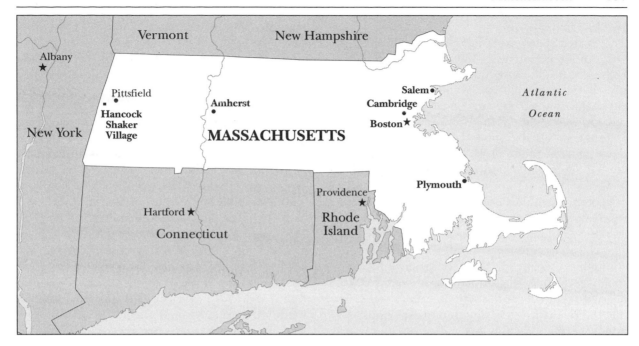

have fainting spells, they accused Tituba of casting spells over them. When Salem reverend Samuel Parris demanded to know who else had been practicing the evil arts, the girls started falsely accusing neighbors of witchery, and soon everyone was accusing everyone else. Nineteen men and women were burned as witches, and nearly 150 more were awaiting trail when authorities in Boston stopped the proceedings. Although the Puritans initiated an atmosphere of intolerance and fear in their society, they must also be remembered for their dedication to hard work and their respect for education; they founded Harvard, the first institution of higher learning in North America.

### The American Revolution

By the mid-1700's Massachusetts was the center of shipbuilding and commerce in the British colonies. The people there were successful, well educated, and accustomed to managing their own affairs. The French and Indian War was won by the British, but at a great cost. To raise more money, Great Britain heavily taxed the colonies. The colonists were particularly upset about this because they were being taxed with no representation in Parliament: "No taxation without representation!" was the frequent cry of colonial protesters. The

merchants of Boston led a boycott of British goods, and Britain responded by stationing troops in the city. One night in March of 1770, mounting tension exploded in a skirmish that became known as the Boston Massacre. Five were killed, the first being a young black man named Crispus Attucks.

On December 16, 1773, a group of Boston men crept aboard three British ships and dumped the tea cargoes in the harbor to protest the high taxes, in what became known as the Boston Tea Party. In April of 1775, the British, intent on quelling the patriots by force, planned to send armed men to Lexington, Concord, and then Boston. Paul Revere, among others, was able to warn the Minutemen, Massachusetts fighters. While the British were able to take Lexington and then Concord in small battles, the patriots were able to defend Boston for a while. Eventually, however, the city succumbed to British force. The Revolutionary War had begun.

The next year, General George Washington took Boston back, chasing the British out of Massachusetts forever. The Treaty of Paris of 1783 granted independence to the colonies. No other colony had contributed more men or money to the war for independence than Massachusetts.

## War and Immigration

The United States went to war with Britain again in 1812 for interfering with American trade, pirating U.S. ships, and forcing Americans to fight the British war with France. Boston, the largest American city of the time, suffered greatly. Boston developed industries to maintain the economy.

In the 1840's, the potato famine in Ireland sent more than one million Irish men and women to the United States, and hundreds of thousands settled in Massachusetts. They found work in the factories of Boston, Lawrence, Lowell, and Worcester. Many residents saw the flood of Irish Catholics as a threat to their Anglo-Protestant society. Discrimination against the Irish was prevalent, and it was not uncommon to see a Help Wanted sign include a No Irish Need Apply slogan. However, any labor was needed eventually as the state became a leader in the American Industrial Revolution. New mills producing textile, paper, boots, and shoes sprang up all over the state.

## The Late 1800's

The Civil War began in 1861, and Massachusetts was the first state to respond, with a regiment of fifteen hundred soldiers. Throughout the war, the state supplied guns, uniforms, and boots to the Union army. When the war was over, the Irish, many of whom served in the war, began climbing the social ladder. They founded businesses, saved money, and bought their own homes. Still, they were discriminated against, and they looked to politics as a way to fight back. In 1880 Hugh O'Brien became Boston's first Irish mayor. In 1892 Patrick Joseph "P. J." Kennedy, son of an East Boston barrel maker, was elected to the state senate. Yet discrimination against Irish, as well as all immigrants, continued.

In the 1880's and 1890's, fresh waves of immigrants poured in. In 1896, U.S. Senator Henry Cabot Lodge, a descendant of Boston's most elite families, sponsored a bill to restrict immigration. He claimed scientific evidence to prove that southern and eastern Europeans were racially inferior and prone to crime. It was vetoed by the U.S. president but signed into law in 1924.

## Economic Hard Times

By 1900 Massachusetts was an industrial state, yet the large mills in the state would not always run smoothly. In 1912 more than twenty-two thousand textile workers staged a strike in Lawrence. There would be other labor problems, and men and women began to organize into unions to fight for better working conditions and higher wages.

After World War I, Massachusetts slipped into recession. When the country fell into the Depression of the 1930's, Massachusetts was hit hard. By 1931 only 44 percent of the state's workers were employed full-time. When World War II began in 1941, Massachusetts factories and shipyards rebounded. The state achieved almost full employment, and thousands of African Americans migrated from southern states to work in the war plants. After the war, the factories fell on hard times yet again. However, another industry, education, led by MIT and Harvard, proved to entice many great minds—and federal grants—to the state. Boston, meanwhile, emerged as a center for banking, insurance, and medicine.

## The Kennedy Dynasty

The son of P. J. Kennedy, Joseph Kennedy graduated from Harvard in 1912 and entered the world of banking. At twenty-five, he became the youngest bank president in the nation. He rose in stature and was eventually named ambassador to England. His political career was ruined, however, when he supported appeasement with German leader Adolf Hitler. Three of his nine children would fulfill his ambitions by going into politics.

In 1960 his son and Massachusetts senator John F. Kennedy became the first Irish Catholic president of the United States. He would not be allowed to finish out his term, however, and the nation grieved when the young president was assassinated in Dallas in 1963. His brother, Robert, was also killed when running for president in 1968. Joseph Kennedy's youngest son, Edward "Ted" Kennedy, served in the U.S. Senate for many years, serving as the patriarch of the ill-fated family. Several of the next generation of Kennedys served in politics as well.

Great politicians and diversity continued to be a strength of the state. Michael S. Dukakis was the first Greek American to be elected governor, in 1972. He later won the Democratic nomination for U.S. president in 1988 but lost the election to George Bush.                                    —*Kevin M. Mitchell*

# Boston Common and Beacon Hill

**Date:** Land for Boston Common purchased in 1634; Beacon Hill built between the 1790's and the 1870's

**Relevant issues:** Colonial America, military history, Revolutionary War

**Significance:** Boston Common is the oldest public open space in the United States. Beacon Hill includes the Massachusetts State House and historic residential areas that were home to some of Boston's leading business, political, and cultural figures.

**Location:** Central Boston; the forty-five-acre Boston Common is bounded by Beacon Street on the north, Park Street on the east, Tremont Street and Boylston Street on the south, and Charles Street on the west, while Beacon Hill is bounded by Beacon Street to the south, Bowdoin Street to the east, Cambridge Street to the north, and the Charles River to the west

**Site Office:**

Greater Boston Convention and Visitors Bureau
Two Copley Plaza, Suite 105
Boston, MA 02116-6501
ph.: (888) SEEBOSTON (733-2678); (617) 424-7664
Web site: www.bostonusa.com

**B**oston Common and Beacon Hill form the historic heart of Boston, the capital of Massachusetts and the leading city of the New England region for more than 350 years. The Common has hardly changed in appearance since it was created in 1634, while the Beacon Hill area, a National Historic Landmark, includes some of the oldest and best-preserved residential streets in the country. Together they show how Boston developed from its foundation to the late nineteenth century, as its citizens, white and black, created a settlement in the European style on what had been the uninhabited peninsula of Shawmut.

## Early History

The first person other than a Native American to settle on Shawmut was not a Puritan, as elsewhere in Massachusetts, but a priest of the Church of England, William Blackstone (or Blaxton). He arrived there in 1625 after the failure of a colony fifteen miles to the south, from which all the other settlers had returned to England. After five years of solitude he invited the Puritans living on the other side of the Charles River to abandon their disease-ridden settlement in favor of Shawmut, which they renamed Boston. In 1634 their town council paid Blackstone thirty English pounds, about one hundred fifty dollars, for his forty-five-acre pasture, which became Boston Common. Blackstone departed for Rhode Island, which was more tolerant than Massachusetts, though he returned in 1659 to find a wife.

The Common came to serve various purposes, as pasture for cows, as a training ground for the militia, and as a place of public executions. The public life of Boston centered on the Common throughout its first century, as the city's population grew from three thousand in 1660 to seventeen thousand in 1740, and it became the largest settlement in the British colonies. British troops camped on the Common when they occupied Boston, beginning in 1768, and in 1775 they set out from it for Lexington and Concord, where the Revolutionary War began. During the War of 1812, all three of the Common's main functions were combined when some cows were accidentally shot during a militia training session. Cows finally left the Common in 1830, and the Great Elm, where the hangings took place, was removed in 1876.

The Granary Burying Ground, separated from the rest of the Common, was started in 1660. The numerous Bostonians buried there, none of whose graves can now be located for certain, include the revolutionary leaders Samuel Adams and Paul Revere, the first American governor of Massachusetts John Hancock, and the five colonials shot by British troops in the Boston Massacre of 1770. Next to the burial ground is the Park Street Church, built in the style of Sir Christopher Wren and opened in 1810, from which William Lloyd Garrison began his campaign against slavery in 1829.

## Beacon Hill

The Beacon Hill district lies directly to the north of the Common. Since 1955 the boundaries of the district have been defined as Beacon Street to the south, Cambridge Street to the north, Bowdoin Street to the east and the Charles River to the west. Two hundred years ago, however, the section between Charles Street and the modern waterfront, now known as the "Flat Side," was all under the Charles River, and the remainder was the so-called Trimountain, a ridge running through the middle of the Shawmut peninsula. Its name derived from its three peaks, Pemberton or Cotton Hill, Beacon Hill, and Mount Vernon. Modern Beacon Hill consists of the remains of the whole Trimountain, and is itself divided into three areas: the Flat Side, the North Slope, and the South Slope.

The first of these, the area between the modern waterfront and Charles Street, was filled in with detritus from all three peaks as they were leveled for building in the 1790's and 1800's. Though there are some distinguished nineteenth century houses on the Flat Side—on Beacon, Brimmer, Lime, and Mount Vernon Streets—it is perhaps most notable for the bookstores, antique stores, restaurants, and bars lining Charles Street; the Charles Street Meeting House, where Frederick Douglass and Sojourner Truth spoke against slavery alongside such white abolitionists as William Lloyd Garrison; and the Hatch Memorial Shell, a concert hall on the waterfront opened in 1928.

The North Slope, the area north of Pinckney Street, was made available for settlement by leveling Mount Vernon. On some maps Mount Vernon was marked as "Mount Whoredom." While most of the Trimountain was unsettled and wild, from about 1725 onward the northern side was the site of brothels and taverns, offering entertainments not available elsewhere in Boston to sailors from ships on the Charles River. The area was officially cleared of brothels and taverns in 1823, but its character was already changing. After 1783, when slavery was outlawed in Massachusetts, it became the center of Boston's free black community. One of the area's oldest houses, built for two free black men, George Middleton and Louis Glapion, in 1795, still stands at 5 Pinckney Street.

### African Americans and Abolitionists

In 1832 William Lloyd Garrison launched the New England Anti-Slavery Society at the African Meeting House in Smith Court, on Joy Street, which had been built in 1806. It is now the oldest remaining black church building in the United States and houses a museum of African American history. In 1834 the black community also opened the Abiel Smith School, nearby on Joy Street, which lasted until the state banned segregated education in 1855, though the building still stands. Also still to be seen is the home, at 66 Phillips Street, of Lewis and Harriet Hayden, who took part in the Underground Railroad network of abolitionists offering aid and shelter to fugitive slaves as they made their way to freedom in Canada.

However, the neighborhood was never exclusively black. In the 1790's Cambridge Street, to the north of Joy Street, attracted some of Boston's elite, including lawyer and politician Harrison Gray Otis, who had the first of his three houses (number 141) built next to the site of the Old West Church, burned down by the British in 1775 and

*The cobblestone Acorn Street on Beacon Hill.* (Greater Boston Convention and Visitors Bureau)

not rebuilt until 1806. The interior of Otis's house has been restored to its early nineteenth century splendor and, like the church, is open to the public. Noteworthy buildings on Pinckney Street, which marks the division between the North and South Slopes, include number 20, where novelist Louisa May Alcott and her family lived until they moved up the social scale to Louisburg Square; number 54, where Nathaniel Hawthorne lived from 1839 to 1842; and number 62, the home of George Hillard, who was in charge of seeking out fugitive slaves at the same time as his wife, presumably without his knowledge, was offering them shelter in a secret attic room.

The South Slope of Beacon Hill was created when the top of Pemberton Hill was replaced by Pemberton Square and the original Beacon Hill became an open space—now the parking lot—next to the Massachusetts State House. (The original Beacon Hill derived its name from the beacons set up on its top, though never lit, in 1634, when the town was threatened by Native Americans, then in 1768, as a symbolic gesture against the British.)

### The State House

The State House was the key to the Trimountain's destruction and the transformation of the South Slope into the wealthiest neighborhood in nineteenth century Boston. In 1795 the city bought what had been John Hancock's pasture, near the top of Beacon Hill, as the site for the new State House. (Hancock's mansion remained, to the west of the State House, until it was knocked down in 1863.) The building was designed by Charles Bulfinch and opened in 1798, in front of a sixty-foot column, commemorating the Revolution, which Bulfinch had also designed. From 1807 to 1810 the area was the subject of litigation between the city, which believed it was common land, and the heirs of John Hancock, who wanted to dig it up for gravel. The heirs won the case, demolished Bulfinch's column, and scooped off the top of the hill to provide nearly fifty acres of landfill in the bay. A copy of the column has since been placed in the parking lot.

The State House that visitors see today is much larger than Bulfinch's building and perhaps, since gold leaf was applied to the dome between 1861 and 1874, more impressive too. A major extension designed by Charles Brigham was opened in 1895,

one hundred years after the laying of the foundation stone, to accommodate the House of Representatives and its famous wooden model of a codfish, leaving the Bulfinch front, still distinguishable by its red bricks, to the Senate. Its chambers share the third floor with the Executive Chamber, the headquarters of the governor and the council, which are not open to the public.

The Great Hall on the second floor was added as recently as 1990 and is now the culmination of walks from the visitors' entrance through the Doric Hall, with its columns and its memorials to John Hancock, George Washington, and Abraham Lincoln; the Nurses' Hall, with its statue of a Civil War nurse and its paintings of historic events in Massachusetts history; and the Hall of Flags, which honors the soldiers of Massachusetts. The historic documents displayed in the Archives Museum, which is also inside the State House, include the colonial charter granted by King Charles I and the Constitution of the Commonwealth of Massachusetts, the oldest written constitution still in effect anywhere in the world.

Also in 1795, anticipating the impact that the opening of the State House would have, Bulfinch joined a group of developers, the Mount Vernon Proprietors, who bought eighteen and a half acres lower down the ridge from the agent of artist John Singleton Copley, who was absent in England. The rising status of the neighbourhood they created can be gauged by the increasing magnificence of the three houses that Bulfinch designed for Harrison Gray Otis, his fellow proprietor. Otis moved from his North Slope house to a more expensive house at 85 Mount Vernon Street (made newly famous when it featured in the 1968 film *The Thomas Crown Affair* and in the television series *Banacek*) and then to his still more expensive final home at 45 Beacon Street. Here he kept a punch bowl always filled for his guests, ate paté de foie gras every morning, and wore clothes trimmed with gold.

### The Boston Brahmins

The land that Bulfinch, Otis, and their colleagues bought lies under the narrow tree-lined streets to the west of the State House. Here lived the so-called Boston Brahmins—the Lowells, the Cabots, the Lodges, and others—who could trace their family trees back to the English settlers and who had come to dominate commerce, banking, law, and medicine in the city. At various times in the nineteenth century the inhabitants also included Julia Ward Howe, the writer of "The Battle Hymn of the Republic" ("Mine eyes have seen the glory of the coming of the Lord . . . "), at 32 Mount Vernon Street and at 13 Chestnut Street; the historian and novelist Henry Adams, who spent his childhood at 57 Mount Vernon Street; Louisa May Alcott (again) at 10 Louisburg Square; Francis Parkman, author of *The California and Oregon Trail*, at 50 Chestnut Street; and Richard Henry Dana, author of *Two Years Before the Mast*, at 43 Chestnut Street.

Beacon Street, running along the northern side of the Common, stands out as perhaps the most exclusive street in this exclusive district. Its oldest houses, those built before 1825, can be distinguished by the presence of purple panes in their windows, the result of the action of sunlight on manganese oxide in the glass. Its leading institution was the Boston Athenaeum, founded in 1807 by Ralph Waldo Emerson and others as a gentlemen's club. Its Italian Renaissance-style interior, containing such treasures as books that belonged to George Washington and paintings by Gilbert Stuart and John Singer Sargent, is now open to the public. Beacon Street's former residents include Robert Gould Shaw, who became famous not for reading or writing books but as the white commanding officer of the black troops of the Fifty fourth Massachusetts Regiment during the Civil War. Their heroism is commemorated in the Shaw Monument, designed by Augustus Saint-Gaudens, which stands opposite the State House. (The regiment is also the subject of the 1989 film *Glory*.)

The last decades of the nineteenth century saw the decline of the manufacturing base of Boston and Massachusetts as the Southern states, with lower wages and taxes, rose from the disaster of the Civil War. The end of the era when a homogeneous Boston elite could isolate itself on the South Slope, away from the newer ethnic groups of the city, can be symbolized by two events that took place in 1897: the dedication of the Shaw Monument and the opening of the first subway in the United States, to take streetcars under the Common. The first station, now a National Historic Landmark, is on Park Street, which passes along the eastern side of the Common to the State House.

## Modern Preservation Efforts

Beacon Hill's integrity as a historic area was threatened in 1947 by a plan to replace its brick sidewalks. After a group of women from West Cedar Street sat down on them to obstruct the plan, public opinion swung in favor of preservation. Beacon Hill has been protected as a historic district of the Commonwealth of Massachusetts since 1955 and as a National Historic Landmark since 1963, so that the external appearance of buildings in the district cannot be inappropriately altered. The Beacon Hill Architectural Commission enforces the rules, forbidding, for example, unsuitable colors for front doors, and maintaining the permanent gas lighting of the streets.

While Boston Common and Beacon Hill are protected as important parts of the city's history, and of the nation's, they are more than merely open-air museum exhibits. The Common is still a busy park where people talk, play, and rest as they did 350 years ago, Beacon Hill remains an attractive residential district though most of the "Brahmins" have moved away, and political business is carried on as usual in the State House. If William Blackstone could return again to Boston he would find solitude impossible to maintain.

*—Patrick Heenan*

## For Further Information:

Amory, Cleveland. *The Proper Bostonians*. New York: E. P. Dutton, 1947. Vividly evokes the lives and opinions of the Beacon Hill "Brahmins," from Harrison Gray Otis through to influential figures still living when Amory wrote the book.

Cooper, Jason. *Historic Boston*. Vero Beach, Fla.: Rourke, 1999. Descriptions of the places where Boston's patriots lived, worked, battled, and argued against British rule. Includes the Massachusetts State House, Faneuil Hall, and the Old North Church.

Lowell, Robert. *For the Union Dead*. New York: Farrar, Straus and Giroux, 1964. The title poem of this collection is a moving meditation on the Shaw Monument and the Common, past and present. It can also be found in many anthologies of modern American verse.

Whitehill, Walter Muir. *Boston: A Topographical History*. 3d ed. Cambridge, Mass.: Harvard University Press, 2000. Outlines the development of the Common, Beacon Hill, and other historic districts of the city. Illustrated with many fascinating contemporary maps and prints.

# Dickinson Homestead, Amherst

**Date:** Built in 1813; designated a National Historic Landmark in 1963; sold to Amherst College in 1965 and, since then, open to the public annually from March until mid-December

**Relevant issues:** Literary history, women's history

**Significance:** No American author is more closely identified with a house than Emily Dickinson is with the Dickinson Homestead. Increasingly reclusive during her last fifteen years, Dickinson seldom strayed from the family dwelling on Main Street in Amherst. After 1883, she left it hardly at all.

**Location:** The Dickinson Homestead is two blocks from Amherst College in Amherst, about twenty miles north of Springfield and seventy-five miles west of Boston

**Site Office:**
The Dickinson Homestead
280 Main Street
Amherst, MA 01002
ph.: (413) 542-8161
Web site: www.amherst.edu/%7eedhouse/intro.htm

No American author is associated more closely with a dwelling than Emily Dickinson, who was born in the Dickinson Homestead on December 10, 1830, and who died there on May 15, 1886. Except for the period from 1840 until 1855, when Dickinson's father, Edward, moved his family to a house on Amherst's North Pleasant Street, the Dickinsons lived at the Homestead, built around 1813 by Emily Dickinson's grandfather, Samuel Fowler Dickinson, an attorney and principal founder of Amherst College.

## The Dickinsons and Their Homestead

When Emily Dickinson died at age fifty-five, she had lived all but fifteen of her years at the Homestead, a red brick, neoclassical structure that underwent various renovations during her lifetime.

Home, particularly the Homestead, was the anchor in her life. It was also the microcosm that provided details for many of the nearly eighteen hundred poems her sister Lavinia found in a cherry chest in her bedroom following her death.

From her birth on December 10, 1830, until 1840, Emily Dickinson lived in the Homestead with her parents, Edward and Emily Norcross Dickinson, and her brother and sister, Austin and Lavinia. The house was bought by David Mack in 1833, shortly before Samuel resettled in Ohio, where he died in 1838. Edward and his family shared the Homestead with the Macks until 1840, when Edward moved his family to a clapboard house on North Pleasant Street. The Dickinsons remained there until 1855, when Edward, a successful lawyer and treasurer of Amherst College, bought the Homestead and returned his family to its ancestral home.

Emily's only protracted absence from Amherst occurred between August, 1847, and the summer of 1848. Following seven years at Amherst Academy, she entered Mount Holyoke Female Seminary in South Hadley, Massachusetts, in August, 1847. Soon, however, she chose to discontinue her studies. She wrote to Austin in 1848: "Home was always dear to me . . . but never did it seem as dear as now." Cheered by the thought that she would leave Mount Holyoke, she returned to Amherst, though to the North Pleasant Street house, not to the Homestead.

From 1855 until she died, Emily lived in the Homestead with her parents and sister. Lavinia, unmarried, remained in the Homestead until her death in 1899. She followed Emily's wish that upon her death her letters were to be burned. Although Lavinia burned many of Emily's letters, about a thousand are extant. Her poems, handwritten and carefully gathered in small books whose left margins Emily stitched to hold them together, fortunately survived. They have established Emily Dickinson as a leading American poet.

## Renovations to the Homestead

The Homestead was originally a typical Federal-style structure. After the Macks sold it back to Edward Dickinson, Emily's now-prosperous father, who had a civic reputation to uphold as he represented his community in the state legislature and his state for one term in the United States Congress, he went about expanding and improving the dwelling. He engaged a Northampton architect, William Fenno Pratt, to design the Evergreens (the house he had built for Austin) and possibly involved him in the renovation of the Homestead. Pratt had recently achieved local celebrity for his design of the Northampton City Hall across the Connecticut River from Amherst.

In the original house, the stairs to the second floor were directly to the left of the front door. A long central hall was created, giving way to a curved staircase leading to the second floor. Later in her life, when guests came to the Homestead, Emily enjoyed sitting on this staircase to listen, unobserved, to the music and conversation that drifted in her direction.

A white cupola was added to the house, reminiscent of the widow's walks one frequently sees in New England. Edward also added a conservatory. Its entry was through the library. This room was among Emily's favorite haunts. She nurtured her exotic plants there, raising such flora as fuchsias, heliotrope, and jasmine.

The Homestead remained in the Dickinson family until 1916, occupied by Emily and Lavinia during their lifetimes. The house was left to Austin Dickinson's daughter, Martha Dickinson Bianchi, when Lavinia died in 1899. Martha rented out the dwelling until 1916, when she sold it to the Parke family. In 1965, two years after it had been designated a National Historic Landmark, Amherst College bought the house.

### Physical Description of the Homestead

The Homestead as it now exists has six rooms, several closets, and a bathroom on the main floor. The second floor has five rooms and four bathrooms as well as several closets. The top floor consists of two rooms, a bathroom, and an attic storage area.

The current tour route includes four rooms on the first floor and three on the second. To most current tourists, the most interesting room in the Homestead is Emily's second-floor corner bedroom. When Martha Bianchi prepared the house for rental to tenants, most of its furniture was removed. The bedroom was refurnished with items from the Dickinson family later, when it was prepared for public access. The house, including Emily's bedroom, is therefore sparsely furnished.

In the bedroom visitors see Emily's small bed against one wall, covered by a white bedspread. One of Emily's paisley shawls is sometimes draped over the end of the bed. A replica of one of her white cotton dresses is displayed in an adjoining room.

Emily Dickinson's bedroom was her refuge from the world. She once brought a cousin into it, locked the door behind them, and, holding up the key, announced, "*This* is freedom!" The room had considerable light in Dickinson's day, although its four large windows are now obscured by the hemlocks outside them. Emily could see the street from her windows. Her reference to the bee as "the little tippler" in one of her most familiar poems, "I Taste a Liquor Never Brewed," is thought to have been evoked when, peering from her window one Saturday night, she saw someone who had drunk too much leaning unsteadily against a lamppost.

### The Evergreens

It is not possible to write about Emily Dickinson and the Homestead without referring also to the Evergreens, the house adjacent to the Homestead that Edward Dickinson built in 1855 for his son Austin to dissuade him from moving to the Midwest. The houses are about three hundred feet apart, their back doors connected by a narrow path. Emily Dickinson described it as "just wide enough for two who love."

For a decade after Austin's marriage in 1856, Emily was close to her brother's wife, Susan Gilbert Dickinson. Some think they had a falling out in 1866 when Susan sent one of Emily's poems to *The Springfield Republican*, which published it without Emily's consent, although this contention has not been substantiated. Emily often trod the path between the two houses, going to the Evergreens to visit her niece and nephews and sometimes to take some of her poems to Susan, who is said to have read over three hundred of them.

Austin's only daughter, Martha Dickinson Bianchi, who lived in the Evergreens until her death in 1943, willed the property to her assistant, Alfred Leete Hampson. He lived there, as did his widow, Mary Landis Hampson, until her death in 1988 at the age of ninety-three. The Hampsons, much immersed in helping to edit Emily Dickinson's poetry, were extremely protective of the Evergreens, elements of which possibly figured in Dickinson's poems. The Hampsons, aware of its

*Poet Emily Dickinson as a young girl. She spent her early childhood and almost all of her adult years at the Dickinson Homestead in Amherst.* (Library of Congress)

ing horse in the now-unused nursery.

Other images in Dickinson's poems have been related to objects in both Austin's house and the Homestead. One scholar has related a sofa in the Evergreens's parlor to the lines in "The Night Was Wide" that read: "How pleasanter—said she/ Upon the Sofa opposite—/ The Sleet—than May, no Thee—." Dickinson uses such objects in subtle ways. She is not writing about a rocking horse or a sofa in the poems cited above but is focusing on broader topics, nature in the latter poem and death in the former. Over one-third of all her poems deal with death. Her imagery, nevertheless, is frequently drawn from the microcosm, including both the Evergreens and the Homestead, out of which she wrote.

Upon Mrs. Hampson's death, according to Martha Bianchi's will, the Evergreens was to be razed to its foundations. Finally, however, because of its significance in Emily Dickinson's life, it was preserved and passed into the Martha Dickinson Bianchi Trust, which is supported by income from the Bianchi estate and by contributions from individuals. The house has been readied for public viewing, probably following a schedule similar to that of the Homestead.　　　　*—R. Baird Shuman*

historic and literary significance, left the property intact during the years they occupied it and maintained an Emily Dickinson room on the first floor.

The Evergreens is important because several Dickinson poems seem to reflect objects Emily saw in the house. This is particularly true of the nursery of her young nephew, Thomas Gilbert "Gib" Dickinson, whose death from typhoid fever in 1883 at the age of eight left Emily so disheartened that her own health failed substantially. She seldom left her bedroom after Gib's death and died less than three years afterward.

Dickinson scholar Masako Takeda suggests that the rocking horse on which Gib played, still reposing in the nursery, perhaps figured directly in the poem "Because I Could Not Stop for Death." The final lines of that poem—"I first surmised the Horses' Heads/ Were toward Eternity"—may have been evoked by the lonely image of the boy's rock-

**For Further Information:**

Berne, Suzanne. "Three Writers' Homes: The Massachusetts Homes of Louisa May Alcott, Edith Wharton, and Emily Dickinson." *The New York Times,* August 30, 1992, travel section, pp. 14-16. Berne demonstrates the role houses have played in the lives and writing of three American authors.

Farmer, Gregory. "The Evergreens: The Other Dickinson House." *The Massachusetts Review* 34, no. 4 (Winter, 1993/1994): 561-564. This short essay written by the Project Manager of The Martha Dickinson Bianchi Trust is an adjunct to Masako Takeda's longer article immediately preceding it.

Farr, Judith, ed. *Emily Dickinson: A Collection of Critical Essays.* Upper Saddle River, N.J.: Prentice Hall, 1996. At least half of the eighteen essays in this collection deal in some way with Dickinson's affinity to the two houses in which she lived.

Ferlazzo, Paul J. *Emily Dickinson.* Boston: Twayne, 1976. Ferlazzo presents interesting insights into Dickinson's need for home, relating some of her emotional problems and reclusiveness to this need.

Johnson, Thomas H. *Emily Dickinson: An Interpretive Biography.* Cambridge, Mass.: The Belknap Press of Harvard University Press, 1955. Despite its age, this thorough biography offers valuable information about the Dickinson Homestead.

Johnson, Thomas H., and Theodora Ward, eds. *The Letters of Emily Dickinson.* Cambridge, Mass.: The Belknap Press of Harvard University Press, 1970. In her letters, Emily Dickinson often reveals her feeling for her home.

Takeda, Masako. "The Evergreens: The Other Dickinson House." *The Massachusetts Review* 34, no. 4 (Winter, 1993/1994): 545-560. This eminent Japanese Dickinson scholar relates the Evergreens to Emily Dickinson's writing and establishes connections between it and the Homestead.

Wheeler, David L. "Seeking Emily Dickinson, Poet, Gardener, Recluse, in the Privacy of Her Home." *Chronicle of Higher Education* 46, no. 10 (October 29, 1999): B2. Wheeler recounts his visit to the Homestead with Martha Ackmann, a professor at Mount Holyoke College, and her American literature students.

# The First Church of Christ, Scientist, Boston

**Date:** Original edifice built from 1893 to 1894

**Relevant issues:** Religion, women's history

**Significance:** As the headquarters of the Christian Science movement, The First Church of Christ, Scientist, in Boston, is also known as The Mother Church.

**Location:** On a fourteen-acre, roughly triangular site between Huntington Avenue, Massachusetts Avenue, and what was once Norway Street, in the Back Bay area of the city

**Site Office:**
The First Church of Christ, Scientist
Visitor Services
175 Huntington Avenue
Boston, MA 02115
ph.: (617) 450-2000
Web site: www.tfccs.com/GV/TMC/

The unique position of The First Church of Christ, Scientist, is marked by the exclusive "The" in its title—branch church buildings elsewhere are called "First Church of Christ, Scientist" or "Second," and so on, without the definite article. The Mother Church consists of two adjoining parts lying on an east-west axis: the smaller "Original Edifice," built from 1893 to 1894 to the plans of a local architect, in a Romanesque style with a bell tower at the eastern end; and The Mother Church Extension, built back to back with it, an imposing domed basilica-type construction completed in 1906 in a mixture of the Byzantine and Italian Renaissance styles. In 1975 a portico was added to the Extension, harmonizing the church buildings with the rest of the complex, the modern part of which was planned and executed in concrete between 1962 and 1975 by the firm of I. M. Pei and Partners. The partners included individuals who later composed the firm of Cossutta and Ponte. The center also includes the neo-classical Christian Science Publishing House building of 1934, the five-story Colonnade Building, the twenty-eight-story Church Administration Building, and the quadrant-shaped, three-story Sunday School.

### Mary Baker Eddy

The directive to begin constructing the original edifice in Boston was given to the Christian Science Board of Directors by the movement's founder and leader, Mary Baker Eddy, in September, 1893. The building was to be finished and ready for use by the end of 1894.

Eddy had been born into a New Hampshire Congregationalist family, the Bakers; she is best known by the last name of her third husband, Asa G. Eddy, whom she married in 1877. Suffering from delicate health, she had long been interested in questions of healing, about which she wrote and lectured, and she had investigated the apparent curative powers of hydropathy, the Graham system, mind cure, suggestion, and homeopathy, among

*The First Church of Christ, Scientist.* (The Christian Science Publishing Society)

### Science and Health

Eddy published in 1875 her primary work on Christian Science, *Science and Health*. Completed later by the addition of the *Key to the Scriptures*, its ideas were considered both by her and her followers to be divinely inspired. The Bible and *Science and Health* constitute the fundamental texts of the Christian Science faith. With the same goals of spirituality and simplicity, Eddy later set out in her *Manual of The Mother Church* (1895) the By-Laws governing the Church. The business of the Church is carried out by the self-perpetuating five-member Christian Science Board of Directors.

Eddy taught and healed according to her "discovery," expecting it to be accepted by and incorporated into orthodox Christianity. When it was not and increasing interest was evident, in 1879 she and fifteen of her followers organized the Church of Christ (Scientist) in Boston, meeting in the early days in private houses and hired halls. On September 1, 1892, Eddy reorganized the church as The First Church of Christ, Scientist, by giving land upon which to build the church to the Christian Science Board of Directors. The plot was on a marshy spit of land called Gravelly Point.

### Building the Original Church

There was a rule that The Mother Church was not to be funded from debts or mortgages, only from money in hand. The story of its construction was marked by a repeated need for ad hoc adaptation to changing circumstances, financial and technical, to reach the goal of completing the church edifice by December 30, 1894.

A stone building was approved and gray New Hampshire granite chosen. Then new laws requiring fireproofing increased the projected cost by over a third. The sum the Board of Directors had at their disposal was far less than the total amount projected. To get permission to start building, estimates had to be obtained and a plan selected and approved by city officials. The problem was not only financial; there were difficulties in getting specifications and estimates from contractors. The permit was finally obtained, and work pro-

others. Her most constant and in-depth study, however, was of the Bible, in particular the cures brought about by Jesus and his disciples. A turning point in her thought occurred in 1866 when, after reading passages in the New Testament about Jesus' healings, she recovered unexpectedly from the nearly fatal effects of a fall. This experience, confirming her theory that disease was a mental phenomenon, inspired her to evolve over a period of years, through study of the Bible, prayer, and demonstration, a spiritual regimen intended to enable students to practice Scripture-based Christianity. In particular, an understanding of the divine laws behind Jesus' healings would aim to shed light on the problem of suffering and evil of all kinds. This spiritual practice, which she called Christian Science, would develop morals, joy, and healing for the difficulties encountered in life, and at the same time cure illness through prayer, without medication, thus demonstrating faith in action, the practicality of God's law of good.

Matter in Christian Science is seen as a human mental construct which yields to an understanding of the spiritual nature of God's creation. According to Eddy, true reality is spiritual. Christ healed sickness and sin and overcame death by his understanding of the spiritual nature of God's creation. Anyone can follow his example, through systematic Bible study, prayer, effort, trials, patience, repentance, and unselfish love, and can progressively and practically prove that the understanding of the nature of God, the divine Mind, or Love, heals.

ceeded with confidence that God would provide.

The pile-driving and foundations contracts were signed on October 19, 1893, and the first stone was laid, on time, on November 8. Work had to be suspended for the worst of the winter, but funds began to flow in again, enough for it to be decided that a start could be made on the walls. The contractors agreed to halt the work if funds failed and then resume again as necessary. Once more, in spite of hitches and delays, materials were obtained and building proceeded. The cornerstone, together with a sealed copper box containing (among other items) one copy of the Bible and one of *Science and Health with Key to the Scriptures* (bound to match), was placed in position on May 21, 1894, and marked with a plaque. So it went, with cash flow problems, workmen's anxiety, and delays. Snow fell early in October and November, 1894, into the still roofless, floorless, windowless church, but impressive energy, persistent prayer, and trust were brought to bear, and the struggle to meet the deadline succeeded. On December 30, 1894, the first Sunday service was held in The Mother Church.

### Architectural Features of the Church

From outside, the gray stone building displays a mixture of rounded and straight window shapes, turrets and chimneys and little arcades, a complicated roof, and a semicircular apselike feature attached to its square tower. Inside there is a vestibule, then a rectangular auditorium with a semicircular balcony, a fresco under the ceiling, rows of pews arranged in an arc in front of the platform with its two readers' desks, and at the rear of the platform the organ, donated by a member of the church in gratitude for a healing. Slender bronze casings instead of wooden frames minimize the darkening effect of narrow Romanesque-style stained glass windows. The stained glass, set mainly around the auditorium, the balcony, and on either side of the platform, includes a rose window representing the raising of Jairus's daughter; another, representing the biblical New Jerusalem, whose four principal sides are discussed in *Science and Health*; rectangular windows depicting such scenes from the New Testament as the raising of Lazarus and the resurrection of Christ; one span of six long, narrow windows representing the six water jugs that figured in the narrative of the wedding at Cana; and two narrow windows depicting lamps

which refer to Psalm 119:105, "Thy word is a lamp unto my feet and a light unto my path."

In the tower off the main vestibule, an apartment known as "Mother's Room" was built—including marble features matching those in the church itself—and carefully furnished for Eddy. The general use by Christian Scientists of the term "Mother" to designate the founder of their movement drew some public criticism, notably from Mark Twain. Eddy decided that "Leader" should be used to describe her role instead. To dispel a sense of personalization, in 1908 she had the Mother's Room closed and dismantled.

### Expansion

With the Christian Science congregation growing rapidly, the original Mother Church's capacity of just under one thousand people soon proved inadequate; by 1905 there had to be three Sunday services to cope with the numbers. In 1902 Eddy called for the building of an extension which, it was decided at the June annual meeting of the movement, should be able to seat four thousand to five thousand people, at a cost of up to two million dollars to be contributed voluntarily by Christian Scientists and others worldwide. By 1903 the rest of the triangular plot on which the original Mother Church stood had been acquired and paid for. The land lay between Falmouth, Norway, and St. Paul Streets. Building was begun early in 1904 and proceeded as more funds were contributed. Because of the nature of the terrain (a landfill site affected by underground tidewater), it was necessary to support the structure on wooden piles, this time more than four thousand of them. The cornerstone was placed at the angle of St. Paul and Falmouth Streets on July 16, 1904. Once again the stone contained copies of the two basic texts of Christian Science, the Bible and *Science and Health*.

Money came in to the building fund from branch churches and individual members, but it was settled that whereas for the original Mother Church individuals had been allowed to donate specific items such as the organ and stained glass windows, the use of donations would now be decided by the Board of Directors. As the June, 1906, deadline approached—the date of the annual meeting—tradesmen labored in shifts around the clock. The essential work was done in time and paid for in stages, with enough money left over for the remaining finishing touches.

The architects for The Mother Church Extension were Charles Brigham of Boston, who had designed the old Boston Art Museum, Solon Spenser Beman of Chicago, and later the firm of Brigham, Coveney, and Bisbee. Eddy, though she never visited the Extension, was involved in some of the planning. A combination of Byzantine and Italian Renaissance style was evolved, using for the walls, around a steel skeleton, New Hampshire granite to match the tone of the older building, and Bedford limestone from Indiana, with Tennessee marble for ornamental features. The extension's twelve bells are housed in the lantern of the 224-foot-high dome, 82 feet in diameter, that forms the apex of the auditorium, with its shape echoed at the north and south ends of the building.

The Mother Church Extension is built onto the western end of the Original Church, along the same east-west line, and symmetrically, so that their respective platforms and organs stand back to back against the middle wall and their vestibules lie one at each end of the double structure.

### Development of the Surrounding Neighborhood

In the decades prior to its most recent development, The Mother Church was surrounded by low rise buildings, street traffic, and a railroad yard. It has taken on a different aspect, as the nucleus of an organic whole, in the public setting created for it by the Christian Science Center's plaza.

The center project got under way in 1962 under the direction of the Christian Science Board of Directors. The Church had already acquired much of the land needed, giving assistance to displaced tenants, and had a justified confidence that the seventy-five million-dollar cost of the center would be covered by voluntary contributions from members and well-wishers.

The architectural scheme was planned by I. M. Pei, a Chinese architect who had studied at the Massachusetts Institute of Technology and designed the glass pyramid at the Louvre as well as Boston's John Hancock Tower. He appointed in overall charge Araldo Cossutta, a graduate of Harvard and of the Paris École des Beaux-Arts, with Vicente Ponte as planning consultant.

Any tendency one might feel to see the juxtaposition of old buildings and new as a sort of two-way architectural irony is prevented by the planners'

obvious regard for the priority and centrality of The Mother Church edifices as the material symbol of a spiritual intention. The colors, textures, and shapes of these edifices, systematically taken up and continued in a modern mode and on a modern scale, are re-created in the bold curving and rectilinear designs of the new buildings, with their concrete colonnades, sweeping futuristic walkways, frameless plate glass windows, and coffered ceilings (which conceal telephone and power lines and air-conditioning ducts).

The 525-foot-long Colonnade Building houses media studios for television, radio, and shortwave radio broadcasting; editorial offices for *The Christian Science Journal*, *Sentinel*, and *Herald*; editorial and publishing offices for *The Christian Science Monitor*, an authoritative international daily newspaper; and a nondenominational Bible Discovery Place for the community, especially young people. The Christian Science Publishing Society is one of the biggest distributors of the Bible around the world. The tall Church Administration Building contains the directors' offices and board room and the church's administrative departments; and the quadrant-shaped three-story Sunday School, for young people up to age twenty, has classrooms and an auditorium seating over a thousand.

Distinct from the administrative buildings is the 1934 Publishing House. In 2000, the Board of Directors announced plans for a multimillion-dollar research library there. Called the Mary Baker Eddy Library for the betterment of Humanity, it would house more than 500,000 documents of the church's founder, as well as exhibits and meeting spaces. The building has always contained a proportioned, thirty-foot, illuminated stained-glass globe, the Mapparium, which allows a visitor to step inside and experience a unified view of the world with 1935 boundaries.

The elements of the complex are situated around and reflected in a rectangular pool 670 feet long, 110 feet wide, and 2 feet deep, bordered along most of its south-east length by flower beds; beyond these is a promenade lined with linden trees. At the eastern end of the reflecting pool is a circular fountain 80 feet in diameter, the size and shape of the extension's dome.

### The Modern Church

The form of religious service used in The Mother

Church is followed in the branch churches. On Sundays (in The Mother Church Extension in the morning and in the Original Edifice in the evening), after an opening hymn, a scripture reading, silent prayer, and praying the Lord's Prayer aloud, two elected readers, one male and the other female without priority by gender, read from the Bible and from related passages in *Science and Health with Key to the Scriptures*. The subject and citations differ each week, the subject being one of a rotating set of topics studied by the congregation during the previous week. There is no preacher, no altar, and no outward form of sacrament, although communion is observed twice a year as silent prayer, without a bread and wine ceremony. Baptism is considered an ongoing purification of thought and action. The first part of the Wednesday meetings is given to readings from the Bible and *Science and Health* on a subject chosen by the first reader; in the second part, members of the congregation bear witness to their experiences of spiritual learning and healing. There are over sixty thousand testimonials, published in church periodicals, to physical and mental cures effected for over one hundred years through Christian Science treatment. In 2000, there were branch churches in over seventy countries worldwide.

*—Olive Classe; revised by Gary A. Jones*

**For Further Information:**

Armstrong, Joseph, and Margaret Williamson. *Building of the Mother Church: The First Church of Christ, Scientist, in Boston, Massachusetts.* Boston: Christian Science Publishing Society, 1980. Contains accounts of the planning and building processes.

Gill, Gillian. *Mary Baker Eddy.* New York: Perseus Books, 1998. New research on all aspects of the founding of Christian Science, including aspects of building the Church edifices.

Marlin, William. "Formed Up in Faith: The Christian Science Center in Boston's Back Bay. . . . " *Architectural Forum*, September, 1973. A detailed and technical account, with plans and photographs, of the center building project up to 1973.

Peel, Robert. *Mary Baker Eddy: The Years of Authority, 1892-1910.* New York: Holt, Rinehart and Winston, 1977. Though partisan, contains some useful factual material about Eddy and the early stages of the Christian Science movement.

# Freedom Trail, Boston

**Date:** 1634-1809

**Relevant issues:** Colonial America, cultural history, military history, naval history, political history, religion, Revolutionary War

**Significance:** The Freedom Trail runs past more than a dozen landmarks in Boston, all related to the role of the city and its environs in colonial times, the American Revolution, and the early days of the United States. The area comprises several cemeteries, including the Granary Burying Ground in which Paul Revere, Samuel Adams, John Hancock, and other key figures of the revolution are interred and Copp's Hill Burying Ground in which lie Puritan leaders Increase and Cotton Mather; the Park Street and Old North Churches, the Old South Meeting House, and King's Chapel and Burying Ground; the Old Corner Bookstore; Faneuil Hall; the Paul Revere House; the Bunker Hill Monument; and the Charlestown Navy Yard, at which is anchored the USS *Constitution* ("Old Ironsides"). The route is marked, in most places, with a red line on the sidewalks of the city, though in a few places it is marked by gray stones on a red brick sidewalk.

**Location:** The trail winds for about three miles through Boston, from Boston Common to the berth of the USS *Constitution* in the Charlestown Navy Yard

**Site Office:**
Boston National Historical Park
Charlestown Navy Yard
Boston, MA 02129-4543
ph.: (617) 242-5644
Web site: www.nps.gov/bost/ftrail.htm

Boston has been called the "Cradle of Liberty" and the "Birthplace of American Independence." Its history is filled with images, names, and phrases graven in the American mind, from the earliest Puritan settlers through the Boston Massacre, the Boston Tea Party, Paul Revere's ride, and the Battle of Bunker Hill. Today, Boston is a history-conscious metropolis—the largest in New England—where three hundred-year old buildings stand surrounded by glass skyscrapers.

## Early History

The first European settler in Boston, called Shawmut (living waters) by the Native Americans, was William Blackstone or Blaxton, who arrived in the New World in 1622 with a group of colonists who settled about fifteen miles to the south. He moved by himself to Shawmut in 1625, after the other colony failed.

Puritans, members of a sect started in the late 1500's by dissenters within the Church of England, arrived in 1630, settling across the river from Blackstone's cottage on a site called Mishawum by the Native Americans. They were the vanguard of more than ten thousand Puritans who would settle in the area over the next decade, driven from England by the major political struggle that developed from their efforts to purify the church of ritual trappings and return to the simplicity of the first Christian congregations. The newcomers renamed the site Charlestown and called the river the Charles, both for Great Britain's King Charles I, who had granted them their colonial charter.

When the Puritans encountered problems with disease and an insufficient water supply, Blackstone invited them to use the springs at Shawmut. They moved across the river and, on September 17, 1630, renamed the area Boston after the English town from which many of them had come. Four years later, Blackstone sold his fifty acres of pasture to the town for thirty pounds and moved to Rhode Island. His pasture became Boston Common, the oldest public open space in the United States.

## Puritan Theocracy

Once settled, the Puritans, who had fled religious intolerance, established a theocracy in which their worldview brooked little variance. They executed individuals with unorthodox religious views and drove out dissenters. Prominent among the leaders of the theocracy was the Mather family. The founder of the clan, Richard (1596-1669), arrived in Boston in 1636 after being suspended from the Anglican ministry. In 1640, he collaborated on the earliest surviving book published in America, The Bay Psalm Book, and in 1646 he drafted the Cambridge Platform, which became the basic organizing document of the New England Congregationalists.

## Increase Mather

Richard's son, Increase (1639-1723), was for almost three decades the leading clergyman in the theocracy. He was the colony's chief diplomat in negotiations with London after Charles II revoked the colony's charter in 1684, a year before his brother, James II, ascended the throne. The original charter had permitted colonists to elect their own governor, and in 1686 Increase Mather was sent to London to argue for the return of the charter and the dismissal of Edmund Andros, the autocratic governor appointed by the king. In 1691, after the overthrow of King James II, Massachusetts secured a new charter and, although the charter did not allow for elections, Queen Mary and her husband, Prince William of Orange, allowed Mather to choose the next governor, William Phips. Increase Mather's son, Cotton, also became a prominent New England clergyman.

Insults visited on the colony by the British Crown did not end with the revocation of its charter. James II ordered the establishment of an Anglican parish in Boston. Since no Puritan would sell the Anglicans land for a church, Governor Andros had difficulty finding a site; finally, in 1687, he seized a corner of the city's oldest burial ground, first used in 1630, the final resting place of many staunch Puritans and a repository of the ornate carvings and unusual epitaphs that are the art and literature in Boston's graveyards.

## The First King's Chapel

On this site was built the first King's Chapel, a wooden structure which quickly became a source of irritation to the colonists. They saw its elegant furnishings, including the first organ to be installed in any church in the British colonies, as symbolic of the churches their forebears had left. They saw its congregants—including royal governors, colonial officials, and military officers—as being too powerful. They saw its presence as a threat to their freedom.

In 1749 the wooden chapel was replaced by a granite structure with an elegant interior. The cornerstone-setting ceremony brought forth a shower of garbage, dead animals, and curses on the celebrants from angry Puritans.

Hostility toward the chapel remained high until the American Revolution, when nearly half its pew holders left with the British Army. In 1785, the re-

*The Paul Revere House, part of the Freedom Trail and the oldest standing structure in Boston. Revere left from this house for his historic ride to Lexington and Concord.* (Greater Boston Convention and Visitors Bureau)

maining congregants of what had come to be called Stone Chapel made it the first Unitarian church in America, combining Unitarian beliefs with liturgy from the Anglican Book of Common Prayer.

### Friction with Great Britain

While the Mathers and other Boston-based theologians spoke out from the city's pulpits, a prosperous merchant-shipping class was developing and increasingly voicing discontent with the king and Parliament. Men such as Samuel Adams, the organizer of the revolution, and John Hancock, the war's banker, spearheaded a movement that would make Boston a center of rebellion. Such local groups as the Sons of Liberty and the Committee of Correspondence organized first resistance to and then open revolt against British-imposed taxes.

A major site of overt friction between Britain and the colonists was what is now called the Old State House. Built in 1713, it was the capitol of the colony, housing not only the royally appointed British officials but also the freely elected Massa-chusetts Assembly, the most radical of the colonial legislatures. Its ground floor was the site of the daily meetings of Boston's first merchants' exchange.

### Moving Toward the Revolutionary War

From the Old State House balcony, the royal governors made their official proclamations; but on July 18, 1776, Colonel Thomas Crafts stood there and read a copy of the Declaration of Independence, newly arrived from Philadelphia. The reading marked the high point of many years of independence-minded activism at the State House.

In 1766 the room where the assembly met became the first governmental meeting place in which a gallery was installed so the public could watch the proceedings. The first proceedings so honored was a debate on the Stamp Act. Thereafter, the gallery provided a place from which crowds could heckle representatives who supported Britain. Because of the assembly's outspokenness, the governor frequently blocked its meetings or forced it to meet away from Boston.

The Old State House ceased being used when the new one on Beacon Hill was completed in 1798. After the old structure deteriorated during the nineteenth century, a citizens' group organized to preserve and restore it. It has been a museum since 1882.

Public opposition to British rule was first voiced in Boston's town meeting hall. The building, completed in 1742, was a gift to the city by Peter Faneuil, a prominent merchant. It was intended as a public market, but the great meeting hall above the market stalls gave it its identity as the "Cradle of Liberty."

Destroyed by fire in 1761, the hall was rebuilt in 1763 in time for a meeting in May, 1764, at which the citizens of Boston denounced the Sugar Act, declaring the principle of "no taxation without representation."

In Faneuil Hall's meeting room, citizens later rallied against the Stamp Act, the Townshend Acts, and the landing of British troops in the colonies. There they created the Committee of Correspondence to exchange news and ideas with other towns and colonies. And there, on November 5, 1773, led by John Hancock, they held the first of the meetings that led to the Boston Tea Party.

After the Boston Tea Party, the British banned town meetings and used Faneuil Hall to house troops. It was then used as a theater, but after the revolution the hall once more fulfilled its donor's stipulation that it always be open for public use. The Marquis de Lafayette was honored there with a banquet after the revolution. Nearly every American war was debated at the hall, as were major issues such as slavery, women's rights, and temperance. In keeping with its role as a bastion of free speech, it served both as the chief rallying place of Boston's active abolitionists and the scene of defense of slavery by Jefferson Davis, the future president of the Confederacy.

Before Faneuil Hall was enlarged in 1806, crowds too large for its confines made their way to the Old South Meeting House, a Puritan church that was the largest meeting place in Boston. Many of the events that led to the revolution took place there.

### The Boston Massacre

One of the earliest of these overflow meetings followed the Boston Massacre of March 5, 1770. What began as a confrontation over a fraudulent barber bill led to a British guard outside the Custom House, across from the Old State House, being surrounded by hundreds of irate citizens. Eight British soldiers and their commander, who went to restore order, were also trapped. The crowd yelled insults and threw snowballs and rocks at the soldiers. Finally, one of the frightened soldiers fired. After a brief flurry of shots, five men were dead or dying and several more were wounded. The first blood of the American Revolution was drawn.

The massacre was the culmination of a series of incidents that grew from the colonists' reaction to the Quartering Acts of 1765 and 1766, under which British soldiers were housed in barracks, public houses, and unoccupied buildings around Boston, and from Bostonian workers' anger over soldiers taking off-duty jobs in the city's industry. In the aftermath of the killings and the meetings at Old South, acting governor Thomas Hutchinson removed the troops from their quarters in the city.

The day after the deaths, the soldiers were charged with murder. They were defended in their October trial by John Adams and Josiah Quincy. Both were anti-British but believed the charges unjustified. Seven of the accused, including the commander, were acquitted, and two were convicted of the lesser charge of manslaughter, branded on the hand, and discharged. The public, however, continued to perceive the event as an attack by bloodthirsty soldiers on peaceful people, and "the massacre" became a crucial event on the road to revolution.

### The Boston Tea Party

The next major incident to fan passions came almost four years later, in response to the Tea Act. The tax on tea was the lone duty Britain left in force when it responded to increasingly violent colonial reaction to its authority by repealing other duties imposed in 1765 and 1767. Late in 1773, some half a million pounds of surplus tea were sent to the colonies. In New York and Philadelphia, merchants refused to accept it. In Charleston, it was stored in warehouses. In Boston, the captains of three tea-filled ships agreed not to unload, but Governor Hutchinson refused to let them leave without paying duty. By law, they had to unload and pay the tax within twenty days of arrival.

Midnight on December 16 was the deadline for the first ship that had anchored. On that day, seven thousand citizens gathered at Old South for a meeting presided over by Samuel Adams. A delegation was sent to make a final plea to Hutchinson, who would not change his mind. After the delegates' report back to the meeting was acknowledged, nearly one hundred members of the Sons of Liberty, dressed as Mohawk Indians, appeared outside the meeting room. Followed by two thousand spectators, they went to the harbor, boarded the ships, and dumped 342 chests of tea weighing a total of sixty tons into the water. Nothing else was damaged.

In retaliation, Parliament closed Boston Harbor, abolished the colony's elected government, and ordered soldiers quartered in civilians' homes.

These acts further united the colonies against British rule.

On April 18, 1775, British troops departed from their camp on Boston Common to seize rebel supplies at Concord. Their plans, devised by General Thomas Gage, Massachusetts's last royal governor, in the Province House, his official residence, were among the worst-kept military secrets ever. When a groom who overheard the plans told Paul Revere, Revere said he was the third person to bring the information.

## Paul Revere

Revere lived in the North End, Boston's oldest neighborhood, then the Island of North Boston, separated from the rest of the city by the Mill Creek. The middle-aged silversmith, who founded the Revere Copper and Brass Company after the Revolution, was an accomplished propagandist and was also an express rider who carried messages for the Committee of Correspondence. He was one of six riders who had warned other ports not to allow tea ships to land their cargoes and also brought the news of the Tea Party to New York and Philadelphia after he spent the night dumping tea into the harbor.

Early in 1775, Revere helped form a committee of patriots to watch the movements of the British troops. On April 16, they noted that the British appeared to be making plans, and Revere made his first ride to Lexington to warn John Hancock and Samuel Adams. After he returned to Boston, Revere and other revolutionary leaders agreed they would hang lanterns in the Old North Church, near his home and possessed of the tallest steeple in the city, to signal the route of the troops if they started to move, just in case he was unable to leave the island. When the soldiers started their anticipated move off the common, the patriots thought, incorrectly, that they were going to arrest Hancock and Adams. Revere asked the church sexton, Robert Newman, to light the lanterns in the steeple. Then Revere set out, as did William Dawes, who traveled by another road to ensure that the message would get through. A third rider, sent from Charlestown, did not reach Lexington.

Revere went by way of Medford, where he awakened the captain of the Minutemen—armed colonists who vowed to show up at any conflict at a minute's notice—and gave a warning at almost every house from there to Lexington, which he reached just after midnight and a half hour before Dawes. After warning Hancock and Adams, the two riders and Dr. Samuel Prescott, whom they had encountered on the way, continued on to Concord. Prescott completed their warning mission after a British patrol stopped the three. Dawes also escaped but did not reach Concord, and Revere was arrested and sent back toward Boston. Outside Lexington, however, a practice volley fired by the militia scared the patrollers and they released Revere, although they kept his horse as the first prisoner of the war.

When the troops from Boston reached Lexington, they kept their rendezvous with history and the Minutemen. The "shot heard round the world" punctuated the confrontation between the British and the colonial forces and marked the formal start of the American Revolution.

After his ride to Lexington, it was almost a year before Revere could return home. It was even longer before his name became famous for the ride rather than his silversmithing. Henry Wadsworth Longfellow heard the story of the ride from a guide when he visited the Old North Church (officially Christ Church in Boston) in 1860 and, a year later, his famous, though not completely accurate, poem was published.

Within days of the fighting at Lexington, colonists were streaming into Cambridge while British reinforcements arrived in Boston. The colonists laid siege to the city but, except for one skirmish and some posturing, little happened until mid-June.

## War Begins

On June 17, two days after George Washington was named commander of the newly designated Continental Army and while he was marching north to take his command, the situation came to a head.

British General Thomas Gage decided that on June 18, his army would land on Dorchester Neck, south of Boston, and sweep around the city. As at Lexington, the colonists learned of the plans in time to circumvent them. They planned to build fortifications on Bunker Hill north of the city and, on June 16, a thousand soldiers advanced, in the end deciding to fortify Breed's Hill instead of its taller neighbor and in so doing creating lasting

*The USS* Constitution, *known as "Old Ironsides," which is anchored at the Charlestown Navy Yards on the Freedom Trail.* (Digital Stock)

confusion about the site of the first great battle of the revolution.

### The Battle of Bunker Hill

When June 17 dawned, the unexpected sight of fortifications confronted the British, but Gage decided it would be easy to take the hill and then continue his planned sweep. The royal troops prepared, perhaps too carefully, spending the morning gathering supplies and loading their packs for the anticipated march while the colonists dug in more securely.

The British rowed across the harbor, set Charlestown ablaze, and then made three assaults on the fortifications. In the first two attacks, they advanced in orderly rows, carrying full packs for the march to come, and lost hundreds of men when the defenders effectively followed their orders not to fire until they saw "the whites of their eyes." Some British units lost 75 to 90 percent of their men, with casualties among the officers, singled out as targets, especially high.

For the third attack, the British troops left their packs behind and were joined by artillery and reinforcements. The colonists, who were almost out of gunpowder, held off the British with rocks and their rifle butts as they made an orderly retreat and left the royal troops in control of the hill. Yet the victory cost the British 1,054 casualties, including 226 deaths, and cost Gage his command. The larger force of the colonists suffered 441 casualties. As one of them said, "I wish I could sell them another hill at the same price."

Fifty years later, the cornerstone for a monument commemorating the Battle of Bunker Hill was laid on the battlefield by the Marquis de Lafayette. Daniel Webster spoke then, as he did when the monument itself, an obelisk, was dedicated in 1843.

On July 3, 1775, Washington took command of seventeen thousand men in Cambridge. He spent the next months training them and awaiting the arrival of cannon. In January, 1776, artillery arrived, and on March 4 it was put in position above Boston.

William Howe, who had replaced Gage, did not want to risk defeat, so he loaded his men and weapons and hundreds of supporters on ships for Nova Scotia. They abandoned the city on March 17.

The next day, Washington marched down the main road into the city, marking the colonists' first victory of the war. Thirteen years later, as president, he returned for a parade down the same road in the day it was renamed in his honor.

### "Old Ironsides"

The USS *Constitution*, better known as "Old Ironsides," was built in Hartt's Shipyard in the North End. It was one of six frigates authorized in 1794 when Congress established a navy. They were built at separate seaports; in 1797 the *Constitution* was the third of the frigates to be launched.

The six were built of live oak, an unusually durable wood found on the sea islands of Georgia. The *Constitution* received its nickname during the War of 1812 after its victorious battle with HMS *Guerriere* when a British seaman observed cannon balls bouncing off its hull and cried, "Her sides are made of iron." The *Constitution* and its crew of 450 amassed an impressive collection of victories during the war and the *Constitution* remained active until 1830, when plans to dismantle the ship were averted by popular sentiment.

In 1800, three years after the *Constitution* was launched, the federal government bought for its first navy yard the land on which Gage's troops had landed to burn down Charlestown and attack Breed's Hill. By that time, Charlestown was largely rebuilt. The community of Charlestown developed into a prosperous suburb and eventually was annexed by Boston.

The Charlestown Navy Yard became one of the two most productive naval facilities in the United States, the other one being the Norfolk Navy Yard in Virginia. It saw its greatest activity during World War II, with as many as fifty thousand workers employed at the yard. In 1943 it built sixty ships, more than it had in all the previous one hundred forty years of its history.

The yard was closed in 1974 and became a historical museum. Two of its most popular attractions are the *Constitution* and a World War II–era ship, the USS *Cassin Young*. The shipyard marks the end of the Freedom Trail.

*—Richard Greb*

**For Further Information:**

Bahne, Charles. *The Complete Guide to Boston's Freedom Trail.* 2d ed. Cambridge, Mass.: Newtowne, 1993. Provides a wealth of anecdotes about early Boston, arranged to follow the sequence of landmarks along the trail.

Cooper, Jason. *Historic Boston.* Vero Beach, Fla.: Rourke, 1999. Descriptions of the places where Boston's patriots lived, worked, battled, and argued against British rule. Includes the Massachusetts State House, Faneuil Hall, and the Old North Church.

Frost, Jack, and Robert Booth. *Boston's Freedom Trail: A Souvenir Guide.* Revised by Shirley Blotnick Moskow. 5th ed. Guilford, Conn.: Globe Pequot Press, 2000. An illustrated guide to legendary landmarks including Faneuil Hall, Quincy Market, the Old North Church, Bunker Hill, and the USS *Constitution*.

Schofield, William G. *Freedom by the Bay: The Boston Freedom Trail.* 2d ed. Boston: Branden, 1988. A guidebook to important sites in colonial Boston. This edition offers a new prologue and epilogue. Includes an index.

# Hancock Shaker Village

**Date:** Founded in 1790

**Relevant issues:** Art and architecture, business and industry, cultural history, religion, science and technology, social reform, women's history

**Significance:** This town was the third of nineteen Shaker religious communities established in New England, New York, Ohio, Kentucky, and Indiana. It was closed in 1960 and reopened in 1961 as a historic site, with twenty original buildings still standing.

**Location:** Five miles west of downtown Pittsfield in western Massachusetts at the intersection of Routes 20 and 41, just one hour from Albany, New York, and three hours from Boston and New York City

**Site Office:**
Hancock Shaker Village
P.O. Box 927
Pittsfield, MA 01202-0927
ph.: (800) 817-1137; (413) 443-0188
fax: (413) 447-9357

Web site: www.hancockshakervillage.org
e-mail: info@hancockshakervillage.org

The Hancock Shaker community in the Berkshire Mountains of western Massachusetts thrived as a nineteenth century American religious community worshiping God, accepting a celibate lifestyle emphasizing hard work, thrift, charity, and simplicity, and committed to equality of the sexes. Closed in 1960 because of declining membership, the Hancock Shaker Village reopened in 1961 as a living history museum dedicated to recounting the past events of the Shaker world to future generations.

### Ann Lee and the Shakers
In 1747 in Manchester, England, James and Jane Wardley created a religious society based on the Quaker values of meekness, simplicity, and pacifism and the French Camisard practices of seizures, trances, and dancing. Their members achieved religious enlightenment from visions and revelations. Because dancing was an important feature of this religious movement's worship service, outsiders called the devotees Shaking Quakers and later Shakers.

In 1758, Ann Lee joined the Shaker religious movement. She married Abraham Standley, as requested by her parents, and gave birth to four children who all died in infancy. In prayer Ann Lee searched for answers to explain the loss of her children, which she interpreted to be a sign of God's displeasure. Revelations that she believed came from God instructed her that God was both male and female; that original sin was sex used for self-gratification, costing humankind purity and righteousness; and that men and women should be treated equally.

Ann Lee's religious devotion led to her persecution in England and imprisonment there on charges of blasphemy. While she was imprisoned, God informed Ann that she was to leave England for the American colonies, where she could practice the faith and gather new members. In 1774 Ann Lee, her husband, her brother, and six other followers sailed from Liverpool and landed in New York City. The members separated for a year and earned money before reuniting in Watervliet near Albany, New York. There, Ann Lee gained converts from among members of the New Light Baptists who were disillusioned when the millennium promised in Revelation failed to occur.

### The Founding of Hancock
In 1783, while on a tour in Pittsfield preaching the Shaker faith, Ann Lee and her followers were attacked; they found safety in the Hancock, Massachusetts, home of Daniel Goodrich, Sr. Although fined twenty dollars for disturbing the peace and told to leave Massachusetts, Ann Lee remained and encouraged the Goodrich, Deming, and Talcott families to form a Shaker community in Hancock. In 1784 these families laid the foundation for the first meetinghouse and began the consecration of their possessions and lands to the Shakers, also known as the United Society of Believers. Although the Hancock Shaker community was nurtured by "Mother" Ann Lee, Hancock was not officially established as a Shaker settlement until 1790, when Calvin Harlow was appointed bishop for Hancock and Tyringham, Massachusetts, and Enfield, Connecticut, and leader of the Hancock brethren. Sarah Harrison was appointed leader of the Hancock sisters.

Hancock's first years were difficult ones for these Shaker farmers, who saw their crops destroyed by frost, pestilence, and drought. Fires destroyed many of their buildings. Membership declined due to deaths caused by fever epidemics and departing members disillusioned with Shaker living, some of whom demanded financial compensation for the land and possessions they had originally donated. However, perseverance and a strong faith eventually turned the community around. By 1803 the Hancock Shakers numbered 142 people, 76 of whom were full church members living on and working 2,000 acres of farmland, growing rye, buckwheat, oats, and hayseed; raising Holstein cattle; and mining iron ore. A new meetinghouse was built along with a gristmill, sawmills, and carding and pulling mills. Economic prosperity was increased by the selling of flat-sided brooms and the packaging and selling on consignment of sixty-nine varieties of seeds from New York to the Chesapeake Bay area.

In 1829 the Hancock Shaker community consisted of six families, with more than 270 members distributed among three orders: the Novitiate Order of new members who resided for a trial period or until they had freed themselves from their entanglements with worldly problems (an East Family, 1792-1911, and a South Family, 1800-1849); the Junior Order of single members who had never been married and those who still wanted some control over their financial and business concerns (a West Family, 1792-1867, and a Second Family, 1792-1920); and the Senior Order of those who had made the total commitment to the Shaker faith, relinquishing all possessions of land, money, and personal family ties (Church Family, 1790-1960, and North Family, 1822-1869). Each family was jointly governed by two elders and two eldresses.

### Revival and Decline

From the 1830's to the 1850's, the Shaker religion went through a period of spiritual revival where members, in returning to the teachings of Mother Ann, underwent mystical experiences. Hancock, renamed the City of Peace, had a revival site located about two miles north of the Hancock property at a mountain named Sinai. There, a fountain stone was placed and engraved with the words "written and placed here by the command of our Lord and Savior Jesus Christ, The Lord's Stone erected upon this Mt. Sinai, May 4, 1843." Fasting, confession, and silent prayer preceded these semiannual pilgrimages to Sinai where Hancock Shakers spoke in tongues, acted out pantomimes, and had the visitation of spirits that transmitted religious communications into written and pictorial form through Shaker members. During one such episode in 1854, Hancock sister Hannah Harrison Cohoon drew the "Tree of Life." The drawing was a draft of a beautiful tree bearing fruit penciled on a large sheet of white paper. The spirit showed Sister Hannah the details concerning leaves, fruit, and colors to be used. Cohoon believed the tree represented a living spirit bearing good fruits—in other words, the Shaker church and its members.

Unfortunately for the Hancock settlement and the Shakers in general, potential members were turned off by their hyper-spiritualism, and Shakers themselves left the religion when their revival led elders to demand that members bow to them and acknowledge their superiority. Declining membership led to the closure of the South Family in 1849, leaving a Hancock membership of just 58 brethren and 135 sisters.

Shaker pacifism during the Civil War further alienated potential members. The West and North

families were dissolved in 1867 and 1869, respectively, leaving only three families in 1870, with a total of ninety-eight members. Continuing membership declines led the Hancock Shakers to offer apprenticeships to outsiders, who helped them to cultivate one thousand acres for growing corn, oats, barley, and wheat; to raise cattle; and to produce brooms, tubs, pails, swifts, a "Hancock" chair, and applesauce for sale. In the hope of attracting new members, the Shakers lifted some severe restrictions, allowing members to plant flower gardens, play musical instruments, travel, have pets, use wallpaper, paint china, frame pictures, and have house plants. Membership still declined.

In 1893 the Bishopric of Hancock was abolished and the Hancock Shakers placed under the ministry of the New Lebanon (New York) Shakers. Further membership declines led to the closing of the East Family in 1911. In 1948 the New Lebanon Shaker community closed, and its members were moved to the Hancock site. The last Hancock brother, Ricardo Belden, died in 1958, leaving just three sisters, Eldress Fannie Estabrook and Sisters Mary Frances Dahm and Adeline Patterson. The Shaker Central Ministry, now in Canterbury, New Hampshire, decided to close the Hancock settlement in 1960.

### Historic Site

Hancock's last trustee, Shaker Frances Hall, actually began the liquidation of the Hancock Shaker site in the 1940's by selling land and buildings or tearing down buildings too old to repair in order to lighten the tax burden. In 1959, 550 acres of Hancock woodland was sold to the state of Massachusetts, to be added to the Pittsfield State Forest in exchange for state maintenance of the Hancock Shaker cemetery. At the time of the 1960 Hancock closure, the property consisted of 974 acres, eleven major buildings, and ten lesser structures. The Hancock property was sold for $125,000 to the Hancock Shaker Village Steering Committee, headed by Laurence and Amy Bess Miller. Eldress Fannie Estabrook, who died in 1960 at age ninety, was the last Shaker buried in the Hancock graveyard. The two remaining sisters were cared for in Pittsfield. Today Hancock Shaker Village is a living museum, open to the public from April to October. The site offers educational programs, workshops, a research library, a publications program, replica reproductions, craft demonstrations, and special events.

## Hancock Buildings and Inventions

Shaker works were prized and valued because they were unadorned, functional, and well made, and displayed a beauty and simplicity that reflected a harmony of work and spirit. Hancock Elders and furniture makers Thomas Damon and Grove Wright constructed 245 cupboards with 369 drawers in the brick dwelling house. Shakers were known for their sense of order and neatness. Brother Damon was also known for the manufacture of the Shaker "table swift," which was used for winding skeins of yarn into balls. When not in use, the "swift" looks like a collapsible folding umbrella. Hancock Shakers developed an adjustable wooden transom for the doors to let air flow though the dwelling house; they also designed a table with a drawer that could be opened from either end and long benches for meeting and dining rooms. Other items attributed to Hancock Shakers include washstands with swinging platforms below them to hold a slop jar or the wastewater from the pitcher and bowl above; close stools that were indoor privies, with tin pipes vented to let odors escape; sliding cupboards (dumbwaiters); and efficient wood-burning stoves. The last Hancock brother, Ricardo Belden, was a noted clock maker.

Among the Hancock Shaker buildings, the most notable structure evidencing Shaker ingenuity was the three-story, round, stone barn constructed in 1826. This structure was built to house fifty head of dairy cattle in a ring of circular stalls to promote efficiency in milking, feeding, cleaning, and the storage of hay. The top floor was used for storing hay and grain. The middle floor housed the cows, with trap doors in the floor to allow manure to be shoveled into the lower pit and hauled away for fertilizer. Other original buildings restored at the Hancock site and open for a tour are the Machine Shop and Laundry (1790), the Meeting House brought from Shirley settlement in 1962 (1792), the Trustee's Office (1800), the Ministry Wash House (1810), the School House (1815), the Brethren Shop (1820), the Sister Shop (1820), the Dwelling House (1830), the Barn and Tan House (1835), the Horse Barn (1850), the Cattle and Equipment Shop (1865), the Ministry Shop (1874-1875), the Poultry House (1878), and the Carriage House (1890). —*William A. Paquette*

## For Further Information:

Andrews, Edward Deming. *The People Called Shakers.* New York: Dover, 1963. Written while Hancock was still one of three active Shaker settlements.

Butler, Linda, and June Sprigg. *Inner Light: The Shaker Legacy.* New York: Alfred A. Knopf, 1985. Fifty-eight photographs of Shaker creations from furniture to boxes and bonnets to songbooks.

Morse, Flo. *The Shakers and the World's People.* Hanover, N.H.: University Press of New England, 1980. A good narrative history about the Shaker experience.

Ott, John Harlow. *Hancock Shaker Village: A Guidebook and History.* Shaker Community, 1976. Both a written and a visual record of the Hancock Shaker community.

Pearson, Elmer, Julia Neal, and Walter Muir Whitehill. *The Shaker Image.* Boston: New York Graphic Society and Shaker Community, 1974. More than 200 photographs with text about the Shakers from 1850 to 1920.

Sprigg, June. *By Shaker Hands.* New York: Alfred A. Knopf, 1975. An illustrated catalog of Shaker inventions written by the then curator of the Hancock Shaker museum.

_____. *Shaker Design.* New York: Whitney Museum of Art, 1986. Catalog for a touring Shaker exhibit of furniture, household objects, tools and equipment, textiles and textile equipment, and graphics.

Stein, Stephen J. *The Shaker Experience in America.* New Haven, Conn.: Yale University Press, 1992. A detailed history about the Shaker movement with commentary about their future ability to survive.

# Harvard Square and University, Cambridge

**Date:** First students admitted in the summer of 1638

**Relevant issues:** Education

**Significance:** This historic and commercial center of the first capital of Massachusetts is dominated

*Harvard University.* (Harvard University, Office of News & Public Affairs)

by the numerous buildings of the oldest university in the United States.

**Location:** Across the Charles River from Boston
**Site Office:**
Harvard Information Center
Holyoke Center
1350 Massachusetts Avenue
Cambridge, MA 02138
ph.: (617) 495-1000

The city of Cambridge began in 1630 as Newtowne, the fortified capital of the Massachusetts Bay Colony, set on a defensible hill with access to the sea along the Charles River. Harvard Square has been its center ever since. The city's Old Burying Ground and its Common lie northwest of Harvard Square, and the winding streets around it retain the original layout of Newtowne. The city has grown enormously and now contains many places of historic interest, such as the Longfellow National Historic Site as well as world-famous academic centers, such as the Massachusetts Institute of Technology (MIT). Among all these features of Cambridge, however, the biggest influence on its history has been the presence of Harvard University, the oldest institution of higher education in the United States and one of the rich-

est and most prestigious universities in the world. Its core buildings are still on the site where it began more than 350 years ago, in Harvard Yard on Harvard Square.

**The Founding of Harvard**
Harvard traces its origins to a meeting in October, 1636, of the Great and General Court of Massachusetts, which decided to provide four hundred English pounds to establish a school or college. In the following year the court chose Newtowne as its location and appointed a board of overseers, half of them magistrates and the other half ministers of the Congregational Church. The overseers then bought the house and a one-acre cow yard from which the modern Harvard Yard expanded. The first master of the college, Nathaniel Eaton, admitted the first students in the summer of 1638. It was at that time that the town was renamed Cambridge for the English university from which Eaton had graduated. In 1639 the new college was named for Eaton's friend John Harvard, who was also a Cambridge graduate and a Congregational minister, and who had died in September, 1638, leaving the college half his fortune and his library of four hundred books.

Within the year Eaton, accused of brutally beating his assistant with a walnut tree cudgel, was dismissed and left the colony with his wife, who had herself been accused of failing to provide the students with sufficient beef. Harvard was empty for a year, until Henry Dunster was appointed president and the students returned to study liberal arts, philosophy, and the "learned tongues" (classical Latin and Greek). It was Dunster who, in 1650, persuaded the general court to grant the charter that still governs Harvard, creating the corporation of teaching staff under the nonteaching overseers.

By 1690, when the theologian Increase Mather was dividing his time between presiding over Harvard and preaching in Boston, the college was admitting around twenty-two students a year. Mather had the charter altered to allow the corporation to be dominated by a majority made up of non-teaching Congregational ministers, but his plans were obstructed, first by the King's Council in London, which wanted power over the college, then by the governor's council in Boston, which wanted to prevent royal interference by taking control itself. Next the King's Council forbade Mather to impose Congregationalism on the members of the corporation. By 1701 Mather had been forced out of Harvard, while some of his fellow conservatives went to New Haven to establish what is now Yale University as a counterbalance to what they saw as the excessive liberalism of Harvard.

This impression of the college was reinforced in 1708 when John Leverett became the first president who was neither a minister of the church nor even a conservative Congregationalist. Leverett allowed students to take private lessons in French and appointed an instructor in Hebrew but otherwise left the curriculum unchanged. In 1720, with the student body reaching around 120, Massachusetts Hall, today the oldest building still standing at Harvard, was added to the existing three buildings in the yard.

### The Great Awakening

Just as the college was growing and acquiring a reputation not only for training ministers, judges, physicians, and other professionals but also for failing to prevent swearing, rioting, and gambling among its students, the religious revival known as the Great Awakening swept through New England, arriving in Cambridge in 1740 through the passionate preaching of George Whitefield, who attacked ministers trained at "godless Harvard." Unlike Yale, Harvard resisted pressure to impose a religious oath on its students, and its teachers issued pamphlets opposing Whitefield's zealotry and his slanders of the college. They also saw to the building of Holden Chapel on a quadrangle inside the yard, between 1742 and 1744. It took more than twenty years to heal the rift between Harvard and Whitefield. Eventually, Whitefield was among those who donated money and books to rebuild the college library after a fire had destroyed Old Harvard Hall in 1765. This disaster occurred just after the opening of Hollis Hall, in 1763, and was followed by the building of what is now called Harvard Hall, in 1766. By extending the number of its buildings and widening its curriculum, Harvard was able to increase its student population little by little, until in 1771 sixty-three students graduated. All examinations were still oral, apart from an essay in Latin.

### The Revolutionary War

Harvard could not avoid the impact of the Revolutionary War. From 1770 to 1773 the General Court of Massachusetts took over Harvard buildings for its meetings. The Meeting House on Watch Hill, inside the yard, was home to the provincial congress of 1774, which took over government from the king's officials, as well as to the convention of 1779, which gave the Commonwealth of Massachusetts what is now the oldest constitution still in force in the United States. It was drafted by John Adams, a Harvard graduate. George Washington formally took command of the Continental Army in Cambridge in 1775, either on Cambridge Common or in Wadsworth House, which was then the residence of the president of the university. As for the college's own activities, from 1774 to 1781 commencement ceremonies were suspended, and from 1775 to 1776 the college was evacuated to Concord, Massachusetts, but otherwise it carried on much as it had before the war.

From 1780 Harvard continued under the terms of the new constitution of Massachusetts. It now became a university, with a board of overseers composed of the governor, lieutenant governor, and council and senate of Massachusetts, along with the ministers of six Congregational churches in Cambridge and nearby. The new board immediately took the next step in Harvard's expansion, the creation of its "Medical Institution," in 1781. This was the first alternative in New England to the traditional apprenticeships to physicians and only the third medical school in the United States. At first it was housed in the yard, but it moved to Boston in 1810 to become the world-famous Harvard Medical School.

### Secularization

By the end of the eighteenth century Harvard University was still mainly what it had been founded to be, a school for ministers and other professionals under the guidance of the government of Massachusetts and the leaders of the Congregational Church. The nineteenth century saw changes in

Harvard's religious atmosphere, its relations with the Commonwealth of Massachusetts, and its educational resources that transformed it into the secular, self-governing and broad-based university of today.

The first breach in Harvard's traditional character came with the appointments of Unitarians as professor of divinity and as president, between 1804 and 1806. As a direct result of this rebuff to tradition, the Congregational church founded its own seminary at Andover, and puritan families in the New England countryside began to send their sons to other colleges. The Harvard Divinity School, founded in 1819, was accordingly dominated by Unitarians. In 1843, perhaps a little belatedly, the rule that the ministers on the board of overseers had to be Congregationalists was abolished, and at last, in 1851, the ministers' seats on the board were abolished altogether. Compulsory attendance at morning prayers continued until 1886, when Harvard became the first American college to abolish it.

Another and different sign of change was the rising cost of studying at Harvard. Annual tuition rose from twenty dollars in 1807 to fifty-five dollars eighteen years later, making it probably the most expensive college in the country, although there were several free scholarships available. Three more halls were built: Stoughton in 1804, Holworthy in 1812, and University in 1814 and 1815, the latter two in granite rather than the traditional brick. From 1814 to 1823, with the Federalist Party in control of the state, Harvard received ten thousand dollars a year in state grants, but after a fierce election campaign, in which Harvard was accused of trying to prevent the foundation of Amherst College, the Jeffersonian Republicans took over the state government, stopped the grants to Harvard, and thus forced the university into a financial independence of the state that has continued ever since.

In 1851 the composition of the board of overseers was reformed. In addition to the removal of the clergy, the president and the treasurer of the university were given membership, the state officials were cut down to just five seats, and thirty seats were now to be elected by the state's house and senate for six-year terms. Finally, only fourteen years later, the state officials were also removed, and the right to elect the thirty other overseers was given to

Harvard graduates meeting in Cambridge on Commencement Day. Harvard had now become a fully autonomous academic community.

### Charles William Eliot's Presidency

Perhaps the greatest single influence on the transformation of Harvard was the forty-year-long presidency of Charles William Eliot, during which the curriculum was gradually expanded and revised beyond all recognition. There were already new professorships in law (1815) and in French and Spanish (1819), and the Lawrence Scientific School had opened in 1847, its three-year program and its relatively low admissions standards indicating the status of science at that time. After fifteen years spent teaching in this school, Eliot became president in 1869 and accelerated the process of modernization. Then came the first professorship of political economy in the United States, in 1871; the Graduate School of Arts and Sciences, in 1872; the Harvard Annex for women students, near Cambridge Common, in 1879, which became Radcliffe College in 1893; and, in 1890, the reorganization of all the teaching in Harvard Yard under the new Faculty of Arts and Sciences.

Eliot was not content simply to increase the number of subjects taught in this faculty. He also wanted to increase students' access to them and therefore broke with tradition by allowing students to choose what courses they would study. Eliot steadily pushed the elective system to the point where, in 1886, the only limits on choice were that courses had to be "liberal" (nonvocational), advanced classes had to follow introductory ones, and students had to avoid conflicting commitments of their time. From Harvard the elective system spread to every large college, including Yale, by 1904. One side effect was the decline of Greek and Latin studies, which had dominated university learning in Europe and the Americas since the Renaissance. The last great academic innovation under Eliot's presidency, the foundation of Harvard Business School in 1908, confirmed Harvard's place among those universities leading the movement away from the lingering medievalism of early nineteenth century education to the involvement of academia in the transformations of the modern world.

Ironically, modernization of the curriculum was accompanied by a revival of medieval architectural styles for the main buildings added to Harvard's stock in Eliot's time. Outside the yard to the north can be found Memorial Hall, an enormous Gothic building, finished in 1878, honoring Harvard graduates killed during the U.S. Civil War, as well as Austin Hall, a Romanesque building designed by Henry Hobson Richardson, who also designed Sever Hall, built in 1880 inside the yard.

## Abbott Lawrence Lowell's Presidency

Eliot's successor, Abbott Lawrence Lowell, was president from 1909 to 1933 and also left his mark both on Harvard and on higher education across North America. From 1914 he overhauled the elective system, introducing the distinction between majors and minors, which is now standard in North American higher education. Perhaps even more important was his courageous stance on academic freedom. When an alumnus made his offer of ten million dollars to Harvard conditional on the removal of Hugo Munsterberg, a philosophy professor who publicly supported Germany even after the United States entered World War I, Lowell refused the gift and kept Munsterberg on the faculty. No doubt it was easier for a president of Harvard than for those in charge of poorer colleges to insist that gifts be unconditional.

The Harry Elkins Widener Library opened in 1913, commemorating a graduate who went down in the *Titanic*. It is now the third largest library in the United States. In 1927 Lowell presided over the relocation of the Fogg Art Museum, founded in 1895, to the east of the yard, on Quincy Street. In the following year he used a gift from Edward S. Harkness to fund the building of undergraduate housing on sites to the south of the yard, toward the Charles River. He also saw to the establishment of the Memorial Church in 1931. It now commemorates Harvard graduates killed in both world wars.

## The Great Depression and World War II

It fell to Lowell's successor, James Conant, to take Harvard through the Great Depression and World War II. Innovations under Conant included the abolition of class attendance records and the university's rank list, the creation of national scholarships to broaden the base of admissions away from New England, and the founding of the educational television station WGBH. After spending most of the

war years at Dumbarton Oaks, supervising research on radar, chemical weapons, and the atomic bomb, Conant returned to Cambridge for an additional seven years, overseeing the introduction of general education courses for undergraduates and restricting Harvard's scientists to undertake only nonclassified research for the federal government.

Even with this restriction in place, government research became a major source of Harvard funding under its next president, Nathan Pusey. By 1963 most of the research in science and engineering was federally funded, as at many other universities. Nor was Harvard immune from the protests that swept campuses in the late 1960's. These peaked in 1969 when a student occupation of University Hall, where personnel files were held, was quickly broken up by police.

Derek Bok became president in 1971, at a time of financial crisis. Federal funding declined from a peak of 40 percent of Harvard's income in 1967 to just 25 percent in 1974, and energy and other costs were rising rapidly. Under Bok, Harvard kept up its tradition of academic innovation, introducing compulsory courses in 1978 to cover the "core" subjects in the curriculum. This helped revive debate about the selection of compulsory subjects, and the view of civilization that they imply, that has continued ever since.

Harvard University has become a very different institution from the college founded by the puritan colonists in 1636. A single house and a cow yard have given place to a sprawling range of buildings in which subjects beyond the founders' imaginations are taught and studied. Architecturally, academically, and—not least—financially, Harvard continues to try to balance tradition and innovation, the heritage of successive generations, and the needs and interests of the contemporary United States and the outside world.

—*Patrick Heenan*

## For Further Information:

Morison, Samuel Eliot. *Three Centuries of Harvard, 1636-1936*. Cambridge, Mass.: Harvard University Press, 1936. Still the standard history of Harvard University. It is also one of the most impressive histories of any university, blending parochial details with wider social changes.
Norton, Bettina A. *Around the Square: An Architec-*

*tural Hunt in the Environs of Harvard Square.* Boston: BAN, 1992. A guidebook to the architecture of Cambridge.

Smith, Richard Norton. *The Harvard Century: The Making of a University to a Nation.* Reprint. Cambridge, Mass.: Harvard University Press, 1998. Brings Morison's story up to date, but with less panache and perhaps too much concentration on the personalities of Harvard's recent presidents.

# Lexington and Concord

**Date:** Concord founded in 1635; Revolutionary War battles fought on April 19, 1775; Minute Man National Historical Park created in 1959

**Relevant issues:** Colonial America, literary history, military history, Revolutionary War

**Significance:** These towns are sites of the first battles of the American Revolutionary War and the homes of the nineteenth century writers Louisa May Alcott, Ralph Waldo Emerson, Nathaniel Hawthorne, and Henry David Thoreau.

**Location:** West of Boston on Route 2-A

**Site Office:**
Minute Man National Historical Park
174 Liberty Street
Concord, MA 01742
ph.: (978) 369-6993; (781) 862-7753
Web site: www.nps.gov/mima/

Concord and Lexington share the distinction of being the places where on one day in 1775 the American Revolution moved from debate and protest about British rule to armed opposition to British troops. Concord has the additional distinction of having been the home of some of the greatest American writers of the nineteenth century.

**Early History**

Neither of these features of the area's later history could have been imagined in 1635, when Concord, the first English settlement in Massachusetts away from the Atlantic coast, was founded at a place known to Native Americans as Musketaquid. It prospered as the shire town (capital) of Middlesex County and as a center for trade with the rest of Massachusetts and for expeditions against the French and Native Americans, its population rising to about 1,500 by 1775. In 1752 and again in 1764 it was even the temporary capital of Massachusetts, when smallpox frightened the lawmakers away from Boston.

In 1774 life in Concord was changed once again by events in Boston. In January, a month after the Boston Tea Party, persons attending the town meeting voted unanimously to join in the boycott of British tea. When the British government ordered the military occupation of Boston, closed the port to shipping, and appointed General Thomas Gage, the commander in chief of the army in North America, as governor of the Massachusetts colony, eight out of ten of the voters in Concord agreed to boycott all British products. The town became the headquarters of the revolution, alternating with Cambridge, when the colonial legislature, defying General Gage, met there as the Provincial Congress in October, 1774, and again in March, 1775. It was the Congress's decision to store arms and provisions in Concord that made it a prime target, first for spies sent out by Gage in March, 1775, and then for military action.

**The Battle of Lexington**

On the evening of April 18, 1775, about seven hundred British troops, known as "redcoats" because of their uniforms, were assembled on Boston Common and ordered to march to Concord. The rebels had spies too and, ironically, the supplies that the redcoats hoped to capture had already been hidden at various places outside the town. Paul Revere was only the most famous of the rebel messengers who spread the word that the troops were coming. When they reached Lexington, a village on the road to Concord, at dawn on April 19, the British were met by 77 rebel fighters, nicknamed Minutemen because they were expected to be ready to fight at a minute's notice. They had been preparing for the encounter for many weeks and were now lined up on the village green.

There is still dispute even now about who fired the first shot. The redcoats ignored their own commander's orders not to fire, and thirty minutes later, when they left Lexington, eight of the rebels were dead and nine injured. It seems that, somewhat surprisingly, the redcoats made no attempt to arrest John Hancock or Samuel Adams, the revolutionary leaders who were both staying in a house only a quarter of a mile from the green.

In the meantime hundreds of Minutemen had assembled at Concord, but they had retreated to the hills by the time the redcoats arrived. They stayed there while the British soldiers searched for weapons (and, incidentally, stole property worth 275 English pounds). Then the colonists advanced toward the North Bridge, where they killed three redcoats, injured others, and forced the rest to run away. Four hours after their arrival the British soldiers marched out of Concord, only to be repeatedly ambushed on the road by a force of about 1,100 rebels until they returned to Lexington in disorder, to regroup and join forces with another one thousand redcoats sent out from Boston. They retreated together, still facing heavy opposition, especially at Menotomy, since renamed Arlington. The Revolutionary War had begun.

**Concord After the Revolutionary War**

After 1775 Concord saw no more fighting but instead became a refuge for rebels fleeing from Boston and Charlestown. They helped to raise the population to nineteen hundred a year after the battle, while men from Concord joined in the siege of Boston, the battle of Bunker Hill, and the assault on Fort Ticonderoga. The inflation that accompanied the war brought economic difficulties to Concord until peace came to the northern colonies in 1780. In 1786 Concord sprang to prominence once again as the only town in eastern Massachusetts where farmers prevented the county court from sitting, in protest against the state's failure to relieve their debts. Unlike in the western counties, however, where similar protests led to Shays's Rebellion, no blood was shed this time in Concord.

The townspeople went on to share in the prosperity of the 1790's, when the French revolutionary wars in Europe gave the neutral American merchants new opportunities. In 1794 the town's leading men, who had formed a Committee of Public Safety during the Revolution, set up a club, the Social Circle, which soon came to dominate the life of Concord, including such new organizations as the Charitable Library Society, founded in 1795. After another depression around the time of another conflict, the War of 1812, Concord returned to prosperity yet again.

**Literary Figures**

"Literary Concord," the home of Emerson, Hawthorne, Thoreau, and the Alcotts, can be said to have begun in the town's Old Manse. This house had been built around 1770 by William Emerson, the minister of Concord's church, who had watched the fighting from its windows but had died in the following year. Ezra Ripley, his successor, married Emerson's widow in 1780 and continued as minister till 1841. In 1832 his stepgrandson Ralph Waldo Emerson (born in 1803) visited Concord and wrote his famous poem about "the embattled farmers" of Concord who "fired the shot heard round the world." Emerson had briefly been a Unitarian minister before visiting Europe and becoming one of the first Westerners to study Oriental religions. In 1834 he came to stay in the Old Manse again in order to compile his lectures on philosophy into his first book, *Nature*, and then lived in what is now called Emerson House until his death in 1882.

The elite Social Circle, which Emerson was invited to join in 1838, frequently held its meetings in this house, but it was also one of the venues for the "Transcendental Club," a looser and more informal group through which Emerson influenced, and was influenced by, his friends Thoreau and Bronson Alcott and others interested in his philosophy, including some of the people who engaged in communal living at Brook Farm, in West Roxbury, Massachusetts, between 1841 and 1847. The Transcendentalist movement that Emerson and his allies thus initiated emphasized self-reliance, both for individuals and for American culture, and brought the ideas of Immanuel Kant and other European philosophers of intuition and individualism to the United States.

Emerson's friend Henry David Thoreau (born in 1817) was the only native of Concord among the four writers whose names are associated with the town. His most famous book, *Walden*, first published in 1854, describes his experiences between 1845 and 1847 when he lived in a one-room cabin near Walden Pond. This was not, as it may seem, an experiment in isolation, for he went into Concord often and many people visited the cabin. Thoreau's aim was to discover what he could learn from simplifying his life down to its essentials, and his determination to realize the Transcendentalist ideal of self-reliance was signalled by his moving into the cabin on July 4. In spite of its fame, however, the book has probably had less impact on the world than Thoreau's essay "Civil Disobedience" (1849), which grew out of his ventures into radical political action. His family's home was a stop on the Underground Railroad, the network of abolitionists that helped runaway slaves reach freedom in Canada, and he spent a night in jail in 1846 after refusing to pay the poll tax in protest against slavery and the war with Mexico. Long after his death (in 1862, from tuberculosis) Thoreau's essay was to inspire the much greater protests of Mahatma Gandhi and Martin Luther King, Jr.

Nathaniel Hawthorne had a more skeptical attitude to Emerson's philosophy, which he satirized in his story "The Celestial Railroad," yet he was on good terms with both Emerson and Thoreau and was just as committed as they were to the pursuit of self-reliance. Born in Salem in 1804, he moved into the Old Manse with his wife Sophia in 1842. Avoiding contact with most Concordians apart from Emerson and Thoreau, he concentrated on writing the stories collected as *Mosses from an Old Manse*. The Hawthornes' time in the house was cut short when, in 1845, Ezra Ripley's son decided to move back into it, and Hawthorne's most famous novels, *The Scarlet Letter* and *The House of the Seven Gables*, were written elsewhere. The Hawthornes moved back to Concord in 1852. This time they lived in a house called the Wayside for a year, spent seven years in Europe, then returned to the Wayside, where Hawthorne died in 1864.

Bronson Alcott, another Transcendentalist thinker and a friend to Emerson, Thoreau, and Hawthorne alike, lived in Concord with his wife and daughters during three separate periods. From 1840 to 1843 they rented a cottage, from 1845 to 1848 they preceded the Hawthornes at the Wayside, which they called Hillside, and from 1857 to 1877 they were in Orchard House. His daughters included Louisa May Alcott, who was to base her most famous novel, *Little Women*, on memories of her life in Concord.

### Impact of the Railroad

The town that these writers, their families, and their friends were familiar with was being transformed even in their lifetimes. The railroad reached Concord in 1844, an event that Emerson responded to, intriguingly, by protesting against the damage it did to the landscape and simultaneously buying extremely profitable shares in it.

Boston was now only one hour away, not four, and subsistence farming rapidly gave way to commercial production of fruit and vegetables, dairy goods, and ice (from Walden Pond). Since then both Concord and Lexington have moved further still from their Puritan colonial origins to become suburbs of Boston.

### Modern Preservation Efforts

There are many physical remnants of the revolutionary and Transcendentalist eras in and around these two historic places. In Lexington the fighting on the Green is reenacted each year on Patriots' Day, the third Monday in April; the house where John Hancock and Samuel Adams were staying is now a museum; and other buildings associated with April 19, 1775, are also open to the public. The Minute Man National Historical Park consists of strips of land running on either side of the Battle Road between Lexington and Concord, together with the area around the North Bridge in Concord itself. The Old Manse, Emerson House, the Wayside, and Orchard House can all be visited, and the graves of all four of the writers are to be found in the town's Sleepy Hollow Cemetery. However, though some of the furniture that Thoreau made for his cabin is displayed in the Concord Museum, alongside many other relics of Concord history, the cabin itself is long gone. Half a mile away from where it stood there is a replica near a parking lot within the Walden Pond State Reservation.

Clearly, there is still much in Concord and Lexington to commemorate those ideals of independence and self-reliance which the Minutemen fought for and which the nineteenth century writers sought to reformulate and express. Thoreau, for one, reminds people that commemorating them is less important than trying to realize them.

*—Patrick Heenan*

### For Further Information:

In addition to the books listed here, the major works of the Concord writers are widely available in various editions.

Brooks, Paul. *The People of Concord: One Year in the Flowering of New England*. Chester, Conn.: Globe Pequot Press, 1990. Uses the events of 1846 as a focus for a study of the relationships among the Alcotts, the Emersons, the Hawthornes, and Thoreau.

French, Allen. *Historic Concord: A Handbook of Its Story and Its Memorials, with an Account of the Lexington Fight.* 2d rev. ed. Concord. Mass.: Friends of the Concord Free Public Library, 1992.

Gross, Robert A. *The Minutemen and Their World.* New York: Hill & Wang, 1992. A detailed and absorbing study of life in Concord around 1775.

# Plymouth

**Date:** Settled in 1620

**Relevant issues:** Colonial America, religion

**Significance:** This town in Plymouth Colony on the coast of Massachusetts was settled by the Pilgrims in 1620. It was folded into the Province of Massachusetts Bay in September, 1691.

**Location:** Southeastern Massachusetts, on Plymouth Bay, eighteen miles southeast of Brockton

**Site Offices:**

Plymouth Plantation
P.O. Box 1620
Plymouth, MA 02362
ph.: (508) 746-1622
fax: (508) 746-4978
Web site: www.plimoth.org

The Pilgrim Society
75 Court Street
Plymouth, MA 02360
ph.: (508) 746-1620
Web site: www.pilgrimhall.org

In 1620, a group of English settlers called Puritans, or Pilgrims, landed ship in what is now Plymouth, Massachusetts. Years before, they had broken away from the Church of England, wishing to "purify" their religious practices, and many of them had suffered persecution at the hands of English officials. Initially, they left England for Leiden, Holland. When a group of merchants and investors agreed to finance a trip to America, the Puritans took the opportunity to settle their own colonies, farm new lands, and worship freely.

**The First Pilgrims**

Before the Pilgrims landed in America, they had spent a month sailing around the Northeast, searching for an ideal place to settle. They finally discovered an area that had plenty of fresh water and clear ground and that seemed to lack the threat of Indians. Earlier expeditions by John Smith and Captain Thomas Dermer reassured the Pilgrims that this area would be a wise choice for a plantation. On December 16, 1620, 102 Pilgrims, those who had survived the laborious trip, anchored their ship, the *Mayflower,* in Plymouth Bay, Massachusetts.

The first few months at Plymouth were grim, as one disaster seemed to follow another. Many Pilgrims remained aboard ship, struggling to survive the cold and the scurvy that had begun to take lives during their journey. In January, a fire destroyed many of their supplies. When summer finally arrived, nearly half of the *Mayflower's* passengers were dead, and not much progress had been made toward building the settlement.

In early March, as the Pilgrims began to prepare the fields for planting, they were visited by Indians, who meant no harm. In fact, they were eager to communicate, having learned English from sailors who fished off the coast. One Indian, Squanto, who owned the lands the Pilgrims planned to cultivate, proved a blessing to the settlers. Until his death two years later, Squanto stayed with the Pilgrims, showing them the best places and methods to farm and fish. As their homes took shape and crops began to grow, the miserable months the Pilgrims had suffered seemed to fade.

**The First Thanksgiving**

Governed by John Carver, Plymouth quickly became a settlement of cooperation and prosperity. Satisfied with the settlement's success, Captain Christopher Jones sailed an empty *Mayflower* back to England. After the autumn harvest, the Pilgrims held a feast along with Indians from the surrounding area, in a celebration that would later be commemorated as Thanksgiving. Carver died soon after and was replaced by William Bradford.

The Pilgrims enjoyed a lush harvest and looked ahead to a secure winter. When England heard word of the Pilgrims' success, however, the investors quickly sent another thirty-six settlers to the colony. Their arrival in November, 1621, dealt a harsh economic blow to the earlier settlers, who shouldered the burden of the newcomers' support. Along with the new settlers, the colony received a series of patents, ensuring the legality of the settlement, but no supplies. As famine raged during the cold winter months, the Pilgrims continued to wait for the now desparately needed supplies from England.

### New Settlers
Instead of supplies, more settlers arrived the following spring and summer, some traveling at their own expense. These men and women were called "particulars" and caused considerable confusion to the economic structure of the settlement. Unlike the Pilgrims, they did not carry the burden of paying off debts and were free to work for themselves; still, the Pilgrims were instructed to provide them with farmland. Bradford agreed to these rules on the basis that the particulars paid an annual tax, were not given political citizenship, and were barred from Indian trade. Not surprisingly, the particulars were dissatisfied and began to complain.

Matters worsened in March, 1624, with the arrival of John Lyford, an Anglican minister. Lyford quickly assumed the role of spokesperson for the particulars, writing letters back to England in protest of Bradford's administration. In addition to fueling unrest within the colony, Lyford's letters caused enough discontent among the English investors to break up the stock company that had financed the settlement. In 1625, Lyford was banished by the Plymouth General Court.

### Breakdown of Communal System of Ownership
The economic structure within the colony was also coming into question. For three years, the colonists used a communal system, but, encouraged by Bradford, they were beginning to see the benefits of private property. In 1627, communal ownership came to an end as land, goods, and stock shares of the settlement were divided among the colonists. As members of this joint-stock company, all adult males (excluding servants) participated in government, shared in a partnership with English investors, and shared in ownership of the plantation and its assets.

Although capitalism inspired initiative and hard work among the colonists, it hindered their ability to pay the annual two hundred pounds the colony still owed to the English creditors. Out of desperation, Bradford decided to pay off the debt, with the help of eleven other "undertakers." In return, the undertakers would receive a monopoly of the Indian trade for six years and an annual tax from the colonists. This plan soured, however, as some of the undertakers began to use debt money for personal investments, most of which failed. Several undertakers, including Bradford, were forced to sell portions of their real estate holdings. The debt was finally paid more than ten years later with the help of Massachusetts intermediaries.

As the colonists struggled to pay the debt, Plymouth's economy was also struggling to prosper. Richer soil was discovered outside the colony, and many settlers left town for other areas. The fishing industry, expected to be a great source of profit, also proved disappointing as few settlers took interest in it. Most of Plymouth's revenue came from beaver skins exported to England.

### Massachusetts Bay Company Puritans
Plymouth's economy sharply expanded in 1629 with the arrival of the Massachusetts Bay Company Puritans. Although the colonization of Massachusetts decreased Plymouth's importance, it provided Plymouth with a nearby market to boost its economy with the sale of livestock and agricultural produce. For ten years, Puritans flooded into New England to escape religious persecution in England. As civil war erupted in Scotland in 1638, Puritans started fighting their cause at home; the great migration nearly halted. As a result, livestock prices plummeted and land grants in Plymouth significantly decreased.

Until the late 1630's, land was distributed (under law of the Mayflower Compact) by the governor and his court of seven assistants. Many colonists opposed this practice, as did the purchasers who had bought out the joint-stock company in 1627 and felt they deserved certain sections of land. Both groups continuously pressured Bradford to amend the system, and in 1639 Bradford came to an agreement with them. The purchasers would select a few tracts of land, and the remaining ungranted land would be distributed to new settlers by the "freemen," or citizens, of the colony. Not until the 1650's did land expansion resume.

### Church and State
Contrary to popular belief, when the colony was founded, the Pilgrims did not want a separate church and state; they believed government con-

trol of religious practices was very important. Though the government tried men for religious offenses, it avoided passing religious legislation until 1650. By that time, dissension had taken the form of a wide variety of practices and beliefs among the colonists. Bradford knew that if religious order were to be kept at all, certain laws needed to exist. In the following years, he attempted to control religious slander, church attendance, and the strict following of the Scriptures. Despite his efforts, religious unity dissipated further, aided by the arrival of Quaker missionaries in 1655.

The Quakers began a fierce attempt to convert the Puritans; opposition to their presence quickly swept through the colonies. For subverting religious and civil authority, the Quakers received severe punishment, yet they continued their struggle. In 1657, Bradford, who vehemently opposed the Quakers, died and was succeeded by Thomas Prence, who held the same convictions. Prence enforced strict laws to rid the colony of Quakers, making illegal almost any dealing with or entertaining of a Quaker.

**Persecution of the Quakers**

When Charles II became king in 1660, he ordered the New Englanders to stop persecuting the Quakers. The overt opposition ceased, causing Quaker missionaries to soften the battle for their cause. In response to the order, Prence penned legislation that eventually bound the colony in a legal commitment to the defense of the established religion. This legislation also led to restrictions on voting privileges. In 1658, the General Court had ordered not only that every man who applied for freemanship must wait a year after his application date but also that no Quaker or Quaker sympathizer could become a freeman. After the new order was handed down, the General Court revised the voting restrictions, adding a high minimum property requirement—twenty pounds. This practice disenfranchised almost one-third of freemen, pushing the colony further away from inclusive democracy.

Despite the importance of religion to the Pilgrims, they had come to America in 1620 without a minister. They believed, like most Puritans, that a clergyman must have a university education, severely narrowing their options. This belief, as well as the influence of the Quakers and Plymouth's attempt to confound sectarianism, made it difficult to find a religious leader. Legislation was passed in 1657 guaranteeing a tax collection be used for clergymen's salary, but colonists opposed the law and most of the small compensation was voluntary. Often, colonists conducted religious services by themselves.

**John Cotton**

Finally, in 1667, John Cotton, a Harvard graduate, was ordained minister by the Plymouth Church and remained there for more than thirty years. Following Cotton, a string of Harvard men settled to preach in other towns within Plymouth Colony. The arrival of men who shared a common education and background indicated that church practices within the colony and, to some extent within the Massachusetts Bay Colony, would become institutionalized.

One of the policies Cotton would immediately create for the Plymouth Church was its procedural requirements for admission. After 1667, applicants would have to make a public "conversion," or statement of their spiritual worthiness, to be later analyzed by the church. (Cotton never refused anyone admission.) Although restrictions appeared to tighten, membership during Cotton's ministry grew significantly. Different churches within the colony borrowed from one another as they formalized their practices, realizing much more congregational freedom than had the Catholic and Anglican churches, with which the Puritans were most familiar.

Although the colony finally began to achieve success in building its church, it never managed major expansion of its economy. Because Plymouth lacked good port facilities, transatlantic trade was difficult. Shipbuilding and ironworks provided some profit, as did sawmills and flour mills. Some men worked as tanners, weavers, coopers, or blacksmiths. Most colonists depended on agriculture, which usually also included the raising of livestock. The demands of agriculture in the colony, as well as the necessity to protect themselves against Indian attack, caused families to organize themselves into small, communal settlements.

Because the colony could not risk the failure of industries important to societal growth, economic life was regulated stringently, including export laws and quality standards for manufactured goods. Certain monopolies existed from town to town, es-

*A replica of the* Mayflower *in Plymouth.* (PhotoDisc)

tablished and supervised by the colony for the common good. Though the colony's economic status remained consistently good, it never reached the level of wealth of the neighboring Massachusetts Bay Colony or Boston.

### Relations with Native Americans

For the first forty years of its existence, the colony had peaceful relations with the Indians. When the Pilgrims first settled, Governor Carver quickly established a friendship with Massasoit, the Wampanoag chief. Friendly relations remained when Carver was succeeded by Bradford. When Bradford died in 1657 and Massasoit in 1660, their successors severed the ties. Trouble began to brew in the early 1660's when the Indians began selling portions of land granted to them by the settlers, often accepting only small amounts of manufactured goods as payment.

To protect the Indians from fraud and exploitation, the General Court forbid the independent purchase of Indian land. The Wampanoag did not understand that the measure was taken for their benefit, and anger grew throughout the tribe. As whites pushed closer to Indian homes and fields, the Indians' angry feelings grew deeper. Adding to the bitterness was Cotton's unending effort to convert them to Christianity. Massasoit's son and successor, Philip, despite his assurances to the General Court, began to act in ways that made many Puritans suspicious of his intentions.

### King Philip's War

In 1672, Prence died and was succeeded by the more moderate Josias Winslow. Winslow immediately heard whispers that Philip was planning an attack on the colony but dismissed the rumors in the hope that Philip would honor his word not to do so. In January, 1675, Winslow was warned in person by Sassamon, an Indian who acted as adviser to Philip. On his way home, Sassamon was murdered by three members of the Wampanoag tribe. The murderers were captured and executed at Plymouth; shortly after, Winslow heard definitive word that Philip had begun to prepare for war.

The first attack occurred on June 20, in the small village of Swansea. As settlers fled, Indians looted and burned their houses. Other tribes joined the Wampanoag, making it obvious that the colony was facing a very serious war. Massachusetts sent missions to nearby tribes, attempted to mediate between Philip and Plymouth, and provided the colony with extra provisions. Situations improved in some areas but got worse in others as the band of Indians, led by Philip, continued to rage through the colony.

On July 16, Plymouth's militia, commanded by Captain James Cudworth, began to pursue Philip, narrowly failing to capture him on several occasions. They were forced to give up as men were needed to bring in the harvest. This allowed Philip to strengthen his troops by spreading the word of war to other tribes in central and western Massachusetts, and King Philip's War soon spread throughout New England. The Indians' offensive did not last long, though, as they were dealing with an organized society that had greater resources and manpower. During the summer of 1676, Indian attacks slowed almost to a halt. Soon after, Philip was killed by a Christian-convert Indian. Rebuilding began at once, and although no town was economically ruined, the war had cost New England numerous casualties and tremendous property loss.

After the war, Plymouth tried to secure Mount Hope, an area formerly occupied by the Wampanoag. They found this annexation difficult, however; no royal charter outlining certain title to their lands had ever been granted. In 1680, after several negotiations with England, they were granted title to the area, yet still no official charter. Governor Winslow took it upon himself to draw up a proposed charter, granting all persons in the colony the same freedoms and immunities allowed to native-born Englishmen. When England replied, it was with a different proposition: the colony would consolidate with Massachusetts and retain Winslow as governor.

With barely a chance to consider the proposal, Winslow died and was succeeded by Thomas Hinckley, who had served under him as deputy governor. At that time, Plymouth was undergoing its own internal reorganization, and much of Hinckley's attention was drawn away from the problems of consolidation. In 1685, Plymouth's first county courts were established, modernizing the colony's entire judicial system.

### Hopes for a Royal Charter

When Charles II died and James II assumed the English throne, Plymouth's hope for a charter quickly faded. James II appointed former New York governor Sir Edmund Andros as new governor of Massachusetts. Soon after, orders were sent to Plymouth, Rhode Island, and Connecticut to report directly to Andros. Not only did this involve great inconvenience for the colonies (Andros was stationed in Boston, forty miles from Plymouth), it also imposed a heavy tax burden on them and took away most of their opportunity to participate in the legislative process. The colonies were greatly distressed and complained bitterly to the Crown. In 1689, the colonies, including Massachusetts, bound together, overthrew Andros, and returned to their former lifestyles.

In 1688, the English entered into war with France in Maine near the present-day Canadian border. As the war pushed its way toward New En-

gland, Plymouth, along with the other colonies, was forced to provide support. The financial strain the war put on Plymouth did nothing to help its confused political state after the successful overthrow of Andros. Holding together a poor, heavily taxed colony in a state of disarray proved too much for Hinckley to handle, especially without the help of a formal charter. By 1690, Plymouth's government had crumbled; in September, 1691, Plymouth Colony became part of the Province of Massachusetts Bay. The colonists did not seem to mind, however; Massachusetts was a strong and wealthy colony, and its government made few changes in their lifestyle. Most important, their religious beliefs and practices remained untouched. Though they had to give up their independent status, the towns in the colony, especially Plymouth itself, finally reached a permanent state of financial, economic, and religious stability.

### Modern Preservation Efforts

Today, museums and landmarks in Plymouth provide many opportunities to trace its history. Plymouth Rock, located on the beach at Water Street, marks the exact spot where the Pilgrims stepped into the New World. Adjacent to the rock sits a full-size replica of the *Mayflower*. Nearby, Coles Hill and Burial Hill house the graves of many seventeenth century Pilgrims, including William Bradford. The Mayflower Society Museum, Plymouth Wax Museum, and Pilgrim Hall Museum display both real and re-created scenes, dramatizations, and artifacts of early Plymouth. Finally, Plymouth Plantation boasts an authentic re-creation of the 1627 Pilgrim village.

Most of Plymouth's independent history has been documented, including the 71 years before the colony was annexed by Massachusetts Bay. After 1691, Plymouth's history blended with the history of Massachusetts, but the story of the Pilgrims and the influence the first settlements had on the shaping of the United States has long been remembered and celebrated. —*Cynthia L. Langston*

### For Further Information:

Bradford, William. *Of Plymouth Plantation.* New York: Alfred A. Knopf, 1952. An official chronicle of the Pilgrim story from 1620 to 1647, told by the second man to govern Plymouth Colony. It is especially helpful as it lends to its historical documentation the perspective of one of Plymouth's most important historical figures.

_____. *Pilgrim Courage.* Edited by E. Brooks Smith and Robert Meredith. Boston: Little, Brown, 1962. Simplifies selected episodes from Bradford's accounts, adding accounts from Edward Winslow, father to Bradford's successor.

Langdon, George D., Jr. *Pilgrim Colony: A History of New Plymouth.* New Haven, Conn.: Yale University Press, 1966. Gives a detailed chronological account of the events that took place at Plymouth Colony from 1620 to 1691.

Nickerson, W. Sears. *Land Ho!—1620.* 1931. Reprint. Boston: Houghton Mifflin, 1997. Tells a somewhat fabricated tale of the *Mayflower*'s construction, navigation, and landing in America.

# Salem

**Date:** Founded in 1673

**Relevant issues:** Business and industry, colonial America, disasters and tragedies, literary history, naval history

**Significance:** This town was the site of the infamous witch trials of 1692. It was also the port of origin for trade with the Caribbean and Asia during the eighteenth and early nineteenth centuries. Many historic buildings from that period still stand in Salem.

**Location:** Sixteen miles north of Boston, bordered by Marblehead, Swampscott, Peabody, and Beverly

**Site Office:**
Salem Chamber of Commerce
32 Derby Square
Salem, MA 01970
ph.: (978) 744-0004
fax: (978) 745-3855
Web site: www.salem-chamber.org

Salem's place in American history has been ensured by the witch trials of 1692; however, its major contribution to America was as a pioneer in trade with Asia in the eighteenth century. With the huge profits from that trade, Salem shipowners and merchants built some of the grandest homes of the time, and a remarkable number of these houses have survived. Some of the most elegant houses in America's Northeast—many of them de-

signed by Samuel McIntire, a master of the Federal style—can be found in Salem, and Chestnut Street is architecturally one of America's most important streets.

## The Founding of the Town

The founding of Salem really began on Cape Ann, in an area near what is now Gloucester. A group of merchants from Dorchester, England—called the Dorchester Adventurers—arrived there in 1623 and 1624 and established a plantation. Everything went wrong. The fishing vessels met various disasters, the price of fish plummeted, and the men fell to bickering.

In 1625, Roger Conant was invited to come from Nantasket to take over the governance of the colony. According to John White, rector of Dorchester's Trinity Church, Conant had a reputation as a "religious, sober, and prudent gentleman"; still, prosperity eluded the enterprise. Some of the settlers returned to England, while others went with Conant to a peninsula called Naumkeag in the autumn of 1626. (*Naumkeag* is an Indian word for "fishing place.")

Back in England, the Dorchester Adventurers agreed to advance money to shore up Naumkeag, but only if a group of trustworthy men could be found to make the voyage there. John Endecott (spelling of the name later changed to "Endicott") took up the challenge. Endecott arrived in Naumkeag on September 9, 1628, as the colony's new governor, accompanied by about fifty people. Roger Conant and three men waded into the water and carried Endecott to land on their shoulders.

Not surprisingly, there arose some conflicts between the old planters and the new settlers, but Conant managed to smooth over the difficulties. In honor of the two groups' compromise, the name of the settlement was changed to Salem (derived from the Hebrew word for "peace").

The first winter after Endecott's arrival was a terrible one. He suffered a personal tragedy when his wife died. The colony was overwhelmed with the problems of diseases imported by those who had made the sea voyage. With no medical facilities, the colony was decimated, with barely enough survivors to nurse the sick and bury the dead.

As the survivors persevered and the years passed, a schism developed between the Salem farmers, whose area became known as Salem Vil-

*The House of the Seven Gables in Salem.* (PhotoDisc)

lage (now Danvers), and the residents of Salem Town. For example, the farmers objected to the heavy burden placed on them by having to share the duties of keeping the night watch. Since some of them lived as far as ten miles from Salem Town, they argued to the Massachusetts' General Court (the colony's legislature) that the duty was unduly onerous. The court exempted from watch duties those living more than four miles away, but Salem Town paid no attention to the verdict, and in 1669 the town sued two farmers for refusing to participate in the watch.

Proximity to the town also played a pivotal role in the villagers' desire to build their own church. Farmers and their families were expected to travel to Salem Town each week for religious services. In March, 1672, the Salem Town meeting allowed Salem Village to erect its own meetinghouse and hire its own minister. After a series of contentious relationships with three ministers (one of whom, William Burroughs, was eventually accused of witchcraft and hanged), the residents of Salem Village engaged Samuel Parris as their minister. It was in his home that the witchcraft proceedings apparently began.

### The Witch Trials

Historians disagree about the source of the bizarre behavior of the ten girls and young women (ages ranged from nine to twenty) who "cried out" various Salem residents as witches. They even disagree on the facts of the inquisition. Chadwick Hansen, who believes that three of those hanged were indeed witches, says that a most important factor in Rebecca Nurse's case was that she was questioned on the same day as Dorcas Good (a five-year-old who confessed to being a witch). Paul Boyer and Stephen Nissenbaum write that Dorcas Good was interrogated on March 23, 1692, and Rebecca Nurse a day later.

According to the Reverend John Hale, a pastor to the nearby village of Beverly and author of a book published in 1702 on the trials, one of the girls suspended an egg white in a glass in an attempt to learn her future husband's occupation, only to be confronted by "a specter in the likeness of a coffin." Two girls in Reverend Parris's household—his daughter, Betty, and his niece, Abigail Williams—subsequently fell ill, as did several of their friends. Parris sought medical attention for them, but the physician was dumbfounded and concluded that the girls were bewitched.

The girls were unable to respond to questions about the source of their torments, leading Mary Sibley, the aunt of one of the afflicted, to persuade Tituba and John Indian (two slaves Parris had brought with him from Barbados) to bake a witch cake—meal mixed with the urine of the afflicted children. After being baked, it was fed to a dog, apparently in the belief that the dog would suffer torments similar to those of the bewitched girls. When Parris learned of this experiment, he denounced Sibley from the pulpit.

The cake apparently unleashed the tongues of the girls, because they were able to identify three tormenters—Sarah Good, Sarah Osborne, and Tituba. According to historian Samuel Eliot Morison, writing in 1936, "At this point a good spanking administered to the younger girls, and lovers provided for the older ones, might have stopped the whole thing." However, such an easy solution was not to be.

On February 29, 1692, the three women were arrested. On the following day, Judge John Hathorne and Jonathan Corwin, members of the provincial legislature, rode from Salem Town and began to question the women. Hathorne behaved more as a prosecutor than an impartial judge, as this passage from his questioning of Sarah Good illustrates:

HATHORNE: Sarah Good, what evil spirit have you familiarity with?
GOOD: None.
HATHORNE: Why do you hurt these children?
GOOD: I do not hurt them. I scorn it.
HATHORNE: Who do you employ, then, to do it?
GOOD: I employ nobody.
HATHORNE: What creature do you employ, then?
GOOD: No creature, but I am falsely accused.

While Good and Osborne protested their innocence, Tituba confessed, in somewhat lurid detail.

She said that the devil who had come to her was "a thing all over hairy, all the face hairy, and a long nose." She described a book he brought with him, in which she had made a mark, and broomstick rides with Good and Osborne. She also reported that the two women had familiars: Good had a cat and a yellow bird, and Osborne had a thing with "wings and two legs and a head like a woman."

The three were sent to jail. Osborne died of natural causes in May. Tituba remained and was eventually sold, because she could not pay the jailer's fees. (One of the additional hardships for the accused was that prisoners were required to pay for their lodging.) Sarah Good was one of those executed.

Two important legal issues were raised in these first hearings. The first (and one that was to haunt the proceedings) was that of spectral evidence—"specters" seen only by those afflicted. For example, Ann Putnam claimed to see a yellow bird on a preacher's hat as it hung on a hook near the pulpit. The bird was visible to no one else. The other issue was whether the devil could assume the shape of innocent persons. While Sarah Osborne denied the charges against her, she speculated that the devil might have assumed her person to torment the children.

During the proceedings, the afflicted girls were in the courtroom and often burst out with reports of attacks by the accused or visions of the accused's familiars.

The first three women named as witches could be described as outcasts: a slave and two old women of dubious reputations. The fourth woman identified as a witch, Martha Corey, was a member in good standing of the church of Salem Village. She had been accused by Ann Putnam, who was the most vociferous of the afflicted girls. The entire Putnam family was involved in accusations against forty-six alleged witches.

The accusations went on, and the jails filled, but there were no trials because, technically, Salem had no government. The Massachusetts Bay Company's charter had been revoked by Charles II in 1684. The Reverend Increase Mather led a commission to England to negotiate a new charter. He returned in May, 1692, with both the charter and the new governor, Sir William Phips, whom he had chosen personally.

One of Phips's first acts was to appoint a special court to deal with the witchcraft accusations. It began its work on June 2 and at that time tried just one person, Bridget Bishop, who was found guilty and hanged on June 10. The jailings, trials, and executions continued until October. During the course of the trials, one of the judges, Nathaniel Saltonstall, resigned, and one of the afflicted girls, Mary Warren, said that her testimony had been false and that the other girls "did but dissemble."

The most controversial of the accusations was that against Rebecca Nurse, by all accounts a woman of great piety. When told that she was under suspicion, Nurse said, "I am as innocent as the child unborn. But surely, what sin hath God found out in me unrepented of, that he should lay such an affliction on me in my old age?" The jury initially found Nurse innocent, but the accusers unleashed hideous cries and one of the judges expressed himself dissatisfied with the verdict. The jury decided to reconsider. When asked to explain a statement she had made, Nurse apparently did not hear the question (being old and deaf) and stood mute. That convinced the jury of her guilt.

On October 3, Increase Mather read to the Boston clergy *Cases of Conscience Concerning Evil Spirits Personating Men*, a direct attack he had written on the concept of spectral evidence. By the end of October, the special court was dissolved and the witch hunt ended.

By its conclusion, nineteen people and two dogs had been hanged, and Giles Corey (husband of Martha) had been pressed to death. No one is sure why he submitted to that incredibly painful end. The sentence resulted from his refusal to enter a plea either of innocence or of guilt; when the court asked him to plead, he had remained silent. Some say that he did so to protect his family's property, since the property of a convicted witch could be confiscated. Others believe that he was denying the court's right to try him.

### An Important Center for Trade

Though the other chapter in Salem's history—that involving trade with Asia—is not so well known, it is far more important in the history of the United States. In 1636, the Reverend Hugh Peter, who succeeded Roger Williams as Salem's preacher, realized that the land in the Salem area was not suitable to farming and that a local industry was needed. Salem fishing boats were soon voyaging to Newfoundland and Cape Cod and bringing back mackerel, haddock, and cod. Though Salem ships were never involved in the infamous Triangular Trade (importing West Indies sugar and molasses to New England, sending New England rum to Africa, and bringing slaves to the West Indies plantations), several Salem fortunes were built on selling supplies (such as cod and horses) to the plantations.

Two men stand out among the early merchants. Philip English (who came from the Isle of Jersey) at one time owned outright or held a share in some twenty vessels trading in Barbados, Suriname, and the Channel Islands. English and his wife were later among those accused in the 1692 witchcraft trials, but they were able to escape to New York. The other prominent merchant was Captain John Turner, who died at age thirty-six after making a fortune in trade with Barbados and building a house later immortalized in Nathaniel Hawthorne's 1851 novel *The House of the Seven Gables*.

The series of acts passed by the British Parliament in the 1760's, which ultimately led to the American Revolution, divided the allegiances of Massachusetts's two major ports. Salem tended to remain loyal to the British Crown, unlike its more radical neighbor, Boston. In fact, the British felt sufficiently safe in Salem to move the seat of the colony's government there. When the General Court met in Salem, however, it supported Boston, and the community staged its own version of the Boston Tea Party. The governor returned to Boston.

During the American Revolution itself, Salem contributed to the maritime war effort in two ways. Over the course of the war, 158 Salem vessels were outfitted as privateers, authorized to capture British ships. Together they seized 458 British vessels. Some ships continued to trade while carrying letters of marque, authorizing them to capture British ships during commercial voyages.

Ironically, the news of peace was not entirely welcome in Salem because of the enormous profits many had realized in privateering. Chief among those was Elias Hasket Derby, whose wartime raids had made him America's first millionaire. Derby's prosperity continued after the war. In 1784, his ship *Light Horse* was the first American vessel in the Baltic, when it called at St. Petersburg with a cargo of West Indies sugar. Two years later, his ship *The*

*Grand Turk* was the first to go from New England to Canton (China) via the Cape of Good Hope. He also sent ships to Calcutta, Bombay, and Manila. Though Derby had made his fortune in government-sanctioned thievery, he forbade his captains to transport slaves on his ships.

The chief rivals of the Derby family were the Crowninshields (though Elias Hasket Derby married Elizabeth Crowninshield and numerous Crowninshields trained on Derby ships). The Crowninshields themselves made history during their travels, though not in so economically rewarding a manner as the Derbys: In 1797, Jacob Crowninshield brought the first elephant seen in America to Salem. He paid $450 for it and charged adults a quarter and children nine pence to see it. The elephant refused to accommodate riders, shaking them off time after time, stole bread from the pockets of spectators, and took the cork from a bottle of porter, which it proceeded to drink. Crowninshield eventually sold the animal for $10,000.

By 1790, Salem, with slightly fewer than six thousand inhabitants, was the sixth-largest city in the United States. Salem ships opened up markets far and wide. A voyage to Sumatra resulted in Salem becoming, for a time, the pepper capital of America. In 1798, Captain Joseph Ropes opened trade in coffee with the Arabian community of Mocha, and by 1805 Salem was importing two thousand pounds of coffee a year.

In 1799, a group of Salem's captains and supercargoes (seagoing business agents) formed the East India Marine Society. Their collections of artifacts from around the world (considerably augmented) are in Salem's Peabody Essex Museum, the oldest continuously operating museum in the United States.

So prominent was Salem that a merchant in Quallah-Battoo thought Salem to be a country—and one of the richest in the world.

Salem never recovered, however, from the War of 1812. In 1807, its overseas fleet consisted of 182 sailing vessels; by 1815, it was down to 57. Joseph Peabody continued to compete in the China trade, but with his death in 1844, Salem's importance as a port ended.

## Home to a Famous Writer

A few years after this decline, Salem's most famous citizen, Nathaniel Hawthorne, came to work in the Custom House (just opposite Derby Wharf). Hawthorne was the great-great-grandson of Judge John Hathorne, who had helped initiate the 1692 witch trials, but the author was so embarrassed by his ancestry that he added a *w* to the family name.

It was at the Salem Custom House that Hawthorne apparently contrived the plot for that most famous indictment of the Puritan culture, *The Scarlet Letter* (1850). In his introduction to that novel, he describes his view from the Custom House and the decay into which the port had fallen: "In my native town of Salem, at the head of what, half a century ago, in the days of old King Derby, was a bustling wharf—but which is now burdened with decayed wooden warehouses, and exhibits few or no symptoms of commercial life . . ."

## Places to Visit

Salem continues to commemorate its two periods of fame in American history. The town logo is Witch City, and the police wear a sleeve patch with a witch on her broomstick highlighted against the moon. The city seal reads *Divitis Indae usque ad ultimum sinum* (to the farthest port of the rich East).

Salem sites associated with the witch trials include Jonathan Corwin's home, also known as the Witch House, on Essex Street. Corwin questioned numerous accused witches at the house. The Witch Museum, housed in a nineteenth century church on Washington Square, presents a dramatization of the trials.

The city's maritime history is evident in the Salem Maritime National Historic Site, which includes the Custom House, related commercial buildings, and Elias Derby's mansion, known as Derby House. Also, the maritime history collection at the Peabody Essex Museum is extensive.

Numerous historic homes, built by shipowners, merchants, and other prominent citizens, still stand in Salem. The section of homes on Chestnut Street between Sumner and Flint Streets is a state historic landmark district. One of the most notable structures on this notable street is Hamilton Hall, designed by Samuel McIntire and completed in 1805. Chestnut Street also boasts a home once occupied by Nathaniel Hawthorne. Other historic homes include six operated by the Peabody Essex Museum; they are located on Essex Street, Hawthorne Boulevard, and Brown Street. One of these, the 1804 Gardner-Pingree House, is among the best examples of McIntire's work.

Salem's most famous house, the House of the Seven Gables, stands at 54 Turner Street and has been restored to appear as it did in Hawthorne's lifetime. For the novel, Hawthorne drew not only on the history of the house—once occupied by his cousin Susan Ingersoll—but also on his own family history; the story concerns persons descended from participants in the witch trials. Other historic structures are on the grounds of the house. One of them is Hawthorne's birthplace, moved there from Union Street.                    —*Elizabeth Devine*

**For Further Information:**

Boyer, Paul, and Stephen Nissenbaum. *Salem Possessed.* Cambridge, Mass.: Harvard University Press, 1976. Reprint. New York: MJF Books, 1997. Explores the sociological aspects of the witchcraft hysteria.

Flibbert, Joseph, ed. *Salem: Cornerstones of a Historic City.* Beverly, Mass.: Commonwealth Editions, 1999. Five regional historians tell the story of Salem by focusing on different aspects of the town's history. Includes seventy color photographs.

Hansen, Chadwick. *Witchcraft at Salem.* Reprint. New York: George Braziller, 1985. Quotes extensively from the trial transcripts.

Hill, Frances. *A Delusion of Satan: The Full Story of the Salem Witch Trials.* New York: Da Capo Press, 1997. Hill, a British novelist and journalist, offers a detailed narrative of the trials.

Lebeau, Bryan F. *The Story of the Salem Witch Trials.* Englewood Cliffs, N.J.: Prentice Hall, 1997. Combines scholarly research with a dramatic narrative.

Morison, Samuel Eliot. *The Intellectual Life of Colonial New England.* Westport, Conn.: Greenwood Press, 1980. Examines the witch trials within the larger context of New England's intellectual history. Originally published as *The Puritan Pronaos* (New York University Press, 1936).

_____. *The Maritime History of Massachusetts, 1783-1860.* New York: Houghton Mifflin, 1921. Reprint. Boston: Northeastern University Press, 1979. Documents the most prosperous days of the Salem seafarers.

Starkey, Marion L. *Devil in Massachusetts: A Modern Inquiry into the Salem Witch Trials.* New York: Alfred A. Knopf, 1949. Reprint. New York: Anchor Books, 1989. A well-researched and readable account of the witch trials.

# Other Historic Sites

## Adams National Historic Site

*Location:* Quincy, Norfolk County
*Relevant issues:* Political history
*Web site:* www.nps.gov/adam/

### JOHN ADAMS BIRTHPLACE

*Statement of significance:* John Adams (1735-1826), first vice president and second president of the United States, lived here from his birth in 1735 until his marriage in 1764. Built in the saltbox style, much of the original fabric remains.

### JOHN QUINCY ADAMS BIRTHPLACE

*Statement of significance:* John Quincy Adams (1767-1848), sixth president of the United States, was born here in 1767. His father, John Adams, had moved here in 1764 and used one room as a law office for several years.

## American Antiquarian Society

*Location:* Worcester, Worcester County
*Relevant issues:* Cultural history
*Statement of significance:* Established in 1812, this organization was the third historical society founded in the United States and is an important repository for early Americana.

## Boston Naval Shipyard

*Location:* Boston, Suffolk County
*Relevant issues:* Business and industry, military history, naval history
*Statement of significance:* From 1800 to 1974, the Boston Naval Shipyard functioned as one of the most important shipyards in the United States. It pioneered modern ship construction and for more than a century manufactured most of the Navy's rope.

## Bowditch Home

*Location:* Salem, Essex County

*Relevant issues:* Science and technology

*Statement of significance:* From 1811 to 1823, this structure was the home of Nathaniel Bowditch (1773-1838), who effected great advances in navigation and helped bring European mathematics to America. He is responsible for *The New American Practical Navigator* (1802).

## Brandeis House

*Location:* Chatham, Barnstable County

*Relevant issues:* Legal history

*Statement of significance:* Louis Brandeis (1856-1941) was appointed to the Supreme Court in 1916 by President Woodrow Wilson. He often stood with Justice Oliver Wendell Holmes against the Court majority.

## Bryant Homestead

*Location:* Cummington, Hampshire County

*Relevant issues:* Literary history

*Statement of significance:* Poet and critic William Cullen Bryant (1794-1878) lived here until early manhood and made his summer residence here in the later years of his life (1865-1878). He composed some of his best-known poems in this house.

## Fruitlands

*Location:* Harvard, Worcester County

*Relevant issues:* Cultural history, social reform

*Statement of significance:* This modest farmhouse served as the home for Bronson Alcott's New Eden (1843-1844), an experiment in communal living modeled on the ideas of this leading education reformer, Trancendentalist, and social philosopher.

## Fuller House

*Location:* Cambridge, Middlesex County

*Relevant issues:* Social reform, women's history

*Statement of significance:* Margaret Fuller (1810-1850), a nineteenth century writer, teacher, intellectual, and reformer, was born here and lived here until 1826. Her *Woman in the Nineteenth Century* (1845) has been called "the first considered statement of feminism in this country."

## Goddard Rocket Launching Site

*Location:* Auburn, Worcester County

*Relevant issues:* Science and technology

*Statement of significance:* Dr. Robert H. Goddard (1882-1945) launched the world's first liquid-propellant rocket here in 1926, setting the course for future developments in rocketry.

## Kennedy Birthplace

*Location:* Brookline, Norfolk County

*Relevant issues:* Political history

*Statement of significance:* John F. Kennedy (1917-1963), the thirty-fifth president of the United States, was born and spent his infancy here, in a house that his father purchased in 1914 and sold in 1921.

## Kennedy Compound

*Location:* Hyannis Port, Barnstable County

*Relevant issues:* Political history

*Statement of significance:* Six acres of waterfront property, containing several Kennedy summer and vacation residences. One of them served as John F. Kennedy's Summer White House.

## Longfellow House

*Location:* Cambridge, Middlesex County

*Relevant issues:* Literary history

*Statement of significance:* Home of Henry Wadsworth Longfellow (1807-1882) from 1837 to 1882. In his day, he was widely regarded as America's greatest poet.

## The Mount

*Location:* Lenox, Berkshire County

*Relevant issues:* Literary history, women's history

*Statement of significance:* Some of the best works of Pulitzer Prize-winning novelist Edith Wharton (1862-1937) were written here, including *Ethan Frome* (1911), set in a rural New England area similar to Lenox.

## Nantucket Historic District

*Location:* Nantucket, Nantucket County

*Relevant issues:* Business and industry

*Statement of significance:* The American whaling industry originated here, and the town of Nantucket remained the leading American whaling port until the 1840's. A number of houses on

Main Street were built by wealthy whale-oil merchants during that period.

## New Bedford Historic District

*Location:* New Bedford, Bristol County

*Relevant issues:* Business and industry

*Web site:* www.rixsan.com/nbvisit/attract/histdist.htm

*Statement of significance:* New Bedford's growth as a whaling port began shortly after the town was established in the early 1760's. In the 1840's, New Bedford superseded Nantucket as the most important U.S. whaling port. The wealth produced by whaling is evident in the structures in the historic district.

## Old Deerfield Historic District

*Location:* Deerfield, Franklin County

*Relevant issues:* Colonial America, western expansion

*Statement of significance:* An early outpost of New England's northwestern frontier, Deerfield was laid out in 1666 and settled a few years later. It was attacked and destroyed several times during French and Indian raids. It is now restored to its colonial appearance.

## Old Ship Meetinghouse

*Location:* Hingham, Plymouth County

*Relevant issues:* Art and architecture, colonial America, religion

*Statement of significance:* Built in 1681, this is one of the oldest English Colonial houses of worship standing in the United States. The name derives from the curved roof timbers, which resemble an inverted ship's hull.

## Olmsted House

*Location:* Brookline, Norfolk County

*Relevant issues:* Art and architecture

*Statement of significance:* From 1883 to 1903, this was the home of pioneer landscape architect Frederick Law Olmsted (1822-1903), who developed New York's Central Park, planned some eighty other urban parks, and was involved in numerous preservation projects.

## The Parsonage

*Location:* Natick, Middlesex County

*Relevant issues:* Literary history

*Statement of significance:* Horatio Alger (1832-1899), a minister and the author of popular rags-to-riches books, spent his summers in this white clapboard parsonage.

## Redtop

*Location:* Belmont, Middlesex County

*Relevant issues:* Literary history

*Statement of significance:* William Dean Howells (1837-1920), author, magazine editor, and influential literary critic at the end of the nineteenth century, wrote some of his most famous novels while residing here from 1878 to 1882.

## Springfield Armory

*Location:* Springfield, Hampden County

*Relevant issues:* Business and industry, military history

*Statement of significance:* Until 1967-1968, this was the U.S. Army's main research and development center and pilot manufactory for small arms. It was formally established as a federal arsenal in 1794.

## Sumner House

*Location:* Boston, Suffolk County

*Relevant issues:* Political history

*Statement of significance:* Charles Sumner (1811-1874) was an outspoken opponent of slavery who represented Massachusetts in the U.S. Senate from 1851 until his death. After the Civil War, he was one of the leading figures in the Radical wing of the Republican Party and played an influential role in foreign affairs.

## Whittier Home

*Location:* Amesbury, Essex County

*Relevant issues:* Literary history

*Statement of significance:* John Greenleaf Whittier (1807-1892), writer, editor, and prominent abolitionist, lived and wrote here from 1836 until his death.

# Michigan

*The State Capitol Building in Lansing.* (Travel Michigan)

# History of Michigan

Michigan's abundant natural resources and access to major waterways, including four of the five Great Lakes, have made it an important area of human activity for more than ten thousand years. The unique geographic situation of Michigan, with the state divided into two separate land masses, has had a profound influence on its history. The southern land mass, known as the Lower Peninsula, developed into a heavily populated area of agriculture, forestry, and industry. The northern land mass, known as the Upper Peninsula, remained sparsely populated but provided important mineral resources.

## Early History

The first inhabitants of the region hunted and fished about eleven thousand years ago. They also made tools from copper found in the Upper Peninsula. This is the earliest known use of metal in the New World. About three thousand years ago, agriculture began to develop in the southwestern part of the Lower Peninsula.

By the time Europeans arrived in North America, Michigan was primarily inhabited by Native Americans belonging to the Algonquian language group. These peoples included the Ottawa, the Ojibwa, the Miami, and the Potawatomi, mostly living in the northern regions. In the south lived the Huron, a Native American tribe belonging to the Iroquois language group. During the middle of the seventeenth century, conflict with other Iroquois peoples to the east drove the Huron and the Ottawa westward. At about the same time, the development of the French fur trade led many Native Americans in northern Michigan to move south.

## Exploration and Settlement

The first European known to have visited the area was Étienne Brulé, who reached the Upper Peninsula from Canada in 1622. Another French explorer, Jean Nicolet, traveled through the narrow strait that separates the two peninsulas in 1634 during a journey from Canada to Wisconsin. The earliest permanent European settlements, located in the Upper Peninsula, were founded by the French missionary Jacques Marquette at Sault Sainte Marie in 1668 and St. Ignace in 1671. During the late seventeenth and early eighteenth centuries, several French missionary, fur trading, and military posts were established on both peninsulas. In 1701 Detroit was founded by Antoine Laumet de La Mothe, Sieur de Cadillac. It soon became the most important French settlement in the Great Lakes region.

During the French and Indian War, a struggle between France and England for control of North America, Detroit was surrendered to the British in 1760. After the war, control of the region went to Great Britain. Fearful that the British would bring many more settlers to the area, many Native Americans united under the Ottawa leader Pontiac. After capturing several British forts in the area, Pontiac's forces laid siege to Detroit for nearly six months in 1763. Pontiac was forced to abandon the siege in October, and the British remained in control.

## Steps to Statehood

Although the end of the American Revolution officially brought the area under American control, the British did not leave Detroit and other military posts until 1796. Michigan was part of the Northwest Territory from 1787 to 1800, when it became part of the newly created Indiana Territory. The Michigan Territory was created in 1805. In the same year, a fire destroyed several buildings in Detroit.

After being rebuilt, Detroit was an important military objective in the War of 1812, a conflict between the United States and England. Detroit was captured by the British in August of 1812 but recaptured in September of 1813. Control of the Great Lakes region was restored to the United States the same month, when American naval forces commanded by Oliver Hazard Perry defeated the British in the Battle of Lake Erie.

Michigan began growing quickly after the war. Settlement was encouraged by the beginning of steamship transportation on Lake Erie from Buffalo to Detroit. The completion of the Erie Canal in 1825, linking the Hudson River to Lake Erie, also

found in the southern part of the Lower Peninsula. In the 1850's, about 85 percent of the population was involved in agriculture.

The pine forests of the northern part of the Lower Peninsula and the mineral resources of the Upper Peninsula were also important parts of the state's economy. Iron, copper, and salt deposits began to be mined in the 1840's. Immigrants from Finland and Cornwall, a region of southwestern England, were involved in the development of the mining industry. An important stimulus to economic growth in the Upper Peninsula was the completion in 1855 of a series of locks at Sault Sainte Marie which allowed ships to travel from Lake Huron to Lake Superior. The growing importance of the northern regions of the state was a factor in the decision to move the capital from Detroit to Lansing in 1847.

led to rapid population growth. From 1820 to 1840, the number of settlers, mostly from eastern states, increased from less than 9,000 to more than 200,000. During this time, many Native Americans gave up their lands or were forced to leave. However, some remained on reservations that still exist.

Michigan reached the population of 60,000 required for statehood as early as 1833. Before statehood could be approved by Congress, however, a border dispute arose between Michigan and Ohio. Ohio claimed lands in the southeastern part of the Michigan Territory. In the Toledo War of 1835, Michigan militia prevented Ohio officials from occupying the area. Michigan eventually gave up the disputed region in return for a large increase in the size of its lands in the Upper Peninsula. It became the twenty-sixth state in 1837.

### Economic Development
Despite an economic depression in the late 1830's, Michigan experienced rapid growth in the two decades after statehood. Many of the new residents were immigrants from Germany, Ireland, and the Netherlands. The vast majority of settlers were drawn to Michigan by the rich, productive soil

### The Republican Party and the Civil War
The Democratic Party dominated Michigan politics from before statehood until the national crisis over slavery in the 1850's. In 1854 antislavery members of the Democratic Party joined with members of the Whig Party and the Free-Soil Party to form the Republican Party in Jackson. The new party would dominate Michigan politics for the next eight decades.

During the Civil War about ninety thousand residents of Michigan fought for the Union, and around fourteen thousand were killed. Among the forces representing Michigan was a regiment of African Americans drawn from several states.

### The Rise of Industry
The late nineteenth century saw the beginnings of modern manufacturing in Michigan. Grand Rapids became a center of furniture making. Kalamazoo dominated the paper industry. The Dow Chemical Company and the Upjohn Company

made the chemical and pharmaceutical industries an important part of the state's economy. Perhaps the most distinctive industry to arise in Michigan at this time was the manufacture of breakfast cereal. This industry, which grew out of health resorts in the state that developed these products as part of a vegetarian diet, is centered in the city of Battle Creek.

By far the most important industry in Michigan during the twentieth century was automobile manufacturing. The industry began in 1901, when Ransom Eli Olds began marketing the Oldsmobile, the first successful American automobile. Inspired by this success, other automobile manufacturing companies soon appeared in the state. Henry Ford organized the Ford Motor Company in 1903 and began manufacturing the highly successful Model T in 1908. The same year, William C. Durant created the General Motors Corporation. Walter P. Chrysler founded the Chrysler Corporation in 1925. These and many other companies made the cities of Detroit, Flint, Pontiac, and Lansing dominant in the automobile industry.

**The Twentieth Century**

During the late nineteenth and early twentieth centuries, large numbers of immigrants from Ireland, Italy, Poland, and other European nations entered the state. At about the same time, African Americans from southern states began to arrive in large numbers. From 1900 to the late twentieth century, the number of African Americans in the state rose from less than sixteen thousand to well over one million. In the last few decades of the century, immigrants also arrived from Latin America, Asia, and the Middle East.

The Great Depression of the 1930's devastated the automobile industry. By 1932 half the industrial workers in Michigan were unemployed. This crisis ended the dominance of the Republican Party in the state. It also made organized labor an important force in Michigan. The entire automobile industry was unionized by the United Automobile Workers by 1941.

World War II revitalized industry in the state as automobile manufacturers turned to making military vehicles. Prosperity continued from the end of the war until the nationwide recession of the 1980's, which brought much higher unemployment to Michigan than to most other states. During the late 1980's and 1990's, the state made efforts to lessen its economic dependence on the automobile industry, particularly by developing technological industries and tourism.

*—Rose Secrest*

# Greenfield Village and Henry Ford Museum

**Date:** Founded in 1929

**Relevant issues:** Business and industry, science and technology

**Significance:** An indoor-outdoor, ninety-three-acre complex that is a museum of U.S. history and technology. Greenfield Village is an outdoor, eighty-one-acre, developed exhibit space containing more than one hundred original homes, factories, and other buildings. Henry Ford Museum is an indoor, twelve-acre exhibit space that displays objects of invention in the fields of transportation, communication, agriculture, industry, domestic life, and the decorative arts. The front of the museum itself is modeled exactly after Independence Hall in Philadelphia. Both Greenfield Village and the Henry Ford Museum were founded by Henry Ford in 1929 as the Edison Institute. The museum complex is an independent, nonprofit, educational institution.

**Location:** The village and museum are located next to each other about ten miles west-southwest of downtown Detroit; the complex is roughly located at the intersection of the Southfield freeway (Michigan 39) and Michigan Avenue (U.S. 12)

**Site Office:**
Greenfield Village and Henry Ford Museum
20900 Oakwood Boulevard
P.O. Box 1970
Dearborn, MI 48124-4088
ph.: (313) 271-1620; (313) 982-6150 (recording)
fax: (313) 982-6250
Web site: www.hfmgv.org

It was typical of Henry Ford both as a man and as an industrialist to go against the grain of common thought and movement. His character was certainly well illustrated by the Ford Motor Company, which Ford founded, in the way that it revolutionized mass production of the automobile. It might be said, however, that nowhere was Ford's uniqueness more apparent than in the museum he founded in 1929—Greenfield Village and Henry Ford Museum (corporately known as the Edison Institute). Ford's purpose seemed simple, yet noble enough: "to give us a sense of unity with our people through the generations, and to convey the inspiration of American genius to our youth . . . " Ford saw in the history of the American people a pioneer spirit and a can-do attitude that enabled Americans to accomplish anything to which they set their minds—no matter how unusual or unconventional. It was on this premise that Greenfield Village and Henry Ford Museum were founded. Ford would create more than just the traditional museum; he would create a link with the past that would embody the American spirit.

### Henry Ford's Vision

In 1926, three years before the opening of the complex, Ford envisioned a two-part museum: One part would show the artifacts of U.S. culture, housed in a mammoth building that would be more reminiscent of one of Ford's factories than of a traditional museum; the other part would replicate a village (as true to an American small town as possible) that would strive to preserve the community aspect of the American past. Ford, as he was wont to do, had defined his goals clearly for this endeavor: "When we are through, we shall have reproduced American life as lived; and that, I think, is the best way of preserving at least a part of our history and tradition." Ford's aim was not merely to show and tell history, but to bring it to life. This achievement is the distinction of Greenfield Village and Henry Ford Museum.

Henry Ford's enthusiasm as a collector of artifacts and a preserver of Americana did not develop overnight. Ford planned very carefully, almost from the beginning of his career, the way in which he could tell the story of the American people and of the American dream. Ford started his collection with his first car, the Quadricycle, built in 1896. He had to repurchase the car because, in the most honored of American business traditions, he had sold it initially for a profit in order to keep his business going; he never sentimentalized his first piece of work until he felt certain that he could afford to do so. It does seem of some interest, however, that although he sold the Quadricycle for two hundred dollars, he managed to buy it back for only sixty-five dollars in 1904.

In 1905, Ford began assembling artifacts from Thomas Alva Edison's life and work; in 1914, he began collecting *McGuffey Readers*, and in 1919, he began building a monument, of sorts, to himself: the preservation of his own birthplace and old family home from Dearborn, Michigan, circa 1860. (Ironically, in 1944, this was the last building he moved to Greenfield Village before his death in 1947.) It was at this point that Ford began in earnest his crusade to bring Americana to Dearborn.

*An assembly line produces Model Ts in Ford Motor Company's Highland Park factory.* (Library of Congress)

By 1924, boxcars of antiques had begun to arrive there; he had arranged storage for them in one of his old tractor plants. In 1927, the very first old building arrived in Dearborn for reconstruction on the future acreage of Greenfield Village—a general store from Waterford, Michigan.

## Ford's Tribute to Edison

It was then that Ford decided to dedicate a part of Greenfield Village to the life and career of his old friend, Thomas Edison. He arranged to move and reconstruct a number of buildings from Edison's Menlo Park, New Jersey, laboratory compound. It was here that many of Edison's greatest inventions, including the light bulb and the phonograph, were researched and developed. Edison's Menlo Park laboratory itself may well have been his greatest invention; from it, the idea of an industrial research center was born. Until this time, inventions had often been developed under haphazard circumstances and solitary conditions. Edison's technique for producing inventions could perhaps be compared to Henry Ford's technique for producing automobiles: mass production in a technically streamlined, organizationally efficient manner, with the purpose of producing the most and the best in the shortest amount of time. Edison had once said that one of his dreams was to produce within Menlo Park one major invention every six months and one minor invention every ten days. At Menlo Park Edison perfected organized technical research, the forerunner of the research and development departments that are now commonplace in large manufacturing companies. Ford realized the significance of his friend's accomplishments and sought to immortalize them by preserving the buildings in which they occurred.

Ford considered this project his most important preservation effort, and it involved Ford's scrupulous care and attention to detail. Much of what had made up the Menlo Park of forty-odd years earlier was in ruins and needed to be painstakingly reconstructed. Ford was equal to this task, and called upon the aging Edison himself to help with the effort. Ford had tons of fragmented materials (boards, bricks, broken bottles, wires, dirt, even an old stump) sent by rail back to Dearborn where they could be pieced together somehow to form a historically correct representation of the Menlo Park laboratory. Ford succeeded, and by the time

of the dedication of Greenfield Village and Henry Ford Museum on October 21, 1929—fifty years to the day after Edison's invention of the incandescent lamp—Edison was ready to inspect the reconstruction of his old compound. After a walk around, Edison pronounced it to be "99 percent perfect." After a perplexed Henry Ford had asked what the problem was, Edison responded, "We never kept it this clean!"

## Ford's Relationship with Edison

Henry Ford's association with Thomas Edison is well chronicled. It was no secret to anyone of Ford's day or even to a modern day visitor to Greenfield Village that Edison's life and work were much revered in Ford's eyes. Ford saw in Edison the Horatio Alger model of the American way of life. It should not be about rank and privilege (as the way of life in Europe was often viewed), but about self-reliance and hard work. Still, in spite of Ford's devotion to Edisonia, he was not without other heroes. There were other Americans whom Ford enshrined at Greenfield Village.

One of these Americans was Noah Webster. Webster is undoubtedly the most notable American lexicographer and philologist who ever lived, yet somehow he escaped much of the recognition that he deserved during his lifetime (1758-1843). The home in which Webster completed *An American Dictionary of the English Language* (1828), and the one in which he lived for twenty years, was brought to Greenfield Village from New Haven, Connecticut, in the 1930's. Ford had heard that plans to raze Webster's home in New Haven were already being carried out when he dispatched a team to rescue it. The house stands now in Dearborn just as it stood in New Haven more than a century ago.

## The Wright Brothers

Orville and Wilbur Wright are granted stature second only to Edison at Greenfield Village. In 1938, both the Wright family home and the Wright Cycle Shop were moved from their original sites in Dayton, Ohio, to Greenfield Village. Orville Wright himself assisted in the move, making every effort to ensure complete originality and authenticity of the interiors and exteriors of the structures. The Wrights belonged to the class of innovative, hardworking industrialists and inventors that Henry

Ford believed to be the backbone of American industrial progress. They were perfect examples of the American work ethic that Ford wanted to showcase at Greenfield Village. As is the case with most of the buildings in Greenfield Village, the Wright brothers' home and bicycle shop evoke not only a sense of the Wrights' particular history, but also a more general sense of the period in which they lived.

## The Village Green

Another part of Greenfield Village that evokes the America of yesteryear is the Village Green and the buildings on or near it. As Henry Ford intended that Greenfield Village be a living example of village life from a bygone era, something would be missing if there were no village green, the hub of the village. Around the green are buildings that formed the very fabric of the American village of the past: a chapel, an inn, a general store, a town hall, a courthouse, and a school. The chapel is the Martha-Mary Chapel, which is still a functional, nondenominational church; the inn is the Eagle Tavern, built in the 1830's in Clinton, Michigan, to serve as a stopping point on the Detroit-Chicago road; the general store is a building that was originally erected in Waterford, Michigan, in 1854; the town hall is reminiscent of those of the early nineteenth century; the courthouse is the Logan County Courthouse (moved from Postville, Illinois), where Abraham Lincoln served as a lawyer in the 1840's; and the school is the Scotch Settlement School, built in Dearborn in 1861. In 1871, Henry Ford began attending this school, which was originally located only about a mile and a half from his home.

## The Henry Ford Museum

In 1928, construction began on the Henry Ford Museum itself. Here was the showcase of Henry Ford the collector, and what he put inside this museum reflects his perception of the genius of America's technological history and the uniqueness of its culture. On September 27, 1928, a cornerstone was dedicated. Thomas Edison thrust a spade that had belonged to the late Luther Burbank (the famed nineteenth century horticulturist, whose birthplace stands in Greenfield Village) into the wet cement of the cornerstone. Edison then put his footprints in the cement and inscribed his name

and the date. This action was meant to symbolize the unity between agriculture and industry, a major theme of the museum. Visitors today may see this stone, enclosed in glass, at the entrance to the museum.

The front section of the museum structure was meant to be a representation of the most American of buildings: Independence Hall in Philadelphia. Even the faults contained in Independence Hall are faithfully recreated in the front of the Henry Ford Museum. In this part of the museum, the American Decorative Arts Galleries are housed. These galleries display items that were used both decoratively and functionally on a daily basis by average Americans of the pre-Revolution era until the end of the nineteenth century. These items include furniture, ceramics, glass, pewter, silver, and textiles.

The rear section of the museum, its largest part, contains the eight-acre Mechanical Arts Hall. This section appears to have followed the functional style of architecture Ford used for his automobile plants. The style is probably no accident; Ford certainly could not have thought of a better way to illustrate a history of mechanized America, containing the tools and products of America's laborers, than by housing them in a space that itself would be representative of mechanized America. The Mechanical Arts Hall contains collections of agriculture, home arts and crafts, industrial machinery, steam and electric power, lighting, communication, and transportation. It is in this area of the museum that period automobiles, trains, airplanes, bicycles, and buggies are displayed. Here is housed even the huge factory generator from Ford Motor Company's famous Highland Park, Michigan, plant, the plant that was Ford's main Model T producer and harbinger of mass production techniques.

Uniting these two sections of the museum is the Street of Early American Shops. In this area are twenty-two examples of eighteenth and nineteenth century American shops and stores with their appropriate wares inside.

Thus the complex illustrates Henry Ford's grand idea of chronicling the U.S. place in the Industrial Revolution and of following the changes in the nation's daily life over its comparatively brief existence. The museum itself is vast, yet accessible. It is also certainly a bit intimidating. It is possible that Henry Ford himself may have thought this sense of the daunting to be appropriate, since it is not unlike the experience of early America itself.

**Opening of the Museum**

On October 21, 1929, Henry Ford was ready to open the doors of his "time machine." For a museum complex this important, Ford decided that no expense should be spared for the opening ceremonies, and that all effort should be made to commemorate the significance of the occasion. Ford drafted a guest list that included such notables as President and Mrs. Herbert Hoover, Thomas Edison, Orville Wright, Eve Curie, John D. Rockefeller, Jr., Will Rogers, Owen D. Young, and Charles M. Schwab. All of them attended and were treated to the first official Greenfield Village and Henry Ford Museum demonstration of living history.

Ford arranged for the Hoovers, the Edisons, and himself and his wife to be transported the last few miles to the dedication in a Civil War-era locomotive that was meant to be a duplicate of the train Edison had served on as a young newsboy in the 1860's. The train pulled up to the same depot where, in 1862, Edison was ejected from a train by a conductor who was not sympathetic to Edison's early scientific experiments. The young Edison had spilled phosphorous on the floor of the train, setting it on fire. Ford moved the train station from Smiths Creek, Michigan, to Greenfield Village, where it still stands today, in use as one of its depots on the Greenfield Village Railroad.

After an afternoon of riding in carriages along muddy streets for an inspection of the progress of the still incomplete museum and village, the guests gathered in the entrance galleries of the museum for a formal banquet. At first, the room the guests occupied was lit only by candles. Edison, however, in a reenactment of the event of fifty years earlier, would change all that. He was chauffeured back to the village by horse-drawn carriage to his old (but newly transplanted and restored) Menlo Park laboratory, where he lit the first electric lamp all over again. In the immediate presence of Hoover, Ford, and NBC radio newsman Graham McNamee, Edison threw the switch that dramatically lit the museum's crystal chandeliers and the houses that stood in the village. McNamee broadcast the event, and Greenfield Village and Henry Ford Museum were inaugurated.

Henry Ford's vision of Greenfield Village and Henry Ford Museum could not have been better realized. He dreamed of a place where one could walk about and see the way one's predecessors had lived, what they had accomplished, and what they stood for. Ford was not interested in documenting a history of the nation's leaders or privileged classes. Ford believed history needed to be viewed from the eyes of the common people. It was only through these eyes, Ford reasoned, that one could see how one's ancestors really lived. Ford is often remembered for stating that "history is bunk." He did say this, but his point is nearly always misconstrued. Ford believed that the "bunk" of history was in the study of wars, of dates, and of politicians; true history to him was the study of the daily lives of common people of bygone eras.

Greenfield Village and Henry Ford Museum wholly embrace this philosophy. There is little evidence at the complex of anything relating to diplomats, but there is certainly something about dairy farmers. Greenfield Village does contain many buildings associated with famous people, but most of those structures represent people who came from humble origins. The vast majority of the exhibits in both the village and museum are symbols of nameless, faceless America. In Ford's eyes, this was America.

Perhaps it is this egalitarianism that makes the Greenfield Village and Henry Ford Museum complex one of the quintessential American museums: It shows the nation's past as it really was and does it in a way that actually puts contemporary visitors there. There is no doubt that the land on which this complex stands has no real historical significance in itself; no battles were fought there, no treaties signed there. There is little doubt, however, that by the nature of what Greenfield Village and Henry Ford Museum are today, modern visitors gain precious insight into the historical significance of the America of yesterday. —*James C. Hart*

**For Further Information:**

Greenfield Village and Henry Ford Museum staff. *The Greenfield Village Guidebook.* Dearborn, Mich.: Edison Institute, 1977. The three books listed below offer very good cursory descriptions, with a somewhat touristy slant, of points of interest and their historical significance. All three books are illustrated.

Henry Ford Museum staff. *An American Invention: The Story of Henry Ford Museum and Greenfield Village.* Dearborn, Mich.: The Museum and Village, 1999. A guide to the museum and village.

_____. *Greenfield Village and Henry Ford Museum.* New York: Crown, 1978.

_____. *Greenfield Village: Preserving America's Heritage.* New York: Crown, 1972.

Wamsley, James S. *American Ingenuity.* New York: Harry N. Abrams, 1985. One of the better books describing both the history of the Edison Institute and the items in its museums. This book is handsomely illustrated and provides an excellent indicator of what the village and museum offer to visitors.

# Mackinac Island

**Date:** Declared a National Park in 1875

**Relevant issues:** American Indian history, business and industry, European settlement

**Significance:** Originally named Michilimackinac, the island was a pilgrimage and burial site sacred to the area's Sioux, Algonquin, and Iroquois inhabitants. In 1634, Frenchman Jean Nicolet became the first European to note the area. Over the next two hundred years, control of the site, and the fur trade centered there, passed repeatedly between France, England, and the United States. With the end of the fur trade in the area, Mackinac briefly became the center of the local fishing industry. In 1875, the island was declared the second National Park; twenty years later, it became a Michigan State Park.

**Location:** In the Straits of Mackinac, which joins Lakes Michigan and Huron and separates the upper and lower peninsulas of Michigan

**Site Office:**

Mackinac State Historic Parks Visitors' Center
P.O. Box 370
Mackinac Island, MI 49757-0370
summer ph.: (906) 847-3328
winter ph.: (231) 436-4100
Web site: www.mackinac.com/historicparks
e-mail: mackinacparks@state.mi.us

The history of the upper Great Lakes region, which in the early days of British and French exploration in North America was the northwestern part of the New World, is dominated by the waters. On the lakes, and on the rivers that flow into them, floated dreams of discovery, wealth, and conquest. They were highways for commerce and exploration, the pathways by which France and Great Britain brought their religion to the native tribes, furs to their channels of commerce, and their battles to each other.

**Early History**

Mackinac (pronounced "mackinaw") Island, a 3.5-square-mile, high-backed piece of land in the middle of the straits joining Lake Huron to Lake Michigan, was at the center of the waters' flow, on the path of Europe's hunt for a water route to China, and in the heart of the fur country that generated substantial interest and principal for the Europeans. As Sault Sainte Marie, fifty miles to the north, was the gateway from Lake Huron into Lake Superior, Mackinac controlled access to Lake Michigan and to exploration of the entire Mississippi River Valley.

The turtle-shaped island of Michilimackinac was a sacred meeting ground to the Native American tribes. Legend said it was there the great spirit, Gitchi-Manitou, made his home among his people. It became sacred to all the tribes, a place to bury their dead and to leave offerings that, if they pleased the spirits, would ensure their prosperity. Gitchi-Manitou, they said, left the island when the white man came, leaving his people under the care of smaller spirits, called Imakinaks.

The island's name has been translated in a variety of ways: as "Great Turtle," as "Place of Dancing Spirits," and as "Turtle Spirits." In any event, it and the region were referred to by the full name of Michilimackinac until after the British took over.

On the shores of the island camped the descendants of the Sioux, the Algonquin, and the Iroquois, the population mirroring the fortunes of the tribes as war and natural trials of famine and disease diminished one tribe's grounds and expanded another's.

The Asseguns, or Bone People, were one of the first to live on the island, having their tribal seat there before 1649. They were displaced by the Ojibwa, called Chippewa by the French, fiercest of the region's tribes. With the Ottawa and Potawatomi, the Chippewa were the remains of one tribe of Algonquin stock that had divided but maintained an alliance. They were driven from the east by the Iroquois, and in turn they pushed the Sioux west to what is now Minnesota and the Dakotas.

### First European Explorers

The first European to pass Michilimackinac came in 1634. Jean Nicolet, traveling at the behest of Governor Samuel de Champlain, had canoes heaped with gifts for the merchants of Cathay (China). Champlain, who had founded the first permanent French colony at Quebec in 1608, was convinced from tales told by the native tribes that the Chinese lived on the edge of a great sea to the west of Lake Huron. While that "sea" later turned out to be the Mississippi River Nicolet's trip was the first of several expeditions through the Straits of Mackinac to find a trade route to the Orient. Although Nicolet was aware of Michilimackinac from tribal legend, and, when passing the island, noted it and the obeisance of the tribesman who were rowing his canoes, he did not stop there. He crossed Lake Michigan to become the first European to meet the tribes of eastern Wisconsin and Illinois, extending French influence to the region.

The next European to reach the Straits of Mackinac, in 1669, was Father Claude-Jean Allouez, a Jesuit missionary. The Jesuits were in the forefront of French exploration and often made first contact with native tribes. They were pathfinders, explorers, mapmakers, recordkeepers, and reporters. For the French, the expansion of their commercial empire was by necessity tied to the expansion of Christianity. The Jesuits were responsible for the first French structures on the island: a cross and a bark chapel, named the Mission of St. Ignace (after St. Ignatius Loyola), which was erected by Father Claude Dablon in 1669.

### Father Jacques Marquette

Father Jacques Marquette, who came to Michilimackinac in 1671, arrived in North America in 1666 and went to Sault Sainte Marie. The next spring, Father Claude Dablon joined him. In 1669, Marquette replaced Allouez at La Pointe at the western end of Lake Superior when Allouez traveled into Lake Michigan to establish a mission at what is now Green Bay, Wisconsin.

At La Pointe, Marquette was given a captive Illinois tribesman by a sick Ottawa he had healed. From this tribesman, he learned of the Mississippi.

Thereafter, he wrote to his superior in Quebec of these new lands to explore and new tribal nations to convert. When the Sioux tribesman at La Pointe rejected his efforts to convert them and threatened war with the Ottawa and Huron who accompanied him, he and his supporters fled back across Lake Superior and he carried on to Michilimackinac. There, he lived for almost a year, conducting services in the chapel built by Dablon. After an isolated winter, Marquette moved to the north shore of the strait, where the Huron built a village, French traders raised cabins, and Marquette built a new mission church also named for St. Ignatius Loyola, from which the town took the name of St. Ignace.

### Louis Jolliet

On December 8, 1672, Louis Jolliet, Nicolet's nephew and an acquaintance of Marquette's from the Jesuit College at Quebec, arrived at St. Ignace with orders that Marquette join him for a voyage to the Mississippi. The following spring, they set off, eventually following the great river to points south of the Ohio. Two years later, on his way back to Michilimackinac along the eastern coast of Lake Michigan, he died. His companions buried him and went on to the island; the following year tribesmen from St. Ignace retrieved his bones. In June, 1677, he was buried under the chapel at St. Ignace.

In 1679, René-Robert Cavelier, Sieur de La Salle, arrived at St. Ignace aboard the *Griffin*, a two-masted cargo ship he had built to further his dreams of a trading empire. The ship, the first to sail Lakes Erie and Huron, arrived there on its maiden voyage, producing awe in the native tribes and anger among traders who disputed La Salle's right to do business there.

The *Griffin* was loaded with pelts collected the year before by voyageurs La Salle had commissioned. It was sent back to Niagara while La Salle and his men continued down Lake Michigan, where the ship was to meet them the following year. It was not until the *Griffin* failed to arrive at the Chicago River that La Salle would realize it had sunk in a storm shortly after setting sail.

By the 1680's, St. Ignace was the center of France's North American enterprise, a way station through which every traveler in the region eventually passed. Surrounding the Jesuit chapel were a

Huron village and the cabins of some fifty French traders and their native wives. An Ottawa camp and a second chapel overlooked the bay. The populace survived on fish, abundant in the straits. Each spring and fall, the beach was filled with the canoes of trappers, traders, and tribesmen from outlying places, and in the summer hundreds camped on the shore. Europe's culture had already changed that of the native, with cloth, iron, guns, and whiskey displacing skins, flint, spears, and self-sufficiency. Scattered villages were left vacant as the tribes clustered around the French stations, even as many of the traders adopted native customs.

### British Intrusion

By 1690 the straits had become a target for the British. Governor Louis de Buade, Comte de Palluau et Frontenac, decided to secure the French position there and sent Louis de la Porte, Sieur de Louvigny, there with one hundred fifty soldiers. Louvigny built Fort de Buade near the St. Ignace mission. Although he said it was to protect the mission and the traders, the military was there to impress the tribes with French might and to regulate the fur trade. The latter failed, as the soldiers themselves began to trade, exchanging garrison supplies for pelts and selling the pelts to unlicensed traders, who in turn sold them to British traders on Lake Superior for shipment to Hudson Bay.

In 1694, Antoine de La Mothe, Sieur de Cadillac, took over the military command, cleaning up the fort and enforcing order. Despite his efforts, however, illegal trade continued. To combat this and centralize fur traffic, France closed all its western posts two years later, revoked trading licenses, and encouraged the tribes to bring their furs to the St. Lawrence, where they had traded years earlier. Cadillac had urged this decision, proposing that a fort be built at Detroit to block English access to the northern region. In 1701, he built Fort Pontchartrain, which attracted Huron, Ottawa, and Potawatomi tribesmen from St. Ignace and Lower Michigan. St. Ignace shrank, and in 1706 the Jesuits withdrew, setting fire to their chapel so it could not be desecrated.

Though the first European settlement at Michilimackinac was no more, the straits continued its centuries-old role as a gathering place. A few French traders and small bands of Native Americans shifted their settlements to the south side, as the British sought to divert trade away from Detroit toward the north.

### French Fortifications

By 1713, the French decided to rebuild a fort at the straits, and in 1715 Constant Le Marchand de Lignery arrived with soldiers and workmen. At this fort, eventually called Old Mackinaw to distinguish it from Ancient Michilimackinac at St. Ignace, the tribes built their brush huts and the priests their chapels. By 1722, there were thirty French families inside the fort and thirty traders' families outside. A band of Chippewa had settled on Michilimackinac Island and came regularly to trade. Commerce and politics flowed through the fort as tribal wars erupted and England and France fought to control the New World.

By 1750, the British were striving to separate Canada from Louisiana. Crossing the Pennsylvania Mountains with packhorses, British traders established a shorter trade route, and one that did not freeze in the winter, and were able to charge less for rum and gunpowder.

At the same time, tribal violence increased with reports of traders being killed, French property being seized by Miami and Ouitenon tribes, and word of plots against French posts by the Shawnee and Miami.

French government incentives to settle in the West attracted few families and an expedition into Ohio by the Canadian-born French commander Pierre Joseph de Céloron de Blainville to win back the tribes was met by chiefs who accepted gifts but refused alliances. Céloron de Blainville found British traders firmly entrenched.

### Coming of the French and Indian War

Meanwhile, at Old Mackinaw, Charles de Langlade, who was born in a Michilimackinac trade house in 1729 to a French trader and the sister of an Ottawa chief and had been accompanying war parties since he was ten, had entered the French Army and devised a way to restore the allegiance of the Ohio tribes to France. In spring 1752, he took a dozen French soldiers and 250 Ottawa and Chippewa warriors, painted for war, to the south. In June, his troop reached Pickawillany, a Miami town whose chief, known to the British as Old Britain, had rejected Céloron de Blainville's overtures three years earlier. The Miami warriors were away

*Fort Mackinac.* (Mackinac State Historic Parks, Mackinac Island)

on a summer hunt. Langlade laid siege to the town and its stockade. After six hours, during which fourteen tribesmen including the chief were killed, he offered to leave if the English traders in the stockade were surrendered. The old men agreed and Langlade took five English prisoners to Quebec, while his raiders went back to Michilimackinac.

The next summer, France sponsored a general council at the Straits of Mackinac with tribes coming from the Canadian prairie, Illinois, and the Wabash. More than twelve hundred warriors gathered and pledged to support the French against the British.

In 1755, British forces, headed by General Edward Braddock, were marching on Fort Duquesne, at the present site of Pittsburgh, while Langlade was gathering Ottawa, Chippewa, and Huron tribesmen. Langlade and two hundred warriors paddled to Fort Duquesne, where they decided to ambush the British on the Monongahela River. They succeeded in routing a superior British force in what was the first battle of the French and Indian War, which paralleled the Seven Years' War in Europe. Langlade went on to command victorious troops in battles against the British over the next four years until the fall of Montreal.

The first Englishman to arrive at the straits after the surrender was Alexander Henry, a young man who had heard that Michilimackinac had the richest supply of furs in the world. Forewarned that he would be killed if the Indians there recognized him as British, he disguised himself. He settled next to Langlade's home and sought to stay secluded, but was betrayed and accosted first by the few French traders left there, and then by the Chippewa, who wanted his trade goods.

Late that summer of 1761, Henry and two other British traders who had arrived were threatened by a band of Ottawa warriors, who demanded to be paid immediately for furs to be delivered the next season. The traders asked for a day to think over the ultimatum and were pleasantly surprised the next morning to see the Ottawa leaving. By noon, British troops had arrived to take possession of the fort, which they formally did on October 1.

As the French and British fought for control of the continent, the Ottawa chief Pontiac saw an opportunity to draw together the Ottawa, Chippewa, and Potawatomi against the British, whose soldiers treated the tribes with contempt, whose traders swindled them, and whose settlers moved onto their lands. In 1763, Pontiac's plan was implemented. On May 10, thirteen of the fourteen forts across the territory were attacked by the Indians. Detroit alone did not fall that day but became the object of a bitter siege. Eventually, when the French support that Pontiac had expected failed to materialize, peace was restored.

At Michilimackinac, to which word of the plan had arrived late due to the long winter, the massacre came three weeks late, on June 2. When news of the victories arrived by drum, the tribes' warriors moved to the fort from the surrounding area. All day, warriors streamed into the trading houses, looking at jewelry and buying knives and hatchets. On the field near the fort, they played baggatiway, a game with webbed rackets and a deerhide ball. The British were toasting the king's birthday and the tribesmen joined in the celebration. Ultimately a ball was lobbed into the fort and the warriors raced to get it, grabbing weapons from their women on the way in and slaughtering the troops and the British traders as the French traders looked on.

Alexander Henry was one of the few to survive, saved by his relationship of brotherhood with the Chippewa chief Wawatam. After a winter in the wilderness with Wawatam and his band, Henry returned to Michilimackinac to find two French traders' houses surrounded by a scattering of Indian lodges. Still threatened, he headed west with a trading canoe to lead a long and adventurous life that he described in a book, published in 1809.

## The British Take Over

It was September, 1764, before the British returned to the straits. Captain William Howard and two companies of the Seventeenth Regiment received the keys to the fort from a trader as the Jesuit priest and a few Indians and traders watched. Over the following months, they rebuilt the fort. There would be ten commanders at the fort over the next thirty-five years, most prominent among them Major Robert Rogers, a hero of the French and Indian War. He took over the fort in 1766, at which time he was also named Superintendent of the Indians. Rogers planned to use the position as a springboard to his dream of claiming the standing twenty thousand-pound award posted by the British Admiralty for discovery of a water route across North America.

Unlike his predecessors, Rogers sought and won the goodwill of the native tribes. Under his orders, an older war veteran named Jonathan Carver set out to explore the Northwest and get to know its tribes, and invite them to a great council at the fort the next year. Rogers's great council brought together tribes from all directions. It included a peace council between the Sioux and Chippewa and trade councils to bind the tribes to Britain. In his comments afterward, Rogers pictured Michilimackinac as Britain's strategic outpost in America and proposed that it be made an independent province. In New York, General Thomas Gage heard reports of Rogers's extravagance and that he planned to establish an independent province, and ordered him relieved of his command and arrested for high treason. He was acquitted but not returned to duty, and eventually died in poverty in London in 1795. Carver, too, died in poverty in London, in 1780, after writing a book on his travels but before it became popular and the source of material to such writers as Vicomte Chateaubriand, Friedrich von Schiller, and William Cullen Bryant.

## The American Revolutionary War

In 1774, the British Parliament created the Province of Quebec, stretching from the Gulf of the St. Lawrence to the Ohio and the Mississippi Rivers. One of its western districts was to be governed from Michilimackinac and, on April 7, 1775, Patrick Sinclair was commissioned the lieutenant governor and superintendent of that district. Because of the American Revolution, it took him until 1779 to claim his post. Until he arrived, Major Arent Schuyler de Peyster commanded the fort, which had scant information about what was going on elsewhere in the country and was besieged by a general shortage of support of any kind. Fort life had been deteriorating since the arrest of Major Rogers. Requests to Quebec for help brought only the advice that the garrison should be self-sufficient.

Sinclair examined the rickety fort he had inherited and the surrounding countryside, and within four days he wrote Quebec pointing out Mackinac Island's natural defenses, fine harbor, and plentiful natural building materials and asking permission to move the fort there. While he awaited formal permission, he put his men to work preparing for the move. In the winter, he had the Church of Sainte Anne de Michilimackinac in the fort yard pulled down, its materials dragged over the frozen strait, and the building reassembled on the island.

Permission arrived in May, 1780, after the spring thaw. That summer, the traders moved their homes, salvaging such necessities as nails, doors, and windows, but it was not until the next year that Sinclair finished bargaining with the Chippewas for purchase of their traditional council and burial grounds at a cost of five thousand pounds. On July 15, 1781, the Eighth Regiment held the last parade at Old Mackinaw and transferred the colors to the island.

As work continued on the new fort, a rumor arose that some of the Chippewas were reconsidering the sale. Sinclair sent to Detroit for artillery. One of these field guns was fired as the ship carrying it entered the harbor. Its echoing report ended all threats.

Meanwhile, questions were developing in Quebec about the amount Sinclair was spending, and three officers were sent to examine his accounts. They found sloppy bookkeeping, and in September, 1782, he resigned. His successor, Captain Daniel Robertson, completed the fort, one of the strongest military sites in the country.

As part of the treaty ending the American Revolution, Fort Mackinac was ceded to the United States. Because of the fort's remote location and the political maneuvering to keep the lucrative fur trade in British hands, however, it was another thirteen years before the American flag flew over Mackinac Island.

**Problems with Indian Communities**

The Native Americans posed a further complication. Though they signed a treaty with the British, the Americans neglected to negotiate with the tribes, treating them as hired mercenaries rather than free agents. The tribes sought to protect their land and continued to fight a guerrilla war until 1794, when General Anthony Wayne won the Battle of Fallen Timbers in northwestern Ohio. As part of the treaty signed the following summer, the tribes ceded substantial lands in the Ohio country to the United States plus such strongholds as Chicago, Detroit, and the Mackinac Island area in exchange for a lump sum payment of twenty thousand dollars and the promise of eight thousand dollars a year in future payments.

The arrival of American troops in October, 1796, did not mark the final change of ownership for Mackinac. Before that change took place, the British, now at St. Joseph's Island in the lower St. Mary's River, made another contribution to the lore of the area. As winter 1811 fell, the inability of the season's final shipload of supplies to reach St. Joseph's left the troops without winter coats. The newly arrived commander, Captain Charles Roberts, went to storekeeper John Askin, requisitioned the pile of brightly colored blankets he had in stock, and had them made into the short, belted coats since known as Mackinaw coats.

**The War of 1812**

As the coats were being made, the Indians of the Wabash country were fighting U.S. troops at Tippecanoe Creek in the battle that unofficially started the War of 1812 and would lead, in July, 1812, to a British assault that would capture Mackinac Island.

To carry out his assignment to capture the island, Captain Roberts claimed the trading schooner *Caledonia*, gathered guns and supplies from the local traders, and recruited three hundred Chippewa, Menomini, Winnebago, and Sioux warriors. They set out on July 16 to cover the thirty-five miles to Mackinac.

Meanwhile at Mackinac, the small garrison toiled quietly, unaware that war had been declared. Concerned by the lack of news and rumors of tribesmen gathering at St. Joseph's, Lieutenant Porter Hanks decided to send Captain Michael Dousman to investigate. Dousman left on July 16, but his boat passed the *Caledonia* on its way to attack the fort and he was captured. He told the British of the weaknesses of the fort, and Roberts, fearing that he would be unable to control the three hundred tribesmen, let Dousman go ashore and warn the townspeople of the danger of massacre. Dousman gathered the townspeople in a stone-walled distillery, while the British landed on a sandy beach behind the fort and began positioning artillery above it. They were already in position by the time the U.S. troops were alerted and preparing to fight. When Lieutenant Hanks saw his position was untenable, he surrendered the fort and its guns, which had been captured from the British at Yorktown in the final battle of the American Revolution.

After the peaceful capture, troops and citizens who would not pledge allegiance to the British were sent to Detroit, those who shifted allegiance remained on the island with life little changed by the new command.

**The Fall of Mackinac**

The fall of Mackinac, with its mythical significance

for the tribes, encouraged them to ally with the British. The Potawatomi attacked Fort Dearborn, at the site of present-day Chicago, massacring its departing residents. Shawnee Chief Tecumseh, with British support, captured Detroit. The following year, with the victory on Lake Erie of U.S. Commodore Oliver Hazard Perry, the tide of the war turned. Tecumseh and the British retreated toward Canada but were caught at the Thames River by General William Henry Harrison, who quickly and decisively defeated them.

Harrison returned to Detroit and embarked for Mackinac, but was turned back by the approaching winter. The winter was harsh at the island, where the troops were building Fort George, a rugged blockhouse to command the entire island on the heights above Fort Mackinac. In the spring, a relief fleet arrived from the British officials on the St. Lawrence, who knew that control of the island meant control of the northern tribes and the northwestern fur trade. In late July, an American fleet from the east arrived at Mackinac.

On July 28, the American ships fired on Fort Mackinac, but they could not tilt their shots high enough and the shells fell harmlessly. Fog set in and the American ships backed off. A week later, they landed at the same spot where the British had landed two years earlier, but had to retreat under heavy fire. Among the dead was Major Andrew Hunter Holmes, for whom Fort George would be renamed after the war.

The battle over Mackinac continued, with subterfuge and fighting, until the British prevailed in mid-August. They still held the straits when the Treaty of Ghent, signed December 24, 1814, ended the war and restored the international boundaries established after the American Revolution. U.S. troops again, and finally, reclaimed Mackinac Island on July 18, 1815.

**Postwar Prosperity**

With the war over, the United States for the first time controlled the area's fur trade. For the next two decades, Mackinac was the northern capital of John Jacob Astor's American Fur Company and the heart of the American fur trade, as it had been the center of the French and British trade and the headquarters for the North West Fur Company, the Mackinac Company, and the South West Fur Company. Astor, a young German immigrant, had

first come to the straits area in 1788 with the help of Alexander Henry, who was then living in Montreal. After his visit to the British posts, he established himself in New York as a fur merchant. In 1808, he founded the American Fur Company to compete with the British merchants. Eight years later, after Congress passed legislation making trade with the Indians the exclusive right of American citizens, he began sending traders throughout the region. By the mid-1820's, he had co-opted all the independent traders in the area and monopolized the fur trade.

Mackinac was now a boomtown, bustling with traders. Missionary fervor also returned to the region. The Mission Church, the oldest Protestant church in the Northwest, was built in 1829, causing consternation among the Catholics and setting the stage for the sects to contend for the souls of the islanders.

The local tribes, meanwhile, had become destitute and dependent on the settlers. Henry Rowe Schoolcraft, geologist, scholar, and Indian agent based in Sault Sainte Marie and Mackinac from 1822 to 1841, dispensed the government's largesse. In 1836, he helped arrange a conference in Washington, D.C., at which tribal leaders agreed to cede substantial lands in Wisconsin and the upper and lower peninsulas of Michigan. In return for nearly twenty million acres, they received two million dollars and perpetual annuities from the government, which also agreed to support schools, shops, and model farms in their villages. The treaty also called for a dormitory to be built on Mackinac Island, where the chiefs could stay when they received the annual support. The first annual disbursement was made in 1836 and continued there for years. In 1841, Schoolcraft moved his family to New York, and in 1845 the Indian Agency was moved to the Apostle Islands in Lake Superior. Schoolcraft's writings provided the inspiration for Henry Wadsworth Longfellow's epic *The Song of Hiawatha* (1855).

With the decline of the fur trade, the economy of the island turned to fishing, which had a short boom period. At the same time, Mackinac Island, which had become a popular resort by 1838, developed as a popular tourist destination. In 1875, Congress reserved the island as the nation's second National Park, and in 1895, the National Park, and the fort, reverted to the state of Michigan.

**Modern Preservation Efforts**

Today, the island is predominantly a tourist destination. Approximately 80 percent of the island is occupied by the Mackinac Island State Park, within which are located the fourteen original buildings of Fort Mackinac (the oldest dates to 1780). The rest of the island is the province of some 550 year-round residents. Automobiles are banned from the island under laws first passed in 1896. The Mackinac State Historic Park also includes two sites on the mainland: Colonial Michilimackinac, located in Mackinaw City, and Historic Mill Creek, an excavated sawmill town from the late eighteenth and early nineteenth centuries, located three miles southeast of Mackinaw City.

—*Richard Greb*

**For Further Information:**

Armour, David A. *One Hundred Years at Mackinac: A Centennial History of the Mackinac Island State Park Commission, 1895-1995.* Mackinac Island, Mich.: Mackinac State Historic Parks, 1995. A history of Mackinac Island and the park. Illustrated with new and old photographs.

Havighurst, Walter. *Three Flags at the Straits: The Forts of Mackinac.* Englewood Cliffs, N.J.: Prentice-Hall, 1966. Takes a detailed look at the flow of events through the Straits of Mackinac, with particular emphasis on the personalities involved and their involvement in westward exploration and the changing balance of power between France, England, and the United States.

Piljac, Pamela A., and Thomas M. Piljac. *Mackinac Island: Historic Frontier, Vacation Resort, Timeless Wonderland.* Portage, Ind.: Bryce-Waterton, 1989. In addition to providing information on current sites, places additional emphasis on the Native American tribes and includes period vignettes of life in the area at various points in its history.

# Other Historic Sites

## Bay View

*Location:* Northeast of Petoskey on U.S. 31, Emmet County

*Relevant issues:* Cultural history, education, religion

*Web site:* www.sos.state.mi.us/history/preserve/phissite/bayview.htm

*Statement of significance:* This site is one of the finest remaining examples of two uniquely American community forms, the Methodist Camp Meeting and the independent Chautauqua. Designed for the first purpose in 1876 as the country's only romantically planned campground, and adapted for the second from 1885 to 1915, Bay View is a major monument of American religious, cultural, social, and educational ideals embodied in an artistically shaped community plan with 437 contributing buildings.

## Cranbrook

*Location:* Bloomfield Hills, Oakland County

*Relevant issues:* Education, social reform

*Web site:* www.sos.state.mi.us/history/preserve/phissite/cranbroo.html

*Statement of significance:* Cranbrook is one of the most important groups of educational and architectural structures in America, a summary of the first half of the twentieth century in the form of a group of buildings. This enclave in Bloomfield Hills, 25 miles from Detroit, was one of the idealist institutions meant to combat shoddy machine-age goods—from the making of beautiful objects to the creation of an architectural setting with details of the finest quality.

## Dow House and Studio

*Location:* 315 Post Street, Midland, Midland County

*Relevant issues:* Art and architecture

*Web site:* www.sos.state.mi.us/history/preserve/phissite/dowalden.html

*Statement of significance:* The architecture of Alden B. Dow (1904-1983) received national attention from his very early career through to his late period, partly because he was closely associated with Frank Lloyd Wright. The body of his work is of rare quality and completeness and remains highly original among the contending forces of twentieth century architecture. The house and studio form his most clearly acknowledged masterpiece.

## Durant-Dort Carriage Company Office

*Location:* Flint, Genesee County
*Relevant issues:* Business and industry
*Web site:* www.sos.state.mi.us/history/preserve/phissite/durantdo.html
*Statement of significance:* From 1895 to 1913, this site served as focal point for the promotional activities of William C. Durant (1861-1947) in both the carriage and the automobile businesses. The Durant-Dort Company played a significant role in financing not only Buick but also General Motors, which he had founded in 1908. His contributions, such as the concept of a large company manufacturing several makes of automobiles, greatly influenced the automobile industry.

## Fair Lane

*Location:* Dearborn, Wayne County
*Relevant issues:* Business and industry
*Web site:* www.sos.state.mi.us/history/preserve/phissite/fairlane.html
*Statement of significance:* Henry Ford (1863-1947) revolutionized American transportation by mass-producing an inexpensive car. The Ford family occupied this fifty-six-room house from 1915 until 1950, three years after Henry's death.

## Fisher Building

*Location:* 3011 West Grand Boulevard, Detroit, Wayne County
*Relevant issues:* Art and architecture
*Web site:* www.sos.state.mi.us/history/preserve/phissite/fisher.html
*Statement of significance:* The Fisher Building (1927) contains some of the most beautiful detailing of any American skyscraper ever built. The Fisher brothers, part of the burgeoning automobile industry in Detroit, intended the building to be a public monument as well as a gift to a more beautiful Detroit. The architect, Albert Kahn, had a national reputation for his industrial buildings but was known in Detroit as well for his commercial, civic, and domestic structures, and this skyscraper is one of his greatest achievements.

## Hemingway Cottage (Windemere)

*Location:* Walloon Lake, Emmet County
*Relevant issues:* Literary history
*Web site:* www.sos.state.mi.us/history/preserve/phissite/hemingwa.html
*Statement of significance:* Ernest Hemingway (1899-1961) spent his boyhood summers from 1904 to 1921 in this one-story frame structure. He began his writing career here, using the setting and his boyhood experiences in some of his stories.

## Highland Park Ford Plant

*Location:* Highland Park, Wayne County
*Relevant issues:* Business and industry
*Web site:* www.sos.state.mi.us/history/preserve/phissite/highland.html
*Statement of significance:* Designed mostly by noted industrial architect Albert Kahn, this plant is considered the birthplace of the moving assembly line. It was in operation from 1910 to 1927.

## Lightship No. 103 "Huron"

*Location:* Port Huron, St. Clair County
*Relevant issues:* Naval history
*Web site:* www.sos.state.mi.us/history/preserve/phissite/huron.html
*Statement of significance:* The 1920 Lightship No. 103, also known by its last official designation, *Huron,* is the only surviving example of a lightship type specifically built for service on the Great Lakes. Lightships were vital partners of Great Lakes shipping, particularly where shoals and reefs far from land could not be safely marked by lighthouses. The Lake Huron station was at the south end of the lake at the entrance to the St. Clair River, on the primary trade route of the Great Lakes. The last lightship to serve on the Great Lakes, No. 103 is now an outdoor exhibit.

## Norton Mound Group

*Location:* Grand Rapids, Kent County
*Relevant issues:* American Indian history
*Web site:* www.sos.state.mi.us/history/preserve/phissite/norton.html
*Statement of significance:* This site contains well-preserved Hopewell mounds of the western Great Lakes region. Norton Mound Group was the center of Hopewellian culture in that area, c. 400 B.C.E. to 400 C.E.

## Pewabic Pottery

*Location:* Detroit, Wayne County

*Relevant issues:* Art and architecture

*Web site:* www.sos.state.mi.us/history/preserve/
phissite/pewabic.html

*Statement of significance:* Founded in 1903 by Mary Chase Perry Stratton, Pewabic Pottery gained national recognition for iridescent glazes as well as their production of architectural tile. An artist of the Arts and Crafts movement, Stratton was concerned with raising the artistic standard of American ceramicists. Her tile installations are in private homes, schools, and churches, as well as in the Detroit Institute of Arts, the Ford Factory in Oklahoma, the Cranbrook Academy of Art, and the Immaculate Conception Cathedral (in Washington, D.C.); her pottery is the only American work displayed in the Smithsonian Institution's Freer Gallery of Art. This building, designed by William Stratton, has been the home of Pewabic Pottery since 1907.

## Quincy Mining Company Historic District

*Location:* Hancock, Houghton County

*Relevant issues:* Business and industry

*Web site:* www.sos.state.mi.us/history/preserve/
phissite/quincy.html

*Statement of significance:* Quincy Mining Company is an outstanding example of the growth and development of the United States copper industry from its earliest years through 1920. Between 1862 and 1882, Quincy ranked first nationally in copper production, making a singular contribution to the Northern effort during the Civil War. Quincy, along with the Calumet and Hecla Mining Company, represents the major elements of the copper industry: mining and mining technology, immigration and ethnic settlement, corporate paternalism and company towns, and labor organization.

# Minnesota

*Minneapolis.* (PhotoDisc)

# History of Minnesota

Reaching farther north than any other state except Alaska, Minnesota was settled more slowly than other states in the center of the United States, which were more accessible to heavily populated eastern states. Despite its isolation, the fertile soils of the south and west, the pine forests of the northeast, and the hardwood forests between these regions eventually attracted settlers. The state's access to Lake Superior, numerous rivers, and countless lakes also brought economic growth to the area. Much of Minnesota remains rural, in sharp contrast to the Twin Cities of Minneapolis and St. Paul near the eastern edge of the state.

## Early History

The earliest people to inhabit the area, known as the Paleo-Indian culture, hunted bison and other large animals more than ten thousand years ago. About seven thousand years ago, the people of the Eastern Archaic culture hunted small and large animals and made tools from copper. The Woodland culture, starting about three thousand years ago, introduced the use of pottery and burial mounds. Starting about one thousand years ago, the Mississippian culture built large, permanent villages located in fertile river valleys and raised corn, beans, and squash.

Both the Woodland culture and Mississippian culture lifestyles lasted until Europeans arrived about three hundred years ago. Until the middle of the nineteenth century, Minnesota was primarily inhabited by the Ojibwa in the north and east and the Dakota in the south and west. Conflicts between these peoples led to the Ojibwa forcing the Dakota to move further southwest in the middle of the eighteenth century.

## Exploration and Settlement

The first European explorers to reach the area were the French fur traders Pierre Esprit Radisson and Médard Chouart, Sieur des Groseilliers, who traveled from Canada through Wisconsin and into eastern Minnesota in 1658. In September of 1679, Daniel Greysolon, Sieur Dulhut, met with Native Americans near Mille Lacs Lake near the center of the region. As a result of this meeting, peaceful relations were established among the French, the Ojibwa, and the Dakota. Dulhut also claimed the area for King Louis XIV of France.

In January of 1680, the French missionary Louis Hennepin began a journey north along the Mississippi River into eastern Minnesota. In April, Hennepin was captured by the Dakota. During his captivity, Hennepin named a waterfall on the Mississippi River the Falls of St. Anthony, near the future site of the Twin Cities. Hennepin was rescued by Dulhut in July.

In 1682 the French explorer René-Robert Cavelier, Sieur de La Salle, claimed the entire valley of the Mississippi River for France. He named this vast area, including western Minnesota, Louisiana. Meanwhile, French fur traders had established the first permanent European settlement in the region in the far north, at Grand Portage. Grand Portage soon became the center of the prosperous fur trade. Among the many noted French explorers who established settlements in the area were Nicolas Perrot, who founded Fort Antoine in 1686, and Pierre Gaultier de Varennes, Sieur de La Vérendrye, who founded Fort Saint Charles in 1731.

## The British and Americans

The wealth generated by the fur trade was part of the struggle for control of North America between France and England that led to the French and Indian War (1754-1763). The British took control of Minnesota east of the Mississippi River after the war. Western Minnesota, with the rest of Louisiana, had been ceded to Spain in 1762 but was returned to France in 1800.

Spain did little to settle the area, but England quickly established the North West Company at Grand Portage to take advantage of the lucrative fur trade. At the end of the American Revolution (1775-1783), eastern Minnesota officially became part of the United States. The North West Company did not leave Grand Portage until 1803, when it moved to Canada. It was replaced by the American Fur Company, established in 1808.

Minnesota. In 1819 Fort Saint Anthony was established as the first permanent American settlement in the area. The site was renamed Fort Snelling in 1825 and went on to become the most important settlement in the area until the middle of the century.

The fur trade began to decline in 1837, with the first in a series of treaties with the Dakota and Ojibwa Indians that ceded large amounts of land to the United States. This encouraged settlers to enter the region and eventually made the lumber industry and agriculture more important than the fur trade.

The Minnesota Territory had about four thousand settlers in 1849, mostly near Fort Snelling. Most of these early settlers were from New England, although many had entered Minnesota from Canada. Within one year, the population jumped to more than six thousand. As the lumber industry grew more important, the population grew even more quickly. By 1857 the number of Minnesota residents, mostly from eastern states, reached more than 150,000.

The majority of new residents settled in the southeast part of the territory, near Fort Snelling. In the same area, St. Paul was founded in 1838 and became the territory capital in 1849. The nearby city of Minneapolis was founded in 1855. Minnesota became the thirty-second state, with much of its western lands removed and added to the Nebraska Territory, in 1858.

Eastern Minnesota became part of the newly created Northwest Territory in 1787. It became part of several different territories as the vast Northwest Territory was reorganized in the early nineteenth century. Between 1800 and 1858, it was part of Indiana Territory, Illinois Territory, Michigan Territory, Wisconsin Territory, and Minnesota Territory.

Meanwhile, the United States purchased Louisiana, including western Minnesota, from France in 1803. From 1834 to 1849, eastern Minnesota was part of Michigan Territory, Wisconsin Territory, the Iowa Territory, again Wisconsin Territory, and Minnesota Territory.

### Becoming a State

During this time, Minnesota remained a sparsely populated area isolated from the rest of the United States. In 1805, a military expedition led by Zebulon Pike failed to locate the source of the Mississippi but did manage to secure lands along a river from the Dakota Indians. In 1818 a treaty with England added a large area of land to northern

### Wars and Industry

Minnesota was the first state to send volunteers to fight for the Union during the Civil War. More than twenty thousand residents of the state served in the war. Meanwhile, Minnesota faced its own violent conflict. In 1862 a rebellion by the Dakotas, confined to reservations within the state, eventually led to more than five hundred deaths within a few weeks. The defeated Dakotas were forced into reservations in western territories. The Ojibwas remained on reservations created for them in the north of the state.

After the Civil War, growth continued at a rapid pace. Germans, Swedes, and Norwegians arrived in large numbers. Other important sources of new immigrants were Finland, Poland, Bohemia, Ireland, France, Canada, the Netherlands, Belgium, Iceland, Denmark, Wales, and Switzerland. During the 1880's, the period of the state's fastest growth, most settlers were homesteaders in western Minnesota or worked in the lumber industry. Flour milling was also a major industry in the Twin Cities, both of which tripled in population during this decade. Mining of iron ore began in 1884 and soon became a major source of income.

### The Twentieth Century

Immigration during the early twentieth century was mostly to the Twin Cities and included Finns, Italians, Slovakians, Croatians, Serbs, Greeks, Jews, Ukranians, Russians, and Hispanics. African Americans from southern states moved to the Twin Cities also. In later years, Asians also immigrated.

Throughout the twentieth century Minnesota tended to be politically independent. It supported traditionally a wide variety of small political parties that influenced the policies of the major parties. The modern Democratic Party in Minnesota incorporates many of the ideas of the Farmer-Labor Party, while the modern Republican Party in the state is influenced by independents.

Loss of natural resources led to changes in the state's economy during the twentieth century. Much of the most valuable lumber was cut by 1920, forcing the industry to turn to other trees. At about the same time, flour milling was moved from Minneapolis to Buffalo. The best iron ore was depleted by the late 1950's. New techniques for using lower-grade iron ore led to a revitalization of the industry in the 1960's, but low-cost imports led to another decline in the 1980's. Despite a decline in agriculture after World War II, agriculture was still the state's largest industry.

The early 1980's brought a drop in crop prices, bringing hardship to farmers throughout the state. However, the nationwide recession of the late 1980's had only a minimal effect on Minnesota. In the 1990's, the state's economy turned to industries such as printing, health care, scientific instruments, chemicals, and recreational equipment.

*—Rose Secrest*

# Fort Snelling

**Date:** Founded in 1819

**Relevant issues:** African American history, legal history, military history, western expansion, World War II

**Significance:** Fort Snelling has never been in harm's way. Its military importance has competed against its scenic location and its historical value. The fort symbolizes both the independence of the state's citizens and their respect and regard for the past.

**Location:** At the confluence of the Mississippi and Minnesota Rivers

**Site Office:**
Fort Snelling History Center
St. Paul, MN 55111
ph.: (612) 726-1171
Web site: www.mhs.org/places/sites/hfs

The site that would become Fort Snelling at the joining of the Mississippi and Minnesota Rivers was a piece of the Louisiana Purchase of 1803 acquired from France. Less than two years later, Lieutenant Zebulon Pike recommended the construction of a fort at the same location. He purchased 100,000 acres of land valued at $200,000 from the Sioux for sixty gallons of whiskey and a few presents worth approximately $200. However, it was not until 1818 that Secretary of War John C. Calhoun decreed that an army fort would be built on the site to contain British threats, pacify the Indians, provide an assembly point for the fur trade, and assure security for a large number of anticipated settlers.

Following recommendations made earlier by Meriwether Lewis and William Clark, Lieutenant Colonel Henry Leavenworth, along with ninety-eight men, their families, and twenty boatmen, arrived in August, 1819, on the south shore of the St. Peters River in Minnesota. Temporary quarters, including a makeshift fort, were built, but severe weather and lack of provisions caused thirty deaths by the following spring. Attempting to improve the location of his campsite, Leavenworth moved to a spring on high ground along the west bank of the Mississippi River. After obtaining a transfer to a more temperate climate in Florida, Leavenworth was replaced by Colonel Josiah Snelling in August, 1820.

### Building the Fort

The construction of a new fort under Snelling's guidance went beyond its original purpose. Few if any frontier forts were as grand as Snelling's creation. It implied permanence. Yet, the duties performed by soldiers stationed there were more similar to those of a police force than a military unit, even though the sheer presence of the fort alone was undoubtedly a strong and obvious symbol of national authority. At first named Fort St. Anthony, it became Fort Snelling in 1827, two years after its completion, as a tribute to Snelling's efforts.

To help overcome the isolation of the fort during the winter, there were dances, theater performances, band concerts, and dinners for some, as well as card-playing for many. A library of four hundred books was established. Marksmanship contests, hunting, and fishing, and skating and sleigh rides in the winter were also popular.

Poor health resulted in a number of personal problems for Snelling. To supposedly cure his ailment, he consumed a combination of opium and brandy. Having allowed dueling at the fort, he announced to his now numerous enemies during his last year that he was willing to duel anyone who challenged him. Duels did take place, as well as allegations of embezzlement against him. Snelling left Fort Snelling in October, 1827, and died the following summer.

During the next three decades ending in 1860, Fort Snelling's military importance diminished. Yet its reputation as a breathtakingly beautiful site grew. It was a popular choice of tourists visiting Minnesota by steamboat up the Mississippi River.

The fort also played an important role in one of the events leading up to the Civil War. In 1836, Dred Scott, a black slave, arrived at the fort with his owner, Dr. John Emerson, recently appointed post surgeon. Ten years later, Scott sued for his freedom, claiming that his residence at Fort Snelling and earlier in Illinois, both of which prohibited slavery, made him a free man. The case was finally decided against Scott in 1857 by the United States Supreme Court. It aroused strong resentment in the North and became an important step toward the Civil War.

When the Minnesota Territory was formed in 1849, many administrative functions carried on at the fort were moved elsewhere by the territorial government. Fort Snelling's decline also included the sale of forty thousand acres to the fort's sutler, Franklin Steele, and Eastern investors in 1858 for ninety thousand dollars, although only one payment of thirty thousand dollars was ever made. Fort Snelling was now in the hands of the Franklin Steele clique. However, a nationwide financial panic ended his plan for selling lots in his proposed city of Fort Snelling.

### The Civil War to the End of the Twentieth Century

The onset of the Civil War, however, had restored the fort's military heritage. It became the mustering and training center for Minnesota troops during the Civil War and the Sioux Uprising. Facilities were expanded so that as many as two thousand men could be accommodated at one time.

Although Steele's investment in the fort had not been paid in full, he claimed that the federal government owed him $162,000 in rent for its use during the Civil War. The contentious issue over ownership of Fort Snelling was finally resolved in 1871, when it was agreed that the government owned fifteen hundred acres contiguous to the fort, and Steele would have title to the remaining sixty-four hundred acres. No money was included in the transaction.

For a time during the post-World War I era, the fort gained the reputation of being the army's country club. Although a summer program, the Citizens' Military Training Camp, required arduous physical and mental participation, there were also horse shows, concerts, athletic contests, and polo matches, as well as facilities including a golf course, tennis courts, a swimming pool, and a hunting club.

The good times ended, however, when World War II broke out in both Europe and Asia. Draftees were processed and examined at Fort Snelling and then sent elsewhere to training camps at a rate of up to 450 men daily. Also, more than six thousand Japanese Americans attended a language and intelligence school at the fort and at nearby Camp Savage.

Although reserve units would remain, Fort Snelling was closed as a regular army post on October 14, 1946. During the late 1950's, the Minnesota Historical Society determined that it was possible to rebuild the fort, thereby promoting a successful effort three years later declaring Fort Snelling Minnesota's first National Historic Landmark. One year later, the state legislature established a 2,500-acre Fort Snelling State Park, and in addition, acquired another vital 320 acres. A major restoration effort took place during the 1970's and early 1980's at a cost in excess of five million dollars.

During the late 1990's and the beginning of the twenty-first century, proposals for a variety of uses of Fort Snelling were under review. They included a Native American charter school for the arts, a liberal arts preparatory academy, and a boarding school for troubled grade school and high school students. A hostel for visitors coming from out-of-state communities was under consideration, as well.

Fort Snelling has survived, and often thrived, on the many changes that it has experienced. It has been most successful in connecting the military with the aesthetic and the historical.

—*John Quinn Imholte*

**For Further Information:**

Hall, Steve. *Fort Snelling: Colossus of the Wilderness.* St. Paul: Minnesota Historical Society Press, 1987. An excellent, well-presented, brief (forty-four pages) account of Fort Snelling.

Luecke, Barbara, and John Luecke. *Snelling: Minnesota's First First Family.* Eagan, Minn.: Grenadier, 1993. A detailed account of Josiah Snelling and his wife, Abigail (Hunt) Snelling.

Ziebarth, Marilyn, and Alan Ominsky. *Fort Snelling: Anchor Post of the Northwest.* St. Paul: Minnesota Historical Society, 1970. A thirty-five-page work in the Minnesota Historical Sites pamphlet series.

# Grand Portage

**Date:** Founded by the French in 1722; named a National Historic Site in 1951 and a National Monument in 1958

**Relevant issues:** American Indian history, business and industry, western expansion

**Significance:** The strategic location of this town was particularly important in the fur trading business from about 1770 to 1790. Today, the site consists of a reconstructed stockade at Grand Portage Bay, as well as reconstituted eight-and-a-half-mile Grand Portage Trail, available for hiking. A reconstructed Ojibwa village is also on this site.

**Location:** Northwest end of Lake Superior (Stockade and Great Hall); Grand Portage Route runs northwest from this point, intersecting U.S. Route 61, until it reaches the site of the former Fort Charlotte at the U.S.-Canadian border

**Site Office:**

Grand Portage National Monument
P.O. Box 668
315 South Broadway
Grand Marais, MN 55604
ph.: (218) 387-2788
fax: (218) 387-2790
Web site: www.nps.gov/grpa/

The Grand Portage area was an important center of commerce from about 1770 to 1800. Christened Grand Portage by the French in 1722, this eight-and-a-half-mile land trail bypassed the unnavigable lower Pigeon River and provided the way for trappers (mostly Native Americans) from the West to get their furs to Eastern and European markets. In the 1770's, it became the headquarters of the North West Company. From here it controlled a fur-trading empire that stretched from the Atlantic to the Pacific. Due to the harsh terrain and the abandonment of the Grand Portage area by the fur traders in the early nineteenth century, no original structures remain. Reconstructions erected since the late 1930's include the Great Hall (where huge banquets were held for those important in the fur trade), a voyageur encampment (voyageurs were those who went west and traded with the natives for furs), and an Ojibwa village.

## Early History

The Grand Portage area had been a crossroads of many cultures even before the arrival of Europeans. In the seventeenth century, the area was claimed by both the Cree and Dakota tribes, who traded actively with each other as well as with tribes such as the Ottawa and Huron, from adjacent areas. Also present were the Ojibwa, although they

*A replica of the fur trading post at Grand Portage.* (Minnesota Office of Tourism)

did not become dominant until many years later. According to Ojibwa legend, the oldest inhabitants of this area were the Maymaygwaysiwuk, small, elusive people who lived underwater and traveled in stone canoes. The Indians left rocks along the banks of Lake Superior as offerings to these creatures.

The Great Lakes provided a superb route to the interior of the North American continent. The main water route west of Lake Superior was the Pigeon River, which leads all the way to Lake Winnipeg. This river and the lakes adjacent to it are all navigable except for a single eight-and-a-half-mile area just west of Lake Superior. Here the Indians carved out a land path they called Kitchi Onigaming, translated by the French as "Grand Portage." Grand Portage was the farthest point west that goods could be delivered by boat from the east, so it became a center of commerce in the important fur trade. The westerners (mostly Indians, along with the Europeans who traded with them) would come to the Grand Portage area every summer and exchange their furs for the goods they needed to sustain themselves through another hard winter.

**First European Explorers**

By the time the first Europeans, the French, arrived in the area, the fur trade was already booming. The French had firmly entrenched themselves in this trade by the late seventeenth century. The French developed a mutually beneficial relationship with the natives and adapted well to Indian social and business customs such as gift giving and pipe smoking. This was a major reason why the Indians chose to fight with the French during the French and Indian War, instead of the British, who were much less interested in adapting their ways to those of the natives. Although Grand Portage became British property at the end of the war in 1763, many French remained to become an integral part of the fur trade under the British.

It was not until the British takeover that Grand Portage achieved the central role for which it is celebrated today. The fur trade continued to grow and, in 1765, the North West Company was founded by British and Scottish businessmen. It dominated the fur trade in the area until the early nineteenth century. The North West Company constructed a stockade at the Lake Superior end of the Grand Portage Trail in 1768, and other buildings soon followed. The most memorable and important of these was the Great Hall, where feasts and gatherings were held when the eastern and western traders met each summer.

## Trade Entrepot

The separate and distinct groups that gathered each summer included Ojibwa traders; the "northmen," those who transported the furs in their canoes from the north and west to Grand Portage; the "pork eaters," who brought the goods for trade from Montreal; the "voyageurs," who carried the goods of the fur trade in boats or on their backs. This last group in particular was romanticized by various nineteenth century writers. Also present at this gathering were the clerks, those who did the menial tasks of counting the furs and sorting them for shipment to the east. These men were quite young and toiled in this difficult area in hopes of getting shares in the company. Those in charge of the gatherings were the owners of the North West Company, who associated only with the clerks and the Ojibwa traders.

The entire trade process took at least a year and sometimes more. Each spring, the goods from Europe and the eastern provinces had to be ready for shipping to Grand Portage. These included food, clothing, cooking implements, and various other goods for the whites and the Indians. When these goods arrived in time for the summer convention, the furs collected over the previous year had to be cleaned and packaged and ready to be shipped east. The voyageurs carried the goods in and out in ninety pound bales, and the outgoing goods were then put in large canoes for delivery to larger ships for eastern shipment. All these bales had to be watertight, as the canoes had to travel over the extremely treacherous Ottawa River.

The company would not be paid for the furs until they were received in Europe, nearly a year after they arrived at Grand Portage. The northmen and

the other workers were, likewise, paid once a year, though they could draw goods and money at the company store against their future wages. (The store always made at least 50 percent profit on the goods it sold.) This arrangement left many of these men in constant debt to the company, a situation that tended to cause discontent.

The northmen and the Ojibwa obtained all of the furs, so it was upon their efforts that the trade was totally dependent. As might be expected, these two groups intermingled over time, and many of the white northmen married Ojibwa women and lived out their days as part of the Indian culture. This intermarriage was also beneficial to their business with the Indians. Because these northmen were totally isolated from the European world for eleven months of the year, their relationship with the natives was even more vital.

## The Revolutionary War

Grand Portage was considered of sufficient importance by the British for them to send an officer and twelve men to guard it during the Revolutionary War. However, these soldiers spent most of their time dealing with labor problems, as the northmen, pork eaters, and voyageurs began to realize that the company was getting wealthy at their expense, while they often ended the year in debt.

In the mid-1770's, a North West Company trader named John Macdonell wrote this description of the Grand Portage trading post:

All the [sixteen] buildings within the fort are . . . made with cedar and white spruce fir split with whip saws after being squared, the roofs are covered with shingles of cedar and pine, most of their posts, doors, and windows are painted with Spanish brown. Six of these buildings are storehouses for the company's merchandise, furs, etc. The rest are dwelling houses, shops, counting houses and mess house. They also have a wharf for loading and unloading.

This same writer gave a brief description of life at Grand Portage during the annual meeting: "[The] Northmen while here live in tents of different sizes pitched at random . . . [this camp is separated from] that of the pork eaters by a brook."

The American Revolution increased traffic at Grand Portage, as the rest of the Great Lakes area was embroiled in war. The British military quickly began taxing and tightly controlling all private trade in the Great Lakes area, requiring, for instance, that all goods be carried on military ships. As a result, smaller traders were mostly squeezed out. Nine Montreal companies, under the leadership of Simon McTavish, merged their resources into the North West Company and, in effect, took almost total control of the fur trade in 1779. These were the prime years of the fur trade at Grand Portage.

### The Ojibwa People

The Ojibwa were a vital part of the fur trade, but their numbers were greatly diminished by the smallpox epidemic of 1781 to 1782. By most estimates, two-thirds of the Indian population died in this plague. The fabric of Ojibwa society never truly recovered from the loss of so many clan leaders, chiefs, artisans, and historians. The fur business was likewise hurt, though those who remained picked up the slack within a couple of years.

By the early 1780's, Grand Portage achieved what seemed a permanent place in the fur trade. There were a number of permanent structures, an Indian village, year-round employment, and great prosperity. With the ending of the Revolutionary War, however, the British made a major error in their land settlement with the Americans. The boundary line was drawn across the middle of the Great Lakes, leaving Grand Portage, along with virtually every other important fur trading post, on the American side. Fortunately for the fur trade, the new American government left things as they were at the trading posts, and allowed them to continue operation as before.

### American Takeover

Meanwhile, disagreements among the principals in the North West Company caused new competitors to come into the market. Among these was John Jacob Astor, who contracted with one of the new companies to import furs to New York. By the early 1790's, the Americans felt the need to take control of the Great Lakes area. The Jay Treaty of 1794 made the Grand Portage area off-limits to the British and, in fact, precipitated their abandonment of Grand Portage. The North West Company decided to reactivate an old French route by the Kaministikwia River and held their last rendezvous at Grand Portage in 1802. Upon leaving, they destroyed all the structures they had built.

Grand Portage next figured in history during the War of 1812, when the Ojibwa and other local tribes joined the British to try to oust some of the American settlers who were encroaching on their land. They were unsuccessful. The Treaty of Ghent ended the war and paved the way for the Americans and British to declare the Grand Portage area a free area for Americans, British, and Canadians, which it remains to this day. The fur trade, however, was firmly entrenched to the north and did not return.

### Nineteenth Century Developments

The mid-1830's found Grand Portage a prosperous fishing station, with twenty Indian employees producing three hundred to five hundred barrels of fish a year. The Panic of 1837 ruined the fish market, however, and all the fisheries were closed shortly thereafter. The 1860's brought a major religious revival among the Indians. In 1865, Our Lady of the Holy Rosary Church was built and is now the house of worship for the oldest Roman Catholic parish in Minnesota.

Trade continued in the Grand Portage area throughout the nineteenth century, though never at the level of the glory days. Scandinavian immigrants began populating the area during the late 1800's. Timber and mining were important sources of income for these people, along with the revitalized fishing business. The forests and the mines were depleted by the early twentieth century, but the fishing business continued until the 1950's when pollution destroyed it. The Ojibwa have continued to live in the area and have opened a gambling casino there.

### Modern Preservation Efforts

Restoration of the site began in the 1920's, when the Grand Portage Trail was reopened. In 1936, a portion of the North West Company depot was reconstructed with funds from the New Deal's Civilian Conservation Corps (CCC). Archaeological research and reconstructions continued until World War II. By the mid-1950's, the reconstructed buildings had fallen into disrepair and remained in decline until 1958, when the area, part of the Ojibwa Reservation, was ceded to the U.S. government. The U.S. Department of the Interior had designated Grand Portage a National Historic Site in 1951 and, after the cession, reconstruction began in earnest. In 1969, lightning and fire destroyed the CCC reconstruction of the Great Hall, and this structure was rebuilt using the best archaeological evidence available.

Excavation continues in the Grand Portage area, and it is hoped that enough evidence will surface so that Fort Charlotte, at the far end of the portage, can also be reconstructed. The many structures that have been reconstructed already, along with the portage route itself, make a visit to the Grand Portage area richly rewarding.

—*Steve Palmer*

**For Further Information:**

Blegen, Theodore Christian. *Minnesota: A History of the State.* Minneapolis: University of Minnesota Press, 1922. Provides little information on Grand Portage, but much on the fur trade in general.

Gilman, Carolyn. *The Grand Portage Story.* St. Paul: Minnesota Historical Society, 1992. By far the best source of information on the site. It includes much detail on the lives of those who worked in the area, both European and Indian, as well as the latest archaeological information.

Holmquist, June Denning. *Minnesota's Major Historial Sites.* 2d ed. Minneapolis: University of Minnesota Press, 1972. Also of interest. Gives a more concise overview of Grand Portage.

Lass, William E. *Minnesota: A History.* 2d ed. New York: W. W. Norton, 1998. With a historical guide prepared by the editors of the American Association for State and Local History. The book covers the fur trade in the early history of the state, but not specifically in Grand Portage.

# Other Historic Sites

## Fitzgerald House

*Location:* St. Paul, Ramsey County

*Relevant issues:* Literary history

*Statement of significance:* F. Scott Fitzgerald (1896-1940), spokesman for the Jazz Age, wrote several stories and his first published novel, *This Side of Paradise* (1920), in this Victorian rowhouse.

## Hill House

*Location:* St. Paul, Ramsey County

*Relevant issues:* Business and industry

*Statement of significance:* From 1891 until his death, this was the residence of James J. Hill (1838-1916), one of the great railroad builders in the American West and one of the leading financiers of the nineteenth century. Known as the "Empire Builder," Hill acquired a number of railroads throughout the Northwest and merged several into the Great Northern Railway Company (1890). His efforts did much to bring the region from St. Paul to the Pacific into the mainstream of American commerce.

## Kathio Site

*Location:* Vineland and vicinity, Mille Lacs County

*Relevant issues:* American Indian history

*Statement of significance:* Occupied from Archaic to historic times (3000 B.C.E.-1750 C.E.), this was the ancestral homeland of the Dakota Sioux at the beginning of the historic period. In 1679, French explorer Sieur Duluth noted the existence of forty Sioux villages in the vicinity. In the mid-eighteenth century, the Chippewa, pressured by the westward expansion of European settlers, drove the Sioux from this area to the west and south, where the Sioux later figured prominently in the history of the Plains and Rocky Mountain states.

## Kelley Homestead

*Location:* Elk River, Sherburne County

*Relevant issues:* Science and technology, social reform

*Web site:* www.mnhs.org/sites/ohkf.html

*Statement of significance:* From 1850 to 1870, this was the home of Oliver H. Kelley (1826-1913), founder of the National Grange of the Order of the Patrons of Husbandry (1867). Kelley, an avowed "book farmer" who advocated experimentation, advanced methods, and increased communications among farmers, founded his organization after seeing firsthand the wretched conditions in the post-Civil War South. The house served as Grange headquarters from 1868 to 1870.

## Kellogg House

*Location:* St. Paul, Ramsey County

*Relevant issues:* Political history

*Statement of significance:* From 1889 until his death, this was the permanent residence of Frank B. Kellogg (1856-1937), lawyer, U.S. senator, and diplomat. As secretary of state (1925-1929), he negotiated the Kellogg-Briand Pact (1928), for which he received the Nobel Peace Prize, and shifted foreign policy away from interventionism.

## Lewis Boyhood Home

*Location:* Sauk Centre, Stearns County

*Relevant issues:* Literary history

*Statement of significance:* From 1885 to 1902, this was the home of Sinclair Lewis (1885-1951), the first American author to be awarded the Nobel Prize in Literature (1930). His novel *Main Street* (1920) was partly based on his impressions of Sauk Centre.

## Mayo Clinic Buildings

*Location:* Rochester, Olmsted County

*Relevant issues:* Health and medicine

*Statement of significance:* The Mayo Clinic Building (1914) was the first building to house both research and diagnosis under one roof, independent of any hospital and dedicated to the private, group practice of medicine; the Plummer Building (1928) represents continuing growth of the concepts first embodied in the earlier building. The form of practice developed by Drs. William J. and Charles H. Mayo has been copied throughout the world and exists today as one of the most common systems of practice in the world.

## Pillsbury "A" Mill

*Location:* Minneapolis, Hennepin County

*Relevant issues:* Business and industry

*Statement of significance:* Of the giant flour mills that made Minneapolis the milling capital of the nation between 1880 and 1930, Pillsbury "A" Mill is the only one standing. The largest, most advanced mill in the world at its completion in 1881, the six-story "A" Mill was the standard by which all other mills of its time were measured.

## Rölvaag House

*Location:* Northfield, Rice County

*Relevant issues:* Literary history

*Statement of significance:* From 1912 until his death, this was the residence of O. E. Rölvaag (1876-1931), Norwegian immigrant and the first American novelist to give a true accounting of the psychological cost of pioneering on the farmer's frontier. His famous trilogy—*Giants in the Earth* (1927), *Peder Victorious* (1928), and *Their Father's God* (1931)—stands in American literature as the most mature and penetrating assessment of the adjustments immigrant pioneers had to make in order to find peace and prosperity in Middle America.

## Soudan Iron Mine

*Location:* Tower, St. Louis County

*Relevant issues:* Business and industry

*Statement of significance:* The opening in 1884 of Soudan Mine, the oldest and deepest in the state, marked the beginning of the exploitation of one of the richest iron ore deposits in the world and the emergence of Minnesota as the leading iron ore producing state in America. The mine remained active until 1962; a number of its original buildings survive.

## Veblen Farmstead

*Location:* Nerstrand, Rice County

*Relevant issues:* Business and industry, social reform

*Statement of significance:* Thorstein B. Veblen (1857-1929), economist, social scientist, and critic of American culture, lived on this farm as a youth and returned often as an adult. The product of an austere agrarian upbringing, Veblen has often been called one of America's most creative and original thinkers.

## Volstead House

*Location:* Granite Falls, Yellow Medicine County

*Relevant issues:* Political history, social reform

*Statement of significance:* From 1894 to 1930, this was the home of Andrew J. Volstead (1860-1947), the man who "personified prohibition." Volstead served in the House of Representatives (1903-1923), where he drafted the National Prohibition Enforcement Act (1919), which became known as the Volstead Act.

## Washburn "A" Mill Complex

*Location:* Minneapolis, Hennepin County
*Relevant issues:* Business and industry
*Statement of significance:* This complex outstandingly represents the growth and development of General Mills, Inc., and the radical transformations of the flour milling industry in the late nineteenth and early twentieth centuries that made it a modern mass-production industry. The Washburn "A" Mill (1874) is the only structure that remains from the original Minneapolis milling complex established by Cadwallader C. Washburn.

# Mississippi

*The State Capitol Building in Jackson.* (Mississippi Tourism Division)

# History of Mississippi

Mississippi's climate has greatly influenced its history. Located in the Deep South of the United States, just above the Gulf of Mexico, Mississippi has long, humid summers and generally short, mild winters. Consequently the growing season throughout the state is more than two hundred days long. In the far South, the growing season can be as long as 280 days. This long growing period, combined with abundant rain, has made agriculture a prominent economic activity. Outside of the hilly region in the north, the soils are finely textured, composed of clays, sands, and other components.

In the nineteenth century, when cotton became a major export crop for the United States, climate and soil tended to make the state heavily dependent on production of cotton. The prominence of cotton, a plantation crop requiring heavy investment of labor, contributed to the development of slavery as a major feature of life before the Civil War. Slavery gave Mississippi a large African American population, and the legacy of slavery produced racial inequality and troubled race relations. Continuing reliance on agriculture also tended to make Mississippi one of the least industrialized and poorest states in the United States throughout the twentieth century.

## Early History

During prehistoric times, the area of Mississippi was populated by people who lived in highly organized farming societies. These societies are known as the Mound Builders, after the great ceremonial earth mounds they constructed. The Mound Builders may be divided into the people of the Hopewell culture, who flourished from about the first century until about 800 C.E., and the people of the Mississippian culture, who lived from about 800 C.E. until about 1500. When the earliest French settlers arrived in what is now the southwestern part of Mississippi, the Natchez Indians were still building mounds, which were used for burials and as sites for public buildings.

By the time of European settlement in this area of North America, there were three major Native American nations in the Mississippi region, as well as a host of small Native American groups. The nation of the Choctaw was the largest of the three. The Choctaw controlled most of central and southern Mississippi. In southwestern Mississippi, the Natchez nation was dominant. In the northern part of what is now the state of Mississippi, the Chickasaw were the largest and most powerful group.

The Choctaw were an agricultural people who lived in thatched-roof cabins made of mud and bark. The Chickasaw were closely related to the Choctaw, and both groups spoke languages of the Muskogean family, but they were traditional enemies before European settlement. The Natchez were the largest and most unified group in the area. However, war broke out between the Natchez and French settlers in the early 1700's. The French joined with the Choctaw to destroy the Natchez in 1729. Some Natchez were sold into slavery, and others were absorbed into other tribes. The Choctaw and Chickasaw continued to live in the Mississippi region, adopting many of the ways of European society. By 1842 though, the U.S. government, under pressure from land-hungry white settlers, forced most of the Native Americans of the Southeast to relocate in Indian Territory in Oklahoma.

## European Exploration and Colonization

The Spanish and the French were the first Europeans to explore the territory of the lower Mississippi River. From 1539 to 1543, the Spaniard Hernando de Soto led an expedition that is believed to have crossed the northern part of the modern state of Mississippi. At the end of the 1600's, the French explorer René-Robert Cavelier, Sieur de La Salle, journeyed down the Mississippi River to its mouth and claimed all of the land drained by the Mississippi in the name of France. La Salle named this huge expanse of territory Louisiana, in honor of King Louis XIV of France.

After the French and Indian War between France and Great Britain, from 1754 to 1763, France ceded all of the French land east of the Mis-

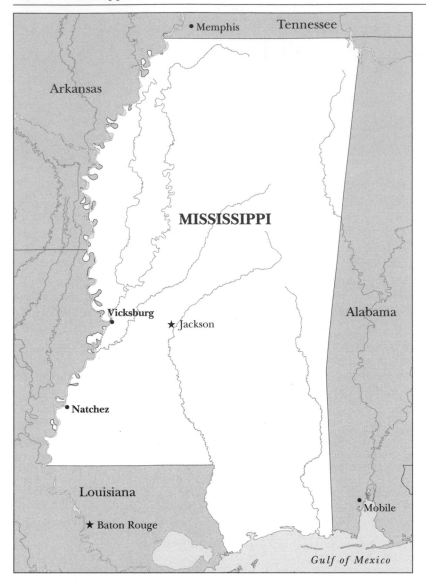

under Spanish rule, revolted against Spain in 1810. West Florida became independent briefly, then it was annexed to the United States. In 1817 Mississippi was admitted to the United States as the twentieth state.

### Cotton and the Civil War

In 1800 there were only 7,600 settlers in Mississippi. By 1820 this number had grown to 75,448. Ten years later, the U.S. Census put the state's population at 136,621. The 1860 census showed a population of 791,305. Much of this rapid growth was due to the immigration of farmers who were looking for land to grow cotton. Cotton was Mississippi's most important crop, and, by the eve of the Civil War, Mississippi produced more cotton than any other state. Although only a small minority of the whites in the state were large plantation owners, owners of the big plantations held most of the economic and political power. Reliance on slave labor meant that the state had a huge slave population, with slaves of African descent far outnumbering whites. Because there were so many people held in bondage, Mississippi's slave laws were among the harshest in the South.

By the 1850's the southern states, which were dependent on agriculture and slavery, were losing control over the U.S. Congress and presidency to the industrialized North. Many southerners believed that the southern way of life, including the institution of slavery, could only be preserved by seceding from the United States. In 1861, after the election of President Abraham Lincoln, southern states began declaring their independence. Mississippi was the second state to secede, and Mississippi planter and former U.S. senator Jefferson Davis be-

sissippi River to Great Britain. Although the British attempted to reserve the land of northern Mississippi for Native Americans and forbade white settlement in that region, white Americans were drawn to the region for its rich soil. In 1783 the Spanish, who had acquired the Louisiana territories from France, took southern Mississippi from the British. In 1798 Spain recognized the northern part of modern Mississippi as territory of the new United States. That same year, the U.S. Congress organized this region as the Mississippi Territory.

American colonists in West Florida, the areas of modern Louisiana and southern Mississippi still

came president of the Confederate States of America.

About eighty thousand Mississippians fought for the Confederacy, and almost one-third of them died in the Civil War. Many counties in Mississippi also saw an internal civil war, as small farmers who opposed secession from the Union organized themselves to fight against the Confederacy. Fighting ravaged the state, and the forces of U.S. general William Tecumseh Sherman were especially destructive in their efforts to defeat the rebellious southerners.

### The Legacy of War and Slavery

Mississippi's history of slavery and civil war led to continuing problems of racial inequality. During Reconstruction, the period following the Civil War when Northern troops occupied the defeated lands of the Confederacy, the state's freed slaves entered political life, although few had sufficient education or experience to hold more than minor offices. By 1875, though, the whites of Mississippi began to retake power. They instituted segregation and, by the early twentieth century, excluded African Americans from public life by laws and terrorism. In some of the counties of the Mississippi Delta, the region where the Mississippi and Yazoo Rivers join together, 80 to 90 percent of the people were African American. Most of them worked as sharecroppers, farmers working the land for a share of the crop, on land owned by whites.

As a consequence of this legacy of slavery, Mississippi became a central battleground of the Civil Rights movement. In 1964, black and white college students working with civil rights organizations traveled to the state for Freedom Summer, to provide educational opportunities to local African Americans and to encourage minority voter registration. After the passage of the Civil Rights Act of 1964 and the Voting Rights Act of 1965, segregation became illegal in the United States, and black Mississippians began to enter public life. By the 1990's, the Mississippi legislature had the highest percentage of African Americans of any state legislature in the nation. Nevertheless, racial prejudice and poverty in Mississippi's black population continued to be problems.

### Economy and Population After the War

Mississippi continued to have an economy based on agriculture well into the twentieth century. However, declining prices for cotton and other agricultural goods contributed to making it the poorest state in the nation by many measures. In 1936 Governor Hugh L. White began an effort to bring industry into the state with his Balance Agriculture with Industry (BAWI) program. World War II helped industrialization, especially in the shipbuilding industry along the Gulf Coast. The period following World War II saw rapid industrialization. By 1990, less than 3 percent of Mississippi's labor force were employed in agriculture, while almost 23 percent were employed in factories. The state's largest areas of employment in the late twentieth century were lumber and wood products, furniture, food products, and the manufacture of clothing.

With the disappearance of agricultural jobs, many black Mississippians left the state. The state's African American population declined from 60 percent of all Mississippians in 1900 to 36 percent in 1990. Most small towns and villages grew smaller or even disappeared after World War II. Most of the state's population growth in this period took place in the urban areas of Jackson, Biloxi-Gulfport, and Pascagoula-Moss Point. By 1990, nearly half of all the people in the state lived in cities.

—*Carl L. Bankston III*

# Natchez

**Date:** Settled by the French in 1716, the British in 1763, the Spanish in 1779, and Americans in 1798

**Relevant issues:** American Indian history, business and industry, Civil War, European settlement

**Significance:** This Southern city is rich in history. It was originally occupied by the Natchez Indians and later colonized by France, England, and Spain. It was an important cotton trade center prior to the Civil War and was occupied by Union forces during the war. Natchez is home to many scrupulously preserved antebellum mansions and other historic sites.

**Location:** Southwestern Mississippi, along the banks of the Mississippi River

**Site Offices:**

Natchez National Historical Park

P.O. Box 1208
Natchez, MS 39121
ph.: (601) 442-7047
Web site: www.nps.gov/natc/

Natchez Pilgrimage Tours
Canal Street Depot
P.O. Box 347
Natchez, MS 39120
ph.: (601) 446-6631
fax: (601) 446-8687
Web site: www.natchezpilgrimage.com
e-mail: tours@natchezpilgrimage.com

Few cities in the United States can claim as many historic treasures as Natchez can. Even fewer have done as much to preserve them. In Natchez today one can find reminders of the area's first known inhabitants, the Natchez Indians; of the early European colonists who built fortifications along the Mississippi River; of the wealthy cotton planters and brokers who built imposing mansions on the bluffs above the river; of the rougher men who plied various trades, legal and otherwise, along the Mississippi and the Natchez Trace; of free black men who made names for themselves even while most African Americans were enslaved; and of the troops who occupied Natchez during the Civil War.

## Early History

The Natchez Indians were a tribe of the Mississippians, who lived all along the river from mouth to source. By 1200 the Mississippians had developed the most advanced Indian civilization located north of Mexico, and by the mid-sixteenth century the Natchez culture had reached its height. The Natchez, like other Mississippian peoples, excelled at agriculture, raising maize, pumpkins, melons, and tobacco. The Natchez also were highly skilled at pottery making. The Natchez had a socially stratified society, with clear distinctions between aristocrats and common people.

The Natchez constructed their Grand Village, the ceremonial and religious center of their culture, along the banks of St. Catherine Creek, within the present-day city limits of Natchez. The tribe was very much entrenched in the area when the first Europeans arrived early in the eighteenth century.

## French Exploration

The French had explored the Natchez area as early as 1701, and by 1714 had established a trading post on land belonging to the Natchez Indians. The Indians were outraged, and they displayed their displeasure by killing several French traders and looting the post. French colonial authorities assigned Jean Baptiste Le Moyne, Sieur de Bienville, to punish the Indians. He ordered the execution of the Indians responsible for the crimes, demanded the return of the stolen goods, and forced the Natchez to build a fort to be occupied by the French. This was Fort Rosalie, completed in 1716, on a bluff overlooking the Mississippi River.

French settlement in the area increased. By 1723 more than three hundred settlers and their slaves lived near Fort Rosalie, and by 1729 the number had grown to 750. They began farming; their crops included tobacco, wheat, indigo, and rice. During this period French authorities created the Natchez District—one of nine subdivisions of the French colony of Louisiana—and chose Fort Rosalie as its capital. The district included the present-day city of Natchez along with lands stretching forty miles to the east.

The Natchez Indians resented the increasing French presence, and they especially feared the possibility of encroachments on their Grand Village. They made war on the French in 1722, but Bienville and his troops put down the uprising. Toward the end of 1729, armed conflict broke out again. The new commander of Fort Rosalie, the Sieur de Chepart, had demanded the Grand Village land as well as monthly supplies of free goods from the Indians; he also told the Natchez to prepare to leave the area for good. The outraged Natchez planned an attack; Chepart apparently had been forewarned, but he refused to make any special preparations for defense on the grounds that the Indians would see this as a sign of weakness. The Natchez attacked Fort Rosalie on November 29; they killed about three hundred Frenchmen and took more than four hundred women and slaves as prisoners. French troops, aided by the Choctaw Indians—traditional enemies of the Natchez—hunted down and decimated the Natchez tribe. For the next several decades, the Natchez District was largely deserted, and the remains of Fort Rosalie were occupied by only a few French soldiers.

## British Rule and the American Revolution

Britain gained control of the Natchez District in 1763, after the resolution of the French and Indian War in North America and the Seven Years War in Europe. The end of the wars also saw Spain take possession of the French colonies west of the Mississippi. The British authorities soon recognized the value of the Natchez area, with its location on the Mississippi River, its fertile soil, and its pleasant climate. Britain made generous land grants to encourage settlement in the area, and farming and commerce grew. As revolutionary fervor took hold in the East, British colonists loyal to the Crown found a refuge in Natchez.

The settlers could not escape the revolution entirely, however. In 1778 the Continental Congress sent a military expedition led by James Willing to bring Natchez residents over to the colonies' side. Willing's men plundered the homes of those who refused to renounce their allegiance to Britain; this action served to make the loyalists even more hostile to the revolutionists' cause. Then in 1779, Spain went to war with Britain, and a force led by Bernardo de Gálvez, governor of Spanish Louisiana, captured Natchez. The British residents were fearful of Spanish rule, and in 1781 they made an unsuccessful attempt to drive out the Spanish. Overall, however, the period in which Spain controlled Natchez was relatively peaceful. Spain's governance of the area, made official by the Treaty of Paris in 1783, was efficient and benevolent.

## Spanish Influence

Spain did not attempt to displace the British population with Spanish settlers, but actively sought to bring Anglo-Americans into Natchez. The Spanish authorities promoted settlement and agriculture through a liberal land grant policy. During the Spanish period, Natchez agriculture focused on the commodity that shaped the Natchez of the nineteenth century: cotton. Natchez tobacco had never matched the quality of the Virginia crop, and indigo production had various drawbacks. So Natchez planters turned to cotton production on a large scale in the mid-1790's. The scale was made possible by Eli Whitney's invention of the cotton gin. The cultivation of cotton also required large amounts of slave labor; by 1798 the population of the Natchez District was 6,900, of which 2,400 were slaves.

During this period Spain and the United States were in negotiations concerning the control of the Natchez District. An ambiguity in the 1783 treaty had led U.S. authorities to believe they had the right to the area, and they had protested through diplomatic channels. In 1795 Spain, wishing to concentrate on problems in Europe, signed a treaty acknowledging the U.S. claim to the area. The Spanish soon had second thoughts, however, and the issue of who owned Natchez remained unsettled until 1798, when Spain finally removed all its military posts from the district.

## Creation of Mississippi Territory

That same year, the U.S. government created the Territory of Mississippi, with Natchez as its capital. The capital was moved to the inland town of Washington in 1802, but Natchez—formally incorporated as a city in 1803—was quickly developing into a center of the plantation economy and an important river port. During this period of development, some notable political and military ventures touched Natchez.

Early in 1807 Aaron Burr, former vice president of the United States, arrived in Natchez along with several boatloads of men. Burr was suspected of planning to foment revolution in the western territories of the United States, or, perhaps, to take Texas and Mexico away from Spain. He was arrested in Mississippi, but the territorial supreme court refused to indict him, believing that Burr's designs were on Mexico rather than the United States. Burr was arrested again near Mobile and was tried for treason and acquitted in Richmond, Virginia.

Militarily, Natchez residents were heavily involved in the War of 1812, especially at the Battle of New Orleans in 1815. One historian reported that nearly all the men of Natchez took part in the battle.

## Cotton Cultivation

Mississippi became a state in 1817, and Natchez was becoming one of its most prominent cities. By this time cotton was unquestionably the leading crop of western Mississippi. Many of the wealthiest cotton planters and brokers soon built majestic homes in Natchez. The rest of Mississippi was populated primarily by small farmers, but the Natchez planter class had the trappings of life that most people continue to associate with the antebellum South—white-columned mansions, luxurious furnishings and clothing, and extensive holdings of land and slaves.

The planter's prosperity was made possible not only by cotton and slavery, but also by Natchez's location on the river and by the advent of steamboat transportation. The *New Orleans* was the first steamboat to serve Natchez, beginning in 1811; Natchez soon became one of the world's leading cotton ports. Land transportation also was important to Natchez commerce. The Natchez Trace, stretching from Natchez to Nashville, Tennessee, had opened as a result of an 1801 treaty with the Chickasaw Indians. The Trace was basically a wilderness path and often hazardous, but it was used by countless settlers and traders on their way to and from Natchez. Some entrepreneurs would make use of both the river and the Trace. One might come

down the Mississippi on a keelboat, sell both one's goods and boat in Natchez, and make one's way back northeast on the Trace.

In Natchez, the boatmen often gathered in a district known as Natchez-under-the-Hill; its name distinguished it from the bluffs on which the planters' mansions sat. Natchez-under-the-Hill became notorious for its rough taverns, gambling houses, and bordellos, and the area was the site of many bloody fights.

**Free Black Residents**

Natchez in this period was home not only to planters, slaves, and boatmen, but also to a number of free blacks and mulattoes. By 1820 most of Mississippi's five hundred free people of color lived in Natchez. The best known of them today, thanks to his extensive diary, is William Johnson. Johnson, a mulatto, was born into slavery in 1809 and freed by

*Monmouth, a plantation in Natchez.* (Natchez Pilgrimage Tours)

his owner in 1820. He became a barber, a popular occupation for free men of color. After an apprenticeship, Johnson operated a shop in Port Gibson, Mississippi, and within a few years he moved to Natchez. Johnson's Natchez barbershop was something of a clearinghouse for the news of the day, and he kept a detailed diary of events. Johnson became a very successful businessman, owning rental property within the city of Natchez, along with farmland just outside town; even though he himself had been freed from slavery, he owned slaves who labored on his property. Johnson's life ended violently; he was shot to death in 1851 as a result of a dispute over the boundaries of his land. A man named Baylor Winn was tried for Johnson's murder and acquitted. Race was a factor in the trial; most people believed Winn was of African descent, but he had lived as a white man and enjoyed whites' legal privileges, one of which was that blacks could not testify against whites in court. The exclusion of this testimony made it difficult to convict him.

The diverse and prosperous community of Natchez could not escape the sectional conflicts of the mid-nineteenth century, but certain of its residents tried. Most of the Natchez planters were opposed to secession and war, and their opposition was based on economics. Not only did they have more to lose in war than did the small farmers; they also, being knowledgable and well-traveled men, realized the North was better equipped for any fight that might come. Many of the planters had even invested their cotton profits in Northern industry. Over their objections, however, Mississippi seceded from the United States early in 1861.

### The Civil War

The Civil War did not bring physical destruction to Natchez. Union forces captured the town in 1862 and began a peaceful occupation. The occupation force made its headquarters at a Georgian-style mansion called Rosalie, named after Fort Rosalie. Located on a high bluff with an excellent view of the Mississippi River, the mansion provided a strategic location for the Union headquarters. General Ulysses S. Grant stayed at the mansion for a brief period; he was followed by General Walter Q. Gresham. Gresham allowed Rosalie's owners, the Andrew Wilson family, to stay there during his occupation, and Gresham was generally so gracious

that he became known as "Natchez's favorite Yankee."

One type of wartime destruction that Natchez could not escape, however, was economic. Many of the planters' cotton fields had been confiscated or burned, and Natchez's stature as a river port had declined. For many years the city was stagnant. By the twentieth century, however, manufacturing had brought some economic revival to Natchez, and tourism had become increasingly important.

### Modern Tourism

Tourism in Natchez focuses on the city's rich history, which is apparent in many well-preserved sites. Touring historic homes is one of the most popular activities among Natchez visitors. Several homes are open for tours year-round, and additional homes are open to visitors during the annual Natchez Spring Pilgrimage. Some of the most notable homes are Rosalie; Longwood, an arresting octagonal house left unfinished after its builder lost his fortune in the Civil War; Monmouth, built by Confederate general John Quitman; Stanton Hall; Dunleith; and Auburn.

Other aspects of Natchez's history are showcased in Natchez-under-the-Hill, which maintains its nineteenth century appearance but now houses upscale restaurants and nightclubs; the William Johnson House, which underwent restoration in the mid-1990's; the Fort Rosalie site, also in the process of being acquired and restored by the National Park Service; and the Grand Village of the Natchez Indians. Going northeast from Natchez, the Natchez Trace Parkway is now a smoothly paved, modern road, with numerous markers explaining events in the area's history.

*—Trudy Ring*

### For Further Information:

Brooke, Steven. *The Majesty of Natchez.* 2d ed. Gretna, La.: Pelican, 1999. A history of Natchez and historic buildings of the region.

Daniels, Jonathan. *The Devil's Backbone.* New York: McGraw-Hill, 1962. Reprint. Gretna, La.: Pelican, 1992. Provides a colorful anecdotal history of Natchez and the Trace.

Davis, Edwin Adams, and William Ransom Hogan. *The Barber of Natchez.* Baton Rouge: Louisiana State University Press, 1954. A profile of William Johnson.

Johnson, William. *William Johnson's Natchez: The Ante-Bellum Diary of a Free Negro*. Edited by William Ransom Hogan and Edwin Adams Davis. Baton Rouge: Louisiana State University Press, 1951. Reprint. Port Washington, N.Y.: Kennikat Press, 1968. Offers Johnson's own words.

Kane, Hartnett T. *Natchez on the Mississippi*. New York: William Morrow, 1947. A slightly dated but still informative overview of the history of Natchez.

Skates, John Ray. *Mississippi: A Bicentennial History*. New York: W. W. Norton, 1979. Includes several sections on important events in Natchez.

Wanner, Glen. *Bicycling the Natchez Trace: A Guide to the Natchez Trace Parkway and Nearby Scenic Routes*. Nashville: Pennywell Press, 1997. Provides excellent background information and detailed information important to cyclists.

# Vicksburg

**Date:** Established as a National Military Park on February 12, 1899

**Relevant issues:** Civil War, military history

**Significance:** This city is part of the Vicksburg National Military Park, a 1,858-acre site which contains all areas involved in the siege of Vicksburg during the Civil War.

**Location:** In western Mississippi, forty-five miles from Jackson, on the banks of the Mississippi and Yazoo Rivers

**Site Office:**

Vicksburg National Military Park
3201 Clay Street
Vicksburg, MS 39183-3495
ph.: (601) 636-0583
Web site: www.nps.gov/vick/
e-mail: vick_interpretation@nps.gov

Vicksburg sits quietly atop a series of bluffs overlooking the Mississippi River. During late 1862 and 1863, this quiet town rapidly became the heart of the Confederacy during the Civil War when Union troops repeatedly tried to capture Vicksburg in order to gain supremacy over river traffic. After more than fourteen months of attempts, Northern forces finally succeeded in breaking the spirit of the town; in retrospect, many identify Vicksburg's fall as the beginning of the end of the South's bid for independence from the United States.

## Early History and Civil War

Vicksburg's earliest history stretches back to 1790, when the Spanish founded Fort Nogales near the present-day site. In 1814, the Reverend Newit Vick chose the current site of the city, high upon bluffs stretching out toward the Mississippi River. When the Civil War began in 1861, Vicksburg was just one of many Mississippi River cities under the control of the Confederacy. Light fortifications guarded the city, but by the summer of 1862 Vicksburg and the surrounding area became the largest Confederate stronghold on the river.

Two events during 1862 set the stage for Vicksburg's rise as a military bastion. In February, Union general Ulysses S. Grant captured Tennessee's Fort Henry and Fort Donelson, leading to complete Union occupation of western Tennessee and the adjoining river. Two months later, Union flag officer David G. Farragut attacked and defeated the supposedly invincible Confederate forts at the mouth of the Mississippi to take New Orleans and control the southern entrance to the river.

As Vicksburg was the only rail and river junction left between Memphis and New Orleans (both now Union controlled), residents and Confederate leaders knew that Vicksburg was the Union's next logical target. If the Union were to gain control, it could isolate the rich Confederate states of Texas, Louisiana, and Arkansas, and the border state of Missouri, which provided not only valuable supplies, but also strong secessionist support. In addition, the Union would control the rail line that connected the large northern cities to the Gulf of Mexico. Knowing that a battle was inevitable, some Vicksburg residents fled, but most stayed to fortify the town. The Confederates rushed troops to Vicksburg. They dug trenches, built guard walls, and constructed batteries of cannon on the bluffs, to cover land invasions and river movements.

## The Union Campaign Against Vicksburg

The Union did strike quickly, sending the same force, under Farragut, that had captured New Orleans to Vicksburg. Boats began arriving on May 18, 1862, to try to take the city by shelling. Four days later, the onslaught began, but little damage was done because of the city's position on the high bluffs.

Farragut realized almost instantly that the city could not be captured by shelling alone, but other tactics were not an option. Troops were unable to land on the west side of the river, due to the flooded river delta. Farragut had been given only two divisions of men, numbering about fifteen hundred. With the city as heavily guarded as it was, landing on the east side would be suicide. Faced with limited options that would yield few results, Farragut retreated back south down the river toward New Orleans.

President Abraham Lincoln and his War Department were unhappy with Farragut's initial showing, and they ordered him to try another attack. This time, another fleet led by Flag Officer Charles C. Davis would meet Farragut and Commander David D. Porter's mortar schooners from the north; the three together would shell the city heavily in the hope of weakening it enough to allow for a land attack.

With only three thousand troops this time, Farragut could do little but sail past the cannon batteries at Vicksburg and begin shelling the city again on June 27. By this time, the Confederate forces in and around the city numbered ten thousand. On July 1, Davis's fleet met up with Farragut and Porter; for more than two weeks they shelled the city, but accomplished little.

To hamper Union activity further, the Confederates launched the gunboat *Arkansas* down the Yazoo toward Vicksburg. The boat sailed for only twenty-three days before being sunk, but it repeatedly hassled and damaged the Union fleet the entire time. Union commanders admitted that a naval assault alone was worthless; but with battle raging on in the east, there were not many troops the Union could spare for a land assault. Also, because of the summer's heat and rampant disease, only eight hundred of Farragut's three thousand troops were available for active duty.

## Naval Bombardment

Over the sixty-seven days that Farragut and Davis stayed within range of Vicksburg, they used between twenty thousand and twenty-five thousand shells, yet the town reported only seven dead and fifteen wounded. After his second failed expedition, Farragut wrote that he believed it would take

between twelve thousand and fifteen thousand troops to take the city over land—a number that in reality was probably much too low.

As Farragut retreated south again toward New Orleans and Davis drifted back north toward Memphis, the Confederates launched a minor land attack against the Union stronghold at Baton Rouge, Louisiana, on August 5, only to be turned back. With the absence of Union gunboats, however, Confederate communication lines that had been cut were once again established, and the South controlled the river from Vicksburg to Port Hudson, Mississippi, a distance of about 250 river miles.

## A New Plan to Take Vicksburg

Lincoln needed a new man to lead a full-scale assault on Vicksburg. In October he appointed Ulysses S. Grant, the taker of the Tennessee forts, to the command of the Department of the Tennessee forces. At the same time, John C. Pemberton, a Pennsylvania-born Confederate commander, was given command of the Department of Mississippi and East Louisiana, which put him in charge of the defense of Vicksburg. The two would cross each other's paths with regularity over the next ten months. As Grant's quest began, his front line extended along the northern border of Mississippi for two hundred miles.

Grant immediately began devising a multipronged attack against Vicksburg. Major General William Tecumseh Sherman would ferry his troops down the Mississippi on (now) Rear Admiral Porter's fleet; Grant himself would drive a division into central Mississippi to confuse Pemberton into thinking he was attacking the city from the rear. Grant hoped he could draw enough of Pemberton's troops away from the city so Sherman's men could overwhelm the rest of the Confederate forces and establish themselves in the hills north of town. The final part of the plan included additional naval support from Farragut, sailing in once again from the south. For the North, the invasion gained even more importance when news came from the east in December—Union troops under Ambrose Burnside had been routed at Fredericksburg, Virginia, summarily ending any Northern hopes in the eastern theater until the spring of 1863.

In late November, Grant's men began to move into central Mississippi; on December 20, Sherman and Porter made their move down the river. With little communication, the river forces assumed Grant was succeeding in his movements, but they were mistaken. Poor defenses at the Union supply depot at Holly Springs, Mississippi, had led to its capture by a group of 3,500 cavalrymen led by Confederate major general Earl Van Dorn. At the same time, another group led by Brigadier General Nathan Bedford Forrest stormed across western Tennessee, interfering with Grant's supply line on the Mobile and Ohio Railroad. With no supplies to back him, Grant decided to abandon his march and retreat, leaving Sherman without any land support. Seeing this, Pemberton brought the troops he had marched eastward to meet the invading Union troops back to Vicksburg to help guard the city.

There was no better news from Farragut. As troops sailed toward Vicksburg from the south, they encountered heavily fortified batteries at Port Hudson. Feeling they could not sail past the batteries without heavy losses, they instead opted to turn back. Without any of the help he thought he would have, Sherman had to go it alone.

### Sherman's Debacle

On December 29, Sherman launched his attack five miles north of Vicksburg at Chickasaw Bayou. The little dry ground available there was heavily covered with Confederate fire from the bluffs. Sherman forged ahead anyway, losing 1,700 men to only 200 for the Confederates. All of his assaults at these northern bluffs were completely repelled, forcing Sherman to retreat northward.

Following the debacle, Sherman was superseded in power by Major General John A. McClernand. In early January, 1863, McClernand led Sherman's former troops and Porter's fleet up the Arkansas River fifty miles from its junction with the Mississippi to attack Arkansas Post, a small Confederate shipping post and military stronghold. The fort was taken, but the attack did little in the long run to weaken Vicksburg.

### Grant Takes Charge of the Assault

After regrouping, Grant launched another set of unsuccessful attempts at taking Vicksburg. On January 31, forty-five thousand of his men set out for Young's Point, twenty miles north of Vicksburg on the west side of the Mississippi. For the next two

and one-half months, Grant tried repeatedly to move his troops across the river onto dry ground where they could launch an attack. The Union troops tried several tacks, including building canals that would bypass the city's batteries, but the waters rose and flooded the delta, swallowing up their work. Making matters worse was the exceptionally rainy winter of 1862-1863 that made any river crossing all the more difficult. By March, disease was spreading, the troops were weary, and some were calling for Grant's ouster.

Pemberton, too, was not without difficulties. Though he was safely on the defensive, he had no idea where Grant would strike next, forcing him to defend a two hundred-mile line around the city in order to cover all the entrances. Covering such a wide area spread his troops very thin. Hampering Pemberton's intelligence even further was the absence of any substantial navy for reconnaissance—Union troops moved freely about the river system and bayous without the Confederates knowing where they were.

For a man swirling in a storm of controversy, Grant devised a daring plan. This time he chose a circuitous route—marching his troops down the west side of the river and making his way through the bayous. Simultaneously, Porter was to sail a group of transport ships pulling supply barges past the dangerous batteries at Vicksburg, meet up with Grant at some point south of the city and transport the troops across the river. After establishing themselves on dry ground east of the river, Grant's troops would loop back toward Vicksburg and attack the city from the rear. To confuse the Confederates, Sherman would launch a phony attack with 1,700 cavalrymen at the northern end of the city.

The daring aspect of the plan was that if the Union troops did make it across the river, they would cut themselves off from any further supplies or communication. After all the other more direct routes had failed, however, Grant had nothing to lose. His plan and early movements went undetected by the Confederates at Vicksburg, who had become complacent following their easy victory over Sherman in December.

The movements of McClernand's corps southward began the operation on March 29. They were to build roads and bridges across the swampy waters in order to facilitate easier movements of the main army. A few days later, Porter and his fleet of six transports, towing twelve barges loaded with supplies headed down the river. Late on the night of April 15 the boats attempted to steal past the batteries under the cover of darkness. They were almost immediately discovered by the Confederates, who lit fires next to the river so the batteries would have a clear shot at the fleet. Even under a massive hail of fire, the boats successfully moved past the city, losing only one transport. Farther down the river, they met McClernand's troops; the main portion of the army followed closely.

Grant first tried to land his troops at Grand Gulf, sixty river miles down from Vicksburg; however, it was too well fortified, and Grant was forced to go elsewhere. He finally found an acceptable landing site at Bruinsburg, about thirty land miles from the city. It was now April 30, nearly seven months from the time Grant had started the Vicksburg expedition.

Pemberton knew that the Union was planning a landing and attack, but could do little. Though there were now more than forty thousand Confederate troops in the area of Vicksburg, the Confederate general was unsure of Grant's plan. He was forced to leave nearly twenty thousand of these men stationed at possible attack points around the city, leaving only twenty thousand troops to roam the area.

To secure his landing, Grant sent McClernand and twenty thousand troops toward Port Gibson, about twelve miles east of the river. There, McClernand met Confederate general John S. Bowen's 7,500 men, beginning what would be the first battle on Grant's march toward Vicksburg. Though severely outnumbered, Bowen's men temporarily resisted the advance; they lost 790 men to the Union's 850 before retreating to Grand Gulf. Fearing obliteration by Grant, the Confederates aban-

*The Illinois Memorial at Vicksburg National Military Park. Each Northern state that took part in the siege has erected a plaque or monument at the park.* (Chris and Judi Irons)

doned the Grand Gulf site shortly afterward, fleeing north to Vicksburg.

By landing at Bruinsburg, Grant had the added advantage of being below the east-west flowing Big Black River. Pemberton's intelligence could not determine whether Grant was heading for the state capital of Jackson or would swing north toward Vicksburg, forcing the Confederate troops to remain thinly fanned out over a wide area. In addition, the Northern troops were protected on their left flank by the river. To aid Grant, a force of cavalrymen led by Colonel Benjamin Grierson was marching simultaneously throughout northern and central Mississippi, disrupting Confederate rail lines, supply lines, and communications.

Grant's next move was indeed toward Jackson—he wanted to take the capital on his way to loop back for the rear assault on Vicksburg. Movements began on May 7. On the way, he met up with a small Confederate force led by General John Gregg at Raymond, a small crossroads town. Gregg's troops numbered only three thousand—they too put up a brave effort before being chased eastward toward Jackson.

### Jackson Falls

Confederate president Jefferson Davis knew of Grant's successful march through Mississippi; to aid Pemberton, he began to send troops led by General Joseph E. Johnston toward Jackson. Grant moved quickly toward the capital, with his troops arriving there from the west and southwest on the morning of May 14. Johnston's men arrived too late; there were only enough Confederate soldiers in Jackson at the time of Grant's arrival to take what supplies they could and flee the city. From then on, Johnston would remain in the eastern portion of Mississippi, trying to assemble enough men to threaten the ever-growing Union force.

Grant ordered the capital destroyed; then his forces turned north. On May 16, they met up with twenty-three thousand of Pemberton's men at Champion's Hill who were moving from south to north, desperately trying to stop the Union march. Fierce fighting continued for four hours before the thirty-two thousand Union troops were able to overcome the Confederates, who retreated toward bridges at the Big Black River. Grant lost twenty-four hundred at Champion's Hill, Pemberton thirty-six hundred. As waves of Union troops moved toward the Confederates at the Big Black, threatening to outflank and trap them, the Confederates retreated to Vicksburg, burning the bridges behind them. The bridges were replaced quickly and the march rolled on.

On May 15, worried about Vicksburg's fate, Davis had summoned General Robert E. Lee to Richmond to discuss strategy. Davis suggested that Lee might want to send James Longstreet south to dislodge Grant, but Lee had another idea. His victory at Chancellorsville that month made him overconfident; he instead persuaded Davis to give the go-ahead for an attack into Pennsylvania, in the hopes of taking Philadelphia and Harrisburg on the way to Washington, D.C. If the Confederates were successful, they would force Grant to come to the aid of the northern capital, thus freeing Vicksburg.

### Grant's Direct Assault

On May 18, Grant's troops arrived in Vicksburg. Confederate battalions had fanned out to fortify all nine possible entrances to the city. Over the next few days, Grant attacked the fortified positions, losing more than four thousand men in the process. Seeing the futility of an all-out assault, Grant opted to wait it out with a blockade, sending the city into a standstill. With Porter's gunboats providing constant shelling and naval cover, he had the city surrounded.

As the siege continued into June, Grant ordered more reinforcements to his rear to protect against an assault from Johnston. As the city's remaining residents and troops starved without supplies, Grant dug in deeper, holding Johnston at bay. With each passing day, life in the city became more difficult—residents were forced to dig shelters in the hills to avoid the constant shelling. Food and supplies were scarce; residents were driven to eating rats and birds for sustenance.

### Vicksburg Finally Falls

His troops weakened by starvation and on the verge of revolt, Pemberton surrendered Vicksburg on July 4, 1863. On the same day, Lee's invasion of the North had been checked at Gettysburg with heavy casualties and a forced retreat south. On July 5, Johnston received word of the city's fall and on July 6, he retreated toward Jackson. The Union now controlled the Mississippi from mouth to source.

The combination of Confederate failures at Vicksburg and Gettysburg in July, 1863, was indeed the beginning of the end for the South; less than two years later the Confederacy would capitulate completely. Vicksburg's residents remained defiant, though; they refused to celebrate July 4 for eighty-one years following their surrender, holding to the end that it was not the Union troops who had won at Vicksburg, but starvation.

### Modern Preservation Efforts

The Vicksburg National Military Park today contains numerous markers explaining the battle and monuments to the men who died there. A Union gunboat, the USS *Cairo*, has been restored and is another feature of the military park. The city of Vicksburg also contains numerous antebellum homes in a variety of architectural styles, and many of these homes played roles in the war. The Duff Green Mansion, a Palladian-style home built in 1856, sustained shelling during the siege and was used as a hospital for both Union and Confederate forces during the siege and for the remainder of the war. McRaven, built in a combination of Frontier, Empire, and Greek Revival styles, also was a hospital and a Confederate campsite. Like many homes in Vicksburg, it bears battle scars and contains shell fragments. The 1840 Cedar Grove Mansion still has a Union cannonball lodged in a parlor wall. Anchuca, an 1830 Greek Revival mansion, was the site of a speech by Jefferson Davis.

—*Tony Jaros*

### For Further Information:

National Park Service, U.S. Department of the Interior. *Vicksburg National Military Park, Mississippi.* Rev. ed. Washington, D.C.: The Service, 1996. A guide distributed by the National Park Service. A good overview of the eighteen-month struggle for the city.

Ward, Geoffrey C. *The Civil War.* New York: Alfred A. Knopf, 1990. A colorful and complete history of the conflict. The book formed the basis for a popular multipart television series.

Wheeler, Richard. *The Siege of Vicksburg.* Reprint. New York: HarperPerennial, 1991. Another detailed account of the battle, with testimony from eyewitnesses and key players.

# Other Historic Sites

## Beauvoir

*Location:* Biloxi, Harrison County

*Relevant issues:* Civil War, political history

*Statement of significance:* From 1877 until his death, this was the residence of Jefferson Davis (1808-1889), president of the Confederacy. Davis spent the last twelve years of his life at Beauvoir writing *The Rise and Fall of the Confederate Government* (1881), which was in part a summation of his life. Beauvoir is an example of the "raised cottage," which takes advantage of the Gulf winds to provide the house with natural ventilation.

## Dancing Rabbit Creek Treaty Site

*Location:* Macon, Noxubee County

*Relevant issues:* American Indian history, western expansion

*Statement of significance:* On September 27, 1830, at Dancing Rabbit Creek, a traditional gathering place of the Choctaw people, an infamous treaty was signed for the removal of the Choctaw people from their homeland. This treaty was the most important of the pacts between the United States and the Choctaw as it resulted in the removal of a large part of the tribe from their traditional Southeastern homeland in present-day Mississippi. The Dancing Rabbit Creek Treaty served as a model for treaties of removal with the Chickasaw, Cherokee, Creek, and Seminole tribes. The treaty led to the extinguishing of all Choctaw title to land east of the Mississippi River owned by the Choctaw nation. It also led to the opening of a vast territory to American settlement.

## Faulkner House

*Location:* Oxford, Lafayette County

*Relevant issues:* Literary history

*Statement of significance:* From 1930 until his death, this two-story Greek Revival structure was the residence of William Faulkner (1897-1962).

Through stories and novels dealing with the decay and sterility of the old aristocracy, the crassness and amorality of the rising commercial class, the burden of guilt in race relations, the endurance and courage of the downtrodden African American, and the incompatibility of nature and organized society, Faulkner is credited with creating a parable of the Deep South. For his accumulated work, he received the Nobel Prize (1950), as well as the Pulitzer Prize (1955 and 1963).

## Highland Park Dentzel Carousel

*Location:* Meridian, Lauderdale County
*Relevant issues:* Cultural history
*Statement of significance:* This wooden carousel (c. 1892-1899) is likely the oldest of the three earliest Dentzel menagerie carousels which remain virtually intact. Over one hundred of these carousels were produced by the Dentzel Company of Philadelphia, founded in the mid-nineteenth century by the son of a German carousel crafter. It is the only one of the three still in a historic "shelter" or carousel house. Built from a Dentzel blueprint, the carousel house is a rare survivor.

## Holly Bluff Site

*Location:* Holly Bluff, Yazoo County
*Relevant issues:* American Indian history
*Statement of significance:* This is the type of site for the Lake George phase of the prehistoric Temple Mound period of the area. The site is important in that it is on the southern margin of the Mississippian cultural advance down the Mississippi River and on the northern edge of that of the Cole's Creek and Plaquemine cultures of the South.

## Jaketown Site

*Location:* Belzoni, Humphreys County
*Relevant issues:* American Indian history
*Statement of significance:* Located in northwestern Mississippi, Jaketown Site is the remains of a complex regional trade center dating from 2000-600 B.C.E., an era known as the Poverty Point period within the Late Archaic prehistory of the United States. Significant as a settlement important in trade in raw materials and manufacture of finished items distributed throughout the Eastern United States, it consists as deeply stratified archaeological deposits, well-preserved earthen mounds, and hidden features which represent extensive and intensive occupation over a long period.

## Lamar House

*Location:* Oxford, Lafayette County
*Relevant issues:* Civil War, political history
*Statement of significance:* From about 1868 to 1888, this was the home of Lucius Quintus Cincinnatus Lamar (1825-1893), Mississippi statesman. In 1861, Lamar resigned his seat in Congress and drafted the Mississippi Secession Ordinance. During the war, he served the Confederacy as a soldier and diplomat; afterward, he was a leading Southern spokesman for reconciliation during Reconstruction. Exponent of Southern industrial progress and leader of the "New South" movement, late in his career Lamar served in the U.S. Senate, as secretary of the interior, and on the Supreme Court.

## Monmouth

*Location:* Natchez, Adams County
*Relevant issues:* Political history
*Statement of significance:* Governor John Anthony Quitman, outstanding Mexican War general, states' rights advocate, and staunch defender of slavery, resided at Monmouth from 1826 until his death in 1858. Monmouth represents Quitman's economic and social status as a wealthy, influential lawyer and planter with a great financial stake in slavery.

## Montgomery House

*Location:* Mound Bayou, Bolivar County
*Relevant issues:* African American history
*Statement of significance:* From 1910 to 1924, this was the residence of Isaiah Thornton Montgomery, who with his cousin Benjamin Green founded the town of Mound Bayou in July, 1887. The community founded by these two former slaves was one of a number of settlements established during the post-Reconstruction period in which African Americans could exercise self-government. The success of Mound Bayou is attributable to its location along the railroad, the fertile Mississippi Delta soil, and the leadership of Montgomery.

## Oakland Memorial Chapel

*Location:* Alcorn, Claiborne County

*Relevant issues:* African American history, education

*Statement of significance:* Constructed in 1838 by skilled black craftsmen, this Greek Revival-style structure symbolizes the importance of Alcorn University as the first African American land grant college in the country. Alcorn was founded in 1871 expressly for the education of African Americans, on the site of Oakland College, which had been established for the education of the white youth of the area. Alcorn's first president was Hiram Rhoades Revels (1827-1901), one of the most distinguished African Americans of the Reconstruction Era.

## Old Mississippi State Capitol

*Location:* Jackson, Hinds County

*Relevant issues:* African American history, political history

*Statement of significance:* Of interest for its architecture, this building's major national significance arises from its association with historical events, the most important of which was the enactment of a comprehensive system of disenfranchisement of African Americans by the state constitution approved in 1890, which was widely emulated by other Southern states. The structure served as the state capitol from 1839 to 1903. Restored in 1959-1960, it now serves as the State Historical Museum.

## Siege and Battle of Corinth Sites

*Location:* Corinth, Alcorn County

*Relevant issues:* Civil War, military history

*Statement of significance:* The 1862 Union victories in the siege (April 28-May 30) and battle (October 3-4) at Corinth, one of the Confederacy's most strategically located railroad junction towns, figured importantly in the ebb and flow of Confederate military fortunes during that year. The Union victory in the latter episode, one of the key events in an overall reversal in the course of the war in favor of the Union, followed a summer during which a string of Confederate victories appeared to presage recognition by the United Kingdom. After the renewed Union successes in the early fall, including that at Corinth, this prospect slipped out of the Confederacy's hands. A number of major Union and Confederate leaders were engaged in the actions at Corinth. Today, among other elements, there remain well-preserved lines of earthworks; batteries; rifle pits; four houses used as military headquarters during the engagements; and the Corinth National Cemetery, where more than 5,600 Civil War interments, most of them unknown, were made.

# Missouri

*The State Capitol Building in Jefferson City.* (Missouri Division of Tourism)

# History of Missouri

Missouri lies almost in the center of the forty-eight contiguous states. It is the southernmost midwestern state. Its eastern boundary is the Mississippi River, its western boundary the Missouri River. It is bordered by eight states. West of Missouri are Nebraska, Kansas, and Oklahoma. To its east are Illinois and Kentucky. Iowa borders it on the north, and Arkansas and Tennessee are on the south. Missouri is about three hundred miles from east to west and about 280 miles from north to south.

The earliest settlers in the area probably lived there more than twelve thousand years ago. By the seventeenth century, the Missouri and Osage Indian tribes were there. The first Europeans in the region were Jacques Marquette, a French missionary, and Louis Jolliet, a fur trader, known to be there in 1673. In 1683 René-Robert Cavelier, Sieur de La Salle, claimed a vast expanse of land, including present-day Missouri, for France, calling it Louisiana after King Louis XIV.

## Early Settlements

The first permanent French settlement in Missouri was Sainte Genevieve, on the Mississippi River south of present-day St. Louis, established in 1735. In 1764, Pierre Laclède and René Auguste Chouteau founded St. Louis, also on the Mississippi River.

In 1762 Spain claimed France's Louisiana Territory and futilely attempted to coerce Spaniards to move there. When the United States became independent in 1776, Spain invited Americans east of the Mississippi to move into Missouri. Substantial numbers of farmers and miners accepted. By 1799 groups of settlers inhabited the area.

In 1800 France reclaimed the Louisiana Territory, which, through the Louisiana Purchase, it sold to the United States for fifteen million dollars in 1803. The Missouri Territory, which included Kansas, had a population of about twenty thousand by 1812. Most settled on land that had been the property of Native Americans, who sought to reclaim it. Various treaties were signed between the indigenous people and the new arrivals, but by 1825, almost no American Indians remained in Missouri.

## The Missouri Compromise

Black slaves came to Missouri as early as 1720, owned by French miners searching for gold and other minerals. These slaves were involved in building Missouri's first cities. Soon southern farmers and plantation owners relocated in Missouri, bringing their slaves with them.

Missouri applied to join the United States in 1818, coming in as a slave state. This would have made for one extra slave state in the country, and the federal government could not sanction an imbalance between slave and free states. The solution was the Missouri Compromise of 1821, which assured that the number of slave states and free states would remain equal. Maine was to be admitted as a free state, thereby permitting Missouri statehood as a slave state. In 1821 Missouri became the twenty-fourth state.

## Early Economy

Missouri's land became fertile when advancing glaciers deposited rich topsoil upon it thousands of years ago. The state also has excellent river transportation in the east and the west. Steamboats carried their cargos to points along the rivers that eventually became thriving ports. Trails running west from Missouri led into the Rocky Mountains, where independent fur traders lived.

Soon there were permanent settlements and thriving towns along the river banks and trade routes. In 1822 the Santa Fe Trail was opened between Independence, in western Missouri, and Santa Fe, New Mexico, then a possession of Mexico. The beginning of the two-thousand-mile-long Oregon Trail was in Independence. When the Gold Rush to California began in 1848, thousands of prospectors passed through Missouri.

The potato famine in Ireland in the mid-1840's resulted in an influx of Irish into Missouri, where they worked on railroad construction or as day laborers. Missouri was growing so fast that extra hands were welcome. By the late 1840's, a wave of

Germans seeking a better life came to the area around St. Louis.

## Slavery

Slavery was a contentious matter in Missouri. By 1860, nearly 115,000 slaves were held in servitude in Missouri, many of them working on farms in the western part of the state. Some 3,600 free African Americans also lived in the state prior to the Civil War, most of them settling around St. Louis.

Dred Scott and his wife, Harriet, were slaves in Missouri. In 1846 the Scotts sued for their freedom, claiming that they were humans, not chattel. Their case reached the U.S. Supreme Court in 1857. The Court ultimately ruled that the Scotts were property owned by the master who had bought them. As such, they had no rights as citizens. This decision enraged northern abolitionists and was one of the crucial factors that led to the Civil War, which started in 1861.

## Missouri and the Confederacy

In 1861 the southern slave states formed the Confederacy, a separate nation with its own government. As a border state, Missouri, despite pressure from many of its slave owners, voted to remain in the Union, although nearly thirty-five thousand Missourians joined the Confederate armed forces.

Months before the war ended, Missouri freed all of its slaves, many of whom remained in the state. At the end of the twentieth century, Missouri had an African American population of nearly 11 percent. During the Civil War, more than a thousand battles were fought in Missouri, which sent more than 150,000 of its men to fight. About 115,000 of these men fought in the Union forces.

## Urban Growth

Missouri's strategic location and access to waterways and major trails resulted in the establishment of towns and cities along trade routes and encouraged urban development. The two cities that emerged as preeminent were St. Louis in the east and Kansas City on the western border with Kansas. Both cities became railroad centers, and Kansas City was known for its stockyards, first established in 1870, which still contribute substantially to its economy.

St. Louis became a major manufacturing center. In 1904 the city held a world's fair that attracted people from around the world. In the same year, St. Louis also became the first U.S. city to serve as the site of the Olympic Games.

By 1990, 75 percent of Missouri's residents lived in urban areas. Chief among these, besides Kansas City and St. Louis, were Springfield, Joplin, St. Joseph, and Columbia, the site of the University of Missouri's main campus, established in 1841.

## Other Factors in the Economy

Agriculture is a major contributor to Missouri's economy. Soybeans are the state's most lucrative crop, but Missouri farms produce sorghum, wheat, and hay as well. Cattle, hogs, and turkeys are also raised.

Its agricultural production notwithstanding, manufacturing became the largest and most important factor in Missouri's economy. Among the major industries located in the state are General Motors and Ford, whose plants produce automobiles and trucks; McDonnell-Douglas, which makes commercial and private airplanes; and the Hallmark Card Company.

Tourism and commerce are also major factors in the economy. Tourists bring more than five billion dollars per year into the state, coming there to sightsee, gamble in the steamboat casinos, and attend the many shows in Branson, where nearly thirty well-known singers own theaters.

### Missouri's Attractions

Besides the riverboat casinos and Branson's theaters, tourists are drawn to the state to view such attractions as the Gateway Arch in St. Louis, designed by Eero Saarinen and opened in 1965, which commemorates St. Louis as the jumping-off point for many pioneers heading into the western frontier.

Tourists also flock into New Madrid, a town on the Mississippi River that in 1811 and 1812 was rocked by three of the worst earthquakes ever recorded in North America. The New Madrid Museum provides detailed information about these earthquakes, which were so destructive they were felt as far away as Washington, D.C., and changed the course of the Mississippi River.

The Ozark Mountains and Lake of the Ozarks in southern Missouri offer excellent recreational facilities. This area attracts both tourists and retirees in large numbers. Tourists also flock into Florida and Hannibal in the north to visit the birthplace of Mark Twain and the town in which he grew up and used as the setting for some of his most popular stories.
—*R. Baird Shuman*

# George Washington Carver National Monument

**Date:** Authorized on July 14, 1943
**Relevant issues:** African American history, education, science and technology
**Significance:** This 210-acre site is the birthplace and childhood home of George Washington Carver, the revered African American agronomist, botanist, chemist, and conservationist. It includes the woodlands and prairie that Carver explored as a boy, along with his birthplace, the relocated house of his foster parents, and the Carver family cemetery.
**Location:** Three miles south of Diamond and seventy miles west of Springfield
**Site Office:**
George Washington Carver National Monument
5646 Carver Road
Diamond, MO 64840
ph.: (417) 325-4151
fax: (417) 325-4231
Web site: www.nps.gov/gwca/

Instituted during World War II when influential politicians realized they needed to lift the morale and motivate the loyalty of African Americans, the national shrine of Carver's birthplace was founded to commemorate the life and work of an outstanding black scientist, educator, and humanitarian. His agronomical discoveries had revitalized an impoverished Southern economy, and his racial views, which emphasized compromise, conciliation, and self-sufficiency, were admired by large numbers of black and white Americans. Although Carver spent only a decade on the Diamond Grove farm, the area and its community had an important influence on the course of his life.

### The Farm and the Boy

The person who would become George Washington Carver was born on the southwest Missouri farm of Moses Carver, a German immigrant and slave-owning Unionist, but the date of his birth is uncertain. In his later life Carver gave 1864 as his birth year, but some scholars locate the event much earlier, in 1860 or 1861, whereas others opt for a later date, 1865. His mother was called Mary by her owners, Susan and Moses Carver, but his father's identity is uncertain. According to Carver's later memory, his father, a slave on a neighboring farm, was killed in a logrolling accident soon after George was born.

As a border state during the Civil War, Missouri contained people who were passionately for and against slavery. Moses Carver, who supported the North, became the prey of "bushwackers," Southern sympathizers who kidnapped Mary and her infant son and took them into Confederate Arkansas (Jim, Mary's older son, escaped this fate by hiding with Moses). With the help of a go-between, Moses

Carver was eventually able to trade a three hundred-dollar racehorse for baby George, but Mary, unable to be found, was assumed to have died. These events occurred around the end of the Civil War, and so freedom and orphanhood came to George and Jim at the same time. The Carvers adopted the boys, and George bore his foster father's last name for the rest of his life (his middle name, Washington, was added much later when he wished to differentiate himself from another George Carver). The boys lived with the Carvers, who treated them as "blood kin," providing them with guidance and affection.

In contrast to his brother, who was robust and tall, George was sickly and short. Some scholars have explained George's stunted growth and high-pitched voice as a result of castration by his kidnappers. In later life he occasionally hinted at a tragic incident in his past that prevented him from marrying. George's frailty exempted him from physically demanding farm chores, but he was able to master such household tasks as cooking, canning, laundering, and crocheting. In his spare time he enjoyed walking in the woods and collecting wildflowers, which he replanted in his own garden. His ability to nurse sick plants to health earned him the sobriquet "plant doctor."

Besides his curiosity about nature, George also exhibited an inquiring mind about reading, music, and art. He received an eclectic religious education from a variety of circuit preachers. His nondenominational faith was nevertheless deep, and he viewed many of his ideas and discoveries as due to divine revelations. Desiring more knowledge than the preachers and the Carver's books could give, George tried to enroll in a local school but was rejected because of his race. However, a one-room school for blacks had been founded in Neosho, the Newton County seat, about eight miles from Diamond. George attended the Lincoln School for Negro Children while living with a black family for whom he did chores in exchange for room and board.

**The Wandering Years**

When George left his boyhood home in the late 1870's in pursuit of an education, he began a peripatetic life through which he would learn who he was and what he was meant to do. He soon became a member of the black migration to free Kansas,

traveling to Fort Scott. Horrified by the lynching of former slaves there, he departed for Olathe, Kansas, where he lived with a black couple, did odd jobs, and continued his schooling. In the summer of 1880, he followed this couple to Minneapolis, Kansas, where he set up a laundry business and attended high school. Exhibiting the versatility that he displayed throughout his life, he also painted pictures, experimented with plants, and played the accordion. After high school he tried a variety of things, including clerking at the Union Depot in Kansas City and successfully applying to a small college in Highland, Kansas. On arrival there, he was crushed to learn that the college did not accept students of his race.

Hearing of opportunities on the Kansas frontier, he traveled to Ness County, where he became a homesteader, building a sod house and attempting to farm his 160-acre claim. Droughts and blizzards doomed his enterprise, and he moved to Winterset, Iowa, where a white couple he met in church encouraged him to enter Simpson College. In 1889, he became the first African American to enroll in this small Methodist college. His ambition was to be an artist, but his art teacher, Etta Budd, encouraged him to pursue his interest in botany by enrolling in Iowa State College of Agriculture and Mechanic Arts where her father was professor of horticulture. Based on her strong letter of recommendation, he was accepted, and in 1891 he transferred to this college at Ames. He did extremely well academically, and his greenhouse work involving cross-fertilizing and grafting plants impressed his teachers. He also tutored the son of an agriculture professor. The father was Henry Cantwell Wallace, who would become secretary of agriculture in the cabinets of Presidents Warren Harding and Calvin Coolidge, and his son, Henry Agard Wallace, would become secretary of agriculture during President Franklin D. Roosevelt's first two terms and, still later, vice president of the United States. Helped by these politicians, Carver was later able to develop successful agricultural extension programs to educate poor black farmers in the South.

Carver's thesis for his bachelor's degree was entitled "Plants as Modified by Man," which described his experiments on hybridization. In 1894, he became the first African American to graduate from Iowa State, and he was offered a position as assistant to Louis H. Pammell, an eminent botanist and authority on mycology. As the first African American faculty member, Carver taught botany to undergraduates and conducted experiments on plants while managing the college's greenhouse. His reports on new species of fungi led to some of them being named after him—for example, *Taphrina carveri*. He also discovered new chemicals that inhibited the growth of harmful fungi on plants. Praised as one of the most brilliant students in the botany department, Carver received his master's degree in 1896.

### Tuskegee Institute

Learning of Carver's achievements, Booker T. Washington, head of the Tuskegee Normal and In-

*A statue at the monument of George Washington Carver as a boy, by Robert Amendola.* (George Washington Carver National Monument)

dustrial Institute for Negroes, invited him to take charge of its agriculture department. Washington was trying to improve the status of African Americans through education, particularly in practical skills. Carver, who shared many of Washington's ideals, accepted his invitation in 1896 and traveled to Tuskegee Institute in Alabama, where he would spend the next forty-seven years of his life.

Carver's early years were challenging since Tuskegee's laboratories were poorly equipped, and he had heavy teaching and administrative responsibilities (he also ran the school's two farms). At first he improvised equipment from whatever was available, but after the state of Alabama funded an agricultural experiment station at Tuskegee, he was able, as its director, to purchase new equipment and begin to use his scientific knowledge of plants and soils to improve the fortunes of Southern farmers. Years of intensive cultivation of cotton and tobacco had depleted the soil of its basic nutrients, causing farmers to sink into debt and increasingly fruitless labor. As a remedy, Carver encouraged farmers to plant peanuts and soybeans. He knew that these plants help restore exhausted soils. He also found that Alabama's soil was well suited to growing sweet potatoes. When farmers followed Carver's advice, peanuts flooded the market, causing prices to drop. Some farmers were tempted to return to cultivating cotton. To prevent this, Carver explored alternative uses for peanuts and sweet potatoes. During his career at Tukegee, he developed more than three hundred byproducts of the peanut, from dyes and soap to milk and cheese substitutes, and over a hundred derivatives from the sweet potato, including flour, molasses, ink, and postage-stamp glue. He freely shared the results of his experiments with the world through his bulletins, making no attempt to amass any personal fortune by patenting his discoveries. However, he did neglect his administrative duties, and this along with personality conflicts with Booker T. Washington led to his removal, in 1910, from the directorship of the experiment station. Carver was not overly disappointed with this decision, since his true interests lay in his educational projects and scientific research.

Although best known for developing derivatives from the peanut and sweet potato, Carver also developed by-products from pecans, soybeans, cowpeas, and plums. He extracted rubber from the milk of the goldenrod and paints from the clays of Alabama. Many of these products were simply curiosities, but those that proved commercially useful helped transform the economy of the South. When Carver first arrived at Tuskegee, the peanut was not even recognized as a crop, but by 1940 it was, after cotton, the second most valuable crop in the South. So impressed was Thomas A. Edison by Carver's inventiveness that he offered the agronomist over $100,000 a year to work for him, but Carver declined the offer, as he did offers from many others, preferring to devote himself to improving the condition of "his people."

In the mid-1930's, Carver became an advocate for chemurgy, the development of new industrial chemical products from agricultural raw materials. In 1937, he met Henry Ford at a chemurgy conference, and a friendship developed between them. In 1941, Ford dedicated the Carver Museum at Tuskegee, and in 1942, he established a nutritional laboratory in Carver's honor in Dearborn, Michigan. These are but a sampling of the many honors Carver received in the late 1930's and early 1940's, but failing health meant that he could attend only some of the ceremonies. When he died from anemia on January 5, 1943, Tuskegee was deluged with letters of sympathy from around the nation. Carver was buried in the institute's cemetery near the grave of Booker T. Washington.

### The Establishment of the National Monument

Shortly after Carver's death, on January 9, 1943, President Roosevelt paid tribute to him in an address before Congress. Senator Harry S Truman then introduced legislation to make Carver's birthplace in Missouri a National Memorial, and members of Congress quickly passed a bill which, on July 14, 1943, was signed into law by the president. Although many white and black Americans genuinely admired Carver, wartime race relations actually constituted the context for the bill's overwhelming support. The government's Jim Crow employment policies and segregated military had created intense discontent among African Americans, hampering efforts to engage black workers and soldiers in the war effort. In lobbying for the bill, Truman tended to ignore the government's segregation policies and emphasize Carver's accomplishments. In rising from slavery and poverty to scientific greatness, Carver was a symbol to all that American democracy worked.

Problems plagued the actual establishment of the monument. The bill's passage did not prevent violent racial conflicts during the summer of 1943. Furthermore, studies by scholars began to destroy the myth of Carver as the world's greatest agronomist who had remade the South's agricultural economy. The National Park Service tried to keep these revisionist interpretations hidden for fear of alienating African Americans. A further complication was the struggle that took place between Richard Pilant, a white Southern professor who had done much to make the Carver memorial a reality and wanted it consecrated to the goal of "race peace," and Sidney J. Phillips, an African American who had successfully raised much money for the underfunded monument and who wanted to operate the memorial as a "model farm." Pilant had the support of African Americans from Tuskegee who feared that Phillips was trying to monopolize control over Carver's legacy. The alliance between Pilant and the Tuskegee professors proved powerful enough to gain control of the monument's administration.

Carver, who hated confrontation and assiduously pursued reconciliation, would not have been happy with the political controversies over his monument. He even chose to separate himself from scientific controversies by not participating in professional meetings of chemists and botanists and by not publishing his discoveries in standard journals of scientific research where they would have been subjected to criticism. Instead, he published his results in bulletins that were directed primarily to farmers, not scientists. Knowing of the legal battles that often followed the patenting of inventions, Carver patented only three of his more than five hundred discoveries, reasoning that God had given him this knowledge, so how could he sell it? Although scholars have sought to reveal the complexities and contradictions in the life and work of this African American scientist, he himself saw his life simply—to use new knowledge to serve humanity, especially the poorest of "his people."

—*Robert J. Paradowski*

**For Further Information:**

Graham, Shirley, and George D. Lipscomb. *Dr. George Washington Carver, Scientist.* Parsippany, N.J.: Julian Messner, 1944. An early example of an idealistic biography intended for young readers.

Holt, Rackham. *George Washington Carver: An American Biography.* Rev. ed. Garden City, N.Y.: Doubleday, 1963. Carver chose Holt to record his life, and this biography benefits from the author's interviews with his subject and his subject's friends and colleagues.

Kremer, Gary R., ed. *George Washington Carver: In His Own Words.* Columbia: University of Missouri Press, 1987. Besides collecting Carver's correspondence and speeches, Kremer has included an extensive bibliography.

Mackintosh, Barry. "George Washington Carver: The Making of a Myth." *Journal of Southern History* 42 (November, 1976): 507-528. The author's controversial thesis is that Carver became famous because white Americans needed an appropriate racial symbol to atone for their prejudice against African Americans as a class.

McMurry, Linda O. *George Washington Carver, Scientist and Symbol.* New York: Oxford University Press, 1981. The author tries to separate the real man from his symbolic portrayals. It is the best scholarly treatment of Carver's life and work, with extensive references in the endnotes to many primary as well as secondary sources.

West, Patricia. *Domesticating History: The Political Origins of America's House Museums.* Washington, D.C.: Smithsonian Institution Press, 1999. The author tells the often politically charged stories of how the homes of such great Americans as George Washington and Thomas Jefferson were first established as museums, and she discusses how the George Washington Carver National Monument became a way of "desegregating" national memory.

# Jefferson National Expansion Memorial, St. Louis

**Date:** Old Courthouse built in 1839; Gateway Arch dedicated in May, 1968; Museum of Westward Expansion completed in August, 1976

**Relevant issues:** Art and architecture, western expansion

**Significance:** This National Historic Landmark is a memorial to President Thomas Jefferson, the Louisiana Purchase, and the westward-moving pioneers of the nineteenth century. It was the first property acquired by the federal government under the Historic Sites Act of 1935. The site includes the Gateway Arch, the Museum of Westward Expansion, and the Old Courthouse. The architects of the Gateway Arch, winners of a 1947 design competition, were Saarinen, Saarinen, and Associates of Bloomfield Hills, Michigan.

**Location:** A T-shaped district in downtown St. Louis bounded by the Mississippi River on the east, the Eads Bridge on the north, the Poplar Street Bridge on the south, and U.S. Interstates 70 and 55 on the west, but also including the grounds of the Old Courthouse (between Market Street, Broadway, and Pine Street) and an undeveloped area in East St. Louis, Illinois, on the eastern bank of the Mississippi

**Site Office:**
Jefferson National Expansion Memorial
11 North Fourth Street
St. Louis, MO 63102
ph.: (314) 655-1700
fax: (314) 655-1641
Web site: www.nps.gov/jeff/

The Jefferson National Expansion Memorial was the first property acquired by the federal government under the Historic Sites Act of 1935. When construction of the Gateway Arch was completed in the late 1960's and the Museum of Westward Expansion opened in 1976, the project fulfilled the dream of a group of St. Louisans to redevelop a section of riverfront along the Mississippi River and simultaneously to memorialize President Thomas Jefferson, the Louisiana Purchase, and the pioneers who explored and settled the American West.

**Early History**

In 1800 the Mississippi River was the western boundary of the United States, and most of the land west of the Mississippi belonged to France, which had just regained it from Spain. Jefferson, who was elected U.S. president that year, wanted to see the young country expand; he wanted free navigation of the Mississippi, and he also feared that French emperor Napoléon Bonaparte had imperial designs on North America. Jefferson sent envoys James Monroe and Robert Livingston to negotiate the purchase of New Orleans from Napoleon, or at least to obtain shipping rights on the Mississippi. The emperor, needing money for military adventures in Europe, agreed to sell the entire Louisiana Territory to the United States for fifteen million dollars in 1803. The purchase agreement defined the territory as "the high lands enclosing all the waters which run into the Mississippi or Missouri directly or indirectly." This encompassed land extending from the Mississippi to the Rocky Mountains, and from the Gulf of Mexico to Canada. The transaction violated laws on both sides. When it had taken the territory back from Spain, France had agreed not to cede it to another nation. Also, Napoléon made the sale without approval of his legislature. On the U.S. part, the Constitution made no provision for expanding the country by purchases of land.

## The Lewis and Clark Expedition

The sale was made, just the same, and the land area of the United States was doubled. Even before the purchase was effected, Jefferson, who had a long-standing curiosity about the western lands, had planned to dispatch explorers on a "Voyage of Discovery" to the area west of the Mississippi. Jefferson had used his great persuasive powers to convince the U.S. Congress to authorize the expedition, even though at that time—late February, 1803—the territory did not belong to the United States. Jefferson selected Meriwether Lewis, who had been his secretary and confidant, to lead the expedition, and Lewis spent the next few months obtaining supplies. In June, Lewis invited William Clark to join him on the trip. Clark was the brother of Revolutionary War hero George Rogers Clark, and a distinguished soldier in his own right. Confirmation of the Louisiana Purchase came on July 3; Lewis spent July 4 celebrating with Jefferson in Washington, and started his move west the following day. In October he met Clark at Clarksville, along the Ohio River in the Indiana Territory. When Lewis and Clark left Clarksville, they had a party of nine men; more volunteers signed on as the explorers moved west.

The party spent the winter of 1803-1804 encamped near a stream they dubbed Wood River, just across the Mississippi from St. Louis and opposite the mouth of the Missouri River. Clark super-

*The Gateway Arch.* (PhotoDisc)

vised the camp and trained the men, while Lewis set up headquarters in St. Louis, where he obtained provisions and made preparations for the journey. St. Louis fur trader Auguste Catha and his half brother, Pierre, were very helpful to Lewis, especially in finding crews of experienced boatmen for the expedition and providing gifts for the explorers to exchange with Indians in the West. Lewis, Clark, and the rest of their party left their encampment on May 14, 1804, and began making their way up the Missouri. Their first stop was at St. Charles, a French settlement twenty miles upriver.

From there they continued deeper into the interior of the country, recording information about the plants and animals they saw. They made numerous side trips, never far from the Missouri River, and encountered various Indian tribes along the way. In September they met a group of Teton Sioux, near the confluence of the Bad and Missouri Rivers in what is now South Dakota. The Indians entertained the white men at banquets, but after a few days some armed Tetons delivered an ultimatum: The explorers could stay with the Sioux or return to St. Louis, but they could not go farther up the Missouri. Clark talked himself out of this predicament, but he never forgave the Tetons, despite evidence that the threat was probably the responsibility of a single chief and did not have the support of the entire tribe.

The party continued up the river and spent the winter of 1804-1805 at Fort Mandan, near an Indian village in what is now North Dakota. The village was inhabited by the Mandan, Minitari, and Amahami tribes. At their winter encampment Lewis and Clark wrote reports of the expedition and organized a shipment of Indian artifacts, animal skins, plant specimens, and other goods to show the president what they had found. They also mapped out the remainder of their journey.

### Sacagawea Joins the Expedition

In the spring a few of the party went downriver with the cargo for President Jefferson, while the rest continued upriver. New members of the exploration party included Sacagawea, a Shosone Indian woman, and her French husband, Toussaint Charbonneau. Lewis and Clark had met the couple during their winter encampment and hired the self-important Charbonneau as an interpreter, but it

was really Sacagawea's facility with Indian languages that they desired. They hired him, in effect, in order to obtain her services. She did prove valuable to the party, while Charbonneau was a hindrance, at one point almost causing one of the boats to sink.

The party continued up to the source of the Missouri and over the Rocky Mountains. In November, 1805, the explorers sighted the Pacific Ocean. They built winter quarters, which they named Fort Clatsop, in what is now Oregon. After three months they began the long trek back, arriving in St. Louis in the autumn of 1806.

### Accomplishments of the Expedition

Overall, the Lewis and Clark Expedition identified twenty-four Indian tribes, 178 plants, and 122 animals. Many of the artifacts sent back by the explorers were displayed in Charles Willson Peale's museum (later the Pennsylvania Academy of Fine Arts) in Philadelphia. The expedition fueled interest in westward migration and established St. Louis as the gateway to the West. Each spring for many years thereafter St. Louis was crowded with parties of emigrants outfitting for the journey across the Great Plains. Tragically, with this western settlement come the displacement of American Indian tribes.

Eventually St. Louis grew into an urban and industrial center, and in 1890 the U.S. Census Bureau announced that there was no more American frontier. Four decades later, various prominent St. Louis citizens became interested in memorializing the pioneers who went west from St. Louis. The memorial itself would be more than three decades in the making.

### Plans for a Monument

Luther Ely Smith, a St. Louis attorney, proposed the idea of a historical monument honoring Jefferson and the pioneers to Mayor Bernard F. Dickmann late in 1933. Smith also saw the monument as a way to revitalize the St. Louis riverfront. Dickmann liked Smith's idea and called a meeting of business and civic leaders to discuss it. Bolstered by a plan presented by local historian McCune Gill, this group transformed itself into a temporary committee and in April, 1934, obtained a state charter as the nonprofit Jefferson National Expansion Memorial Association.

Following an abortive attempt to secure a thirty million-dollar congressional appropriation, the association focused instead on creating a federal commission to study the project's feasibility. On June 15, 1934, President Franklin Roosevelt signed a joint resolution establishing the United States Territorial Expansion Memorial Commission with fifteen members: three each chosen by the president, the Senate, and the House of Representatives, and six from the association. The National Park Service was designated to develop the memorial and opened an office in St. Louis in 1936.

The commission decided on a mix of federal and municipal funding for the project. The complicated procedure for approving federal public works expenditures, political opposition to a St. Louis bond issue, and resistance from property owners in the area delayed the project for several years. Finally, in 1940, funding was in place, and all the land needed for the memorial had been acquired and began to be cleared. By this time it had been decided to include the Old Courthouse within the memorial. The courthouse, dating from 1839 (with major additions in the 1850's) was the site of several historic events. Dred Scott filed suit for his freedom there in 1847; Ulysses S. Grant freed his only slave there in 1859; and Virginia Louisa Minor sued for the right to vote there in 1872. The building ceased being used as a courthouse in the 1930's.

Buildings that had to be cleared from the memorial area were demolished by 1942. By then, the United States was deeply involved in World War II, so development of the memorial slowed, although some renovations were made to the Old Courthouse. Toward the end of the war, the memorial association revived a plan, first proposed in 1933, to hold a national architectural competition to design the memorial.

### Saarinen's Arch
The competition opened in 1947 and drew 172 entries. The winner, announced in 1948, was Eero Saarinen, whose design called for a stainless steel arch, symbolizing a gateway and incorporated into a plan that included a monumental stairway down to the river, two museums, a tree-lined mall, a campfire theater, and a village of pioneer houses.

Again, there were delays in federal funding for the memorial. It was not until 1954 that President Dwight D. Eisenhower authorized $5 million for preliminary elements of Saarinen's design. In 1958 the federal government increased the total authorization to $17.25 million, to be supplemented by city funds left from the bond issue of the 1930's.

Saarinen had redesigned the memorial in 1957, shifting the arch and cancelling plans for one of the museums and the reproductions of pioneer buildings. Site preparation began in 1959, and Saarinen began to make working drawings so construction could begin. Saarinen did not live to see his project completed, however; he died of a brain tumor in 1961 at age fifty-one.

### Construction Begins
The first concrete was poured for the arch's foundations in 1962, and the first stainless steel section put in place early in 1963. The north leg of the arch opened in July, 1967, and the south leg in March, 1968; Vice President Hubert H. Humphrey dedicated the arch in May, 1968. A temporary Museum of Westward Expansion opened in June, 1967, with the permanent museum completed by August, 1976. Renovation of the Old Courthouse was finished in 1986, and the site was named a National Historic Landmark in 1987. In addition to the courthouse, the site includes another historic building, the Old St. Louis Catholic Cathedral, dating from 1834.

The future of the Jefferson National Expansion Memorial as an important part of St. Louis's cultural life seems well assured. The people of the city have embraced the Gateway Arch with increasing affection, and each year about two and a half million visitors come to the site; about one million ride to the top of the arch. The words "arch" and "gateway" and depictions of the arch have been employed by a large number of local businesses and organizations. Over the Fourth of July holiday the grounds of the memorial serve as home to an annual fair that draws several million people. In 1984, President Ronald Reagan signed a bill expanding the boundaries of the memorial to a section of the East St. Louis riverfront, which awaits development.
—*Steven P. Gietschier*

### For Further Information:
The Jefferson National Expansion Memorial Archives, located in the Old Courthouse, hold the

public records concerning the memorial, plus a large number of reports, documents, and clippings. Especially helpful are "A History of the Gateway Arch" by Michael A. Capps, a former Jefferson National Expansion Memorial historian and the administrative history of the site written in 1984 by Sharon A. Brown. There also have been numerous editions of Lewis and Clark's journals.

Cheek, Larry. *Eero Saarinen: Architect, Sculptor, Visionary.* Edited by Sandra Scott. St. Louis: Jefferson National Expansion Historical Association, 1998. A biography of the architect.

Hawke, David Freeman. *Those Tremendous Mountains.* New York: W. W. Norton, 1980. A helpful account of the Lewis and Clark Expedition.

Hosmer, Charles B., Jr. *Preservation Comes of Age: From Williamsburg to the National Trust, 1926-1949.* 2 vols. Charlottesville: University Press of Virginia, 1981. Of less value but still useful. Hosmer emphasizes the role of National Park Service personnel and deplores the demolition of the site's original buildings in the name of historic preservation.

Temko, Allan. *Eero Saarinen.* New York: George Braziller, 1962. The standard biography of the architect.

# Mark Twain Boyhood Home, Hannibal

**Date:** Built around 1843 and occupied by Mark Twain's family until 1853

**Relevant issues:** Art and architecture, cultural history, literary history

**Significance:** Mark Twain lived in this house through the formative years of his youth. Decades later, his memories turned back to those years and he wrote the most popular boys' story of all time, *The Adventures of Tom Sawyer* (1876), setting it in a village like that of his own youth and giving Tom a home almost identical to his own. During the twentieth century, his boyhood home came to be regarded as an icon of nineteenth century America and helped make Hannibal a major tourist stop.

**Location:** At 208 Hill Street in Hannibal, a Mississippi River town about 150 miles, by water, north of St. Louis

**Site Office:**
Mark Twain Home Board
208 Hill Street
Hannibal, MO 63401
ph.: (314) 221-9010
Web site: www.hanmo.com/hcvb (Hannibal Convention and Visitors' Bureau)

When Mark Twain left Hannibal, Missouri, in 1853, he was not quite eighteen years old, and less than half of his young life he had spent living in what later became famous as his boyhood home. Despite the comparative brevity of his residence in that house, the building came to occupy a special place in American cultural history, both because of Mark Twain's fame and because Hannibal—which styles itself "America's Hometown"—is perceived as an archetype of small-town America. The years that Mark Twain did spend in the house were important ones, and when he later approached middle age, his thoughts increasingly went back to those years. His now-classic depictions of early nineteenth century America center on idealized memories of Hannibal and his boyhood home. Millions of people visited the house during the twentieth century. Many—perhaps most—hoped to capture the nostalgic flavor of the simpler and more innocent world depicted in *The Adventures of Tom Sawyer.*

**The Clemens Family in Hannibal**

Born Samuel Langhorne Clemens, Mark Twain was the sixth of seven children of a proud but impoverished Virginian, John M. Clemens, and Jane Lampton Clemens, who had come to Missouri in the mid-1830's in the hope of finding prosperity. The Clemenses first settled in the tiny inland hamlet of Florida, where Sam was born on November 30, 1835. Disappointed by Florida's failure to provide business opportunities and devastated by the death of a daughter there, the family relocated to nearby Hannibal, a steamboat stop on the Mississippi River, around the time that Sam turned four. Apart from summers spent on an uncle's farm near Florida, Sam lived in Hannibal without interruption until 1853. He never lived there again, but he did revisit the town at least seven times over the next half century.

In 1819, two years before Missouri became a state, Hannibal was founded on a site well placed

*Mark Twain stands in front of his boyhood home in 1902.* (Arkent Archives)

No original plans or pictures of the boyhood home exist, but late twentieth century research and reconstruction work discovered that the house originally had two stories in the front and one in the rear. The Clemenses either enlarged the house while they occupied it or its plans were modified in the midst of its original construction to add more upstairs rooms. In any case, Sam and his younger brother, Henry, shared a rear second-story room, from which they could see the river and climb out a window for nocturnal adventures. At times, their sister Pamela used the downstairs parlor—which also served as a bedroom—to teach piano, and their older brother, Orion, published a newspaper out of an annex to the house.

Although the head of the family, John Clemens, earned the community's respect as a lawyer and civic leader, he never found the business success he sought. His family's fortunes—always precarious—fell even lower when he died in early 1847. His widow managed to get the family back into the boyhood home, but Sam's formal education gradually gave way to full-time employment, and he learned the printing trade while working for local newspapers, including his brother's. In June, 1853, he left Hannibal for good. After working as a journeyman printer in the East, he became a steamboat pilot in 1857 and worked on the lower Mississippi until the Civil War ended commercial river traffic. He then went west, where he became a newspaper reporter and wrote sketches under the pen name "Mark Twain." After his first travel book, *The Innocents Abroad,* made him famous in 1869, he married and settled in the East. By 1871 he was becoming a gentrified New Englander in the Nook Farm community of Hartford, Connecticut.

Meanwhile, Pamela Clemens had married in 1851 and moved to St. Louis, where her home would become Sam's base on return visits to Missouri. In the fall of 1853, Orion moved to Muscatine, Iowa, accompanied by Henry and their mother, Jane. Each of them later returned to Hannibal, but only after they died—for burial.

amid a developing transportation network pointing toward the western frontier. The Clemenses arrived there in 1839, shortly after Hannibal was incorporated. Though it had but a thousand residents, it seemed poised for rapid growth. It did, indeed, eventually become a prosperous transportation and manufacturing center, but not until after the last Clemens had left.

The Clemenses lived in several different Hannibal houses, all of which were on or near Main and Hill Streets, several hundred yards west of the river and about the same distance south of Holliday's Hill—a prominent landmark that *The Adventures of Tom Sawyer* would later immortalize as "Cardiff Hill." Soon after arriving, John Clemens purchased a large Hill Street lot that he subdivided, while reserving the plot on which he had a small wood-frame house built for his family. Exactly when the house went up is not known. However, the Clemenses were living in it by 1844. They stayed there until 1853, except for an interval in 1846-1847, when financial problems forced them to board in the upstairs apartments of a drugstore down Hill Street. That building, still standing, later became known as the Pilaster House.

Killed in a steamboat accident in 1858, Henry was originally buried alongside John Clemens in Hannibal's Baptist cemetery. In 1876—the year that *The Adventures of Tom Sawyer* was published—Mark Twain had his father's and brother's remains moved to Hannibal's newer Mount Olivet Cemetery, where his mother, Orion, and Orion's wife were later buried. (Mark Twain himself is buried in Elmira, New York.)

**Later Residents of the Boyhood Home**

After the Clemenses left Hannibal, their home became a rental property. City directories published every other year in the late nineteenth century show the names of different occupants in the house in almost every edition. During one period, the house appears to have been a restaurant. In 1882 it was occupied by an African American family—a fact that Mark Twain noted in *Life on the Mississippi* (1883), which includes a nostalgic account of his return visit to Hannibal in 1882.

When Mark Twain paid his final visit to Hannibal in 1902, he had his picture taken directly in front of the old family house. On that occasion he remarked that each time he returned to the house, it seemed to grow smaller; if he came back one more time, he feared, it would be only a birdhouse. His remark was long interpreted as being merely a reflection of his changed perceptions after decades of living in a palatial mansion in Connecticut. However, when the Hannibal house was being restored in 1990, it was discovered that Mark Twain had not merely imagined that it was smaller; it *was* smaller in 1902 than it had been when he lived in it.

**The Boyhood Home in Fiction**

Mark Twain became a novelist only after making his reputation as an author of travel books and humorous sketches. His first novel, *The Gilded Age: A Tale of To-day* (1873), he wrote in collaboration with his Hartford neighbor Charles Dudley Warner. That book's first eleven chapters contain an embroidered history of how the Clemens family came to Missouri and offer a memorable depiction of frontier conditions there in the 1830's. After publishing *The Gilded Age*, Mark Twain turned to writing about his own past. In 1875 he published, in *The Atlantic Monthly*, a vivid memoir of his years as a steamboat pilot that he later expanded into *Life on the Mississippi* (1883). Around that same time he wrote *The Adventures of Tom Sawyer*, his first novel without a collaborator.

Untroubled by the moral issues raised in the more complex *Adventures of Huckleberry Finn* (1884), that earlier book is—as Mark Twain himself described it—simply a "hymn to boyhood." It puts Tom, and his friend Huck, through a series of exciting adventures that conclude with an extraordinarily satisfying triumph. Along the way, Tom displays large measures of rascality, brilliance, and heroism—qualities that ensured the book's universal and lasting appeal. In what is probably the book's most famous episode, for example, Tom tricks his friends into paying him to whitewash a fence.

The house in which Tom lives with his Aunt Polly so closely resembles Mark Twain's boyhood home that passages in *The Adventures of Tom Sawyer* and other stories provided useful clues that helped in the real house's restoration. The fictional St. Petersburg of the Tom and Huck stories also closely resembles the Hannibal of Mark Twain's youth: from its position on the Mississippi River to its nearby limestone cave. One of the most dramatic episodes in *The Adventures of Tom Sawyer* occurs toward the end, when Tom and his girlfriend, Becky Thatcher, get lost in a labyrinthine cave south of St. Petersburg that is modeled on a real cave south of Hannibal.

**Restoration**

By the time of Mark Twain's death in 1910, his boyhood home had fallen into such disrepair that it was slated for demolition. A year later, however, a community leader named George A. Mahan bought the house, had it refurbished, and donated it to the city. Since 1912 it has been a public museum. For twenty-five years, a caretaker lived on its second floor, and visitors were allowed to inspect only the first floor, where memorabilia were displayed. In 1937, with the help of the federal Works Progress Administration (WPA), a permanent museum was built next to the house. It provided living quarters for the caretaker, making it possible to open to visitors the rest of the house, which was refurbished with WPA help. Meanwhile, the city of Hannibal created a permanent commission to maintain the house. In 1990 that commission became the Mark Twain Home Board, which leased the house and several other properties to the Mark Twain Home Foundation, a semiautonomous nonprofit body that still maintains the home.

Never strong to begin with, the house suffered under the traffic of the literally millions of visitors who tramped through it after 1912. In 1984 its interior was closed to visitors, and an exterior viewing platform was built along its west side, permitting visitors to peer inside through windows. Meanwhile, ambitious plans were made to restore the house to its original condition. Around that time the discovery of an 1883 photograph of the house showed ground-level and second-story rear rooms that had disappeared some time before Mark Twain's 1902 visit. Under the direction of curator Henry Sweets III, a careful study of the house and grounds revealed its original layout and suggested that a chimney collapse may have been the reason that the rear rooms were removed after 1883.

In 1990-1991, the house was placed under a protective cover and taken apart, down to its interior beams. After its foundation was correctly aligned, its entire structure was strengthened and then rebuilt to resemble its appearance when Mark Twain's family lived in it.

In addition to the house and the museum—to which a downtown branch was added in 1999—the Mark Twain Home Foundation maintains the nearby Pilaster House, in which the Clemenses briefly lived, and a small building that served as John Clemens's law office. The section of Hill Street on which the boyhood home stands has been transformed into a pedestrian arcade, along which visitors can find both authentic and purely commercial evidences of Mark Twain's legacy. Although a sign beside the boyhood home proclaims the spot to be the very place where Tom Sawyer got his friends to whitewash the fence for him bewilders many visitors, management of the boyhood home and museum meets high standards of objectivity and professionalism.

*—R. Kent Rasmussen*

**For Further Information:**

Fishkin, Shelley Fisher. *Lighting Out for the Territory: Reflections on Mark Twain and American Culture.* New York: Oxford University Press, 1997. Examines darker aspects of Hannibal's history, which the town ignores while celebrating a sanitized legacy of Tom Sawyer.

"Hannibal, Missouri: Mark Twain's Hometown, America's Hometown." www.angelfire.com/mo2/hannibal2/home.html. Web site containing pictures and information on the boyhood home, as well as links to other Hannibal and Mark Twain Web sites.

Powers, Ron. *White Town Drowsing.* Boston: Atlanta Monthly Press, 1986. Written while Hannibal was preparing to celebrate Mark Twain's sesquicentennial, a penetrating look at Mark Twain's legacy by a former Hannibal resident.

Rasmussen, R. Kent. *Mark Twain A to Z.* New York: Oxford University Press, 1996. General reference work containing lengthy entries on the boyhood home, Hannibal, and other related subjects.

Sweets, Henry H., III. "Mark Twain Boyhood Home." In *The Mark Twain Encyclopedia,* edited by J. R. LeMaster and James D. Wilson. New York: Garland, 1993. Concise history of the house by its curator. Other articles in the encyclopedia cover related subjects.

Twain, Mark. *The Adventures of Tom Sawyer.* Berkeley: University of California Press, 1982. Authoritative, corrected edition of the novel, prepared by the Mark Twain Project at Berkeley.

# St. Joseph

**Date:** Named in 1843

**Relevant issues:** Cultural history, western expansion

**Significance:** This city, the fifth-largest in Missouri, was the base for the Pony Express and its starting site during the 1860's. It was also an important point of departure for emigrants heading west on the Oregon and California Trails, and it was the city where the outlaw Jesse James last lived and was killed.

**Location:** In northwestern Missouri, along the bluffs of the eastern bank of the Missouri River, fifty-five miles northwest of Kansas City

**Site Office:**

St. Joseph Convention and Visitors' Bureau
109 South Fourth Street
P.O. Box 445
St. Joseph, MO 64502
ph.: (816) 233-6688

The city of St. Joseph began life as the Blacksnake Hills trading outpost of the American Fur Company in 1826, when the firm sent Joseph Robidoux III to open a fur-trading station there. Robidoux purchased the outpost from the company in 1830.

### European Settlement Begins

In 1836, Sauk, Mesquakie, and Ioway Indians sold a strip of land north of Robidoux's post to the United States, which then annexed it to the state of Missouri as slave territory, contrary to the Missouri Compromise of 1820. Slaveholders began pouring into the new territory, many of them from Virginia, Tennessee, Indiana, and Ohio, and a farming community developed. Robidoux's post became the principal trade center for the newcomers. The farmers raised hogs and cattle and grew tobacco and hemp with the help of their slaves, establishing the only tobacco market west of the Mississippi. In 1843, Robidoux renamed the former company outpost St. Joseph, after his patron saint.

St. Joseph's population increased rapidly following James Wilson Marshall's discovery of gold at Sutter's Mill, California, in 1848. Marshall had left for California from St. Joseph, and the next year many forty-niners stopped off on at the town on their way west via the Oregon and California Trails. The town prospered as the miners were joined by other travelers passing through on their way to settle the West.

### Supply Depot to Western Pioneers

St. Joseph, with a population of one thousand, became a major supply depot and outfitter for the fifty thousand gold seekers passing through in 1849 alone. Its meat packing and livestock industries were created to feed the hungry travelers, and the town was a last stop in "the states" for wagons, saddles, provisions, and pack animals. One hundred twenty-three new buildings were constructed in St. Joseph in 1849 along the city's center, some still standing, including the notable Robidoux Row, one of the first examples of row houses in the West. That spring fifteen hundred wagons crossed the Missouri by ferry to Indian territory to begin the journey west.

Many of the emigrants made St. Joseph their point of departure because the town was slightly to the north and west of the other major Missouri outposts of the time—Westport (today a part of Kansas City) and Independence. Traveling through St. Joseph therefore cut a few days' time off the journey to California. A cholera outbreak in Westport and Independence in 1849 sent even more travelers through St. Joseph on their way west.

Each spring for the next twenty-five years, thousands of travelers left St. Louis by steamboat bound for St. Joseph, where they disembarked and spent weeks outfitting for the trip west. They built tent cities, where they lived until the prairie grass reached four inches so their oxen could graze along the route. They then ferried across the Missouri. The crossing itself cost five dollars per person and fifty cents for each animal. Besides this, travelers paid about one hundred dollars for a wagon and one thousand dollars to outfit for the trip, huge sums at the time.

### Trails to the West

The travelers then followed the St. Joe Road across the northeast corner of what is now Kansas for ten to thirteen days until the trail joined up with the Oregon Trail at what is now Marysville, Kansas. Later on the trail, travelers branched off to Portland, Oregon, or Sacramento, California.

St. Joseph residents feared many of the emigrants, whose ranks included many gamblers and troublemakers. City council members even hired night guards to protect the citizens. Some 350,000 to 550,000 people eventually traveled west via the Oregon Trail. The ferry landing from which they departed to Indian territory across the Missouri River still stands in Riverfront Park.

When gold was discovered in Colorado in 1859, setting off the Pikes Peak gold rush, another wave of travelers surged through the town. St. Joseph solidified its status as a major point of departure for those traveling west with the completion of the Hannibal and St. Joseph Railroad that same year; Joseph Robidoux drove a final golden spike for the railroad, which carried the first passenger train across Missouri. The town was not only the final western railroad stop, but also the eastern terminus of the Central Overland, California, and Pikes Peak Express Company stagecoach line.

### Stagecoaches and the Pony Express

As the city where the railroad met the stagecoach line, St. Joseph was a natural point of origin for the

Pony Express. The service ran from St. Joseph to Sacramento, California, from April 3, 1860, to November 20, 1861.

The Russell, Majors, and Waddell firm, owner of the Central Overland, California, and Pikes Peak Express stagecoach line, started the Pony Express, with operations based in St. Joseph's Patee House Hotel, a luxury hotel of the time and now St. Joseph's only National Historic Landmark. At the time, the Central Overland stagecoach line carried passengers from St. Joseph to Salt Lake City, but it was experiencing financial difficulties. The firm needed the money that the government supplied to those lines that carried mail. They started the Pony Express to show that it was possible to deliver mail expediently via the Central Overland route and thereby secure a government mail contract for its stagecoach line.

The service especially hoped to get mail and telegraph messages more quickly to the growing number of people in California who ached for news from the East but were separated by the vast, sparsely populated western territories. Another group far from home, the gold miners in the Pikes Peak region, also were clamoring for letters and newspapers.

At the time, Russell, Majors, and Waddell competed with the Butterfield Route, a more southerly stagecoach route that the government favored for the delivery of mail to and from the Pacific coast. There were hostile Indians and inhospitable desert areas along the Butterfield Route, but the winters were less severe along this path than on the northern Central Overland trail. Therefore, residents in the northern cities such as Salt Lake City were lucky to receive mail once a month.

### Coming of the Telegraph

By this time, the telegraph lines had reached as far west as St. Joseph. Russell, Majors, and Waddell knew that the transcontinental telegraph would become a reality in the near future, and that it would make the Pony Express obsolete, but they hoped to secure the $600,000 government mail contract by then. Because their stagecoach line stopped at Salt Lake City and the stations were too far apart for Pony Express purposes, the company first had to spend $100,000 building relay stations.

Advertisements about the Pony Express appeared in papers in the East and West, telling read-

ers that beginning April 3, 1860, riders would carry telegraphic dispatches from New York to Sacramento in ten days and letters in thirteen days. The charge for the service was a whopping five dollars per half ounce. The Pony Express promised to pick up mail weekly (quickly changed to semiweekly due to demand) and deliver it in about half the time taken by the previous routes through the Isthmus of Panama or the Butterfield line.

### Operating the Pony Express

Applicants for the dangerous two thousand-mile route, more than two-thirds which ran through territory held by hostile Indians, were encouraged to be at least twenty years old, weigh less than 125 pounds and, preferably, be orphans. Every rider was required to sign a pledge stating:

> I do hereby swear before the great and living God that during my engagement, and while I am an employee of Russell, Majors and Waddell, I will under no circumstances use profane language; that I will drink no intoxicating liquors; that I will not quarrel or fight with other employees of the firm, and that in every respect I will conduct myself honestly, be faithful to my duties, and so direct all my acts as to win the confidence of my employers. So help me God.

The company bought five hundred of the best horses it could find, paying one hundred fifty to two hundred dollars for each at a time when an average horse cost about fifty dollars. Many riders owed their lives to the Pony Express's swift horses, which could outrun those of the Indians. Relay stations for the riders were constructed every ten to twelve miles, following the stagecoach routes along the Oregon and California Trails.

A train brought mail from the East to St. Joseph, where riders began the trip to Sacramento, whence mail was taken by boat to San Francisco. Each rider's stint was sevety-five to one hundred miles a day at top speed; this generally entailed seven stops at relay stations to change to a fresh horse. At the end of the run, riders were allowed a brief rest before returning back east with mail.

Eighty young men who lived along the trail from St. Joseph to Sacramento signed up with the new Pony Express. Soon after the initial thrill, however, many riders dropped out, unable to withstand the

*The Pony Express Monument in St. Joseph.* (St. Joseph Convention and Visitors Bureau)

next three hundred miles, much of it along the south bank of the Platte River. From here, the rider went steadily westward, passing Chimney Rock, Nebraska, on the way to Fort Laramie, Wyoming. Here, the trail entered the foothills of the Rockies, and then went over the mountains, through South Pass, and on to Fort Bridger and Salt Lake City. The trail passed into Carson City, Nevada, through Placerville, California, and on through Folsom to Sacramento. The worst part of the journey lay between Salt Lake City and Sacramento, an area that was a vast desert.

### Supplying the Pony Express

The St. Joseph store owned by Israel Landis made many of the saddles used by the riders. These saddles had a special leather covering called a *mochila*, onto which four padlocked mailboxes, called *cantinas*, were placed, two on each side. The rider's legs fit between the boxes. Mail pouches were never used on the Pony Express. The *mochilas* negated the need for saddle changes. At each relay station, the rider would simply transfer the *mochila* to a fresh horse already saddled and bridled; only two minutes were allowed for the transfer. At the end of the route, a station keeper would unlock the box.

In St. Joseph, the horses were kept at the Pikes Peak Stables, built from 1858 to 1861 and now reconstructed and containing blacksmith and wheelwright shops as part of the Pony Express National Memorial. It was from here that the first westbound rider embarked.

The Pony Express ceased operations after only nineteen months, mainly because of the advent of the telegraph. Financial troubles also contributed to the company's demise. The cost of feeding and keeping the horses in some of the remote, mountainous, and, at certain times of year, snowy areas of the West had not been counted in the owners' equation, and the federal government was unable

toll taken by the day-to-day pounding along the trail.

The first rider, who was most likely Johnny Frey, was seen off from St. Joseph amid the roar of a cannon, a cheering crowd, and a brass band. The rider carried forty-nine letters, several newspapers, and five private telegrams, including a telegram from President James Buchanan congratulating the sponsors of the Pony Express. The event was covered by reporters dispatched from newspapers across the country.

The Pony Express route ran northwest through Kansas to Fort Kearny, following the same path the Mormons used when they traveled to Salt Lake City in 1847 and the same route as the gold seekers of 1849. The trail then ran through prairies for the

to pay its bills for postal delivery. When the last rider left on November 20, 1861, the company was bankrupt.

## Demise of the Pony Express

The Overland Stage Company began daily mail service from St. Joseph to California that same year. The service, owned by Ben Holladay, followed the same central route across the country. Holladay sold the business in 1866 to Wells Fargo and Company, which moved the stage terminus west with the building of the transcontinental railroad.

Business in St. Joseph slackened during the Civil War but picked up in the late 1860's, when Texas cattle ranchers began herding their livestock to the railroad terminus at St. Joseph. A bridge was completed across the Missouri River in 1873, and in 1887 the St. Joseph Stock Yards Company was formed.

## Outlaw Jesse James

St. Joseph's most famous resident had nothing to do with the Pony Express or cattle ranching, however. He was an outlaw—Jesse James. His house still stands at 1318 Lafayette Street, where James lived with his family under the alias of Tom Howard until his death in 1882.

James had learned to kill during the Civil War as a member of William Clarke Quantrill's Raiders, a group of Confederate guerrillas from Missouri who ambushed federal soldiers and raided towns in the neighboring Union state of Kansas. Jesse's brother, Frank, was an original member of the Raiders and participated in their sack of Lawrence, Kansas, in which two hundred buildings were burned to the ground and one hundred fifty men were killed. In retaliation for this raid, federal soldiers came to Jesse's home in occupied Missouri and demanded to know the whereabouts of Quantrill's men. When the family refused to furnish the information, Jesse's stepfather was tortured and nearly killed; Jesse, his mother, and his sister were imprisoned. Upon their release, Jesse himself joined Quantrill's guerrillas, likely as revenge for what had been done to his family.

Quantrill's irregulars proved perfect training for a life of robbing and killing. The men were constantly on the move, ruthlessly striking and leaving just as quickly. In Quantrill's group, Jesse met the Younger brothers—Cole, John, James, and Rob-

ert—who, along with Jesse's brother, Frank, would be his partners in crime in years to come.

After the Civil War, Jesse turned outlaw and began robbing banks, trains, and stagecoaches. He was a fugitive when he came with his family to St. Joseph. He and Frank were the only members of their gang who had escaped from the disastrous Northfield, Minnesota, raid of 1876. The Younger brothers were seriously wounded, captured, and sentenced to prison, and three other gang members died in the foiled bank robbery. Undaunted, Jesse continued to rob and kill, using his new home in St. Joseph as a base of operations.

Robert Ford, a member of Jesse's gang, had decided to betray him when he learned there was still a ten thousand-dollar reward on Jesse's head. Apparently unaware of Ford's plan, Jesse invited him to take part in a bank robbery in Platte City. Ford and his brother Charles went to stay with Jesse in St. Joseph to prepare for the robbery. The next day, when Jesse was unarmed, Robert shot him in the back of the head. The Ford brothers were themselves betrayed by the law officers to whom they had planned to deliver Jesse. They were arrested and convicted of murder and conspiracy. Robert Ford was sentenced to be hanged but was pardoned by the governor. He was later shot and killed by a member of Jesse's gang.

## Modern Preservation Efforts

The house where Jesse James died has been restored with period furnishings and is open to the public. The Buchanan County Courthouse, where the Ford brothers were tried, is still in use by the county. It is one of the largest county government compounds in Missouri.

Beginning in the 1870's, St. Joseph, aided by its many railroads entered another heyday as a wholesale supplier to the West. As new wealth poured into the city, Victorian mansions were built. Between 1888 and 1893, Harvey Ellis designed many homes in St. Joseph in the Richardsonian Romanesque and Chateauesque styles, working at the local firm of Eckel and Mann. The American National Bank and the Police Station in St. Joseph, along with numerous residences, are showcases of this Midwestern genius.                    —*Sharon Bakos*

## For Further Information:

Bradley, Glenn. *The Story of the Pony Express.* Chicago: McClurg 1913. Reprint. Ann Arbor, Mich.: Gryphon Books, 1971. A shorter, yet encompassing, account of the Express.

Chapman, Arthur. *The Pony Express*. New York: Chapman Square, 1932. An excellent historical account of how the Pony Express started, how it was run, and the true adventures of the riders.

Davis, Robyn L. *St. Joseph, Missouri: A Postcard History*. Charleston, S.C.: Arcadia, 1999. A pictorial history of the town that consists mostly of illustrations.

Ghent, W. J. *The Road to Oregon: A Chronicle of the Great Trail*. Longmans, Green, 1929. Reprint. St. Clair Shores, Mich.: Scholarly Press, 1971. A comprehensive account of the Oregon Trail.

Settle, William A., Jr. *Jesse James Was His Name*. Lincoln: University of Nebraska Press, 1966. A thorough, scholarly biography of James.

# Other Historic Sites

## Anheuser-Busch Brewery

*Location:* St. Louis, St. Louis County

*Relevant issues:* Business and industry

*Statement of significance:* Representative of the influence of German immigrants on the beer-brewing industry in America, this company, begun in 1852 by Eberhard Anheuser who in 1865 was joined by his son-in-law, Adolphus Busch, pioneered the use of new methods of production and distribution, including the invention of the refrigerated railroad car. These buildings, dating from the last quarter of the nineteenth century, are of brick, ornamented on the exterior with gargoyles and other figures.

## Arrow Rock

*Location:* Arrow Rock, Saline County

*Relevant issues:* Western expansion

*Statement of significance:* The Missouri River crossing at Arrow Rock, noted by French cartographers (1723) and by Meriwether Lewis and William Clark (1804), figured prominently in the very early trail-breaking expeditions that opened the West. In 1817, a permanent ferry was established at what was to become the starting point for the traders from Old Franklin and Boon's Lick who operated on the Santa Fe Trail.

## Bingham House

*Location:* Arrow Rock, Saline County

*Relevant issues:* Art and architecture

*Statement of significance:* From 1837 to 1845, this was the residence of George Caleb Bingham (1811-1879), American portrait and landscape painter. Bingham preserved with realism human characteristic scenes of old-time Missouri life. It was during his years at Arrow Rock that he began his sketches of the Missouri River and frontier life around him that developed into his famous "genre" paintings.

## Carrington Osage Village Sites

*Location:* Horton vicinity, Vernon County

*Relevant issues:* American Indian history

*Statement of significance:* Occupied from about 1775 to 1825, this was the last dwelling place of the Big Osage Indians in southwest Missouri, prior to their removal to a reservation in Kansas. The site was visited in 1806 by Zebulon Pike. Because of the large number of trade goods found here, the site illustrates the rapid acculturation of the Big Osage.

## Clark House

*Location:* Bowling Green, Pike County

*Relevant issues:* Political history

*Statement of significance:* From 1899 until his death, this was the residence of James Beauchamp Clark (1850-1921), who served as Speaker of the House of Representatives (1911-1919). "Champ" Clark played a major role in the campaign to replace House Speaker Joseph G. Cannon and was Woodrow Wilson's leading competitor for the Democratic presidential nomination in 1912.

## Erlanger House

*Location:* St. Louis, St. Louis County

*Relevant issues:* Health and medicine

*Statement of significance:* From 1917 until his death, this was the home of Joseph Erlanger (1876-1965), graduate of The Johns Hopkins Medical School and one of the leading American physiologists of the first quarter of the twentieth century. He shared the 1944 Nobel Prize in Medicine or Physiology for his discovery of the electrical nature of the human nervous system.

## Fort Osage

*Location:* Sibley, Jackson County
*Relevant issues:* American Indian history, business and industry
*Statement of significance:* Established in 1808 by General William Clark (1770-1838) for the protection and promotion of trade with the Osage Indians, Fort Osage was one of the most successful of twenty-eight trading houses operated from 1795 to 1822 under the U.S. government's factory system. The fort served as the point from which distances were measured by the Federal Survey of 1825.

## Goldenrod

*Location:* St. Louis, St. Louis County
*Relevant issues:* Cultural history, naval history
*Statement of significance:* One of two remaining examples of the modern era of showboats that ended in the 1920's, *Goldenrod* (1910) is the largest and most elaborately decorated of the showboats. Originally seating fourteen hundred, it provided entertainment in the form of minstrel shows, vaudeville, or serious drama. Today, it continues in its role as a showboat.

## Graham Cave

*Location:* Mineola, Montgomery County
*Relevant issues:* American Indian history
*Statement of significance:* At the time of the 1949 excavations of the site, remains found here, dating to 8000 B.C.E., were among the earliest known for the Archaic Period. The remains from Early and Middle Archaic times give the site its importance and illustrate a merging of Eastern and Plains influence in Missouri.

## Joplin Residence

*Location:* St. Louis, St. Louis County
*Relevant issues:* African American history, cultural history
*Statement of significance:* From 1900 to 1903, this was the residence of Scott Joplin (1868-1917), one of America's significant composers. His work with the musical genre later known as ragtime provided important foundations for modern American music, combining elements of Midwestern folk and African American melodic rhythmic traditions within the structural contexts of Western European musical forms.

## Laura Ingalls Wilder House

*Location:* Mansfield, Wright County
*Relevant issues:* Literary history
*Statement of significance:* From 1896 to 1957, this was the home of Laura Ingalls Wilder (1867-1957), famous author of the *Little House* series. These books, considered international classics by specialists in children's literature, tell of Wilder's life on the frontier as her family homesteaded in Wisconsin, Kansas, Minnesota, and South Dakota and illustrate the struggles and hardships as well as the joys of pioneer life encountered by Laura as a young girl between the ages of five and eighteen (1872-1885). Wilder began writing at the age of sixty-five; her books have been translated into twenty-six languages.

## Missouri Botanical Garden

*Location:* St. Louis, St. Louis County
*Relevant issues:* Cultural history, science and technology
*Statement of significance:* Established in 1859, this is the oldest functioning botanical garden in the country. Its founder, Henry Shaw (1800-1889), intended the seventy-five-acre garden to serve two functions: to provide the public with the ornamental delights of plants as well as educating the average citizen in basic botany and horticulture; and to serve the pure or basic science objective of conducting botanical research according to the highest standards of the discipline.

## Pershing Boyhood Home

*Location:* Laclede, Linn County
*Relevant issues:* Military history, World War I
*Statement of significance:* From 1866 to 1877, this was the home of John Joseph Pershing (1860-1948), career Army officer. In 1917, as commander of the American Expeditionary Force sent to Europe, he exercised the greatest authority of any American general since Ulysses S. Grant and organized the largest army in American history to that time; his forces were an important factor in ending the war there. In 1919, Congress made

Pershing General of the Armies, the first American to achieve that rank. Later, as Chief of Staff, he laid the groundwork for the reorganization and modernization of the Army which would prepare it for World War II.

## Sainte Genevieve Historic District

*Location:* Sainte Genevieve, Sainte Genevieve County

*Relevant issues:* European settlement

*Statement of significance:* An old French river town, Sainte Genevieve has retained much of the atmosphere of its missionary fur trading, mining, and military eras.

## Shelley House

*Location:* St. Louis, St. Louis County

*Relevant issues:* African American history, legal history

*Statement of significance:* Half of a typical St. Louis two-family flat built in 1906, the Shelley House is important in African American history and in law. It served as the home of the plaintiffs in the landmark case *Shelley v. Kraemer* (1948), in which the United States Supreme Court ruled unconstitutional the enforcement of racial restrictive covenants in housing. Extending beyond racial distinctions, the *Shelley* decision is of importance to all Americans of ethnic and minority heritage.

## Tower Grove Park

*Location:* St. Louis, St. Louis County

*Relevant issues:* Cultural history

*Statement of significance:* Officially opened to the public in 1872, Tower Grove has been characterized as the largest and best preserved nineteenth century Gardenesque-style city park in the United States. This formal landscape architecture style features winding paths, symmetrical features, intense planting, and the use of architecturally elaborate gates, pavilions, and houses; it differs from the much more numerous Picturesque landscapes of Frederick Law Olmstead and others. The 285-acre tract in the south central part of the city, along the adjacent Missouri Botanical Gardens, was a gift to the city of St. Louis by merchant philanthropist Henry Shaw (1800-1889), who was largely responsible for its design.

## Truman Farm Home

*Location:* Grandview, Jackson County

*Relevant issues:* Political history

*Statement of significance:* Working here from 1906 to 1917, future president Harry S Truman (1884-1972) developed abilities that served him throughout his career, such as the knowledge of farming that shaped his federal farm programs and enhanced his appeal to farmers in the close-fought election of 1948.

## Truman Historic District

*Location:* Independence, Jackson County

*Relevant issues:* Political history

*Statement of significance:* From 1919 until his death, this area was associated with Harry S Truman, thirty-third president of the United States. The district centers around the residence of former president Truman and forms a corridor along North Delaware Street linking the house with the Truman Library, which adjoins the district on the north.

## Utz Site

*Location:* Marshall, Saline County

*Relevant issues:* American Indian history

*Statement of significance:* Located on bluffs overlooking the Missouri River, this site was occupied from c. 1400 C.E. to the late 1700's. Probably the principal village area occupied by the Missouri Indians at the time of their first contact with Europeans, Utz is noted by French explorers, beginning with Père Jacques Marquette, whose 1673 map placed "Messourit" Indians here.

## Washington University Hilltop Campus Historic District

*Location:* St. Louis, St. Louis County

*Relevant issues:* Cultural history, sports

*Statement of significance:* The district is associated with the Louisiana Purchase Exposition held in 1904 and the third in the modern series of Olympic Games held in conjunction with the exposition. The exposition was the largest in area and scope of world's fairs up to that date. The early buildings here, although not specifically designed as exposition structures, are the largest extant group from the heyday of world's fairs.

## Watkins Mill

*Location:* Excelsior, Clay County

*Relevant issues:* Business and industry

*Statement of significance:* Built in 1859-1860 as the central feature of a self-sufficient community on Missouri's western frontier, Watkins Mill is probably the best preserved example of a mid-nineteenth century woolen mill. Not only the building but also the rare machinery and the voluminous business records have been preserved.

## Westminster College Gymnasium

*Location:* Fulton, Callaway County

*Relevant issues:* Political history

*Statement of significance:* On March 5, 1946, at the gymnasium of this small liberal arts college, British statesman Winston S. Churchill (1874-1965) delivered his now-famous speech "Sinews of Peace," in which he gave his analysis of the postwar world. He spoke of the destruction caused by war and pleaded for a strong United Nations based on a firm Anglo-American alliance; he cautioned against nuclear proliferation and the threat of Soviet expansion. "From Stettin in the Baltic to Trieste in the Adriatic," he declared, "an iron curtain has descended across the Continent."

## White Haven

*Location:* Grantwood Village, St. Louis County

*Relevant issues:* Political history

*Statement of significance:* Significant because of its long and close association with Ulysses S. Grant (1822-1885), White Haven was the home of his wife, Julia Dent Grant. The Grants met and courted here, they lived here for a short period in the 1850's, and it was to here that Grant originally planned to retire, before the political scandals of his administration and financial difficulties made that impractical.

# Montana

*The State Capitol Building in Helena.* (Travel Montana/Donnie Sexton)

# History of Montana

Montana, one of the six Rocky Mountain states, lies directly south of the Canadian provinces of Saskatchewan and Alberta. To its east are North and South Dakota. Wyoming lies south of it, and Idaho borders it to the south and west. It is 570 miles from east to west. From Canada in the north to Wyoming in the south is 315 miles.

With an area exceeding 147,000 square miles, it ranks fourth in size among the fifty states. With a population density of 5.5 people per square mile, Montana ranks forty-fourth among the states in population. Montana lost population between 1980 and 1990 but experienced a slight population upsurge during the 1990's.

The Rocky Mountains dominate the western two-fifths of the state. The eastern three-fifths consist mostly of rolling hills and plains. The climate is dry and, in winter, extremely cold. Summers are hot. The rich soil of the plains, the hot summers, and the long summer days in this latitude are ideal for agriculture.

## Early History

When French Canadian explorers first visited the area, it had already been inhabited by humans for more than nine thousand years. Evidence exists of cultures that date to 8000 B.C.E. Among the native tribes in the area were the Arapaho, Assiniboine, Blackfoot, Cheyenne, Crow, Kalispel, Kutenai, and Salish Indians.

In prehistoric times, dinosaurs roamed Montana. A nest of duck-billed dinosaur fossils was discovered there in 1978. In 1988 the most complete skeleton of a tyrannosaur ever unearthed was discovered. The earliest human inhabitants hunted bison and other indigenous animals with spears.

## Early Exploration

The earliest known explorers to reach Montana were François and Louis Joseph de La Vérendrye, French Canadian brothers who arrived in 1743. Montana became part of the United States in 1803 through the Louisiana Purchase.

Explorers Meriwether Lewis and William Clark, guided by a young American Indian woman, Sacagawea, crossed the territory in 1805 en route to America's northwest coast. They returned in 1806 on their trip east. A Spanish trader, Manuel Lisa, established the Missouri Fur Company and went on a trading expedition up the Yellowstone River. In 1807 he established Montana's first trading post, Fort Manuel.

The following year Canadian David Thompson established a trading post on the Kootenai River and, in 1809, founded Salish House near Thompson Falls. By 1829, both the Hudson Bay Company and the American Fur Company traded in this area.

Montana's rivers and low mountain passes encouraged transportation. The second longest river in the United States, the 2,315-mile-long Missouri, begins in Montana. Other rivers—the Jefferson, the Madison, the Gallatin, and the Yellowstone—criss-cross the state.

By 1850 fur traders had overhunted and exploited Montana to the extent that most of the fur-bearing animals had been killed. Whole herds of bison, fox, and deer were wiped out by voracious traders.

## The Discovery of Gold

When gold was discovered in California in 1848, thousands of easterners rushed across the country seeking instant wealth. Meanwhile, residents of Montana searched for gold in their area. In 1862 John White discovered small gold deposits at Grasshopper Creek. By 1863 more than five hundred miners had come there.

Soon a gold strike was made nearby. A settlement, Virginia City, which by 1865 had ten thousand inhabitants, sprang into being. Gold was discovered at Last Chance Gulch, where its discovery spawned another city, Helena. Meanwhile, rich veins of copper and silver were found around Butte in the Rocky Mountains.

Lawlessness soon became a considerable problem. Gangsters robbed stagecoaches of the gold and silver they transported. During 1863 one gang

killed more than one hundred people. In the following year, vigilantes captured and hanged more than twenty such criminals, thereby reducing crime substantially.

Miners flocked into the area as well as merchants, who arrived with their families to open stores and to establish an infrastructure. Cattle ranchers came to eastern Montana. In 1863 schools were opened in Bannack and Nevada City.

### The Road to Statehood

Congress created the Montana Territory in 1864. In 1875 Helena became its capital. American Indian uprisings raged. In 1876 the Sioux and Cheyenne Indians killed Lieutenant Colonel George Armstrong Custer in the Battle of the Little Bighorn, but in 1877, Chief Joseph of the Nez Perce tribe surrendered, ending the American Indian wars that plagued the territory. By 1880, Montana's Native American population was deployed to seven American Indian reservations within the territory.

In 1880 the Utah and Northern Railroad laid tracks across Montana, enabling Montanans to ship produce and cattle to eastern markets. Montana's first bid for statehood in 1866 was premature because the state had a very small population, little access to eastern markets, and continuing problems with American Indian wars. Because the expansion of the railroad into the state resulted in the population quadrupling within a decade, a constitutional convention was called in 1884, and statehood was again requested but refused for political reasons.

In 1889 President Grover Cleveland signed an enabling bill guaranteeing that if North Dakota, South Dakota, Washington, and Montana submitted acceptable constitutions, statehood would be granted. Montana held a constitutional convention in July of that year, offered a constitution to its electorate, and was granted statehood in November, 1889, becoming the forty-first state. In 1894 Montana voters chose Helena as the capital.

### Copper Mining in Montana

Although early prospectors found gold and silver around Butte, it was copper that brought the greatest wealth to Montana. Marcus Daly, seeking silver in the area, discovered one of the richest copper deposits in the world and in 1881 opened his copper mine in Anaconda. William Clark soon opened a copper operation nearby in Butte.

The copper found here was so abundant that Butte Hill was nicknamed "the Richest Hill on Earth." The copper industry attracted immigrants, mostly from Great Britain, to work in the mines. Daly established the Anaconda Copper Mining Company, and in 1926 Clark's Butte holdings were sold to that corporation.

## Montana Politics and Education

The two powerful copper barons who emerged from the Butte-Anaconda area, Marcus Daly and William Clark, were business and political rivals. They engaged in a heated campaign to have their own towns declared capital of the state, with Clark prevailing. Each owned the newspaper in his respective town.

Clark was elected to the U.S. Senate in 1891 but resigned when a scandal, perpetrated by reports accusing him of bribery in Daly's newspaper, the *Anaconda Standard*, cast doubt upon Clark's integrity. He was, nevertheless, elected to the Senate when he ran again in 1900.

Montana was the first state to elect a woman to Congress. Jeannette Rankin was elected in 1917 and served for two years. She served again from 1941 to 1943. Rankin was the only member of Congress to vote against the U.S. entry into World War I in 1917 and into World War II in 1941.

Montana's first constitution, ratified in 1889, was replaced when a constitutional convention called in 1972 produced a new constitution, narrowly ratified by the electorate and put into effect in 1973. This constitution combined more than one hundred state agencies into fifteen departments, whose heads report to the governor. In 1974 the constitution was amended to change the annual sixty-day legislative session to a ninety-day session to meet in odd-numbered years.

Montana prides itself on valuing education. Its 1990 literacy rate of 92 percent is 5 percent above the national average. Seventy-five percent of Montanans are high school graduates, whereas the national average is 67 percent.

## Industrial Expansion

Natural gas was discovered in Glendive, near Montana's eastern border, in 1913. This was an important discovery because where there is natural gas, there is usually oil. It was not until 1950, however, that vast oil deposits were discovered on the Montana-North Dakota border. Oil revenues spurred the state's faltering economy. The strip mining of bituminous coal in the eastern part of the state also helped to advance Montana's economy, changing the nature of the plains considerably. Nevertheless, the Montana plains are among the most prolific producers of wheat in the United States.

In 1955 the Anaconda Aluminum Company began operation in Columbia Falls in northwestern Montana. In 1983, however, the once-powerful Anaconda Copper Mining Company, having depleted the area around Butte, suspended mining operations.

## Natural Disasters

Between 1917 and 1920, Montana suffered greatly from droughts that caused many farmers and cattle ranchers in eastern Montana to fail. In 1929 another drought began that again devastated eastern Montana and lasted for several years, during which the economic contractions of the Great Depression also affected that state's economy. During 1935, Helena was struck by more than one hundred earthquakes. Although no lives were lost, property damage was severe.

With federal aid, Montana strove to avert the devastation earlier droughts had inflicted upon the state. Although Flathead Lake, which covers two hundred square miles, is the largest fresh water lake west of the Mississippi River, it proved insufficient to provide irrigation during droughts. In 1934 Montana began a dam building project that, in 1940, culminated in the creation of the four hundred-square-mile Lake Peck and several other artificial lakes that provide irrigation and hydroelectric power for Montana's farms and cattle ranches.

*—R. Baird Shuman*

# Butte

**Date:** Founded in the 1860's
**Relevant issues:** Business and industry, political history
**Significance:** Famous for its copper production, Butte dominated world output from 1877 to 1920; its mining heritage resulted in designations as Montana's first Cultural Heritage Area and a National Historic Landmark District of 4,500 civic, residential, mining, and business structures.
**Location:** 5,765 feet above sea level on a plateau of the northern Rocky Mountains of southwestern Montana on the western slope of the Continental Divide; at the crossroads of Interstates 15 and 90, sixty-five miles southwest of Helena

**Site Office:**
Butte Chamber, Visitor, and Transportation Center
1000 George Street
Butte, MT 59701
ph.: (800) 735-6814; (406) 723-3177
fax: (406) 723-1215
Web site: www.butteinfo.org
e-mail: butteinfo@butteinfo.org

Butte began its existence as a gold placer camp in the 1860's only to carve out its place in mining history two decades later as a preeminent copper town, which grew to dominate world production from 1887 to 1920. As Butte came of age it became recognized for both its mining barons—and their "war of the copper kings" waged over "the richest hill on earth"—as well as its miners, whose labor organizations brought Butte a designation as the "Gibraltar of Unionism." After the mining industry was consolidated, labor and management faced off in a series of conflicts while Butte's residents—to counter the political and economic domination of Anaconda Copper Mining Company—looked for leadership to various third parties and labor organizations, including the Socialist Party, which governed the community from 1911 to 1914. By the time copper production peaked in Butte in 1920, however, the power of third parties and unionism in Butte had been squelched.

**Early History**
Butte was neutral territory frequented by a variety of intermountain Indian tribes before gold prospectors began flocking to the area in the 1860's. In 1864, the year Montana became a separate U.S. territory, the first placer mine was established near Butte, but within a few years the gold was played out; by 1870 Butte had nearly faded into obscurity. A few miners such as William Farlin believed there were riches remaining in Butte's quartz deposits, and in 1874 Farlin gave rise to a new mining era after removing ore rich in silver and copper from his Asteroid claim. William A. Clark, an investor with interests in banking and mining, provided the financing for Farlin to develop his claim about the same time that Clark, who would later become known as one of Butte's copper kings, purchased and began developing a trio of his own claims.

By 1876 silver ore had been successfully treated for profitable extraction, and Butte City, named for the nearby conical peak Big Butte, was home to one thousand residents. That year Marcus Daly, who would soon become Clark's archrival, arrived in Butte to inspect properties for possible development by the Walker brothers, Salt Lake City entrepreneurs. Daly bought and then managed the Alice Mine for the Walkers. By the end of the decade, a two hundred-foot-deep shaft had been sunk at the Alice Mine, a twenty-stamp silver mill was relocated from Utah to Butte, and the Washoe process for treating ores, first developed at Nevada's famous Comstock Lode, was introduced into local mining operations. Meanwhile at the request of Daly, the Colorado & Montana Smelting Company in 1879 constructed a Butte smelter, found indispensable in treating the area's minerals with their high concentrations of arsenic.

During the 1870's, while Clark was bringing in investors from Colorado, Andrew Jackson Davis, another banker-miner, courted East Coast capitalists who needed copper to service markets for electrical conduits. Davis invested in several Butte properties including the Lexington Mine, which became a great silver producer and helped him become Montana's first millionaire as well as owner of Butte's First National Bank. By 1881 Davis had sold his Lexington Mine for one million dollars, formed the Parrot Silver and Copper Company and built a smelter.

While Butte's mine owners were developing necessary technology, its miners were organizing, and in 1878 Aaron C. Witter, credited as the father of Montana unions, helped found the Butte Workingmen's Union, later renamed Butte Miner's Union (BMU). The BMU successfully fought off a threat by owners to reduce wages and soon became the West's most recognized labor organization, able to guarantee workers a daily minimum wage of $3.50.

**The Anaconda Mine**
In 1880 Daly sold his interest in the Walker mines and purchased the Anaconda Mine, first developed for silver by Michael Hickey who named the property after General Winfield Scott's military strategy of surrounding the enemy with a snakelike grip. Daly and others discovered that the quartz of Butte was richest in silver near the surface, while

erosion had left copper sulfide hundreds of feet deep. The Anaconda Hill area of the Butte mining district contained great seams and veins of copper.

To develop the Anaconda Mine, Daly sought the backing of powerful San Francisco tycoons, including George Hearst, the father of newspaper baron William Randolph Hearst. With his financiers Daly organized the Anaconda Copper Mining Company (ACM) and began accumulating dozens of mining properties in Butte, as well as timberlands and coalfields to provide fuel and lumber for his mining operations. By 1883 Daly's Anaconda Mine workers had driven a mine shaft 650 feet deep, where they found a copper vein that widened to 100 feet and represented the richest body of copper sulfide yet discovered. The following year Daly built a massive copper reduction works and his own smelter, the Washoe, twenty-six miles west of Butte on Warm Springs Creek, giving birth to a town Daly named Anaconda.

## Multiethnic Community

By 1885 the increasing need for workers had brought Butte a population of twenty-two thousand. Both Daly and Clark imported miners by the thousands. Many of Daly's crews were Irish. In the mid-1880's Cornishmen began to arrive in Butte, and numerous other nationalities came as well, including Italians, Serbians, Croatians, French Canadians, Finns, Scandinavians, Lebanese, Chinese, Mexicans, Austrians, Germans, and black Americans. During this period of population growth, which continued through World War I, Butte became known as one of the country's toughest towns and was famous for its gambling dens, brothels, and round-the-clock saloons.

With the community growing, workers in many of Butte's industries followed the miners' lead in forming unions, and in 1886 these organizations joined together as the Silver Bow Trades and Labor Assembly. Despite tensions between English and Irish workers, the BMU itself grew in force and won the closed shop for Butte mines by 1887, the year silver production peaked in Butte. That year Montana came of age as a copper mining center, producing more than seventy-eight million pounds of copper—with fifty-eight million pounds alone extracted from the Anaconda Mine.

## War of the Copper Kings

The so-called War of the Copper Kings began in earnest in 1888 when Daly began using his money and power to thwart Clark's election as a congressional territorial delegate to represent Montana, which became a state the following year. The initial impetus for the Clark-Daly feud is not certain; it is known that Clark and Daly had worked together in 1884 at Montana's constitutional convention and along with Helena businessmen C. A. Broadwater and Samuel Hauser became known as the "Big Four" of the Democratic Party.

There were obvious differences between Clark, who had been educated at the Columbia School of Mines and later sought the prestige of both wealth and national political office, and Daly, a self-educated Irish immigrant with an instinct for ore and a vision of creating a fully integrated copper company. In 1888 Clark, who lost each of his bitterly fought bids for a seat in Congress, and Daly employed similar campaign tactics, though. With Clark running the *Butte Miner* and Daly the *Anaconda Standard*, the War of the Copper Kings initiated the use of newspapers as political vehicles. They launched twelve years of election campaigns to advance the interests of the mine owners, campaigns dominated by massive street parties financed by the two copper kings, with whiskey and gold the principal campaign tools.

## Decline of Silver and Rise of Copper

The Panic of 1893 and the repeal of the Sherman Silver Purchase Act, which ended the use of silver as legal tender, helped strengthen Butte's copper industry while wiping out the remains of silver mining in the community. As Butte's reputation as a copper community continued to grow, so did the reputation of its labor organizations, and in 1893 miners throughout the West met in Butte and formed the Western Federation of Miners, with the BMU named Local Number One.

In 1894 the second round of the Clark-Daly feud was waged over a statewide runoff vote to determine Montana's capital, with Daly supporting the town he founded, Anaconda, while Clark adopted Helena's cause. Ultimately Clark claimed victory and became a hero in Helena after the two copper barons spent nearly three million dollars to influence voters. Throughout the remainder of the 1890's Clark continued his drive for political office.

In 1899 Clark was elected by the Montana Legislature to represent his state in the U.S. Senate, but the Senate, which was lobbied heavily by Daly, refused Clark a seat, citing alleged campaign improprieties.

In 1899 Daly agreed to sell his Anaconda Company to Standard Oil in a deal that created the giant copper trust, Amalgamated Copper Mining Company, and made Daly the new corporation's president for a brief period. Amalgamated began absorbing its local competitors, and by 1900, the year Daly died, the company was responsible for half of the U.S. output of copper.

## The Election of 1900

The election campaign of 1900-1901 marked a major turning point in the copper king wars. Clark formed an alliance with another mining baron, Fritz Augustus Heinze, and Heinze and Clark fused together a number of political factions under the Democratic Party banner—in what the Amalgamated-controlled *Anaconda Standard* called the "Heinzeantitrustboltingdemocraticlaborpopulist ticket"—to oppose the newly created copper trust, which backed anti-Clark candidates. Clark wanted a friendly state legislature that would send him to the U.S. Senate.

To win the support of labor, Clark and Heinze granted their workers a long-sought-after eight-hour workday and challenged Amalgamated to follow suit; the company refused and labor threw its support to Clark's faction. Clark won his seat in the U.S. Senate. Soon after the election Clark and Heinze went their separate political ways, and once in Washington Clark proved to be a staunch conservative, serving one term that lasted through 1907.

With Clark in Washington, D.C., Heinze was left as the lone independent mine owner who could challenge the domination of the expanding copper trust. Heinze had originally come to Butte in 1889; he had an engineering degree from the Columbia School of Mines and begun working as a surveyor for the Boston and Montana Company at the age of twenty. In 1892-1893 Heinze opened the Montana Ore Purchasing Company and constructed a large smelter to handle ores of independent companies at reduced rates, making him a favorite of smaller mine owners. He later purchased and leased properties near Amalgamated claims; they became the cause of legal disputes.

## The Apex Law

Heinze launched his own five-year battle with Amalgamated in 1898 when he began taking advantage of the Apex Law, which provided that an owner of a claim on which a vein of ore apexed, or touched the surface, could follow that vein wherever it led. Heinze bought off local judge William A. Clancy to ensure favorable rulings in lawsuits filed by Anaconda and had his workers dig deep crosscuts from his claims into Amalgamated's claims. Heinze's tactics set off an underground war between his and Amalgamated's miners; the fighting resulted in the deaths of two men in a dynamite blast.

In 1903 Heinze—who had at his disposal small quantities of stock from various of the newly merged Amalgamated subsidiaries—played his final card and filed suit claiming that the copper trust was built through illegal acquisitions that did not have the approval of minority stockholders. In 1903 Clancy ruled in favor of Heinze in a decision that threatened to strip Amalgamated of much of its power. Amalgamated responded by shutting down most of its operations, locking out fifteen thousand workers, and then demanding that Governor Joseph Toole call a special legislative session to pass a groundbreaking law allowing for the removal of a biased judge from a case. Toole was faced with either appearing the victim of obvious corporate coercion or causing his state economic turmoil; he chose the former, and on November 10, 1903, the Montana Legislature passed a Fair Trials Bill. Heinze quickly lost his political power, and in 1906 he sold his mining operations to Amalgamated in a deal worth about twelve million dollars.

## Challenging Anaconda

In the absence of a mine owner who championed worker rights, Butte flirted with a number of labor and political organizations that provided miners some hope of countering the power of the consolidated copper company. Between 1905 and 1920 liberals and laborers were involved in a succession of organizations, including the Industrial Workers of the World (IWW), a far left-wing group of labor insurgents known as Wobblies; the Socialist Party, which advocated public ownership of companies; the American Society of Equity, which championed marketing and purchasing cooperatives; and the

Nonpartisan League, which advocated state-owned banks and grain elevators and urged increased taxation of the copper trust. In 1906 the IWW held its founding convention in Chicago, and Butte sent the country's biggest delegation.

In 1910 Clark sold his remaining Butte mining properties to Amalgamated (which again became Anaconda Copper Mining Company that year), giving ACM complete control of Butte mining. Setting the stage for the remaining battle to be fought over Butte—a contest between labor and management—was the rise in popularity of the Socialist Party, which advocated improved living conditions and honest government.

### A Short-Lived Socialist Government
In 1911 Butte elected its first Socialist city officials, including Unitarian minister Lewis Duncan, who won the mayoralty. Between 1912 and 1914 Duncan's party came to control the city council as well, and Butte became one of the largest U.S. cities ever to be governed by Socialists.

During their brief reign the Socialists helped improve the conditions of working-class neighborhoods, building sidewalks and paving streets while also implementing health codes for local businesses. Nonetheless, frustrations with the mines' working conditions, which had been deteriorating since 1906, led to a split among miners, and by 1914 the BMU was divided among a conservative faction, generally supportive of the company, and a liberal faction, including workers affiliated with the IWW.

Those frustrations exploded in June, 1914, during the city's annual Union Day celebration, when most union members—sympathetic with the liberal wing of labor—boycotted the parade, watching from sidewalks as only a few hundred BMU members marched. Union insurgents, angered at the "rustler card," or work permit, system, which in effect allowed the company to blacklist workers, assaulted those marching in the parade, sacked the union hall, and threw union records out the window and onto the street. A new union was quickly formed, and ten days after the parade the old Miners' Union Hall was destroyed by dynamite.

By August, 1914, a company employment office had been dynamited as well, and ACM was refusing to recognize either the new or the old union. Throughout the summer of 1914 the city appeared on the brink of anarchy. Finally, in September, Governor Samuel V. Stewart declared martial law and the National Guard was sent in to patrol Butte's streets. Following a grand jury investigation of the summer's incidents, Duncan and his sheriff, Tim Driscoll, were charged with failure to protect the property of Butte's citizens and removed from office following impeachment proceedings. Within two years the Socialist Party had all but disappeared from Butte.

### The Crisis of 1917
By 1917, Butte's population had mushroomed to 100,000. The community's population as well as its copper production peaked that year while World War I brought to a head workers' bitterness over labor conditions. In the five years preceding 1917 trade agreements had lapsed and not been renewed, collective bargaining had been eliminated in favor of bargaining with individual workers, and an open shop—with workers not required to be union members—had replaced the closed shop. The result was that the IWW moved into Butte in larger numbers to take up the slack in labor leadership.

In June, 1917, the worst hard-rock mining disaster in U.S. history occurred when the Speculator Mine exploded into a fire, after a carbide lamp accidently ignited frayed and oil-soaked electrical insulation. More than 160 miners were killed in the incident, with the loss of lives sparking a spontaneous strike, the beginning of four years of labor unrest. In the wake of the disaster a new organization, the Metal Mine Workers Union, was formed to lead the strike, and by the end of that month fifteen thousand workers had abandoned their jobs.

In July, IWW leader Frank Little came to Butte, and after making a series of antiwar, anticorporation speeches the liberal leader was kidnapped from his boardinghouse, tied to the back of a car, and dragged to the outskirts of town where he was hanged from a railroad trestle. The 1917 strike came to an end a few weeks after Little's burial, with the arrival of U.S. military troops.

### Continuing Labor Struggles
Between 1918 and 1920 the IWW led three more strikes in Butte, all of which were eventually halted after federal troops—which occupied the city six times between 1914 and 1920—were called in to

ensure order. During a strike in April, 1920, company guards at the Neversweat Mine fired into a crowd of picketers, killing one and wounding fifteen more, the climax of labor violence in Butte. In January, 1921, when the last troops pulled out of the mining city, unionism and socialism had been drained of much of their power. In retrospect, many Butte historians have agreed that the federal government, along with labor conservatives, broke the back of third parties and unions, which did not win back the closed shop until the New Deal era.

### Open-Pit Mining

In the 1920's ACM began reducing its activities in Butte, opting for investments in Chile and other countries, and Butte's population began diminishing. The Depression of the 1930's, coupled with the increased use of mining machinery and foreign competition, brought a slump to Butte and fostered the development of open-pit mining practices, less labor-intensive than underground mining. Open-pit mining began with the opening in 1955 of the Berkeley Pit, which became the world's most formidable truck-operated open-pit copper mine. The excavation of Berkeley Pit and other nearby projects ultimately changed the face of Butte, eliminating hundreds of homes, apartments, boardinghouses, bars, and corner groceries that once dominated Butte's east side; in the process entire neighborhoods vanished.

During the early 1970's the government of Chile expropriated ACM's South American mining operations, and in 1977 the company, which had lost more than $1 billion, sold its Butte assets to the Atlantic Richfield Company (ARCO). That same year Butte and Silver Bow County merged, creating Butte-Silver Bow, which increasingly looked to supplement the local mining economy with tourism and new industries associated with environmental reclamation. In 1982 ARCO closed the Berkeley Pit and shut off its underground pumps, causing the pit to be flooded. In 1983 ARCO shut down all mining operations in Butte, which had over the course of a century yielded $22 billion in copper, gold, and silver, mostly for outside investors.

In 1985, Montana Resources, owned by millionaire businessman Dennis Washington, acquired all former Anaconda properties but subsequently sold those assets in 1987 to Montana Mining Properties, which reopened several historic underground mines and began to explore for lead, silver, and zinc. In 1993 the Montana House and Senate approved legislation designating Butte as the first Cultural Heritage Area in the state, citing its contribution to the nation's industrialization and its history of hard-rock mining and smelting.

### Modern Preservation Efforts

The Butte area has been well preserved, with enough of the city's turn-of-the-century structures remaining to give visitors a sense of the community's historic involvement with frontier capitalism and mining. Butte's National Historic Landmark District includes the city's uptown area and portions of residential areas and is highlighted by copper king mansions, mining sites and structures, famous business and civic buildings, and a brothel (finally closed in 1982) located in the Butte's former red-light district.

Butte's legacy is further preserved by the nearby World Museum of Mining, the motorized Neversweat and Washoe Railroad which departs from the museum for a six-mile run through historic neighborhoods and mine sites, the Butte-Silver Bow Public Archives, and the Mineral Museum at the Montana College of Mineral Science and Technology, founded in 1893.     —*Roger W. Rouland*

### For Further Information:

Calvert, Jerry W. *The Gibraltar: Socialism and Labor in Butte, Montana, 1895-1920.* Helena: Montana Historical Society Press, 1988. Traces the threads of socialism and progressive parties in Butte from their impetus to their decline. Calvert tends to side with labor and his book has a decidedly socialistic bent.

Gutfeld, Arnon. *Montana's Agony: Years of War and Hysteria, 1917-1920.* Gainesville: University Presses of Florida, 1979. Suggests that the Anaconda Copper Mining Company posed serious threats to American freedoms in attempting to reduce labor's power.

Malone, Michael P. *The Battle for Butte: Mining and Politics on the Northern Frontier, 1864-1906.* Seattle: University of Washington Press, 1981. Provides a more thorough treatment of the economic and political battles waged over Butte Hill. Tends to side with labor.

Malone, Michael P., Richard B. Roeder, and William L. Lang. *Montana: A History of Two Centuries.*

Rev. ed. Seattle: University of Washington Press, 1991. Offers a chapter detailing the relationship between copper and politics in Butte and another chapter outlining the progressive movement in the community.

Marcosson, Isaac F. *Anaconda*. New York: Dodd, Mead, 1957. Offers a boosteristic view of the giant copper company from Anaconda's point of view; the book includes very little history from the 1906-1920 period.

Shovers, Brian, Mark Fiege, Dale Martin, and Fred Quivik. *Butte and Anaconda Revisited: An Overview of Early-Day Mining and Smelting in Montana*. Billings, Mont.: Bureau of Mines and Geology, 1991. Provides an objective overview of Butte's history as a mining town, treating the development of the mining industry in depth.

Woodbury, Richard. "The Giant Cup of Poison." *Time* 151, no. 12 (March 30, 1998): 4. This article discusses the environmental crisis facing this region as a result of acidic mining residues from Butte's Berkeley Pit copper mine.

# Little Bighorn

**Date:** Battle fought on June 25, 1876

**Relevant issues:** American Indian history, disasters and tragedies, military history

**Significance:** The Little Bighorn Battlefield National Monument includes the site of the Battle of the Little Bighorn, Custer National Cemetery, the Reno-Benteen Battlefield, Medicine Tail Ford, and the site of an Indian village.

**Location:** Within the Crow Reservation in southeastern Montana, one mile east of Route 1-90 (U.S. 87) and eighteen miles north of Hardin; connected with the Black Hills and Yellowstone National Park on U.S. Route 212

**Site Office:**

Little Bighorn Battlefield National Monument
P.O. Box 39
Crow Agency, MT 59022
ph.: (406) 638-2621
fax: (406) 638-2623
Web site: www.nps.gov/libi/

Inside the two million-acre Crow Reservation, which encompasses most of Bighorn County between Hardin and the Wyoming state line, stands one of the most important historical sites in the United States. The Battle of the Little Bighorn was one of the last attempts of the Plains Indians to protect their land and traditional way of life against annexation and assimilation by the whites. It also immortalized George Armstrong Custer as a hero to the nation, even though his defeat and death in the battle represent one of the greatest disasters in American military history.

**Early History**

In the mid-nineteenth century, the presence of about 225,000 Indians on the Great Plains and Rocky Mountains seemed likely to impede the westward expansion of the white population. Yet the influx of miners and cattlemen, and the later construction of the transcontinental railroad, rapidly transformed the lives of all the Indian tribes of the West. The traditional hunting and gathering life of the Indians was not compatible with a settled agricultural and industrial economy, especially after white hunters all but destroyed the immense buffalo herds that were essential not only for food but for housing, fuel, and weaponry. The spread of European diseases among the Indians made resistance even more difficult; four epidemics of smallpox between 1835 and 1860 and an outbreak of cholera in 1849 had devastating effects.

The plains, mountains, and deserts of the West presented extremes of topography and climate that the U.S. Army had not encountered in the East and gave the Plains Indians certain advantages during the military confrontations. Their raids and ambushes had to be sporadic since they needed to seek food, and they were vulnerable when they retired to their lodges for the winter. Custer, for one, saw the advantages of launching ruthless dawn raids on Indian villages during the winter months. While the army was less mobile than the Indians, it could feed itself with less effort and could campaign throughout the year.

**White Pressure on the Plains Indians**

The pressures on the Plains Indians intensified after 1850, when the United States made territorial gains following the Mexican War. Wagon trains of emigrants flooded the plains, destroying the grasslands and making the traditional hunting of the buffalo herds increasingly difficult. The government attempted to bring the situation under control by establishing agencies to feed the Indians, and at Fort Laramie in 1851 government officials persuaded several tribes to move to reservations under new treaties. This change in policy signified the collapse of the "permanent Indian frontier," as the Indians granted unrestricted transit rights along the main trails and allowed the government to build forts in their territory. In return the Indians were promised fifty thousand dollars' worth of goods each year for fifty years. This was later reduced to fifteen years by Congress without the Indians' consent.

The government now intended to keep the Indians away from the white travel routes and settlements by restricting them to reservations. The reservation policy was designed not only to restrict the Indians geographically but to "civilize" them as well

*The battlefield where George Armstrong Custer and his troops were defeated by the Sioux.* (PhotoDisc)

through such institutions as reservation schools. The whites' belief in the superiority of their religion, education, and technology made them unable to respect the traditional Indian way of life or seek any compromise with it. Not even the Civil War could slow the advance westward. Mineral strikes throughout the West brought whites into areas previously considered Indian domain. During the war, the ranks of the prospectors were increased by Northerners evading the draft and by refugees from the destroyed farmlands of Kansas, Missouri, and northern Arkansas.

**Events Leading to Little Bighorn**

The origins of the 1876 campaign that culminated in the Battle of the Little Bighorn lay in the Black Hills of Wyoming and South Dakota. The Black Hills, considered sacred by the Sioux and used as a main hunting ground by both the Sioux and Cheyenne, had been granted to these tribes by the U.S. government in 1868 as part of their reservations. In 1873 the Northern Pacific Railroad sent out surveyors to prepare routes in unceded territory, only to run into opposition from Sitting Bull and the Sioux. In 1874 an expedition under Custer found gold in the Black Hills of Wyoming. The U.S. Army tried halfheartedly to halt the flow of miners, but by 1875 thousands were swarming the hills. The miners had violated the treaty guarantees, and the government, not wanting to face a public outcry, attempted to buy the hills from the Sioux. In September government negotiators offered the Sioux six million dollars, which the Sioux rejected. The army then gave up any pretense of trying to prevent the rush of prospectors, and the Sioux and Cheyenne began to move beyond the borders of their reservations and to encroach into the lands of the Crow tribe.

The government proclaimed that those Sioux and Cheyenne who remained outside the reservations would be treated as hostile. The decision was made easier since some of the Indians had already broken the Fort Laramie treaties by raiding white settlements in Montana, Wyoming, and Nebraska. The Sioux and the Cheyenne failed to heed the government's ultimatum. In 1876, under Sitting Bull and Crazy Horse, they had several skirmishes with the army before gathering near the Little Bighorn River in June. By doing so they issued a challenge not only to the U.S. Army but also, once again, to the Crow Indians, for the site of this Sioux and Cheyenne settlement was on their reservation.

### Custer's Seventh Cavalry

Brigadier General Alfred Terry was the officer in overall command of the Third Army sent out to deal with the Sioux and Cheyenne. While he led one column, including six hundred men of the Seventh Cavalry under Custer, west from Fort Abraham Lincoln in the Dakota Territory, General George Crook led another column north from Fort Fetterman in Wyoming, and General John Gibbon led the third column from western Montana. Crook's column was pushed back by more than a thousand Sioux and Cheyenne at the Rosebud Valley on June 17, but Gibbon's and Terry's columns successfully rendezvoused on June 21. Custer was ordered to take his men into the Little Bighorn Valley from the south, leaving the bulk of the combined columns to come in from the north.

Custer and his men reached the Sioux and Cheyenne settlement on June 25 and began their attack. Intelligence reports had underestimated the number of Indians waiting for them: There were more than ten thousand, including up to four thousand warriors. Custer divided his men into three, with Major Marcus Reno and Captain Frederic Benteen commanding one battalion each, leaving Custer with only 225 men under his direct command. The Indian warriors rapidly repelled Reno's and Benteen's battalions away from the settlement and up onto the riverside bluff to the south, where they remained under attack through to the evening of June 26. They could hear the gunfire and see the smoke of the battle to the north, but could not prevent it. Custer and his 225 men were surrounded by some twenty-five hundred Indian warriors under Crazy Horse, who killed all of them. Only about fifty Indians were killed in the battle, though a larger number probably died later of wounds they received there.

### The Controversy over Blame

Controversy still continues over who was to blame for the massacre on the Little Bighorn. Reno and Benteen were officially exonerated of blame for the deaths of Custer and his troops. However, many historians argue that they could and should have tried harder to move north from the bluff and come to Custer's rescue. Mari Sandoz has argued quite convincingly in her book *The Battle of the Little Bighorn* that Custer's strategy was seriously flawed from the beginning. First, he had been warned by his scouts, Indian and white, that a large council would be held at Bear Butte as in previous summers, bringing together several lodges of the Sioux, Northern Cheyenne, and Arapaho. He gravely underestimated the odds, simply assuming he would be victorious. Secondly, Custer's column was sent to scout rather than attack; he had no reinforcements of infantry, cavalry, or Gatling guns. To make matters worse, he divided this small force into three parts, perhaps to reserve more glory for himself.

Chief Sitting Bull, the spiritual leader of the Sioux who did not take part in the battle, said that Custer was a "great chief" but also a "fool who rode to his death." Not surprisingly, the U.S. government and American public opinion could not agree with Sitting Bull's assessment, and made Custer into a national hero. His remains were interred at West Point in 1877, and a National Cemetery was established in 1879 on the battle site in order to protect the soldiers' graves.

### Government Reaction to the Battle

Meanwhile, the War Department reacted to the humiliating defeat of the Seventh Army by sending one-third of the entire U.S. Army to Montana. In October, 1876, the boundary of the Sioux reservation was altered to exclude the Black Hills. After the eventual defeat of the Sioux and Northern Cheyenne in 1877, they were forced onto a number of cramped reservations. Cattlemen and farmers quickly poured into the vacated plains, and in Montana the Crow, who had trusted the U.S. government and some of whose warriors had fought alongside Custer, saw their reservation boundaries altered too.

The Battle of the Little Bighorn was a watershed of the Indian wars. By the mid-1880's there were 187 reservations, covering a total of 181,000 square miles and home to 243,000 Indians. Government bureaucracy grew accordingly; in 1850, the Indian Bureau had only three hundred officials, but by the 1880's there were twenty-five hundred. The Sioux, who had long dominated the northern plains from the Minnesota River to the Bighorn Mountains and from the upper Missouri to the Platte and Republican Rivers, fought longer and harder than any other Plains tribe, only to succumb to violent defeat at Wounded Knee in 1890, the year when the frontier was officially declared to have vanished.

### Modern Preservation Efforts

In 1940 the Custer Battlefield National Cemetery was transferred from the War Department to the National Park Service, and six years later the cemetery officially became the Custer Battlefield National Monument. In 1983, a brush fire swept across the battlefield site, and archaeological excavations on the newly exposed land recovered over four thousand artifacts, including large quantities of spent rounds and cartridge cases. Ballistic science and computer technology were combined to analyze the movement of individual weapons taking place during the battle and thus to prove that the Indians repeatedly attacked the soldiers as they stayed in their initial battle positions.

The National Monument was unusual in being dedicated to the losers of a battle rather than to the victors. Indian activists spent decades pointing out this irony, in their attempts to have a monument placed at the battlefield to the Sioux and Cheyenne who died there. (Such a monument has still not been built.) They also campaigned for many years to have the name changed from the Custer Battlefield National Monument to Little Bighorn Battlefield National Monument. This change took effect in December, 1991.

Some whites had expressed sympathy for the Sioux and the Cheyenne long before the name was changed. The words of William F. "Buffalo Bill" Cody, who had served with Terry as chief army scout, still stand as a statement of the significance of the battle: "The defeat of Custer was not a massacre. The Indians were being pursued by skilled fighters with orders to kill. For centuries they have been hounded from the Atlantic to the Pacific and back again. They had their wives and little ones to protect and they were fighting for their existence."

—*Monique Lamontagne*

### For Further Information:

Cox, Kurt Hamilton. *Custer and His Commands: From West Point to Little Bighorn.* London: Greenhill, 1999. A biography of Custer and descriptions of nineteenth century U.S. Army uniforms, equipment, and cavalry. Illustrated.

Hagan, William T. *American Indians.* 3d ed. Chicago: University of Chicago Press, 1993. An excellent study of four centuries of white/Indian relations.

Lavender, David. *The Great West.* Boston: Houghton Mifflin, 1965. Provides an introduction to the history of the frontier.

Sandoz, Mari. *The Battle of the Little Bighorn.* Reprint. Lincoln: University of Nebraska Press, 1978. Offers critical insight into Custer's ambitions, as well as a detailed account of the battle.

# Other Historic Sites

## Bannack Historic District

*Location:* Dillon, Beaverhead County

*Relevant issues:* Business and industry, political history

*Statement of significance:* This was the first territorial capital and the site of Montana's first gold discovery in 1862. The remaining buildings are of frame and log construction, typical of a frontier boomtown.

## Chief Joseph Battleground of Bear's Paw

*Location:* Chinook, Blaine County

*Relevant issues:* American Indian history

*Statement of significance:* This is the site of the battle in which Chief Joseph (c. 1840-1904) and more than four hundred Nez Perce Indians surrendered to the United States Army (1877). The Bear's Paw surrender signaled the close of the Nez Perces' existence as an "independent Indian people." Henceforth, they lived as a group of displaced persons—in the white culture, but certainly not of it.

## Chief Plenty Coups Home

*Location:* 0.5 mile west of Pryor, at the intersection of BIA roads #5 and #8 (Edgar Road), Big Horn County

*Relevant issues:* American Indian history

*Statement of significance:* This was the homestead of Chief Plenty Coups (c. 1849-1932), also called Aleekchea'ahoosh, one of the last and most celebrated traditional chiefs of the Crow Indians. It includes the house of Chief Plenty Coups, an adjacent log store operated by the chief, and the Plenty Coups Spring, a site of historic and cultural significance to the Crow people. Chief Plenty Coups established the homestead in 1884 and lived there until his death in 1932, making his political career of more than a half a century one of the longest of any chief. One of the most important Native American leaders of the transitional period and an ambassador and negotiator for the Crow, Chief Plenty Coups advocated the adoption of those aspects of American culture necessary to succeed on the reservation while maintaining traditional Crow religious beliefs and cultural values.

## Going-to-the-Sun Road

*Location:* Glacier National Park, West Glacier, Flathead County

*Relevant issues:* Science and technology, western expansion

*Statement of significance:* An essential step in making large scenic reservations accessible to the motoring public without unduly marring landscape scenery or natural systems was the initiation of "landscape engineering." When it was begun, Going-to-the-Sun Road was the most ambitious road construction project ever undertaken by the Bureau of Public Roads and the National Park Service (NPS). The extreme terrain and conditions, as well as the newness of the administrative agreement between the two federal bureaus, made the road a laboratory of innovative road engineering practices and policies. While building the road, the NPS and the Bureau of Public Roads developed the construction standards and the cooperative administra-

tion that characterized future road construction not only in National Parks but on other federal lands and, after 1933, in State Parks as well.

## Grant-Kohrs Ranch

*Location:* Deer Lodge, Powell County

*Relevant issues:* Business and industry

*Statement of significance:* John Grant, the original owner of the ranch, starting in 1853, is sometimes credited with founding the range-cattle industry in Montana. Conrad Kohrs, who bought the ranch about 1866, was among the foremost "cattle kings" of his era.

## Great Falls Portage

*Location:* Great Falls, Cascade County

*Relevant issues:* Western expansion

*Statement of significance:* The Lewis and Clark Expedition undertook an eighteen-mile, thirty-one-day portage at Great Falls, one of the most difficult ordeals of their westward trip.

## Pictograph Cave

*Location:* Billings, Yellowstone County

*Relevant issues:* American Indian history

*Statement of significance:* This is one of the key archaeological sites used in determining the sequence of prehistoric occupation on the northwestern Plains. The deposits indicate occupation from 2600 B.C.E. to after 1800 C.E.

## Pompey's Pillar

*Location:* Pompey's Pillar, Yellowstone County

*Relevant issues:* Western expansion

*Statement of significance:* This massive natural block of sandstone was a major landmark on the Lewis and Clark Expedition. William Clark's signature, carved on its surface, is still visible.

## Rankin Ranch

*Location:* Helena, Lewis and Clark County

*Relevant issues:* Political history, social reform, women's history

*Statement of significance:* This was the residence, from 1923 to 1956, of Jeannette Rankin, the first woman elected to the U.S. House of Representatives (1916). She served two terms, 1917-1919 and 1941-1943. Best remembered for her pacifism, Rankin played an important role in the women's rights and social reform movements.

She was the only member of the House to oppose the declaration of war against Japan in 1941.

## Russell House and Studio

*Location:* Great Falls, Yellowstone County

*Relevant issues:* Art and architecture

*Statement of significance:* Charles M. Russell (1865-1926), one of the best-known twentieth century painters of western subjects, occupied this house from 1900 to 1926.

## Traveler's Rest

*Location:* Lolo, Missoula County

*Relevant issues:* Western expansion

*Statement of significance:* This campsite is where Meriwether Lewis and William Clark stopped before crossing the Bitterroot Mountains on their 1805 trip west and on their return the next year.

## Virginia City Historic District

*Location:* Virginia City, Madison County

*Relevant issues:* Business and industry, political history

*Web site:* montana.avicom.net/virginiacity

*Statement of significance:* This was the territorial capital of Montana (1865-1875) and the site of one of the greatest gold strikes in the West (1863).

# Nebraska

*The State Capitol Building in Lincoln.* (P. Michael Whye/Department of Economic Development, Nebraska Division of Tourism)

# History of Nebraska

Nebraska's eastern and northeastern borders are defined by the Missouri River, across which lie Iowa to the east and South Dakota to the north. It is 462 miles across Iowa to its extreme western border at the Wyoming state line. West and south of the state is Colorado. From the northern border at the South Dakota line to the southern border at the Kansas line is 210 miles. With a land mass of 77,358 square miles, Nebraska ranks sixteenth in size of the states, although, with 1,656,870 residents in 1997, it ranked thirty-eighth in population. In 1990, it had a population density of about twenty people per square mile.

Nebraska is considered one of the midwestern states, although it is at the western extreme of the Midwest. Its climate is semiarid, with hot, dry summers and very cold winters. Because glaciers pushed topsoil into the area as they advanced south more than two million years ago, the soil, called till, is fertile. However, droughts sometimes lead to dust storms that blow away some of the richest topsoil from thousands of acres.

**Early History**
Human habitation of the Nebraska area is estimated to have begun more than ten thousand years ago. Ancestors of the bison roamed the plains, supplying settlers with food and fur, from which they fashioned clothing and shelters in the form of tepees. They used animal bones to make buttons and such instruments as knives.

The largest mammoth skeleton ever recovered was found near North Platte. This animal, resembling an elephant, was nearly fourteen feet tall. When the Ice Age arrived more than two million years ago, many of these animals disappeared and eventually became extinct. At the end of the Ice Age, however, some animals, including bison and mammoths, survived, and the ancient people who lived in the area hunted them with spears. These people also farmed and made pottery.

By the 1500's, Native Americans, notably the Omaha, Oto, Pawnee, and Ponca, occupied the area, living in villages and raising crops of beans, corn, and squash. The Arapaho, Cheyenne, Comanche, and Sioux were more hunters than farmers. Living in tepees, they roved the plains hunting for animals, mostly bison. The largest Native American group at this time was the Pawnee.

**Early European Exploration**
Even before Europeans reached what is now Nebraska, Spanish explorers who had traveled to Texas, Oklahoma, Kansas, and Missouri had claimed for Spain all of the land they had visited and a great deal of land north and west of it that they had not seen. By 1541 both Francisco Vásquez de Coronado and Hernando de Soto had laid claim to much of this land for Spain.

In 1682 René-Robert Cavelier, Sieur de La Salle, had claimed much of the same land for France, naming the whole vast area between the Mississippi River and the Rocky Mountains Louisiana, in honor of King Louis XIV of France. It was not until 1803 that the United States, through the Louisiana Purchase, bought all of this land from France for fifteen million dollars.

Meanwhile, in 1714 Etienne Veniard de Bourgmont, a French explorer, made his way into the Missouri River Valley of Nebraska. Spanish forces were known to have been in the state in 1720, when they clashed with some of the natives, who soundly defeated them. Almost two decades later, in 1739, brothers Paul and Pierre Mallet crossed Nebraska, following the course of the Platte River.

The area was so sparsely populated that its development was slow. It was not until 1823 that the first white settlement was established at Bellevue on the Missouri River in the eastern part of the region. The United States Army had built Fort Atkinson on the Missouri's west bank four years earlier.

The Oregon Trail passed through Nebraska, so a steady stream of people who set out during the 1840's to seek their fortunes in the West passed through the area. These early travelers, however, had to keep moving because the government had designated Nebraska as an Indian territory and, at that time, would not permit further white settlement there.

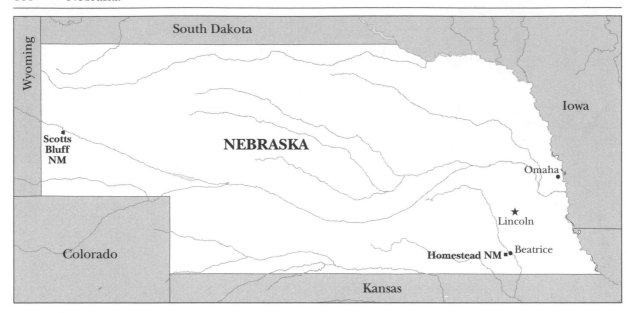

## The Homestead Act

By 1854 the federal government, in enacting the Kansas-Nebraska Act, made Kansas and Nebraska territories. Nebraska was now opened to anyone, mostly Europeans, who wished to settle there. In the same year, Omaha was founded.

The Homestead Act of 1862 gave families or any male over age twenty-one 160 acres of land that would become theirs after five years if they settled on it and improved it. This bonanza attracted so many people that by 1867 Nebraska had sufficient population numbers to justify statehood. With many of its residents still living on the prairie in sod houses, Nebraska became the thirty-seventh state in 1867. Lincoln became its capital. In 1871 the University of Nebraska was founded at Lincoln.

## The Early Homesteaders

Life was not easy for most of the homesteaders who were given land in Nebraska. The winters were long and harsh. Driving winds howled outside as residents huddled in drafty homes, many of which had been fashioned from squares of sod cut from the prairie. Wood for stoves was scarce.

During the long winters, hungry animals, particularly wolves, roved the prairie looking for food and putting the settlers, particularly small children, at risk. Until the late 1870's, there was the added threat of attacks by hostile American Indians, which subsided somewhat after the Sioux chief

Crazy Horse surrendered at Fort Robinson, where he was murdered in 1877. These were difficult times for people living on the prairie.

## Water Problems

The eastern part of Nebraska always received more precipitation than the west, but droughts were common throughout the state, ruining agriculture. Permanent damage was done to the land as dust storms blew valuable topsoil away. A particularly devastating blizzard in 1888 resulted in the deaths of more than two hundred people in Nebraska. Floods in springtime plagued the areas along the Missouri and Platte Rivers.

It was not until late in the nineteenth century that Nebraska farmers began to irrigate their fields with water obtained from great reservoirs that had been constructed along the Platte. In 1895, largely at the instigation of the Populist Party that had been established three years earlier, the state set up a Board of Irrigation. In 1902 the U.S. government passed the Reclamation Act, which provided money for the development of irrigation projects.

Modern Nebraska faces significant water problems: On their way to Nebraska the state's rivers are siphoned by other states, depriving Nebraska of much-needed water. So great has been the problem that Nebraska has had to tap its aquifer, the subterranean water in porous rocks and gravel, that is not renewable. The use of pesticides and other agricultural chemicals has polluted much of Nebraska's water, including its aquifer.

**The Nebraska Economy**

Nebraska is known for having the lowest unemployment rate of any state in the United States for many years. During World War I, Nebraska farms supplied much of the food that the armed forces required, and forty-eight thousand Nebraskans went off to serve their country in the war. Wheat and corn production was strong, as was the production of sorghum and soybeans. The state was prosperous until the late 1920's, when two coincident factors ruined the economy.

The stock market crash late in 1929 changed the economic picture all over the United States. Banks and businesses failed. People lost their life savings and their homes. Factories closed and armies of people were unemployed nationwide. Despite this economic chaos, farmers, who were usually self-sufficient, might have been expected to survive economically.

During the early 1930's, however, severe droughts plagued the Midwest, reducing farm production to all-time lows. Nebraska, like many other midwestern states, found itself hit hard by the Great Depression. In 1934 Nebraskans voted to establish a one-house legislature to speed up legislation and to cut costs. This unicameral system persisted.

More than sixty thousand desperate Nebraskans were forced by the economic meltdown to leave the state and find work elsewhere. By the end of the 1930's, Nebraska's weather had improved measurably, so farming again became profitable. War industries came into the state during World War II, bringing factory jobs. As rainfall increased substantially during the 1940's, farmers were again producing record crops.

**The Move away from Farms**

After World War II, Nebraska's farms were bigger, but there were fewer of them. Many independent farmers sold their land and moved into cities and towns. Large agricultural corporations moved into the state, swallowing up small farms and turning agriculture into a much more specialized and scientific pursuit than it had once been. Omaha became a center for food processing. In 1953 the first frozen dinners in America were produced there.

By 1960 Nebraska had more city dwellers than rural inhabitants. By 1994 Omaha and Lincoln had only about a 2 percent unemployment rate. In the 1990's about half of Nebraska's workforce of 800,000 were employed in sales or service occupations. Some 200,000 people were employed in sales and telemarketing, centered in Omaha. Another 200,000 worked as doctors, nurses, lawyers, bankers, insurance agents, automotive repair people, and other service personnel. The local, state, and federal governments offered employment to another 150,000. The state had one public school teacher for every fourteen students enrolled, which is much higher than the national average.

Despite the move to urban areas, Nebraska still has more than fifty thousand farms; farms and ranches occupy 90 percent of the state's land. In the western part of Nebraska, which is not suited to farming, the great grasslands provide excellent grazing for cattle, which are produced there in large numbers. —*R. Baird Shuman*

# Homestead National Monument

**Date:** First homestead granted on January 1, 1863

**Relevant issues:** Western expansion

**Significance:** This National Historical Landmark is the site of the first claim made under the Homestead Act of 1862, made by homesteader Daniel Freeman. Also on the site is the Freeman School, a one-room brick schoolhouse, and the Palmer-Epard Cabin, built on a nearby homestead in 1867. The park's visitors' center contains displays including photographs of sod homes and tools used by the settlers.

**Location:** Four and one-half miles west of Beatrice and about forty miles south of Lincoln

**Site Office:**
Homestead National Monument of America
8523 W. State Highway 4
Beatrice, NE 68310
ph.: (402) 223-3514
Web site: www.nps.gov/home/

The Homestead National Monument commemorates the settlement of the Great Plains in the last half of the nineteenth century by pioneers who claimed land under the provisions of the Homestead Act of 1862. This legislation offered free land to those willing to settle the vast, unfarmed territories of the West. Though there were some strings attached, the offer was good enough that nearly twenty million acres were claimed in Nebraska alone.

### Settling the Louisiana Purchase Lands

When Thomas Jefferson bought the Louisiana Territory from Napoleon in 1803, he was ridiculed by some for paying too much. In retrospect, this fifteen million-dollar deal was perhaps the greatest bargain in history. The entire Mississippi Valley and tributary lands were included in this huge parcel, and some historians have suggested that Napoleon, soon to go to war with England, felt he would lose the land in a settlement with the British anyway. It is hard to imagine the United States gaining the world prominence it eventually achieved had a foreign power continued to control this area.

Although America tried continually to settle this vast area, by the 1850's much of the midwestern plains still appeared to be wilderness. As early as 1825, Senator Thomas Hart Benton of Missouri had proposed free government land grants to expedite development, and in 1852 the antislavery Free-Soil Party called for free land for settlers. By 1854, the first bill reflecting these demands was introduced in Congress. There was great support for this concept all through the West, though some easterners (primarily farmers) were opposed.

At first, it was thought that cheap land would be enough to lure sufficient settlers. By 1859, Nebraska lands were offered at $1.25 an acre. However, this charge was made retroactive to those who had already settled the land. The uprising by these settlers caused great problems among the new arrivals. In the end, most of the original settlers were allowed to stay, but the publicity of the whole incident was rather bad.

### The First Federal Homestead Act

Congress passed a homestead act of sorts in 1860. This required settlers to pay twenty-five cents an acre for the land. President James Buchanan, however, refused to sign the bill and it never went into effect. Finally, on May 20, 1862, President Lincoln, a longtime supporter of the homestead movement, signed the Free Homestead Act, to take effect on January 1, 1863. Under its provisions, any man or woman twenty-one years old or any head of a family could have 160 acres of land. To achieve ownership, he or she had to live on the land for five years and pay about eighteen dollars in fees. Some historians believe that this act provided more benefit to the American people than any other passed by Congress.

Daniel Freeman, then a Union soldier at home on leave, was granted the first homestead on January 1, 1863. The land office was not to open until January 2 (New Year's Day being a holiday), but the huge throng of land claimees agreed to

*The Freeman School, Homestead National Monument.* (National Park Service)

let soldier Freeman be the first. They persuaded the head clerk at the office to open for a few minutes on January 1 to take care of Freeman, as he had to leave to return to his regiment. The land he claimed is on Cub Creek in Gage County, Nebraska, about five miles northwest of Beatrice. This is now the site of the Homestead National Monument.

Thus began the great homesteading drive that continued until the beginning of the twentieth century. Over a million people claimed and received more than 120 million acres of land under this program. It is interesting to note, though, that approximately 48 percent of the land claimed was never actually transferred to the claimees. There is little doubt that the region's harsh terrain and weather played a large role in this statistic.

### Homesteading the Great Plains

In many parts of the Great Plains, there was very little forestation. Those settlers who had the means could purchase wood to construct their homes. Many of these structures were rough log cabins, but some were slightly more elaborate. Those who could not afford wood, or those who lived far from a forest, often built homes of sod. The construction process was described by Cass G. Barns, a physician who served the Nebraska area in the late nineteenth century:

> The first step in making a new home would be to select the location and then choose the best low spot where the sod would be thickest and strongest. A breaking plow was used to turn over furrows on about half an acre of ground, using care to make the furrows of even width and thickness so that the home wall would rise evenly. A spade was used to cut the furrow into sod bricks about three feet long. A float made of planks or the forks of a tree or even the wagon drawn by horses or oxen, was used to transport the sod bricks to the building place. The first layer in the wall was made by placing three-foot-wide bricks side by side around the foundation except where the door would be located, carefully breaking joints. When the first row was placed, the cracks were filled with fine dirt and two more layers placed on top. . . . Every third course was laid crosswise of the others to bind them together. This process was followed till the walls were high enough to take the roof. A door frame had been set on the ground and built

around with sods and two window frames placed higher up in the wall, one by the door and the other opposite on the other side of the house. The wall was then carefully trimmed to symmetrical proportions by the use of a sharp spade.

The roof was usually made of a wood frame with metal sheeting. Some of the better "soddies" had plank floors and glass windows, but this was the exception rather than the rule.

Other settlers lived in dugouts, usually located by the sides of mountains or ravines. These would resemble lean-tos and sometimes were almost totally underground. Some homes, in fact, were completely underground, with only a stovepipe and door to show their location. The settlers who lived in such homes existed with very few possessions or luxuries. A stove for cooking was often the main furnishing. (Because wood was so scarce, the settlers used buffalo chips for fuel.) Handmade beds were sometimes present, though sleeping on the dirt floor was more common. Despite these hardships, the sod houses and dugouts were home. One settler later wrote, "The wind whistled through the walls in winter and the dust blew in summer, but we papered the walls with newspaper and made rag carpets for the floor, and thought we were living well."

Virtually all these people engaged in farming. Many had farmed previously elsewhere, but the differences in climate and soil often made their transition difficult. The prairie tallgrass had to be cleared before crops could be planted. Ordinary cast-iron plows proved unable to cut through the tough, root-woven sod, so the steel grasshopper plow was invented. The harsh weather in many areas of the Midwest also made the farms somewhat less than sure bets. Rain was scarce, and traditional crops such as oats, barley, and wheat repeatedly failed; by default, corn became the staple crop. These problems, combined with the fact that few of these settlers had much capital with which to buy implements, livestock, working animals, or other necessary items, made the failure rate of these farms nearly 50 percent. Many did make a go of it, however, and some became quite prosperous.

The settlement figures for the state of Nebraska illustrate the yearly trends of homestead claims. In the first year (1863), 349 claims were made covering 50,775 acres. The height of homesteading was in 1885 when 11,293 claims were made totaling 1,748,841 acres. Even by 1900, the end of the homesteading era, 3,141 claims were made for 456,855 acres. And from 1863 to 1900, 141,446 homesteaders claimed 19,820,201 acres of Nebraska land.

### End of the Homesteading Era

By the turn of the century, many hundred of thousands of settlers were working their lands all over the Midwest, and the great sea of tallgrass had all but vanished from the prairie. In 1934, the homesteading era officially came to an end with the repeal of the Homestead Act. Two years later, the federal government decided to commemorate this great migration with a public memorial. President Franklin D. Roosevelt signed a bill on March 19, 1936, making that first homestead claim by Daniel Freeman a public memorial park.

### Modern Preservation Efforts

This historic homestead is now a National Monument and has been expanded to include other historic structures. Among these is the Freeman School, named either for Daniel Freeman or for Thomas Freeman, whose kiln fired the building's bricks. Built in 1872, it served as a school, church, and general meeting place for the community until 1967. This school also provoked a historic court case involving the separation of church and state. Daniel Freeman filed suit in 1899 to prevent religious instruction in public schools. The school board denied his challenge, but the Nebraska Supreme Court agreed with him in their decision of October 9, 1902; the U.S. Supreme Court would not take this position for some time. The school has now been restored to its original appearance.

Also on the Homestead National Monument Site is the Palmer-Epard Cabin, built in 1867. It was moved to its present location for display purposes in 1950. This cabin is constructed of mixed hardwoods and homemade brick set in lime mortar. It is currently furnished to illustrate life in the 1880's.

Another restoration is the one hundred acres of tallgrass prairie within the park area. Planted with the region's native tallgrass and mantained, in part, through controlled burnings, the prairie now looks just as it would have to the settlers when they arrived to build their homesteads.

—*Steve Palmer*

### For Further Information:

Barns, Cass G. *The Sod House.* Lincoln: University of Nebraska Press, 1903. Reprint. 1970. Gives firsthand descriptions of how the homesteaders lived.

Neill, Edward. *Dahkotah Land and Dakohtah Life.* Philadelphia: J. B. Lippincott, 1859. A scarce but interesting title.

Olson, James. *History of Nebraska.* 3d ed. Lincoln: University of Nebraska Press, 1997. Covers the subject of homesteading in Nebraska.

Sheldon, Addison Erwin. *Nebraska: Old and New.* Chicago: University of Chicago Press, 1966. Another book on homesteading in Nebraska.

Wollaston, Percy. *Homesteading.* New York: Lyons & Burford, 1997. The author, who was born in 1904, describes his experiences growing up homesteading in Montana.

# Scotts Bluff National Monument

**Date:** Established in 1919

**Relevant issues:** Western expansion

**Significance:** Scotts Bluff, in western Nebraska, was a visible geological landmark for thousands of European immigrants who traveled westward on the Oregon Trail from 1843 to 1869, and for Pony Express riders from 1860 to 1861. The landmark bluff became a National Monument during the presidency of Woodrow Wilson.

**Location:** Two miles west of Gering, Nebraska, on State Highway 92

**Site Office:**
National Park Service
P.O. Box 27
Gering, NE 69341
ph.: (308) 436-4340
Web site: www.nps.gov/scbl/

Scotts Bluff offers a commanding view over the surrounding area. The summit rises seven hundred feet above its base and was created by the erosive action of the North Platte River. Scotts Bluff, the Pony Express, and the Oregon Trail inspired a noted American artist, William Henry Jackson (1843-1942).

## Major Landmark on the Oregon Trail

Scotts Bluff is memorable primarily as one of several distinctive geological landmarks on the Oregon Trail located along the southern banks of the North Platte River in Nebraska. Thousands of European immigrants streamed westward over the Great Plains toward new homes via the Oregon Trail between 1843 and 1869, and often mentioned Scotts Bluff in their diaries. During the peak travel year, 1852, approximately fifty thousand immigrants made the trip. The end of the long, slow, monotonous trek across the plains and the welcome start of the upward road to Wyoming and the mountains of the West were signaled by a sequence of physical landmarks along the Platte River in western Nebraska: Jail Rock, Courthouse Rock, picturesque Chimney Rock, Castle Rock, and, finally, Scotts Bluff. The North Platte River cut close to the base of Scotts Bluff, such that two passes to the south of the bluff (Mitchell Pass and Robidoux Pass) had to be followed by those traveling onward to Fort Laramie in Wyoming. From 1864 to 1867, the lives of European immigrants were guaranteed by a small military outpost, Fort Mitchell, located just west of Mitchell Pass.

### The Pony Express and Technological Change

From April, 1860, through October, 1861, the romantic but short-lived Pony Express experiment, which utilized parts of the Oregon Trail, used a route that traversed the Scotts Bluff region via Mitchell Pass. Under a U.S. government contract, the Pony Express company provided transcontinental mail service from Missouri to California. Young riders galloped cross-country in one hundred-mile segments, changing from exhausted to fresh horses every fifteen miles at regularly spaced Pony Express stations. Messages were carried from one end of the route to the other in approximately a week's time. Three Pony Express stations were located in the neighborhood of Scotts Bluff: one near Chimney Rock (Station No. 34), a second near present-day Melbeta, Nebraska (the Ficklin's Springs station, Station No. 35), and a third, the Scotts Bluff site (Station No. 36), believed to have been located near old Fort Mitchell. The Pony Express failed economically after October 24, 1861, when the first transcontinental telegraph made possible virtually instantaneous communication. Investors in the Pony Express company lost money, and the three stations in the Scotts Bluff area immediately became obsolete.

On May 10, 1869, eight years after the failure of the Pony Express, the first transcontinental railroad was completed, and wagon traffic on the Oregon Trail ceased almost immediately. People and goods were subsequently transported by rail more quickly, more safely, and more economically to the Far West than was ever possible via wagon over the Oregon Trail. The new route connecting the Union Pacific and the Central Pacific Railroads went fifty miles south of Scotts Bluff. No longer a visible landmark for most westward travelers, Scotts Bluff National Mon-

*Scotts Bluff National Monument.* (PhotoDisc)

ument symbolizes westward European expansion and a bygone era in the history of transcontinental transportation and communication.

**Inspiration for a Noted Artist**

William Henry Jackson (1843-1942) documented the westward expansion of European settlers in hundreds of drawings, paintings, and photographs. Jackson's works evoke romantic images of European pioneers, Pony Express riders, and the vast landscapes of the western United States, including Chimney Rock and Scotts Bluff. His atmospheric—and often mythic—images were, like those of Frederic Remington (1861-1909), widely published in popular, mass-circulation magazines, and instrumentally contributed to the European cultural understanding of the American West in the late nineteenth and early twentieth centuries.

**Places to Visit**

Scotts Bluff National Monument, open all year, features an interpretive museum, hiking trails, and an automobile road to the summit. The museum exhibits a noteworthy collection of art by William Henry Jackson. Chimney Rock National Historic Site is nearby. 　　　　　　*—Michael R. Hill*

**For Further Information:**

Franzwa, Gregory M. *Maps of the Oregon Trail.* Gerald, Mo.: Patrice Press, 1982. This atlas of detailed maps includes the Scotts Bluff portion of the Oregon Trail and is especially useful to anyone planning to retrace the westward treks of the early European immigrants.

Hales, Peter B. *William Henry Jackson and the Transformation of the American Landscape.* Philadelphia: Temple University Press, 1988. Detailed, thoughtful, and well-illustrated assessment of Jackson's artistic accomplishments and wider cultural influence.

Harris, Earl R. *History of Scotts Bluff National Monument.* Gering, Nebr.: Oregon Trail Museum Association, 1962. A concise account of the development and administration of the national monument from its establishment in 1919 through 1961.

Jackson, William Henry. *Time Exposure: The Autobiography of William Henry Jackson.* New York: G. P. Putnam's Sons, 1940. Reprint. New York: Cooper Square, 1970. Folksy narrative of the frontier artist's life and adventures in the American West.

Mattes, Merril J. *The Great Platte River Road: The Covered Wagon Mainline via Fort Kearney to Fort Laramie.* Lincoln: Nebraska State Historical Society, 1969. Major work on the place of Scotts Bluff and the Oregon Trail in the history of westward expansion by European settlers, includes extensive bibliography of first-person overland narratives.

_____. *Scotts Bluff National Monument.* National Park Service Historical Handbook 28. Washington, D.C.: U.S. Government Printing Office, 1983. A compactly written guide and the best single source for information on Scotts Bluff.

Mattes, Merril J., and Paul Henderson. "The Pony Express: Across Nebraska from St. Joseph to Fort Laramie." *Nebraska History* 41, no. 2 (June, 1960): 83-122. Describes the location and history of Pony Express stations, including the Scotts Bluff Station, from 1860 to 1861.

# Other Historic Sites

## Bryan House

*Location:* Lincoln, Lancaster County

*Relevant issues:* Political history

*Statement of significance:* From 1902 to 1922, Fairview was the home of William Jennings Bryan (1860-1925), lawyer and politician. Bryan won the Democratic presidential nomination in 1896 at the age of thirty-six and was twice again (1900, 1908) the losing nominee of his party. Later, he served as secretary of state under President Woodrow Wilson (1913-1915).

## Cather House

*Location:* Red Cloud, Webster County

*Relevant issues:* Literary history

*Statement of significance:* From 1884 to 1890, this was the home of Willa Cather (1876-1947), an author who wrote primarily of the West and Southwest. Many of Cather's best-known writings deal with her life in Red Cloud, where she lived in her youth.

## Coufal Site

*Location:* Cotesfield, Howard County

*Relevant issues:* American Indian history

*Statement of significance:* Coufal (1130-1350 C.E.) is a major village of the Central Plains tradition. Earth lodges of the prehistoric Indians of the Itskari Phase have been excavated here, bridging the gap between late prehistoric villagers and the origins of the Pawnee.

## Father Flanagan's Boys' Home

*Location:* Boys Town, Douglas County

*Relevant issues:* Social reform

*Statement of significance:* In 1921, Father Edward Joseph Flanagan (1886-1948) established his home for homeless boys on a farm outside Omaha. This "City of Little Men" led in the development of new juvenile care methods in twentieth century America, emphasizing social preparation in what has become a recognized prototype for public boys' homes worldwide.

## Fort Atkinson

*Location:* Fort Calhoun, Washington County

*Relevant issues:* Western expansion

*Statement of significance:* Fort Atkinson (1820) is one of the line of forts ("The Permanent Indian Frontier") established to guard the western U.S. frontier and to protect U.S. fur trade from English competition. Headquarters of the Upper Missouri Indian Agency, it was abandoned in 1829; only archaeological remains survive.

## Fort Robinson and Red Cloud Agency

*Location:* Crawford, Dawes County

*Relevant issues:* American Indian history

*Statement of significance:* In 1873, the U.S. government moved Chief Red Cloud and his large band of Cheyenne, Arapaho, and Sioux to the White River area; nearby Fort Robinson was established in 1874 to protect government employees and property. The fort served as a base for Army campaigns against several groups of Native Americans, including the 1876 campaign against the Powder River Sioux. After 1919, the fort became a major quartermaster remount depot.

## Hazard

*Location:* Omaha, Douglas County

*Relevant issues:* Military history, naval history, World War II

*Statement of significance:* One of two surviving Admirable Class fleet minesweepers, the largest and most successful class of American minesweepers, *Hazard* (1944) was fitted for both wire and acoustic sweeping and could double as an antisubmarine warfare and antiaircraft ship. The Admirable Class vessels were also used for patrol and escort duties. *Hazard* first served in this capacity, escorting a convoy from San Francisco to Pearl Harbor and then running with convoys to Eniwetok and Ulithi. In March, 1945, it was sent to Okinawa, where it first performed antisubmarine patrol before sweeping the area off Kerama Retto in keeping with the minesweeper's slogan No Sweep, No Invasion.

## Leary Site

*Location:* Rulo, Richardson County

*Relevant issues:* American Indian history

*Statement of significance:* This large prehistoric village and burial area of the Oneota Culture was first noted by Meriwether Lewis and William Clark in 1804.

## Norris House

*Location:* McCook, Red Willow County

*Relevant issues:* Political history

*Statement of significance:* From 1899 until his death, this two-story house was the property of George W. Norris (1861-1944), Progressive Republican. Norris served in the U.S. House (1903-1913) and Senate (1913-1943) and was a key supporter of the establishment of the Tennessee Valley Authority.

## Picotte Memorial Hospital

*Location:* Walthill, Thurston County

*Relevant issues:* American Indian history, health and medicine, social reform

*Statement of significance:* This hospital was built by

Dr. Susan La Flesche Picotte (1865-1915), the first Native American physician, who pioneered in providing health care for Native Americans. Picotte was born on the Omaha Indian Reservation, the youngest child of Chief Joseph La Flesche (Iron Eye), the last recognized chief of his tribe and a strong advocate of integration. Picotte was educated at the Hampton Institute in Virginia and received her medical degree from the Woman's Medical College of Pennsylvania. She returned to the Omaha Reservation in 1890 as physician at the government boarding school, ultimately becoming physician for the entire tribe, serving as well as teacher, social worker, adviser, and interpreter. Picotte was an active advocate for temperance and Omaha Indian rights.

## Pike Pawnee Village Site
*Location:* Guide Rock, Webster County

*Relevant issues:* American Indian history, western expansion

*Statement of significance:* This is generally accepted as the Pawnee village where Lieutenant Zebulon Pike, on his mission to secure the new territory in the Plains acquired under the Louisiana Purchase, caused the American flag to be raised and the Spanish flag lowered in late September, 1806. Archaeological evidence corroborates the identification.

## Robidoux Pass
*Location:* Gering, Scotts Bluff County
*Relevant issues:* Western expansion
*Statement of significance:* Robidoux Pass was a significant landmark on the Oregon Trail. In 1848, an Indian trader named Robidoux established a trading post near this natural landmark on the old Oregon Trail. This route fell into disuse after the opening of Mitchell Pass in 1851.

# Nevada

*The State Capitol Building in Carson City.* (Nevada Commission on Tourism)

# History of Nevada

Nevada is mostly arid, its desert terrain broken up by a series of mountain ranges. Part of the Great Basin region, it lies between Utah to the east and California to the west. Nevada's geography has deeply influenced nearly every principal aspect of its economy and society. Nevada's history would hardly have been the same without its laws, all influenced by geography, governing gambling, personal and corporate taxation, and marriage and divorce—even prostitution, which, unique among American states, it permits in sparsely populated counties.

The role of the state's geography is most apparent in that, unlike its neighbors, especially California, Nevada has few hospitable natural areas for human settlement. The proximity of populous, wealthy California, however, provides an abundant source of tourism. This fact gave legalized gambling in Nevada an irresistible appeal. Gambling revenues, in turn, allow the state to dispense with state income tax, which now helps to persuade large numbers of retirees, many of them Californians, to settle in the state, especially in the Las Vegas area.

Nevada has had incredible wealth beneath its surface, though virtually all of its mining bonanzas have turned to busts, at least temporarily. Even with the precious metals and other minerals in the state, Nevada's population did not exceed one million until the 1980's; at the end of the twentieth century its population was still fewer than two million.

### Early History

Human society in Nevada extends as much as ten thousand years into the past. Before the arrival of white settlers, American Indian peoples, including the Shoshone, Northern Paiute, and Washoe tribes, inhabited the region. In the eighteenth century, Spanish explorers were the first Europeans to visit the area. Spanish interest in the territory waned, however, after the report of Father Francisco Silvestre Vélez de Escalante, who accompanied an expedition, commented negatively on the area's steep, dry character.

By the early nineteenth century, Canadian and American explorers had arrived. Some were seeking animal furs, and others led scientific expeditions, such as John C. Frémont in the 1840's. Frémont's systematic research of the area and reports on his findings provided the federal government its first systematic account of the region and stimulated interest in the West among easterners. However, the harsh terrain was inhospitable to settlers, and those who passed through Nevada's deserts and mountains were usually on their way to kinder environs. One of the immigrant parties that crossed Nevada was the Donner Party, which in 1846-1847 became snowbound while attempting to cross the Sierra Nevada west of Reno, resorting to cannibalism to survive.

There appear to have been fewer conflicts between settlers and American Indians than in neighboring territories. The settler population was sparse and grouped in only a few locations, so that contacts with American Indians were fewer. That did not mean there was no conflict, however. For example, in 1855 when Mormons arrived in Las Vegas (Spanish for "the meadows") to convert Paiute Indians and supply travelers on their way to Salt Lake City from the Pacific, they found themselves attacked by American Indian raiding parties. Three years later, they abandoned their adobe fort.

In the 1870's, in accordance with federal American Indian policy, reservations were established, the largest of which were the Pyramid Lake Reservation, north of Reno, and the Walker River Reservation, southeast of Reno. These and a number of other smaller reservations, numbering fewer than a dozen, are scattered around the state.

### From Territory to State

The United States acquired the land of modern Nevada, along with other territory in 1848, after the signing of the Treaty of Guadalupe Hidalgo ended the Mexican-American War. In 1850, when New Mexico and Utah were established as territories, Nevada's land was incorporated into the new Utah Territory, administered from Salt Lake City by the Mormon regime.

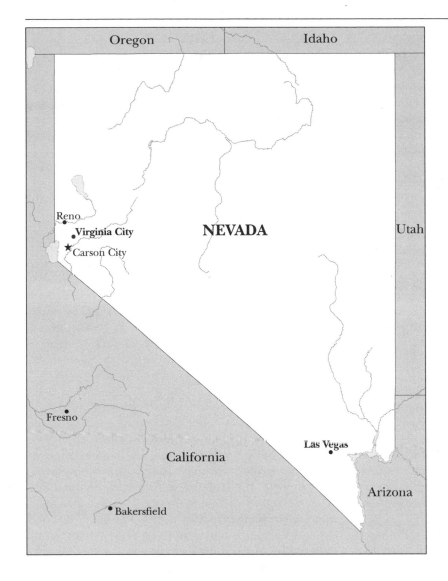

Those seeking their fortunes in the gold fields of California undertook the first great trek through Nevada in 1849-1850. Their numbers led to the first white settlement in present Nevada, when Mormons from Salt Lake City established Mormon Station (later called Genoa), southeast of Carson City. The establishment was obliged to close in 1857, when Mormon leader Brigham Young recalled them, fearful of an attack by U.S. Army troops during a dispute with the federal government. Young had proposed a new state to be formed called "Deseret" but was turned down by the government. Non-Mormons who flocked to the area two years later, who generally opposed living under Mormon rule, tried to set up a provi-sional territorial government, but Washington, D.C., refused to recognize it.

Miners began pouring into Nevada in 1859, when a rich silver lode was discovered, according to one story, by siblings Ethan and Hosea Grosh near Virginia City but credited to Henry T. P. Comstock, who assumed the brothers' claims after they mysteriously died. This strike, which resulted in the extraction of some $400 million in silver, brought thousands of adventurers into Comstock and the surrounding area. Nearby Virginia City became the site's de facto capital, scene of fabulous luxury as well as lawless behavior, as fantastic fortunes were extracted from the ground. Among the invaders from California was the young Samuel Langhorne Clemens, better known later as Mark Twain, who had become a reporter for Virginia City's *Territorial Enterprise*. Twain chronicled the raucous life of the era in his book *Roughing It* (1872). By the 1870's, however, wasteful mining methods and the demonetization of silver by the U.S. government, which lowered its price, combined to diminish the silver rush, and by 1898, Comstock was all but abandoned.

Although settlers were unsuccessful in their first attempt at establishing a territory, events were moving in their favor. Lawlessness needed to be curbed, but, perhaps more important, the Civil War looming early in 1861 directed Washington, D.C., to ensure the loyalty of the West. Accordingly, Nevada became a territory in 1861. The next step to statehood was the writing of a constitution. After voters rejected a first constitution in 1863, a second version—this time without objectionable mining taxes—was accepted the following year. Although the territory was unqualified for statehood because its population was too small (6,857 in 1860), President Abraham Lincoln needed votes in the Senate to pass constitutional amendments and was anxious to add more. Accordingly, the entire text of the new constitution was sent to Washington, D.C., for approval in the longest telegram up to then ever sent, at the astronomical cost of $3,416.77. The territory was made a state in 1864.

The formal institutions of government followed the lead of other states in splitting executive powers into a number of elective offices. This policy had the effect of keeping power out of the hands of a single chief executive, and it reflected traditional American, especially western, distrust of executives, whether kings or presidents. The legislature is bicameral. Five justices sit on the Supreme Court of Nevada, all elected to six-year staggered terms. Nine district courts, with thirty-five district judges serving six-year terms, and a series of municipal courts, complete the judicial system.

**Economy and Society**
Life in the new state improved by the arrival in 1868 of a transcontinental railroad, a more satisfactory communications link than the Pony Express. In the 1870's the economy went sour when the nation turned to the gold standard and silver was no longer used in coins. Cattle and sheep ranching now assumed prominence in the state's economy. Mining in the state revived after 1900 with new gold, silver, and copper discoveries. Moreover, the mining boom stimulated railroad building. In 1905 the Union Pacific Railroad constructed tracks from Salt Lake City to Los Angeles through Las Vegas. Prosperity had its dark side, too, as early in the century violent strikes took place, pitting workers against mining companies.

Mining boomed again when the nation entered World War I in 1917, but after the war demand fell off and declined in the 1920's. When the Depression came in 1930, to stimulate the economy the state legalized gambling, which had been outlawed since 1909. To attract more visitors, it also relaxed marriage and divorce laws, in time making a "Nevada divorce" a household term. Mining revived once more in the late 1930's and 1940's, as federal spending for war materiel increased.

**Postwar Developments**
After World War II society and economy in Nevada changed dramatically. Contrary to some expectations, the demand for minerals remained high in the postwar years. First, big-time gambling was inaugurated with the opening in Las Vegas of the Flamingo Hotel, built and financed by organized crime. By the mid-1950's dozens of large casinos had opened in Las Vegas and Reno, drawing gamblers and vacationers from throughout the nation with headline entertainment and inexpensive food and accommodations.

Second, the federal government dramatically increased spending in the state, opening an Air Force base north of Las Vegas and a bombing range, including a site for testing atomic weapons. In addition, irrigation projects brought water to make the desert bloom. By the 1980's a controversy had broken out between the state and the federal government, which owns 87 percent of the state's domain, over use of federal land for storing atomic waste. In the 1990's the state lost key court decisions over the matter, and the federal government began creating storage facilities for nuclear waste.

**Recreational Mecca**
In the 1960's, the threat of organized crime to the state's gaming industry led Nevada to change its laws, allowing public companies to open casinos in the state. The advent of well-financed commercial gaming in the state was to revolutionize the industry. Gamblers, some of them very rich, began to arrive from all over the world. By the 1980's and 1990's casinos had adopted a policy of attracting families, and significant expansion of the tourist industry took place. Reno and neighboring Lake Tahoe prospered, and Las Vegas became an international center of postmodern architecture. Its cavernous casino-hotels, some designed with a touch of whimsy, often made thematic reference to lost civilizations, such as ancient Egypt and Rome, or to contemporary cities, such as New York and Paris.

The state also attracts increasing numbers of retirees. Las Vegas in particular, with its mild winter climate and proximity to Southern California, became a mecca for retirees. Other factors attracting retirees and others was housing made inexpensive by an inexhaustible supply of cheap land, stretching endlessly into the desert and the absence of a state income tax, made unnecessary by gambling revenues.
—*Charles F. Bahmueller*

# Las Vegas

**Date:** Incorporated in 1911
**Relevant issues:** Art and architecture, business and industry, cultural history, western expansion
**Significance:** Legalized gambling, neon lights, and outrageous architecture come together to make this city one of the most popular tourist destinations in the United States.
**Location:** The southeast corner of Nevada
**Site Office:**
Las Vegas Chamber of Commerce
3720 Howard Hughes Parkway
Las Vegas, NV 89109-0937
ph.: (702) 735-1616
fax: (702) 735-2011
Web site: www.lvchamber.com

According to a survey by the United States Travel Industry Association at the end of the twentieth century, 38 percent of all U.S. residents had visited Las Vegas, most drawn by the allure of easy money. There is, however, more to the city than slot machines, roulette wheels, and flashy showgirls. The fertile valley surrounding the Las Vegas Strip has historically been used as a safe oasis for westbound settlers, a missionary outpost, and an important stop on the railroad line. Even today, Las Vegas continues to undergo a metamorphosis, shifting from it historical role as "Sin City" to a family-friendly playground that just happens to have a few casinos.

## The Founding of the Town

According to archaeologists, Native American tribes of Anasazi and Patayan occupied what would become the Las Vegas Valley at different times before the arrival of European settlers. Spanish traders arrived in the early 1700's, seeking a safe route for transporting their goods between Mexico and California. This trek, know as *jornado de muerta* (journey of death), crossed hundreds of miles of inhospitable desert and unforgiving mountain passes.

It was not until the winter of 1829-1830 that Rafael Rivera became the first person of European ancestry to reach the valley while scouting a route for New Mexico merchant Antonio Armijo. The area became known as Las Vegas, Spanish for "the meadows," and was later used as a resting point for Spanish and Mexican settlers traveling between Santa Fe and Southern California.

While Rivera may have been the first European to reach the valley, credit for its "discovery" is commonly ascribed to John C. Frémont of the U.S. Topographical Corps. Frémont included the valley on his maps of the area, making it an important and lifesaving stop for many westbound settlers. Frémont, who once traveled with legendary explorer Kit Carson, wrote:

> After a day's journey of 18 miles, in a northeasterly direction, we encamped in the midst of another very large basin, at a camping ground called Las Vegas—a term which the Spaniards use to signify fertile or marshy plains. . . . Two narrow streams of clear water, four or five feet deep, gush suddenly with a quick current, from two singularly large springs; these, and other waters of the basin, pass out in a gap to the eastward. The taste of the water is good, but rather too warm to be agreeable; the temperature being 71 in the one and 73 in the other. They, however, afford a delightful bathing place.

The U.S. Congress printed twenty thousand copies of Fremont's 1845 map, and the new route between Mexico and California became known as the Old Spanish Trail.

The valley's first settlement was established by a group of Mormon missionaries in 1855. Led by William A. Bringhurst, the missionaries spent two years trying to convert the Las Vegas Paiutes and provide a safe haven for religious pilgrims traveling between California and Utah. Mormons believed that American Indians, or Lamanites, were descendants of the people of ancient Israel, and it was the responsibility of Mormons to convert Lamanites to their own religion. So many used this route that the Old Spanish Trail was known by many to as the Mormon Road, and a portion of their original fort still stands at Las Vegas Boulevard and Washington Avenue.

Relations between settlers and Native Americans, which had begun in a peaceable manner, became strained when food grew scarce. The Mormons' attempts at teaching farming to the Paiutes were hampered by drought and soil that proved to be too alkaline for most crops.

The discovery of lead at what would later be called Mount Potosi further strained the mission's

*The Las Vegas Strip.* (Corbis)

In 1905, the Las Vegas Valley became one of the primary stops on the newly finished rail line linking Southern California and Salt Lake City, Utah, and the railroad auctioned over one thousand lots to land speculators and eager settlers. Las Vegas became an incorporated city and adopted its first charter on March 16, 1911. The new city had approximately eight hundred inhabitants and covered 19.18 square miles. For the next twenty years, the railroad would surpass farming as the city's most valuable industry.

**Sin City**

The year 1931 was a pivotal one for the city. First, gambling was legalized in the state of Nevada on March 19. Las Vegas issued six gambling licenses the following month, the first going to the Northern Club on historic Fremont Street. Second, liberalized divorce laws led to the establishment of long-term resorts or "dude ranches," which gave those hoping to end their marriages a place to stay while establishing their six-week residency as required by law. These ranches would later evolve into the massive hotel and casino resorts seen today. Finally, construction began on the Boulder Dam in 1931, bringing the population of the area to more than ten thousand. Those construction workers needed entertainment, and the first gambling establishments opened in downtown Las Vegas on Fremont Street.

El Rancho Vegas was the first resort on what is traditionally known as "The Strip," but it was not until notorious gangster Bugsy Siegel opened the Flamingo casino in 1946 that Las Vegas began to attract national attention. No ordinary gambling joint, the Flamingo featured an outdoor pool and a casino lined with palm trees. Though the enterprise was a success, Siegel defaulted on his loan from the infamous New York gang Murder, Incorporated, and was gunned down in his mistress's

resources, when Mormon leader Brigham Young ordered laborers away from their farms and into the mines. The mine was ultimately abandoned as unworkable in early 1857, and many of the Las Vegas missionaries were allowed to leave a few months later. The mission was officially disbanded in the fall of 1858.

The State Land Act of 1885 offered settlers the chance to purchase sections of land at $1.25 per acre, and, despite the poor soil, agriculture became the main industry of the valley for the next twenty years. In addition, minerals and precious metals were discovered in the surrounding hills in the late nineteenth century.

Beverly Hills home the following year. El Rancho Vegas burned to the ground in 1960. Nevertheless, gambling and entertainment quickly became the town's main industry in the years following World War II. Siegel's death only increased the town's notoriety, and the Flamingo served as a prototype for the glitzy gaming palaces that followed.

Eccentric billionaire Howard Hughes purchased several casinos in the late 1960's, giving the gambling business an air of respectability. In 1967, the state legislature passed a law allowing public corporations to obtain gambling licenses, and gradually major corporations replaced private owners. By 1975, annual gaming revenues had reached one billion dollars.

Ironically, the city that owes a portion of its heritage to liberal divorce laws developed a thriving secondary industry—marriage. A license is all that is required; there is no counseling or waiting period. Clark County issued more than one hundred thousand wedding licenses in 1996.

### Lady Luck Gets a Facelift

Nevada enjoyed a monopoly on casino gaming until 1978, when casinos were legalized in Atlantic City, New Jersey. Although Las Vegas remains a major convention center, competition from legalized gambling in other states and on Mississippi River steamboats and Indian reservations has forced the casinos and the surrounding city to broaden their appeal. The focus shifted from seedy to squeaky-clean in the late 1980's as family-friendly theme resorts rapidly replaced the old-style traditional casinos. The facelift worked; according to the Las Vegas Convention Center and Visitors Authority, the hotels are filled to 95 percent capacity on an average weekend.

Las Vegas resorts became "brighter" and "bigger," the two most important words in the race to attract the tourist dollar. By mid-1999, Las Vegas boasted the top ten largest hotels, and eighteen out of the top twenty, in the United States. Examples of the new "attraction" casinos include the Excaliber, which mixes slot machines with live jousting amid a medieval theme. When it opened in 1990, Excaliber was the world's largest resort hotel. The Luxor followed in 1993, featuring a giant pyramid with an atrium large enough to hold nine Boeing 747's and topped by a spotlight made up of forty-five Xenon lights. Also in 1993, the MGM Grand

Hotel and Casino opened, taking over the top slot as the world's largest resort with more than five thousand rooms. Soon, other nongambling spectacles included a sea battle (Treasure Island), roller coasters (New York, New York and Stratosphere), and a show based on the television and film franchise *Star Trek* (Las Vegas Hilton).

The race was not without casualties, as many of the "classic" casinos had to be razed to make room for the new, multiblock megaresorts. The Dunes was imploded in 1993, followed by the Landmark (1995), the Sands (1996), the Hacienda (1996), and the Aladdin (1998).

### Places to Visit

For an updated taste of old-fashioned glitter, tourists can visit the Fremont Street Experience, four blocks of historic downtown Las Vegas closed to automobile traffic in favor of a pedestrian promenade. There, visitors can shop, gamble, and enjoy roving entertainers, topped by a light and sound show with more than two million lights and half a million watts of sound. There are shows every hour on the hour at dusk through 11:00 P.M. and at midnight on Fridays and Saturdays.

In a similar vein, the Neon Museum is dedicated to preserving Las Vegas signs, putting them on display for all to enjoy. Historic signs currently on display on Fremont Street include the lamp from the Aladdin and the Hacienda Horse and Ride.

Considered one of America's "Seven Civil Engineering Wonders," Hoover Dam is located thirty miles southeast of Las Vegas and contains enough concrete for a two-lane paved road stretching from San Francisco to New York City. Lake Mead, created by the dam, provides water to cities as far away as Los Angeles and San Diego. The visitors' center is located in Boulder City and open every day of the year except Thanksgiving and Christmas.

—*P. S. Ramsey*

### For Further Information:

Land, Barbara, Myrick Land, and Guy Louis Rocha. *A Short History of Las Vegas.* Reno: University of Nevada Press, 1999. A comprehensive overview of the city's history from its frontier origins to 1999.

Littlejohn, David, ed. *The Real Las Vegas: Life Beyond the Strip.* New York: Oxford University Press, 1999. A series of essays that offer a glimpse of the

Las Vegas that lies beyond the glitter of the casinos.

McCracken, Robert D. *Las Vegas: The Great American Playground.* Reno: University of Nevada Press, 1997. Provides a detailed look at the evolution of the city of Las Vegas.

Odessky, Dick. *Fly on the Wall: Recollections of Las Vegas' Good Old, Bad Old Days.* Las Vegas: Huntington Press, 1999. Details life in Las Vegas from the 1950's through the 1970's.

Sheehan, Jack, ed. *The Players: The Men Who Made Las Vegas.* Reno: University of Nevada Press, 1997. Covers some of the city's most influential citizens.

Venturi, Robert, Denise Scott Brown, and Steven Izenour. *Learning from Las Vegas.* Cambridge, Mass.: MIT Press, 1977. Describes the architectural development of the Las Vegas Strip and its effects on American culture.

# Virginia City

**Date:** First claim made in 1859

**Relevant issues:** Business and industry, western expansion

**Significance:** This nineteenth century mining boomtown, the leading city in Nevada for twenty-five years, helped advance Nevada's territorial status to statehood.

**Location:** In northwestern Nevada; twenty-four miles southeast of Reno via U.S. 395 and Route 17 and sixteen miles northeast of Carson City via U.S. 50 and Route 17

**Site Office:**
Virginia City Chamber of Commerce
P.O. Box 464
Virginia City, NV 89440
ph.: (775) 847-0311

In 1859, thousands of Californians began invading Mount Davidson in northwestern Nevada, searching for a share of the Comstock Lode, a rich vein of gold and silver. By 1860 several mining camps had been converted into three small towns, Silver City, Gold Hill, and Virginia City, site of the northern section of the lode. During two decades of mining, the colorful frontier town would extract more than four hundred million dollars in gold and silver. The vast treasure at Comstock pushed San Francisco ahead of its competitors in world commerce, hastened Nevada's elevation to statehood, and enriched the U.S. Treasury. Virginia City was a forerunner of many successful boomtowns—Boise, Idaho; Helena, Montana; and Leadville and Denver, Colorado—which attracted persons from diverse ethnic and professional backgrounds. It also served as the cornerstone for a new society that linked the Atlantic and Pacific coasts. The area between the Sierra Nevada and the Rockies became indispensable to the nation.

**Early History**
Before 1859 few miners explored the rocky, sagebrush-covered canyons of northwestern Nevada, then known as Washoe. Most simply used the Carson River Valley below Lake Tahoe as a place to rest on the way to California. In 1850, on Mount Davidson's southern slope, several prospectors found traces of gold along the banks of a creek, and named the gulch Gold Canyon. Sparse amounts of the precious metal also had been found at Six-Mile Canyon, a gulch to the north of Mount Davidson. The difficulty of sifting gold from the area's dense black mud discouraged any formal operations during the mid-1850's. Less ambitious miners staked out small placer claims along the creek, making only three to four dollars a day, just enough to scrape by. Placer refers to the mineral deposits found near a body of water, lode to the primary vein of ore.

**The Comstock Lode**
Located between both gulches, at an altitude of 6,400 feet, was the Comstock Lode. In the early spring of 1859 a prospector named James Fennimore, or "Old Virginny," Finney, reached the head of Gold Canyon and staked his claim on top of a knoll. Henry T. P. Comstock and several other men staked claims beside Fennimore's, following the regulations for placer mining—fifty by four hundred feet per man. Soon the men began raking in twenty dollars a day atop Gold Hill, and they founded a small town named after the lucrative knoll.

Comstock happened to stake his claim above the southern end of the lode. At the head of Six Mile Canyon, Patrick McLaughlin and Peter O'Riley discovered the northern end of the same lode, but Comstock claimed he owned the source of their gold, a spring atop Gold Hill. After Comstock threatened to keep them from digging, McLaughlin and O'Riley agreed to a new partnership with Comstock and his associate, Emanuel Penrod.

For two weeks the four men extracted as much gold as they could. Because their gold was "contaminated" with a pale metal substance, it sold for only eight dollars an ounce, half the price of California gold. Nonetheless, their daily profits soared, into hundreds of dollars. After a curious settler took a sample of the pale dust to be analyzed in Grass Valley, California, the miners discovered they had been throwing away silver—$3,000 a ton, plus $876 in gold. At a time when "good" ore brought $100, $3,876 was an astronomical figure.

## The Washoe Gold Rush

The race to Washoe began. The financial panic of 1857 had created hard economic times in the East and Middle West. The unemployed traveled west for a better life, while in California, a surplus of prospectors and miners moved eastward. Comstock, O'Riley, McLaughlin, and Penrod, however, had shifted the status of their claim from placer to lode, entitling them to more land—a 1,500-foot share which they named the Ophir Mine. One night, legend says, as James Fennimore drunkenly staggered near the Ophir Mine, he tripped, dropped his whiskey bottle, and watched it shatter. He exclaimed "I christen this ground Virginia!" one explanation given for the name, Virginia City.

*The Fourth Ward School in Virginia City.* (Nevada Commission on Tourism)

Columns of stakes, frame shanties, and canvas tents greeted the fortune-seekers who arrived; many had to turn back, because the available claims were snapped up quickly. Some newcomers, called "developers," bought out claims at very low prices. Since many prospectors were interested in a quick return, and unwilling to take on risky investments, most only skimmed the surface of claims. After making a modest profit from a placer claim, the prospector would sell out to developers, who reaped the greatest profit.

### Exploitation of the Comstock

For two decades the Comstock was explored and approximately thirty ore bodies were found. In 1873 the largest vein, the "Big Bonanza," was discovered. The mines produced $1 million worth of metal in 1860, $6.24 million in 1862, and $15.79 million in 1864. Later figures varied, but the highest yield occurred in 1876 with $38.57 million, after miners extracted the greater part of the Big Bonanza. The Comstock output eventually reached $400 million dollars worth of gold and silver, or a block of ore equal in size to a modern freight car.

The area around the Comstock was dominated by its major industry. An underground network of mines required a large labor force, specialized equipment, mills, railroad yards, and foundries. There were problems with water, finance, and government. In 1859 and 1860, there was no political control. The Gold Hill Mining District had elected a justice of the peace and a constable, and established a code of conduct, but it was completely ignored.

### Creation of Nevada Territory

On January 18, 1861, the Utah territorial legislature passed an act which incorporated Virginia City. With the organization of the Nevada Territory, new acts of incorporation were passed in December, 1862, and February, 1864, the latter establishing a mayor-council government. Virginia City's growing wealth precipitated Nevada's statehood in 1864. Consequently, on March 4, 1865, the Nevada legislature approved a more thorough act which provided for the election of a mayor, a board of four aldermen, a recorder, a treasurer, an assessor, and a chief of police. The aldermen were responsible for creating other offices, levying and collecting taxes, and fixing license fees on billiard

tables and saloons. Only five years after the Comstock discovery, Virginia City had transformed Nevada.

To facilitate the import of machinery and supplies, and the export of ore, a railroad was built from Virginia City to Carson City in 1869. Most of the twenty-one-mile railway was blasted through solid rock. Later construction extended the curving railroad north, to the Central Pacific at Reno.

### Boom Times in Virginia City

By 1870 the quality of life in Virginia City was comparable to that of eastern cities. The railroad delivered loads of furniture, ornamental woodwork, and stone for an opera house and the luxurious International Hotel, unrivaled between Chicago and San Francisco. First-class restaurants, theaters, churches, and schools afforded most of the citizens a comfortable lifestyle. The population of the Gold Hill-Virginia City area reached a peak of twenty-five thousand in the 1870's.

Despite its riches, Virginia City was negligent in offering fire protection. Most of the wooden buildings were close to one another, the water supply was inadequate, and the firefighters were inexperienced volunteers. The most disastrous fire struck during the city's most booming period. On October 26, 1875, a fire started in a lodging house and quickly spread to the business district. A strong wind, or "Washoe zephyr," fanned the inferno westward, from the center of the city to the mine buildings. The fire burned four hundred feet down the Ophir shaft, destroying the hoisting works.

Before the blaze was snuffed out, it had destroyed three-quarters of the town, and forced the temporary closing of three major mines, the Consolidated-Virginia, the California, and the Ophir. Two thousand people were left homeless. Cyrenius B. McLellan, a famous Nevada artist, lost most of his work. Several important buildings were saved: the Fourth Ward School, the Presbyterian church, a brewery in Six-Mile Canyon, Piper's Opera House, and the mansion of Robert N. Graves, superintendent of the Empire Mine.

Within a matter of months, however, the city rebuilt its businesses, mines, and homes, constructed a second water line, and improved its hydraulic system. By 1880 the rebuilt city was host to an array of businesses: twenty-two restaurants, twelve lodging houses, ten boarding houses, thirty-nine groceries, fifteen butcher shops, six furniture stores, seven tailoring establishments, seven millinery shops, six dry goods stores, eight pharmacies, and eleven dairies.

## Multiethnic City

Virginia City's population encompassed a wide variety of ethnic groups. Most of them formed national societies. The largest group, the Irish, formed three military companies—the Emmet Guard, the Sweeney Guard, and the Scarsfield Guard. Germans participated in several bands and the Turnverein societies, which met each Sunday at Von Bokkelen's Beer Gardens. Each August, the Scottish Caledonian Society sponsored a "Gathering of the Clans." The Italian Benevolent Society held picnics and balls, while many of the English performed in a choir and orchestra.

Mexicans, Chinese, Indians, and blacks were subject to discrimination, but they formed their own institutions and gradually assimilated into the social fabric of Virginia City. Blacks organized a Masonic lodge, a Baptist church, and an African Methodist Episcopal church. There were unsuccessful attempts to set up black schools, but by 1880 the public schools were educating black, Chinese, and Indian children.

## Virginia City Vice

During the day Virginia City may have resembled a stable, cosmopolitan community, but at night the "Queen of the Comstock" was a frontier mining town like no other. An extensive red-light district flourished amid noisy saloons, gambling houses, and pool rooms. Stage celebrities such as Sarah Bernhardt, Lillian Russell, and Lotta Crabtree entertained packed theaters. Drinking was a common pastime for miners. Some men consumed a quart of whiskey a day, causing one observer to say, "Heavy drinking was the curse of the Comstock." In 1880, 200,000 gallons of alcohol were shipped by railroad to Virginia City. The arrest rate in Virginia City was high; the most common charges included drunk and disorderly conduct, disturbing the peace, fighting, and sleeping on the sidewalk.

News about the notorious mining town spread quickly, attracting many visitors. The most prominent visitors included presidents Benjamin Harrison, Rutherford B. Hayes, and Ulysses S. Grant; politicians James G. Blaine and Schuyler Colfax; Civil War generals Philip Sheridan and William Tecumseh Sherman; the inventor Thomas A. Edison; the famous minister Henry Ward Beecher; the agnostic Robert Ingersoll; humorist Artemus Ward; and suffragist Susan B. Anthony. Samuel Langhorne Clemens started using his pen name, Mark Twain, as a reporter for the *Territorial Enterprise*, Virginia City's leading newspaper.

In 1866 the miners formed a union and soon established relatively fair working regulations: an eight-hour shift and a daily salary of four dollars for underground work. The miners' wages were among the highest in U.S. industry during the 1860's and 1870's, but their working conditions were frightening. In 1867 a photographer named Timothy O'Sullivan exposed the nether world of the Comstock in a haunting portfolio. His eerie pictures showed miners engaged in lonely, arduous work in a place that was, as he said, "hundreds of feet below daylight."

## Dan De Quille

One of the first writers to describe the miners' environment was William Wright, alias Dan De Quille, a reporter and editor for the *Territorial Enterprise*. In 1876 De Quille finished a major reference piece about the Comstock, *The History of the Big Bonanza*. He provided a vivid description of a silver mine:

> Almost the first thing that attracts our attention upon entering the place is the mouth of the main shaft. We see rushing up through several square openings in the floor great volumes of steam. This steam appears to be hissing hot, and rushes almost to the roof of the building. We are surprised to see men coolly ascending and descending the very heart of these columns of steam.

De Quille himself braved the underground descent.

> At the depth of from 1,500 to 2,000 feet the rock is so hot that it is painful to the naked hand. In many places, from crevices in the rock or from holes drilled into it, streams of hot water gush out. In these places the thermometer often shows a temperature of from 120 degrees to 130 degrees.

In April, 1877, the *Territorial Enterprise* reported that miner John Exley slipped into a pool of water that had reached a temperature of 160 degrees. He sank waist-deep for only a few seconds, but his burns were so severe that he soon died.

### Conditions in the Mines

Iron cages used for transporting men, timber, silver, and debris presented several dangers. An arm, leg, or head extended beyond the speeding cage was ripped off instantly. Sometimes timber or tools fell down a shaft. In 1880, at the surface of the New Yellow Jacket Mine, a cage containing steel drills caught on an obstruction and spilled its contents. After falling half a mile, the drills struck eight men in another cage, killing five and injuring three. In a bizarre accident, a dog failed to leap across a shaft, plummeted three hundred feet, and landed on two men, killing them.

Most deaths resulted from falls down the deep shafts. As miners were hoisted to the surface after a day of exhaustive work, sometimes a man became faint, fell out of the cage, and ricocheted to the bottom. Other miners would have to retrieve the remains. Numerous men were killed in cave-ins, a likely event if the timbers supporting the shafts were not installed properly. In addition, the thick sheets of clay in the Comstock swelled when exposed to air, causing the timbers to buckle under the pressure. Sometimes groaning timbers warned the men of a cave-in up to a day or two beforehand. Nevertheless, miners had to continue working. Of the perhaps ten thousand men who worked in the underground Comstock, at least three hundred were killed and six hundred maimed or disabled.

As the digging continued, larger pumps were needed to stem the increased flooding, and more tunnels were dug eastward to allow water—which reached ever-hotter temperatures as the mines went deeper—to drain down Mount Davidson. Engineer Adolph Sutro devised an extensive deep tunnel system to facilitate the effort, but the system was not finished. By 1882, the mine shafts had reached a depth of three thousand feet. The suffocating heat was so severe that miners were unable to work more than fifteen minutes out of every hour. Gloves had to be worn as protection from the heat of the wooden pick handles, and an average worker consumed ninety-five pounds of ice a day. Officials of the U.S. Mint questioned the advisability of keeping the mines open, given the difficult working conditions and the fact that the yield had lessened severely.

### Decline of Virginia City

By the late 1870's Virginia City was on a downhill slide, and by the end of the century mine production was averaging half a million dollars a year. Mining continued on the Comstock for decades with new refining processes, but most efforts yielded modest returns. The mines shut down in 1942, as the U.S. Government considered gold and silver as nonessential to World War II production.

The Comstock left a rich legacy—about twenty millionaires, and hundreds of other wealthy individuals, including those who speculated on the mines in the San Francisco stock market. John W. Mackay, who arrived in Virginia City as a poor miner, left with a tremendous fortune and founded the Postal Telegraph Company. John Percival Welch started his career as a stone mason, became superintendent of a mill, and later served in the U.S. Senate for thirty years. George Hearst, father of newspaper publisher William Randolph Hearst, got his start in mining at the Comstock. He made huge profits with a share of the Ophir and went on to make greater fortunes at the Homestake gold mine in South Dakota and the Anaconda copper mine in Montana. Comstock and his original partners were beset by personal problems and bad business decisions, but many other mine owners became successful capitalists or politicians. The Comstock also proved invaluable to the mining industry: superintendents, foremen, mechanics, carpenters, and miners used their experience and skills to open new mines elsewhere in the United States, Canada, and overseas.

### Modern Preservation Efforts and Tourism

After World War II, a new industry—tourism—sparked life into Virginia City. Lucius Beebe, a New York columnist and railroad buff, prompted the tourist boom when he moved to Virginia City in 1950. Beebe restored a fading mansion, named one of his railroad cars after the town, and revived the *Territorial Enterprise* in the style of Mark Twain. Renovations were also completed at Piper's Opera House and the Fourth Ward School; museums, antique shops, and mansions offered tours and various exhibits. Publicity soared in the 1950's with the debut of *Bonanza*, a popular television series set near Virginia City. The show revolved around a group of cattlemen rather than miners, but it increased interest in Virginia City just the same.

Virginia City offers dozens of fully restored, historic buildings to present-day visitors. The three-story, Second Empire-style Fourth Ward School is home to a visitor center and history museum. Historic homes include the Mackay Mansion, which was occupied—at different times—by George Hearst and John Mackay; the Chollar Mansion, originally built over the Chollar Mine; the Savage Mansion, built by a mining company of that name; and the Castle, built by Robert N. Graves, superintendent of the Empire Mine.

The *Territorial Enterprise* building houses the Mark Twain Museum, a collection of memorabilia affiliated with the city's leading newspaper. The oldest saloon in town is the Old Washoe Club, where the "bonanza kings" celebrated their lucrative business deals. The Way It Was Museum offers mining artifacts, photographs, and various exhibits, including a model of the Comstock Lode directly below Virginia City. Other important public buildings that have been preserved include the Miner's Union Hall and the Storey County Court House.                     —*Richard Trout*

**For Further Information:**

Ellen, Mary, and Al Glass. *Touring Nevada: A Historic and Scenic Guide.* Reno: University of Nevada Press, 1983. Supplements a descriptive one-day tour of Virginia City with historical background. For those interested in visiting the Queen of the Comstock.

Elliot, Russell R. *History of Nevada.* 2d ed. Lincoln: University of Nebraska Press, 1987. A broader view of Virginia City. Political, economic, and social issues are meticulously explored as Elliot reveals the Comstock's pervasive influence on Nevada and the West.

Hinckle, Warren, and Fredric Hobbs. *The Richest Place on Earth: The Story of Virginia City and the Heyday of the Comstock Lode.* Boston: Houghton Mifflin, 1978. A narrative account of the wild characters and escapades of Virginia City. Thoroughly researched, the dramatic yet light-hearted tale is more colorful than most sources. Hobbs's expressive line-drawings are amazingly faithful to the story's tone.

Toll, David W. *The Complete Nevada Traveler: The Affectionate and Intimately Detailed Guidebook to the Most Interesting State in America.* Virginia City, Nev.: Gold Hill, 1998. A guidebook offering anecdotes about the locations covered, including Virginia City. Includes maps and illustrations.

Twain, Mark. *Roughing It.* 1871. Rev. ed. Berkeley: University of California Press, 1993. This embellished memoir of Mark Twain's years in Nevada provides the most vivid depiction of Virginia City during its flush times ever published.

Wallace, Robert. *The Miners.* Alexandria, Va.: Time-Life Books, 1976. Takes a penetrating look at the rise and fall of the Comstock in Chapter 2, "A Lode to Outshine King Solomon's Mines." Assisted by old photographs and maps, Wallace vividly describes the physical and mental ordeals of being a miner. The reader gains an excellent understanding of the layout, technology, and complex workings of a mine.

# Other Historic Sites

## Fort Churchill

*Location:* Weeks, Lyon County

*Relevant issues:* Western expansion

*Statement of significance:* Established in the Carson Valley as a result of the Paiute War of 1860, this adobe fort (1860-1871) provided protection for the emigrant trail to California and the lines of communication that went along with it: the Central Overland Mail Route, the Pony Express, and the projected transcontinental telegraph.

## Fort Ruby

*Location:* Hobson, White Pine County

*Relevant issues:* Civil War, military history, western expansion

*Statement of significance:* Constructed in 1862, Fort

Ruby was a temporary emergency post and was a critical defense link for transportation and communication services connecting the Union states of the East and the West at the onset of the Civil War. The fort also protected immigrants on the Overland Trail from Indian attack.

## Hoover Dam

*Location:* Boulder City, Clark County

*Relevant issues:* Science and technology, western expansion

*Statement of significance:* Begun in June, 1933, and dedicated September, 1935, two years ahead of schedule, this concrete arch-gravity storage dam is among the largest and earliest of the Bureau of Reclamation's massive multiple-purpose dams. By providing electric power, flood control, and irrigation water, this dam made increased levels of population and agricultural production in large areas of the Southwest feasible, affecting not only lands near the river but also urban centers such as Los Angeles.

## Newlands Home

*Location:* Reno, Washoe County

*Relevant issues:* Political history

*Statement of significance:* From 1890 until his death, this large shingle-style house was the home of Francis Griffith Newlands (1849-1917), congressman (1892-1903) and senator (1903-1917) for Nevada. Newlands was the author of the Reclamation Act of 1902, which placed the federal government in the irrigation business, opening up vast areas of the West to farming.

# New Hampshire

*Autumn in New Hampshire.* (PhotoDisc)

# History of New Hampshire

Part of New England, New Hampshire is one of the original thirteen states. When the glaciers that once covered the North American continent retreated in the area now known as New Hampshire, they left behind a hard, gray granite rock called gneiss, which is why New Hampshire is called the Granite State. The state is relatively small: Its longest distance is 180 miles from north to south, and is ranked forty-fourth in land area among states. Bounded by Canada in the north, its other borders are the New England states of Massachusetts, Maine, and Vermont. New Hampshire has a small coastline, stretching only eighteen miles, with Portsmouth serving as the state's only harbor. Because of the state's relatively small amount of arable land, farms produce mostly dairy and poultry products. The impressive water power available made New Hampshire attractive to industrialists in the early 1900's, and manufacturing is still an important segment of the state's economy. With fiercely independent people whose state motto is Live Free or Die, this traditionally conservative state is one of the few without a state income tax.

Before 1800 New Hampshire was home to the Ossipee, Nashua, Pennacook, Piscataqua, Squamscot, and Winnipeaukee Indians. These people, known collectively as the western Abenaki, belonged to the eastern branch of the Algonquian family, a large group of tribes related by similar languages and customs. They lived in wigwams and were primarily hunters and gathers, living off the area's fertile fishing waters and hunting grounds. The encroaching European settlements drove most of the early settlers off the land by the late 1700's. Native Americans comprised 0.2 percent of the population in 1990.

### Early Exploration
Viking Leif Eriksson and other Norse sailors most likely explored some of New Hampshire during their travels in 1000. Explorer Martin Pring was at the mouth of the Piscataqua in 1603. In 1605, British captain George Weymouth landed in Maine, kidnapped five Abenaki men, and took them back to England. Upon meeting the tribesmen, King James I agreed to sponsor a settlement there. In 1620 he formed the Council for New England which gave out land grants, the first going to Captain John Mason, "the founder of New Hampshire." The following year, David Thompson started the first known English settlement in New Hampshire, now known as Rye. He headed a company that organized fishing and trading.

### Religious Conflict
In 1636 the Reverend John Wheelwright was banished from Massachusetts for his religious beliefs. Wheelwright was an Antinomian who believed that Christians do not need to observe moral laws if they are saved by God. Ironically, the Puritans, who had fled England because they were persecuted for their religious beliefs, had little tolerance of other religious philosophies.

Wheelwright turned down an offer from Roger Williams to come to Rhode Island because he wanted to establish a new colony. He went by boat as far as the site of present-day Portsmouth, New Hampshire. It was there that he and a settler named John explored further west and established the village of Exeter and the Laconia Company, a joint-stock company.

In the same year, Massachusetts encouraged Puritans to settle nearby Hampton. Tension quickly erupted between the Antinomians and the Puritans. Both New Hampshire and Massachusetts granted townships within New Hampshire territory. It took the Revolutionary War against Great Britain to unite the two factions for a greater cause.

### The Wentworth Family
The Wentworths were New Hampshire's most influential family throughout much of the 1700's. In 1717 the king of England appointed John Wentworth, a wealthy, self-made merchant, lieutenant governor of New Hampshire. At the time a single royal governor administered both Massachusetts and New Hampshire.

When John Wentworth died in 1730, his son Benning worked to separate from Massachusetts. In 1740, the King's Council established a boundary

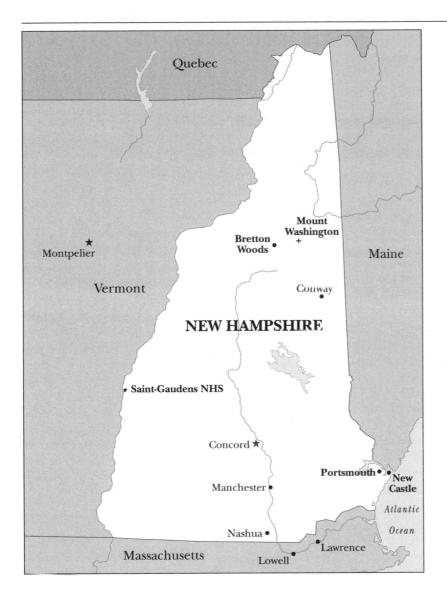

## Revolution

In what some historians consider the first revolutionary act against Britain, four hundred New Hampshire men stormed the British fort at New Castle and carried off arms and ammunition in 1774. The following year the Revolutionary War began, and New Hampshire was represented in every important battle. Portsmouth's shipbuilding industry naturally grew significantly as naval vessels were needed to aid the war.

About four thousand of the state's men fought in the war. Another three thousand men served the cause by privateering: These men sailed the coast capturing British supply ships and seized their cargoes for the American army. Those at home did not have to suffer invasions—New Hampshire was the only one of the original thirteen states British armies never attacked.

## The New State

New Hampshire was the first state to adopt its own constitution, in 1776, and also the first of the original thirteen states to call a convention to write a better one. In 1784 the permanent state constitution was adopted.

In 1808 the state's seat of government moved to Concord. Like most of the country's population, New Hampshire's at this time was mainly made up of farmers. When the Industrial Revolution came to New England in the 1830's, it caused an upsurge in economic activity downriver from Concord in Manchester, which soon became the economic center of the state.

The first commercial buildings to appear were sawmills, which processed lumber, and gristmills to grind grain. The rivers in the Merrimack Valley provided great power, and soon the area developed

and the following year appointed Benning Wentworth as the first independent governor of the providence. Like his father, he was a loyal representative of the Crown. His devotion to England was unpopular with most citizens, who found the king's taxes unjust, and he resigned from office in 1766. His nephew, John Wentworth, was the new royal appointee. He too tried to keep New Hampshire on the side of Britain, and in 1774, he dissolved the assembly for speaking of revolution. The colonists took matters into their own hands, and in June of 1775, Governor Wentworth was forced from office, ending 160 years of colonial rule in New Hampshire.

into one of the world's leading textile centers. The millworkers labored long hours, usually under dangerous conditions. The workers had no bargaining power to speak of, as in 1840's the mill owners had an influx of cheap labor: Ireland's potato famine had driven many of that country's poorest to the shores of America, many ending up in New Hampshire. Wages remained low and working conditions harsh.

### Favorite Sons and Civil War

One of the country's most gifted orators and famous politicians, Daniel Webster was born in Salisbury, New Hampshire, in 1782. After graduating from Dartmouth College, he was New Hampshire's state representative from 1813 to 1817. Webster eventually moved to Massachusetts, however, representing that state in both houses of Congress.

In 1852 New Hampshire lawyer and former state representative Franklin Pierce came out of retirement to become the Democratic nominee for president. He was elected and was then the youngest president ever to serve. His inexperience lead to several botched political moves, and in 1854 he backed the Kansas-Nebraska Act, which repealed the Missouri Compromise. Many historians believe that this act reignited the slavery issue on a national level and pushed the country quickly toward Civil War, which began in 1860.

During the Civil War, New Hampshire was fortunate again as no battles were fought on its soil. Yet the citizens were staunch defenders of the Union, and nearly half the state's population at the time, thirty-nine thousand men, fought in the war.

### The Twentieth Century

When the new century began, more people in New Hampshire made their living from manufacturing than from agriculture. Labor unions began forming in the factories, and a labor reform bill passed in 1907 that limited the workweek for women and children to fifty-eight hours.

The United States entered World War I in 1917, and New Hampshire citizens fought again in large numbers. The Portsmouth Naval Shipyard built warships, including submarines. After the war, the 1920's brought the beginning of years of decline for New England textile milling, and the state entered an economic slump that would worsen

through the Depression and only start to get better at the beginning of World War II.

Frank Knox, publisher of Manchester's *Union Leader*, was appointed secretary of the Navy. Production rapidly went into high gear at the Portsmouth Naval Shipyard making U.S. submarines—at one point during the war, two a week. About twenty thousand men and women worked in the yard.

### The Primary State

In 1913, New Hampshire state legislators moved the date of their election year primary and began a long tradition of being the first primary of every political season. After World War II, presidential primaries became more important, as they were seen as a testing ground for potential candidates. The eyes of the nation focus on New Hampshire during this time every four years. Other states, jealous of the attention, have tried to move their primaries up, and New Hampshire has responded by passing a law dictating that their primary will be held the Tuesday before any other state's.

Since 1952 no president has been elected without first winning the New Hampshire primary—until 1992, when U.S. senator Paul Tsongas won the primary but later lost the nomination to Bill Clinton.
—*Kevin M. Mitchell*

# Mount Washington Cog Railway

**Date:** Started service in August, 1869
**Relevant issues:** Business and industry, science and technology
**Significance:** The Mount Washington Cog Railway was the first such railway ever constructed, and it became the model for other cog railways around the world. It continues to attract thousands of tourists and sightseers every year.
**Location:** Bretton Woods; the base station on the western side of the mountain is reached by an access road that turns northeast from Route 302 just north of Crawford Notch in Coos County
**Site Office:**
Mount Washington Cog Railway
Route 302
Bretton Woods, NH 035899

ph.: (800) 922-8825, ext. 5; (603) 846-5404
Web site: www.cog-railway.com

Neither the hiking trails nor the automobile road offers the traveler such a carefree and scenic trip up Mount Washington as does the unique cog railway, in operation since 1869 except between 1943 and 1945. Thousands of tourists including celebrities like President Ulysses S. Grant (1822-1885) and showman P. T. Barnum (1810-1891) have made the 6.2-mile, three-hour round-trip to the summit over the years. Barnum called the view from the top "the second greatest show on earth." Current ridership numbers eighty thou-

sand per season. The summit of Mount Washington, at 6,288 feet, is the highest point in New Hampshire, and the third highest point in the United States East of the Mississippi. The mountain rises near the town of Bretton Woods, about 25 miles north of Conway, in the White Mountain National Forest. The mountain was one of the first features of its kind to be noticed by European settlers in the seventeenth century, since clear weather permits the peak to be seen from the Atlantic Ocean, 75 miles east.

Darby Field ascended Mount Washington in 1642, accompanied by two Native Americans, in whose language the mountain was called Agio-

*Every year, thousands of sightseers travel up and down Mount Washington on the cog railway.* (The Mount Washington Cog Railway, Bretton Woods)

cochook. His feat was recorded in the journal of Massachusetts governor John Winthrop (1588-1649) and is the earliest recorded ascent by a settler from the Old World.

## Construction of the Cog Railway

The idea for the Mount Washington Cog Railway came from Sylvester Marsh (1803-1884), of Campton, New Hampshire. Inspired by his hike up Mount Washington in 1857, Marsh put together a proposal for a cog railway, brought it before the state legislature in 1858, and was granted a charter. Work was begun on the tracks and on the first engine with its vertical boiler—originally named Hero. By May, 1866, Hero (now renamed Old Peppersass because of its resemblance to a sauce bottle) was in operation on the mountain, and although the tracks did not yet extend to the summit, the first passengers were able to take a short ride on August 29, 1866. By July, 1869, the tracks had been extended to the summit, supported by trestles, including the 300-foot-long Jacob's Ladder. Most of Jacob's Ladder was blown down in the Great New England Hurricane of 1938, but it was quickly rebuilt.

The cog railway has two outer tracks but differs from an ordinary railroad in the use of two inner rails joined by evenly spaced cross members in a ladderlike configuration. A large gear on the engine is turned by steam power so that its teeth engage the rungs of the "ladder" and force the train along upgrades that average 25 percent, but approach 37 percent in some spots. The passenger car is pushed upward by the engine behind it, but on the return trip, the engine goes first. For safety, the wheels all have independent brakes and a ratchet mechanism that prevents them from turning backwards. The engine and the passenger car are not coupled, and may separate slightly at times. The passenger seats are flipped over to give the passengers a clear downhill view during the descent. A round trip requires the burning of about one ton of coal and the conversion of one thousand gallons of water into steam. The train stops at an elevation of 3,800 feet to take on additional water from the Waumbek tank. (The name is the American Indian word for the White Mountains.) The tank gets its water from a well that has been drilled on the site. Until 1910 wood rather than coal was used as fuel. Old Peppersass remained in operation for twelve years, and then was removed from service and exhibited in various places. It made one last trip in 1929 but was wrecked on the way down the mountain.

After the death of Sylvester Marsh, the Mount Washington Cog Railway was owned by the Concord and Montreal Railroad for 10 years, and then by the Boston and Maine Railroad until 1931, when it was bought by Colonel Henry N. Teague.

## Places to Visit

Marshfield Station at the base of the railway offers food and souvenirs, and houses a museum. Old Peppersass is displayed outside. A fire in 1998 destroyed the old station, but not the new one. An overnight hotel stay can be enjoyed at the Summit House atop Mount Washington, and nearby one can visit the observatory of the U.S. Weather Bureau, where the world's record wind speed of 231 miles per hour was recorded on April 21, 1934.

—*John R. Phillips*

## For Further Information:

Bray, Donald H. *They Said It Couldn't Be Done.* Dubuque, Iowa: Kendall/Hunt, 1984. Story of the cog railway, with emphasis on the technical side.

Burt, Frank Allen. *The Story of Mount Washington.* Hanover, N.H.: Dartmouth, 1968. Covers earliest times until 1960. The author's grandfather once published a newspaper at the summit.

Douglas, W. O., and K. Revis. "The Friendly Huts of the White Mountains." *National Geographic* 120, no. 2 (August, 1961): 205-239. Supreme Court Justice William O. Douglas hiked in the Presidential Range, photographing the scenery and staying at Appalachian Mountain Club huts.

*New Hampshire: A Guide to the Granite State.* Boston: Houghton Mifflin, 1938. Dated but very thorough guide to the state, with about a page devoted to the Cog Railway.

Poole, Ernest. *The Great White Hills of New Hampshire.* New York: Doubleday, 1946. White Mountains and their history, including many of the old Native American names.

Teague, Ellen C. *I Conquered My Mountain.* Canaan, N.H.: Phoenix, 1982. The autobiography of a former owner and operator of the Mount Washington Cog Railway.

# Portsmouth and New Castle

**Date:** Portsmouth incorporated in 1653; New Castle received a royal charter in 1693

**Relevant issues:** Business and industry, colonial America, naval history

**Significance:** This historic city and town were elemental in the settlement and organization of the New World, particularly for major contributions to U.S. naval and private shipbuilding. Recent years have seen a rejuvenation of the local economy, in part based on tourism for the many original colonial buildings. Portsmouth is site of the internationally recognized Strawbery Banke outdoor museum.

**Location:** Portsmouth is situated on the Atlantic Ocean at the mouth of the Piscataqua River, a fifteen-square-mile area halfway between Boston, Massachusetts, and Portland, Maine, one hour from either along interstate highway I-95; New Castle is a one-square-mile island just off Portsmouth's east coast

**Site Office:**

City of Portsmouth Chamber of Commerce
1 Junkins Avenue
Portsmouth, NH 03801
ph.: (603) 431-2000
Web site: www.cityofportsmouth.com

At the mouth of the Piscataqua River along New Hampshire's seacoast, the city of Portsmouth and the island town of New Castle are present-day celebrations of a much earlier New England. Pioneer settlements of immigrants from the Old World, these maritime centers boast a colorful history of considerable significance to the birth of the United States.

From the mid-nineteenth century through the mid-twentieth century, the Portsmouth area endured continually eroding economic standing, in part due to an unsteady market for shipping products in the wake of advancing transportation modes. However, the past few decades have seen a wholesale turnaround of the region's fortunes, as civic leaders have invested in the restoration of Portsmouth's often glorious past. Today, the region thrives in a rich atmosphere combining commerce with culture and the flavors of New England.

## Early History

In 1603 England's Queen Elizabeth I selected twenty-three-year-old seafarer Martin Pring to explore this part of the New World, which was then considered the northern part of Virginia. The young captain, commissioned to scout merchant business for the future in the wildlife of the American shoreline, guided his two ships, the *Speedwell* and the *Discoverer*, past several of Maine's rivermouths before settling on the entrance to the Piscataqua River. Pring specifically sought the root of the indigenous sassafras tree, which was coveted for its alleged healing powers; finding none, he traveled south to a place he named Whitson's Harbor. Several years later, this area took on the more familiar nickname of "Plymouth Rock."

Pring was the first to record a detailed description of the Piscataqua's link with the Atlantic Ocean. In England, curiosity arose among opportunistic men with a penchant for exploration. In 1614, Captain John Smith, sent by British merchants, mapped the coast of the New World from Maine's Penobscot Bay to Massachusetts's Cape Cod. At the Piscataqua, he dubbed the string of islands now known as the Isles of Shoals "Smith's Isles."

## Smith Names New England

Smith's notes show that he foresaw a time when the bountiful New World would provide a home to adventurous immigrants, where "every man may be master and owner of his own labour and land. . . . I would rather live here than anywhere." On Smith's return to England, Prince Charles instructed the explorer to name the area "New England."

For nine years after Smith's visit, the region hosted summertime trappers and fishermen from overseas, men who anchored in coves and set up temporary living arrangements on offshore islands. Then in 1623, three years after the settlement of Plymouth, Scotsman David Thompson brought seven men on the *Jonathan* to become the first residents of what is now the Portsmouth area. They chose a point called Pannaway (now known as Odiorne Point, in neighboring Rye), on Little Harbor, where they built a common quarters they called Piscataqua House.

After trading provisions with Plymouth's Miles Standish, Thompson became enamored of an island near Plymouth which he named after himself.

There he relocated with his wife and infant son, and there he took ill and died, leaving the remaining settlers of Piscataqua House at a loss for leadership.

### John Mason's Colony

The Englishman John Mason, formerly the governor of Newfoundland, seized this opportunity to secure from the Plymouth Company not only partial control of Pannaway, but also a grant of six thousand acres leading inland from Pannaway, as well as all islands within three miles of its shore.

Mason's venture differed from those of other settlers in that he sought not a refuge from political and religious strictures, but a prosperous land holding to be peopled with workers in his debt. Mason remained in England, at his estate in Hampshire County known as Portsmouth; he and co-owner Sir Ferdinando Gorges sent acting governor Walter Neale and ten stewards to oversee the pro-

ductivity of seventy-eight colonists. The group arrived in shifts throughout the year 1630, on the vessels the *Pide-Cowe* and the *Warwick*.

After an initial group stayed a short time at Piscataqua House, Mason's colonists broke ground for their community on a spot two miles from Pannaway, facing north at the mouth of the river with a strawberry-covered hill rising from water level. The settlers named the area Strawbery Banke. Here the carpenter Humphrey Chadbourne led a team of builders in erecting Great House, their center of activity, around which they built water wells, a blacksmith shop, a sawmill, and a fort equipped with four cannons. Although Great House no longer remains, today the Strawbery Banke district has been revivified as an "outdoor museum," home of several historic houses benefiting from a multimillion-dollar preservation project which ended the looming threat of urban demolition.

*A replica of the HMS* Bounty *sails into Portsmouth.* (AP/Wide World Photos)

The people of Strawbery Banke sent beaver, mink, and marten skins to London, and they began to fell the area's most sturdy trees for use as sail masts, an activity that would prove to be most profitable in years to come. However, Mason was not inclined to have his settlers plant fields of wheat or corn in the name of self-sufficiency; instead he continued to provide them with cattle and foodstuffs sent from the mother country, and he encouraged the workers to use their time digging for silver and gold in addition to gathering pelts and timber. The Strawbery Banke settlers worked for Mason in a feudal arrangement common to the English of the era, and all reports indicate that he was generous to them. In 1634 Mason's partner Gorges sold his stake in the colony to Mason, who promptly named his six thousand-acre land grant "New Hampshire" and announced his intention to finally join his settlers overseas. He died before he could do so, however.

## Strawbery Banke After Mason

Mason's death in 1635 was a blow to Strawbery Banke's progress: His widow refused aid to the colony, and some of its members devised their own means of survival. Two stewards drove one hundred head of cattle to Boston and sold them for their own profit, and many others of the colony stole away with supplies and tools. In an effort to keep the community from further fragmentation, the remaining members wrote and signed a pact called the Combination. Two decades of growing pains at Strawbery Banke were effectively dismissed when documentation was destroyed in 1652, presumably in an effort to give the settlement a fresh, less argumentative start. It is known, however, that the year 1640 saw a grant of fifty acres made to a minister of the Church of England (which differed in its religious views from those of the Congregational churches of neighboring Massachusetts). Also in 1640, Strawbery Banke saw fit to construct its first jailhouse. In 1641 New Hampshire was annexed to Massachusetts.

In 1652, Strawbery Banke was home to fifty families. At a town meeting it was decided to change the name of their settlement to Portsmouth, after the late John Mason's estate. Development on Strawbery Banke had cleared the hill of its strawberries, and the new name was fitting for the seafaring community. In 1653 Portsmouth was incorporated as a town, despite the protest of Mason's grandson Robert, who still wished to lay claim to the land grant.

By then the region was realizing great successes from the export of its forest products. New Hampshire's white pine trees, more than one hundred feet tall and rigidly straight, were ideally suited for ship's masts. Consequently, shipbuilding became Portsmouth's leading industry. The area's chief factories were long, thin buildings called "rope walks," in which rope for ships was spun. Though Portsmouth enjoyed great wealth from trade with England and the British West Indies, many loggers in favor of free trade were angered by the so-called Pine Acts of the Crown decree, which forbade woodsmen from chopping down trees claimed for the Royal Navy.

## Friction with England

This displeasure with the demands of the mother country was an early indication of separationist sentiment. Portsmouth was developing its own identity as a growing hub, at once creating an aristocratic class of merchants and businessmen, a middle class of tradesmen, and a working class at least partly made up of religious and criminal castoffs from other colonies. New Castle, then also known as Great Island or Sandy Beach, was particularly lively, with a motley crew of tavern patrons and fishermen; on this island without a bridge to the mainland, the prison for the entire province was located. New Castle received its royal charter in 1693.

In 1663 shipwright Richard Jackson built the house that still bears his name. The oldest existing residence in Portsmouth, the Jackson House provided a home for three centuries of his descendants before being turned over to the Society for the Preservation of New England Antiquities. Recognizable by its small, seventeenth century-style leaded glass windows, the house may be seen by appointment.

## Seventeenth Century Prosperity

For one hundred years the Portsmouth area solidified its status as one of the busiest and most important ports on the Atlantic coast. In 1679, the town (along with Dover, Hampton, and Exeter) separated from the Commonwealth of Massachusetts and became a royal province. English shipbuilders whose income was declining at home frequently relocated to the flourishing town, where during the decade of the 1690's they often found themselves besieged by North American Indian allies of the French in isolated battles of King William's War.

The first regular stagecoach in America, at a cost of three dollars per passenger, ran from Boston to Portsmouth, adding to the New Hampshire city's increasing prominence. The town became the seat of the provincial government of New Hampshire, with Benning Wentworth serving as the first royal governor during the years 1741 to 1766, the first of three Wentworths to do so. His residence, the Wentworth-Coolidge Mansion on Little Harbor Road, still stands and can be viewed today; its bedroom wallpaper dates to the original decoration of the house.

### Coming of the American Revolution

During the 1760's, England's Stamp Act aroused the ire of New World colonists. Taxes were applied to all contract transactions, including land deeds, marriage licenses, wills, diplomas, bonds, and newspaper advertising. Portsmouth's residents led the way in repudiating the act. On October 31, 1765, the *New Hampshire Gazette* was published with black borders and, claiming that Liberty was dead in New Hampshire, declared an end to its publishing to denounce the tax. (The paper, in fact, published into the twentieth century before folding, at one point owning the distinction of being the oldest continuously published newspaper in the country.) Portsmouth's Sons of Liberty staged a symbolic funeral march, carrying a coffin inscribed with the epitaph "Liberty, Aged 145 Years" to its grave, then replacing a female figure representing Liberty with a copy of the Stamp Act before burying the casket.

By now unrest between rebellious colonists and those loyal to the mother country was growing fierce. Portsmouth's role in this unrest made history on December 13, 1774, when the colonists learned of a British decision to cut off exports of gunpowder and military supplies to America. During the night, four hundred Sons of Liberty seized Fort William and Mary on Great Island before British reinforcement could arrive. Five guardsmen were subdued and the patriots, under the command of John Sullivan and John Langdon, made off through shallow waters with one hundred barrels of gunpowder. The powder was hidden in nearby Durham and later transported to Boston's

Bunker Hill just in time for the monumental battle between the colonists and British that occurred on that site.

Governor Wentworth put forth a call for British loyalists in Portsmouth, a call that went resoundingly ignored. The town's revolutionary action at Fort William and Mary (now known as Fort Constitution) would prove to be one of the first open acts of rebellion toward England.

### Portsmouth at War

During the Revolutionary War, the legendary naval captain John Paul Jones commanded the Portsmouth-based vessel *Ranger*. As the war reached its conclusion, he was promised the largest ship in the American navy, the *America*, which was under construction in Portsmouth. When the new United States government decided to award the *America* as a gift of gratitude to its French allies, Jones ceremoniously launched the ship in Portsmouth Harbor, an event witnessed by all five thousand Portsmouth residents of the day. Awaiting construction of the ship during the fall of 1782, Jones had lived at an inn on Middle Street, which still stands; the John Paul Jones House is now property of the Portsmouth Historical Society.

When the first president of the young nation announced plans to tour his states, Portsmouth took the honor of being the first stop on his itinerary. George Washington's visit in 1789 prompted the townspeople to line up alphabetically by title of occupation, as the president paraded down Congress Street accompanied by seven hundred cavalrymen. Among his destinations during his four-day stay was the home of Governor John Langdon, the exquisite architectural detail of which delighted the appreciative president. A signer of the Declaration of Independence, Langdon went on to join the U.S. Senate; his house is now under the care of the Society for the Preservation of New England Antiquities.

These were among Portsmouth's most glorious years. After the turn of the century, although its shipbuilding industry continued to thrive, a number of unfortunate events undermined the community's prosperity. Lucrative trade with England and the West Indies had been eradicated by the Revolution, and the area's timber profits declined as virgin forests in New Hampshire's interior were tapped. In 1808 the seat of New Hampshire's government was moved from Portsmouth to Concord, which became the state capital. Compounding these obstacles, a huge fire blazed through some of Portsmouth's oldest buildings in 1813.

### Shipbuilding Center

Still, the first half of the nineteenth century was tremendously prosperous for shipbuilders based in Portsmouth. In 1800 the Portsmouth Naval Shipyard was established by the U.S. government, guaranteeing jobs in that industry for what was at the time the fifteenth-largest port in the nation. The popularity of the fleet style of ship called the clipper benefited Portsmouth's builders, who crafted many of the country's finest. Not until the mid-century advent of the steamship and the railroad, which together displaced much of the demand for sailing vessels, did Portsmouth's economic base begin to see a marked decline. Wrote native son Thomas Bailey Aldrich, "The running of the first train from Boston to Portsmouth . . . was attended by a serious accident. . . . This initial train . . . ran over and killed—LOCAL CHARACTER."

The Portsmouth Naval Shipyard, located on Seavey's Island at the mouth of the Piscataqua, has brought plentiful hope—but also despair and ignominy—to the area. In 1815 its first federal ship, the seventy-four-gun *Washington*, was launched, a symbolic illustration of the yard's potential as a cornerstone of Portsmouth's fortune. In a more sober portrait, hundreds of prisoners of the Spanish-American War were incarcerated there in the summer of 1898, thirty-one of whom died in captivity; buried in the shipyard's cemetery, their bodies were exhumed in 1916 and returned to Spain.

In 1905 President Theodore Roosevelt chose the Portsmouth Naval Shipyard as the site for peace negotiations between the two sides of the Russo-Japanese War. The *Portsmouth Herald* boasted that "an epoch-making period in the history of

*The Wentworth-by-the-Sea hotel in New Castle.* (AP/Wide World Photos)

Portsmouth and the world has begun," and indeed, the city enjoyed certain international acclaim for its role in the event. The Treaty of Portsmouth was signed at the shipyard on September 5 of that year, with other ceremonies taking place at the prestigious hotel in New Castle known as Wentworth-by-the-Sea.

Beginning with World War I, the shipyard benefited from the U.S. government's interest in submarine technology, a field previously monopolized by two private companies. Submarine production at the Portsmouth Naval Shipyard has seen more than 130 completed projects to this day. However, in addition to its triumphs, the shipyard has often been the victim of an unpredictable market for oceangoing vessels. For years, thousands of workers at the shipyard could never be sure whether their services would be needed, a hardship that contributed to an unstable local economy. Defense cuts in the 1960's threatened the very existence of the Portsmouth Naval Shipyard; today, its productivity has stabilized.

### Modern Preservation Efforts

For much of the twentieth century, Portsmouth, which had incorporated as a city in 1849, endured a standstill in its growth as commerce sped by on Interstate 95 between Maine and Massachusetts. The "delicacy of design" in its architecture noted by the U.S. Federal Writers' Project fell into years of neglect and disrepair. Ethnic enclaves divided the city, with Greeks on Fleet, Hanover, and Vaughan Streets; Italians in the North End; Polish on McDonough, and a melting pot on the South End, whose "Puddle Dock" section grew particularly dilapidated. The stately homes on Middle Street were, for a time, some of the last vestiges of Portsmouth's once-proud bearing.

Beginning in the 1950's, however, with the help of several historical organizations, the community has been transformed to a mix of its old-time splendor and modern-day innovation. Today Portsmouth's Market Square, at the union of Market, Daniels, Pleasant, and Congress Streets, is a thriving commercial district that retains much of the "Dickensian" charm of its past. Portsmouth's narrow avenues and antique shops add to the atmosphere; neon-lit storefronts have been replaced with hand-lettered signs. The once-decaying waterfront strip is now the city treasure, featuring the

widely recognized Theatre by the Sea as well as a number of the fine restaurants. New Castle's Fort Constitution, used by the U.S. military during the War of 1812, Spanish-American War, World War I, and World War II, was named to the National Register of Historic Places in 1973. The fort had undergone extensive renovation in 1808, and much of that construction is visible today. The fort is open for tours year-round. Another historic military installation that may be toured at New Castle is Fort Stark, built in 1794 (replacing a 1775 structure) and modified during the War of 1812.

—*Aruna Vasudeuan*

### For Further Information:

Brighton, Raymond. *They Came to Fish.* Reprint. Portsmouth, N.H.: Randall-Winebaum Enterprises, 1979. Definitive text on the region. Available locally.

Federal Writers' Project. *New Hampshire: A Guide to the Granite State.* Boston: Houghton-Mifflin, 1938. Dated but helpful.

Hertz, Sue. "Time and Tide in Portsmouth." *Boston Globe Sunday Magazine,* April 24, 1983. Provides an intriguing look at the clash between Portsmouth's tourism-minded renovators and residents who lament the influx of newcomers.

Sammons, Mark J., ed. *Strawbery Banke: A Historic Waterfront Neighborhood in Portsmouth, New Hampshire.* Portsmouth, N.H.: Strawbery Banke, 1997. An official guidebook available locally.

Winslow, Ola Elizabeth. *Portsmouth: The Life of a Town.* New York: Macmillan, 1966. Written with juveniles in mind but nonetheless indispensible in its wealth of information concerning Portsmouth's colonial days.

# Saint-Gaudens National Historic Site

**Date:** Established in 1965

**Relevant issues:** Art and architecture, cultural history

**Significance:** The site honors the achievements of America's most celebrated sculptor and coin designer. It is the place where Augustus Saint-Gaudens planned and prepared much of the work that established his reputation. The park includes a studio, a gallery displaying his 1907 coin designs, and other exhibits reflecting the sculptor's work and life.

**Location:** Cornish, a rural community in the extreme northern region of the state, accessible from U.S. Interstate 89 and New Hampshire Route 12A

**Site Office:**

Saint-Gaudens National Historic Site
Rural Route 3
P.O. Box 73
Cornish, NH 03745
ph.: (603) 675-2175
fax: (603) 675-2701
Web site: www.sgnhs.org

Augustus Saint-Gaudens is recognized as America's most successful and one of its most prolific sculptors. There are some who compare him to the renowned French sculptor, Auguste Rodin. For more than sixty years after his death on August 3, 1907, Saint-Gaudens was largely forgotten or dismissed by American art critics, but in 1969, a National Portrait Gallery exhibit of his bas-reliefs began a reappraisal of the artist and created a new interest in his work.

### Early Life and Training

Saint-Gaudens was born in Dublin, Ireland, on March 1, 1848. His father, Bernard Saint-Gaudens, was a French shoemaker who moved to Dublin in the mid-1840's and married Mary McGuinness, Augustus's mother. To escape the Irish famine of the late 1840's, the family immigrated to New York City in September, 1848.

As a young boy, Augustus showed artistic interest and talent, and at age thirteen he was apprenticed to a cameo cutter and also attended art classes at Cooper Union and the National Academy of Design in New York City. Six years later, he went to Paris to study under a prominent sculptor, Francois Jouffry. After three years in Paris, Saint-Gaudens moved to Rome where, for five years, he studied classical architecture. It was in Rome that he received his first minor commissions. In 1877, Saint-Gaudens married Augusta Homer, an American art student he had met in Italy.

In 1876, a year before his marriage, Saint-Gaudens earned his first major commission, a monument to Civil War hero Admiral David Glasgow Farragut. When the Farragut Monument was unveiled in Madison Square, New York City, in 1881, there was resounding critical acclaim. Art critics praised the way in which Saint-Gaudens blended allegory and realism. The positive reaction heralded a distinguished career.

### New Hampshire Residence

The 1881 Farragut Monument led to a stream of commissions for Saint-Gaudens and, as his career advanced, he established a summer residence in Cornish, New Hampshire, in 1885. He first rented and then purchased a house that he named Aspet after the town in which his father was born. Aspet became his permanent residence from 1900 until his death in 1907.

On the land around Aspet, Saint-Gaudens built several studios where many of his sculptures were created. He had one large studio, carved out of an old hay barn, to accommodate the work of the assistants he brought to Cornish. The work in Cornish consisted principally of modeling and plaster casting. The plaster casts were then sent by train to foundries in New York. Saint-Gaudens's many assistants prepared the casts according to his instructions. The master himself visited Cornish only periodically until 1900. He spent much of his time teaching regularly in New York and giving advice on such major undertakings as the Columbian Exposition of 1893 and the preservation of Washington, D.C., architecture. Interspersed with this activity there were frequent trips to Europe for "artistic renewal."

### Artistic Community

From 1890 through 1907, Cornish, New Hampshire, was one of the most active artistic communities in North America. Many of the most famous artists of the era followed Saint-Gaudens to Cornish. Among the numbers were architect Charles Platt, dramatist Percy MacKaye, sculptors Paul Manship and Louis Saint-Gaudens (Augustus's brother), and painters Deforest Brush and Kenyon Cox. In the center of this vibrant assembly stood Saint-Gaudens, who was always viewed as the reason the community existed. By the early 1890's, the commissions that Saint-Gaudens received for memorial sculptures had made him an industry upon which the economy of Cornish depended. In 1905, to honor Saint-Gaudens, the art colony produced a play, *A Masque of Ours*, whose set included a temple. The temple was later re-created in marble and is at the Saint-Gaudens burial site.

With Saint-Gaudens's death in 1907, the other artists soon began to leave Cornish. It once again became an isolated village with few permanent residents.

**The Work**

Although his 1907 gold coin designs and his many smaller works are exquisite, Saint-Gaudens is best known for his major monument sculptures. Scattered across the United States as well as Ireland and Scotland, these bronze memorials stand as the most obvious testimony to his brilliance. All his works are arresting for their detail and graceful lines. Critics disagree about which are the best of his memorials, but among those most often cited are *Lincoln: The Standing Lincoln* in Lincoln Park, Chicago; the *Memorial to Mrs. Henry Adams* in Rock Creek Cemetery, Washington, D.C.; and *The Colonel Robert Gould Shaw Memorial* in Boston Commons. The Shaw monument required fourteen years to complete and is frequently referred to as Saint-Gaudens's "Symphony in Bronze." While largely unfamiliar to Americans, Saint-Gaudens's *Memorial to Robert Louis Stevenson* in Edinburgh and his monument in honor of Irish hero Charles S. Parnell in Dublin, Ireland, are also considered to be superior efforts.

There are some critics who complain that Saint-Gaudens tried to do too much, or that he relied to an excessive degree on his assistants. The consensus, however, is that Saint-Gaudens was not only the first true American sculptor, but that his work places him in the upper echelon of artists regardless of time or place.         —*Ronald K. Huch*

**For Further Information:**

Dryfhout, John. *The Works of Augustus Saint-Gaudens.* Hanover, N.H.: University Press of New England, 1982. Essential reading for those with a serious interest in Saint-Gaudens's work.

Hureaux, Alain Daguerre, ed. *Augustus Saint-Gaudens, 1848-1907: A Master of American Sculpture.* New York: Somogy Editions D'Art, 1999. Color catalog of Saint-Gaudens's work featuring two 1999 European exhibitions. Includes eleven essays by art scholars.

Saint-Gaudens, Homer, ed. *Reminiscences of Augustus Saint-Gaudens.* 2 vols. Reprint. New York: Garland, 1969. Edited by Augustus's son, these reminiscences are sometimes interesting but not very enlightening.

Taft, Lorado. *The History of American Sculpture.* Reprint. New York: Arno Press, 1969. Suggests that American sculpture really began with Augustus Saint-Gaudens.

Tharp, Louise Hall. *Saint-Gaudens and the Gilded Era.* Boston: Little, Brown, 1969. Puts Saint-Gaudens in the context of late nineteenth century American culture.

Wilkinson, Burke. *The Life and Works of Augustus Saint Gaudens.* San Diego: Harcourt, 1985. A highly readable account of Saint-Gaudens's life that tries to correct some misconceptions.

# Other Historic Sites

## Albacore

*Location:* Portsmouth Maritime Museum, Portsmouth, Rockingham County

*Relevant issues:* Naval history

*Statement of significance:* Albacore (1953), an experimental, diesel-electric submarine represents a revolution in naval architecture. Designed to be a true submarine, in which surface characteristics are subordinated to underwater performance, it was much quieter, faster, and more maneuverable than any earlier submarine. Through a series of tests of various configurations it provided the model for all future U.S. Navy and most foreign submarines.

## Bartlett House

*Location:* Kingston, Rockingham County

*Relevant issues:* Colonial America, political history

*Statement of significance:* From 1774 until his death, this was the home of Josiah Bartlett (1729-1795), physician, Revolutionary patriot, and signer of the Declaration of Independence and constitution for New Hampshire. Bartlett also served as chief justice and governor of the state.

## Canterbury Shaker Village

*Location:* Canterbury, Merrimack County

*Relevant issues:* Religion

*Statement of significance:* Designed, built, and inhabited by Shakers for two hundred years, Canterbury Shaker Village is considered among the most intact and authentic of the surviving Shaker villages—the largest, most successful, and best known of America's nineteenth century communal utopian societies. The stark harmony of the well-ordered, practical structures of this village illustrates well the Shaker principle of simple beauty through function.

## Chase Birthplace and Boyhood Home

*Location:* Cornish Flat, Sullivan County

*Relevant issues:* Political history

*Statement of significance:* From 1808 to 1816, this was the childhood home of Salmon P. Chase (1808-1873), who served Ohio in the U.S. Senate (1849-1855, 1861) and as governor (1855-1859) and the nation as secretary of the Treasury (1861-1864) and chief justice (1864-1873). In the latter capacity, he presided over the impeachment trial of President Andrew Johnson.

## Cummings House

*Location:* Silver Lake, Carroll County

*Relevant issues:* Literary history

*Statement of significance:* This white clapboard farmhouse is associated with one of the most innovative poets of the twentieth century, E. E. Cummings (1894-1962). From 1923 until his death, "Joy Farm," set in an unspoiled rolling, wooded countryside, was the summer home of Edward Estlin Cummings.

## Frost Homestead

*Location:* Derry, Rockingham County

*Relevant issues:* Literary history

*Statement of significance:* From 1900 to 1909, this thirteen-acre farm was the home of Robert Frost (1874-1963), one of the few twentieth century poets to command both critical respect and wide readership. Frost authored eleven volumes of poetry and on four occasions won the Pulitzer Prize in poetry (1924, 1931, 1937, and 1943).

## Harrisville Historic District

*Location:* Harrisville and vicinity, Cheshire County

*Relevant issues:* Cultural history

*Statement of significance:* Harrisville is an exceptionally well-preserved industrial community of the early nineteenth century. Its complex of mills, stores, boardinghouses, dwellings, churches, and other buildings is virtually intact.

## Jones House

*Location:* Portsmouth, Rockingham County

*Relevant issues:* Naval history, Revolutionary War

*Statement of significance:* For two years (1781-1782), this large rectangular two-and-a-half-story wood boardinghouse was the residence of John Paul Jones (1747-1792), Scottish-born American naval officer and hero. While here, Jones supervised the construction of *America*, a ship of the line for the Continental Navy.

## Langdon Mansion

*Location:* Portsmouth, Rockingham County

*Relevant issues:* Political history, Revolutionary War

*Statement of significance:* Erected in 1784, this home, one of the great Georgian houses of America, was the residence of Governor John Langdon (1741-1819), a leading figure in New Hampshire mercantile, military, and political affairs for more than forty years. Langdon served as a delegate to the Constitutional Convention in 1787 and as the first president pro tempore of the United States Senate. His house was built by local craftsmen who derived details from architectural guidebooks by British author Abraham Stone.

## MacDowell Colony

*Location:* Peterborough, Hillsborough County

*Relevant issues:* Cultural history

*Statement of significance:* Established in 1908 as a living memorial to Edward MacDowell (1861-1908), one of the first Americans to be recognized as a composer of serious music, the colony—forty-two buildings on four hundred acres of forest and meadow land—has since become known internationally as a retreat where men and women gifted in the arts enjoy ideal conditions for creative work.

## Mount Washington Hotel

*Location:* Bretton Woods, Coos County

*Relevant issues:* Business and industry, political history

*Statement of significance:* This was the largest spa (352 rooms) in the White Mountains when it opened in 1902. Built in Spanish-Renaissance style, it is a large wooden frame, Y-shaped structure with two five-story octagonal towers. Its isolation and scale made it the choice location of the 1944 Bretton Woods Conference, an international gathering of economists, lawyers, and politicians to chart a blueprint for the world's monetary system. The World Bank was established at this conference.

## Pierce Homestead

*Location:* Hillsborough, Hillsborough County
*Relevant issues:* Political history
*Statement of significance:* From infancy until his marriage in 1834, this two-story frame and clapboard house was the home of Franklin Pierce (1804-1869), fourteenth president of the United States. Pierce held office during one of the most critical periods (1853-1857) of the antebellum generation; during his tenure, the apparent calm of the Missouri Compromise of 1850 gave way to the Kansas-Nebraska Act of 1854, "Bleeding Kansas," and the renewed sectional storms which resulted in the Civil War.

## Sullivan House

*Location:* Durham, Strafford County
*Relevant issues:* Military history, Revolutionary War
*Statement of significance:* From 1764 until his death, this two-story, L-shaped wood structure was the home of John Sullivan (1740-1795), a major general during the War for Independence and one of George Washington's ablest officers. In December, 1774, leading four hundred Portsmouth Sons of Liberty, Sullivan captured Fort William and Mary at the entrance of Portsmouth Harbor, appropriating its weapons and stores for the patriotic cause.

## Webster Family Home

*Location:* West Franklin, Merrimack County
*Relevant issues:* Political history
*Statement of significance:* From 1800 until the end of his days, The Elms served Daniel Webster (1782-1852) as a home, vacation retreat, and experimental farm. The gravesites of his parents and four brothers and sisters are located here.

# New Jersey

*The beach in Atlantic City.* (PhotoDisc)

# History of New Jersey

Situated on a relatively narrow strip of land between the Atlantic Ocean and the Delaware River, New Jersey has been one of the most densely populated areas of the nation since the early years of the United States. Bordering the large cities of New York City to the northeast and Philadelphia to the southwest, New Jersey was heavily urbanized and industrialized at an early date but still retains scenic seacoasts and wilderness areas.

### Early History

About six thousand years ago, the Delaware, a Native American people also known as the Lenni-Lenape, arrived in the region between the Hudson River and the Delaware River. The Delaware practiced agriculture, hunted, fished in the rivers, and gathered shellfish from the Atlantic Ocean. Not long after European colonists established settlements in the area, the Delaware, reduced greatly in numbers by newly introduced European diseases, sold their native lands and moved westward. By the middle of the nineteenth century, the Delaware were removed to Oklahoma, where many of their descendants reside today.

The first European to reach New Jersey was the Italian navigator Giovanni da Verrazano. Working for the French, Verrazano explored the Atlantic coast from North Carolina to Canada in 1524. During this voyage, Verrazano entered what is now Newark Bay. In 1609, the English navigator Henry Hudson, working for the Dutch, explored what is now Sandy Hook Bay.

### Colonization

Despite this early exploration, settlement of the area began slowly. Although Dutch trading posts were founded on the Hudson River as early as 1618, and Swedish trading posts on the Delaware River by 1638, the first permanent European settlement was not founded until 1660. This settlement, known as Bergen, was founded by the Dutch at the present site of Jersey City. The Dutch, who had taken control of the Swedish trading posts in 1655, retained ownership of the colony until 1664, when an En-

glish fleet sailed into New York Harbor and took control of the Dutch colonies of New York and New Jersey without a fight.

King Charles II of England granted all the lands between the Connecticut River and the Delaware River, including New York and New Jersey, to his brother, the duke of York and Albany. The duke (later King James II) in turn granted the region between the Hudson River and the Delaware River to John Berkeley and George Carteret, two friends and allies of the king. This area was divided into East Jersey and West Jersey in 1676, when Berkeley sold his share of the land to a group of Quakers. The Quakers took possession of West Jersey, while Carteret retained control of East Jersey.

East Jersey was mostly settled by Puritans from Long Island and New England. The Quakers purchased East Jersey in 1682. In 1702 English Queen Anne united the two colonies under royal rule and placed them under the administration of the governor of New York. In 1738, New Jersey became a separate colony from New York, with Lewis Morris serving as its first governor.

### Revolution

Located between the two important colonial cities of New York City and Philadelphia, New Jersey soon became an important area of transportation, with more roads than any other colony. During the American Revolution (1775-1783), New Jersey's strategic position between these two vital cities led to more than one hundred battles in the area.

The British, who had captured New York City in late 1776, drove American troops commanded by General George Washington out of New York and New Jersey into Pennsylvania. Early on the morning of December 26, 1776, Washington crossed the Delaware River into New Jersey and captured Trenton. Although Trenton was recaptured by the British on January 2, 1777, Washington won another victory at Princeton the next day. These early successes, although not decisive, prevented the American war effort from failing during the early years of the Revolution. A later American victory on June 28, 1778, when Washington attacked British

forces withdrawing from Philadelphia at Monmouth Court House, helped maintain a stalemate in the northern states, allowing the Revolution to continue until more critical victories in the southern states led to the end of the war.

After the war, Princeton served as the capital of the United States for brief periods in 1783 and 1784. New Jersey played a key role during the convention in Philadelphia in 1787 that created the U.S. Constitution. The New Jersey Plan, which advocated equal representation for each state, was combined with the Virginia Plan, which advocated representation based on population, to create the Senate and the House of Representatives. New Jersey ratified the Constitution on December 18, 1787, officially becoming the third state. It was the first state to ratify the first ten amendments to the Constitution, known as the Bill of Rights, on November 20, 1789.

### Industry and Transportation

Although first noted in colonial days as a highly productive area for agriculture, hence the nickname of the "Garden State," New Jersey quickly became one of the first states to develop an industrial

economy. The process began during the American Revolution, when New Jersey supplied much of the iron needed for cannons and ammunition. In 1791 Alexander Hamilton founded the nation's first industrial town at Paterson, located at the Great Falls of the Passaic River, which supplied water power.

Much of the success of industrial growth during the early nineteenth century was due to improvements in transportation. During the 1830's, a series of canals linked the Hudson River and the Delaware River, allowing easier transport of goods between New York City and Philadelphia. During the same period, railroads began to appear in the state. An early industry that developed in New Jersey due to the transportation revolution was the dyeing and weaving of cloth. The textile industry would remain important to the state's economy.

### The Civil War and Immigration

Its central position between northern states and southern states, combined with economic ties to southern states, made New Jersey one of the most divided states during the Civil War (1861-1865). The Democratic Party in the state included many Peace Democrats, who advocated an end to the war through negotiation with the Confederacy. The Republican Party demanded complete victory over the Confederacy. This early struggle was reflected in later years, when the two parties continued to share almost equal power in the state. Although the military draft was strongly opposed in 1863, New Jersey supplied large numbers of troops and manufactured goods to the Union. After the war, many politicians opposed granting civil rights to African Americans, who were not allowed to vote in New Jersey until 1870.

Meanwhile, the first of many waves of immigration to the state brought many Germans and Irish to New Jersey in the 1840's. Immigrants during the late nineteenth century mostly arrived from southern and eastern Europe, particularly Italy, Russia, Poland, and Hungary. The increase in population, particularly in urban areas, combined with an increased demand for manufactured goods, continued the industrialization of the state. One of the largest factories in New Jersey was founded by Isaac M. Singer, who opened a sewing machine plant in Elizabeth in 1871. Other thriving industries at this time included oil refining along the Hudson River and pottery manufacturing in Trenton. Newark became one of the most prominent industrial cities in the state, with a variety of manufacturers as well as an important insurance industry.

### The Age of Wilson

New Jersey rose to prominence in national politics in the early years of the twentieth century. Woodrow Wilson, president of Princeton University since 1902, was elected governor in 1910. The success of his progressive policies led to his election as president of the United States in 1912. During his first term in office, Wilson was active in promoting legislation that reformed national economic policies. Reelected in 1916, Wilson helped to establish the League of Nations after World War I, winning him the Nobel Peace Prize in 1920.

In sharp contrast to Wilson's idealism, local politics in New Jersey were often highly corrupt. The most notorious of the state's political bosses was Frank Hague, who ruled Jersey City from 1917 to 1947. Hague was famous for his boast that "I am the law." Although reforms diminished the power of political bosses, New Jersey continued to have a reputation for political corruption and organized crime.

### The Twentieth Century

World War I made New Jersey a center of shipbuilding and munitions manufacturing. The war also prevented German chemicals and pharmaceuticals from reaching the United States, and New Jersey became a leader in these industries. Chemical production continued to be the most important industry in the state. After the Great Depression of the 1930's, New Jersey's economy recovered during World War II, when aircraft manufacturing became a major industry in the state, along with a revival in the making of ships and armaments.

World War II also brought many African Americans to New Jersey. The 1950's and 1960's saw large numbers of Puerto Ricans enter the state. After Fidel Castro established a Communist government in Cuba in 1959, many Cubans immigrated to New Jersey. Later decades saw an increase in the number of immigrants from Asia and the Middle East.

After a recession in the 1970's and early 1980's, New Jersey's economy shifted from manufacturing to service industries. Unemployment dropped from 10 percent in the middle of the 1970's to 4 percent in 1988. Despite a strong economy in the 1990's, New Jersey faced the problems of crime, poverty, and pollution, which were inevitable for any heavily urbanized state.   *—Rose Secrest*

# Cape May

**Date:** Constructed between 1850 and 1910

**Relevant issues:** Art and architecture, cultural history

**Significance:** A National Historic Landmark, the city of Cape May is a well-preserved nineteenth century oceanfront resort community. It contains approximately six hundred public and private buildings constructed between 1850 and 1910, with most built between 1878 and 1890.

**Location:** At the southernmost tip of New Jersey, starting point of the Garden State Parkway, with entrance to the town from the parkway via Lafayette Street; most of the Historic District, at the center of town, is roughly bounded by Washington Street, Perry Street, Beach Avenue, Howard Street, and Franklin Street, although other historic sites are scattered beyond these borders throughout the town

**Site Office:**
Mid-Atlantic Center for the Arts
1048 Washington Street
Cape May, NJ 08204
ph.: (800) 275-4278; (609) 884-5404
Web site: www.capemaymac.org

Given all that Cape May has been through, it is a wonder that it is still standing: For more than a century, the oceanside resort town, located at New Jersey's southernmost tip, has weathered a series of devastating fires, powerful storms, and speculative land developments that, by all rights, should have rendered it a ghost town several times over. Thanks to the dedicated efforts of preservationists, helped along by Cape May's natural attractions of a pleasant climate and beautiful beaches, the town has survived, with much of its Victorian-era charm intact. In fact, Cape May has today become a popular tourist destination for those longing to see its beautiful oceanfront, its preserved Victorian architecture, and its special events and seasonal festivals, qualities that have helped to make—and sustain—this community as the nation's oldest seashore resort.

## Modern Preservation Efforts

Listed on the National Register of Historic Places and designated as a National Historic Landmark city, Cape May today boasts more than six hundred preserved nineteenth century structures. Nearly all were built between 1850 and 1910, with most constructed between 1878 and 1890. Among the preserved buildings are private residences, hotels, and churches, some of which were designed by such famed architects as Frank Furness and Samuel Sloan. Many of these structures continue to fulfill their original purposes, as is the case with many of Cape May's guesthouses. These charming turn-of-the-century inns have been authentically restored, right down to the period furniture and decorative appointments.

Most of Cape May's preserved structures are located at the town's center. They can be perhaps best seen on guided walking or trolley tours sponsored by the Mid-Atlantic Center for the Arts, the organization responsible for spearheading most of Cape May's preservation efforts. These tours even provide access to the interiors of some of the structures. Those wishing to view Cape May on their own can walk through the historic district, although visitors should be aware that many of the buildings are privately owned and not open to the public.

Visitors can find some of the best examples of preserved Victoriana along Hughes Street, called by one travel guide "the prettiest street in town." Other architectural treasures can be found along nearby Columbia Avenue, Howard Street, Gurney Street, Ocean Street, Beach Drive, Congress Place, and Perry Street. Particularly noteworthy are the Chalfonte Hotel at 301 Howard Street, built in 1876 and the oldest continuously operated hotel in Cape May, and the Emlen Physick House and Estate at 1048 Washington Street, a once-abandoned mansion that helped spark much of the community's preservation drive.

The land on which Cape May is located is at the southern point of New Jersey, where the Atlantic Ocean meets Delaware Bay. While this land for all practical purposes resembles a cape, it is technically an island, cut off from the "mainland" by a creek and canal that run the width of the peninsula.

These progressive influences were limited, however, as most of Cape May's structures reflected the simple styles that had been in vogue at mid-century. Charming though it may have been, however, this architectural conservatism contributed to Cape May's decline as a resort. By the turn of the century, Cape May had become a "country town by the seashore," as one author described it. Those seeking resorts with more glitz, glamour, and activity began flocking to such stylish locales as Saratoga, Newport, and Atlantic City. With the elimination of legal gambling in 1897 and legal liquor in 1899, Cape May lost two of its last remaining attractions.

Ironically, the architectural conservatism that helped bring about Cape May's decline would be the spark behind its later rebirth. Many years would pass, however, before this regeneration occurred.

## Early History

Sir Henry Hudson is credited with being the first European to arrive in the area. He noted the cape's existence while on a 1609 exploration voyage. However, Hudson made no claim to the land. In fact, no such claim was made for another twelve years, when Dutch seaman Captain Cornelius Jacobsen Mey sailed by while on a voyage for the Dutch East India Company. Mey, whose name was later Anglicized to May, claimed the land for the Netherlands and bestowed his own name upon it. He believed the land possessed great beauty and tremendous potential for development. He was right, but his thinking was several hundred years ahead of its time. Cape May would develop, but without much influence from the Dutch.

In the years following Mey's claim, a few Dutch settlers followed, but most of the area's early population growth, beginning in about 1638, came from transplanted New Englanders. These resettled Yankees moved to the area in hopes of developing a whaling industry. As time passed, the whaling industry did not live up to expectations, so many of the new arrivals and their descendants took to farming for a living. By 1660, the area came under English control, prompting most of the Dutch settlers to leave; they either moved west to Delaware or north to New Netherland (which would quickly become New York).

Little changed over the next century. Whaling and farming sufficiently sustained the residents of Cape Island, as the area was known then. On June 20, 1766, a small but significant event took place that would ultimately set the region on a new course. Robert Parsons, a Cape May farmer, placed an advertisement in the *Pennsylvania Gazette*, enticing summer vacationers to come enjoy "the healthful benefits of bathing in local waters." The ad further went on to invite "paying guests" to his spacious home. So it was that Cape May's tourist industry was born.

## Long History as a Vacation Spot

Although the *Pennsylvania Gazette* advertisement was the first known document to solicit the business of paying visitors, vacationers had been summering at the cape on a more informal basis for some time. The Kechemeche Indians, for example, had been coming to Cape May for many years to get away from the inland summer heat. The cape was a popular destination for such escapes because, as a peninsula, it received the cooling breezes of both the ocean and the bay.

In the ensuing years, word gradually spread about Cape May. Development was slow at first, but after the War of 1812, the community entered a period of steady growth. In addition to its sparkling beaches and beautiful weather, Cape May had another advantage in its proximity to the major population centers of the time—one hundred fifty miles from New York, eighty miles from Philadelphia, and one hundred twenty from Washington, D.C. Even though land routes to the area left much to be desired (as they did in much of the country at that time), the cape was readily accessible by water, and this significantly helped fuel Cape May's growth.

## Increasing Popularity Among Travelers

With the emergence of sailing ship (and later steamboat) service to the cape, visitors began flocking to this new vacation destination. Initially, the journey by boat from most major nearby ports took

*Visitors can tour Cape May by trolley.* (New Jersey Commerce & Economic Growth Commission)

two or three days. A voyage of such duration was still a far more attractive option than an equally long and far more uncomfortable journey over land by horseback or stagecoach, the most common modes of land transport available at that time.

With the arrival of more and more tourists, the Cape May landscape began to change. What had been a sparsely populated farming and fishing community was being transformed into a bustling resort town. With the number of tourists quickly eclipsing the number of guestrooms available in the homes of local residents, hotels began springing up, with nearly two dozen in place by 1850.

Cape May's growth as a resort community also led to growth in the town's land area and permanent population. This expansion brought with it a corresponding increase in public construction and infrastructure development. A school was built in the 1830's, and two churches, one Methodist and one Presbyterian, were erected in 1843 and 1844, respectively. Simultaneously, the street system developed and expanded, resulting in a formal surveying in 1850. In 1851, the town was officially incorporated as the city of Cape Island. In the years that followed, additional public buildings were constructed, such as a city hall, a firehouse, a post office, and several additional churches.

As Cape May's street system took shape, there was also new residential development. At first, residential lots were sold primarily to townspeople. By the 1850's, an increasing number of lots were sold to out-of-towners seeking to build vacation cottages. Well-to-do tourists who once sought accommodation in the hotels gradually began to seek refuge from them by building their own housing. With the emergence of this trend, Cape May was on the way to being owned largely by seasonal residents.

By the 1850's, Cape May's reputation as a resort was well established. For the next fifty years, it would be a favorite vacation destination of both the well-off and the well-known. Presidents Abraham Lincoln, Franklin Pierce, Ulysses S. Grant, Chester A. Arthur, Benjamin Harrison, and James Buchanan all spent time here before, during, and/or after their terms in office. Other dignitaries, such as composer John Philip Sousa and industrialist Henry Ford (who once even raced one of his automobiles against Louis Chevrolet along Cape May's beachfront), also visited.

## Boom-and-Bust Cycles

Cape May was not without its problems. A series of events launched the town into a pattern of boom-and-bust cycles that caused fits and starts in Cape May's growth and evolution. The first major blow came in 1856, when Cape May was at the height of its popularity. A railroad line connecting the nearby blossoming resort town of Atlantic City with Camden, a New Jersey suburb of Philadelphia, was completed. As the new resort grew, it gradually began siphoning off business from Cape May. Five years later, when the nation was plunged into the upheaval of the Civil War, development in Cape May came to a virtual standstill.

The decline was not to last forever. In 1863 a railroad line was built to Cape May, bringing renewed interest in development. This trend gained momentum after the Civil War, especially for residential construction. New subdivisions were established, greatly accelerating the building of new homes, particularly tourist cottages.

Just as growth was beginning to take off, a devastating (and suspicious) fire struck Cape May in August, 1869, destroying a number of hotels, a portion of the business district, and other structures. This setback was overcome in a period of rebuilding and new growth that lasted for several years. Then came the financial panic of 1873, which brought development to a halt. Growth resumed in 1875 and continued steadily, although less robustly, until 1878, when an even more devastating fire swept through the resort, virtually leveling the town.

Unlike the aftermath of the 1869 fire, reconstruction following the 1878 fire proceeded slowly. This was largely due to the restrained development plans put in place during that period. Instead of erecting new, modern structures, hotel developers and homeowners who lost buildings in the 1878 fire constructed facilities that were only slightly updated versions of their forerunners. These "new" buildings—mostly revamped editions of 1860's-style structures, with few modern twists—gave Cape May a look that was considered decidedly "old-fashioned" for the time.

## Architectural Conservatism

The conservative architectural nature of the reconstructed buildings did much to inhibit Cape May's future growth. While the area's quaint ambiance may have appealed to its established (and aging) tourist base, it did little to attract new, younger vacationers. It also did little to encourage the purchase of residential lots in the area's new subdivisions, which were located increasingly farther from the center of town. This lack of interest, combined with inadequate local ground transportation, helped prompt the failure of most of these new real estate developments. Cape May had begun to decline.

Why had Cape May's architecture become stuck in a time warp? In part it was because Cape May persisted in viewing itself as a small town (despite its success in attracting tourists from far and wide), and small towns were slow to adopt innovation at that time in U.S. history. It also may be partly due to all the changes that Cape May had been through in the last half of the nineteenth century—and the fact that its conservative, established residents were more willing to embrace the familiar than experiment with new ideas.

Cape May's architectural conservatism during the last half of the nineteenth century was perhaps most attributable to the architects who worked in the town. Many received their first commissions in Cape May in the mid-1860's, around the time the railroad line was completed and "new" development began. Many of these architects were also well along in their careers, past the point where they were willing to attempt much innovation in their projects. As a consequence, they largely adapted and reproduced the prevailing architectural styles, a practice that endured throughout the remainder of the nineteenth century (and even into the early twentieth century at one firm) in Cape May.

Like the developers who gave them their commissions, most of the architects who worked in Cape May at that time were from Philadelphia. The most prolific of these architects was Stephen Button, who arrived in Cape May in 1863 at age fifty and at the height of his career. Button had distinguished himself in the Philadelphia architectural community as a proponent of designs that reflected clean, simple, classic lines, much like those in the 1850's clapboard structures that dominated Cape May when he arrived in town. Button employed this vernacular style of architecture in his more than forty designs over the next three decades. From the time of his first commission until his death in 1897—even through the reconstruc-

tion periods following the 1869 and 1878 fires—his style would persist, making an indelible mark on the community and profoundly influencing the designs of other architects and builders who worked in town.

Despite the overwhelming impact of Button and his contemporaries, not all of Cape May's architecture conformed to a uniform aesthetic during this period. Indeed, there were some attempts at striking out in new directions. High Victorian influences began creeping in during the late 1870's, as evidenced by such structures as the Emlen Physick House and Estate, a design of Frank Furness, built in 1878. The Queen Anne style also appeared in the 1880's and 1890's, as seen in some of the area's cottages and in architectural add-ons fitted to more conventionally styled structures.

## Attempt at Rejuvenation

A last-ditch effort at reviving the area's fortunes came just after the turn of the century with plans for a new development called New Cape May. Located east of the established Cape May community, this speculative venture called for the construction of residential and resort properties, along with an industrial seaport.

Plans for residential development in the land east of Cape May were initiated as early as 1891, but nothing materialized, due to the lack of buyer interest. Plans for the new development were launched in 1901-1902, but financing and construction problems, coupled with widespread skepticism about the viability of this overly ambitious project, led to its eventual downfall in 1915.

The collapse of the New Cape May project marked the beginning of a nearly fifty-year period of virtual inactivity in the area. Some new permanent housing was built after World War II, and a few new hotels were constructed. Little of significance happened until 1962, when nature intervened. A severe wind called a northeaster lashed Cape May, submerging much of the town under water and later burying it under sand. The storm severely damaged many of the town's now-decrepit structures and nearly wiped out the beaches, which had been gradually eroding for some time. Cape May's future was clearly in doubt.

Given the extensive damage from the storm, many local business owners and developers "wanted to bulldoze everything that was left," according to

*One of Cape May's historic inns.* (New Jersey Commerce & Economic Growth Commission/Scott Barrow)

ble modern resort community. Over the course of the next two decades, those plans were realized through the restoration and preservation of more than six hundred nineteenth century buildings. Although the preservation process was initiated in the mid-1960's, it received a big push in 1969, when the entire town of Cape May was entered on the National Register of Historic Places. It was further aided a year later with the establishment of the Mid-Atlantic Center for the Arts (MAC), the organization that has coordinated much of Cape May's preservation efforts ever since. Then in 1979, after many long years of hard work, Cape May received the additional distinction of being named a National Historic Landmark. Indeed, Cape May had come back to life.

Today Cape May is once again a popular vacation destination. Weekend and seasonal tourists visit the area to see the beautifully restored buildings and to partake of the MAC-sponsored architectural tours. Some also come for the town's many special events, such as a summer music festival, a spring tulip festival (in honor of the Dutch sea captain who discovered Cape May), an autumn Victorian festival, and a Christmas festival. Some even come for what attracted Cape May's original tourists—its beautiful oceanfront and lovely summer weather.

Cape May's rebirth and continued viability are direct results of the effort that dedicated preservationists have put into the community to ensure its continuance. The town has weathered much and still survived, thanks largely to those who would not let it die.                                        —*Brent Marchant*

one account. For a time, with the incentive provided by a $2.3 million grant from the U.S. Department of Housing and Urban Development (HUD), it looked as though they just might get their wish. Before the plowing began, HUD ordered an architectural survey of the area, which revealed a wealth of historic information about the surviving structures. The Cape May preservation movement was thus born.

### New Redevelopment Plans
In the ensuing years, redevelopment plans were drawn up to preserve and renovate Cape May's historic structures, while restoring the area as a via-

### For Further Information:
Boslough, John. "The Landmark Hunter." *Historic*

*Preservation*, April, 1986. A brief but detailed look at one woman's role in Cape May's historic preservation movement. This article examines the work of Carolyn Pitts, an architectural historian for the National Park Service, whose career in helping to preserve the nation's historic structures got its start in Cape May. While the article is focused on Pitts, it does provide insight into the town's rescue from the wrecking ball and its rebirth as a historic landmark community.

Dorwart, Jeffrey M. *Cape May County, New Jersey: The Making of an American Resort Community*. New Brunswick, N.J.: Rutgers University Press, 1992. Another option in the same vein as Thomas and Doebley's book below.

Thomas, George E., and Carl Doebley. *Cape May: Queen of the Seaside Resorts*. 2d ed. Philadelphia: Associated University Presses, 1998. Updated and enlarged edition. A substantive historical account about Cape May and its architecture. This comprehensive text, liberally illustrated with many period photographs and drawings, provides detailed histories of the resort and its structures.

# Edison National Historic Site

**Date:** Estate and laboratory declared a National Historic Site in 1954

**Relevant issues:** Science and technology

**Significance:** This is the site of the Glenmont estate, which Thomas Alva Edison purchased in 1886 and which served as his home until his death in 1931. In 1887, Edison began construction of a laboratory on land adjacent to the estate; the laboratory served as his "Invention Factory" for forty-four years and produced more than half of his 1,093 U.S. patents. The estate and the laboratory were declared a National Historic Site in 1954; it was closed on June 6, 1999, to make improvements to some historic spaces and to install new exhibits and temperature and humidity controls, with a scheduled reopening in the spring of 2001.

**Location:** A short distance from the Garden State Parkway and U.S. Interstate 280

**Site Office:**
Edison National Historic Site Visitor Center
Main Street at Lakeside Avenue
West Orange, NJ 07052
ph.: (973) 736-0550
fax: (973) 736-8496
Web site: www.nps.gov/edis/

In 1886, the year that Thomas Alva Edison purchased the Glenmont estate, his final home and the site of his largest laboratory, he was already well established as the preeminent inventor in the United States. He had made his mark originally for his work in the telegraph industry, and then "electrified" the world by solving the problem of the incandescent light bulb and creating a system for bringing electrical resources to the office and home. In his biography of Edison, Robert Conot observed that

> Edison was a lusty, crusty, hard-driving, opportunistic, and occasionally ruthless Midwesterner, whose Bunyanesque ambition for wealth was repeatedly subverted by his passion for invention. He was complex and contradictory, an ingenious electrician, chemist, and promoter, but a bumbling engineer and businessman. The stories of his inventions emerge out of the laboratory records as sagas of audacity, perspicacity, and luck bearing only a general resemblance to the legendary accounts of the past.

**Edison the Inventor**
After Edison's first big break, the 1871 invention of the universal stock printer, which allowed remote brokers' offices to keep in close contact with the central transmitters of the financial exchanges, he had enough money to open his own inventor's shop in Newark, New Jersey. These Newark years saw his attentions focused on the telegraph and a string of patents for receiving and sending messages faster and more clearly. Most of these patents revolved around the automatic repeating telegraph and the quadraplex telegraph. The patents also took him in and out of various partnerships for manufacturing and using the machines he created.

One such company was the Gold and Stock Company, a subsidiary of Western Union. To work the transmitters for its network, the Gold and Stock Company trained young girls, one of whom was sixteen-year-old Mary Stilwell. Edison courted her and they were married on Christmas Day, 1871. The next day he was back at work, the first of many examples of his obsession with invention. Mary and Thomas Edison had three children—Marion, Thomas Jr., and William. Over the years of her marriage, Mary's behavior became erratic and her health deteriorated until she died in August, 1884. It was discovered that she had a brain tumor.

Though rich and famous, Edison was not prepared to care for his children alone. In 1885, he met Mina Miller while at the World Industrial and Cotton Centennial Exposition in New Orleans. Mina's father, Lewis Miller, was the inventor of the first efficient grass mower and made a fortune manufacturing it and other implements. A fervent Methodist, Miller helped found the Sunday school movement and was active in the Chautauqua continuing education movement. As Conot described it, "When Edison was obsessed with an idea, he could not rest until he followed it to success—and he was now obsessed with Mina." Edison courted Mina across the eastern half of the United States until he won over both her and her family. They were married in February, 1886, and spent part of their honeymoon in Fort Myers, Florida, because Edison was building a laboratory there.

### Edison at Glenmont

When Edison was looking for a home for his new bride, a New York real estate firm offered him the Glenmont estate in Llewellyn Park, a private, aristocratic community in West Orange, New Jersey. Llewellyn Park was one of the new suburban communities that developed once rail transportation allowed the wealthy to live in the country and commute to their city offices. Realizing this potential, Llewellyn S. Haskell acquired three hundred acres along the eastern slopes of the Orange Mountains and laid out more than one hundred private estates on this land, contouring the roads around the hills and setting aside open fields and woodlands as parks.

Glenmont was one of the largest estates in Llewellyn Park and today is one of its oldest homes still standing. Architect Henry Hudson Holly designed the Glenmont grounds and house in 1880 for Henry C. Pedder, a New York businessman. The Queen Anne-style mansion was made from brick and timber. In 1886, Glenmont was on the market

because Pedder had been caught embezzling. The money he had poured into the estate had been skimmed from the funds of Constable's, a fashionable New York City department store. Before Pedder was caught, he had spent more than $300,000 on paneled and bronzed walls, elaborate stained-glass windows, and uncommon furnishings, including $40,000 worth of greenhouses, a $15,000 stable, and a toilet that one ascended to as a throne. The list of furnishings ran thirty-five pages. The house was on the market for only $235,000, and Edison was a man who knew a bargain and one who could do things in grand fashion. It was also a chance to ensconce his wife in a house on the order of her parents' home. He raised $150,000 from his assets and acquired an $85,000 mortgage for the remainder.

Thomas and Mina Edison moved into Glenmont in the spring of 1886. Three children—Madeleine, Charles, and Theodore—were born at Glenmont over the next twelve years. Edison used Glenmont as a country home for retreat and relaxation, hosting friends and dignitaries, including Charles Lindbergh, Helen Keller, John Pershing, George Eastman, Herbert Hoover, Woodrow Wilson, and Henry Ford.

An artificial pond in front of the house was used as an ice-skating rink during the winter by the Edisons. Edison built the garage in 1907 using poured concrete in a precast iron mold, a technique he explored as a method for use in low-cost housing construction. The garage had a gas pump, a battery charger, and a turntable that facilitated parking. A chauffeur lived on the second floor. Glenmont's grounds also contained a family swimming pool, a kitchen garden, a greenhouse and potting shed, a barn that housed a small flock of chickens and several milking cows, and a gardener's cottage (another structure made of poured cement). There were also fruit trees and flower beds. All this was maintained by a full-time staff.

There was an implicit understanding between Mina and Thomas Edison that he was master of his laboratory and Mina was to run the household. The inventor's workweek was a full six days, so he was never really at Glenmont except for Saturday night and all day Sunday. Usually, he spent his time in an upstairs sitting room where he and Mina had desks. This became what today would be called a family room. The children would be around constantly, playing as Edison read. Occasionally, he would participate in the children's games, but he would always change the rules to his advantage. Conot writes that "he was, indeed, treated like an absolute monarch. Mina had an ironclad rule that whatever Edison wanted, Edison got." According to Ronald W. Clark in *Edison: The Man Who Made the Future*, Edison's lifelong credo was work first, family second. His children had fond memories of their time with him at the estate. His daughter Madeleine later wrote,

> My father was the man who drew pictures for me of beautiful if slightly angular ladies, which I did my best to copy; who thought a spectacular thunderstorm or a brilliant rainbow sufficient excuse to wake us from our first sleep and bundle us out of our cribs to see it; he was the man who telephoned Mother almost every evening from the "Lab" to "send down lunch for seven—we'll be working all night"; the man who played Parchesi with us strictly according to his own rules—now there was an invention for you!—and who had remarkably efficient attacks of indigestion whenever there was a party. The remarkable part was that they always occurred before, and not after, the festivities.

**A Poor Businessman**

In fact, Edison was constantly working himself in and out of fortunes and debts. His parents had lived hand to mouth at times, and he himself had knocked about as an itinerant telegrapher through his teens and early twenties. Now that his inventions had established his fame and fortune, he attempted to ensure his family's security by paying off the mortgage on Glenmont, transferring it along with $200,000 in bonds into Mina's name.

Erected in 1887, the nearby laboratory complex, with its teams of workers, became the prototype for the modern industrial research laboratory. Edison envisioned the laboratory during his convalescence from pneumonia and pleurisy in the winter and spring of 1886-1887. During his long convalescence, Edison developed the idea of placing his laboratory close to home. The design he had in mind indeed seemed the extravagant dream of someone in delirium. It would be, in the words of Robert Conot, "an inventor's dream, a laboratory of grand design, such as the world had never seen before. It would be so complete as to contain everything required for any experiment in chemistry,

electricity, or physics." Edison immediately set some of his assistants to work on purchasing property near the foot of the hill on which Glenmont was located. He contracted Henry Hudson Holly, Glenmont's architect, to design the buildings. Construction costs were first estimated at $38,000, but before completion Edison's investment had reached $150,000.

The foundations were laid in the spring of 1887 but the construction of the site never went smoothly. Demanding perfection, Edison was never completely satisfied. Slowly the site took shape and the main building was operational by the end of the year. Still, Edison continued tinkering with the site and was reluctant to invite the newspapers and magazines for a public showing. He soon added ancillary structures around the main building. In addition to the forty thousand square feet of the lab, Edison had added four buildings, each one hundred by twenty-five feet, for metallurgy, chemistry, woodworking, and galvanometer testing. This last building was constructed without iron so that no magnetic action could throw off the instruments. However, streetcars started running by the place within two years, interfering with the instruments.

Edison stocked the laboratory with every conceivable supply. According to Conot,

> He bought $6,300 worth of chemicals and a supply of every metal in existence, including the entire stock of the American Nickel Works. He ordered hog bristles, porcupine quills, tanned walrus hide, skins of every known animal, a pound of peacock tails, five pounds of hops, fifty pounds of rice, every kind of grain, a dozen bulls' horns, a dozen walrus tusks, twenty-five pounds of marlin.

He reused materials from his previous plants, which required one chemist to spend his hours identifying the contents of hundreds of bottles without labels.

Edison hired an equally unusual array of workers for his laboratory. He tended to hire young, inexperienced men or learned immigrants, both groups willing to work for his relatively low wages.

Once products were developed and perfected at Edison's "Invention Factory," they were placed into mass production at the factory buildings that sur-

brought to the consumer markets.

The products Edison developed at West Orange included a disc phonograph, improved cylinder phonographs, a dictating machine, the nickel-iron-alkaline storage battery, the motion picture camera and projector, a talking motion pictures system, the kinetophone, the fluoroscope, ore-milling machinery, improved electrical generators, and a line of household appliances. The Black Maria, the world's first building constructed expressly as a motion picture studio, was part of the laboratory complex from 1893 until 1903. Today visitors to the site can walk through a replica of the studio.

The laboratory complex stayed in operation past Edison's death in 1931. It was a model for the modern private research and development laboratories, such as those run by Bell and Westinghouse. Perhaps this was Edison's greatest invention—a site for spirited and prolonged general research, in which each new product is used as a stepping stone toward the next discovery.

### Modern Preservation Efforts

Today the National Park Service preserves the laboratory and Glenmont estate with much of the apparatus, furnishings, and memorabilia intact from the days when Edison had to be cajoled from his beloved laboratory to dinner with Mina. Glenmont's twenty-three rooms are furnished as they were when Edison and his wife lived there. A video theater features Edison's 1903 motion picture *The Great Train Robbery.* Thomas and Mina Edison, who were first buried at Rosedale Cemetery in Orange, New Jersey, are interred in a gravesite at the rear of the house. In 1962 their children arranged for their remains to be brought back to Glenmont.               *—Bob Lange*

*Thomas Alva Edison.* (Library of Congress)

rounded the research laboratories. This extensive factory complex employed thousands of people, reaching a peak of about ten thousand in 1919-1920. The West Orange laboratory was the most productive of Edison's workplaces in terms of the quantity of patents and products developed. More than half of his 1,093 patents were submitted from West Orange. Although his most famous work was initiated at Menlo Park, New Jersey—the incandescent light bulb and the attendant materials for electric power distribution—Edison was still amazing the world with the myriad devices he

**For Further Information:**

Clark, Ronald W. *Edison: The Man Who Made the Future.* New York, G. P. Putnam's Sons, 1977. Quite useful in its presentation.

Conot, Robert. *A Streak of Luck.* New York: Seaview Books, 1979. Contains a wealth of detail, its research coming from more than a million and a half documents stored at the West Orange laboratory. Conot's presentation is somewhat convoluted: Its chapters focus on particular periods but jump back and forth to specific years.

Israel, Paul. *Edison: A Life of Invention.* New York: John Wiley & Sons, 2000. A more recent biography of Edison.

# Morristown

**Date:** Founded in 1739

**Relevant issues:** Business and industry, colonial America, naval history, Revolutionary War, science and technology

**Significance:** Named for New Jersey's first governor, Lewis Morris, Morristown was the site of two critical winter encampments of General George Washington's Continental Army during the American Revolution; it was also a key point of defense due to its proximity to major cities and iron mines. Morristown is the site of Speedwell Iron Works, where much of the SS *Savannah* (the first steamship to cross the Atlantic Ocean) was built and where Samuel F. B. Morse and Alfred Vail debuted telegraph technology in 1838. It has a long history of well-to-do residents—at one time, Morristown claimed more millionaires than any comparably sized area in the world.

**Location:** Centered in the upper half of the state, roughly twenty-five miles west and north of Newark; on both banks of the Whippany River, along the Watchung Mountain range; U.S. Interstate 287 passes Morristown to the east

**Site Office:**

Historic Morris Visitors Center
6 Court Street
Morristown, NJ 07960
ph.: (973) 631-5151
Web site: www.morristourism.org

Morristown holds a place of paramount distinction in the annals of the American Revolution. In terms of hardship and endurance, the winter encampments of General George Washington's troops in Morristown rival those that took place in the more legendary Valley Forge. In Morristown, members of the Pennsylvania Line staged a near-disastrous mutiny to protest their wretched conditions. Also in Morristown, the court-martial of the traitorous General Benedict Arnold took place. Despite these obstacles, however, Morristown came to symbolize the determined efforts of the colonists to break with British rule. Near the war's end, a successful defense of the site against Loyalist troops demoralized the British.

In the nineteenth century, Morristown developed a reputation as the home of an elite class. Iron-mining fortunes and an increasingly convenient commute to some of the East Coast's busiest metropolitan areas combined to make Morristown a favorite bedroom community of the rich. The Speedwell Iron Works was instrumental in the preparation of the SS *Savannah*, the first steamship to cross the Atlantic Ocean, and it was the site of the first demonstration of Samuel F. B. Morse's and Alfred Vail's telegraph system. Today, Morristown retains much of its colonial heritage and its industrial-era affluence in its preserved homes and federally supported historic parks and sites.

**Early History**

In 1710, groups of colonists from New Jersey and New England began to move westward from Newark toward the Watchung Mountains, enticed by the rich supply of iron ore that the region's Lenni-Lenape Indians called "sucky-sunny." One party settled at the foot of Mount Kemble, along the narrow Whippany River, in a small valley that came to be known as the Hollow. They named their village West Hanover, welcoming newcomers whose homes spread to the tablelands above the Hollow; this central area became the site of Morristown Green.

When the growing community around West Hanover saw fit to create its own body of government to eliminate the wearisome trek to Trenton, prominent figure Jacob Ford led a movement to secede from Hunterdon County and form a new county. Reassigned as Morris County, the area was named for New Jersey's governor at the time, Lewis

Morris, a popular leader who had been elected by a unified East and West New Jersey in 1738. Ford hosted the first meeting of Morris County court at his tavern, presiding as justice over a session that renamed his village Morristown and made it the seat of county government. By 1741, the township had a log church, and by 1755 the county court could move from Ford's tavern into its own courthouse.

With an average of two settlers per square mile, Morris County stretched across the area that currently comprises Morris, Sussex, and Warren Counties. During the 1750's, Sussex temporarily separated from Morris, but its courts returned in 1757 when they were disrupted by Indian uprisings along the Delaware Valley. Morristown was the center of commerce and public affairs for the hamlets of Bottle Hill (later Madison), Chatham, Chester, Dover, German Valley, Mendham, Pompton, Rockaway, and Whippany; however, its relatively small populace kept it from acquiring a seat in the New Jersey State Legislature until 1772.

In 1750, a British edict barring colonists from operating certain types of mills aroused Morris County's ironmasters, who defied the mother county's ordinance. The increasingly successful businessmen of the region were not willing to sacrifice their lucrative trade. Evidence suggests that this early act of rebellion toward the British was less ideological than financial: Some of the most flagrant violators of this British law later declared themselves Tories during the American Revolution.

**Morristown During the Revolutionary War**

The events that would make Morristown an important Revolutionary War site began early in 1777. Following his storied crossing of the Delaware River, Washington and his troops encountered a surprise attack at Princeton on January 3 from a small detachment of British soldiers. Nearly defeated by the ambush, the general rode to the front line to regroup his shaken men, and they killed, wounded, or captured four hundred of the British. The majority of British commander Lord Charles Cornwallis's men had been asleep at Trenton awaiting battle there, unaware of Washington's move toward Princeton. Unable to reach Princeton before the battle there had ended, Cornwallis assumed that Washington was en route to New Brunswick, where much of the American military

cache was stored. Washington instead turned north and set out for Morristown, again outwitting his counterpart.

From January through May, 1777, Washington's army camped at Morristown. Cornwallis predicted that Washington "cannot subsist long where he is," correctly assessing the debilitating conditions the American general would face but not the perseverance of his corps. Morristown proved to be a stronghold for the Americans, naturally suited for defense in wartime with the fortress-like Watchung Mountains to the south and east and the nearly impenetrable Great Swamp to the south. Additionally, the hills to the north of the town were brimming with as many as eighty iron forges to equip the Continental army with shovels, axes, and cannonballs. This essential function of the forges allowed for exemption from military service for the forge workers. Finally, the taste for colonial rebellion among the region's civilians was acute, and the army was welcomed.

Still, the winter months were difficult, as ranks were diminished by completed tours of duty, and an epidemic of smallpox gripped the town. Both of Morristown's churches were converted to hospitals, and Washington was compelled to prescribe an unproven inoculation method in order to subdue the virus. Jacob Ford and his son, Jacob Jr., both died early in 1777, depriving the community of two important leaders at a time of crisis. Jacob Ford, Jr., had operated New Jersey's first gunpowder mill.

Throughout this first winter in Morristown, Washington stayed at Jacob Arnold's Tavern, while his troops occupied the Loantaka Valley. Fifty huts of log, woodchips, and mud were erected in the valley two and one-half miles from the center of Morristown, among farms without fences that would impede the soldiers' movement.

Wartime inflation coupled with the damaging counterfeiting activities of the British led to exorbitant rates for goods in the colonies—beef was fifteen cents per pound and butter, forty-five cents. Garments, too, were costly, prohibitively so given the meager wages of the enlisted men. Washington lamented that "a wagonload of money will scarcely buy a wagonload of provisions."

**Washington's Second Stay in Morristown**

Washington and his four thousand troops ended

*The Ford Mansion in Morristown.* (Morristown National Historical Park)

their first stay in Morristown in May, 1777, when they moved twenty miles to the south, to Middlebrook, New Jersey, seven miles northwest of the British post at New Brunswick. Two years later, as the war dragged on, they returned to camp at Morristown. Arriving during December, 1779, regiments from Providence, Rhode Island, and Danbury, Connecticut, broke ground at Jockey Hollow on the outskirts of town; gradually joined by as many as twelve thousand men, they settled in for a winter that would prove to be even more grueling than the first.

With a total of twenty-eight snowfalls, that winter of 1779-1780 was recorded as the worst of the eighteenth century. A particularly devastating January blizzard killed scores of men who were temporarily housed in tents, burying them under drifts as high as six feet. Many of the destitute men reportedly had only a pair of trousers or a blanket to shield them from the elements.

Washington and his advisers were lodged three-quarters of a mile from the Morristown Green at the Ford Mansion, where Jacob Ford, Jr.'s widow and her four children moved into two rooms to accommodate the commander in chief and his party of fifteen. (The elegant Ford Mansion, begun in 1772 and standing today, has been restored for viewing and has a comprehensive historical museum on its grounds.) At the mansion, Martha Washington greeted the ladies of the town's elite society while knitting a stocking, gently suggesting that "American ladies should be patterns of industry" to support the campaign for independence; one socialite wrote that she "never felt so ashamed and rebuked in my life."

The court-martial of Washington's trusted major general Benedict Arnold had taken place in December, at Morristown's Dickerson Tavern. After an unsuccessful attempt to win command of West Point, Arnold had notified British lieutenant general Sir Henry Clinton of the impending arrival of French allies in the colonies. Arnold's action was indicative of Washington's ongoing difficulties in forging seamless support for the independence movement.

There were, however, bright spots during Washington's second sojourn in Morristown. Colonel Alexander Hamilton successfully wooed his future bride, Elizabeth Schuyler, daughter of General Philip Schuyler. He often courted her at the house now designated the Schuyler-Hamilton House (built in 1760, located at 5 Olyphant Place, and today operated by the Daughters of the American Revolution as a museum). Noblemen from overseas who supported the colonists' cause were feted at Morristown: The Marquis de Lafayette brought news of the imminent arrival of the French fleet and of the birth of his son—George Washington Lafayette. On April 28, 1780, the untimely death of Spain's ambassador Don Juan de Miralles became an occasion to commemorate the bond between his country and the colonies. As he was buried among diamond-studded accessories, his lavish funeral required guardsmen to deter thievery.

Despite signs of unity across the colonies and in Europe, however, the men of the Continental army continued to suffer without proper rations or clothing, and their wages were paid in Continental currency, which was nearly worthless. At Jockey Hollow, the soldiers' village was nearly complete by mid-February, but by then hundreds of men had already been lost to the weather. The sixteen-square-foot huts constructed by the Continental troops (re-created at the Jockey Hollow Visitors' Center) were arranged in fours along the road to the Grand Parade Field, with officers' huts lined to the rear. Southwest of town, on the northern crest of Mount Kemble, the men began construction of a fort to house military supplies. Because the fort faced the town, not the approaching valleys, subsequent generations came to believe that Washington's men were ordered to build "Fort Nonsense" simply to keep their idle hands busy. Today, the site is marked by a granite monument.

In April, 1780, the detachment of Continental troops known as the Pennsylvania Line was stung by a surprise raid by the British. Their commander was mortally wounded, and several of Morristown's homes were burned to the ground; of the fifty prisoners taken, five or six were officers. Throughout

that spring, threats of other attacks by the British were commonplace, as Washington's base in Morristown dwindled in numbers when several brigades were detached to help defend a ravaged South Carolina.

## Dissension in the Continental Army

Desertion was rampant among the nearly starved soldiers, and on May 25, 1780, men of regiments from Connecticut, Pennsylvania, and New York were ordered to dig graves for eleven captured deserters who had been condemned. That night, men of the Eighth Connecticut "Nutmeg" Regiment, part of the Second Connecticut Brigade, refused to disperse after the traditional evening parade, replying with sarcasm to their commanding officers' threats. Legend has it that one enlisted man, expecting court-martial after an argument with a commander's adjutant, banged the butt of his musket on the ground and cried, "Who will parade with me?" The First and Second Connecticut Brigades banded together to march in protest, doing so without a leader, in order to leave no one vulnerable to court-martial. Pennsylvania troops, nearly tricked in the dark into surrounding the Connecticut men, realized the ploy and declared an intention to join in the mutiny.

After a disorderly series of angry confrontations, the men were finally dissuaded by two popular officers, Colonel Return Jonathan Meigs and Lieutenant Colonel John Sumner. Appeased by promises—a slaughtered herd of cattle for their consumption, a sympathetic ear for their concerns, and four ounces of rum for each man—the disgruntled soldiers were brought back into the fold. The following day, ten of the eleven men scheduled for execution were granted reprieves: The eleventh, found guilty of forging one hundred discharges, was hanged.

## Von Knyphausen's Assault on Morristown

On June 6, 1780, following the British triumph at Charleston, South Carolina, Hessian lieutenant general Wilhelm von Knyphausen led an army of six thousand redcoats from Staten Island into New Jersey in a bid to put an end to the war. Men from General William Maxwell's New Jersey Brigade and the Third New Jersey Militia faced Knyphausen's troops near Connecticut Farms (now Union), determined to protect the Hobart Gap through the

Watching Mountains toward Morristown. Though greatly outnumbered, the Continental forces undermined Knyphausen's march from snipers' cover behind trees and fences. In retreat, the British set fire to much of Connecticut Farms, and one of their riflemen fired through a window and killed the wife of the Reverend James Caldwell as she huddled with her baby. The British forces were chased back to Elizabethtown by the furious Continentals.

Seventeen days later, after Washington had ordered much of the military's supplies removed from Morristown to Pennsylvania, Knyphausen again launched an assault toward Morristown. The Continental army, better prepared for this second attack, summoned five thousand members of the New Jersey militia to match the numbers of the British and their allies at Springfield. It was reported that the Americans were buoyed by the widower Reverend Caldwell, who passed out Watt's Hymnals to use as cannon wadding, shouting, "Give 'em Watt's boys!" Springfield burned, but Knyphausen was forced to retreat to Staten Island after suffering between four hundred and five hundred casualties.

For the rest of 1780, Washington's men were spread out in a thin line from Morristown to West Point. At idle encampments, their attentions once again turned to their lack of sufficient supplies. Out of their frustrated deprivation comes the tale of Tempe Wick. Tempe, the teenaged daughter of a farmer in Jockey Hollow, was accosted by members of the Continental army, who attempted to confiscate her horse. In defiance, she fled for home, and hid her horse for three weeks in a bedroom to thwart ransacking troops. The Wick House, built in 1746, can be seen today at its site adjacent to the Jockey Hollow Visitor Center.

That act of mischief on the part of the colonial troops foreshadowed a much more troubling insubordination: In Morristown on New Year's Day, 1781, the Pennsylvania Line turned on its officers in mutiny and set off for Philadelphia to lodge their grievances. Their woeful conditions seemed even worse in contrast with the prosperity in Morristown, which, according to one historian, flowed "with milk and honey, or more pertinently, hard cider and applejack." Two thousand well-organized mutineers killed one officer and wounded many others, holding the well-respected General "Mad Anthony" Wayne at the point of a bayonet. Met near Trenton

by messengers of the British commander Clinton, who sought to enlist the mutinous Continentals, the Pennsylvanians hanged the messengers to deny the implication that they were traitorous. In Philadelphia, the Continental Congress did not hesitate to meet the mutineers' demands for better conditions. Many men were granted early discharges, and in a show of faith, many more reenlisted. Not long thereafter, the army's station in Morristown was abandoned for good, as Washington prepared for his final campaign to end the war.

## After the Revolution

Morristown was considerably quieter after the war, and it was not until the first decade of the nineteenth century that the area's economy received a boost, from the institution of toll roads that improved routes of trade. Morristown and Elizabethtown were connected by a toll road—which irked frugal residents so much that they paved a so-called shunpike along a parallel route. In 1806, another significant roadway, the Morristown-Phillipsburg turnpike, was chartered.

Although the iron industry was the backbone of the region, it seemed destined for collapse because of the depletion of forests—which provided wood needed to fire forges—and rising transportation costs. Morristown schoolteacher George P. Macculloch rescued the industry when he designed an ambitious canal linking Morris County to Pennsylvania's abundant coal fields. By August, 1831, the canal—dug entirely by hand—was complete, incorporating lock systems to convey cargo ships over the mountains. (Today, the Macculloch Hall Historical Museum at 45 Macculloch Avenue is housed in a Federal-style mansion built around 1810 by its namesake.) Ironically, the New Jersey Iron Works in nearby Boonton effectively doomed the Morris Canal before it was completed, when that company began turning out parts for the railroad industry, which would render the canal obsolete.

Morristown's Speedwell Iron Works, dating to the Revolution, enjoyed one of its finest moments in 1819 when the site produced the drive shaft and other major parts of the SS *Savannah*, which became the first ship to cross the Atlantic under steam power. Later, Speedwell earned a different place in history when it provided the grounds for the first electromagnetic telegraph transmission. Alfred Vail, the son of Speedwell owner Judge Stephen Vail, joined with his partner Samuel F. B. Morse to demonstrate their invention on January 6, 1838, at Speedwell. Alfred Vail, a student at New York University, had seen a rudimentary demonstration given by Morse at the school and had procured the financial backing of his father for the project. "A patient waiter is no loser" was the message Alfred Vail sent, in the dot-and-dash format known today as the Morse code, across two miles of wire laid around the mill.

The Vail family moved the iron works to Brooklyn, New York, in 1873: In 1908 the mill buildings at Speedwell were lost to fire. Remaining in the custody of the Vails' descendants until 1955, the property was sold into years of neglect until a benevolent buyer resurrected the site. Today, Historic Speedwell, located at 333 Speedwell Avenue, consists of nine buildings, including the cotton factory where the telegraph was introduced and the Vail home (the latter featuring an early version of a central heating system). There are also three historic houses—the L'Hommedieu House, circa 1820; the Moses Estey House, circa 1787; and the Ford Cottage, circa 1800—which were relocated from the center of Morristown when they were threatened with demolition during the 1960's. A few of the buildings are not currently open to the public, but Speedwell's exhibits of nineteenth century instruments are numerous, and the factory is a National Historic Landmark.

### Arrival of the Railroad

On January 29, 1835, the Morris and Essex Railroad began operation, reaching Morristown by New Year's Day 1838. The train eventually won the nickname "The Millionaires' Express," as some of the wealthiest businessmen of the era took up residence in Morristown in part because the railroad made the commute to New York City convenient. By 1874 Morristown was being compared with New-

*The Wick House in Morristown.* (Morristown National Historical Park)

port, Rhode Island, in terms of affluence; by the early twentieth century, as many as ninety-two millionaires (fourteen worth more than ten million dollars) dwelt within three miles of the Morristown Green, an astonishing figure given that the entire population of the town numbered 11,267.

Members of Morristown's elite achieved their status in the life insurance business, in the stock market, and in railroading. Their opulent homes ranged from thirty-room "cottages" to veritable castles that imitated the styles of Europe, crowned by the one hundred-room Hamilton Twombly estate called Florham, a name derived from Florence and Hamilton. In 1899, Mr. and Mrs. Twombly, whose combined assets reportedly reached seventy million dollars, were granted their wish that the nearby village of Afton be renamed Florham Park. Fairleigh Dickinson University now occupies the estate.

In addition to the rich, artists and writers were attracted to Morristown's beauty and luxuriance, among them the authors Bret Harte and Rudyard Kipling, the painter A. B. Frost, and the cartoonist Thomas Nast, who created the political symbols of the Republicans' elephant and the Democrats' donkey.

Idyllic conditions, however, were not everlasting. The first country club operated by women, the Morris County Golf Club, was wrested from its founders by men two years after its inception in 1894. In 1903, many of Morristown's most prominent socialites were embroiled in a highly publicized power struggle in the town, and in 1906 many more were implicated in an investigation into corruption in New York's insurance industry.

### Modern Preservation Efforts

The iron mines, which enjoyed a short revival during and immediately following World War II, now lie dormant. Many of the turn-of-the-century estates are no longer in existence, and others have been converted to other uses. In the early 1960's, conservationists unsuccessfully protested against the proposed route of Interstate 287. The highway now runs adjacent to the historic Ford Mansion.

Conservationists won a dispute with New York's Port Authority in 1959, when the authority sought to destroy the Great Swamp south of Morristown to make way for an airport. Three thousand acres of the swampland were purchased and donated to the federal government for use as a National Wildlife Refuge. Moreover, the sites of Washington's Morristown encampments form the nation's oldest designated National Historical Park, dedicated on July 4, 1933. Preserved estates like the Fosterfields Living Historical Farm (with its Gothic Revival mansion on Kahdena Road) and the Frelinghuysen Home and Arboretum (at 53 East Hanover Avenue) are testimonies to the enduring natural grace of the region.      —*James Sullivan*

**For Further Information:**
Cunningham, John T. *New Jersey: America's Main Road.* Rev. ed. Garden City, N.Y.: Doubleday, 1976.
_____. *This Is New Jersey.* 4th ed. New Brunswick, N.J.: Rutgers University Press, 1994. Cunningham made a career of chronicling New Jersey's history as the author of books such as these.
Federal Writers' Project. *New Jersey: A Guide to Its Present and Past.* New York: Viking, 1939. This work by the Works Progress Administration is dated but nonetheless useful.
Fleming, Thomas. *The Forgotten Victory: The Battle for New Jersey—1780.* New York: Reader's Digest Press, 1973. A comprehensive study concerning Morristown's involvement in the American Revolution.
Miers, Earl Schenck. *Crossroads of Freedom: The American Revolution and the Rise of a New Nation.* New Brunswick, N.J.: Rutgers University Press, 1971. Another comprehensive study of Morristown and the American Revolution.
Stein, Alan. *War Comes to Morristown: The Impact of the Revolutionary War upon a Small Village, 1775-1783.* Morristown: Washington Association of New Jersey, 1998. The companion book to an exhibit that opened in 1995 in the museum of Morristown National Historical Park.

# Paterson

**Date:** Founded in 1791
**Relevant issues:** Business and industry
**Significance:** This industrial city, at 8.44 square miles, was founded as the site of the first planned industrial community in the United States by Society for Establishing Useful Manufactures (SUM), chartered by Alexander Hamil-

ton. Its designer was Pierre Charles L'Enfant. The township was created in 1831; it became the Passaic County seat in 1837 and received a city charter in 1851. Great Falls of the Passaic was named a National Landmark in 1967, and Paterson is the site of the first U.S. Historic Industrial District.

**Location:** On the Passaic River fourteen miles north of Newark in Passaic County; approximately twenty-three miles from midtown Manhattan, New York City

**Site Office:**

Great Falls Visitor Center
65 McBride Avenue
Great Falls Historic District
Paterson, NJ 07501-1715
ph.: (201) 279-9587

The third-largest city in New Jersey and the seat of Passaic County, Paterson was the first planned industrial community in the United States. Situated on a bend in the Passaic River, Paterson's most prominent natural phenomenon— and one of the nation's first tourist attractions—is the seventy-seven-foot Great Falls, which provided the water power that made Paterson "the silk capital of the world" and the birthplace of a number of industrial innovations, including America's first locomotive, the Colt repeating cylinder revolver, the first practical submarine, and the engine of Charles A. Lindbergh's famous airplane, *The Spirit of St. Louis.* Paterson is also important in the history of the labor movement; it is the site of both the first factory strike and the first company lockout in the United States. The industrial city was also the philosophical focal point of William Carlos Williams's five-book poem, *Paterson.*

Designed as a corporation rather than a city, Paterson has experienced recurrent economic booms and busts throughout its history. It traditionally has been dependent upon one major industry—alternately cotton, railroad locomotives, silk, and airplane motors. More recently, its economy has diversified to include textile dyeing and the manufacture of chemicals, electronic parts, small machines, toys, dolls, cosmetics, and paper products. Yet, Paterson's economy has remained precarious, and in the 1990's major revitalization and renovation efforts were under way for the downtown area and historic district.

**Early History**

In 1679 the Dutch acquired the tract of land in what was to become Paterson, attracted to the area by the Lenni-Lenape Indians' description of the Great Falls, which they called To-ta-wa. More than one hundred years later, Treasury Secretary Alexander Hamilton also was impressed by the potential water power of the falls, and in November, 1791, the area was selected as the site of a model factory town by the Society for Establishing Useful Manufactures (SUM). Chartered by Hamilton six months previously, SUM was a private support group established as part of a plan to encourage development of independent American industry and wean the fledgling nation from foreign industrial products. While SUM did not accomplish this goal, it did serve to stimulate the textile industry in Paterson. That year the settlement was named after William Paterson, governor of New Jersey, signer of the Declaration of Independence, and a stockholder in SUM. Governor Paterson signed the controversial charter, which some critics believe led to government corruption in Paterson for centuries to follow and contributed to the city's decline.

The charter, as approved by the New Jersey legislature, exempted the company from county and township taxes and gave it the right to hold $4 million in property and $1 million in stock, improve rivers, build canals, charge tolls, raise $100,000 by lottery, lay out and govern a six-square-mile section to be incorporated as a town, and engage in manufacturing. Major Pierre Charles L'Enfant, designer of Washington, D.C., was commissioned to plan the industrial community. SUM fired him two years later, claiming his extravagant designs were delaying the building of a raceway. Only his 1796 design, which took water from above the Passaic Falls, was used.

By the end of 1792, SUM had acquired between seven hundred and eight hundred acres of land, above and below the Passaic Falls, out of which Paterson grew. The settlement was reported to have no more than ten houses and fifty people at the time. In 1794, SUM built a small cotton mill on Mill Street on the middle raceway. This was Paterson's first factory, the first cotton center in New Jersey, and the second such center in the country. The original four-story stone building, forty feet by ninety feet, was equipped with twenty-five spinning jennies and sixty single looms operated by an oxen-

*William Carlos Williams, who published a five-book poem called* Paterson.
(Irving Wellcome/New Directions)

powered treadmill, as the raceways were not yet completed. Cotton manufacturing and machinery were so important to Paterson at this time that it was known as "the Cotton City." Later, silk, linen, jute, hemp, wool, and smaller cotton plants took the place of the mill.

### The First Labor Lockout in U.S. History
In 1794 SUM built a waterpower mill for making cotton cloth with facilities for one of the country's first calico printing shops. That same year, disgruntled calico printers became disorderly and caused the mill to close its doors—the first lockout in American history. SUM closed the mill in 1796

and the following year, SUM collapsed as a result of the lockout, a disastrous business venture, and financial mismanagement. Paterson's population, which had grown to five hundred, returned to fewer than fifty. SUM was reorganized in 1814 when the Colt family took over the organization. Although the reorganization led to a business boom—assisted by the War of 1812, which cut off the import of manufactured goods from Europe—some regarded the company as a dictatorship under the Colts.

In 1828, mill owners changed the lunch hour of the thirteen-and-a-half-hour workday from noon to one o'clock, in the supposed interest of the health and comfort of its child workers. Cotton workers abandoned their looms in protest, asking that the noon lunch hour be restored and that the workday be reduced to twelve hours. The cotton workers' walkout was the first American factory strike. Paterson mechanics, carpenters, and masons also walked out in solidarity—the first recorded sympathy strike in the United States. The strike was a partial success; the noon lunch hour was restored, and, more important, the community took note of its workers' concerns.

In 1835, under the leadership of the Paterson Association for the Protection of the Laboring Classes, twenty mills closed as workers struck for an eleven-hour workday. The strike ended six weeks later when a compromise was reached.

### Inventions
Paterson was named a township in 1831. That year, Morris Canal opened, reaching into the Pennsylvania coal fields. A year later, the first tracks were laid for the Paterson and Hudson River Railroad. In 1837, Thomas Rogers built one of the country's first steam locomotives, the *Sandusky*, modeled af-

ter an English import, in John Clark's Paterson machine shop. Mechanics from England and New England came to Paterson to begin manufacturing locomotives. For the next fifty years, nearly half of America's locomotives were produced in Paterson. Rogers Locomotive Works manufactured the chief train-hauling locomotives of this era, including the Civil War's *General* and *Texas*, as well as the first locomotives to lead transcontinental trains through the Rocky Mountains. By 1888, 5,871 engines were manufactured in Paterson for use throughout the hemisphere. By the end of the century, Paterson produced 80 percent of the locomotives manufactured in the United States. At this time, Paterson was the fastest-growing city on the East Coast; its population increased by about 50 percent every decade.

In 1835, Samuel Colt patented the world's first successful repeating cylinder revolver. The following year, when Paterson became the Passaic County seat, he established the Patent Arms Manufacturing Company in Paterson, known as "the Gun Mill," where he began manufacturing his Colt "Paterson."

In 1838, in the same mill, Samuel Colt's brother, Christopher, opened Paterson's first silk weaving plant. The venture was not prosperous, and it was abandoned a few months later. The following year, the Colt factory also stopped manufacturing its revolvers when peace following the Seminole War forced a shutdown. The Gun Mill had produced 2,850 revolvers.

Silk production in Paterson resumed in 1843, when George Murray and John Ryle, who bought out Christopher Colt's interest, founded the Pioneer Silk Company. In 1851, Paterson received its city charter. By 1865, the new city was processing two-thirds of the country's silk imports, and by the late 1880's, it was dubbed "Silk City" and its silk products were shipped worldwide.

In 1878, Irish American schoolteacher and inventor John P. Holland tested his fourteen-foot submarine in the Passaic River, about two hundred yards north of the Great Falls, where it sank after its first trial. Holland eventually kept the underwater boat down for twenty-four hours, but it sank in the mud of the river bank, where it remained submerged for nearly fifty years. The submarine is on display in the Paterson Museum. In 1881, Holland produced the thirty-one-foot *Fenian Ram*, which was built for a crew of three, powered with a one-

cylinder combustion engine, and traveled at a maximum speed of nine miles an hour—but lacked a periscope. Launched from Staten Island, it remained submerged one hundred feet below the surface for an hour, then collided with a ferry at Weehawken. *Fenian Ram* was later salvaged and is on display in a small plaza in Paterson's Westside Park. In 1893, the U.S. government awarded a contract to Holland for his submarine design. The Navy began using its first submarine, the *Holland*, seven years later. Holland began producing his submarines through his own company, the J. P. Holland Torpedo Boat Company.

**Paterson in the Twentieth Century**

By 1900, Paterson was the fifteenth largest city in the United States and one of the nation's leading industrial centers. Two years later, however, the city was devastated by a series of major natural disasters. On February 8 and 9, 1902, a fire destroyed more than five hundred buildings in the center of the city, including the entire Paterson business district. Jersey City and Hackensack firefighters stopped the fire a mile from its origin. Less than a month later, on March 2, the Passaic River flooded the downtown area, destroying bridges, homes, and buildings. Several months later, a tornado tore through Paterson, uprooting trees, destroying houses, and cutting off city services.

The city recovered, and eight years later, as the silk industry peaked, Paterson employed twenty-five thousand workers who wove nearly 30 percent of the country's silk in three hundred fifty plants. Then, three years later, on January 23, 1913, a bitter five-month strike began in Paterson's Henry Doherty Silk Mill. Under the leadership of the Industrial Workers of the World (IWW), more than twenty-four thousand men, women, and children walked out of Paterson's silk mills, calling for an eight-hour workday, an end to child labor, improved working conditions, and a halt to mill owners' plans to increase the number of looms tended by each worker from two to four. On February 15, employers declared a lockout. Picket lines were led by IWW's William "Big Bill" Haywood, Elizabeth Gurley Flynn, Carlo Tresca, and John Reed. From January to July, there was violent picketing, 2,837 arrests, and a shooting, in which one picketer was killed. For this worker, Haywood led a funeral procession of fifteen thousand.

During the strike a group of Paterson workers walked sixteen miles to New York in a solidarity movement—to which New York workers reciprocated with a return trip to Paterson. On May 1, fifty strikers' children were transferred to New York City to be fed and to send a message addressing Paterson's alleged inability to provide relief to its citizens. On June 7, the "Paterson Pageant" rally, organized by Reed, was held in New York City's Madison Square Garden. Although workers returned to their looms defeated in July, the walkout was Paterson's greatest strike and an important struggle in New Jersey and labor history.

In 1924, twenty thousand Paterson silk workers again fought unsuccessfully against the four-loom system. In 1933, Paterson silk workers' and dyers' unions won the first strike in years, increasing pay from twelve and thirteen dollars weekly to eighteen and twenty-two dollars weekly in the silk mills, and from as low as twenty cents per hour to sixty-six cents per hour in the dye plants. As a result of the 1933 strike, Paterson dyers became part of the largest union in New Jersey. However, another silk and dye strike the following year was not as successful.

In 1933, Charles Roemer, a former Paterson city attorney, sued to have SUM dissolved, claiming that it had violated its charter. The case came before the New Jersey Supreme Court in 1936, and SUM lawyers won the case. In 1946, SUM finally dissolved, more than one hundred fifty years after it was chartered. Some charged that SUM had doomed Paterson from the beginning. Writer Christopher Norwood asserts, "Since 1796, [SUM] had broken the provisions of an all too provident charter; it had obviously violated antitrust laws; it had corrupted the government of New Jersey." Norwood blames SUM for what he calls "a total failure in that the city's structure—its economy, government, and natural resources—had no relation to its citizens." Norwood further accuses SUM of tampering with the water supply of the Great Falls: "Toward the end of [SUM's] reign, [it] began diverting 75 million gallons a day out of a normal flow of 87,500,000, changing the cascade into a polluted trickle."

### The "Vilest Swillhole in Christendom"
The "meek Falls of the Passaic" described almost two hundred years earlier by Alexander Hamilton, had become, for Rutherford, New Jersey's poet, William Carlos Williams, "the vilest swillhole in Christendom." The Passaic River served as the thread that linked the complex components of William's philosophical five-book poem, *Paterson*, published between 1946 and 1958. Williams saw Paterson as a prototypical American city of hope and despair, triumph and defeat. The poem is noted for its overriding metaphor that "man in himself is a city." Considered one of the major philosophical poems of the twentieth century, *Paterson* was said to have provoked a literary explosion against materialism and machinery.

World War II served to revive Paterson's economy, and some regarded the years from the war to the early 1950's as a temporary renaissance for Paterson. In the postwar years, however, Paterson, like many cities during this period, experienced a decline in local industry. Paterson's Wright Aeronautical went from a wartime peak of sixty thousand employees to five thousand, after which the company moved to the suburbs. Paterson's reign as "the silk capital of the world" ended as silk was replaced by synthetic fabrics such as rayon.

In the 1950's, U.S. Department of Housing and Urban Development (HUD) programs supplied Paterson with funding for better housing, schools, and other services. Yet, some felt that HUD—like SUM—acted as yet another conglomerate that limited Paterson's power. In the 1960's, Paterson was rocked by race riots—including one in 1967, in which twenty-seven people were killed. By the 1970's the city had become infamous for its crime, drug problems, and government corruption.

### Modern Preservation Efforts
In 1967 the Great Falls became a registered National Landmark; four years later, the 89-acre area between Spruce and Market Streets was designated the Great Falls Historic District. The district was subsequently expanded, and in 1976 President Gerald Ford declared the entire 119-acre district the first federally designated National Historic Industrial District. The district's focal point is the Paterson Museum, located in Thomas Rogers's former locomotive shop and showcasing Paterson's industrial, political, and cultural history.

As Paterson observed its bicentennial in the 1990's, major renovation and revitalization efforts were under way for the city, including construction of the Roe Federal Building and the Passaic County

Administration Building; renovation of the railroad station and traffic signalization; replacement of city and street signs; renovation of Cooke Mill and planned development projects in the historic district, where former mill buildings would be converted into offices, medical clinics, retail establishments, and residences; and the Center City Project in downtown Paterson, where a two-block complex of offices, retail shops, restaurants, a hotel, and the twenty-two thousand-square-foot, five hundred-seat "Silk City Stadium" would be built. The completion in the early 1990's of the Route 19 Interchange into Paterson facilitates access into the revitalized historic district, which city developers, leaders, and boosters called "the key to Paterson's future," in the hope that the city's economy would also be revitalized as it moved into the twenty-first century.                        —*Shawn Brennan*

**For Further Information:**
Iozia, Joseph. *Discovering Paterson in the Civil War.*

Hightstown, N.J.: Longstreet House, 1996. A history of Paterson and the Seventh New Jersey Infantry Regiment in the Civil War.
Kenyon, James Byron. *Industrial Localization and Metropolitan Growth: The Paterson-Passaic District.* Chicago: University of Chicago, 1960. This research paper is a finely detailed case study of Paterson's industrial development with many historical photographs, charts, graphs, and statistics.
Norwood, Christopher. *About Paterson: The Making and Unmaking of an American City.* New York: Saturday Review Press, 1974. A critical commentary on the city's economic, political, and social development, with a special focus on SUM.
Tripp, Anne Huber. *The I.W.W. and the Paterson Silk Strike of 1913.* Urbana: University of Illinois Press, 1987. A detailed account of the history of the Industrial Workers of the World, with emphasis on the Paterson silk workers' strike of 1913.

# Other Historic Sites

## Atlantic City Convention Hall
*Location:* Atlantic City, Atlantic County
*Relevant issues:* Cultural history
*Statement of significance:* This hall is the remaining edifice that best recalls the city's historic heyday as a seaside resort. It is the largest structure on the Boardwalk and is significant in the history of large-span structures, containing, when it was built, the largest room with an unobstructed view and the largest pipe organ in the world. It is also the scene of the Miss America pageant.

## Botto House
*Location:* 83 Norwood Street, Haledon, Passaic County
*Relevant issues:* Business and industry, political history, social reform
*Statement of significance:* On January 27, 1913, eight hundred workers at one of the largest silk mills in the silk manufacturing capital of the country walked off the job, in a dispute over job security, low wages, long hours, and poor working conditions. Soon, twenty-five thousand men, women, and children who worked in the mills also rebelled. From the balcony of this two-story rectangular block stone house, leaders of the Industrial Workers of the World (IWW, the "Wobblies") rallied workers during the Paterson Silk Strike (1913), a salient event in the American labor movement.

## Boxwood Hall
*Location:* Elizabeth, Union County
*Relevant issues:* Political history
*Statement of significance:* Elias Boudinot (1740-1821), president of the Continental Congress (1782), purchased Boxwood Hall in 1772 and owned it until 1795. In that year, he sold it to Jonathan Dayton (1760-1824), the youngest signer of the Constitution, who was then Speaker of the U.S. House of Representatives. Dayton resided here until his death.

## Cleveland Home
*Location:* Princeton, Mercer County
*Relevant issues:* Political history
*Statement of significance:* From 1897 until his death, Westland was the residence of Grover Cleveland

(1837-1908), president of the United States (1885-1889, 1893-1897). Cleveland retired to this stucco-covered stone house at the end of his second term.

## Craftsman Farms

*Location:* Parsippany, Morris County

*Relevant issues:* Art and architecture

*Statement of significance:* Craftsman Farms is the former home and school of Gustave Stickley (1858-1942), one of the leaders of the Arts and Crafts movement in America. Established in 1908, the farm-school was in operation until 1915. Stickley produced a new architectural style and a strikingly simple kind of furniture that profoundly influenced taste at the beginning of the twentieth century. His belief in a simple design, natural materials, and careful craftsmanship gave a lasting legacy to American architecture, interior design, and aesthetics.

## Einstein House

*Location:* Princeton, Mercer County

*Relevant issues:* Science and technology

*Statement of significance:* From 1936 until his death, this was the home of Albert Einstein (1879-1955), German-born theoretical physicist and Nobel Prize winner (1921). Einstein is best remembered for his achievements in three theoretical directions: the special theory of relativity, the general theory of relativity, and unified field theory.

## Fortune House

*Location:* Red Bank, Monmouth County

*Relevant issues:* African American history, social reform

*Statement of significance:* From 1901 to 1915, this was the home of T. Thomas Fortune (1856-1928), the crusading African American journalist who articulated the cause of black rights in his newspapers at the turn of the twentieth century.

## Great Atlantic and Pacific Tea Company Warehouse

*Location:* Jersey City, Hudson County

*Relevant issues:* Business and industry

*Statement of significance:* From its beginnings in 1859 as a leather and tea importing business in New York to its position as the nation's largest retailer by the mid-twentieth century, A&P outstandingly symbolizes every major phase of chain-store history in America. The A&P Warehouse is a little-altered, nine-story, reinforced concrete structure that between about 1900 and 1929 formed part of a manufacturing and distribution center for the New York-New Jersey-Long Island area.

## Hadrosaurus Foulkii Leidy Site

*Location:* Haddonfield, Camden County

*Relevant issues:* Science and technology

*Statement of significance:* Discovered by William Parker Foulke in October, 1858, *Hadrosaurus foulkii Leidy* was the first relatively complete dinosaur skeleton found in North America, and, in fact, anywhere in the world. Realizing the spectacular nature of his find, Foulke called upon Dr. Joseph Leidy and Isaac Lea of the Academy of Natural Sciences of Philadelphia for assistance in evaluating the fossils. Presentation of this discovery to the scientific world revolutionized the understanding of dinosaurs.

## Hangar No. 1, Lakehurst Naval Air Station

*Location:* Manchester Township, Ocean County

*Relevant issues:* Aviation history, disasters and tragedies

*Statement of significance:* Commissioned in 1921, Lakehurst Naval Air Station became the hub of naval lighter-than-air activity; it was the home port for the Navy's rigid airships *Shenandoah, Los Angeles, Akron,* and *Macon.* In addition, it was the only stopping place in the country for commercial airships, and, in 1937, was the scene of the crash of the German zeppelin *Hindenburg.*

## Henry House

*Location:* Princeton, Mercer County

*Relevant issues:* Science and technology

*Statement of significance:* This was the home of Joseph Henry (1797-1878), who did important research in the field of electromagnetism and served as the first secretary of the Smithsonian Institution (1846-1878) and president of the National Academy of Sciences (1868-1878). Henry lived in this two-story brick house while he taught (1832-1846) at what became Princeton University.

## Horn Antenna

*Location:* Holmdel, Monmouth County

*Relevant issues:* Science and technology

*Statement of significance:* The Horn Antenna, at the Bell Telephone Laboratories, is associated with the research work of two radio astronomers, Dr. Arno A. Penzias and Dr. Robert A. Wilson. In 1965, while using the Horn Antenna, Penzias and Wilson stumbled on the microwave background radiation that permeates the universe. This discovery—the most important in modern astronomy since Edwin Hubble demonstrated in the 1920's that the universe was expanding—provided evidence that confirmed the big bang theory of the creation of the universe. In 1978, Penzias and Wilson received the Nobel Prize in Physics.

## Lawrenceville School

*Location:* Lawrenceville, Mercer County

*Relevant issues:* Art and architecture, education

*Statement of significance:* A rare, surviving example of the successful collaboration of architects and landscape planners, this school, which pioneered progressive education, retains its historic appearance as almost no other private school in the country. Designed by Peabody and Stearns of Boston and landscape architect Frederick Law Olmsted on the English system of classrooms, residences, and dormitories placed around a central green, the campus effectively blends into and enhances the town that surrounds it.

## Monmouth Battlefield

*Location:* Freehold, Monmouth County

*Relevant issues:* Military history, Revolutionary War

*Statement of significance:* The Battle of Monmouth (June 28, 1778) marked the combat debut of the American Army after the hard winter's training at Valley Forge. Here, on a hot summer day, George Washington's troops attempted to disrupt British General Henry Clinton's march to Sandy Hook following the British evacuation of Philadelphia.

## Morven

*Location:* Princeton, Mercer County

*Relevant issues:* Political history

*Statement of significance:* Morven, a mid-eighteenth century Georgian residence, was the birthplace and home of Richard Stockton (1730-1781), a signer of the Declaration of Independence, lawyer, and judge. It served as the official residence of New Jersey's governors between 1954 and 1982.

## Nassau Hall

*Location:* Princeton University, Princeton, Mercer County

*Relevant issues:* Colonial America, education, military history, Revolutionary War

*Statement of significance:* Completed in 1756, Nassau Hall was the first important collegiate building of the Middle Colonies and served as the prototype of many subsequent colonial college structures. During the Revolution, it was used as a barracks and hospital and was the scene of the last British stand during the Battle of Princeton.

## Old Barracks

*Location:* Trenton, Mercer County

*Relevant issues:* Colonial America, military history, Revolutionary War

*Statement of significance:* This two-and-a-half-story fieldstone structure is the only surviving barracks of five erected by New Jersey's colonial legislature to house troops during the French and Indian War. At different times during the Revolution, American and British soldiers and Hessian mercenaries were quartered here; Hessians were here on Christmas, 1776, when George Washington crossed the Delaware and surprised the Trenton garrison.

## Paulsdale

*Location:* Mt. Laurel Township, Burlington County

*Relevant issues:* Social reform, women's history

*Statement of significance:* Paulsdale was the childhood home of Alice Paul (1885-1977), a leader in the woman suffrage movement and advocate of women's rights. Paul's strong Quaker upbringing influenced her views on the equality of the sexes and molded her for work she was to accomplish: securing passage of the Nineteenth Amendment in 1920; drafting the Equal Rights Amendment in the 1920's and working for its passage; and including the sex equality clause in the United Nations Declaration of Human Rights.

## Princeton Battlefield

*Location:* Princeton, Mercer County

*Relevant issues:* Military history, Revolutionary War

*Statement of significance:* George Washington's victory here helped raise the morale of the colonists at a time when the Continental army had suffered a series of defeats. It is now a State Park.

## Prospect

*Location:* Princeton, Mercer County

*Relevant issues:* Political history

*Statement of significance:* From 1902 to 1911, this house, built in the Tuscan villa style, was the residence of Woodrow Wilson (1856-1924). Wilson lived at Prospect during a period significant both for his presidency of Princeton University and the beginning of his political career.

## Red Bank Battlefield

*Location:* National Park, Gloucester County

*Relevant issues:* Military history, Revolutionary War

*Statement of significance:* On October 22, 1777, Fort Mercer, an earthen fort erected to guard the river approach to Philadelphia, was successfully defended by Americans in the Battle of the Red Bank. Their victory delayed the opening of the Delaware River as a route of supply for General William Howe's army, which had occupied Philadelphia on September 26.

## Sandy Hook Light

*Location:* Sandy Hook, Monmouth County

*Relevant issues:* Naval history

*Web site:* www.nps.gov/history/maritime/sandyhk .html

*Statement of significance:* When erected in 1764, the tall, white structure at Sandy was the fifth lighthouse built in America, and today is the oldest standing light tower in the United States. Built of brick on a masonry foundation, it rises eighty-eight feet above the water.

## Seabright Lawn Tennis and Cricket Club

*Location:* Rumson, Monmouth County

*Relevant issues:* Sports

*Statement of significance:* Seabright Lawn Tennis and Cricket Club (organized in 1877 and incorporated in 1886) is the among the oldest continuously active tennis clubs in the country. Over the years, Seabright has been host to many of the best-known American and international amateur tennis players. The Seabright Invitational Tournament, held annually from 1884 to 1950, became a major event on the eastern U.S. tennis circuit and the traditional prelude to the national championships.

## Stanton House

*Location:* Tenafly, Bergen County

*Relevant issues:* Social reform, women's history

*Statement of significance:* From about 1868 to 1887, this two-story, white Victorian frame house was the residence of Elizabeth Cady Stanton (1815-1902), an early proponent, philosopher, and leader of the women's rights movement. Stanton delivered the call for female suffrage at the Seneca Falls (New York) Convention of 1848.

## Whitman House

*Location:* Camden, Camden County

*Relevant issues:* Literary history

*Statement of significance:* From 1884 until his death, this two-story, plain frame house was the home of Walt Whitman (1819-1892), the "Poet of Democracy."

# New Mexico

*The Chapel of Our Lady of Guadalupe, Santa Fe.* (American Stock Photography)

# History of New Mexico

New Mexico's arid climate and southwestern geographical position have deeply influenced its history. Known as the "Land of Enchantment," the state's high altitudes, clear air, and colorful mountains and deserts attract artists and tourists alike. Its lack of water, however, makes large-scale settlement difficult, and its proximity to Mexico has long been a factor in making its culture a Spanish-American hybrid. Added to these ingredients, the state's large American Indian population and late—1912—achievement of statehood give New Mexico a unique flavor.

**Early History**

American Indians have lived in New Mexico for perhaps twenty-five thousand years. Evidence shows that they hunted in northeastern New Mexico about ten thousand years ago. Later, the Mogollons settled near the modern Arizona border, eventually building villages. The Anasazis, another ancient people, lived in "Four Corners," where Colorado, Arizona, New Mexico, and Utah meet, and created one of the most developed civilizations of the time. The Pueblo Indians are descendants of the Anasazis. In about 1500 B.C.E. the Navaho and Apache Indians arrived; Ute and Comanche tribes arrived shortly afterward.

**Exploration**

The Spanish conquistador Hernán Cortés invaded Mexico in 1519. Nine years later, another Spaniard, explorer Álvar Nuñez Cabeza de Vaca, became shipwrecked off the Texas coast. When he finally made it to Mexico City in 1536, his reports of large wealthy cities sparked interest in further exploration. In 1538 Franciscan friar Marcos de Niza set out exploring and within a year returned with tales of golden cities larger than Mexico City.

Spanish authorities chose Francisco Vásquez de de Coronado, then twenty-nine, to explore the region. He set out in 1540 with more than 1,600 men but in two years had found no opulent cities. His travels did increase Spain's geographical knowledge of the region, however, and profoundly influenced the future.

After later expeditions, the Spanish finally decided in 1598 to found a colony in the region, with the capital at San Juan de las Caballeros, near the Chama River. In 1609 the capital was moved to Santa Fe ("holy faith"). The Spanish treated the American Indians harshly. Missionaries made inroads into their traditional culture, while secular rulers set up a system of forced labor tantamount to slavery. A revolt in 1680 left hundreds of Spaniards dead; the remainder fled. Twelve years later the Spanish reconquered the region, and for the next 125 years, the two sides lived in relative peace.

After 1821, however, Mexico gained its independence from Spain. Traders and trappers had been making uninvited forays into the New Mexico area, but now, with the suspicious Spanish gone, they were welcome. Also in 1821 American trader William Becknell established the Santa Fe Trail, over which millions of dollars of goods would travel until replaced by transcontinental railroads. New Mexico's Indians and the Mexicans themselves rebelled against the government in 1837 but were crushed. In 1841 Texas, which had become an independent republic, invaded the region, but this effort also failed.

Matters changed again, this time decisively, after the United States and Mexico went to war in 1846. Troops led by General Stephen W. Kearny occupied New Mexico with little difficulty. After American victory in 1848, New Mexico, along with a huge swathe of territory that included much of California, Colorado, Utah, Nevada, and Arizona, came under American rule. The stage was set for the future state to emerge.

**Becoming a Territory**

It took sixty-four years for New Mexico to join the American Union as a separate and equal state. Much conflict and agonizing over statehood lay ahead. First, in 1850, New Mexico, which then included Arizona, was organized into a territory. In 1853 the Gadsden Purchase added new land on the southern border. Yet statehood was little more than a dream. The region had too few inhabitants—

about sixty thousand in 1850—to become part of the Union. While in time thousands of Americans came to live there, the territory's Mexican character drew hostility from certain forces in Congress. The fact that most inhabitants were Roman Catholic added to the distrust of the suspicious East.

Moreover, New Mexico, along with Arizona and other western regions, was a violent place, plagued with serious American Indian problems and often equally serious Anglo-American problems, in the form of range wars and general lawlessness. From the 1850's to the 1880's, when the last dangerous American Indian menace succumbed to peace and outlaws such as Billy the Kid were laid to rest, New Mexico was truly the Wild West.

### Civil War

The territory experienced the Civil War in 1862, when an army of Texas Confederates commanded by General Henry J. Sibley invaded from the east.

Sibley defeated a Union force at Valverde, more than one hundred miles south of Albuquerque on the east side of the Rio Grande, and advanced north toward Santa Fe and Albuquerque. His army was then to head north to Colorado and its gold regions around Pikes Peak and Denver. They never made it, however, because when they reached Glorieta Pass and Apache Canyon, near Santa Fe, Union soldiers turned them back in a battle sometimes called "the Gettysburg of the West."

### Conflict

In 1863 Congress organized the territories of Arizona and Colorado, in the process reducing the size of New Mexico. After the Civil War ended in 1865, cattle ranchers, sheepherders, and others flocked to the state in search of prosperity or adventure. Affairs were hardly fit for the pursuit of wealth, however, since conflicts broke out repeatedly among settlers. Some of the worst of the hostilities came in the late 1870's in a county southeast of Albuquerque. The Lincoln County War saw cattlemen and others battling for political control. In this "war," Billy the Kid, a teenage bandit who survived only until age twenty-one, murdered twenty-one men before being shot by Sheriff Pat Garrett. To end the bloodshed, in 1878 the territorial governor pardoned the fighters. Over the next decade other territorial governors helped establish order.

Establishing peace between settlers and American Indians, however, was another matter. Apache chief Victorio led many murderous raids against his enemies until his death in 1880. Control was passed to Geronimo, last of the warring Apache warrior chiefs. Geronimo surrendered repeatedly, only to escape and regroup his army. In September, 1886, he finally surrendered after receiving personal assurances of safety from President Grover Cleve-

Map of New Mexico showing: Utah, Colorado, Arizona, Texas, Mexico. Cities and sites: Durango, Farmington, Aztec Ruins NM, Chaco Culture NHP, Taos, Los Alamos, Bandelier NM, Gallup, Zuñi Pueblo, Grants, Santa Fe, Ácoma Pueblo, El Morro NM, Albuquerque, Mountainair, Salinas Pueblo Missions NM, NEW MEXICO, Gila Cliff Dwellings NM, Silver City, El Paso.

land. Geronimo lived on to convert to Christianity and participate in President Theodore Roosevelt's inauguration in 1905.

### New Mexico Economy

With peace established, economic progress could proceed. Without American Indian depredations, cattle ranching prospered. Mineral wealth had been discovered and would continue to be discovered well into the next century. Between 1880 and 1890 the population swelled by more than one-third, to just more than 160,000. By 1910, though New Mexico was still not a state, the population had more than doubled again, to 325,000.

As in much of the West, the advent of the transcontinental railroad changed life in New Mexico. When the first train entered in 1878, products such as cattle could be easily and cheaply transported east. The territory experienced a boom in cattle and mining products. New Mexico's economy, however, was handicapped by a lack of water; annual rainfall is less than ten inches. Sheriff Pat Garrett inaugurated far-reaching irrigation projects.

### Statehood

New Mexicans desired statehood, but by 1901 this goal had not been accomplished, despite many attempts. Congress feared allowing a seemingly foreign territory to gain precious votes in the Senate. The territory appeared too Mexican for full membership. The Spanish-American War (1898) allowed the territory to demonstrate its loyalty. Lieutenant Colonel Theodore Roosevelt recruited many of his Rough Riders in New Mexico, and they proved their trustworthiness. Finally, in 1910 Congress passed a statehood bill, and two years later New Mexico entered the Union.

The state constitution, adopted in 1911, is considered conservative in comparison to other western states, since it omits the initiative, referendum, and recall, which allot extra powers to the electorate. Instead, all legislative power lies in the bicameral legislature. Along with a governor, a lieutenant governor, and five other executive officers, officials are elected to four-year terms. They may hold office no more than two successive terms. Members of the upper house serve four-year terms; lower-house members serve two-year terms. Provisions guaranteeing voting rights and education for Spanish-speaking people can be changed only by three-fourths of the legislature and three-fourths of the electorate.

### Two World Wars

The state was soon called upon again for military service, and its soldiers fought in World Wars I and II. The postwar period proved problematic, however, as a long drought wreaked havoc with the state's economy. Livestock prices sank, ranchers went bankrupt, and banks collapsed. Providentially, however, new mineral wealth was discovered, and new businesses appeared. When Carlsbad Caverns became a National Park in 1930, a focal point for tourism was born. Water projects begun in the 1920's eventually brought significant acreage under cultivation. While there was limited capacity for these supplies to be increased, New Deal projects during the Depression continued making inroads into this chronic problem.

Like those of neighboring states, New Mexico's economy gained considerably during World War II, when federal spending increased dramatically. A secret project begun at Los Alamos turned out to be development of the world's first atomic bombs. The first atomic explosion lighted up the New Mexico desert at Trinity, near Alamogordo, in 1945.

### Postindustrial Society

New Mexico's postwar economy grew on the strength of federal spending, especially for defense. Key areas were research on the military, peacetime uses of nuclear power, and experiments with rockets. This effort was assisted when uranium was discovered in the state in 1950. In the 1960's, coal production rose markedly; New Mexico's power supply is generated primarily from coal burning.

New Mexico's economy and society dramatically changed with its passage from an industrial to a postindustrial and high-tech economy, with service industries far outweighing manufacturing, construction, agriculture, and mining in both income produced (70 percent) and number of employees (81 percent). In the 1990's the state ranked among the nation's leaders in nuclear and space research.

*—Charles F. Bahmueller*

# Ácoma Pueblo

**Date:** First inhabitants probably arrived between 1075 and 1200 C.E.

**Relevant issues:** American Indian history

**Significance:** This Native American village at the top of a mesa known as the Rock of Acuco is one of the oldest continuously occupied sites in the continental United States.

**Location:** Forty-five miles southwest of Albuquerque, off U.S. Interstate 40 in northwestern New Mexico

**Site Office:**
Pueblo Cultural Center
2401 12th Street NW
Albuquerque, NM 87104
ph.: (800) 766-4405; (505) 843-7270

Ácoma Pueblo is impressive for both its physical grandeur and its inhabitants. The pueblo, also known as Sky City, sits atop a 357-foot-high mesa and is barely visible from below. A modern road takes tour buses to the top, but an ancient stone stairway also remains at the site. The pueblo is still home to a small number of the Ácoma people, making it one of the oldest continuously inhabited sites in the United States. Its inhabitants have withstood the encroachments of a variety of outside cultures.

**Early History**

The origins of Ácoma Pueblo and its residents are somewhat mysterious; there is great variance of opinion concerning just how long the area has been inhabited. Many scholars believe the first inhabitants arrived anywhere from 1075 to 1200 C.E. The Ácomas themselves say their ancestors arrived earlier; different legends put the habitation at about 600 C.E. or even before the time of Christ. The word "Ácoma" means "a place that always was." The Ácomas also dispute scholarly claims that the habitation resulted from migrations. They say that they have always lived on the mesa and have welcomed nomadic tribes there. Another opinion, however, is that the Ácomas migrated from Mesa Verde in southwestern Colorado. The Ácomas, this theory goes, were often in conflict with other tribes, so they chose to live on the top of the mesa because of its defensive advantages. Whatever the truth may be, Sky City was once home to thousands of Ácomas, a tribe of the Keres Indians.

The earliest written records of the Ácomas come from Spanish explorers. The first Europeans to have contact with the Ácomas were Hernando de Alvarado, the Franciscan friar Juan Padilla, and their party of soldiers, who in 1540 were dispatched by Francisco Vásquez de Coronado to explore the area east of Zuñi Pueblo, which is near the western edge of present-day New Mexico. Alvarado was impressed by Ácoma Pueblo. "The city was built on a high rock," he wrote. "The ascent was so difficult that we repented climbing to the top. The houses are three and four stories high. The people [are] of the same type as those in the province of Cíbola [Zuñi], and they have abundant supplies of maize, beans, and turkeys like those of New Spain." This encounter between the Spaniards and the Ácomas was, by most accounts, peaceful.

Coronado was disappointed in his search for riches in the area that is now New Mexico, and his army returned to Mexico in 1542. Rumors of wealth to be had in the area, however, continued to abound, leading another Spanish party to venture there in 1581. It was organized by a Franciscan, Agustín Rodríguez, and included soldiers commanded by Francisco Sánchez; it made contact with several pueblos, including Ácoma. One member of the party, Hernando Gallegos, recorded a brief description of Ácoma, saying the mesa contained about five hundred houses three or four stories high.

**Antonio de Espejo's Expedition**

A member of another expedition in the following year, Antonio de Espejo, described a well-developed society at Ácoma, which he estimated had more than six thousand residents. He observed that the residents engaged in farming fields a few miles from the pueblo and diverted a river to irrigate these fields. The people of Ácoma engaged in trade with nearby communities, exchanging salt, game, and hides for other goods. The Ácomas were cordial to Espejo and treated him to performances of juggling and ceremonial dances.

Still, some Ácomas were suspicious of the Spaniards, and that suspicion was justified: The Spaniards were bent on conquest. The Ácomas did not wish to be conquered, so eventually the encounters between the Spanish and the Ácomas turned violent.

Espejo found evidence of gold mines west of Ácoma, in what is now Arizona, and his reports fueled the Spaniards' desire to explore and conquer the land they called New Mexico. The Spanish authorities assigned this task to Juan de Oñate, who set out from Mexico in April, 1598, with a party of soldiers, their families, and a few Franciscans. They visited several pueblos and arrived at Ácoma in late October, then held a ceremony in which the Ácomas were asked to pledge obedience to the Spanish Crown. Oñate and his party then moved on, but another group, led by Juan de Zaldivar, his nephew, soon followed. When this group arrived early in December, the Ácomas were initially friendly, but then attacked the Spaniards and killed thirteen of them, including Zaldivar.

A party of seventy men, led by Juan de Zaldivar's brother, Vicente, came to Ácoma on January 11,

1599, intending vengeance. Three times, the Spaniards asked the Ácomas to accept them peacefully. Because these efforts proved unsuccessful, Vicente de Zaldivar ordered his troops to attack the pueblo the next day. A three-day battle ensued, with the Spaniards emerging victorious and taking more than five hundred Ácomas as prisoners. The adults among the prisoners were sentenced to slavery.

There were further Spanish explorations in New Mexico during the next several years. The Ácomas' relations with the Spaniards were peaceful but aloof, and their community was rather isolated. This isolation changed in 1629, when a priest named Juan Ramírez arrived at Ácoma. He was well liked by the Ácomas and helped them rebuild the pueblo, which the Spanish had set afire during the battle in 1599. He also oversaw the construction of the San Esteban del Rey Mission, which still stands

*Ácoma Pueblo.* (Mark Nohl/courtesy *New Mexico Magazine*)

at Ácoma. The Ácomas gradually adopted the Catholic religion and Spanish agricultural methods. This situation was not to last forever.

## Growing Resentment of the Spanish

Resentment of the Spaniards by the native peoples of New Mexico led to the Pueblo Revolt of 1680; Ácoma's distance from the other pueblos meant that it was not heavily involved. Evidently the Ácomas supported the goals of the revolt, as one account says they burned all the Christian emblems at the pueblo and killed their priest, Lucas Maldonado, one of Ramírez's successors.

Following the revolt, Spain made several attempts at reconquest. An expedition led by Don Diego de Vargas arrived at Sky City in November, 1692. The Ácomas at first refused the Spaniards admittance, but surrendered after the Spanish force climbed the mesa. There were battles between the Spanish and various native tribes over the next few years, and the Spanish reconquest of New Mexico forged ahead; a major event was the surrender of Taos Pueblo in 1696. A few isolated skirmishes followed, but the reconquest was complete by 1699.

During the eighteenth century the small mission staff at Sky City converted many Ácomas to Christianity. The Ácomas continued farming, although increasing drought made this enterprise difficult. Disease decreased the Ácoma population during this period; the Spanish also blamed Apache raids. Whatever the causes, the population of the pueblo was estimated at fewer than one thousand near the end of the century. At this time the Ácomas had distinguished themselves as blanket makers; their blankets were said to be the finest in New Mexico. Pottery making was another significant craft. In the late eighteenth century, Ácomas began assisting the Spaniards in raids against the Navajo Indians.

## Under Mexican Rule

When Mexico won its independence from Spain in 1821, the Ácomas' way of life changed very little. The Mexican government accepted the Ácomas as citizens, and the Ácomas went on farming and hunting. Like the Spanish before them, the Mexican authorities continued to have trouble with the Navajo. Whether or not the Ácomas assisted the Mexicans in their battles is not documented, but it is possible they did assist. Some authorities, however, claimed the Ácomas were "in collusion" with the Navajo.

When the Mexican War broke out in 1846, U.S. troops occupied New Mexico; when the war ended, the Treaty of Guadalupe Hidalgo brought the territory into the United States, and the Ácomas had to deal with yet another government. U.S. military engineers who surveyed Ácoma Pueblo were impressed with the residents' agriculture and craftsmanship. There were threats to the Ácomas' way of life. There were land disputes with Mexicans and with other native tribes, including the Lagunas.

## Under U.S. Rule

The U.S. Indian agent for the territory supported, in theory, the rights of the Ácomas and other peaceful pueblo dwellers to retain their traditional lands and to receive assistance with trade and agriculture; in practice, however, U.S. authorities were not able to keep out encroaching settlers. Boundary disputes continued throughout the nineteenth century. Finally, in 1913, the U.S. Supreme Court ruled that the Ácomas and other pueblo dwellers were protected against unauthorized settlement on their lands. By this time the Ácomas had lost much of their traditional land. In 1948 they began working on legal action to seek compensation for the land losses; the proceedings were lengthy. In 1970 the U.S. government agreed to pay the Ácomas slightly more than six thousand dollars.

Growing crops and raising livestock, especially sheep, remained principal activities of the Ácomas until World War II. Since then, the increasing dryness of their land has made agriculture less feasible. More and more Ácomas live and work away from the pueblo, particularly in the nearby villages of Acomita and McCartys, with the pueblo now functioning as something of a ceremonial home. For the handful of Ácoma families who live at Sky City, tourism has become important. They allow visitors to take guided trips around the pueblo; the mission church also is open for touring. At the foot of the mesa there is a visitor center that features an extensive, permanent exhibit of Ácoma pottery.

—*Thomas B. Ford and Trudy Ring*

## For Further Information:

Minge, Ward Alan. *Ácoma: Pueblo in the Sky.* Rev. ed. Albuquerque: University of New Mexico Press, 1991. A thorough and sympathetic examination of the Ácomas, their history, and their culture.

Sedgwick, Mrs. William T. *Ácoma, the Sky City.* Cambridge: Harvard University Press, 1927; reprint, Chicago: Rio Grande Press, 1963. An extensive work, but, perhaps because of its age, is a bit precious in its language and somewhat condescending toward Native Americans.

Sturtevant, William. *Handbook of North American Indians.* Washington, D.C.: Smithsonian Institution, 1983. Contains detailed sections on the Ácoma people.

# Aztec Ruins

**Date:** Named a National Monument in 1923 and a World Heritage Site in 1987

**Relevant issues:** American Indian history

**Significance:** This monument, on twenty-seven acres, is devoted to Anasazi pueblo ruins dating from the twelfth through thirteenth centuries; it includes six major archaeological sites, partially excavated, and the only fully reconstructed Anasazi kiva (ceremonial chamber).

**Location:** On the Animas River in northwestern New Mexico, just north of the town of Aztec; fourteen miles northeast of Farmington, New Mexico, or thirty-five miles southwest of Durango, Colorado, on U.S. Interstate 550

**Site Office:**

Aztec Ruins National Monument
P.O. Box 640
84 County Road 2900
Aztec, NM 87410-0640
ph.: (505) 334-6174
Fax: (505) 334-0640
Web site: www.nps.gov/azru/
e-mail: azru_front_desk@nps.gov

One of the best-selling books of the 1840's in the United States was *The Conquest of Mexico* by William Prescott. The American imagination was fired by Prescott's account of central Mexico's magnificent Aztec Empire and its destruction by the Spanish. When American scouts came upon a number of ruins in the United States' southwestern territory during that period, ruins of great age that indicated the existence of some impressive civilization, these European Americans preferred to believe them the work of the Aztecs, rather than of the ancestors of the local Indian tribes. One of these sites, in northwestern New Mexico, was thus named Aztec Ruins. Thirty years later settlers arrived in the area and founded a town they called Aztec, after the ruins.

**Anasazi Civilization**

Throughout the Four Corners area of the American Southwest, in the land drained by the San Juan River, a great civilization did in fact exist and reached its height there in the twelfth century, disappearing by the end of the thirteenth century. This civilization, known today by the Navajo name Anasazi ("ancient ones"), developed the style of dwelling house now called pueblo (Spanish for "village"). They built breathtaking cliff dwellings in such places as Mesa Verde, Colorado, and Canyon de Chelly, Arizona, and expansive structures in river basins sites such as Chaco Canyon, New Mexico. These were the builders of the impressive ruins on the bank of the Animas River, centuries before the Aztec Empire arose and farther north than the Aztec civilization ever spread.

**Early Exploration of the Ruins**

To the first white settlers of Aztec, the ruins were a curiosity, an impediment to agriculture, and a convenient source of building supplies. The ruins appeared as large mounds of building debris covered with the accumulated sand and dirt of centuries, overgrown with vegetation. They briefly drew the attention of anthropologist Lewis H. Morgan in 1878; he surmised a relationship with the ruins of Chaco Canyon. Then in 1881, a local schoolmaster took a group of his students on a exploration of the ruins. They broke through the crumbling masonry walls and found themselves in a mazelike series of long-buried rooms. To their surprise they found skeletons along with pottery artifacts. The interest of the community was aroused, and soon the ruins were a frequent target for artifact-hunters and vandals. Finally in 1889 the property was purchased by John R. Koontz, who kept the vandals out. A few years later Warren K. Moorehead was allowed to survey but not dig the ruins. At the same time archaeologists were beginning to excavate other Anasazi ruins in the region and seek information about their culture.

In 1916 the new owner of the site, H. D. Abrams, agreed to allow an excavation. To direct the project

*A kiva at Aztec Ruins National Monument.* (Mark Nohl/courtesy *New Mexico Magazine*)

which lasted from 1916 to 1921, the American Museum of Natural History selected Earl H. Morris. Morris was a native of the region, educated at the University of Colorado, and familiar with various Anasazi sites. Because of the proximity of the town of Aztec, he had a ready supply of laborers, townspeople who both needed the money he offered and took a personal interest in what was happening to "their" ruins.

Morris decided to work on the large western mound, dubbed the West Ruin. Clearing of the ruin was the first and one of the most arduous tasks. Once the vegetation was gone, the impressive size of the ruin was apparent. It spanned some 360 by 280 feet in a roughly rectangular structure, built around a central courtyard 180 by 200 feet. As the excavation progressed, a complex of 353 rooms was revealed. The pueblo contained 221 interconnected rooms on the ground level, 119 rooms on a second story, and 12 rooms on a third. There were 29 small kivas, probably for individual clan use, and, in the courtyard, a Great Kiva for the use of the community.

## Construction of the Ruins

The pueblo's design indicates an awareness of the importance of solar orientation; the highest wing of the pueblo was on the north, with only minimal ventilation openings in the wall. The lowest part of the structure faced south, to permit the winter sun to warm all of the building. The north wing had five and sometimes six rows of rooms from its south wall to its north. The east wing was five rooms deep; the still-uncleared west wing, seven rooms deep. The south wing, a single-story bowed structure, was one room deep.

The construction was very similar to that found at Chaco Canyon sites, although the stonework was not as fine because the local sandstone did not break as cleanly. The walls were filled with a rubble core, then faced with shaped blocks of sandstone set in alternating courses of thick and thin stones. In some places the rows included alternating colors as well, the final effect clearly intended to be aesthetically pleasing. The veneer blocks were not bonded to the core, causing an intrinsic weakness in the structure. Finally the sandstone surface was thickly covered with mud plaster. The Anasazi accomplished this impressive construction without metal technology, without wheeled transportation, and without draft animals.

### Early Occupation Periods

The evidence that Morris and his team uncovered in the West Ruin at Aztec, in the form of varying construction styles, pottery styles, and similarities to other sites, made clear one significant fact in the history of the site: It was occupied twice, by two culturally different groups of Anasazi, separated by a period of perhaps fifty years. The striking similarity in building techniques to those at Chaco Canyon convinced Morris that the builders of the West Ruin were somehow related to the Chacoans. Recent aerial archaeological surveys have revealed the existence of an extensive network of roadways radiating out from Chaco Canyon. Aztec may have served as a satellite community, providing both living space and surplus food to the highly populated Chaco center. Tree-ring dating of beam samples from the pueblo indicated that the original beams were cut between 1111 and 1115, with a few more dating to 1124. This dates the West Ruin to a period only forty years after the construction of Pueblo Bonito at Chaco Canyon. Evidence of migration from Chaco Canyon suggests that the Chacoans left Aztec Ruins only about fifty years after its construction.

The presence of Mesa Verde-style pottery, intramural burials, and construction techniques in refurbished areas of the pueblo indicates a later occupation by people from the north. Tree-ring dating of remodeling beams indicates that they were cut between 1220 and 1260, with most cut between 1225 and 1252.

### The Disappearance of the Anasazi

The evidence from Aztec Ruins suggests that the disappearance of the Anasazi from the entire Four Corners area by the end of the thirteenth century was not due to a single mass exodus but rather occurred in several waves of migration. Tree-rings have revealed that a long and serious drought affected the whole Colorado Plateau from 1130 to 1190, a disaster for an agricultural people like the Anasazi. The Chacoans, although possessing a large and complex culture based at Chaco Canyon, apparently moved further south at an early date, by the late twelfth century, and the people at Aztec went with them.

The Mesa Verdians left their cliff-top fields and cliff dwellings and moved south but paused in the abandoned pueblo they found on the bank of the Animas River. The river may have permitted them to continue their agricultural efforts longer. There they modified the building and the kiva to suit their own taste, and added new buildings as well. It was probably they who built the East Ruin, still unexcavated. Another drought, which lasted from 1276 to 1299, may have precipitated their departure from the region. They stayed until the end of the thirteenth century, when they too moved farther south, to the Santa Fe River, where the descendants of the Anasazi, the Pueblo Indians, live today.

### Anasazi Building Methods

It is not known how the Anasazi were able to build their multistory walls when they had no technological means of raising building materials. Most probably it was a matter of human labor hauling stones and baskets of mortar up ladders in the interior, with masons working from temporary platforms, debris piles, or nearby roofs. It is possible that there may have been exterior balconies as well, since there is some inconclusive evidence for one on the north wall.

The walls of the interior rooms were also plastered; some of this material still remains. Usually the rooms were covered with an uncolored clay tempered with sand. In some rooms there was a red-tinted wainscoting against gypsum-white upper walls; there also were some rooms with incised or painted patterns for decoration. In one room white hand prints decorate the ceiling beams.

The excavators found nineteen of the original room ceilings in the West Ruin intact. The ceilings were elaborate constructions, supported by large pine or juniper beams that spanned the rooms. Over these beams poles of pine, juniper, or cottonwood were closely laid perpendicular to the beams. These were sometimes topped by a willow matting laced with yucca, perhaps partly decorative, perhaps to protect the occupants from falling dust. The final layer was of juniper splints covered with a thick deposit of tamped earth; this would form either an exterior roof or the floor of an upper room.

There were no windows as such in the pueblo. Ventilation was provided by small openings in the outer walls, or by ventilation shafts to those openings. Rooms in the deep interior that lacked fresh air apparently were used primarily for storage, with the exterior, better-ventilated rooms used for habitation. Ladders were used for access to one floor from another; door openings were placed a foot above floor level to protect floor-level hearths from drafts. A few doorways were built in room corners; the feat required considerable engineering skill.

A number of rooms had been abandoned to other uses and became trash dumps. In some, human remains were found as well, at times buried in the floor in shallow graves, at other times simply placed on the floor. Burial within abandoned rooms was typical of the late period of culture at Mesa Verde; this evidence would become important to Morris's interpretation of the Ruins.

### Rich Diversity of Artifacts

A rich diversity of stone and bone tools, shell beads, and jewelry was found within the West Ruin, along with several hundred intact pieces of pottery. Some were utilitarian pots, intended for cooking; some were decorated. Perishable artifacts such as wooden arrow shafts and bows, snowshoe frames, cradleboards, ladders, various types of basketry, moccasins, yucca sandals, and reed-stemmed cigarettes were also found, telling archaeologists much about the character of life in the pueblo.

In 1921, as the end of the dig grew near, Morris determined to excavate a great depression in the courtyard, which he believed to be a kiva, a subterranean ceremonial chamber. Excavation proved him correct. This kiva was much larger than those the excavators had found within the pueblo; it was forty-one feet in diameter. Great Kivas were known from the Chaco Canyon area, but this one held a surprise. Around its rim at ground level were fourteen arc-shaped chambers, each with an exterior doorway, each connected to the kiva proper by ver-

tical wall slots with embedded rungs. Like most other kivas, the Aztec Great Kiva is laid out on a north-south axis. The central surface room on the north is larger than the other thirteen, with special features, including what seems to be an altar, and a stairway to the kiva chamber.

On the kiva floor Morris found the remains of four massive masonry pillars, each three feet square, footed on four stacked slabs of limestone lying at the bottom of a hole, the limestone in turn bedded on a lignite foundation. Clearly these pillars were intended to support a great weight. Because there were no pilasters around the circular wall, but only two benches, Morris deduced that the Great Kiva had been covered by a giant circular flat roof rising ten to twelve feet above the level of the courtyard. He decided that a central square of beams resting on the four pillars had supported at least twenty-three beams radiating like spokes from the center to the exterior walls. Over these the Anasazi would have lashed layers of saplings and juniper splints and covered them with a thick layer of earth. When completed, the roof would have weighed about ninety tons, all supported without the use of securing nails, tenons, or pegs.

Morris was unable to complete his excavation of the West Ruin before his funds ran out and the museum called a halt. About a quarter of the ruin was left covered.

### Modern Preservation Efforts

On January 24, 1923, Aztec Ruins was declared a National Monument by presidential proclamation. Most of the land was donated by the American Museum of Natural History, and some was purchased from the heirs of H. D. Abrams and from other property owners. Consisting of 27.1 acres, the site is now administered by the National Park Service.

Because the removal of covering debris invariably exposes a site to decay, the American Museum of Natural History had provided funding for the preservation and stabilization of the ruins as they were excavated; this was a very innovative approach for the time. Walls were supported and capped in cement, intact ceilings were covered with roofs, and extensive drainage systems were set up. Repairs and stabilization were, and are, a continuous problem. The Great Kiva was particularly subject to erosion and decay, and concerned local citizens persuaded the federal government to act. It was decided not merely to repair but to reconstruct the Great Kiva. Earl H. Morris returned to supervise the work, which began in 1933. It was the ultimate test of his theory of roof construction. The Great Kiva at Aztec Ruins is still the only building of its kind ever restored.

Exploratory work was done on the East Ruin in 1957. It seemed to be in a state of preservation similar to that of the West Ruin; workers found thirteen intact ceilings on the west edge of the mound. The building style suggests that this pueblo was built by the Mesa Verdians at the same time that they were remodeling the West Ruin pueblo.

In 1953 park archaeologists excavated the Hubbard Mound, a site northwest of the West Ruin. They found three increasingly substantial layers of construction, all from the Mesa Verdian period. The third and final layer proved the most interesting. Three concentric masonry walls rose some twelve feet around a central space sixty-four feet in diameter. Spaces between the walls had been divided into twenty-two small chambers, into which there were no doorways. Entrance must have been through ceiling hatchways. In the center of the circular courtyard was a kiva three feet below the ground. None of the walled chambers connected to it. A similar circular structure was found located to the east of West Ruin. The ceremonial nature of these structures seems apparent, but their exact use remains a mystery.

Today the visitor to Aztec Ruins can tour some of the rooms in the West Ruin, enter the Great Kiva restored to its original appearance, and view the Hubbard Mound. Other mounds on the site remain unexcavated.                          —*Elizabeth Brice*

**For Further Information:**

Corbett, John M. *Aztec Ruins National Monument, New Mexico.* Washington, D.C.: National Park Service, 1963. A straightforward account of the park and its history.

Lister, H., and Florence C. Lister. *Aztec Ruins on the Animas: Excavated, Preserved, and Interpreted.* Albuquerque: University of New Mexico Press, 1987. Provides a thorough description of the excavation of Aztec Ruins by Morris and others and includes many photographs of the work in progress.

Thybony, Scott. *Aztec Ruins National Monument.* Tucson, Ariz.: Southwest Parks and Monuments Association, 1992. A brief history of the park and of the Pueblo Indians.

# Bandelier National Monument

**Date:** Named a National Monument on February 11, 1916

**Relevant issues:** American Indian history

**Significance:** The Pajarito Plateau is an elevated area of volcanic rock called tuff (hardened volcanic ash) and basaltic lava thrown out thousands of years ago by a great volcano. The surface of the plateau is crossed by deep gorges cut by streams running east to the Rio Grande valley. One of the largest and most accessible of these valleys is Frijoles Canyon, the site of numerous ruined structures and cliff dwellings built mostly between 1200 and 1400 C.E. by the Anasazi, ancestors of modern-day Pueblo Indians.

**Location:** Nearly fifty square miles on the Pajarito Plateau west of the Rio Grande; the main part of the site is about forty-six miles west of Santa Fe on Route 4, while the separate Tsankawi section of the monument, a large unexcavated Indian ruin on a high mesa, is eleven miles north from Bandelier on Route 4

**Site Office:**

Bandelier National Monument
HCR-1, Box 1, Suite 15
Los Alamos, NM 87544
ph.: (505) 672-0343
Web site: www.nps.gov/band/

Some knowledge of the dramatic geologic history of the Bandelier site is necessary to understand the physical changes to the land that made possible human habitation, the remains of which are of such compelling interest to modern visitors. The monument is on the east side of the Jemez volcanic field in northern New Mexico. This was a large group of volcanoes active within the last ten million years, part of the Rio Grande Rift formed by the movement and spreading of tectonic plates. This rift now containing the Rio Grande, runs generally north to south from central Colorado to Mexico and has been characterized by active faulting and volcanism.

Constant volcanic activity led to massive, catastrophic eruptions 1.4 and 1.2 million years ago. More than twenty-four cubic miles of ash and molten lava covered the area east of the eruptions with a thick layer of hardened ash intermixed with fragments of volcanic glass and lava. The explosions left the remains of large craters now known as the Valles Caldera and the smaller Toledo Caldera, immediately west of the monument within sight of New Mexico Route 4. Their rims form the Jemez Mountains. Meanwhile the lava and hardened ash thrown out by the eruptions formed a flat, sloping shelf between the volcanoes and the Rio Grande Rift. This shelf became known as the Pajarito (little bird) Plateau.

The Bandelier Monument occupies about fifty square miles of the more than three hundred square miles of the Pajarito Plateau. Like the rest of the plateau, the monument is crossed from west to east by a series of deep canyons, in order from north to south: Frijoles Canyon, Alamo Canyon, Capulin Canyon, and Sanchez Canyon. Intermixed with these on the eastern side of the monument are shorter canyons such as Lummis, Hondo, and Medio. All of the canyons were cut by streams running east to the Rio Grande. The streams provided well-watered settlement and agricultural sites in the canyons for Indians fleeing drought in the western lowlands. The Indian settlement in the Frijoles Canyon is a major feature of the Bandelier National Monument.

**First Human Inhabitants of the Region**

The distant ancestors of the modern Pueblo Indians can be traced back to groups of hunter-gatherers who lived in northwestern New Mexico and along the Rio Grande during the so-called Archaic period from around 5500 B.C.E. to about 400 C.E. Their lifestyle was based on gathering a variety of vegetation and hunting game with stone knives and arrowlike darts hurled by an *atlatl* (throwing stick). Radiocarbon dating of numerous campsites in these areas and on the southern Pajarito Plateau, including the site of the Bandelier Monument, reveals that human occupation occurred around 1750 B.C.E., 670 B.C.E., and 590 B.C.E. The periods of occupation involved constant movement from campsite to campsite in search of fresh game and better selections of plant food. These ancient people did not build perma-

nent settlements. Archaeological remains reveal that they had a variety of cooking procedures such as stone boiling, in which heated rocks were dropped into a watertight basket sealed with pitch. In this way the Archaic Indians could cook without the use of fireproof ceramic utensils, which were not yet widely developed.

The era between 600 and 1200 C.E. has been labeled the Developmental period, and was characterized by a change from hunting and foraging to increasing reliance on agriculture. Corn, beans, and varieties of squash were among the staple crops; however, the limited archaeological research on the Pajarito Plateau has not yet defined the extent to which these early agriculturists farmed in the Bandelier area. Permanent dwellings such as circular pit houses dug into the ground together with small rectangular masonry structures were in use by the tenth century. Natural or excavated caves in hillsides were also used when available.

**The Anasazi**

Beginning around 1175 C.E., a migration of Anasazi Indians from the west began to occur, caused by drought in former living areas and the search for higher-yield farming grounds. This is now known as the Coalition phase. The well-watered and fertile canyons of the Pajarito Plateau, including Frijoles Canyon, proved to be popular settlement sites, as was part of the Rio Grande valley. Stone axes, the bow and arrow, and more developed ceramic pottery appeared. Settlements ranged from one-room structures to larger fifteen- to twenty-room sites usually accompanied by a round subterranean space known as a kiva, where meetings and religious ceremonies were held. The basic social grouping was a household of up to four families, with some sites containing several such households living together. The evidence for social groupings, however, must be inferred from archaeological remains since the Indians were not literate until the coming of the Spanish in the sixteenth century.

Starting around 1300 or 1325 C.E., the archaeological remains indicate that significant cultural changes occurred in the Pajarito and Rio Grande areas both north and south of Frijoles Canyon. These changes are believed to represent the presence of new Indian populations and more intensive occupation as well as developments and adaptations among the older settlement groups. This new era is known as the Classic phase. One change was the appearance of Rio Grande glazeware pottery, an improvement over the earlier Santa Fe carbon-painted ceramics. Settlement patterns expanded to sites of from two hundred to as many as eight hundred ground-floor rooms. According to archaeologists Richard C. Chapman and John V. Biella,

> The southern classic population had evolved a social and economic system that allowed considerable residential flexibility. . . . Family units or households of related families could freely relocate from one part of the northern Rio Grande region to another in response to local fluctuation in climate that affected crop yields.

Indians of this period, which lasted until roughly 1525 C.E., dispersed to small sites during the growing season then congregated at larger sites during the winter. Other improvements included the building of agricultural terraces, checkdams, small-scale irrigation systems, and networks of trails between the larger pueblos. Ceramic manufacturing centers appeared, although the possible existence of trade networks is still conjectural. The major ruins of the Frijoles Canyon settlements, which might have been a focal point of trade, were excavated in the late nineteenth and early twentieth centuries, when modern excavation procedures and analytical techniques were unknown.

Scattered artifacts have been found that indicate some occupancy of Bandelier itself as far back as 9500 B.C.E. However, the most productive period of Bandelier settlement occurred from early 1200 C.E. until the Indians abandoned the Bandelier during the 1500's to move to pueblos (towns) along the Rio Grande. Numerous cliff houses and caves were built in all of the canyons. Those in the Frijoles Canyon have been the most studied and, in some cases, excavated by archaeologists. The Frijoles Canyon is also the most accessible to visitors and the site of the visitors' center maintained by the National Park Service.

**Archaeological Sites**
A number of important ruins and cliff dwellings are within walking distance of the visitor center.

One of the major ruins in the Frijoles Canyon is just to the east—a large circular pueblo site on the valley floor called Tyuonyi, an Indian name meaning "meeting place." The site includes the remains of around three hundred masonry rooms covered with adobe plaster and built around a large circular plaza nearly one hundred fifty feet in diameter. The rooms are arranged in four to seven concentric rings around the plaza and may have originally been two or even three stories in some sections. Three kivas were dug into the northeast side of the plaza, and a single large kiva has been excavated just down the canyon.

Steep cliffs of tuff with slopes of accumulated rock and debris at the base are found on the north side of Frijoles Canyon. Small houses, known as talus houses, were built for about two miles along the base of the cliff and, together with the caves, were used as dwellings. The longest section of these talus houses, stretching about seven hundred feet, is called the Long House and is considered a typical pueblo cliff dwelling of the time. It is made up of five separate clusters of rooms. Each cluster is believed to have housed a group of related families forming a clan. Fragments of elaborate plaster decorations on Long House walls can still be seen. Also, a large variety of rock art, figures of people and animals, and religious symbols can be found in cave rooms adjacent to many of the talus houses. These petroglyphs were incised into the walls using sets of dots, circles and lines, later colored for better visibility. West of the Long House is a ceremonial cave, a cavern in the north cliff 160 feet above the canyon floor. It contains a kiva and about twenty rooms and can be reached by ladders and a trail cut in the rock.

In addition to these easily accessible ruins, the Bandelier Monument covers some twenty-five thousand acres of parallel canyons separated by narrow mesas that can be reached only by foot and horse trails. This area contains some interesting prehistoric sites such as one with carvings of two mountain lions, which is a sacred shrine to some Indians down to the present day. A few miles from the lions is a large cave known as the Painted Cave, which is covered with colored pictographs. Tsankawi, a separate portion of the monument, is reachable by driving about eleven miles north on New Mexico Route 4. This site includes a pueblo ruin believed to have been occupied during the fif-

*Bandelier National Monument.* (Mark Nohl/courtesy *New Mexico Magazine*)

teenth and sixteenth centuries. This would have been near the end of Indian occupation of the Pajarito, but the site has not yet been intensively studied. In fact, much of the Pajarito Plateau and the Bandelier Monument has not been closely surveyed by experts. Much research remains to be done.

### Departure of the Anasazi

The Anasazi seem to have abandoned Frijoles Canyon and the southern Pajarito Plateau by the early sixteenth century, probably because of drought. The first Spanish explorations of the area in the mid-sixteenth century found little evidence of current Indian occupation. By then most of the Indians had moved to pueblos along the Rio Grande, many of which are still inhabited by descendants of the Bandelier and Pajarito settlers. Spanish colonization began around 1600 C.E. and was characterized by the brutal enslavement of the Indians. The famous 1680 Pueblo Revolt drove the Spanish from New Mexico, although they were back by

the end of the century. Bandelier thereafter saw only occasional Indian settlement by sheep herders and small family groups of farmers and hunter-gatherers.

Some logging was carried out by American companies during the late nineteenth and early twentieth centuries. During World War II, the Los Alamos Laboratory was established a few miles from the Bandelier site. Because of security concerns during the work on the atomic bomb at Los Alamos, the Bandelier Monument was taken over by the army for the duration of the war.

### Adolph F. Bandelier

The importance of the Pajarito Plateau in the search for information about the early Indian culture of the Southwest was originally dramatized by a single remarkable individual. Adolph F. Bandelier was born in Switzerland in 1840 and came to the United States as a boy. He grew up in St. Louis and worked in his father's banking business. Bored by business life, he undertook a new career as an anthropologist and ethnologist at the age of forty. Interested in the Southwest, in 1880 he became the first researcher to study the ruin-filled canyon in Pajarito, which he called Frijoles. Though he lacked academic training, Bandelier was a careful observer with a passionate and somewhat romantic desire to study prehistoric societies. His investigations in New Mexico between 1880 and 1892 led to the publication of his *Journals* and, in 1890, a novel about prehistoric life in the Frijoles Canyon called *The Delight Makers*. The novel was a best-seller and remains in print to this day. The *Journals* remain a useful reference source for Pueblo Indian society and the ancient ruins he studied.

Bandelier's publications helped to inspire the prominent ethnologist Edgar Lee Hewett to take an interest in the Pajarito. Hewett carried out studies and excavations during the years before World War I. Equally important, he was worried about vandalism and the theft of artifacts from the area, and he encouraged the U.S. government to take some action. In 1915 the Department of Agriculture proposed that a national monument be created there, and in 1916 President Woodrow Wilson issued a proclamation establishing Bandelier National Monument. The monument was managed initially by the U.S. Forest Service until 1932, and subsequently by the National Park Service. During the early 1930's the Civilian Conservation Corps, a depression-era federal work program, constructed a visitors' center, a lodge, and, in 1935, a road leading into the monument. Except for the army takeover from 1943 to 1945, Bandelier National Monument has been continuously open to the public. The monument's sixty-five miles of maintained trails and its variety of impressive and significant ruins continue to provide absorbing views of the early Indian culture of the Pajarito Plateau.

—*Bernard A. Block*

**For Further Information:**
Bandelier, Adolph F. *The Delight Makers*. 1890. Reprint. New York: Harcourt Brace Jovanovich, 1971. Of particular interest as a primary source.
_____. *The Southwestern Journals of Adolph F. Bandelier*. Edited by Charles H. Lange and Carroll L. Riley. 4 vols. Albuquerque: University of New Mexico Press, 1966-1984. Written between 1880 and 1892. Another excellent primary source on the area.

Barry, Patricia. *Bandelier National Monument*. Tucson, Ariz.: Southwest Parks and Monuments Association, 1990. A history of the park and of Pueblo Indians. Includes illustrations and maps.
National Park Service. *Bandelier National Monument, New Mexico*. Harpers Ferry, W.Va.: Author, 1941. A somewhat dated but informative and still useful survey of the monument.
Noble, David G., ed. *Bandelier National Monument: Geology, History, Prehistory*. Santa Fe, N.Mex.: School of American Research, 1980. Contains a series of well-illustrated essays on the monument with good coverage of its geologic and cultural history.
Rohn, Arthur H. *Rock Art of Bandelier National Monument*. Albuquerque: University of New Mexico Press, 1989. Offers a scholarly and very well illustrated survey of the remains of ancient Indian rock art. Many of the illustrations are in color.
Stuart, David E. *The Magic of Bandelier*. Santa Fe, N.Mex.: Ancient City Press, 1989. Discusses the anthropological history of Bandelier in some detail, with emphasis on specific sites within the monument. The book is well illustrated with an index and a brief bibliography.

# Chaco Canyon

**Date:** Became a National Monument in 1907; expanded and renamed a National Historical Park in 1980
**Relevant issues:** American Indian history
**Significance:** This large, prehistoric pueblo community, trading center, and ceremonial site flourished circa 900-1180 C.E. The thirty-four-square-mile park contains one of the largest collections of ancient pueblo ruins in the southwestern United States. Chaco Canyon was the hub of a four-hundred-mile network of roads connecting it with numerous outlying communities, usually called outliers. The size and intricacy of its architecture, the sophistication of its agricultural irrigation system, and evidence of artistic, economic, and astronomical endeavors indicate this was an advanced ancient civilization, sometimes called the "Chaco Phenomenon." Abandoned for unknown reasons in the twelfth century, its existence first became

known to the outside world in 1849 when it was discovered by a U.S. Army expedition.

**Location:** Northwestern New Mexico, about 175 miles northwest of Albuquerque; the southern entrance is located sixty-four miles north of Interstate 40 on Route 57

**Site Office:**
Superintendent
Chaco Culture National Historical Park
P.O. Box 220
Nageezi, NM 87037
ph.: (505) 786-7014
Web site: www.nps.gov/chcu/

A millenium ago, an advanced civilization flourished amid the stark desert of Chaco Canyon in northwestern New Mexico. Its people were farmers, pottery makers, and sun worshipers, but above all they were builders. From 900 to 1115, the Anasazi (a Navajo word for "ancient ones") created nine large multistory structures within the canyon, known as the Great Houses of Chaco, plus four more in the immediate area. The largest of these towns, Pueblo Bonito, had more than six hundred fifty rooms and covered three acres in a D-shaped structure. While there are numerous ruins of ancient pueblo dwellings throughout the southwestern United States, the Great Houses of Chaco were unusual because of their high ceilings, intricate masonry patterns, and sheer size.

**Building of Chaco Canyon**
Most of the construction at Chaco Canyon took place between 900 and 1115, with a sudden surge of activity starting around 1075. Construction of Pueblo Bonito, for instance, began in the early 900's, but its east and west wings were added around 1075. These were massive projects, with construction of Pueblo Bonito's east wing alone requiring an estimated 193,000 worker hours. About half of the work involved quarrying sandstone and cutting and transporting trees. Approximately 100,000 pounds of sandstone had to be cut by hand from the nearby cliffs to construct one small room; researchers estimate that one of the Great Houses, Chetro Ketl, required fifty million pieces of sandstone to be cut. Each of the Great Houses also required as many as 200,000 wooden beams for roof support. That the Chacoans were able to harvest sufficient trees for these projects is remarkable,

considering that the nearest forests were at least twenty miles away.

The magnitude of these structures is reflected in early estimates of the peak population of Chaco Canyon. These estimates ranged from 4,400 to 25,000. Recent archaeological studies indicate that many rooms in Chaco's structures were used for storage, not residential purposes, and the population probably never exceeded 2,000. Still, scientists believe there were more people than Chaco Canyon's cropland could support. Numerous sites have been found where turquoise jewelry was made, suggesting that many Chacoans concentrated on craft work that they traded for food and other items brought into the canyon by others.

Besides large quantities of turquoise, excavations have uncovered painted black-on-white cylindrical vases, tools with inlaid decorations, drilled beads, rings, copper bells, and macaw skeletons. Scientists believe that the evidence of metal and macaws shows that Chacoans were trading with people far to the south, in what is now Mexico.

**Chaco Culture**
Chaco also was distinguished by a sophisticated agricultural irrigation system that captured and distributed the area's scarce rainfall and an extensive network of roadways to connect the canyon's villages with dozens of outliers. More than one hundred fifty Great Houses have been identified outside Chaco Canyon, connected to the canyon hub by numerous roads, usually from twenty-six to forty feet across, that run in straight lines for miles with only a few sharply angled "dogleg" turns. The existence of the roads has been known since the late nineteenth century, yet the full extent of the road system was not discovered until the 1970's, when aerial photography was systematically used to find about four hundred miles of roads, only one hundred miles of which are inside the park.

These studies have illustrated that the Chaco culture extended well into what are now Arizona, Utah, and Colorado. Given the widespread nature of Chaco culture, some scientists believe that Chaco Canyon was much more than a place where people lived and goods were stored and traded.

Analyses of trash mounds at Chaco have found a huge amount of broken pottery, suggesting that breaking pots was part of some ceremonial ritual.

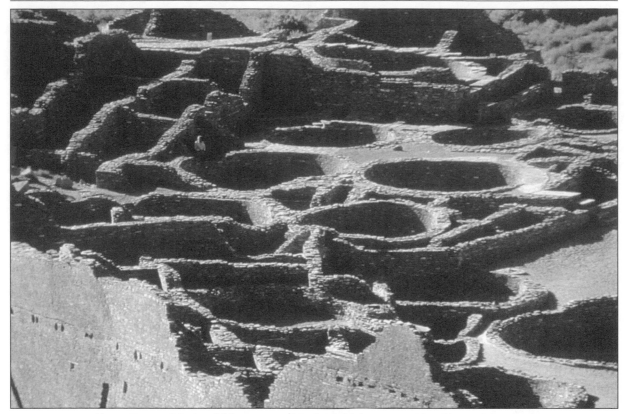

*Chaco Canyon National Monument.* (Mark Nohl/courtesy *New Mexico Magazine*)

Clear evidence of Chaco's importance as a religious or cultural center is shown by numerous circular ceremonial chambers called kivas, including at least eighteen Great Kivas that measure up to 63.5 feet in diameter. These centrally located Great Kivas could accommodate dozens of people, perhaps even the whole town. There were dozens of smaller kivas, including at least thirty-two at Pueblo Bonito alone.

What the Anasazi built here during such a brief period was the center for what is often called the "Chaco Phenomenon," an economic, social and religious system that extended far beyond the canyon and today's park boundaries. The Chaco Phenomenon was the apogee of centuries of human life in the canyon, going back to nomadic hunters who roamed the area five thousand to seven thousand years ago. Around the first century c.e. the population grew larger and more stable as farming developed. By the 600's and 700's, a culture called the Basketmakers developed. These people were known for their basketweaving and pottery. A new

pattern called the Pueblo culture emerged between 750 and 800; this was marked by flat-roofed homes made of mud, rock, and poles. As the population increased during the mid-900's, the buildings became larger and more substantial, with masonry walls and underground kivas. By the late eleventh century, with such structures as Pueblo Bonito, Chetro Ketl, and Pueblo del Arroyo Chaco buildings had reached their maximum size.

Besides the more obvious large ruins, recent studies of the Chaco area have identified more than twenty-five hundred archaeological sites, ranging from prehistoric rock art to small, two-room structures. In the San Juan basin, at least sixteen thousand archaeological sites dating as far back as the Paleolithic era have been discovered, and some scientists believe that this area is the largest archaeological resource in the United States, with an estimated a quarter of a million potential sites. During the ten-year Chaco Project, an intense archaeological survey that ended in 1981, more than 308,000 artifacts were found. These artifacts included 255,000 pottery fragments, 2,254 stone tools, and more than 7,000 ornaments and mineral pieces.

By 1180, Chaco Canyon was largely abandoned, perhaps because of a lengthy drought. It was occupied briefly in the 1200's by people from nearby Mesa Verde and reinhabited in the 1700's by the Navajo, who remain in the surrounding area today. The site was marked on early Spanish maps, probably a mispronunciation of *tse koh*, the Navajo word for "rock canyon." However, Chaco Canyon remained unexplored until its discovery in 1849 by Lieutenant James H. Simpson, a U.S. Army topographical engineer who was surveying Navajo country.

## Archaeological Research

The first major excavations took place in 1896, led by Richard Wetherill, a one-time cow rancher turned archaeologist who discovered the ruins of Mesa Verde, Colorado, in 1888. Financed by Fred and Talbot Hyde, two wealthy New York brothers, Wetherill participated in the Hyde Exploring Expedition, which excavated 190 of Pueblo Bonito's rooms over the next four years. Critics charged that the expedition had vandalized the ruins for profit, and the federal government ordered a stop to the excavation. It is unclear whether the charges were true, but the controversy resulted in passage of the Antiquities Act of 1906 to preserve Chaco and other ancient ruins. The following year, President Theodore Roosevelt signed legislation to establish Chaco Culture National Monument.

In 1921, the National Geographic Society sponsored the first major scientific investigation of Chaco, led by Neil M. Judd, curator of American archaeology at the Smithsonian Institution. He found that the Anasazi had built and rebuilt Pueblo Bonito several times over the years, with four distinct styles of masonry. This expedition also found that nearby Pueblo del Arroyo, 400 feet southwest of Pueblo Bonito, contained 284 rooms and 14 kivas. Pueblo del Arroyo's masonry was similar but the handiwork and materials were inferior to its larger neighbor. "Pueblo Bonito stands today a fitting memorial to its unknown and long-forgotten inhabitants," Judd wrote. "It stands a monument to their primitive genius, to their tenacity of purpose, to their ambition to erect a communal home in which each resident should find

a deep and permanent interest."

During the next forty years, many of Chaco Canyon's lesser ruins were excavated, and a broader understanding of its culture developed. Sites that received attention included Chetro Ketl, a third giant pueblo near Pueblo Bonito. It is shaped like a capital letter *E* with a wall, now almost completely buried, enclosing the plaza within. Its longest side is more than 450 feet and its entire perimeter measures 1,540 feet. Like Pueblo Bonito, Chetro Ketl has intricate masonry, with layers of large stones alternating with small pieces to create a banded effect. One reason Chaco Canyon's masonry is so distinctive is that it was made from a relatively hard variety of rock called Cliff House Sandstone, which could be chipped and ground with precision.

Within the plaza of Chetro Ketl, archaeologists found a huge Great Kiva, averaging 62.5 feet in diameter. It has been called the most important structure excavated north of Aztec Mexico. The base of a timber roof support was still in place, measuring 26.5 inches in diameter. This is the largest log ever found in Chaco, and its presence indicates a significant accomplishment, as the Chacoans had to transport it from miles away by hand. Archaeologists found that this Great Kiva had several more layers under the first terrace, with the original floor 12 feet below the top floor. At this level, they found ten sealed niches in the wall. Each contained turquoise pendants and strings of beads containing a total of seventeen thousand beads.

The largest Great Kiva is on the other side of Chaco Canyon. Measuring 63.5 feet in diameter, Casa Rinconada is the only Great Kiva that stands apart from any of the Great Houses or smaller structures. Archaeologists do not know whether it served the nearby villages or the entire canyon. Its most unusual feature was a 39-foot underground passageway leading into the chamber. This would have allowed participants in whatever rituals took place to enter the kiva without being seen by spectators.

## The Anasazi Calendar

A significant discovery in recent years is that the Chaco Anasazi developed a sophisticated solar calendar, probably for ceremonial and agricultural purposes. Known today as the Sun Dagger, it was discovered in 1977 by Anna Sofaer, an artist from

Washington, D.C. Atop the 430-foot Fajada Butte near the park's south entrance, she found three upright slabs of sandstone, about six to nine feet high, leaning against the cliff. These slabs allow sunlight to pass through in a vertical pattern. Behind them are two spiral petroglyphs (rock carvings) on the cliff; at summer solstice, she found that the narrow shaft of light bisected one spiral's center precisely at noon. Other distinctive light patterns marked the equinox and winter solstice, and it is believed that the Sun Dagger also was used to predict lunar eclipses. Unfortunately, little more than a decade after its discovery, it became apparent the slabs had shifted, and the Sun Dagger no longer accurately marked the summer solstice. Visitors to the site may have caused erosion that allowed the slabs to move, and the site is now off limits to the public.

In 1980, after research showed the Chaco system covered a much larger area than originally thought, Congress passed legislation to protect thirty-three of Chaco's outliers from the area's extensive energy exploration and development. The bill also renamed the canyon and outlying sites as the Chaco Culture National Historical Park.

—*Paul Merrion*

**For Further Information:**

Frazier, Kendrick. *People of Chaco: A Canyon and Its Culture.* Rev. and updated ed. New York: W. W. Norton, 1999. A thorough and highly readable review of Chaco Canyon's ancient history through the eyes of archaeologists who explored its structures and complex social order.

Lekson, Stephen H., Thomas C. Windes, John R. Stein, and W. James Judge. "The Chaco Canyon Community." *Scientific American*, July, 1988. Worth reading for its illustrations, details, and insights is this article by four archaeologists who worked together for more than ten years studying Pueblo Alto and other Chaco Canyon Structures.

Matlock, Gary. *Enemy Ancestors: The Anasazi World with a Guide to Sites.* Flagstaff, Ariz.: Northland, 1988. A more thematic approach is taken by Matlock. He covers the natural environment, culture, and history of the Chaco culture and provides information for visitors interested in serious appreciation of Chaco Canyon and other Anasazi sites in the area.

# El Morro

**Date:** Proclaimed a National Monument on December 8, 1906

**Relevant issues:** American Indian history, European settlement, western expansion

**Significance:** This natural outcropping or mesa of sandstone carries inscriptions dating from prehistoric times to the early twentieth century by people who have lived there and by those who passed by. It is also called Inscription Rock.

**Location:** Forty-two miles from the Grants exit of U.S. Interstate 40 to the site entrance via New Mexico State Road 53; fifty-six miles from the Gallup exit of U.S. Interstate 40 to the site entrance, also via New Mexico State Road 53

**Site Office:**
El Morro National Monument
Route 2, Box 43
Ramah, NM 87321-9603
ph.: (505) 783-4226
Web site: www.nps.gov/elmo/

El Morro thrusts some two hundred feet from the floor of the New Mexican desert and seems solid and stalwart, with castle-like embattlements. At first glance, it looks like the hundreds of other mesas in the U.S. Southwest. However, El Morro is not what it seems to be. It is hollow, actually V-shaped, with a box canyon carved into its center. This canyon can be seen from the top of what has come to be known as Inscription Rock, so named because people, from prehistoric times to about 1906, carved messages into the soft sandstone. Normally, the inscriptions in the sandstone would have eroded away over the centuries, but not at El Morro. This mesa has a cap of hard rock, which has protected the inscriptions to a large degree.

### Mysteries of El Morro

One of El Morro's mysteries is the identity of the prehistoric people who carved petroglyphs, or rock art, of mountain sheep, bear claws, and people into the rock some seven hundred years ago. Another mystery is how they built two fortified villages atop the rock. The only clue as to how they ascended and descended from their stronghold is well-weathered toe holds. The top of the mesa also contains several cisterns that can hold rainwater, but some water must have been carried up from the feature that made El Morro such a well-visited spot: a pool of fresh water in the middle of the desert. The pool is formed from runoff rain and melted snow and is seldom dry. It was on an ancient trail between the Indian villages of Zuñi and Ácoma.

The Zuñi have named the larger mesa-top town A'ts'ina, meaning "writing on the rock." The ruins suggest that the pueblos there rose as high as three stories and enclosed five hundred rooms. Some fifteen hundred people were housed there, and by 1990, sixteen rooms and two kivas, or sunken ceremonial chambers, had been excavated. One of the kivas is unusual because it is square (most extant kivas are round).

## The Anasazi People

The builders of the city are believed by modern archaeologists to have been a people called the Anasazi, hunter-gatherers who moved into the area some two thousand years ago. Even nineteenth century Indians knew nothing of the Anasazi writings. The Anasazi are usually referred to by archaeologists as ancestors or predecessors to the Zuñi and other Pueblo Indian tribes. Today's Zuñi still consider the mesa and its cities as sacred places.

Atop El Morro, the Anasazi gradually changed from hunter-gatherers to middlemen trading with neighboring peoples of the Southwest. The Anasazi themselves grew corn and other products in irrigated fields, harvested the crops, and stored the surplus in sealed rooms in the pueblo. As builders, the Anasazi used the flat sedimentary rock that surrounded them as building materials. A mixture of clay and pebbles was used as mortar. The buildings were cool in summer and warm in winter.

After building the pueblos in the late 1200's, the people left suddenly. Many historians ascribe their flight to a drought that afflicted the area from 1276 to 1299, but the evidence is obscure. The exodus could also have been due to invasion by the Athabascan to the north or by other pueblo peoples.

*Inscription Rock at El Morro National Monument.* (Mark Nohl/courtesy *New Mexico Magazine*)

The pueblo ruins not too distant at Sand Canyon contain burned kivas and the remains of bodies with their skulls crushed.

## The Arrival of the Spanish

By 1517, Spaniards had reached Mexico and Florida; A'ts'ina was soon to bear inscriptions by a new people and receive three new names. The first dated inscription by a Spaniard was made in 1605, but archaeologists believe other, undated Spanish inscriptions preceded it. Some might have belonged to the party of Francisco Vásquez de Coronado, who most likely passed by El Morro in 1540 during his search for the fabled golden cities of Cíbola.

The site first appears in an outside record in 1583 in the journal of Diego Pérez de Luxán, who stopped there twice that year as part of a company led by Antonio de Espejo. He gave the site its first Spanish name, El Estanque del Peñol (the pool by the great rock). The site would be visited by Spaniards again in 1598, when Captain Gaspar Pérez de Villagrá accidently fell into the pool after becoming lost in an October snowstorm. After several days he was found and rescued by his men. Villagrá went on to publish his account of this experience in his verse history, *Historia de la Nueva México*, published in 1610. The story of his encounter with El Morro was also noted by Juan de Oñate, governor of New Mexico, to whom Villagrá was brought after his rescue:

> Captain Villagá arrived, being brought in by three soldiers who had gone to round up horses which the snow storm had scattered and found him almost dead at El Agua de la Peña, without horse or arms, and not having eaten for two or three days.... Only the mercy of God prevented him from perishing.

Oñate thus gave the mesa its second Spanish name, El Agua de la Peña (the water by the rock).

It was Oñate who carved the first known dated inscription at El Morro. It reads:

PASO POR AQUI EL ADELANTADO DON JUAN DE OÑATE DEL DESCUBRIMIENTO DE LA MAR DEL SUR A 16 DE ABRIL DE 1605 (The governor Don Juan de Oñate passed by here from the discovery of the Sea of the South on April 16, 1605)

The Spaniards had been looking for a route from the interior to the "South Sea," or Pacific Ocean, for some time. Historians believe that if Oñate discovered anything on his 1604-1605 expedition, it was the Gulf of California. Many of the subsequent Spanish inscriptions begin with the literary convention *paso por aquí*, or "passed by here."

Some of these inscriptions tell of expeditions to punish or avenge the killings by Indians of priests and Spanish officials. Contrary to Oñate's written orders, Spaniards robbed, killed, and enslaved Indians. The Indians finally rose in rebellion in 1680 and massacred the Spaniards. Twelve years later, the conquistadores returned. An inscription by the commanding general reads, "Passed by here was General Don Diego de Vargas who conquered for our Holy Faith and the Royal Crown all New Mexico at his own expense in the year 1692." Like many conquistador carvings, it contained more bombast than truth. New Mexico was hardly tamed. An inscription dated 1716 reads, "Passed this way Don Feliz Martinez, Governor and Captain General . . . to the reduction and conquest of Moqui [Hopi Indians]." At some point the name of the site was changed to El Morro (the headland).

About 1730, the number of Spanish carvings began to decline, indicating less travel, perhaps because of fear of attacks by Indians. There was a brief spurt of travel and rock signatures in the reign of King Carlos III of Spain (1759 to 1788). After that, the number of inscriptions faded along with the Spanish Empire.

## American Intrusions

The time was approaching for the new invaders: Americans. In 1803 the United States acquired a vast, undefined area known as the Louisiana Territory, bounded roughly by the Mississippi River and the Rocky Mountains. This acquisition brought U.S. surveyors such as Lieutenant Zebulon Montgomery Pike to New Mexico in 1806 to define Louisiana's western boundary. American traders and mountain men had been infiltrating New Mexico for some time. Neither group was welcome by the Spanish or, later, by the Mexicans, who acquired New Mexico when they gained independence from Spain in 1821.

This hostility could explain the ambiguity of the one El Morro inscription of the period: "O. R. 1836." Whoever carved it had the ego to memorialize himself in rock but did not want Mexican authorities to know who wrote it. One mountain man, and later soldier, who probably saw Inscription Rock many times beginning in 1829 was Kit Carson. Someone, possibly Carson himself, inscribed his name on the rock and dated it 1863.

Ten years after the anonymous scout left his initials, the United States and Mexico went to war. In 1848, the Treaty of Guadalupe Hidalgo ceded California and much of the Southwest, including parts of New Mexico, to the United States. El Morro was now U.S. property. The U.S. Army sent expeditions into Zuñi country almost immediately. Lieutenant James H. Simpson of the U.S. Army Topographical Engineers and artist Richard Kern arrived at El Morro in September, 1849. They were so impressed with what they saw that they stayed two extra days copying the inscriptions. Simpson also named the site "Inscription Rock" in his report. Like so many before them, they could not resist the temptation of adding their own mark there. They carved their names in neat, legible letters: "Lt. JH Simpson USA & RH Kern Artist visited and copied these inscriptions, September 17th 18th 1849." (Ironically, they left the letter "R" out of the word "inscription" and had to caret it in afterward.) They are the first known Americans to carve their names upon Inscription Rock.

American soldiers came to El Morro again. In 1857, the U.S. Army Camel Corps arrived. The camel experiment had been planned for some time by Major Henry C. Wayne and Edward ("Ned") Beale. Beale at that time was superintendent of Indian affairs in California, an old friend of Kit Carson, and a lieutenant in the U.S. Navy. He hoped the camels, designed by nature for desert survival, would solve the problem of transporting California-bound Americans across the deserts of the Southwest. Beale's name is inscribed on El Morro, as is that of P. Gilmer Breckinridge, who was in charge of the camels in 1857. Beale had carved his name sometime earlier. The U.S. Army Camel Corps became extinct when Confederate soldiers captured its base at Camp Verde, Texas.

In 1858, two persons on a wagon train took the time to engrave the only names known to be those of women: "MISS A. E. BALEY" and "MISS A. C. BALEY." In 1868, surveyors for the Union Pacific Railroad examined the trail past El Morro but decided on a route twenty-five miles north instead. By

1906, the government declared El Morro a National Monument and prohibited any more "guest signatures."

Today visitors can get acquainted with El Morro at a visitors' center and take two self-guided trails. Inscription Rock Trail passes the carvings at the base, and Mesa Top Trail takes the more energetic visitors to the top. The latter is two miles round trip, steep, and requires sturdy shoes, water, and stamina.
—*James Lahey*

**For Further Information:**

Dodge, Bertha S. *The Road West: Saga of the 35th Parallel.* Albuquerque: University of New Mexico Press, 1980. Mentions many appearances of El Morro in New Mexico history.

*El Morro Trails: El Morro National Monument, New Mexico.* Globe, Ariz.: Southwest Parks and Monuments Association, 1998.

Park, Edward. "El Morro: Story in Stone." *National Geographic*, August, 1957. Covers El Morro.

# Gila Cliff Dwellings

**Date:** Established as a National Monument on November 16, 1907

**Relevant issues:** American Indian history

**Significance:** These five caves were inhabited by the Mogollon people until the thirteenth century.

**Location:** On Route 15, forty-two miles north of Silver City

**Site Office:**
Gila Cliff Dwellings National Monument
Route 11, Box 100
Silver City, NM 88061
ph.: (505) 536-9461, 536-9344
Web site: www.nps.gov/gicl/

Southwestern New Mexico has long been known not only for its beautiful scenery but also for the many archaeological sites that have preserved the rich cultural heritage of pre-Columbian America. The Gila Cliff Dwellings National Monument, situated in the isolated canyon of the West Fork of the Gila River inside the 3.3-million-acre Gila National Forest, is one of these sites. The word "Gila" possibly derives from an Apache word meaning "mountain."

## Early History

The people who inhabited these dwellings and whose culture flourished in the area between 300 B.C.E. and 1300 C.E. have become known as the Mogollon, a name taken from the mountain range on the modern border between Arizona and New Mexico, which cuts through the Gila National Forest. This range in turn was named for Don Juan Ignacio Flores Mogollón, who in the early eighteenth century was governor of the Spanish colony of Nueva Mejico (New Mexico), which then extended to the California coast.

Archaeologists have concluded that the Mogollon culture was closely linked with the Mesoamerican civilizations of Mexico and Central America. These civilizations were the first in the Americas to develop skilled farming and organize highly developed societies. Starting around 3500 B.C.E., their knowledge was transferred into the desert region to their north, where the Cochise people, believed to have been present since approximately 6000 B.C.E., had mostly likely been forced to abandon hunting after exhausting the limited supply of game. The Cochise initially lived among the cliffs and caves of the mountains but later built underground pit houses. It was from the Cochise that the Mogollon were to develop, along with the Hohokam, who farmed along the Gila River between 100 B.C.E. and 1500 C.E., and the Anasazi, who settled in the Four Corners region (Utah, Colorado, Arizona, and New Mexico) between 100 B.C.E. and 1300 C.E.

The rugged mountain villages of the Mogollon were usually located near streams. Using tools made of wood and stone, they cultivated corn, beans, squash, tobacco, and cotton. Their pit houses were built of log frames, set into holes ten to sixteen feet long and two to five feet deep, roofed with reeds, saplings, and mud, and linked to the surface by ramp-like passages. The largest of these houses, now known as kivas from a Hopi word meaning "old house," were mostly used for ceremonies or meetings, or, as has recently been suggested, for steam baths, from all of which women were probably excluded. There were also food storage pits lined with stones to protect against rodents. As the making of pottery jars became widespread, these storage houses became rarer.

The earliest Mogollon pottery, from around 300 B.C.E., was made from coiled and polished clay that turned brown and red when fired. It seems that it was not until between 600 and 900 C.E. that intricate colors and designs were introduced. The most famous of

*Gila Cliff Dwellings.* (Mark Nohl/courtesy *New Mexico Magazine*)

this later type are the black-on-white pots made by the Mimbres, a subculture of the Mogollon, around 900 C.E. Clothmaking was also an important part of the culture; blankets were made from yarn taken from animal fur and cotton.

### The Mogollan, Hohokam, and Anasazi Cultures

The overlap among the Mogollon, Hohokam, and Anasazi cultures has made it difficult to define their distinctive characteristics and their evolution. It is true that they shared agricultural practices, pit houses, and coiled pottery. However, the differences among them can be shown clearly in the development of architecture. In this respect the Anasazi culture seems to have had considerable influence on the other two. The Anasazi began to build above ground after 750 C.E., developing a new style of building using masonry to construct houses several stories high, now known as pueblos (from the Spanish word for "village"). Rather than doors or windows these houses had entrance-holes in their roofs, making the houses secure against attack. Ladders were used to connect each floor. Around 1000 C.E., however, the Anasazi switched to building pueblos inside the cliffs, perhaps because they wanted to protect themselves against raids from other villages.

There is considerable archaeological evidence to suggest that both types of Anasazi dwellings influenced Mogollon architecture once the Mogollon, too, began constructing houses above ground after 1100. According to the tree-ring dating of the roof beams found inside them, the Gila Cliff Dwellings were built around 1280. They consist of five caves, containing a total of forty-two rooms. Earthen roofs were built inside the caves, as well as stone walls that can still be seen today in the larger caves. The T-shaped doors of the dwellings are a strong indication of Anasazi influence.

The Mogollon appear to have used these dwellings for only about twenty years, abandoning them around 1300. It has been suggested that an influx of the Anasazi into the area may have forced many of the Mogollon to move northward, toward the land now occupied both by the Zuñi (descendants of the Mogollon), and by the Hopi (descendants of the Anasazi). During the thirteenth century, the Hohokam and the Anasazi also abandoned their cliff dwellings. One theory suggests that severe droughts starting around 1200 and affecting the whole Southwest region may have forced all three peoples to go farther afield to find better sources of food, perhaps even to return to hunting. A second theory postulates that the Mogollon had to fight for their territory against the Gila and Mimbrenos Apache groups who settled in the Silver Creek area near the Gila Cliffs.

### The Apache

The Apache arrived in the Southwest between 800 and 1000 C.E. from what is now western Canada. They soon adopted farming but did not make much cloth or pottery, tending instead to obtain these items through trade or pillage. Most of their bands lived in wickiups, dome-shape structures made of grass. For four hundred years after the departure of the Mogollon it was the Apache who controlled the area around the cliff dwellings. The Navajo, who arrived in southwestern New Mexico around 1050 C.E., may also have contributed to the mass migration of the cliff dwellers and desert farmers. In 1598 the Spanish explorer Juan de Oñate established the colony of Nueva Méjico (New Mexico). The Spanish inflicted great hardships on their new subjects, who rebelled against them in an uprising known as the Pueblo Revolt and drove them out of New Mexico in 1680, only to see them return in 1692.

The Apache were reluctant to accept the Spanish as their masters but did not join in the uprising. Instead they went on conducting raids on the Spanish settlements and hiding out in the nearby caves, including the Gila Cliff Dwellings. The Apache remained a constant irritant to the Spanish until 1821, when New Mexico came under the authority of a newly independent Mexico. This arrangement lasted only twenty-seven years, until the Treaty of Guadalupe Hidalgo, which transferred the region and its inhabitants, the Zuñi, the Hopi, the Apache, and the Navajo, to the United States. These peoples' understandable suspicion of this occupation by another foreign power turned to outright hostility with the influx of prospectors and miners seeking gold in the Mogollon Mountains during the late 1860's.

From the 1860's to the 1880's chiefs such as Mangas Coloradas, Victorio of the Mimbrenos Apache, and the legendary Geronimo of the Chiricahua Apache led revolts against the Americans. It was during the uprisings of 1881-1886 that

Geronimo and his warriors took refuge in the canyon of the Gila Cliff dwellings. Geronimo had grown up in the area and knew the mountains and canyons well. The Americans managed to quell the rebellions and forced many of the Indians of the Southwest onto the reservations that still exist today.

**Archaeological Research**
From the late 1870's archaeologists began to excavate ruins in Arizona and New Mexico. The archaeologist Adolph F. Bandelier followed the Gila River south from Arizona until he came upon the ruins of the Mogollon dwellings in the Gila Cliffs in 1884. Bandelier concluded that the caves had been inhabited by a group connected in some way to the Hopi or Zuñi. In 1907 President Theodore Roosevelt signed a bill that designated the cliff dwellings as a National Monument. The half million acres surrounding the monument were designated as the Gila Wilderness Area by the federal government in 1924, the first such area of preserved wilderness in the United States.

It was not until the 1920's and 1930's that the inhabitants of the caves began to be seen as a distinct group. The term "Pueblo Indians," which had come to be applied to the Hopi and Zuñi in reference to their traditional buildings, was extended to the earlier inhabitants of the region until the 1930's, when certain archaeologists began to use clearer terminology for each culture. Research carried out by such institutions as the Museum of New Mexico and the Gila Pueblo in Arizona made enormous advances in the study of prehistoric Indians. The archaeologists at Gila Pueblo at this time established concretely the existence of two distinct cultures: the Hohokam, with the largest explored site at Snaketown, Arizona, and the Mogollon of Arizona and New Mexico.

Although the Gila Cliff Dwellings are not as spectacular as the Mesa Verde of Colorado, they are among the few remnants of the region's past to have been preserved. The dwellings have generated insights into a sophisticated culture that flourished more than a thousand years ago, and they can still evoke admiration for a people who survived in an inhospitable terrain without any of the advanced technologies that help to sustain the inhabitants of New Mexico today.

—*Monique Lamontagne*

**For Further Information:**
Chilton, Lance, et al. *New Mexico: A New Guide to the Colorful State.* Albuqerque: University of New Mexico Press, 1984. Provides an informative general history.

Cordell, Linda S., and G. Gumerman, eds. *Dynamics of Southwest Prehistory.* Washington, D.C.: Smithsonian Institution Press, 1989. A collection of insightful essays that highlight the debate among archaeologists about the development of the early peoples of the Southwest.

Martin, Paul. *Digging into History: A Brief Account of Fifteen Years of Archaeological Work in New Mexico.* Reprint. Chicago: Natural History Museum, 1969. A detailed study of a Mogollon site at Reserve, New Mexico, not far from Gila Cliffs. Outlines the way of life of the Mogollon people.

# Los Alamos

**Date:** Atomic bomb tested on July 16, 1945
**Relevant issues:** Science and technology, World War II
**Significance:** Because of its isolation, the federal government in November, 1942, chose Los Alamos to be the site for the construction of the first atomic bomb. The atomic bombs that destroyed Hiroshima and Nagasaki in August, 1945, were assembled there. Since its beginning, the University of California, under contract with the Atomic Energy Commission, has continuously operated at this site in its research in atomic energy. Today, a community has grown up around the Los Alamos Laboratory.
**Location:** An incorporated city and county in north-central New Mexico, situated on a 7,300-foot plateau thirty-three miles northwest of Santa Fe
**Site Office:**
Los Alamos National Laboratory
P.O. Box 1663
Los Alamos, NM 87545
ph.: (505) 667-5061
Web site: www.lanl.gov
e-mail: www-core@lanl.gov

In mid-1942, the U.S. government, hoping to bring an end to World War II, stepped up its efforts to develop an atomic bomb. The military situation looked grim for the United States and its allies in its all-out war with Germany, Japan, and Italy. The country had not fully recovered from the shock of the Japanese attack on Pearl Harbor in late 1941, and Japan was still in control of the Pacific Ocean. Meanwhile, American troops were pinned down in North Africa. Although it had lost important battles at El Alamain in 1942 and Stalingrad in 1943, Germany still looked as if it could win the war.

### The German Bomb Threat

The Allies, moreover, had evidence that German scientists were working on an atomic bomb of their own. The Allies' suspicions were aroused when they learned that Germany had stopped the sale of uranium, a vital element in the bomb, from the rich mines of Joachimsthal, Czechoslovakia, a region under its control. The Allies' fears were confirmed by Albert Einstein, Edward Teller, and Leo Szilard, refugee scientists from Europe, who a few years earlier had written to President Franklin D. Roosevelt, warning of the enormous threat posed by German development of the atomic bomb.

President Roosevelt took the scientists' warning seriously and on October 12, 1939, created the secret Advisory Committee on Uranium. The United States had officially entered the race for the bomb. The committee consisted of three government officials: Lynan Briggs, director of the National Bureau of Standards, and as such, the government's senior scientist; and two other military officers, representing the army's and navy's ordinance divisions. To conduct basic research on the atomic bomb, the committee, on the advice of scientists Szilard, Teller, and Eugene Wigner, acquired four tons of graphite and fifty tons of refined uranium ore.

By 1940, the facts of fission were common knowledge not only to the Germans but to other physicists throughout the world as well. British and American scientists judged it unwise to continue publishing new results. At the urging of Teller, Szilard, and Wigner, the Allies implemented a self-imposed news blackout and began working to develop an atomic bomb to be used in the war.

In building an atomic bomb, the Allies were faced with a major challenge—finding enough uranium, fission's vital material. With the Joachimsthal mines in German hands, the Allies turned to another large source: Belgium's African colony of the Congo. In June, 1940, twelve hundred tons of high-grade ore were transferred by freighter from the Congo via Belgium to New York City and a Staten Island warehouse for storage. Before the war's end, the United States would receive over twenty additional ore shipments from the Congo. The Allies, however, were taking no chances. At about the same time, they began to produce plutonium (Pu-239), which they believed would be superior to the uranium isotope (U-235).

### Building a Bomb

By December, 1942, a Chicago-based group of scientists under the direction of Enrico Fermi succeeded in producing the world's first human-made nuclear chain reaction. There was still no fissionable material for building the atomic bomb because the construction of the plants at which the materials were to be produced had not yet begun.

Additional research also had to be done to supply missing information crucial to making the atomic bomb. Responsibility for the secret research program was assigned to the U.S. Army Corps of Engineers—its code name, "Manhattan Project." Put under the direction of Dr. J. Robert Oppenheimer, the project eventually involved a workforce of over 100,000 persons and took nearly three years to complete. It was located in New Mexico and served, in the words of I. I. Rabi, as "the first line of defense of the United States." This was the beginning of the Los Alamos Laboratory, or Project Y.

Los Alamos Laboratory is located on the Pajarito Plateau of New Mexico's Janoy Mountains. The area's first permanent settlers, mostly farmers, arrived in the area about 1911. It also became the site of a tuberculosis convalescent center, which attracted people from the industrial East. From 1918, the Los Alamos Ranch served as a school for young boys. The school thrived, and by the 1930's it had forty-five students.

### Oppenheimer and Los Alamos

Robert Oppenheimer's summer home was across the valley from Los Alamos, and he would often visit the school. Asked to advise the corps on the selection of the atomic bomb research laboratory a few years later, the noted scientist recommended the Los Alamos site. When the military officials inspected Los Alamos, they concluded that it did indeed offer many advantages. It could adequately accommodate the thirty scientists expected to work on the project, and the land could be easily acquired in secrecy. Los Alamos was large and isolated; experiments could be conducted under secure and safe conditions.

In December, 1942, the U.S. government used condemnation proceedings to close the school. The property had to be vacated by mid-February, 1943. The government appropriated more than forty-five thousand acres from government agencies, mostly the Forest Service, and made plans to buy approximately nine thousand privately owned acres. The residents were never told why they were being forced to move. In all, thirty farm families were evicted and their farmland appropriated.

The U.S. government paid $275,000 for the boys' school. The school's owner, A. J. Connell, thought it was worth at least $400,000, and went to court. At the end of 1943 a federal court ruled that Connell should receive $375,000 and $7,884 in interest. The settlement and the way the government conducted the confiscation made Connell bitter. He later wrote to a former headmaster of the school, "There are many sides to the taking of Los Alamos. They stopped a growing concern in the middle of its operation, which could not be moved."

In January, 1943, the government selected the University of California to operate the laboratory at Los Alamos, and soon after, the university signed a contract with the Manhattan Engineering District of the Army. By early spring the project was ready to begin operation.

**Life at Los Alamos**

Life was difficult for the scientists who took the challenge of developing an atomic bomb at isolated Los Alamos. Security was so tight that not even the scientists' wives were told what their husbands were doing at the laboratory. Housing, moreover, was substandard and always in short supply. As historian Hal Rothman describes the situation,

> Except for the row of home cottages that previously housed the ranch school faculty and had been reserved for the royalty of the world of science, most people lived in green, barracks-like, military-built, four-unit apartments. The water

tower, a fixture in southwestern towns, was the only identifying feature of the community.

There was little in the way of entertainment, never enough water, censorship of outgoing mail, and insufficient telephone lines. The project was surrounded by barbed wire and armed guards. The first resident dentist did not arrive until 1943, while the local hospital was not established until 1944. Oppenheimer later recalled, "The notion of disappearing into the desert for an indeterminate period and under quasi-military auspices disturbed a good many scientists and the families of many more." As Richard Rhodes explains in his book *The Making of the Atomic Bomb,* "The hardships only mattered because they slowed the work. Oppenheimer had sold [the Los Alamos assignment] as work that would end the war to end all wars and his people believed him."

Los Alamos was a place cloaked in anonymity. No one could use the word "physicist," and everyone was known as an "engineer." Famous scientists were given pseudonyms. Niels Bohr, for example, was known as "Nicholas Baker," and Enrico Fermi as "Henry Farmer." During the entire war, all incoming mail was addressed simply to "P.O. Box 1663, Santa Fe, New Mexico."

In this austere setting, the scientific team at Los Alamos set out to design the atomic bomb. The theoretical basis of building a bomb was already understood, but much of the technological work remained. The problem was how to build a bomb that would get its explosive energy from the fusion of either uranium 235 or plutonium 239. To do this, the scientists had to prepare two fissionable core materials. So in 1943 the government began building a separation plant at Oak Ridge, Tennessee. The project took two years to complete. Plutonium gradually became available in small amounts varying from micrograms to grams. By late 1943, the government had decided that the only way it could evaluate the results of an atomic bomb explosion was to test the one being constructed. Too much was still unknown about the weapon. So the government launched what became known as Project Trinity.

**Testing the Bomb**

On September 7, 1944, the committee chose a site near Los Alamos to test the bomb, known as the

*Los Alamos Scientific Laboratory circa 1945.* (AP/Wide World Photos)

Jornada del Muerto (journey of death). Bleak and isolated, Jornada, a part of the Alamorgordo Bombing Range, was located about two hundred miles from Los Alamos. The closest inhabitant lived twelve miles away.

Before the actual bomb was exploded, and to prepare for the real test, the scientists scheduled a smaller, trial explosion using one hundred tons of TNT and one hundred curies of fission products for May 5, 1945. The date eventually had to be changed to May 7 so additional equipment could be installed. The trial run, when it finally took place, was itself spectacular. The orange fireball generated by the blast was seen as far away as the Alamorgordo base ten miles away. Kenneth Bainbridge, Trinity's project director, commented, "No one who saw it could forget it, a foul and awesome display."

Nevertheless, scientists working on the project, including Oppenheimer himself, wondered if the real bomb would work. So many questions still remained unanswered, including the big one: Had anything been overlooked?

In the months following the trial run, plans for the final test proceeded. Observation planes made passes over the test site to simulate the dropping of the bomb. Plutonium was stockpiled. Meanwhile, high-ranking observers began to assemble in New Mexico, including William L. Laurence of *The New York Times*, the sole reporter allowed to document the atomic bomb's development.

The big date for the test was July 16, 1945. General T. F. Farrel, an observer, described the mood as the countdown continued: "The scene inside the shelter was dramatic beyond words. It can be safely said that most everyone present was praying. Oppenheimer grew tenser as the seconds ticked off. He scarcely breathed. He held on to the post to steady himself."

Then at 5:29:45 A.M. Mountain War Time, the bomb exploded, creating a brilliant burst of light and a multicolored cloud that pushed and billowed upward. The light illuminated the landscape. The spectacle was seen in Santa Fe as well as Albuquerque and El Paso. One man thirty miles away in Carrizozo recalled, "It sure rocked the ground. You'd have thought it went right off in your backyard."

It would be weeks before the measurements taken of the test would be corroborated and interpreted, but it was immediately apparent that the test was a success. The Allies now had the power to crush Japan and end the war.

Three weeks after the Trinity test, on August 6, the crew of the bomber *Enola Gay* dropped an atomic bomb on the Japanese city of Hiroshima. Three days later, another Trinity-type bomb exploded near another Japanese city, Nagasaki. Within days, the conflict with Japan had ended. World War II was over, the Cold War was about to begin.

Today at Los Alamos a community has grown around the laboratory where the atomic bomb was built. That laboratory is still operated by the University of California under contract with the Atomic Energy Commission for research in atomic energy.

—*Ron Chepesiuk*

**For Further Information:**

Purcell, John. *The Best Kept Secret: The Story of the Atomic Bomb.* New York: Wingard Press, 1963. An early but still reliable work.

Rhodes, Richard. *The Making of the Atomic Bomb.* New York: Simon & Schuster, 1986. Perhaps the most thorough and reliable book about Los Alamos.

Rothman, Hal. *On Rims and Ridges: The Los Alamos Area Since 1980.* Lincoln: University of Nebraska Press, 1992. Puts the Los Alamos laboratory in historical context.

Schroyer, Jo Ann. *Secret Mesa: Inside Los Alamos National Laboratory.* New York: John Wiley & Sons, 1998. The history of the laboratory and early nuclear weapons research.

# Salinas Pueblo Missions

**Date:** Established as a National Monument in 1980

**Relevant issues:** American Indian history, European settlement

**Significance:** Administered by the National Park Service, this was once a major trading center and is now the site of mission ruins and Indian

pueblo ruins that have survived since the villages were abandoned in the 1600's.

**Location:** Mountainair, one block west of the U.S. 60 and New Mexico 55 junction; about eighty miles south of Albuquerque

**Site Office:**

Salinas Pueblo Missions National Monument
P.O. Box 517
Broadway and Ripley
Mountainair, NM 87036
ph.: (505) 847-2585
Web site: www.nps.gov/sapu/

Salinas Pueblo Missions National Monument, situated in the central New Mexican town of Mountainair, is really three monuments: the ruins of Abó, Gran Quivira, and Quarai stand as reminders of Indian communities that have been abandoned since the 1600's. The region's communities were a bridge between the prehistoric Pueblo Indian cultures and the later cultures that arose from contact with Europeans. The ruins there also bear witness to a combination of styles reflecting the architecture of both the Pueblo Indians and the Spanish Franciscans.

**Early History**

The overlapping of two southwestern Indian cultures in the Salinas Valley planted the seeds for the Salinas Pueblos. Until the tenth century, the Mogollon culture dominated the region, its first dwellers subsisting as hunters and gatherers. At first living in pit houses, they later built aboveground homes known as *jacales*, pole dwellings covered with adobe plaster.

By the late 1100's, the nascent pueblo communities got their start with the arrival of the Anasazi from the Colorado Plateau. Their stone and adobe dwellings were home to the society later discovered by Spanish settlers.

By 1300, the Anasazi culture was flourishing. Their homes developed into large stone complexes surrounding plazas dotted with kivas (round, sunken ceremonial chambers). The villagers' sartorial choices reflected the trade of the time: turquoise and shell jewelry, breech cloths, bison robes, antelope and deer hides, as well as decorative cotton and yucca blankets.

The blending of Anasazi and Mogollon cultures evolved into the Abó, Gran Quivira, and Quarai so-

*Gran Quivira, Salinas National Monument.* (Mark Nohl/New Mexico Economic & Tourism Department)

ley in 1581, Abó was a prosperous community along a passage opening to the Rio Grande Valley. It flourished as a trading post for the Pueblo and Plains Indians, where salt, beans, squash, maize, and pinon nuts were exchanged for hides, flints, and shells. Mountainair at one time was dubbed the "Pinto Bean Capital of the World." By the seventeenth century, the population had swelled to at least 100,000.

In 1598, Juan de Oñate, who eventually became governor of New Mexico, led a group of soldiers to the area to establish a permanent colony. There he came upon a valley dotted with pueblos along the eastern side of the Manzano Mountains. Oñate declared that salt—which was abundant in the region—was "one of the four riches of New Mexico." Salt was valuable worldwide for trading and was a key element for the Spanish in smelting silver. The Spanish named the place Salinas, meaning "salt mines."

Oñate's troops, however, did not make a good first impression: Soldiers riled the Indians by trying to collect from them tribute to the Spanish crown. Once Oñate became governor, he sent his nephew, Vicente de Zaldivar, to lead a troop of men to find the South Sea (the Pacific Ocean). Stopping at Gran Quivira, Zaldivar demanded corn. The villagers gave him stones instead. Zaldivar went onward with his expedition, but he was so incensed that his uncle Oñate rushed to the pueblo with fifty armed men.

Oñate demanded that the residents of Gran Quivira give him their handwoven cotton blankets, and they reluctantly presented about a dozen to him. The next day, the governor ordered his troops to set a corner of the pueblo on fire and shoot at a crowd of residents. In the melee that ensued, at least five Indians died, two men were captured and eventually hanged, and others suffered injuries. Throughout the events, Oñate had been talking through an interpreter. He began to suspect that the translator was not speaking in the best interests of the Spaniards. Although Oñate was not sure, he

cieties. Quarai, now the smallest of the three monuments, was once home to early Indians who made their living through farming and trade. Abó first became the site of Mogollon pit houses around 1150. The community was distinguished by the gray paste pottery they made, which later gave way to the Anasazi's glazed, painted pottery. The early pueblos of Gran Quivira were formed in concentric circles using masonry and mortar work. Another pueblo was eventually built on top of the original rooms.

### Arrival of the Spanish
When the Spaniards first set foot in the Salinas Val-

nonetheless had the interpreter hanged. The initial resistance of the Indians to the Spanish soon gave way to reluctant acceptance.

### Roman Catholic Missionaries

During the 1620's, the Franciscans under Francisco de Acevedo and Francisco Fonte began converting some of the eight hundred residents of Abó. By the end of the decade, the friars had begun constructing the community's first church. The ruins of the San Gregorio de Abó Church are among the few remaining examples of medieval architecture in the United States. The red sandstone and mud mortar ruins are situated on the hilly land of Abó, ten miles west of Mountainair, against the backdrop of the Manzano Mountains. The church walls were supported on one side by two exterior buttresses and a fifty-foot-high bell tower. An Indian kiva was discovered when the mission was excavated. Some believe that Indians had built the kiva surreptitiously but had to destroy it when it was discovered by a Spanish priest.

The mission at Quarai, a village eight miles north of Mountainair, amid cottonwoods and the Manzano Mountain wilderness, was established by Friar Estéban de Perea in the 1620's. In 1630, he and Friar Juan Gutierrez led the pueblo women and children in building the Church of the Immaculate Conception. Today, the red sandstone walls of the church ruins rise forty feet high. The church was adjacent to a monastery, underneath which a kiva was discovered when the structure was excavated.

### Surviving Ruins

Twenty-six miles south of Mountainair is the pueblo of Gran Quivira, once home to fifteen hundred people, making it the largest of those abandoned by the Indians. Only the isolated ruins remain today. The origins of the village's name remain unknown. Oñate named it Pueblo de Las Humanas, or the Pueblo of the Striped Ones, after the Indian residents who had stripes painted on their noses. After it had been abandoned, it was confused with Quivera, the mythic city of gold and silver that Francisco Vásquez de Coronado had sought in vain.

The ruins include two mission churches, the Chapel of San Isidro and the Mission of San Buenaventura. San Isidro was built between 1630 and 1636 and destroyed during an Apache raid about forty years later. San Buenaventura was started in 1659 but was never used or finished. The massive church building stretched 138 feet long, with walls that were 5 feet thick. The writer Charles F. Lummis described the ruins in the late 1800's as "an edifice in ruins, it is true, but so tall, so solemn, so dominant in that strange, lonely landscape, so out of place in that land of adobe box huts, as to be simply overpowering. On the Rhine it would be a superlative, in the wilderness of the Manzano it is a miracle." The ruins are distinguished by their blue-gray limestone. A number of kivas, as well as seventeen house mounds, are at the site. While excavating and repairing the ruins, researchers discovered small reservoirs and ditches used for irrigation.

While the area was burgeoning with trade and construction, tension was escalating with the Spanish settlers—particularly from their attempts to convert the residents to Christianity. The cultural differences between the Spanish missionaries and the Pueblo priests were vast. To the pueblo leaders, the Christian ideal of an individual relationship with one god was incomprehensible. The Pueblo Indians' religious customs—which included costumed dancers sending messages to their various gods—were equally bewildering to the Franciscans. The Spanish banned the native ceremonies, but the Indians continued them in secret. In turn, the Spanish burned and filled some of the belowground kivas where the Pueblo Indians had conducted many of their sacred rites.

### The Pueblos, the Apaches, and the Spanish

Adding to the Pueblos' troubles, the Apaches started pillaging them for food and herds of livestock. The Apaches had become more and more frustrated with the Pueblo Indians, whom they considered accomplices of the Spanish in their ongoing raids among the unconverted Indians for slaves to send south to work in the mines of Mexico.

Despite the tension that had existed between them, during the 1660's the Pueblos joined forces with the Apaches to plan a revolt against the Spanish. The plan was discovered before the uprising could be carried out, and the person who organized it was put to death.

The combination of drought and widespread famine during the 1660's and 1670's devastated the

Salinas pueblos. At Gran Quivira alone, 450 people starved to death. The Spanish settlers had brought with them European diseases that swept through the pueblos, killing off still more of the residents. During the 1670's the Salinas missions and pueblos were entirely abandoned; surviving Indians moved in with relatives in other pueblos. The new church that had been started at Gran Quivira was never finished. The emptying of the pueblos was so sudden that the communities became known as the "the cities that died of fear."

**Pueblo Revolt of 1680**
The friction that had been simmering for so long eventually boiled over into the Pueblo Revolt of 1680, which occured to the north of Salinas and temporarily drove the Spanish out of New Mexico. In the aftermath, the Piro and Tompiro Indian survivors of the Salinas pueblos moved south to El Paso, Texas. There they adopted the culture of their new Indian neighbors, making them the only group among the Pueblo Indians to permanently lose their language and homeland.

In 1821, Mexico wrested control of New Mexico from the Spanish, and governed the territory for the next twenty-five years. The loose reins that Mexico assumed during that period resulted in a surge of raids by the Navajo and other tribes on the Pueblos.

In 1853, Major J. H. Carleton stopped at Abó while on an expedition to the Salinas district. "The tall ruins standing there in solitude, had an aspect of sadness and gloom," he wrote. "The cold wind . . . appeared to roar and howl through the roofless pile like an angry demon."

In 1909, Gran Quivira was proclaimed a National Monument. In 1980, the two state monuments of Abó and Quarai were combined with Gran Quivira as Salinas Pueblo Missions National Monument. The park headquarters and orientation center are situated in the Shaffer Hotel in Mountainair.                              —*Laura Duncan*

**For Further Information:**
Hewett, Edgar L., and Reginald G. Fisher. *Mission Monuments of New Mexico.* Albuquerque: University of New Mexico Press, 1943. Offers a colorful, thorough description of the history surrounding the various monuments of the state. The extremely detailed descriptions of renovations at the end of the book are, however, now out of date.
Jaffe, Matthew. "The Enchanted Road: Las Cruces to Albuquerque." *Sunset* 199 (October, 1997): 34-35. This article describes a back-road route that passes through Salinas Pueblo National Monument.
Kenner, Charles L. *A History of New Mexican-Plains Indian Relations.* Reprint. Norman: University of Oklahoma Press, 1994. Examines the often contentious relations between the Spanish settlers and Indians.
Simmons, Marc. *The Last Conquistador.* Norman: University of Oklahoma Press, 1991. Offers a more detailed look at the expeditions of Juan de Oñate throughout the Southwest.

# Santa Fe

**Date:** Founded in 1610
**Relevant issues:** American Indian history, European settlement, military history, western expansion
**Significance:** Santa Fe is the oldest city to become a state capital in the United States.
**Location:** In the north central part of New Mexico; the capital city is about sixty miles northeast of the state's largest city, Albuquerque, and is ninety miles south of the Colorado border
**Site Office:**
Santa Fe Convention and Visitors Bureau
P.O. Box 909
Santa Fe, NM 87504-0909
ph.: (800) 777-2489; (505) 984-6760
Web site: www.santafe.org

Although Santa Fe, established in 1610, is well known as the oldest city continuously used as a territorial or state capital in the United States, the area actually has a much longer history of civilization. It was populated by various Pueblo Indian villages between 600 and 1425 C.E., but then was abandoned for reasons that are not understood. Actually, archaeologists have found evidence of ancient peoples inhabiting the region just southwest of what is now Santa Fe as early as 3000 B.C.E. to 600 C.E. At the end of this period, these people turned from foraging to farming. This phase of existence of the northern Rio Grande area was called the developmental period and lasted until about 1200. Early sites from this era are scarce, while later sites are more easily found.

### Early History

During the coalition period, from 1200 to 1325, the Santa Fe area underwent a huge growth in population. Archaeologists offer two reasons for this: Some attribute the growth to an influx of people from neighboring areas who left their homes because of climate and cultural changes, while others believe it was due to improved farming techniques and other advances that transpired because of a larger local population. According to historian David Grant Noble, the people began to congregate in larger communities during this period, and their villages featured "multiroom masonry or adobe houseblocks built around plazas and include characteristic round, subterranean kivas."

Next came the classic period, from 1325 until 1600, which was marked by the use of mineral-paint glazes instead of vegetable or organic paint on pottery. The pottery itself was thick and porous, known as biscuit ware. During the early part of this period, the population seemed to thrive and used techniques like gridded gardens and check dams to conserve soil and water. However, in the latter part of the classic period, around 1425, the Pueblo Indians disappeared from the area. Santa Fe was again populated by the Pueblos 250 years later, but Spanish troops promptly ousted them when they arrived to settle the area.

### Arrival of the Spanish

The Spanish settlement of La Villa de Santa Fe in 1610 began with a classic showdown between church and state. This situation was in part set up by the history of ecclesiastical and civil leaders in Spain. As they had viewed their victory over the Islamic Moors to be a holy crusade, so the kings of Spain now saw their conquest of the New World as a holy mission to Christianize the Native American population. Therefore, when Pedro de Peralta set out to found La Villa de Santa Fe, he was accompanied by numerous clergy. Initially, Governor Peralta shared power harmoniously with the local missionaries, at that time led by Friar Alonso de Peinado at their ecclesiastical headquarters in Domingo Pueblo. Trouble began in 1612, when Friar Isidro Ordóñez arrived with twelve new mis-

sionary recruits from Mexico City and claimed to have orders to relieve Peinado of his duties. These orders were later deemed fraudulent, but this discovery was made only after Ordóñez had irrevocably changed the history of Santa Fe.

The first sign of trouble came almost immediately upon Ordóñez's arrival, for he declared he had orders that the soldiers and settlers who wanted to leave could return to Mexico. This announcement was in direct conflict with Peralta's efforts to strengthen the settlement. Ordóñez's plan was to drive Peralta and the government out of Santa Fe so that it could become exclusively the province of the mission, and he tried many tactics to undermine the governor. The next serious dispute between the two men came in May, 1613, when the friar tried to interrupt the governor's annual tax collection of corn and blankets from the Indians because it fell too close to the Feast of the Pentecost. The two men argued over whose authority ruled in the matter; Ordóñez ultimately displayed a document naming him the agent of the Holy Office of the Inquisition for New Mexico and threatened to excommunicate the governor if he did not call off the tribute collection. When Peralta refused, Ordóñez made good on his threat. Later he absolved Peralta, but the incident set the stage for later scuffles.

That summer, Peralta made a failed attempt to banish Ordóñez to the Santo Domingo ecclesiastical headquarters and lost the support of many settlers when another friar ended up shot and wounded in the argument. This scene gave Ordóñez the upper hand, and he and his followers laid a trap for Peralta. When Peralta tried to return to Mexico City to tell the viceroy of Ordóñez's actions, Ordóñez and his men arrested the governor and his entourage. Peralta remained imprisoned for eight months before escaping, but Ordóñez tracked him down and arrested him again.

Finally, after a new governor, Bernardino de Ceballos, was appointed, Peralta was allowed to return to Mexico City, where he reported to Spanish officials his treatment at the hands of Ordóñez. Peralta had papers to prove his accusations, and Ordóñez was summoned to Mexico City and reprimanded. The conflict between these two leaders lay the foundation for continuing trouble between church and state for the next seventy years.

*The Inn at Loretto, Santa Fe.* (American Stock Photography)

### Peralta's Legacy

Peralta left another lasting legacy to Santa Fe. It was under his leadership that the construction of the Palace of the Governors began in 1610. It is the oldest public building in continuous use in the United States. The Palace of the Governors was New Mexico's state capitol until 1860, and Confederate forces used it as their headquarters in 1862. It became the centerpiece of the Museum of New Mexico in 1913.

The Palace of the Governors also was the refuge for the Spaniards during a ten-day siege in the Pueblo Revolt of 1680. The revolt was the culmination of years of Indian resentment over the injustice of the Spanish colonial occupation. On August 10, 1680, the revolt began when the Pueblo Indians killed Friar Juan Baptista Pio. Settlers from the outlying villages fled to Santa Fe or Isleta. The Indian warriors attacked the outlying villages and then moved toward Santa Fe, on whose outskirts they were spotted on August 13.

That day, one of the Indian leaders approached the barricaded walls of Santa Fe and tried to negotiate with the governor, Antonio Otermín, to secure a surrender from the Spaniards. Otermín turned him away and suggested the Indians give up their fight. The rebels began burning the buildings surrounding Santa Fe, and Spanish soldiers left the city's walls to fight back. Soon, the rebels succeeded in cutting off the Spaniards' water and food supply, and the Spaniards were held captive within the city walls for nine days.

On August 20, Otermín convinced the desperate settlers that they had no choice but to fight their way out of the compound. Striking at dawn that morning, the settlers were able to surprise and drive off the rebels, who suffered severe losses. The next day, the people of Santa Fe decided they must abandon their city before the rebels returned; Otermín led more than one thousand men, women, and children from Santa Fe to Isleta. When they arrived, they found Isleta abandoned, too, its townspeople having fled for El Paso. After Otermín and the villagers left Santa Fe, the Indians celebrated by tearing down churches, turning the governor's palace into a pueblo, and washing baptized Indians in soapweed in order to purify them.

### Reconquest of Santa Fe

In 1693, Don Diego de Vargas led a group of one

hundred soldiers, citizens, Indian auxiliaries, and two friars to reconquer Santa Fe. After cutting off their water and bringing up a small cannon and mortar, Vargas was able to convince the natives to make peace. He conducted a ceremonial repossession of the city, but actual reoccupation would come much harder. Vargas requested five hundred settler families to recolonize Santa Fe, but only seventy Spanish families braved hunger and an early winter to approach the villa in October, 1693. As they arrived, it became clear the Pueblo Indians had no intention of vacating their homes. On December 29, 1693, a new battle began. Unlike the Pueblo Revolt, in which Indians from the different pueblos united against the Spanish colonists, this time the Indians were not unified. The Pecos Pueblo Indians joined the settlers against the Santa Fe Pueblo Indians, and the Spanish settlers gained the upper hand. By the next day, the Spanish had seized the villa.

A century later, Santa Fe was still not a city. The 1790 census showed that about half the heads of households were farmers. The census also showed a highly multiethnic society. Spanish heritage was valued; those with pure or mostly Spanish ancestry enjoyed higher social positions. The Spanish developed a complex system of racial classification, known as the *castas*, to categorize those of mixed descent. This castas system was rejected when Santa Fe made its transition from colony of Spain to extension of Mexico in 1821. In that year, Mexican revolutionaries declared themselves independent of the kingdom of Spain. The Mexican government also liberalized or abolished strict Spanish prohibitions on foreign trade. Mexico desired foreign goods, so American merchants brought their trade to Santa Fe and enjoyed brisk sales.

### The Santa Fe Trail

Thanks to this new revenue stream, the Santa Fe Trail opened as an avenue for commerce. It had been established as a route from Santa Fe to St. Louis by a French pathfinder named Pedro Vial in 1792. William Becknell, who became known as "Father of the Santa Fe Trail," brought the first wagon of goods to Santa Fe on November 6, 1822. The American traders enriched Santa Fe not only with their goods, but also by paying custom duties, which supported the area's military efforts.

In May, 1846, the United States declared war on Mexico, dividing New Mexico's loyalties. Although American trade was virtually the region's only business and financial support, New Mexico's governor, Manuel Armijo, was obliged, as a general in the Mexican army, to fight the United States. On August 15, as U.S. General Stephen W. Kearny approached the Apache Canyon with his invading Army of the West, Armijo sent his citizen army to block them and followed them himself the next day with his presidial army. When he got to the canyon, he decided to surrender, and Kearny and his troops marched into Santa Fe to claim it for the United States.

On August 23, Kearny began construction of Fort Marcy behind the Palace of the Governors. One hundred soldiers and thirty-one Mexican brick masons built the ten-sided structure, and within three months it was defensible. At this point, Kearny appointed well-known trader and Taos resident Charles Bent as governor. His tenure ended a few short months later, with his murder on January 19, 1847, by a group conspiring to overthrow the Americans. The Taos Rebellion was put down within days and marked the last time American authority was challenged in New Mexico.

### New Mexico Applies for Statehood

In 1850, New Mexico applied for statehood at the prompting of President Zachary Taylor and other antislavery politicians, who thought New Mexico's lack of slavery could boost the antislavery vote in Congress. Texans, who were proslavery and held that New Mexico was part of their state, prepared to invade New Mexico. The Compromise of 1850 stipulated that both Arizona and New Mexico would be organized as a single territory with no congressional vote. The compromise also said the new territory would not take a stand on slavery until it became a state, which did not happen for another sixty years.

In 1912, New Mexico achieved statehood as the forty-seventh state in the Union, ending sixty-two years of territorial status. Although a minority of the state's 327,301 citizens supported statehood, the minority was active and vocal. It included politicians who aspired to a U.S. Senate seat, land owners who hoped that investors would be lured to the new state and would increase the value of real estate, and some progressive citizens.

## Modern Preservation Efforts

Today, visitors to Santa Fe will see a wealth of remains of the city's cultural and historical past. The Plaza has been the center of life in Santa Fe for almost four hundred years. Other famous sites include the End of the Trail Monument, which honors pioneers who made it to the end of the eight-hundred-mile Santa Fe Trail; the Palace of the Governors, which is now a museum of cultural history; the Museum of Fine Arts and seven other museums; the circular Capital Building; the Chapel of San Miguel, whose foundations were laid in 1610, making it one of the oldest churches in the United States; and the Loretto Chapel. Another famous church is the Chapel of Our Lady of Guadalupe. Built in 1795, it is considered the oldest shrine to the Virgin of Guadalupe in the United States. Equally fascinating are Santa Fe's adobe houses, most of them built in the eighteenth century.

Within one hundred miles of the city, about twenty Pueblo Indian villages show tourists a glimpse of an eight hundred-year-old way of life. The famed Santa Fe Opera is located just north of Santa Fe near the pueblos of the Tesuque and Nambé. It has produced more world premiere performances than any other American opera company. The Indian Market, hosted by the Southwestern Association on Indian Affairs every August, is the nation's largest and most prestigious American Indian art show. —*Lisa Collins Orman*

## For Further Information:

Noble, David Grant, ed. *Santa Fe: History of an Ancient City.* New York: School of American Research, 1989. A highly readable collection of writings by some of Santa Fe's most famous historians and archaeologists.

Simmons, Marc. *New Mexico: A History.* New York: W. W. Norton, 1977. Somewhat drier than Noble's work above but fuller in detail on the city's Spanish and Indian heritage. Together, the books provide a rich understanding of Santa Fe's most famous historical events and an appreciation for the ethnic and cultural diversity of the city.

Wilson, Chris. *The Myth of Santa Fe: Creating a Modern Regional Tradition.* Albuquerque: University of New Mexico Press, 1997. Covers the modern history of Santa Fe and the developments in culture and tourism in the twentieth century.

# Taos

**Date:** Spanish trading post founded in 1615;
**Relevant issues:** American Indian history, art and architecture, cultural history
**Significance:** This artists' and ski resort town in New Mexico was inhabited originally by Native Americans and later by Spanish settlers. The Taos Pueblo has been home to Taos-Tiwa Indians for one thousand years.
**Location:** Northern New Mexico, at the base of the Sangre de Cristo Mountains; seventy miles northeast of Santa Fe
**Site Office:**
Taos County Chamber of Commerce
229 Paseo del Pueblo Sur
Post Office Drawer 1
Taos, New Mexico 87571
ph.: (800) 732-8267; (505) 758-3873
Web site: www.taoschamber.com
e-mail: info@taoschamber.com

At the base of the Sangre de Cristos Mountains in northern New Mexico lies the community of Taos, where Native American and Spanish influences remain strong centuries after the first settlers arrived there. The town's rich history and distinctive culture are still apparent in its terra-cotta colored adobe buildings, restored haciendas, narrow streets, and pueblo dwellings.

## Early History

Paleo-Indians are believed to be the first people to have visited the Taos area, more than nine thousand years ago, passing through after hunting the buffalo that were prevalent in northern New Mexico. Throughout the Taos area there are prehistoric ruins dating from 900 C.E., when farmers and hunters known as the Pit House People permanently settled in the area. The Pit House People were so named because they dwelled in round pits that they had dug into the ground. At first they built storage areas for their crops of beans, corn, and squash, but later expanded the buildings by adding rooms for their families. By 1200 C.E. the Pit House People had started organizing their buildings into small communal dwellings known as pueblos, to avert the constant attacks by Plains Indians for food and slaves, and to serve as a site for trading with other tribes. The Taos Pueblo serves as

*The Old Spanish Mission in Taos.* (Library of Congress)

a reminder of those early settlers; it is one of the oldest continually inhabited communities in the United States, one of New Mexico's nineteen Native American pueblos still in existence.

The pueblo's two main buildings, divided by the Taos River, are believed to have been built sometime between 1000 and 1450 c.e. With adobe walls made of mud and straw, the pueblo has maintained its traditional appearance for hundreds of years. For nearly one thousand years, Taos-Tiwa Indians have lived at the site.

### The Arrival of the Spanish

Europeans first set foot in Taos in 1540, when Captain Hernando de Alvarado was exploring the area for Francisco Vásquez de Coronado's expedition. By 1615, Spanish settlers had founded a trading post in Taos, attracted by the well established Taos trade fairs, abundant water, and timber. For decades Spanish settlers and the Indians farmed and created a system of irrigation using ditches that is still used today.

It was not a peaceful coexistence, however. Under a Spanish program to "civilize" them, the Indi-

ans were forbidden to practice their native religion. Men who were caught engaging in any kind of religious ceremonial were whipped and sometimes killed.

Eventually, tensions erupted into what became known as the Pueblo Revolt of 1680. The battle left some seventy Spaniards dead in Taos, including two missionaries and a number of children. Survivors were driven from the area. The revolt freed the villages of Spanish influence, allowing for a period of peace that lasted twelve years.

In 1692 Don Diego de Vargas conquered New Mexico for Spain, reestablishing colonial rule. Conflict between the Spanish settlers and the natives continued to percolate for the next several years. In 1694, Vargas led a storming of the Taos Pueblo, returning again two years later to quell a revolt by that community.

### Spanish-Indian Wars

The battles between the Spanish and the Indians resulted in the construction of buildings for protection. Many of these architecturally distinctive buildings still stand. For instance, four miles south of town is the Ranchos de Taos, a farming and ranching community that dates back to Spanish settlers of 1716. The hallmark of the area is the San Francisco de Asis Church, which was originally built by the Franciscans in the late 1700's and fortified to ward off raiding Apaches, Utes, and Comanches. With its thick adobe walls, twin towers, and gargantuan buttresses, the church has served as inspiration for the works of Georgia O'Keeffe, Ansel Adams, and other painters and photographers.

## Taos Becomes a Trading Hub

In 1739, French traders and trappers began using Taos as a stopping point for bartering along their way to Santa Fe. That trade with the French helped build up the arms supply of the Comanches and Apaches. Despite a local proclamation forbidding the sale of firearms to Indians, in 1748 Comanches attacked several Taos farms using firearms sold to them by the French. Many lives were lost, and a number of Spanish women and girls were taken captive.

While some Comanches attacked pueblos, others were peacefully bartering goods at Taos. By 1750, the Taos Pueblo had become a hub for Indian trade fairs and the winter home for trappers. Repeated attacks by the Plains Indians caused the population of the Taos valley to drop. There were so many battles during that era that each New Mexican governor's term was marked and recorded by his campaigns against the Indians.

In 1760 and 1761, the Comanches launched a new string of attacks that besieged Taos for several years. The battles left the area abandoned. When Mexico took control of the territory in 1821, a new group of traders flocked to Taos and Santa Fe, giving birth to the Santa Fe Trail. By 1826, Christopher "Kit" Carson and other famous mountain men had made their homes in Taos, attracted by the abundance of beavers for trapping. Still standing and open for public view is Carson's twelve-room adobe home, where he and his wife lived for more than twenty-five years. The living room, bedroom, and kitchen are furnished in the style of the mid-1800's. The adjacent museum is brimming with art and artifacts from early New Mexican history.

When Mexico lost New Mexico to the United States in 1848, the Pueblo Indians at first welcomed the freedom from Spanish and Mexican bondage.

Their friendliness quickly turned into resentment, then outrage, toward the U.S. government.

## Revolt Against American Rule

In 1847, Mexican rebels and Taos Indians launched a revolt. A group of Indians and Mexicans rushed the house of territorial governor Charles Bent, shot him with arrows, scalped him, and left him to die. The adobe home where Bent was murdered has been well preserved and made into a museum that still contains his family's possessions and furniture.

The rebels who killed the governor went on to raid other houses in the Taos area. They tortured and killed as many as twenty Anglo settlers, including the U.S. district attorney. Eventually the rebels met the Army of the West, as it was officially called, in Taos Canyon. During predawn hours at Taos Pueblo, U.S. soldiers blew apart the church where the rebels were holed up, killing one hundred and fifty Indian and Mexican revolutionists. Ten U.S. soldiers had been killed and fifty-two wounded. After a quick, informal trial, leaders of the rebellion were hanged in Taos. The remains of the church where the revolt ended still stand.

## American Settlers

The arrival of U.S. settlers also weakened the Apaches and eventually forced them into accepting living on reservations. The Santa Fe Trail had cut through their terrority, bringing thousands of miners and ranchers into the area. By 1870, the Apaches' farmland was occupied by white settlers. The Apaches responded by turning to the Santa Fe Trail to raid ranches, farms, and wagon trains. They stole the settlers' horses, mules, and burros so they could increase their mobility. The raids earned the Apaches a reputation as the most dreaded warriors of the Southwest.

Under pressure from the U.S. Army and weakened by hunger and tuberculosis and other diseases, the Apaches agreed to live on reservations. Today, the tribe lives along wooded mesas and sagebrush valleys, earning much of its income from gas, oil, minerals, timber, and ranching.

Nestled in the center of the village of Taos is the two hundred-year-old Plaza that is lined by shops and galleries. Near the Plaza is the Taos Inn, a hotel whose adobe walls, antique-filled guest rooms, and hand-loomed rugs typify New Mexican design. Although many works are recent creations of local artists, parts of the inn's structure are nearly four hundred years old.

Because of a number of fires that swept through the city, none of the Plaza's buildings date back earlier than the nineteenth century. A flag continues to fly in the center of the plaza as a symbol of Kit Carson and others raising the Union flag during the Civil War.

## Subjugation of the Navajos

While some have lauded Carson as a hero, the Navajo Indians do not hold him in that regard. In 1863, Carson, made a colonel in the U.S. Army, was assigned to launch a successful battle against the Navajos, ending their reign of supremacy in the Southwest. Rather than risk losing to the strong fighters on their own terrain, Carson decided to starve them out of their home territory. He led his troops and some Ute Indians to wipe out the Navajos' supply of sheep and horses, burn their crops, and cut down peach orchards.

By 1865, the Navajos were slowly starved into surrendering. More than eight thousand had been driven from their homes to march three hundred miles to Bosque Redondo, east of Santa Fe. Many of the elderly Navajos were too weak to make the "Long Walk," as it later became known, and were left to die.

Most of those who survived the journey to Bosque Redondo suffered disease and poor living conditions due to crop failure, undrinkable water, and poor soil. A quarter of the Navajos who had been imprisoned there died. Outrage over the conditions there eventually resulted in the signing of a peace treaty with the Navajos in 1868. The Treaty of 1868 allowed them to return to their old country, where they were granted a 3.5 million-acre reservation.

## Growing Colony of Artists

While the history of Taos is marked by conflict between the whites and Indians, the last century has been distinguished by the influx of artists to the area. In 1898, New York illustrators Bert Geer Phillips and Ernest Blumenschein were traveling to Mexico when a broken wagon wheel took the pair on a detour to Taos. They stayed, and their example provoked a influx of artists; eventually, Taos became a notable artists' colony. The influx of artistic immigrants helped fill the underdeveloped land of northern New Mexico that had for so long been sparsely populated. The low cost of living and picturesque mountains, mesas, and desertland drew scores of struggling artists to Taos, including perhaps the most well-known, Georgia O'Keeffe.

In 1912, the Taos Society of Artists formed and mounted traveling exhibitions that enjoyed international acclaim. The Taos colony, largely painters, flourished until 1942, when the combined forces of the just-ended Great Depression and beginning of World War II brought an end to the organized artist community.

Artists were still lured to the area's mountains, adobe buildings, and wide open land. In 1952, local artists formed the Taos Artists' Association. In the 1990's, the area was brimming with more than eighty art galleries. Taos' cultural institutions, preserved historic buildings, and nearby ski slopes have made it a popular destination for travelers.

—*Laura Duncan*

## For Further Information:

Dutton, Bertha P. *American Indians of the Southwest.* Albuquerque: University of New Mexico Press, 1983. Gives a good overview of historical and more recent tribal affairs, arts and crafts, and distinguishing cultural and social characteristics of the Southwest Indians. Dutton, an anthropologist, tends to describe events with sympathetic leanings toward the Native Americans.

Gattuso, John. *Insight Guides: Native America.* Boston: Houghton Mifflin, 1993. Offers a bit more balanced and certainly a more up-to-date look at the history and contemporary affairs of American Indians.

Gibson, Arrell Morgan. *The Santa Fe and Taos Colonies.* Norman: University of Oklahoma Press, 1983. Concentrates on the influx of artists into the area between 1900 and 1942, the era that has long marked the culture of Taos and Santa Fe.

Hemp, Bill. *Taos: Landmarks and Legends.* Los Alamos, N.Mex.: Exceptional Books, 1996. A guidebook to the Taos region. Includes descriptions of historical buildings and local legends.

Weber, David J. *On the Edge of Empire: The Taos Hacienda of los Martinez.* Santa Fe: Museum of New Mexico Press, 1996. A history of Taos and New Mexico haciendas that profiles the Severino Martinez House (1761-1827).

# Other Historic Sites

## Big Bead Mesa

*Location:* Near Ojo del Padre, Sandoval County

*Relevant issues:* American Indian history

*Statement of significance:* Occupied from about 1745 to 1812, this is an impressive fortified Navajo village site. After moving into the Big Bead Mesa region, the Navajos established a stronghold that menaced the pueblos of Laguna and Ácoma and formed an alliance with the Gila Apaches. The site is an important representative of patterns of trade and raiding that characterized Navajo relations with Pueblos, Apache, and Hispanics.

## Folsom Site

*Location:* Folsom, Colfax County

*Relevant issues:* American Indian history

*Statement of significance:* The archaeological discoveries at this site confirmed theories of the early advent of humans in America.

## Georgia O'Keeffe Home and Studio

*Location:* Abiquiu, Rio Arriba County

*Relevant issues:* Art and architecture

*Statement of significance:* Georgia O'Keeffe (1887-1986) occupies a pivotal, pioneering position in American art. She created her own style by adapting early modernist tenets to quintessentially American motifs. Her stark paintings of cattle skulls bleached by the desert sun are familiar to all. From 1949 until her death, O'Keeffe lived and worked here at Abiquiu. The buildings and their surroundings, along with the views they command, inspired many of her paintings, and continue to provide great insight into her vision. The home and studio are maintained by the Georgia O'Keeffe Foundation and are open to the public.

## Glorieta Pass Battlefield

*Location:* Santa Fe, Santa Fe County

*Relevant issues:* Civil War, military history

*Statement of significance:* In February, 1862, a Confederate brigade of 2,500 Texans marched up the Rio Grande Valley, with the intention of driving through Albuquerque and Santa Fe, and on to Denver; 1,300 federal soldiers moved to intercept them. The armies met at Glorieta Pass in the Sangre de Cristo Mountains. The Battle of Glorieta Pass (March 26-28, 1862) ended a Confederate invasion of New Mexico that threatened to seize a large part of the Southwest.

## Hawikuh

*Location:* Zuñi, Valencia County

*Relevant issues:* American Indian history, European settlement, Latino history

*Statement of significance:* Established in the 1200's and abandoned in 1680, the Zuñi pueblo of Hawikuh, largest of the "Cities of Cíbola," was the first pueblo seen by Spanish explorers. In 1539, the black scout Estevan became the first non-Indian to reach this area; he was killed by the people of Hawikuh as he entered their city. The next year, when the Coronado Expedition reached the fabled pueblo, they found not gold but a small, crowded, dusty sandstone village.

## Lincoln Historic District

*Location:* Lincoln, Lincoln County

*Relevant issues:* Cultural history, Western expansion

*Statement of significance:* This is one of the best preserved of the cowtowns that sprang up along the cattleman's frontier in the years following the Civil War. To it drifted cowboys, badmen, gunfighters, rustlers, soldiers, and famous lawmen; it was the scene of courtroom battles, public executions, and gunfights. Disputes over water, government beef contracts, and grazing rights led to the armed conflict known as the Lincoln County War of 1878, which ended in a three-day gun battle on the streets of Lincoln.

## Mesilla Plaza

*Location:* Las Cruces, Dona Ana County

*Relevant issues:* European settlement, Latino history

*Statement of significance:* Mesilla was founded in 1848 by the Mexican government to bring Mexican citizens from territory recently ceded to the United States into Mexican domain; by the terms of the Gadsden Purchase Treaty (1851), the town became part of the United States. The town retains the flavor of a Mexican village.

## Raton Pass
*Location:* Raton, Colfax County
*Relevant issues:* Civil War, military history, western expansion
*Statement of significance:* In 1821, Raton Pass was "opened" for wagon traffic to Santa Fe by Captain William Becknell. The pass played a crucial role in Brigadier General Stephen Watts Kearny's conquest of New Mexico in 1846, and the Colorado Volunteers' stanching of the Confederate invasion in 1862. From 1861 to 1865 much of the traffic to Santa Fe crossed the Pass, as Confederate raiders and the threat of attack by some Southern Plains Indians halted traffic over the Cimarron Cutoff.

## Seton Village
*Location:* Santa Fe, Santa Fe County
*Relevant issues:* Cultural history
*Statement of significance:* The Village grew up around the forty-five-room "castle" built by Ernest Thompson Seton (1860-1946), artist, author, scientist, and one of America's greatest naturalists. Seton was chair of the committee that brought the Boy Scout movement to the United States; he served as Chief Scout and wrote the first Scout manual.

## Trinity Site
*Location:* Bingham, Socorro County
*Relevant issues:* Military history, science and technology
*Web site:* www.wsmr.army.mil/paopage/pages/trinst.htm
*Statement of significance:* Here, on the bleak and barren desert of the Jornada del Muerto, the world's first atomic device was exploded on July 16, 1945, at 5:29:45 A.M.

## Village of Columbus and Camp Furlong
*Location:* Columbus, Luna County
*Relevant issues:* Military history
*Statement of significance:* On March 9, 1916, approximately 485 Mexican revolutionaries under the command of General Francisco "Pancho" Villa (1878-1923) crossed into the United States and attacked the sleeping border town of Columbus, killing ten civilians and eight soldiers. Without consulting the Mexican government, President Woodrow Wilson ordered a punitive expedition, led by General John J. Pershing, into Mexico to capture Villa and prevent further raids across the international border.

## Watrous (La Junta)
*Location:* Watrous, Mora County
*Relevant issues:* Western expansion
*Statement of significance:* Here, at the settlement of La Junta de los Rios Mara y Sapello, the Mountain and Cimarron Cutoff Routes of the Santa Fe Trail joined. Wagon trains organized here before entering hostile Indian territory. In 1879, the Santa Fe Railroad laid out the present town of Watrous to the east.

## White Sands V-2 Launching Site
*Location:* White Sands Missile Range, Dona Ana County
*Relevant issues:* Aviation history, science and technology
*Statement of significance:* This site is closely associated with U.S. testing of the German V-2 rocket, the origins of the American rocket program, and the leadership of Dr. Wernher von Braun (1912-1977). The V-2 Gantry Crane and Army Blockhouse here represent the first generation of rocket testing facilities that would lead to U.S. exploration of space.

## Zuñi-Cíbola Complex
*Location:* Zuñi, Valencia County
*Relevant issues:* American Indian history
*Statement of significance:* A series of sites on the Zuñi Reservation, containing house ruins, kivas, pictographs, petroglyphs, trash mounds, and a mission church and convent. They have proven to be an important source of material for ethnological studies of the early Zuñi, Mogollon, and Anasazi cultures. They include the Village of the Great Kivas, Yellow House, Hawikuh, and Kechipbowa.

# New York

*The State Capitol Building in Albany.* (New York State Economic Development)

# History of New York

Dominated by the nation's most heavily populated city, New York has been an area of economic and political importance since the earliest years of the United States. Its position between the Atlantic Ocean and the Great Lakes made it a major area of population movement to the west, and New York City attracts emigrants from around the world.

## Early History
The first humans to reside in the area arrived about ten thousand years ago and hunted bison and other large game. Thousands of years later, the culture known as the Mound Builders grew crops in southwestern New York. By the time Europeans arrived in the New World, the Atlantic coast was inhabited by the Mohegans and the Munsees, members of the Algonquian language group. Farther inland resided the Onondaga, the Oneida, the Seneca, the Cayuga, and the Mohawk tribes, members of the Iroquois language group. In 1570, these five peoples united into the Iroquois League, a powerful confederation that dominated the area for two centuries.

## Exploration and Colonization
The first European to visit the area was the Italian navigator Giovanni da Verrazano. Working for the French, Verrazano explored the Atlantic coast from North Carolina to Canada, including New York Harbor, in 1524. The French explorer Samuel de Champlain journeyed from Canada to northern New York and reached Lake Champlain in 1609. The same year, the English navigator Henry Hudson, working for the Dutch, sailed up the Hudson River about as far as the modern site of Albany.

Despite this early exploration, settlement of New York began slowly. The Dutch established Fort Orange, later known as Albany, in 1624 as the first permanent European settlement in the area. The next year they established New Amsterdam, later known as New York City, on Manhattan Island. By 1650, the Dutch colony had about one thousand residents. In 1664 an English fleet sailed into New York Harbor and captured the colony without a fight. At this time the area contained about eight thousand colonists, including Dutch, English, French, Germans, Finns, Swedes, Jews, and African slaves.

The colony was granted by English King Charles II to his brother, the duke of York and Albany, later King James II. After approving a charter adopted by the colonists in 1683, James II revoked it when he became king in 1685. Instead, he united New York and the colonies of New England to the north under a single administration. Strong resistance to the unification of the colonies led to a rebellion in 1689, after a political crisis in England forced James II to abdicate. Jacob Leisler, the leader of the rebellion, controlled New York until 1691, when the new king, William II, sent in a new royal governor, who had Leisler hanged for treason.

The next several decades brought conflict between the French and the English in the area. The French made a number of raids from Canada into central and northern New York, limiting settlement beyond Albany. An important factor in England's ability to retain control of the colony was an alliance with the Iroquois League. The struggle for control of North America led to the French and Indian War (1754-1763), which ended with the English in firm control of New York. The war also weakened the power of the Iroquois League, which ceded much of its land to the colonists.

## Revolution and Population Growth
The British victory in the war encouraged settlement of the area. By the start of the American Revolution (1775-1783), New York had a population of 163,000. About one-third of the battles of the Revolution took place in New York. American forces under Ethan Allen captured Fort Ticonderoga, in the northeastern part of the colony, in 1775. The British captured New York City in 1776 and recaptured Fort Ticonderoga in 1777. One of the most important events in the war took place in New York on October 17, 1777, when British general John Burgoyne surrendered his army at Saratoga, between Fort Ticonderoga and Albany. This American victory, often considered the turning point in

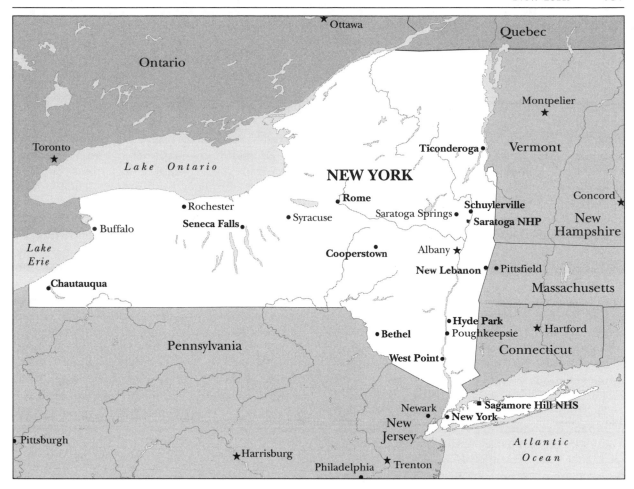

the Revolution, helped bring France into the war against the British.

New York adopted it first state constitution on April 20, 1777, with Kingston, located between Albany and New York City, as the first state capital. After the war, New York City served as the capital of the United States from 1785 to 1790. It became the most populous city in the nation in 1790. New York officially became the eleventh state of the Union in 1788, when it ratified the U.S. Constitution. The state capital was moved to Albany nine years later.

Migration to the state from New England made New York the second most heavily populated state in 1800 and the most heavily populated state in 1810. The opening of the Erie Canal between the Hudson River and Lake Erie in 1825, linking New York to new territories in the west, contributed to the state's rapid growth.

**The Civil War and Tammany Hall**

New York abolished slavery in 1827 and was a center of the antislavery movement. Although the state was firmly on the side of the Union during the Civil War (1861-1865), violent draft riots in New York City in 1863 led to two thousand deaths, including those of many African Americans. Despite this crisis, the war was generally good for the state's growing economy.

Meanwhile, New York City became a stronghold of political corruption with the rise of Tammany Hall. This group had been founded in 1789 to represent the interests of the middle class against the policies of the Federalist Party. It later evolved into an organization that dominated the Democratic Party in New York City, giving it control of the city government. Tammany Hall reached its greatest power in the middle of the nineteenth century, when William Marcy "Boss" Tweed took control in

1857. Tweed stole millions of dollars from the city treasury. Tammany Hall lost much of its power when Tweed was arrested in 1872, but it continued to have an influence in city politics well into the twentieth century.

### Economic Growth and Immigration

New York's position as one of the most economically important states in the nation began soon after statehood. Dairy farming, long the most important agricultural activity in the state, was established before the American Revolution. Poultry and egg production, as well as fruit and vegetable farming, also began at an early date. Such agricultural pursuits would remain important parts of the state's economy.

Investment and finance, which began with the founding of the New York Stock Exchange in 1817, would remain centered in New York City's Wall Street. The textile industry began in the 1820's. International trade was also established at an early date, with New York handling half of the nation's imported goods as early as 1831.

The first railroad in the state was completed in 1831. The growth of the New York Central Railroad Company throughout the nineteenth century was a major factor in the rise of industry in the state. After the Civil War, during the so-called Gilded Age, rapid economic growth created many millionaires and led to the founding of nationally important companies such as Westinghouse, General Electric, and Eastman Kodak.

Meanwhile, the first of many waves of immigration brought large numbers of Germans and Irish to New York in the 1840's. During the late nineteenth century, new residents from around the world arrived, particularly from eastern and southern Europe. New York's Ellis Island was the center of immigration in the United States from 1892 to 1943.

Large numbers of African Americans began to arrive in New York during World War I, followed by an even larger number during and after World War II. New York's African American population rose from less than 5 percent in the early 1940's to more than 20 percent by the end of the century. During the 1950's and 1960's, large numbers of Puerto Ricans arrived in the state. Later decades brought an increase in immigration from Asia and the Middle East.

### The Twentieth Century

New York, long dominant in national politics, began a new era with the election of Franklin Delano Roosevelt as governor in 1928. Roosevelt's policy of increased government spending on social services, particularly after the stock market crash of 1929 and the Great Depression, continued when he served as president of the United States from 1933 to 1945. This trend continued in New York City after World War II, leading to a financial crisis in 1975, when federal funds of $4.5 billion were needed to protect the city from bankruptcy.

In 1970 California surpassed New York in population. Between 1970 and 1980, New York was one of the few states to decrease in population. Despite a decline in manufacturing during the same decade, the rise of service industries led to economic growth in the late 1970's and 1980's. This growth came to a sudden halt in late 1987, when a stock market crash led to a recession. In addition to economic problems, New York City faced an increase in racial violence in the late 1980's and early 1990's. Although New York City managed to improve its image as a center of crime and poverty in the late 1990's, it still faced numerous challenges in the twenty-first century.
—*Rose Secrest*

# Brooklyn Bridge

**Date:** Officially opened on May 24, 1883

**Relevant issues:** Art and architecture, science and technology

**Significance:** The Brooklyn Bridge is the first suspension bridge in history to use steel cables, thus heralding the use of steel as a building material and setting the stage for the development of the skyscraper in the twentieth century. It made possible and inevitable the consolidation of New York and Brooklyn—at that time separate cities—into the nation's greatest metropolis. Signaling the shift from rural to urban society, it has served as the source of inspiration for many artists and writers and has become a cultural symbol of the American ideal of progress and industry.

**Location:** Spans the East River between downtown Manhattan near City Hall and downtown Brooklyn's Civic Center

**Site Office:**
New York City Department of Transportation
40 Worth Street
New York, NY 10013
ph.: (212) 442-7033
Web site: www.ci.nyc.ny.us/calldot

Though the history of the Brooklyn Bridge can be said to begin with the dream of its designer, German-born engineer John Augustus Roebling (1806-1869), the idea of a bridge linking the separate cities of New York and Brooklyn was proposed before Roebling was born. As early as 1800, Jeremiah Johnson, later a general in the War of 1812, expressed an interest in seeing a bridge built on the East River. By 1811, the feasibility of such a structure was promoted by Thomas Pope. In his *Treatise on Bridge Architecture* (1811), the freelance builder proposed a kind of cantilevered arch that could be suspended over a large expanse of water. Pope was convinced that such a project was feasible based as it was on purely mathematical principles. The main problem with Pope's idea was the use of the traditional building materials of the era: wood and iron.

As technology advanced in the nineteenth century, however, new materials became available. The era of wood was passing, and a technological revolution was beginning to replace the heavy, inflexible iron with stronger, more tensile steel. John Augustus Roebling came at the right time to take advantage of the change.

**The Builder**
Born in Muhlhausen, Germany, in 1806, Roebling studied engineering and graduated from the Royal Polytechnic Institute of Berlin in 1826. Influenced by the idealism of the philosopher Georg Wilhelm Friedrich Hegel (1770-1831) and his doctrine of self-realization and personal freedom, Roebling took a job as assistant engineer, hoping to build a new type of bridge he had been reading about. During the three years he worked in Westphalia, a German province, however, he was not given the freedom to pursue his interests. Too much bureaucracy and too many restrictions prompted him to immigrate to the United States in 1831. In America he felt he would be free to build what he wanted.

Ironically, his first enterprise in America was not as an engineer but as a farmer. He and a group of fellow immigrants bought land near Pittsburgh, Pennsylvania, and established a farming community named Saxonburg. In 1837, however, Roebling became a naturalized citizen and returned to engineering. By now the civil engineer was becoming a favored professional as American society became dependent on more efficient transportation systems like canals and railroads. Private construction companies were proliferating to fill the need.

By 1840, Roebling was working as a civil engineer surveying portage railroads, which connected waterways when mountains blocked passage through canals. By this system, trains were hauled up a mountain or similar obstruction by means of a stationary engine at the top. Strong ropes attached to the engine pulled up the cars. The ropes, however, made of hemp, often frayed and broke. The system was thus expensive and often dangerous. Applying his idea of a new type of bridge to the system, Roebling designed cables made of twisted wire, which was stronger, lighter, and more durable than twisted hemp.

By the late 1840's, Roebling had sold the farm and moved to Trenton, New Jersey, on the Delaware River, where he designed and manufactured his own cable on his own machines in his own factory. He was also building bridges.

His first great bridge—and the prototype of his masterpiece—was the Niagara River Bridge, completed in 1855. Spanning the river just below the falls, the bridge was a two-level suspension-type able to support a railroad. With it, Roebling became the most important and best-known masterbuilder of the suspension bridge. As an engineer, he was honest, demanding, and eminently practical. He had proven that such a bridge was both technologically and economically sound. It was large enough to allow great ships to pass beneath and, because it was anchored to both sides of the river, it kept the waterway clear.

With the completion of the Niagara River Bridge, John Augustus Roebling's defining achievement as an engineer was about to be launched. The popular account suggests that the idea of building the Brooklyn Bridge came to him one winter day when he found himself stranded for a long time on a ferryboat on the East River clogged with ice. Such scenarios were not all that uncommon. Bad weather, especially in winter, often kept commuters—particularly those who lived in Brooklyn but worked in

Manhattan—at home. Commerce between the two cities often came to a standstill. Since Brooklyn was situated on Long Island, it was commutable only by boat, and goods were more expensive on both sides of the river. Sensing a growing economic need and aware of the possibility of meeting it, Roebling wanted to construct a "parabolic truss," a suspension bridge that would throw a steel wire span across the river. Supported by granite towers on each side of the river, the bridge would he able to carry pedestrians by means of a walkway and, more important, it could allow the passage of goods and people by means of a roadway and a railway system.

Throughout the late 1850's, Roebling promoted his idea largely by letters to newspapers and influential businessmen and politicians. Though the idea gradually began to take hold, the advent of the Civil War in 1861 put a temporary halt to the plan. After the war, in 1865, the New York Bridge Company was formed and John Augustus Roebling, the bridge's staunchest and ablest supporter, was made chief engineer of the project in 1867.

In the master plan that he submitted to the company board, Roebling emphasized the stability and safety of the bridge made possible by his introduction of a system of triangular stays, or trusses, supporting the steel cables that would hold up the sixteen hundred-foot span of roadway. The bridge would not fall, he predicted, even if the main cables snapped. The roadway, in turn, would be strong enough to bear high winds and the demands of commercial traffic, especially trolleys and a railroad. The entire span would weigh approximately five thousand tons.

The towers that anchored the span drew conflicting reactions from architects and critics. Some saw them as aesthetic failures because of the eclectic nature of the design: elongated gothic arches cut into the block of rough-textured granite. Others viewed the functional nature of the design as being softened by the arches. In this view, the arches incised into the masonry emphasized the traditional building style, while the steel wire span attached to the towers bespoke the style of the modern era. The bridge was seen as a synthesis of stone and steel, a kind of "cathedral of industry."

*The Brooklyn Bridge.* (PhotoDisc)

## The Builder's Son

John Augustus Roebling was not to see his dream fulfilled. While surveying a site on the Brooklyn side of the river, he was struck by an oncoming ferryboat. His leg was pinned against the pilings and was shattered. Within a few weeks he contracted tetanus and suffered a slow, painful demise. He died on July 22, 1869.

His son, Washington Roebling, was now entrusted with bringing his father's work to fruition. The young Roebling had graduated as an engineer from Rensselaer Polytechnic Institute in 1857 and immediately started working with his father. He was working closely with him on the practical design elements of the Brooklyn Bridge, and it was natural that he should take over the project.

Washington Roebling did more than merely carry out his father's design. Certain practical problems had to be overcome during the day-to-day operations, and the younger Roebling designed some methods of preparing the site of the bridge itself. From the first day of actual digging, January 2, 1870, Roebling supervised the lighting and ventilation system of the caissons—huge, watertight chambers (about ten feet high by fifty feet square) into which air was pumped and within which the workers could dig the footing under the river. These pneumatic caissons were a relatively new innovation, and Roebling himself had gone down into the caissons, notably on the Brooklyn side where the first footings were to be.

It was while helping to put out a fire in one of the caissons in December, 1870, that Roebling first contracted "caisson disease," commonly known as "the bends," a condition characterized by intense muscular pain and respiratory problems. His attacks worsened over a period of three years as he spent many days and nights supervising the work in the caissons. By 1873, he was a virtual invalid. For the next ten years he supervised construction from his bedroom window in his house in Brooklyn. Looking through a telescope and binoculars he dictated orders to his assistants. He even trained his wife Emily who, besides acting as courier, became his on-site eyes and ears and his most valuable assistant.

From the first day when actual digging began to the opening day ceremonies, the Brooklyn Bridge took thirteen years and five months to build.

## Places to Visit

Many of the cultural and historical areas of New York City can be seen on foot. Starting on the Brooklyn side of the bridge, one can walk to the section known as Brooklyn Heights, a fashionable part of the borough. Well-maintained brownstones and large, elegant homes and churches sit along quiet, tree-lined streets that remind one of what life must have been like in the late nineteenth century. Located in the borough are the homes of some great American writers, such as the poet Walt Whitman, who lived there while he was editor of the newspaper *The Brooklyn Eagle*, and twentieth century novelists such as Thomas Wolfe and Truman Capote.

Walking over the Brooklyn Bridge is one of the unique experiences of life in New York City. From the pedestrian walkway just above the traffic lanes, one can see the entire lower bay, including the Statue of Liberty, the skyscrapers of lower Manhattan, and the ships and private small boats that ply up and down the East River.

On the Manhattan side, City Hall sits at the foot of the bridge. From there one can explore the downtown area, including the financial district and such places as the New York Stock Exchange on Wall Street. Near the beginning of Broadway is historic Trinity Church, built before the American Revolution and in whose churchyard rests the grave of Alexander Hamilton. Nearby is Federal Hall where George Washington took the oath as president. Down by the battery—the southern tip of Manhattan—is Fraunces Tavern where Washington bade farewell to his troops at the end of the Revolution.

Farther uptown, following Broadway, is a series of ethnic conclaves including Chinatown, the largest of its kind in the Western Hemisphere. Little Italy, on Mulberry and Mott Streets, lies adjacent to Chinatown, and beyond are blocks of iron-fronted buildings and former tenements characterizing the district known as the Lower East Side. Many of New York's immigrants lived in this district during the nineteenth and early twentieth centuries.

—*Edward Fiorelli*

## For Further Information:

Ellis, Edward Robb. *The Epic of New York City.* New York: Coward-McCann, 1966. Chapter 29 provides an excellent discussion of the building of the bridge. Written in a very readable, popular style.

McCullough, David. *The Great Bridge.* New York: Simon & Schuster, 1972. The most comprehensive account of the building of the bridge. Highly detailed, replete with information from primary manuscript sources and contemporary newspaper accounts.

Mann, Elizabeth. *Brooklyn Bridge: A Wonder of the World Book.* New York: Mikaya Press, 1996. A monograph presenting a clear, concise account geared mainly toward younger readers.

Trachtenberg, Alan. *Brooklyn Bridge: Fact and Symbol.* Chicago: University of Chicago Press, 1965. Discusses the history of the bridge as a cultural symbol of American ideals.

Weigold, Marilyn E. *Silent Builder: Emily Warren Roebling and the Brooklyn Bridge.* Port Washington, N.Y.: Associated Faculty Press, 1984. Deals mainly with Washington Roebling's wife and her life before, during, and after the construction of the bridge.

# Central Park

**Date:** Work on the site began in 1857; first phase opened in 1858

**Relevant issues:** Art and architecture, cultural history, social reform

**Significance:** Central Park was the first artificially landscaped public park in the United States. Its success helped establish landscape architecture as a legitimate vocation and cemented the career of its designers, Frederick Law Olmsted (1822-1903) and Calvert Vaux (1824-1895). First opened in 1858, the park has provided an outdoor refuge, recreational facilities, and cultural events for New York City's residents ever since.

**Location:** Mid-Manhattan, bordered by 60th and 110th Streets and Central Park West and Fifth Avenue

**Site Office:**
Central Park Conservancy
The Arsenal, Central Park
New York, NY 10021
ph.: (212) 315-0385
Web site: www.centralparknyc.org

With over eight hundred acres of lush green lawns, sparkling ponds, and shaded walkways, Central Park has provided New York City dwellers with playing fields, bridle paths, bicycling and jogging trails, and winter skating and sledding since just before the American Civil War. Viewed by some as a pastoral retreat and by others as a haven for crime, the park has often been the center of controversy. Nevertheless, it remains one of New York City's major attractions, visited by over twenty million people annually.

### Park Origins

Early nineteenth century New York City was a maze of streets and alleys and a jumble of commercial and residential buildings that many considered an unattractive place to visit or live. In the 1840's, to help counter that reputation, city residents began to debate the merits of constructing a large public park. In 1811, the city had designated 450 acres for park squares, but by 1838, that acreage had been reduced to 120. Many of New York's wealthy families traveled extensively in Europe, where cities like London and Paris boasted beautifully landscaped parks. These New Yorkers, eager to overcome America's reputation for boorishness and rough living, adopted many European customs. In the hope of establishing their city as an international cultural center, many of them also began to advocate the development of a park like those they enjoyed in their travels.

In an 1844 editorial in the *New York Evening Post,* William Cullen Bryant (1794-1878) suggested such a park. Mayor Ambrose Kingsland formally proposed the idea in 1851, when he asked the city council to appropriate public funds to purchase Jones Woods, 150 undeveloped acres bordering the East River between 68th and 77th Streets. Andrew Jackson Downing, a prominent landscape architect and the editor of the respected gardening journal, *Horticulturalist,* protested that this site was too small and suggested instead a park of at least 500 acres. In 1853, after months of debate, the state legislature authorized the city of New York to acquire more than 700 acres in the center of Manhattan, to be paid for with a combination of general taxes and an assessment on nearby property owners.

The land chosen for the new park lay between Fifth and Eighth Avenues and stretched from 59th

*Central Park.* (NYC & Company Convention and Visitors Bureau)

Plan. Their plan called primarily for a pastoral landscape in the English romantic tradition, that embraced nature's wilderness—albeit often artificially constructed out of the park's rocky, swampy land. It also included, however, several more formal gardens such as the Mall and Bethesda Terrace. Designed to be a place where city dwellers could forget their urban surroundings, the plan included borders of trees to hide the city from view. Four sunken transverse roads that allowed crosstown traffic to travel through the park undetected further excluded urban intrusions. Pedestrian, vehicular, and equestrian traffic streams within the park were innovatively separated by a clever series of bridges and tunnels that allowed park goers to move without interruption throughout the grounds. In April, 1858, the commission chose Olmsted and Vaux's Greensward Plan from thirty-three entries as the official design. With few exceptions, it has served as the blueprint for the development of Central Park ever since.

With a design in place, work on the park began in earnest. The commission named Olmsted as chief architect and appointed Vaux as his assistant. Following on the heels of the nationwide financial Panic of 1857, construction proved a boon to the local economy by providing jobs to nearly twenty thousand workers. The site underwent a massive transformation. Workers blasted and removed rocks, drained swamps, and spread tons of fertilized topsoil. By 1873, when the park was finished, nearly five million cubic yards of organic material had been moved into or out of the park. Planting also took place on a monumental scale, with workers setting in place countless hardy perennials and between four and five million trees and shrubs, representing over six hundred varieties.

to 106th Street. In 1859 this original site was enlarged to include the land between 100th and 110th Streets, bringing the park's total acreage to the present 843. The site was predominantly uneven, rocky, and swampy. Except for Seneca Village, a mostly African American settlement on the west side of the proposed park, it was primarily home to the city's castoffs—squatters and immigrants who farmed, raised pigs, and boiled bones. In 1855, the city began the task of evicting and compensating these people in preparation for work on the site. In 1857, the state legislature appointed the first Central Park Commission and charged it with the development of the park. Shortly thereafter, commission members hired Frederick Law Olmsted, a journalist, as the park's first superintendent. His primary duty was to oversee the clearing of the future park's grounds, which began on August 12, 1857.

### The Greensward Plan

In October, 1857, the newly created commission offered a two-thousand-dollar prize in a competition for the park's design. Olmsted and Calvert Vaux, an English-born architect, decided to collaborate on an entry they called the Greensward

**Evolution of the Park**

The park opened in phases; the first users were ice skaters on the partially filled Central Park Lake in December, 1858. Walking paths on the Ramble, a beautifully and intricately landscaped hillside just north of the lake, opened in June, 1859, and the first of several sections of park roads opened in November of that year. During construction, and for the first several years of operation, users could only enter the park during official hours through one of eighteen gates, each guarded by a gatekeeper. Olmsted, who had strong views about how the park should be used, compiled several rules and regulations that were posted prominently throughout the park. They included restrictions against walking on any grassy area not labeled as a commons and allowing dogs to run loose. In order to enforce these regulations, he organized and trained a special force of park guards. These heavy restrictions, while widely enforced in the park's early years, were slowly removed or revised in the last third of the century. When the park first opened, for example, boat rentals, music, and beer sales were all banned on Sundays. By 1877, however, the last of these Sabbath restrictions was lifted when concerts were at last permitted on Sunday, the only free day for many of the city's working-class citizens. By the end of the century, Olmsted's special park guard had merged with the metropolitan police force, turning the park into just one more city jurisdiction.

Many of these changes were the work of the Tammany machine that controlled New York City politics in the 1870's. The Tweed Charter, passed in 1870, transferred the supervision of the park from the Board of Commissioners to a new board under the authority of the city's Department of Public Parks. While the new system's more flexible attitudes encouraged more people than ever to use the park, they also neglected much needed park maintenance. Olmsted, forced out of his position in 1878 after several disagreements with the new commission, expressed his disgust over park deterioration and the politicization of its control in an 1882 pamphlet entitled *The Spoils of the Park*. Vaux's resignation from park management in the next year signalled the end of an era for Central Park.

From the first days of construction, debate over what kind and how many buildings to allow in the park has been frequent and heated. Olmsted and Vaux, who believed that the park should contain few buildings, included only a few structures, all designed by Vaux: the Ball Players' House (1869), the Dairy (1870), the Workshops (1871), a stable (1871), and Belvedere Castle (1871). With the exception of Belvedere Castle, which was built to grace the more formal grounds of the Mall, each of these buildings provided a specific service to park goers or workers. In subsequent years various other buildings have been proposed and their merits debated. Significant additions to the park include the zoo, the Metropolitan Museum of Art, and the Tavern on the Green. Playgrounds, tennis courts, ice skating rinks, and the Delacorte Theater have also been completed. The only building left standing today that predates the park is the 1848 Arsenal at 64th Street and Fifth Avenue, saved by the Greensward Plan for museum space.

Since the end of the Olmsted/Vaux era, the park has endured a series of declines and renewals. Vaux's one-time partner and successor, Samuel B. Parsons, Jr., shared much of the designers' vision. After his 1911 departure, the park began a serious decline. Park grounds suffered as maintenance became careless; several varieties of trees and shrubs disappeared throughout the next several decades. During the Great Depression, the city allowed the unemployed to build squatter colonies within park boundaries. When Fiorello La Guardia (1882-1947) became mayor in 1934, he appointed Robert Moses (1889-1981) as park commissioner, a post he held until 1960. Moses provided much needed stability and continuity to park management, and during his tenure, the park was largely restored. During the second half of the twentieth century, despite a brief period of decline in the 1970's, a well-maintained, beautifully restored Central Park, provided a natural refuge to an ever more crowded Manhattan.

**Visiting the Park**

Despite the political infighting, the disputes about correct park usage, and the roller coaster of decline and renewal, the public has always enjoyed Central Park. Some of the most visited sites include the Sheep Meadow, a vast green lawn popular for picnics and sunbathing that derives its name from the sheep that grazed there until 1934. The nearby Sheepfold, a building designed by Jacob Wrey Mould and built in 1870, housed the sheep at

New York • 805

night. After their departure, the building was remodeled and became the famous Tavern on the Green. Strawberry Fields, a tribute to John Lennon, who lived in the renowned Dakota apartment building across from the park's west side, also draws large crowds. The Carousel, a popular attraction since 1870, still rings with the shouts of happy children. The formal gardens, including the Mall and the neighboring Bethesda Terrace, remain favorites with the park's many visitors. Free stage productions and concerts are offered frequently in the summer at the Delacorte Theater and the Great Lawn.

While it is best to avoid the park at night, except for planned events, the gates are no longer in place and the park is open at all times. Good maps and guidebooks are widely available and should be consulted by first-time visitors. —*Jane Marie Smith*

**For Further Information:**

Beveridge, Charles E., and David Schuyler, eds. "Creating Central Park, 1857-1861." In *The Papers of Frederick Law Olmsted,* Vol. 3. Baltimore: The Johns Hopkins University Press, 1983. A well edited compilation of Olmsted's voluminous reports and correspondence. Includes an informative introduction and biographical directory of key participants, as well as much of the Greensward Plan, the original design for the park.

Kinkead, Eugene. *Central Park, 1857-1995: The Birth, Decline, and Renewal of a National Treasure.* New York: W. W. Norton, 1990. Kinkead, a writer and editor at *The New Yorker* for nearly 60 years, provides an insightful overview of the evolution of the park.

Putnam, Karen, and Marianne Cramer. *New York's Fifty Best: Places to Discover and Enjoy in Central Park.* New York: City & Co., 1999. Putnam, president of the Central Park Conservancy, and Cramer, a former Central Park planner and landscape architect, provide a guide to both popular and lesser-known sites in the park.

Reed, Henry Hope, and Sophia Duckworth. *Central Park: A History and A Guide.* New York: Clarkson N. Potter, 1967. Reed, a former curator of the park, offers an occasionally biased insider's overview of the park's history from its conception through the mid-1960's.

Rosenzweig, Roy, and Elizabeth Blackmar. *The Park and the People: A History of Central Park.* Ithaca, N.Y.: Cornell University Press, 1992. An award-winning, comprehensive social history of the park and its development. Considered by many scholars to be the seminal work on the park's history.

"Welcome to Central Park." www.centralpark nyc.org. A wealth of information including a history, photos, schedule of events, and contact information.

# Chautauqua

**Date:** Established in 1874; constructed mostly from the 1870's to the 1920's

**Relevant issues:** Education, religion, social reform

**Significance:** This National Historic District and National Historic Landmark is listed on the National Register of Historic Places. The 750-acre enclosed educational institution and residential community was built on the site of an old Methodist camp meeting. The residential and public buildings are in a variety of styles ranging from Victorian to Art Deco.

**Location:** Complex in southwestern New York, bounded by Chautauqua Lake, North and Lowell Avenues, and New York State Route 17-J

**Site Office:**
Chautauqua Institution
P.O. Box 28
One Ames Avenue
Chautauqua, NY 14722
ph.: (800) 836-2787; (716) 357-6200
fax: (716) 357-6369
Web site: www.chautauqua-inst.org

Tucked into the southwestern corner of New York State lies an institution that President Theodore Roosevelt reportedly described as being "typical of America at its best." For more than a century, the Chautauqua Institution has been a popular, influential, and eclectic center of learning, culture, and recreation. Its summer programs in the fine and performing arts, philosophy, religion, current events, sports, and other disciplines have long attracted national and international audiences to hear the words and works of noted instructors and performers. Providing the backdrop for

*The Chautauqua Institution.* (NYC & Company Convention and Visitors Bureau)

high ceilings, wide verandas, and wicker outdoor furniture.

Chautauqua's public buildings, constructed mostly between the 1870's and the 1920's, are primarily brick and stone structures that reflect a wide variety of styles. At Chautauqua's cultural and geographic center is the 5,500-seat amphitheater, built in 1893 and still home to many of the institution's performances and special events. Other public structures of note are the Italian-style Miller Bell Tower, which was built in 1911 and still chimes every quarter hour; the art deco Norton Memorial Hall, built in 1929, one of Chautauqua's more "modern" structures; and the Hall of Philosophy, built in 1903, an open-air auditorium that serves as the site of many of Chautauqua's lectures.

this unique educational oasis is a charming turn-of-the-century community in an idyllic setting along the shores of Chautauqua Lake.

Today, the Chautauqua Institution continues its tradition of rich and varied programs, annually welcoming more than 180,000 visitors to its nine-week seasonal schedule of performances, classes, and special events. The 750-acre enclosed complex, bounded by fencing and the lake shore, also serves as home to 7,500 permanent residents.

### Architecture

Architecturally, Chautauqua features a mixture of residential and public buildings interspersed among parks and informal open spaces, with many buildings constructed along narrow, automobile-free, tree-lined streets. Its Victorian era charm has been well preserved, earning the institution designations as a National Historic District and a National Historic Landmark, as well as a listing on the National Register of Historic Places.

Chautauqua's closely spaced turn-of-the-century residences—affectionately referred to as "cottages"—are mostly two-story frame houses with pastel gingerbread appointments. These and other vintage structural elements can also be found proudly displayed at the Athenaeum Hotel, a sprawling architectural grand dame known for its

### Early History

The history of Chautauqua is as rich and diverse as its programs and architecture. Founded in 1874 as a summer training assembly for Sunday school teachers, Chautauqua quickly evolved into an institution with a broader scope and agenda. To a certain degree, this evolution occurred because conditions at the time made such growth favorable. To an even greater degree, however, the institution's expansion and development resulted from the vision of its two founders, Lewis Miller and the Reverend John Heyl Vincent. To understand how Chautauqua came to be what it is today, one needs some background on the impact of these influences.

In the years following the Civil War, the United States was at a turning point in its development as a nation. With the war over and westward settlement nearly complete, the nation was leaving behind its nearly hundred-year-old childhood and adolescence, heading at last into young adulthood. Many Americans had finally moved beyond their preoccupation with simply "putting down roots." Indeed, these once-fragile roots had begun to take hold and grow as the nation's onetime-frontier communities began evolving into established population centers.

Because people no longer had to worry as much about mere day-to-day survival, they had more free time. As a result, their thoughts and attention began turning to other matters. Particularly important was a new hunger for knowledge. Likewise, there was a growing desire for entertainment and recreation. Developed as the nation was becoming, however, its educational system and entertainment outlets had not kept pace. So the question became, how were these needs to be fulfilled?

### The Chautauqua Movement

A newfound interest in the nation's spiritual institutions was also beginning to develop. The horrors of the Civil War caused many to seek refuge in the stability offered by religion. This development, in turn, prompted increased interest in religious education. As with secular education, however, inadequate structures were in place to address this need. Thus a push for Sunday school reform began sweeping the nation.

It is in the light of these conditions that one must examine the impact of Miller and Vincent in their establishment of Chautauqua. Their innovative ideas not only helped to address America's new needs but also led to the birth and growth of their beloved institution.

Lewis Miller was a successful inventor, manufacturer, and businessman from Akron, Ohio. He was also a devoutly religious man. He served as superintendent of the Sunday school program of his hometown parish, the First Methodist Church of Akron, and even designed its Sunday school building. In addition, Miller was a trustee of the Chautauqua Camp Meeting Association, which sponsored a popular religious revival each summer at Fair Point, New York, a Methodist campground on the shore of Chautauqua Lake and later the site of the Chautauqua Institution.

John Heyl Vincent was a young, zealous Methodist minister who had a strong aptitude for teaching, even at an early age. During his initial postings, he began to incorporate some experimental and unorthodox approaches in his Bible study and Sunday school classes. For instance, Vincent used maps to provide a geographical context to sites of important biblical history, and he also sometimes conducted his classes in relaxed outdoor settings.

These methods, unusual though they were, quickly became popular and garnered the attention of church leaders, who appointed Vincent general agent of the Methodist Sunday School Union. Upon assuming his new post, however, Vincent discovered that there was an inadequate number of knowledgeable, properly trained instructors available to fill all the vacant Sunday school teacher slots. To fill these vacancies and help promote uniform instruction, Vincent envisioned the development of a standardized approach to training Sunday school teachers, a method similar to those used for training public school teachers. Soon local institutes for Sunday school teacher training began springing up, but Vincent saw them as limited in duration and scope. He believed there had to be a better way.

The plans for a better way began taking shape when Miller and Vincent finally met. Miller enthusiastically embraced Vincent's ideas, and the two set out to put them into practice. First, there was a desire to overcome the inherent shortcomings of the local institutes by conducting training for a more extended period at a centralized location. To help make this plan more attractive to would-be participants, Miller proposed using one of the innovations Vincent employed in his early classes—that of holding the event in a relaxed, natural setting. With that in mind, the duo set out to find a suitable location.

Miller's affiliation with the Chautauqua Camp Meeting Association provided an established connection to a suitable site. So it was that Fair Point was selected as the meeting location. The first Sunday School Teachers' Assembly was held in 1874, and Chautauqua was thus on its way to being born.

### Selection of Chautauqua's Site

Prior to the first assembly, Vincent was admittedly reluctant about Miller's site suggestion. Vincent took a more scholarly approach to religion than was practiced in the camp meetings of the time. Specifically, he objected to the extreme emotionalism that characterized such events. He did not want the influences of a camp meeting intruding upon his training assembly, and he was concerned that people might unwittingly come to associate his program with an event that he so strongly disliked. By giving the program a different name and an agenda significantly different than one would find at a camp meeting, Vincent and Miller believed they could adequately differentiate their event.

Perhaps the main difference between the assembly and a camp meeting was the content of the program. Miller and Vincent clearly established the assembly as an outlet for Sunday school teacher training and not as a religious revival. More than that, the duo proposed distinguishing the assembly by incorporating programs that covered more than just theological issues. Specifically, Miller and Vincent sought to include recreational activities and secular educational programs. While these influences were not readily apparent in the first assembly, they were added in subsequent years and quickly became an integral part of the summer program.

In part, Miller and Vincent decided to include recreation and secular education as attendance incentives; after all, such programming helped meet the nation's growing demand for these activities. Moreover, Miller and Vincent's decision reflected an important view they both held dearly: that instruction in worldly topics and activities necessarily had to coexist with religious education programming. It is because of this outlook that Chautauqua evolved into the institution it later became.

**Early Success**
The success of the first assembly launched Miller's and Vincent's brainchild into a period of explosive growth even they had not anticipated. To help sustain their fledgling institution, Lewis Miller and John Heyl Vincent charged a gate fee to visitors entering the enclosed Fair Point compound, a practice that remains in effect to this day. The fee did not appear to hinder attendance. Thanks to an ever-expanding schedule of educational and recreational programs—made possible by the funding provided by the gate fee—Chautauqua quickly became a vacation destination for thousands. Whether they traveled over land or by steamboat up the twenty-two-mile-long Chautauqua Lake, they came in droves to take part in the Chautauqua experience.

In 1877, the community of Fair Point legally changed its name to Chautauqua. In the years that immediately followed, the community embarked upon a major expansion program that would earn Chautauqua a reputation as an institution synonymous with the concepts of educational enrich-

ment, enlightenment, and tolerance. In fact, over the next quarter century, what had begun as a twelve-day training program conducted under canvas tents would expand into a full-fledged, eight-week summer school offering more than two hundred courses taught in a variety of permanent buildings. Individuals who subscribed to this way of life and learning came to be known as "Chautauquans," regardless of whether they resided in or even visited the upstate New York facility. In short, Chautauqua had become a truly American phenomenon.

The first courses added at Chautauqua covered topics related to the program's original curriculum, such as biblical history, biblical geography, and Hebrew. By 1879, five years after the first assembly, courses in secular topics were added, such as languages and public education. Not long thereafter, additional courses were developed in history, music, and science.

As Chautauqua's reputation spread, so did its impact on American education. Some of this impact resulted from programs whose reach extended beyond the institution's grounds. The most notable of these was the Chautauqua Literary and Scientific Circle (CLSC), established in 1878. This reading and discussion group was established to provide members with a well-rounded education in a broad variety of topics. Its four-year program, complete with examinations and the chance to earn a diploma, made the CLSC a sort of "everyday college," as Vincent once termed it.

**Spread of the Movement**
What set the CLSC apart most from other programs was that it was not confined to the institution's grounds. Rather, reading groups under the CLSC aegis were established in communities across the country. With an initial enrollment of 8,400—far in excess of Vincent's expectations—the CLSC quickly grew, and within twenty years, there were nearly ten thousand groups in existence throughout the United States and Canada.

The success of the CLSC prompted the development of similar programs, such as a series of correspondence courses. These courses were dropped in 1900, however, as colleges and universities, drawing upon the Chautauqua model, began developing similar programs, usurping the role Chautauqua once played in this form of education.

Not all of Chautauqua's programs involved education. As a popular vacation destination, it developed extensive recreational activities. With its lakeside location, Chautauqua was an ideal spot for boating, fishing, and swimming. Other diversions included croquet, lawn tennis, and cycling. By 1886, interest in physical education had grown so strong that a school devoted to it was established. The most popular sport at Chautauqua in the 1880's and 1890's was that new American pastime, baseball. Chautauqua's contingent in this endeavor was captained by a young Yale University divinity student who would one day gain renown in the sports world, Amos Alonzo Stagg.

Indeed, famous people were becoming commonplace at Chautauqua. Well-known and respected speakers began flocking to Chautauqua to present lectures on various topics. Initially these lecturers came primarily from religious quarters, but soon Chautauqua was attracting educators from great American universities, famed authors, noted scientists, social reformers, and political leaders. Even Presidents Ulysses S. Grant, Rutherford B. Hayes, James A. Garfield, and Theodore Roosevelt could not resist the draw of Chautauqua.

**Expansion of Facilities**

As Chautauqua's programs grew and expanded, so did its need for facilities. In 1879, the first amphitheater and hall of philosophy were dedicated; these structures were later replaced by newer facilities (in 1893 and 1903, respectively) that bore the same names and still stand today. Two years later, the Athenaeum Hotel, considered by one author "comparable to the best summer resort hotels of the day," opened for guests. This was followed in 1886 by the Pier Building, which welcomed visitors arriving by boat—for years as often as every hour—until its replacement by a newer structure in 1916. Various educational halls followed, as did the CLSC Alumni Hall, opened in 1891.

Permanent residences began springing up, too. The old camp meeting tents were quickly replaced by clapboard cottages. Down by the waterfront, the cottages took on somewhat more lavish form, described by one author as "sprawling summer homes with landscaped lawns." Some of these homes were owned by famed industrialists of the era, such as Henry Heinz and Clement Studebaker. With the coming of these more permanent residences, Chautauqua began to develop its own modern infrastructure, including electric lights, paved walkways, a water works, and modern sanitation.

In any successful endeavor, imitators are sure to follow, and Chautauqua was no exception. Within a few years of the assembly's founding, traveling and permanently settled "chautauquas" began springing up around the country. The imitators genuinely seemed to be establishing their programs more out of emulation and respect for the original institution than as a means to profit from its innovations. In fact, many of the imitators sought and received the advice and assistance of Miller, Vincent, and their growing team of colleagues. However, Chautauqua maintained no official relationship with these upstart entities, other than some CLSC chapter affiliations.

Why did the new chautauquas arise? In large part, they came about as the result of the difficulty of travel at the time. Although transportation had improved markedly by the 1880's and 1890's, travel was still difficult, and Chautauqua's somewhat remote location did not make the pilgrimage any easier. Thus the new chautauquas arose to help fulfill the education and entertainment needs of those unable to make the journey to upstate New York.

**New Locations**

Some of the new chautauquas had permanent locations, such as Winona Lake, Indiana; Bay View, Michigan; Lakeside, Ohio; and Boulder, Colorado. By the turn of the century, between one hundred fifty and three hundred such institutions had been established. However, as one historian wrote, establishing a permanent chautauqua required "initiative, vision and capital," and few communities had all three at their disposal. For this reason traveling chautauquas evolved to help bring education and entertainment to communities that otherwise could not afford them.

Few of the imitators enjoyed the success, notoriety, and influence of the original institution, which some came to affectionately call the Mother Chautauqua. Many imitators flourished well into the 1920's, but over time most faded from the scene, with only a few left by the 1940's.

As the United States headed into the twentieth century, the nation's world view began to enlarge. Such events as the Spanish-American War, the U.S.

annexation of Hawaii, and the Klondike gold rush caused Americans to turn their attention toward matters other than themselves. Meanwhile, social reform movements at home, such as those involving women, labor, and juveniles, gave Americans challenges to face in their own backyard.

### The Movement in the Twentieth Century

In light of all these new developments, the time had come for Chautauqua—which had successfully developed a reputation for addressing what was on the cutting edge of the American mind—to respond. It did so by sponsoring programs that covered these topics and featured noted speakers. In 1902, for example, Chautauqua presented a weeklong program on social settlement issues, highlighted by an address given by Jane Addams. Similarly, in 1907, Chautauqua hosted a conference on social unrest. True to the Chautauqua tradition of promoting tolerance, the conference featured presentations by both old-line conservatives and Socialists.

Interest in world affairs grew markedly with the onset of World War I, and Chautauqua again responded. Neutrality and preparedness were frequent lecture topics, as evidenced in an address given by a young assistant secretary of the navy named Franklin D. Roosevelt. The institution's bookstore was also fully stocked with publications addressing the new overseas crisis.

Although current events have continued to this day as an important part of Chautauqua's programming, the end of the war freed Chautauqua to refocus its attention on subjects for which it had become best known. One area that benefited greatly during this period was musical programming.

### Music and New Programs

Music had been a part of Chautauqua's curriculum from nearly the beginning, but it experienced some of its greatest advancements during the 1920's. In 1920 and 1923, for example, the New York Symphony presented concert series that extended throughout much of the Chautauqua summer season. In 1926, the Rochester Opera Theater presented a repertoire of Gilbert and Sullivan operettas and other works. In 1929, the institution established the Chautauqua Symphony Orchestra and the Chautauqua Opera, both of which still perform today.

The 1920's saw other developments, too, such as an aggressive building program. In 1924, Chautauqua marked the opening of Smith-Wilkes Hall, the Hall of Missions, and a summer school dormitory. In 1929, the art deco Norton Memorial Hall was opened as the site of many of Chautauqua's musical and theatrical performances.

By 1932, the nation's economic realities had caught up with Chautauqua. The Great Depression was having its impact. Crowds began to decrease, and by the close of the 1933 season, it was unclear whether there would be a 1934 season. The massive debt that Chautauqua had taken on to finance its construction program, coupled with declining revenues from visitor attendance, left Chautauqua financially strapped. So the institution went into receivership.

### Rejuvenation During the Great Depression

In 1934, there was renewed hope for Chautauqua. The Chautauqua Reorganization Corporation was established to raise funds to clear the institution of its debt of $800,000. Friends and followers rallied to the cause, launching a sweeping "Save Chautauqua" campaign that helped the institution become financially sound by 1936. A year later, the Chautauqua Foundation was established to ensure the institution's perpetuation and to avoid the financial troubles of the past.

In later decades Chautauqua continued the traditions it established during its founding years. The crowds still come to hear the lectures, attend the concerts, and take advantage of the many recreational opportunities. It also continues its world affairs programming, having sponsored a series of five widely heralded conferences on U.S.-Soviet relations during the 1980's. Of particular note was a 1987 conference that brought two hundred Soviet families to Chautauqua to live with American families for a week.

Chautauqua may not be a typical American resort, but for those who relish the past, seek diversity, and continue to adhere to Reverend Vincent's belief that "education ends only with life," this uniquely American institution is without equal.

—*Brent Marchant*

### For Further Information:

Campen, Richard N. *Chautauqua Impressions: Architecture and Ambience.* Reprint. Chagrin Falls,

Ohio: S. W. Campen, 1997.

Gould, Joseph Edward. *The Chautauqua Movement: An Episode in the Continuing American Revolution.* New York: State University of New York, 1961.

Irwin, Alfreda L. *Three Taps of the Gavel: The Chautauqua Story.* 3d ed. Chautauqua, N.Y.: Chautauqua Institution, 1987.

Kostyal, K. M. "An Enduring Tradition." *National Geographic Traveler,* May/June, 1993. An exploration of present-day Chautauqua.

Morrison, Theodore. *Chautauqua: A Center for Education, Religion and the Arts in America.* Chicago: University of Chicago Press, 1974.

Noffsinger, John S. *Correspondence Schools, Lyceums, Chautauquas.* New York: Macmillan, 1926. Examines the history, content, and impact of these three American educational movements. A clear but brief history of the "traditional" Chautauqua facility is presented, along with discussions on such "modern" alternatives as the CLSC and the traveling chautauquas.

Orchard, Hugh A. *Fifty Years of Chautauqua.* Cedar Rapids, Iowa: Torch Press, 1923. Provides a detailed history of the Chautauqua imitators that arose in the years following the original institution's founding. The opening chapter provides a clear, concise history of the New York State facility's establishment, while subsequent chapters provide comparable accounts of the namesake entities that arose in Chautauqua's wake.

Richmond, Rebecca. *Chautauqua: An American Place.* New York: Duell, Sloan and Pearce, 1943. A comprehensive history of the Chautauqua Institution up to the time it was written. Although occasionally flowery in its tone and lacking in its presentation of certain facts, the book nevertheless provides a thorough treatment of the subject.

Simpson, Jeffrey. *Chautauqua: An American Utopia.* New York: Harry N. Abrams/Chautauqua Institution, 1999. A history of Chautauqua Institution.

Vincent, Reverend John Heyl. *The Chautauqua Movement.* Boston: Chautauqua Press, 1886. Includes an introduction by Lewis Miller. Libraries with comprehensive historical collections may contain this work written by Chautauqua's founders. Features an account of Chautauqua's early days in the words of those innovators who started it all.

# Cooperstown

**Date:** Incorporated in 1786

**Relevant issues:** Cultural history, literary history, sports

**Significance:** A graceful, well-kept village in the northern Catskill Mountains, Cooperstown was the home of writer James Fenimore Cooper, and the town and surrounding area provided the setting for two of his novels. Cooperstown also is the site of the National Baseball Hall of Fame and Museum, which draws about 400,000 visitors a year. Within the city limits are three other museums—Fenimore House, dedicated to Cooper and local history; the Farmers' Museum and Village Crossroads; and the Larry Fritsch Baseball Card Museum. Just outside of town are the Cherry Valley Museum, illustrating life in the area in the eighteenth and nineteenth centuries; the Corvette Americana Hall of Fame; and the Petrified Creatures Museum of Natural History.

**Location:** On the south shore of Otsego Lake in central New York, approached by Route 28 from the south, Route 80 from the north, and Route 20 east to west, all rural two-lane highways; approximately seventy miles due west of Albany, thirty miles south of the New York State Thruway, and two hundred miles northwest of New York City

**Site Office:**

Cooperstown Chamber of Commerce Information Center

31 Chestnut Street

Cooperstown, NY 13326

ph.: (607) 547-9983

fax: (607) 547-6006

Web site: www.cooperstownchamber.org

e-mail: info@cooperstownchamber.org

One cannot help but wonder how a town this small wound up with so many museums. Only about 2,000 people live in Cooperstown, and no more than 2,800 have ever lived there at a time, yet within the village itself are four museums and three more are located nearby. Somehow, the New York State Historical Society, with many more populous and popular places from which to choose, has picked Cooperstown for its headquarters. Protecting the past is one of Cooperstown's major industries. Though many large cities could say as much about the past, few have profited from it so well.

## Early History

This passionate interest in Cooperstown's history could be said to have begun in 1823 with the publication of *The Pioneers* by James Fenimore Cooper. It was a history of Cooperstown disguised as a novel. The town was only thirty-three years old (three years older than Cooper himself), but it was already looking back in wonder.

Cooper's father, Judge William Cooper, bought the land on which he founded the town at a sheriff's sale in 1785. At that time there was nothing but wilderness and game for miles around. Little was known about the land besides the name of its previous owner—George Croghan—and not much besides a hut remained from his tenancy. During the American Revolution, the Continental Army under the direction of General James Clinton had built a rough road to Lake Otsego, and a dam where the lake fed the Susquehanna River. George Washington had toured the area. Otherwise, there was no sign of humans having ever lived there.

Humans had lived there—arrowheads and burial mounds have been discovered in the area—but no other record of their stay remains, except for the tales told by the son of the founder. Judge William Cooper incorporated the town in 1786, and brought the rest of his family to the wilderness from New Jersey in 1790. James was a year old.

There were fifty others living in Cooperstown in 1790, when Judge Cooper sold off forty thousand acres of land in sixteen days, most of it in parcels of one hundred acres. The people who bought were poor, but Cooper extended credit to them. He gave each tenant seven to ten years to pay for the land, and, unlike most landowners of the time, he sold to them outright, so that while they were in his debt, they were also landowners themselves. Wealthy himself, he was also able to extend credit for the basic necessities to the poorer settlers, and in this way the town was built: The people in it had a stake in its success, and the land around it became populated with small family farms.

Cooper also founded Otsego County, and the town became the county seat. He wrote a book about the experience called *A Guide in the Wilderness*. He was an active and often vociferous participant in New York state politics, causing the arrest of the founder of New York's public school system, Jedediah Peck, when Peck urged the repeal of the Alien and Sedition Law, and championing Aaron Burr, the controversial former vice president who outdueled Alexander Hamilton and was acquitted of treason charges. Judge Cooper made as many enemies as he did friends in the hurly-burly of early American politics, and was killed by an unknown attacker after a political meeting in Albany in 1809. His youngest son James was ten years old.

## James Fenimore Cooper

The young James Fenimore Cooper was sent away to school, first to private school at Albany, and then, when he was thirteen, to Yale. After being expelled three years later for a prank, he joined the crew of a merchant ship and, subsequently, the navy, but resigned after marrying in 1811. His wife, Susan DeLancey, was from one of the New York's first families, and in 1817, after a few years in Cooperstown, the couple moved closer to her family in Westchester. Cooper settled down to a life of leisure, but was unable to stay settled for long. He started writing in 1820.

He began writing about Cooperstown three years later, taking his father's legacy and turning it into legend. *The Pioneers* introduced the world to "Judge Temple" of "Templeton," but, more important, it introduced the world to Natty Bumppo, the good scout also called "Leatherstocking." Through this character, to whom Cooper returned for five novels, the story of the taming of the American frontier was first told to readers in Paris and Vienna. Cooper was the first American author to enjoy world renown. Leatherstocking roamed through time and the countryside, returning to his youth and the area around Cooperstown in *The Deerslayer* in 1841. Cooper himself returned to Cooperstown in 1834, after living much of his adult life in Westchester, New York City, and Europe. His was not a happy return.

Cooper quarreled with the townspeople over items both large and small, but his principal troubles grew from a contest over a piece of the family property. Three Mile Point on Otsego Lake had become a popular spot for the local people to picnic, but Cooper tried to put a stop to that. His action drew bitter criticism from the press, both in and outside the town. He fought back, bringing suits

*The Baseball Hall of Fame in Cooperstown.* (Cooperstown Chamber of Commerce)

that helped codify the principles of American libel law, and he won. His right to privacy on his land was established, but he became the most unpopular man in town. He died in 1851, and his house, Otsego Hall, burned down two years later. A statue stands on the spot today, and he is buried with his wife in the Christ Church cemetery.

Although most of the village also burned down in 1862, it was rebuilt soon after. Cooperstown attracted a sizable number of notable men for a town its size. Samuel Nelson, who sat on the U.S. Supreme Court from 1845 to 1872, lived there, as did the originator of the "dime novel," Erastus Beadle. Though in 1838 James Fenimore Cooper had predicted future popularity for Cooperstown as a resort, no one could have predicted that events later said to have taken place in 1839 would lead to the renown that the village enjoys today. The Leatherstocking books are still read, but Cooperstown is never mistaken for Templeton; when Cooperstown is mentioned now, it is baseball that comes to mind.

It is a strange coincidence that America's first literary figure, and its first and most literary sport, would originate in the same out-of-the-way place. Stranger still, in both, fiction proves stronger than fact.

### Origins of Baseball

Baseball was not invented by Abner Doubleday, nor was the first game played in Cooperstown. Doubleday himself never said he had invented baseball, though the town assented to the claim made on its behalf by a committee headed by Albert G. Spalding (president of the Chicago baseball team), and chaired by Abraham G. Mills, the fourth president of baseball's National League. In the latter half of the nineteenth century, baseball became recognized as the American national game, but no one could pinpoint where, or how, it began. Spalding wanted to prove the game was American in origin, and was instrumental in establishing a seven-man commission, headed by Mills, which would find out, once and for all, where the game started. Mills conducted a very limited investigation beginning and ending in 1907.

Basing his opinion on the testimony of a former resident of Cooperstown named Abner Graves, who said he thought he remembered Doubleday introducing the game to the boys of the town, maybe in 1839, maybe in 1841, Mills declared the case closed even before the commission had issued its final report. Grave's testimony was his only evidence.

Mills had known Doubleday during the Civil War, when Doubleday was a major general in the Union army. Until he made his report, Mills had never mentioned anything about Doubleday's supposed association with baseball. Doubleday himself had written three books, one of which described his early boyhood, and had not touched on the invention of baseball. No one can be certain that Doubleday was ever even in Cooperstown, although if he had been there in 1839, he was already past boyhood. He was enrolled at West Point by then.

A more likely explanation of the origins of baseball is that it evolved from the English game of rounders. A game called "base-ball" is illustrated in a book printed in London in 1744, and the same book was reprinted throughout northeastern America later in the century. A compilation of children's games published in America in 1829 describes the rules of rounders, which were similar to the rules of baseball, and in 1835 a book published in Rhode Island described the rules of rounders but renamed the game baseball. In 1839 another book, published in New Haven, laid out the baseball field.

Despite this evidence to the contrary, the theory of spontaneous American invention in Cooperstown won the day. The changes this myth brought to Cooperstown did not come until thirty years after the findings of the commission, but change when it came was dramatic.

### The Baseball Hall of Fame

The two-room National Baseball Hall of Fame and Museum opened on June 12, 1939, the centennial of Abner Doubleday's alleged "invention." Babe Ruth was there, and Cy Young, and Honus Wagner, and other baseball giants, joined by multitudes of fans and politicians who later congregated at Doubleday Field to watch an all-star game played by the legends in attendance.

A few years earlier, the editor of two of the local papers, Walter Littell, had told his friend Stephen C. Clark that he had seen a mangled leather baseball supposedly used by Doubleday. According to Littell, Clark paid five dollars for the beat-up ball, and plans for the Hall of Fame were launched. The New York state legislature sent a committee to Cooperstown in 1937, and the committee found that Cooperstown was indeed the "birthplace of baseball" and recommended a celebration of the centennial of its birth, in 1939. The state spent ten thousand dollars to advertise the event and put up road signs to direct the faithful to the little town. The shrine was validated by an act of Congress, and a commemorative stamp was issued by the U.S. Postal Service. The first members of the Hall of Fame were inducted in the 1939 ceremonies.

Since 1939 the Hall of Fame has been expanded far beyond its two-room beginnings. A wing was added in 1950, and the Hall of Fame Gallery was built in 1958 to house the bronze plaques bearing the likenesses of the outstanding baseball players who have been chosen for membership. The Hall of Fame Library was added ten years later, and a third wing, which doubled the size of the complex, was completed in 1980. The complex includes numerous displays of artifacts, photographs, and memorabilia from throughout the history of baseball.

Stephen C. Clark's family had been in Cooperstown since just before the Civil War, and had made a great impact in a variety of ways. The first Edward Clark, Stephen Clark's grandfather, bought property there in 1854; he was a principal partner in a new company that would make a fortune manufacturing sewing machines—I. M. Singer and Company. In the first third of the twentieth century, Stephen Clark's brother, Edward Severin Clark, used his part of the family fortune to build up Cooperstown. He built the "cow palace," a huge barn, in 1918, and Fenimore House, which is now a museum, in 1932. Fenimore House was built on property once occupied by James Fenimore Cooper. Edward S. Clark also built a luxury hotel, the Otesaga, and the Alfred Corning Clark Community Gymnasium, named for his father. After Edward died in 1933, these properties were administered by Stephen, who used them to transform the village.

Stephen Clark gave Fenimore House to the New York State Historical Association, donated the cow palace and other barns that became the Farmer's Museum, and played a primary role in bringing the Hall of Fame to Cooperstown. His brother Edward had started the Mary Imogene Bassett Hospital; Stephen increased its endowment, making it one of the largest rural hospitals in the country. Stephen also founded the Clark Foundation, which helped to start the Glimmerglass Opera Theater in 1975. He brought the New York State Historical Association to Cooperstown in 1939, housing it first on Main Street and moving it in 1945 to Fenimore House. Edward Clark was known in Cooperstown as "The Squire," but it was Stephen Clark who had the central role in the remaking of Cooperstown from a small town with a history into a small-town history center.

### Modern Cooperstown

In the 1990 census, 2,180 residents of Cooperstown were counted. Some among them work at the Hall of Fame, and others operate businesses related to it. Some of the descendants of the area's farmers and artisans recreate the nineteenth century at the Farmer's Museum, where the Cardiff Giant, one of America's greatest hoaxes, lies in state. The town's literary history is preserved at the library in Fenimore House, where the painting *Peaceable Kingdom*, by Edward Hicks, is displayed. The Corvette Americana Hall of Fame covers the 1950's through the 1990's, displaying Corvette automobiles in dioramas and film clips with blaring music accompanying the presentation. Boats tour Otsego Lake, with guides pointing out the places familiar from Cooper's novels, and the trolley, built in 1990, still fills up with passengers on Main Street. The town seems as eternal as the surrounding mountains, a place where history and legend are an old, contented couple: cozy and virtually indistinguishable.

—*Jeffrey Felshman*

### For Further Information:

Cooper, James Fenimore. *The Chronicles of Cooperstown.* Cooperstown, N.Y.: H. & E. Phinney, 1838. A history of the town. In addition, Cooper's *The Pioneers* (1823) and *The Deerslayer* (1841) are still in print.

Jones, Louis C. *In Cooperstown.* Cooperstown: New York State Historical Association, 1982. The rough edges of Cooperstown's development have been smoothed over, yet they do not go unmentioned. Its paeans to Cooperstown's charm and beauty appear to be sincerely felt.

Seymour, Harold. "How Baseball Began." In *The Armchair Book of Baseball*, edited by John Thorn. New York: Charles Scribner's Sons, 1985. First published in the *New York Historical Society Quarterly* in 1956, this was the signal work in debunking the myth of baseball's beginnings. A must read for baseball fans.

Taylor, Alan. *William Cooper's Town: Power and Persuasion on the Frontier of the Early American Republic.* New York: Vintage Books/Random House, 1996. A history of Cooperstown and a biography of James Fenimore Cooper.

# Eleanor Roosevelt National Historic Site

**Date:** National Historic Site established by Congress in 1977 and opened on October 11, 1984

**Relevant issues:** Political history, social reform, women's history

**Significance:** This site was the retreat of Eleanor Roosevelt from 1925 to 1945. From the time of her husband's death in 1945, it was her home until her death in 1962. As a retreat and home, it sustained her and provided her with a nurturing environment for personal and intellectual development.

**Location:** In the Hudson River Valley seventy-five miles north of New York City in Hyde Park, two miles east of the home of Franklin Delano Roosevelt

**Site Office:**
Eleanor Roosevelt National Historic Site
4097 Albany Post Road
Hyde Park, NY 12538
ph.: (914) 229-9422
Web site: www.nps.gov/elro/

The Eleanor Roosevelt National Historic Site is also known as Val-Kill after the Dutch name for "valley stream." Franklin D. Roosevelt added this

*Eleanor Roosevelt's bedroom at Val-Kill in Hyde Park.* (Richard Cheek/Eleanor Roosevelt National Historic Site)

number of adult children who vexed her and made the home a turbulent one.

At fifteen Eleanor was sent to England for schooling at Allenswood, a school whose headmistress, Marie Souvestre, believed in bringing out the best in the young women under her supervision. Within this environment Eleanor flourished. She became a leader among the young women, a friend one could count on, and the favorite of Souvestre. At Allenswood, Roosevelt was schooled to become independent and useful. Above all, however, she was taught to be compassionate. At seventeen, after finishing her course of study, Roosevelt returned to New York City where she sought to put her learning to use. She volunteered to teach at a settlement house which offered aid and education to recent immigrants who resided in tenement houses on the Lower East Side of Manhattan.

In addition to her volunteer work, Roosevelt did what was expected of a young woman of her wealth and class, making her debut into New York society. During one of the social events to which she was invited, she became reacquainted with her fifth cousin, Franklin Roosevelt. She impressed him with her graceful bearing and fine mind. She took him to the Lower East Side and showed him the destitution of the poor residents there. This was a world to which he had never been exposed during his sheltered youth. This event established a pattern in the Roosevelts' relationship—Eleanor discovered the poor and disadvantaged and revealed their suffering to Franklin. The two married in 1905.

site to his family's Hyde Park estate in 1911, and the family used it for scenic outdoor activities. In 1925 Franklin Roosevelt gave lifetime rights to the property to Eleanor. Val-Kill, to Eleanor, was her special place, where, she said, "I used to find myself and grow" and "I emerged as an individual." This National Historic Site is a reminder of Roosevelt's personal growth as well as her towering accomplishments as a humanitarian.

### Eleanor Roosevelt's Early Life

Eleanor Roosevelt was born in 1884 in New York City. Her parents were Elliott Roosevelt and Anna Hall Roosevelt. The Roosevelts were a large and prominent family which included Theodore Roosevelt, Eleanor's uncle and president of the United States from 1901 to 1909. Though her family was wealthy, Eleanor's early years were marked by adversity. She was orphaned at a young age by her mother's death from diphtheria and her father's subsequent death from complications of alcoholism. Eleanor was particularly desolate at the loss of her father, who had treated her very lovingly. She was then looked after by her grandmother, Mary Hall, at Hall's estate at Tivoli, New York. Though Hall had Eleanor's best interests at heart, she had a

### Eleanor's Marriage and Motherhood

Eleanor and Franklin resided in New York City while Franklin completed law school at Columbia University and later worked as a lawyer. In 1910 Franklin was elected to the New York state senate.

During these early years of their marriage Eleanor gave birth to Anna in 1906, James in 1907, and Franklin Jr. in 1909. She was grief-stricken when Franklin Jr. succumbed to influenza at seven months. Ten months later, Elliott was born. Franklin was named assistant secretary of the navy in 1913, and the couple moved to Washington, D.C., where the second Franklin Jr. was born in 1914, followed by John in 1916. Eleanor remembered that during the entire first decade of their marriage, she either was pregnant or had an infant or toddler in her care. Eleanor also had obligations, arising from her husband's position, such as following a strict schedule of social visitation to wives of cabinet members and members of Congress. Though naturally shy, she performed her social rounds conscientiously.

Eleanor's world fell apart in 1918, when she discovered that her husband was romantically involved with her social secretary, Lucy Mercer. Eleanor considered divorce but was persuaded to reconcile with her husband. After this blow, the marriage never fully recovered. Eleanor determined to lead a more independent life for herself. During the early 1920's, she joined the League of Women Voters, the Women's Trade Union League, and the women's division of the Democratic Party. There were no more children.

In the summer of 1921 Franklin was stricken by polio. Despite his mother's desire that he retire to Hyde Park, Eleanor fought to keep her husband active in politics. She was successful in keeping the Roosevelt name before the public. At the same time that she was encouraging her husband to resume his political career, Eleanor continued to build a life independent of FDR. Intrinsic to this quest was the establishment of her own special place.

### A Retreat at Val-Kill

The impetus to build a retreat at the part of the Hyde Park estate called Val-Kill came in August of 1924. Two of Eleanor's friends, Marion Dickerman and Nancy Cook, had joined the family for a picnic. When the three friends regretted that Hyde Park would be closing soon for the winter, Franklin suggested that the women build a cottage at Val-Kill so they could come year-round. He offered them several acres for their lifetime use. As FDR put it, "My Missus and some of her female political friends want to build a shack on a stream in the back woods and want, instead of a beautiful marble bath, to have a stream dug out so as to form an old-fashioned swimming hole."

The "shack" was a stone cottage built in 1925. Franklin helped architect Henry Toombs design the two-story structure in Dutch Colonial style. Cook and Dickerman moved into the cottage and made it their permanent residence until 1947. Eleanor visited on weekends, holidays, and during the summer. In 1926 the three women were joined by a fourth, Caroline O'Day, in a project to aid the upper New York State farmers. They founded Val-Kill Industries, an artisans' workshop where farmers could supplement their incomes by making simple Shaker-style furniture, pewter pieces, and weavings. The workshop was constructed in 1926. The idea behind the establishment of the industry was that if the farmers were given a way to supplement their inadequate incomes, they would not be forced to move to the city, which the women felt to be a less healthy environment. Eventually the industry fell victim to the Depression and when the factory closed, Eleanor converted the building into two apartments for herself and her private secretary, Malvina "Tommy" Thompson. There were two living rooms, a dining room, seven bedrooms, a dormitory for young people, two large porches downstairs, and a sleeping porch upstairs. This home, the only one which actually belonged to her, brought the greatest happiness to Eleanor.

Franklin was elected governor of New York in 1928. Eleanor continued her activities in the women's division of the Democratic Party and further honed her political skills. When FDR was elected president of the United States in 1932, Eleanor feared that her own interests would suffer. Just the opposite happened. Eleanor Roosevelt became a spokesperson for the underprivileged in society. She became a champion of racial justice and rights for women. She was highly energetic and traveled widely, becoming the compassionate representative of her husband to people throughout the United States. In addition, she would continue her role as acute observer and report conditions in the country to him. When World War II began, she continued her good works, and traveled throughout the globe bringing comfort to the troops overseas.

### Eleanor's Permanent Home

After FDR's death in 1945, Eleanor Roosevelt took up permanent residence at Val-Kill. The home of Franklin D. Roosevelt at at Hyde Park was turned over to the government, but Val-Kill was not part of the bequest. Though Eleanor again had thought her public life would end, she continued to serve her country in many roles. She was appointed by President Harry S Truman as a member of the delegation to the United Nations, an organization she strongly supported. As chairperson of the Commission on Human Rights she was the driving force behind the United Nations Declaration of Rights. Roosevelt considered this to be the greatest work of her life.

Val-Kill was a busy place in the seventeen years that Eleanor lived there after Franklin's death. She entertained guests ranging from heads of state such as Nikita Khrushchev and Jawaharlal Nehru to students from foreign countries. She had an annual picnic for students from a nearby school for disadvantaged boys and involved her grandchildren in this endeavor. Though Roosevelt entertained frequently, she lived a simple lifestyle, often doing her own daily shopping. She frequently left her guests on their own to enjoy walking, playing tennis, boating, and swimming while she attended to her writing. Though she often traveled she always tried to stop by and greet picnickers while at home. One of the visitors to Val-Kill was Democratic presidential nominee John F. Kennedy, who, upon becoming president, reappointed Roosevelt to the U.N. delegation and appointed her chairperson of the President's Commission on the Status of Women, the last important role of her life. Though Roosevelt also had a place in New York City, Val-kill was the special nurturing place where she felt most comfortable.

### Places to Visit

At the Eleanor Roosevelt National Historic Site are the furnished home of Eleanor Roosevelt (Val-Kill Cottage), the Stone Cottage, a rose garden, a cutting garden, and a playhouse. It is located two miles east of the home of Franklin D. Roosevelt. At his estate are two sites of interest: the home of FDR and his presidential library and museum. Also in the vicinity is the Vanderbilt mansion.

The home of Franklin D. Roosevelt is called Springwood, and it has original furnishings and family portraits. The gravesites of the president and First Lady are in a rose garden on the estate.

The Franklin D. Roosevelt Library and Museum was the first presidential library to be established. It contains the personal as well as official papers of the former president. The holdings also include memorabilia, movies, and an extensive collection of photographs. Franklin Roosevelt and his mother donated sixteen acres at Hyde Park for the establishment of this institution.

The Vanderbilt Mansion in Hyde Park, New York, is a graceful structure built in the Beaux-Arts manner. It has furnishings of the period, a formal garden, and a beautiful view of the Hudson River.

*—Bonnie Ford*

**For Further Information:**

Cook, Blanche Wiesen. *Eleanor Roosevelt, 1884-1933.* New York: Viking Press, 1992.

_____. *Eleanor Roosevelt, 1933-1938.* New York: Viking Press, 1999. The first two volumes of the most exhaustive biography of Roosevelt.

Goodwin, Doris Kearns. *No Ordinary Time: Franklin and Eleanor Roosevelt—The Home Front in World War II.* New York: Simon & Schuster, 1994. Documents the wartime White House interestingly and well.

Lash, Joseph P. *Eleanor and Franklin.* New York: W. W. Norton, 1971.

_____. *Eleanor: The Years Alone.* New York: W. W. Norton, 1972. Lash was a close friend of Eleanor and provides personal insights in these two volumes.

Roosevelt, Eleanor. *The Autobiography of Eleanor Roosevelt.* 3 vols. New York: Da Capo Press, 1992. This publication of Roosevelt's work includes the three volumes of her autobiography.

Youngs, J. William T. *Eleanor Roosevelt: A Personal and Public Life.* New York: Longmans, 2000. A superb brief biography.

# Empire State Building

**Date:** Construction commenced on March 17, 1930; building opened on May 1, 1931

**Relevant issues:** Art and architecture, business and industry, science and technology

**Significance:** A grandiose monument to unregulated private capitalism, the building repre-

*The Empire State Building.* (Corbis)

The site of the Empire State Building was formerly that of the old Waldorf-Astoria, in its day, New York City's largest, most luxurious hotel. According to legend, the hotel came to be built because of a feud between two members of the socially prominent and wealthy Astor family whose mansions stood on the site. Resentful that his aunt, the formidable Mrs. William Backhouse Astor, had assumed the title of *the* Mrs. Astor, her nephew, William Waldorf Astor, feeling that as he was the head of the family that title rightfully belonged to his wife, got his revenge. He had a luxury hotel called the Waldorf erected on the site of his mansion on the 33d Street corner. As anticipated, the aunt would not tolerate living next to a commercial establishment. She sold out and another luxury hotel, called the Astoria, was erected on the site of her mansion. The hotels were then combined to create the Waldorf-Astoria. A family feud gave birth not only to the hotel but also to a full-block frontage building lot on Fifth Avenue—a rarity in New York real estate.

### The Search for a Profitable Project

The Empire State Building was the inspiration of John Jakob Raskob (1879-1950), a shadowy financial genius who had made a fortune devising a plan whereby consumers could buy General Motors automobiles on the installment plan. In 1928, he had been financial adviser to Alfred E. Smith (1873-1944), the four-time New York governor, in his bid for the presidency—which Smith lost. Raskob now had available an unemployed but highly popular former governor with extensive executive experience and political connections.

Raskob was looking for a project to occupy his time and to make money. He was aware of the publicity the Woolworth Building, constructed in 1913 at a height of 792 feet, gained from being the world's tallest building. Raskob came upon the idea of constructing a speculative office building, and in order to attract tenants, would make it the

sented an expression of faith in American business enterprise in the 1920's.

**Location:** The West Side of New York City, on Fifth Avenue between 33d and 34th Streets

**Site Office:**

Empire State Building
Information Desk
350 Fifth Avenue
New York City, NY 10118
ph.: (212) 736-3100
fax: (212) 967-6167
Web site: www.esbnyc.com
e-mail: info@esbnyc.com

world's tallest building. It was to be named the Empire State Building. Former governor Smith joined Raskob in forming a company for the purposes of erecting and managing the building. During the spring and summer of 1929, Raskob laid the groundwork—obtaining both title to the Waldorf-Astoria site and the necessary financing. He had the architect, William F. Lamb of the architectural firm Shreve, Lamb, and Harmon, draw up designs. On August 29, 1929, Alfred E. Smith announced the creation of a company that would build an office building of eighty stories, 1,000 feet high—the tallest in the world. The announcement spurred to action Walter P. Chrysler, who had been erecting a building nearby in competition with the Bank of Manhattan Building for the title of the world's tallest building. At 927 feet, the Bank of Manhattan Building was taller by 2 feet than the Chrysler. Chrysler won the contest through an astonishing feat. In October of 1929, his architect had raised through the top of the Chrysler Building a secretly constructed stainless steel spire, which increased the total height of the building to 1,048 feet, surpassing in height not only the Bank of Manhattan Building but also the projected Empire State Building. Raskob then had his architect add five stories to the Empire State Building, raising the total to eighty-five and the height to 1,050 feet—2 feet higher than the Chrysler Building. Then, for added security, Raskob had his architect add a 200-foot lantern tower to the building, raising its height to 1,250 feet. In a clever publicity move, the tower lantern was projected as a dirigible mooring mast, although no dirigible ever would or ever could be moored to it. It was the tower lantern that made the building distinctive, even unique. If the Woolworth Building was New York City's Cathedral of Commerce, the Empire State Building would be its lighthouse—as famous as the legendary lighthouse called the Pharos at Alexandria, one of the Seven Wonders of the Ancient World.

### Built in Record Time

Once the plans were in final form, Raskob and Smith went to work on the details of construction, which demonstrated their organizational ability, their political connections, and their financial resources.

The building site proved ideal. It was entirely solid granite or schist. Complicated and expensive shoring was unnecessary. The construction contract was given to Starrett Brothers and Eken, who had constructed the Bank of Manhattan Building in record time. They got the Empire State Building contract largely because Paul Starrett, principal of the firm, assured Raskob and Smith that his firm had no equipment available for the job. Because of the nature of the construction, new equipment, as well as new building methods, would have to be devised.

Excavation began on January 22, 1930; construction started on March 17, 1930; the cornerstone was laid by Alfred E. Smith on September 17, 1930. The magnificently constructed old hotel did not go easily. In the desire to get the new building started, no attempt was made at salvage; large sections of the old building, with woodwork and fittings still attached, were cut away with acetylene torches and dumped into the Atlantic Ocean. Working without interruption even during the bitter winter of 1930-1931, the building went up at the astonishing rate of approximately a story a day. The building was finished ahead of schedule. The total construction time was one year and forty-five days.

Probably never in the history of the world has a building of such size and quality been erected in so short a period of time. The stock market crash of October 29, 1929, which deepened an economic depression already underway, proved an unanticipated advantage in the construction of the building. Capital, labor, and supplies became increasingly available at steadily decreasing costs. The final cost of the building was $24,718,000—about half its projected cost of $43,000,000.

### The Finest, Most Durable Materials

Sponsor, architect, and builder were agreed that only the finest materials were to be used both within and without, and the building was to benefit from the latest developments in building technology and the science of metallurgy. The seventy-three elevators rose and fell at speeds up to 1,400 feet per minute. Advances in metallurgy made available stronger and lighter steels and improved specialty metals such as cast aluminum and chrome-nickel steel. The building was clad in fine Indiana limestone cut to size at the quarry. Sections of the sixty thousand tons of steel used in construction were made to precise specifications in Pittsburgh and delivered still warm to the site. The use of less expensive cast aluminum and chrome-nickel steel for much of the exterior not only cut the cost of construction by eliminating more costly stone, but resulted in a stone cubic foot to building cubic space ratio four times greater than customary. The frames of the 6,500 windows were painted with a tomato-red rust preservative. The awe-inspiring lobby was sheathed in costly marbles imported from Germany and Spain.

## An Aesthetic Success, a Commercial Failure

The opening ceremonies were held May 1, 1931. President Herbert Hoover in the White House pressed a button that illuminated the building. Thousands admired the innovative beauty of the great building, but neither the ebullience of Smith nor the optimism of Raskob could mask the pervasive influence of the terrible depression that was searing the American psyche. Construction had come to a standstill, and most of the thousands of workers who had toiled so splendidly on the building were now either unemployed or on bread lines. The rental market, too, was dead or dying. Despite the best efforts of Smith and Raskob, the building was only about 30 percent rented—and then mostly to small renters. Fifty-six floors remained vacant, bravely lit up at night so as to give the impression of occupancy. The only bright spots were the observatories on the 86th and 102d floors that continued to turn large profits. The use of the lantern tower, first for radio and then for television antennae, would also contribute to the profitability of the building.

## A Disillusioned Sponsor

Alfred E. Smith served as president of the new building, but time took its toll. With inadequate revenues because of unrented space, the building faced bankruptcy, which was only staved off by Raskob's financial manipulations. The election of 1932, which gave the presidency to Franklin D. Roosevelt, also gave Smith hope that he would be given an important position at the federal level. Roosevelt, however, disliked Smith, and even though he used much of Smith's social agenda as governor of New York for his own New Deal legislation, never offered the former governor a position. The once "Happy Warrior" grew increasingly embittered and gradually faded from public view, even abandoning his beloved Democratic Party.

Smith died in 1944 and did not live to witness the spectacular crash on July 25, 1945, of a B-25 bomber into the side of the Empire State Building at the seventy-fourth floor. Even though the crash did minimal damage, quickly repaired, to the building, it killed fourteen people.

## An Unfulfilled Dream but a Beloved Landmark

Although east 34th Street never became the new commercial center Raskob had hoped, for the Empire State Building this was an advantage. The building continued to stand in splendid isolation, visible for miles around. By 1950 it was fully rented and profitable. New Yorkers and visitors alike have taken the building to heart. They love and admire it, and even after it was superseded as the world's tallest building in 1970 by the mundane World Trade Towers to the south, the Empire State Building still stands tall in imagination. The building was designated a New York City landmark in 1981, listed on the state and National Registers of Historic Places in 1982, and recognized as a National Landmark in 1986. More importantly, the Empire State Building serves as the symbol of New York City around the world, and its observatories remain one of the city's main tourist attractions.

—*Nis Petersen*

## For Further Information

Bryant, David. "Margaret Bourke-White; Lewis W. Hine: The Empire State Building." *Library Journal*, February 1, 1999, p. 82. The writer discusses the contents of two books of spectacular photographs of the Empire State Building by the greatest photographers of the time.

Burrough, Bryan. "Emperors of the Air." *Vanity Fair*, May, 1995, p. 120-129. A somewhat racy account of three present-day real estate tycoons who are attempting to gain control of the famous building.

Heller, Steven, Sarah J. Freymann, and Steven Schwartz. *The Empire State Building Book*. New York: St. Martin's Press, 1980. Contains an easy-to-follow account of the actual construction of the building.

Langer, Freddy, ed. *Lewis W. Hine: The Empire State Building*. New York: Neues, 1998. A capsule history accompanied by facts and figures that have made this Art Deco landmark so famous.

Levy, Donald S. "Monuments of the Age." *Time*,

December 7, 1998, p. 121. The author analyzes how five major monuments, including the Empire State Building, define the twentieth century.

Tauranac, John. *The Empire State Building: The Making of a Landmark.* New York: St. Martin's Griffin, 1995. The first book-length treatment of the famous building by a noted architectural historian.

Willis, Carol. *Building the Empire State.* New York: W. W. Norton, 1998. An eyewitness account through a meticulously kept in-house notebook details the innovative building process.

# Fort Stanwix and Erie Canal Village

**Date:** Original fort existed from 1758 to 1784

**Relevant issues:** American Indian history, business and industry, colonial America, European settlement, military history, Revolutionary War

**Significance:** Fort Stanwix National Monument is a replica of an eighteenth century post that supervised military affairs and Indian relations in this region between 1758 and 1784. British soldiers built and manned the post during the French and Indian War, and American soldiers occupied it during the War for Independence. It is managed by the National Park Service, U.S. Department of the Interior. The Erie Canal Village is a living museum that recreates life along the Erie Canal during the early nineteenth century. It includes historic buildings moved to that site from within a fifty-mile radius of Rome. It is owned by the city of Rome and managed by the Rome Historical Society.

**Location:** In the Mohawk River valley of central New York, 108 miles west of Albany and 42 miles east of Syracuse; a key junction in the inland water routes that connect the Great Lakes and the Atlantic Ocean

**Site Offices:**

Fort Stanwix National Monument
112 East Park Street
Rome, NY 13440
ph.: (315) 336-2090
Web site: www.nps.gov/fost/

Erie Canal Village
5789 New London Road
Rome, NY 13440
ph.: (315) 337-3999
fax: (315) 339-7755
Web site: www.eriecanalvillage.com

Rome, New York, is the site of one of the most important cultural and commercial crossroads in the northeastern United States. Long before Rome was founded in 1786, the terrain it occupies connected the Atlantic seaboard to the Great Lakes. To the east of Rome, the waters of the Mohawk River flow toward Albany, where they meet the Hudson River and continue southward until they empty into the Atlantic Ocean at New York City. To the west of Rome, Wood Creek, Oneida Lake, and the Oswego River open a path to Lake Ontario and the Ohio and Mississippi River valleys. Since pre-Columbian times, the inhabitants of North America have met, traded, and fought over this important passage to the continent's interior. Its strategic location accounts for two of Rome's historic sites, Fort Stanwix National Monument and the Erie Canal Village.

**Early History**

During the colonial era, the Mohawk Valley's inhabitants called the site of Rome the Oneida Carrying Place. "Oneida" referred to the Iroquois nation of the same name whose homelands included this important junction; "Carrying Place" described this location's role as a portage in the trade route between the Hudson River and Lake Ontario. European fur traders from Albany and Schenectady sailed on the Mohawk River in broad flat-bottomed boats, or bateaux, loaded with clothing, tools, arms, liquor, and food. Near the headwaters of the Mohawk they carried their boats and goods across a stretch of level ground, the site of present-day Rome, until they reached Wood Creek. Their journey ended at Oswego, a British trading post on the southeastern shore of Lake Ontario. There they engaged in annual summer markets, trading goods with Indians from the Great Lakes region for animal pelts to be exported back to Europe.

In the colonial era, everyone wishing to move quickly between the Great Lakes and the eastern seaboard had to pass through this important portage. As its name implies, local Indians controlled the Oneida Carrying Place for most of the colonial period. The Oneidas, one of the six Indian nations in the powerful Iroquois Confederacy, allowed their colonial neighbors to use this portage, but they resisted European domination. Tensions between fur traders and their Indian customers often resulted from this arrangement. At a meeting to discuss Indian affairs in 1754, Albany traders complained to the New York governor about Indians at the Carrying Place who forcibly stopped the traders and threatened harm if not paid exorbitant wages for assistance in transporting their goods. Such a strategic location certainly encouraged competition as well as cooperation among peoples who relied on this portage for their livelihood.

The intensity of that competition resulted in outright hostilities during the French and Indian War of the 1750's. In this climactic struggle between the British and French empires in North America, the Oneida Carrying Place played an important role. For the British, it was a vital link in preserving communication and supply lines between Albany and Oswego, and at the war's outset they built several posts to defend the Carrying Place. A combined French and Indian force destroyed one of these posts, Fort Bull, in March, 1756. A few months later, Oswego also fell to a French assault. British commander Daniel Webb retreated from the Carrying Place, burning the remaining British posts there so they would not fall into French hands.

### Fort Stanwix

Except for a devastating attack on the colonial settlement at German Flats in November, 1757, the French never acted on their opportunity to invade the Mohawk valley. Thus, in 1758 British commander in chief James Abercromby ordered one of his officers, John Stanwix, to occupy and refortify the Oneida Carrying Place. The Oneidas agreed to the army's presence on the conditions that the British restore trade with the Indians and destroy the post at the war's end. British and American soldiers built Fort Stanwix quickly between August and November, 1758. Ironically, its importance to the war effort declined almost immediately with British victories on the Ohio and Great Lakes frontiers in 1759 and 1760. As the war moved elsewhere, British commanders reduced the size of Fort Stanwix's

garrison until it included only fifty men in 1761.

Fort Stanwix remained a center of controversy even after British victory in the French and Indian War. With the arrival of peace, British military officers discovered they had two other problems: resentful Indians and restless colonists. The Indians, while they welcomed and often depended upon British trade, did not relish British claims to possession of the Carrying Place. When the British failed to destroy Fort Stanwix as promised, they irritated the local Oneidas. The mounting expenses of maintaining the North American army, however, finally convinced British administrators to abandon the fort along with many other frontier posts in 1767.

Fort Stanwix's last important role in British colonial policy came a year later, when the crown's Indian Superintendent, Sir William Johnson, convened a treaty there with the Iroquois and several other Indian nations. One of the British army's tasks in North America was mediating disputes between Indians and western settlers. In the 1768 Treaty of Fort Stanwix, Johnson negotiated a new boundary line between the Indians and colonists. The Iroquois also surrendered lands in the Ohio River valley highly coveted by colonial land speculators, including Johnson. This treaty angered many of the Indians inhabiting the ceded territory and led to renewed hostilities in 1774.

### The Revolutionary War

After falling into neglect and disrepair, Fort Stanwix returned to prominence in the American Revolution. When war broke out in 1775, the Mohawk valley's inhabitants were sharply divided. Loyalists gravitated toward the Johnson family. Sir William Johnson had died in 1774, but representation of the crown's interests passed to his son John Johnson and nephew Guy Johnson. In May, 1776, John Johnson led a group of loyal New Yorkers into Canada to avoid arrest. With the Johnsons out of the way, the patriots wasted no time in occupying the crumbling remains of Fort Stanwix. They rebuilt the old post with the assistance of a French engineer in the winter of 1776-1777 and negotiated an alliance with the local Oneidas. In March, 1777, Colonel Peter Gansevoort took over command of the fort. Some patriots now called it Fort Schuyler, in honor of Philip Schuyler, a prominent New Yorker.

*Fort Stanwix.* (Eastern National)

on Sunday, August 3, 1777. Colonel Peter Gansevoort commanded about seven hundred men inside the fort, which also protected local families and laborers. According to legend, Gansevoort greeted the enemy by raising an improvised version of the Stars and Stripes over the fort. The Continental Congress had approved the design for the flag a few weeks earlier, and if the legend is correct, then the siege of Fort Stanwix would mark the first time the Stars and Stripes flew over U.S. troops in battle. Subsequent scholarship, however, has debunked this claim, noting that it would have been impossible for news of the congressional flag resolution to reach the isolated fort by the time the siege began. The flag legend apparently dates to a local nineteenth century retelling of the story, and has no contemporary evidence to support it. St. Leger offered the outnumbered Americans an opportunity to surrender with his protection, but Gansevoort declined.

St. Leger tried to coax the Americans out of the fort. Gansevoort refused to budge, since he expected reinforcements to turn the British back. Those reinforcements were supposed to arrive in a militia force from Tryon County under the command of General Nicholas Herkimer. Tryon County had been split by divided loyalties, and some patriots suspected Herkimer himself of British sympathies. Not wanting to fuel such rumors, Herkimer led eight hundred militiamen and sixty Oneida Indians toward Fort Stanwix shortly after the siege began. St. Leger learned of Herkimer's advance and sent a force of Indians and New York Loyalists under John Johnson's command to intercept him.

The Loyalists and Indians waited in ambush for Herkimer's troops about five miles east of Fort Stanwix, where the road to the fort passed through a deep ravine. On the morning of August 6, some of the fiercest fighting in the War for Independence occurred at this site in the Battle of Oriskany. Herkimer's leg was shattered in the action

These measures to occupy and defend the Oneida Carrying Place paid off for the patriot cause during the pivotal campaign of 1777. In that year, the British planned to subdue New York by marching one army south from Canada and another east along the Mohawk River. The two armies would converge at Albany, quelling the rebellion in the Upper Hudson and Mohawk valleys along their way. Once in Albany, they would be poised to cooperate with the forces of Sir William Howe, the British commander in chief who had already occupied New York City. The British expected this campaign to secure New York, isolate New England from the rest of the colonies, and deliver a fatal blow to the American rebellion.

While General John Burgoyne led his army south from Canada, Colonel Barry St. Leger assembled a force that marched east from Oswego. St. Leger's army was made up of about one thousand British-allied Indians and eight hundred European soldiers, including British regulars, German infantrymen, French-Canadian militiamen, and New York Loyalists. The only major obstacle in their path to Albany was Fort Stanwix.

**The Siege of Fort Stanwix**

St. Leger's army initiated its siege of Fort Stanwix

and he later died, following amputation of the limb. Although the patriots sustained heavier casualties, the Loyalists and their Indian allies abandoned the field first. Herkimer's force, however, was too decimated to press on to Fort Stanwix.

## The Battle of Oriskany

The fort, however, did benefit unexpectedly from the Battle of Oriskany. A sortie of 250 men that went out to assist Herkimer came upon the encampments of the Loyalists and Indians then doing battle at Oriskany. With the enemy gone, these soldiers from the fort ransacked the camps and took a few stragglers prisoner. This surprising twist in the day's events strengthened Gansevoort's resolve and disheartened the Loyalists and Indians returning from battle. Many of the Indians assisting St. Leger abandoned the siege after suffering such heavy losses and finding their provisions destroyed.

Making the best of a rapidly deteriorating situation, St. Leger offered surrender terms to the fort again on August 9. Gansevoort declined, stating "it is my determined resolution, with the forces under my command, to defend this fort and garrison to the last extremity, in behalf of the United American States, who have placed me here to defend it against all their enemies." St. Leger bombarded the fort with his artillery to no avail. Within two weeks he received word from his informants that a much larger patriot reinforcement was marching from the east under the command of Benedict Arnold. Realizing that his dwindling forces could not maintain the siege and engage Arnold's troops at the same time, St. Leger opted for retreat. Abandoning much of his equipment, the British commander headed back to Oswego on August 22, just one day ahead of Arnold, who arrived at Fort Stanwix with one thousand additional troops.

The importance of the Americans' stand at Fort Stanwix became evident the following October, when General John Burgoyne surrendered his army to American forces at Saratoga. Without the assistance of St. Leger, Burgoyne had been unable to sustain his invasion from the north. The Mohawk and Upper Hudson valleys remained under patriot control, and the British campaign for 1777 fell apart. In Paris, Benjamin Franklin carried news of Saratoga to the French court, cementing the alliance that turned the war in American favor.

## After the Revolution

After playing such a prominent role in 1777, Fort Stanwix slipped once again into the background. Patriot forces continued to garrison it, but hostilies moved out of the northern states. In 1784, the fort hosted another Indian treaty, this time between the Iroquois nations and the United States. The Iroquois, like many of the region's inhabitants, had suffered severely during the war; some of the confederacy's nations had supported the patriots, while others had assisted the British. As a result, the diplomatic power of the Iroquois had been undermined, and the victorious Americans treated them as a conquered people. At the 1784 Treaty of Fort Stanwix, the Iroquois ceded much of their native homelands to the United States and New York. For the Indians, Fort Stanwix became a symbol of the commercial and military intrusions that made them strangers in their own land. The fort was gradually abandoned until it was demolished in 1830.

In 1935, Congress recognized the site of Fort Stanwix as a National Monument. Thirty years later, the city of Rome began to excavate the site in preparation for reconstructing the fort. Today the reconstructed fort matches as closely as possible its features and dimensions in 1777, including buildings, fortifications, and grounds. It contains historic furnishings, and its exhibits include artifacts recovered from the site. Programs and demonstrations sponsored by the National Park Service re-create life at the fort during the Revolutionary era.

## The Erie Canal

The Erie Canal Village, like Fort Stanwix, re-creates life in Rome at a time when it made important contributions to the nation's development. In 1817, ground was broken in Rome to begin construction of the Erie Canal, ushering in a transportation revolution in nineteenth century America. The Erie Canal was started in Rome for the same reason that Fort Stanwix was built there in 1758: to take advantage of the region's natural link in the nation's waterways. In Rome, the canal eliminated the need for a "Carrying Place," thereby reducing the cost and time of shipping goods between the Great Lakes and the Atlantic Ocean.

When the Erie Canal was completed in 1825, it cut across 363 miles of western New York, from Buffalo to Albany. The engineering marvel of its time, it was forty feet wide and four feet deep, with eighty-three locks and eighteen aqueducts to handle the 565-foot difference in elevation between the Hudson River and Lake Erie. A system of tributary canals developed around it, connecting Lake Ontario to the north with the Susquehanna River valley of Pennsylvania. This expansion in interior waterways sparked dramatic population and economic growth in western New York, as farmers could now sell their produce to larger and more distant markets at a much cheaper rate.

The Erie Canal Village was established in 1973 at the site of the Erie Canal's groundbreaking on July 4, 1817, to re-create life and work along this famous waterway. The village began with horse-drawn packet boat rides along a restored section of the old canal. It has since expanded to include several historic buildings moved from the surrounding area, including a tavern, school house, blacksmith shop, church, and canal store. The site also includes the New York State Museum of Cheese, which features exhibits on the dairy industry that sprang up in rural New York alongside the Erie Canal. Fort Bull Park, the site of a British post during the French and Indian War, is also located within the village, as is the Clarence C. Harden Museum, featuring canal-era carriages and farm equipment. Visitors to the Village may take a ride on the *Chief Engineer*, a replica of an original Erie Canal packet boat, as well as a steam locomotive, which gradually replaced the canal as the nation's most important form of commercial transportation. The Erie Canal Village also hosts a variety of craft programs and seasonal activities. —*Timothy J. Shannon*

**For Further Information:**

Clark, Andrew L. *The Wabash and Erie Canal: The Lower Divisions.* Mount Vernon, Ind.: Windmill, 1999. A history of the Wabash and Erie Canals.

Luzader, John, Louis Torres, and Orville W. Carroll. *Fort Stanwix: History, Historic Furnishing, and Historic Structure Reports.* Washington, D.C.: Government Printing Office, 1976. A comprehensive study of Fort Stanwix.

Manley, Henry S. *The Treaty of Fort Stanwix, 1784.* Rome, N.Y.: Rome Sentinel, 1932. For readers interested in Fort Stanwix's role in Indian relations.

Scott, John Albert. *Fort Stanwix (Fort Schuyler) and Oriskany.* Rome, N.Y.: Rome Sentinel, 1927. A detailed account of the siege of Fort Stanwix and the Battle of Oriskany.

Shaw, Ronald E. *Erie Water West: A History of the Erie Canal, 1797-1854.* Reprint. Lexington: University of Kentucky Press, 1990. Covers the Erie Canal and its role in western New York's development.

# Fort Ticonderoga

**Date:** Original fort existed from 1755 to 1781

**Relevant issues:** Military history, Revolutionary War

**Significance:** Present-day Fort Ticonderoga is a restored eighteenth century military post that guarded the portage between Lake Champlain and Lake George. Between 1755 and 1781, French, British, and American soldiers garrisoned the fort, which was of great strategic significance in the French and Indian War (1754-1760) and the American Revolution (1775-1783). Since 1909, the Fort Ticonderoga Museum has been open to the public as a private, nonprofit educational institution. Its facilities include the restored fort, museum collections, and the Thompson-Pell Research Center, a library specializing in eighteenth century American warfare.

**Location:** On the southwestern shore of Lake Champlain in northeastern New York; two miles east of town on Route 74 and eighteen miles east of exit 28 on U.S. Interstate 87

**Site Office:**

Fort Ticonderoga
Fort Road, Box 390
Ticonderoga, NY 12883
ph.: (518) 585-2821
fax: (518) 585-2210
Web site: www.fort-ticonderoga.org
e-mail: fort@fort-ticonderoga.org

Fort Ticonderoga is located on a small peninsula where the waters of Lake George flow by way of the La Chute River into Lake Champlain. These two lakes are part of a grand inland waterway connecting New York and Canada. It begins with the St. Lawrence River, which carries water from the Great Lakes into the Atlantic Ocean. From Montreal on the banks of the St. Lawrence, an eighteenth century traveler could place his canoe in the Richelieu River and paddle south to the head of Lake Champlain. After navigating this large lake, which forms the modern boundary between New York, Vermont, and Canada, the traveler would arrive at Ticonderoga and carry his canoe overland to Lake George to avoid a series of waterfalls in the La Chute River. From there he could continue south, and after another short portage, reach the Hudson River, which would eventually deposit him in New York City before it emptied into the Atlantic Ocean. Thus, the entire distance between Montreal and New York City, covering more than 380 miles, could be traversed with minor interruptions by the waters of the channel.

In the wars of the eighteenth century, the channel provided a path for invasion and conquest by waterborne armies. Ticonderoga, because it controlled the passage between Lake Champlain and Lake George, was a hotly contested region: whoever controlled it also controlled the flow of people and goods to the north and south. At the outset of the French and Indian War, French soldiers from Canada fortified this portage, and it took the British several tries and one infamous defeat to dislodge them. In May, 1775, the colonists' first offensive operation in the American Revolution took place here when Ethan Allen's Green Mountain Boys captured the small British garrison stationed at the fort. Ticonderoga remained a flashpoint in the Anglo-American conflict until General John Burgoyne's defeat at Saratoga in 1777.

### Early History

Long before the arrival of Europeans, the native inhabitants of this region used the portage between Lake Champlain and Lake George. The Iroquois called it "Ticonderoga"—meaning "between two lakes"—and traversed it when trading or warring with Indians to the north. The first European to visit Ticonderoga was Samuel de Champlain, the French explorer who accompanied a group of Canadian Indians warring with the Iroquois in 1609. Champlain left Quebec with eleven other Frenchmen and more than three hundred Indians, but as the group moved further into enemy territory, it dwindled to only three Frenchmen and about sixty Indians. Near Ticonderoga, Champlain and his party encountered a war party of about two hundred Iroquois. In the ensuing battle, the French-

men held back until they could use their firearms to full effect. Startled by the European strangers and their weaponry, the Iroquois quickly withdrew. In his diary Champlain wrote about his great victory, but little did he realize how quickly European technology and interests would enter into the age-old rivalries surrounding Ticonderoga.

During the next one hundred fifty years, Ticonderoga remained an avenue for commerce, diplomacy, and occasionally war. As the European empires in North America took shape, French merchants in Montreal and their Dutch counterparts in Albany traded across this route. Imperial powers in London and Paris prohibited such interaction, but Indians along the New York-Canadian frontier carried furs from Montreal to Albany in exchange for clothing, tools, weapons, and rum. The French established posts at the northern end of Lake Champlain, and the Albany Dutch pushed north to the southern shore of Lake George, but most of the Champlain Valley remained a middle ground of Indians and Europeans plying their wares. Occasionally tensions flared, and a raiding party or army would pass through Ticonderoga to wreak havoc to the north or south. Schenectady and Saratoga, two outlying settlements of Albany, suffered devastating attacks by French and Indian forces in 1690 and 1745 respectively, while the British launched unsuccessful invasions of Canada through the channel in 1691 and 1746.

### British-French Rivalry in the Region

The escalating tensions between the British and French in North America led the French to extend their hold on Lake Champlain. In 1731, they built Fort St. Frédéric at Crown Point, another important peninsula on the southwestern shore of Lake Champlain only sixteen miles north of Ticonderoga.

The French and Indian War broke out in 1754. In 1755, in the aftermath of George Washington's 1754 defeat in the Ohio Valley, the British began fortifying the northern approaches to New York. Construction began first on Fort Lyman (named for the colonel of the Connecticut regiment doing most of the work) near the falls of the Hudson River, on the site of earlier Forts Nicholson (1709) and Lydius (1731-1745). After William Johnson's victory in the Battle of Lake George on September 8, 1755, the British provincials began to build an advanced post near the site of the battle. Johnson ordered the two posts named for the king's sons, Forts Edward and William Henry, and the adjacent lake for the king himself.

Ticonderoga was the most important terrain between Crown Point and Lake George. Both armies had reconnoitered the strategic Ticonderoga peninsula during the summer of rising tensions in 1755. The French succeeded first in occupying the position. The peninsula was fortified by troops on the retreat from the debacle at Lake George. On September 20, 1755, Governor-General Philippe de Rigaud, Marquis de Vaudreuil, gave orders to young engineer Michel Chartier de Lotbinière to begin laying out a fort. It was called Fort Vaudreuil at first, but the vernacular name for the peninsula, Carillon, stuck better than a courtier's effort to flatter his patron. Legend has it that "Carillon" came from the bell-like chiming sound from the nearby waterfall, but recent scholarship has shown that the name actually derives from a Franco-Spanish retired officer and fur trader, Phillippe de Carrion du Fresnoy. The French continued to work on this structure during 1756 and 1757, cementing their hold on Lake Champlain.

**The French and Indian War**
The British, who suffered numerous defeats along the New York frontier in the early years of the war, did not challenge the French position at Ticonderoga until 1758. William Pitt's plan for the 1758 "Irruption into Canada" called for General James Abercromby, the British commander in chief in North America, to lead an army of 20,000 provincials and an additional 7,000 regulars into Canada by way of the Champlain Valley. The several colonial governments were unable to raise their quotas of men, however, and Abercromby marched toward Carillon with roughly 16,000 men. He enjoyed a five-to-one superiority over the French garrison at Carillon, which was commanded by the Marquis de Montcalm. Shortly after the British forces landed at the northern end of Lake George on July 6 and began their brief march to the fort, one of Abercromby's most important field commanders, Lord George Howe, was killed in a skirmish with some French troops. This loss deprived Abercromby of an important source of advice; he had depended on Howe for all the logistical and tactical planning for the campaign.

Abercromby believed the French numbers to be stronger than they were, and reports by French soldiers captured by the British on July 6 caused him to fear reinforcement by members of an expedition to the Mohawk Valley led by Chevalier de Lévis, which was racing to come to the assistance of Montcalm and Carillon. Abercromby made the decision to attack. On the morning of July 8, 1758, he sent his troops into a frontal assault against the French entrenchments that guarded the approach to the fort. Abercromby and his engineer, Matthew Clark, had developed a carefully crafted plan to bring artillery into position so that it could open flanking fire upon the French lines in precise coordination with the assault by the massed British troops at 1:00 P.M. The boats delivering the artillery got lost, however, and fell under heavy French fire. They withdrew, leaving the massed British troops unsupported by artillery. The errors and confusions multiplied. Rather than assembling in silence for the coordinated mass attack, the first British troops to arrive before the French lines opened fire. What was to have been a coordinated attacked by roughly ten thousand men disintegrated into a series of uncoordinated, unsupported attacks for six hours across the breadth of the French lines. Without modern means of rapid communication, the plan of attack fell apart disastrously. The British sustained heavy casualties—although proportional to those of the French—yet failed to breach the French lines. Abercromby retreated quickly to the southern end of Lake George, and Pitt's well-laid plans for the invasion of Canada never got past Montcalm at Ticonderoga.

Abercromby paid for this botched attack with his job. The following year found Jeffrey Amherst in charge of British operations in North America and facing the same task of dislodging the French from Ticonderoga. Amherst collected an army of about eleven thousand soldiers in Albany and started north in June, 1759. The garrison at Carillon, about four thousand strong, had orders to abandon the fort once the enemy appeared, since the French could no longer spare the men and supplies necessary to maintain it. When Amherst and his forces arrived in late July, the French followed orders and retreated, blowing up the fort's powder magazine in their wake. The resulting explosion did considerable damage to the magazine in the Southeast Bastion and to the East Barracks. Most of

*Fort Ticonderoga.* (Fort Ticonderoga Museum)

tia officer named Benedict Arnold brought plans before the Committee of Safety for attacking Ticonderoga and using its guns in the siege of Boston. In Connecticut, another militia officer named Samuel Holden Parsons drew up similar plans. In the Vermont country southeast of Lake Champlain, Ethan Allen organized his irregular patriot force, the Green Mountain Boys, for the same task.

In May, the Green Mountain Boys joined with the men recruited from Massachusetts and Connecticut, making a total of about two hundred men. Arnold and Allen agreed to share the command, but Allen quickly dominated the expedition because his Green Mountain Boys dominated the force.

the rest of the fort remained intact, however, if somewhat damaged by fire. British provincials were able to make repairs in short order, once the fires were put out, but the East Barracks and powder magazine were never rebuilt.

The British finally had their toehold on Lake Champlain, and from Ticonderoga they continued northward to conquer New France. In 1759 and 1760, Amherst's men repaired the fort and rechristened it Fort Ticonderoga, but with British victories farther north, its importance faded. For the remainder of the war, Ticonderoga remained a communications and supply link between Albany and Canada. After the fall of Quebec, the British reduced the number of troops there to a mere handful. By the early 1770's, contemporaries were reporting that the fort was in a ruinous state with a garrison of only forty-two men.

## The Revolutionary War

In April, 1775, Fort Ticonderoga was a poorly manned frontier post crumbling in disrepair. The importance of its location within the channel, however, had not changed. Thus, shortly after the battles of Lexington and Concord, colonial forces hatched schemes to capture Ticonderoga and invade Canada. In Massachusetts, a Connecticut mili-

In the predawn hours of May 10, this small army stole across the lake to Ticonderoga and surprised the British garrison, easily overpowering the sentries and other soldiers asleep in their barracks. Captain William Delaplace, the fort's commander, appeared after being roused by Allen's calls to "come out, you old rat." When Captain Delaplace asked under what authority Allen acted, the quick-tempered patriot responded. "In the name of the Great Jehovah and the Continental Congress." Faced with no other choice, Delaplace surrendered the fort, and the patriots had easily won their first offensive operation of the American Revolution.

During the rest of 1775, the colonists used Ticonderoga as a base for extending their grip on Lake Champlain. The day of Allen's victory, the patriots also seized Crown Point and its garrison of thirteen men. Shortly thereafter, Arnold captured a British schooner at the head of the lake. In the fall, the colonists launched their invasion of Canada. The army of the Northern Department in the autumn of 1775 was commanded by Major General Philip Schuyler, with Brigadier General Richard Montgomery as second in command. Schuyler fell ill as the army began to lay siege to St. Johns. He returned to Ticonderoga to manage the northward flow of supplies, and Montgomery took over field command, including the successful sieges of Chambly (October 18, 1775), St. Johns (November 2, 1775), and Montreal (November 13, 1775). The British, however, managed to turn back the American assault on Quebec, and the year ended with the colonists removing Ticonderoga's guns and transporting them and the guns from Crown Point east to assist George Washington in the siege of Boston.

The defeated and desperately ill American army retreated from Canada and began to dig in at Ticonderoga in June, 1776. The army, commanded by Schuyler and then by Horatio Gates, began fortifying the peninsula and the opposite shore in what is now Vermont. The French lines were rebuilt, and the old French fort was strengthened as the western anchor of American defenses. An eastern anchor was built at Mount Independence, so named after the army received the news of Congress's declaration in late July, 1776.

The successful defense of Ticonderoga—which, to officers on both sides, meant the narrow pass in the lake in addition to the old fort—in the autumn of 1776 cannot be understood without attention to both posts on opposite sides of Lake Champlain, as both fell under the same command and supply structure. By October, as Canadian governor Sir Guy Carleton's eight thousand-man combined army-navy force came pouring south after the Valcour action, the American defenders numbered some thirteen thousand. After Carleton withdrew, however, the American army withdrew as well. Gates headed to Philadelphia to lobby Congress, and Colonel Anthony Wayne was appointed commander of some three thousand ill, ill-fed, and ill-equipped troops at Ticonderoga. Many of his men spent the terrible winter of 1776-1777 in tents pitched on the old French lines, surrounded by the relics of Abercromby's army. Wayne wrote that Ticonderoga "appears to be the last part of the world that God made & I have some ground to believe it was finished in the dark." He reported that his soldiers, for want of better vessels, drank out the plentiful skulls available on the battleground and pitched their tents with "the shin & thigh bones of Abercrombies men."

## Benedict Arnold

Both the British and the colonists realized the value of naval supremacy on Lake Champlain, and both sides spent most of 1776 building ships. Benedict Arnold commanded a fleet that included a sloop, three schooners, and numerous smaller lakecraft. His fleet was built in Skenesborough (now Whitehall) and rowed north to Ticonderoga, where the ships were masted, rigged, and outfitted. One of Arnold's gunboats, *Philadelphia*, now preserved in the Smithsonian Institution's National Museum of American History, was armed with a seventeenth century Swedish bow-gun from the Ticonderoga artillery complement. The British constructed a larger flotilla at the north end of the lake to assist in a planned invasion of New York to be commanded by Carleton. On October 11, Arnold's fleet engaged in a four-hour battle with the larger British fleet near Valcour Island, in the north end of the lake. The outnumbered colonists fought bravely and executed a brilliant retreat under cover of darkness. The British, however, caught up with Arnold as he headed south and inflicted more damage on the Continentals.

Of the fifteen ships originally under Arnold's command, only four returned to Ticonderoga; the rest were either sunk or abandoned. The British regained control of Lake Champlain, but the Continentals had bought precious time. Arnold's fleet had delayed Carleton's advance. Carleton's armed naval vessels probed the strength of the American lines at Ticonderoga from less than a mile away and then withdrew north in early November, 1776. The colonists' cause had survived another year.

In the campaign of 1777, the British returned in force to challenge the Continentals' hold on Ticonderoga. This time the invading army was led by General John Burgoyne, who had orders to march from Canada to Albany and secure the Champlain Valley on his way. Burgoyne had more than seven thousand British regulars and German mercenaries in his command. The colonists at Ticonderoga, led by Major General Arthur St. Clair, were powerless to stop Burgoyne's advance without a naval presence on the lake.

Burgoyne arrived at Ticonderoga in early July. He had brought sufficient artillery to subdue the Continental forces, and he ordered a battery installed atop Mount Defiance, a hill overlooking the fort from the south. The Continentals thought such a task impossible because of Mount Defiance's steep elevation, but Burgoyne proved them wrong. After learning that the guns were in place, St. Clair conferred with his officers on July 5 and decided to vacate the fort without a fight. The Continentals retreated in great haste, scampering across a bridge that night to the Vermont side of the lake. (Burgoyne's German troops considered this floating bridge, which had been built during the late winter of 1777, to be one of the engineering wonders of the New World.) St. Clair later faced a court-martial for his decision, but the court exonerated him because of the general assumption that Ticonderoga could not be defended against enemy artillery installed on the elevations around it.

### Fall of Fort Ticonderoga to the Americans

The British held Ticonderoga briefly during the summer and fall of 1777 as Burgoyne continued his march south. It served as a convenient spot for holding American prisoners of war and an important link in British supply lines. Hoping to distract Burgoyne, Continental general Benjamin Lincoln ordered a raid on the fort in September, 1777. Colonel John Brown led a small force that accomplished little other than freeing some American prisoners and capturing some British soldiers. After Burgoyne's surrender at Saratoga in October, the British burned Ticonderoga and retreated northward. The fort once again fell into the colonists' hands, but they failed to garrison it for the remainder of the war. In 1780 and 1781 British officers and soldiers stopped briefly at Ticonderoga while engaging in sporadic warfare and peacemaking along the New York-Canadian frontier. A small force led by British General Barry St. Leger in 1781 was the last to use the fort as a military base. Washington visited Ticonderoga in July, 1783, during the long wait for a treaty of peace to be concluded. In September, 1783, the United States officially acquired the fort and garrison grounds by the Treaty of Paris ending the war. In 1785, the federal government turned over to the states unneeded military posts—thus turning over Ticonderoga to New York State.

### The Fort After the Revolution

In 1790, the state legislature assigned the fort and garrison grounds to the Regents of the University of the State of New York. In 1802, the legislature confirmed action by the Regents and granted an undivided interest in the property to Columbia University, in New York City, and Union College, in Schenectady, the two institutions of higher learning in New York State. After the War of 1812 ended, pressures for settlement on the western shores of Lake Champlain prompted the two colleges to "cash in" their land endowment. William Ferris Pell, a prominent New Yorker with an interest in the Champlain Valley, seems to have leased the garrison grounds for some years and then, in 1820, purchased the property and the ruins of the fort. In 1826, Pell constructed a building known as the Pavilion near the fort, with the King's Garden nearby; this house later became a hotel, although there is some reason to think that it was intended as a hotel from the outset. In any case, after the opening of the Champlain Canal in 1823, heritage tourism increased rapidly. The Pavilion became a hotel on the "Northern Tour" after William Ferris Pell's death in 1839.

Since 1826, the destiny of Fort Ticonderoga has been linked to the presence and future of the Pavilion, the imposing Greek Revival summer home built in the shadow of the fort on the shore of the lake. For nearly two centuries, the fort and the Pavilion together have shaped the sensibilities of millions of American and Canadian travelers about the meaning of their common history and landscape.

The ideological connections between the house and the fort are rooted in the early nineteenth century affinity for sublime landscapes enhanced by ruins. At Ticonderoga, the sublime wilderness of the Adirondacks meets the picturesque landscapes of the Hudson River. Thomas Cole's earliest signed oil painting, *Gelyna: A View from Ticonderoga*; James Fenimore Cooper's great novel *The Last of the Mohicans*, describing the French setting off to attack Fort William Henry from Fort Carillon; and William Ferris Pell's summer home and landscaped grounds, the Pavilion—all three created in 1826—are significant documents of the first formal American landscape aesthetic.

Locals used the old fort as a quarry and salvage yard, taking its stone, window frames, and other materials for their homes, cellars, and barns. In 1904, English architect Alfred C. Bossom (later Lord Bossom of Maidstone) began planning the restoration of Fort Ticonderoga. In 1908, Stephen H. P. Pell began work on the restoration of the fort. Pell received much support, especially financial support, from his wife, Sarah G. T. Pell, a pioneering preservationist, philanthropist, and suffragist. While Pell and Bossom restored the fort, she and Bossom restored the Pavilion. She also worked on the restoration of the King's Garden with Marian Cruger Coffin, the first woman to graduate with a degree in landscape architecture in the United States. In 1909, Fort Ticonderoga was opened to the public in a ceremony attended by President William Howard Taft and other dignitaries. Work continued through much of the twentieth century, with reconstruction of the fort's walls, buildings, and grounds.

### Modern Preservation Efforts

Today, Fort Ticonderoga and its eighteenth century "dependencies"—Mount Defiance, Hope, and Independence; the Carillon Battlefield; the Pavilion; and the King's Garden—are preserved and managed by a private, nonprofit educational association. It offers the public a museum devoted to the lives of soldiers, civilians, and Indians in this region during the eighteenth century. In addition to its collections, the fort hosts tours, reenactments, demonstrations, and other special programs related to life and culture in the colonial Champlain Valley. Scholars may also use the Thompson-Pell Research Center, a library of thirteen thousand volumes specializing in manuscripts and published resources related to the French and Indian War and the American Revolution. Along with nearby historical sites at Crown Point and Fort William Henry, Fort Ticonderoga offers visitors an excellent opportunity to experience life in the Champlain Valley at a time when European soldiers, colonists, and Indians struggled to control one of the most important natural highways in North America.

—*Timothy J. Shannon; revised by Nicholas Westbrook*

### For Further Information:

*Bulletin of the Fort Ticonderoga Museum,* 1927-    . This illustrated scholarly journal provides primary sources and strong interpretations of the fort's history. Copies are found in most major university libraries and in state historical societies in the Northeast. Back issues and subscriptions are available.

Hamilton, Edward P. *Fort Ticonderoga: Key to a Continent.* 2d ed. Ticonderoga, N.Y.: Fort Ticonderoga, 1995. A comprehensive study of Ticonderoga that provides much analysis of its role in the French and Indian War and the American Revolution.

Pell, Stephen H. P. *Fort Ticonderoga: A Short History.* Reprint. Ticonderoga, N.Y.: Fort Ticonderoga Museum, 1990. Another brief history of the fort.

# Franklin D. Roosevelt, Home of

**Date:** Hyde Park first settled by Europeans about 1700; Roosevelt born on January 30, 1882

**Relevant issues:** Cultural history, political history

**Significance:** The village of Hyde Park was the birthplace of Franklin D. Roosevelt (FDR), the thirty-second president of the United States. His home, now a National Historic Site, reflects the culture of his formative years that shaped his personality and political beliefs and substantially accounted for his presidential leadership.

**Location:** Eighty-five miles north of New York City on the Hudson River

**Site Office:**
Home of Franklin D. Roosevelt National Historic Site
519 Albany Post Road
Hyde Park, NY 12538-1997
ph.: (914) 229-9115
Web site: www.nps.gov/hofr/

The village of Hyde Park, New York, sits on a bluff on the east side of the Hudson River. In 1867 James Roosevelt, father of Franklin D. Roosevelt (FDR), purchased a seventeen-room house and several hundred acres about a mile south of the village to replace his previous house a few miles farther south that a fire had destroyed. At the time, large estates lined the bluff for miles overlooking the Hudson. Between this new Roosevelt estate and the village of Hyde Park were the Newbold and Rogers estates, the latter a seventy-room mansion in Romanesque style. In 1898, Frederick W. Vanderbilt built a Renaissance-style mansion of fifty rooms and a gatehouse only a block north of the center of the village. Hyde Park owed its existence to the nearby estates; as late as 1925 fewer than nine hundred persons lived in the village.

## James and Sara Roosevelt and Springwood

Mr. James, as everyone called him, named his estate Springwood and ran it like an English gentleman. When, as a widower, Mr. James married Sara Delano in 1880, a similar family background had prepared her well for the life at Springwood. There, on January 30, 1882, she gave birth to Franklin D. Roosevelt, the future thirty-second president.

Until he was fourteen years old, Master Franklin lived in a world deeply rooted in a distinctive way of life that provided him with love, attention, status, security, and role models. It was an ordered world in which everyone knew her or his place and responsibility. Life at Springwood included a cook, a nurse and governesses, maids, a gardener and a greenhouse, a coachman, and workers who farmed the extensive estate. Master Franklin's playmates included, in addition to visiting relatives, Mary Newbold from the adjoining estate and the two Rogers sons. Until he left for Groton School, private tutors educated him.

His parents, their relatives, and their friends evaluated individuals and events by standards of honesty, public morality, and a belief in noblesse oblige. Despite business affairs in New York City and extensive foreign travels, James and Sara Roosevelt most cherished their Hyde Park home and their self-assigned roles of an English country squire and a patrician matron who were responsible for setting examples of how persons of their class should live. The Roosevelt wealth, while substantial, was more modest than that of the Rogers and Vanderbilt families, and the Roosevelt consumption was far less conspicuous, although they did travel by private railroad car.

Mr. James maintained a relationship with Hyde Park. He sat on the school board, served a two-year term as supervisor for the town, and for decades served as vestryman at St. James Episcopal Church. Although the majority of voters tended to vote Republican in the village and township, Democrats in 1892 celebrated the election of Grover Cleveland as president; they organized a torchlight parade and march to Springwood in honor of Hyde Park's most prominent Democrat.

An understanding of life at Springwood and, to a lesser extent, its setting in Hyde Park is essential to understanding FDR personally and politically. Scholars, almost unanimously, have concluded that Roosevelt's greatest contributions as president were his ability to inspire confidence across the country and his belief that the federal government had a positive responsibility for the general welfare of the nation. Most biographers also agree that FDR's ability to inspire stemmed from a personality anchored in his own sense of security and that his belief in governmental stewardship reflected a principle embedded in the values of James and Sara Roosevelt.

FDR's four years at Groton reinforced the values he absorbed at home. James had carefully selected Groton because the headmaster, Endicott Peabody, was an Episcopalian clergyman who ran his school on a philosophy of an enlightened English boarding school. Throughout his life FDR identified Endicott and Fanny Peabody as second only to his parents in their influence on his life.

## FDR and a Political Career

For the six years after he graduated from Harvard in 1904, FDR attended Columbia University Law School. He married Eleanor Roosevelt, his fifth cousin, in 1905 and worked for a law firm in New York City. Neither the law nor the city satisfied FDR, so in 1910 he eagerly accepted the Democratic Party's nomination for state senator from the mid-Hudson Valley district. A political career based in Hyde Park appealed to him. He won the election and embarked on the profession that characterized the remainder of his life.

After James died in 1900, Sara managed the Springwood estate as closely as possible in the manner of her husband. FDR, however, wished to control property of his own. In 1911 he purchased 194 acres adjoining Springwood to the east. The first year he planted 8,000 evergreen trees; by 1928 the number had increased to 65,000, and by the time of his death he had planted more than 300,000 trees. Throughout his political career he called himself a tree farmer. Clearly FDR's conservation programs and policies as governor and president had antecedents in Hyde Park years earlier. FDR added other land to his holdings, became a landlord, and maintained friendships in the community.

FDR made his most important and lasting impact on Springwood in 1915 and 1916, when he planned and contracted for a fundamental remodeling of the house his father had purchased. By

*The home of Franklin D. Roosevelt in Hyde Park.* (Richard Cheek/Home of Franklin D. Roosevelt)

FDR's penchant for native fieldstone resulted in several buildings of that material. In 1924, he helped plan a stone cottage on his land for his wife so that she could meet with friends in her own home. It would be almost two miles east of the Big House, as local residents called Sara's house. The Dutch Colonial style that FDR picked for Eleanor's house, known as Val-Kill, indicated his strong identification with his Dutch ancestors and the Dutch who settled much of the Hudson Valley. In 1927 Sara, in keeping with her son's preference for native fieldstone and Dutch Colonial architecture, built a small library of that material and style in the village in honor of her late husband.

1915 Eleanor and Franklin had four children; their fifth child arrived in March, 1916. The seventeen rooms in the house simply could not accommodate his family with its nurses and maids and house servants. Only when FDR insisted that he would build his own house did Sara consent to the changes.

The remodeled house bore little resemblance to the original. A raised roof added a third floor to the center of the house, and the south and north wings added still more rooms. When finished, the house contained thirty-five rooms, eight of them for servants, and nine baths. Native fieldstone from stone walls on the estate covered the two wings, and stucco coated the central portion of the house. A large library-living room filled the entire first floor of the south wing and mirrored FDR's interests. Bookshelves held his vast leather-bound book collection, and cabinets held his stamp collections. Each end of the room featured a marble fireplace. Over one hung a portrait of FDR's great-great-grandfather, and over the other a portrait of his great-grandfather. At Christmas a large tree with live candles stood in the center of the room. FDR so loved the room that in 1937 he wrote funeral instructions that would place his casket in front of one fireplace so that he could spend the night before burial in his favorite spot.

Like his wife, FDR enjoyed a more private atmosphere than the Big House provided. In 1938 he started construction on what he called his Top Cottage. Located on a hill east of Eleanor's stone cottage, the one-level Dutch Colonial structure of fieldstone offered a spectacular view of the Hudson, more than two miles to the west. Except for two crossing highways and the railroad tracks along the river, the fields and woods between Top Cottage and the river all belonged to the Roosevelts.

In 1940 FDR dedicated Hyde Park's three new fieldstone schools named in his honor. The next year he dedicated the new fieldstone post office.

**The Legacy**
Late in his second term FDR decided to build a library near the Big House to hold his family records, official papers, and mementos of his time in office. He donated sixteen acres of land, and private citizens donated the money for construction. FDR designed the stone Dutch Colonial building. The museum portion of the library opened in 1941, but FDR maintained a study in the archives portion, where he held meetings and gave four of his fireside chats. The museum exhibits include

FDR's car, with its hand controls, in which he enjoyed driving around his estate and Hyde Park village. Every president after FDR has followed his example and built a presidential library.

Sara Roosevelt died in September, 1941, and thereafter FDR maintained the house exactly as she left it. Two years later he donated the house and thirty-three acres to the government with the proviso that his family be permitted to live there after his death. In November, 1945, seven months after his death, the family relinquished their rights and the National Park Service assumed administration of the property.

The village and town of Hyde Park form part of Dutchess County, whose residents of that time usually elected Republican candidates. In FDR's seven political campaigns, Hyde Park village voters gave him a majority in only his two races for the state senate in 1910 and 1912 and his 1930 race to win reelection as governor. On election nights, Hyde Park supporters kept up a long tradition of calling on FDR to help celebrate his victories. Hyde Park, with a population of a few thousand at the time FDR died, became a suburban community during the following decades. FDR's legacy, however, defines Hyde Park.

The only president ever elected to third and fourth terms, FDR led the nation through its greatest economic depression and through World War II. At Springwood he proudly entertained such houseguests as the king and queen of Great Britain, the crown princess of the Netherlands, and British prime minister Winston Churchill. As president he often returned to Hyde Park for weekends and vacations. To a degree matched by few other leaders, FDR assimilated family tradition and a place, Hyde Park, into his personality and transmitted them to the nation.

### Places to Visit

In Hyde Park the National Park Service administers as National Historic Sites the home of Franklin D. Roosevelt and the home of Frederick W. Vanderbilt. Approximately two miles from the Roosevelt Home, the National Park Service administers the Eleanor Roosevelt National Historic Site. The National Archives operates the Roosevelt Presidential Library. The Hyde Park post office contains a large mural depicting local scenes from different time periods. —*Keith W. Olson*

### For Further Information:

Burns, James MacGregor. *Roosevelt: The Lion and the Fox*. New York: Harcourt, Brace & World, 1956. One of the finest biographies of any American. Covers FDR's first two terms. Volume 2, *Roosevelt: Soldier of Freedom* (1989), continues the study.

Graham, Otis L., Jr., and Meghan Robinson Wander. *Franklin D. Roosevelt His Life and Times*. Boston: G. K. Hall, 1985. A treasure of essays of varying lengths about Roosevelt, other individuals, events, and programs.

Maney, Patrick. *The Roosevelt Presence*. New York: Twayne, 1992. A short, insightful, well-written biography.

Roosevelt Library. www.fdrlibrary.marist.edu.

Ward, Geoffrey C. *Before the Trumpet: Young Franklin Roosevelt*. New York: Harper & Row, 1985. A rich narrative of family history and biography of FDR, stopping after his wedding in 1905.

_____. *A First-Class Temperament: The Emergence of Franklin Roosevelt*. New York: Harper & Row, 1989. Continues his study, covering the years 1905 through election as governor in 1928.

# Grant's Tomb

**Date:** Completed in 1897

**Relevant issues:** Civil War, military history, political history

**Significance:** The General Grant National Memorial, commonly called Grant's Tomb, is the largest mausoleum in the United States. It honors the memory of Ulysses S. Grant, head of the Union armies in 1864 and 1865 and president of the United States from 1869 to 1877.

**Location:** Riverside Drive and 122d Street in the borough of Manhattan, New York City

**Site Office:**

General Grant National Memorial
Riverside Drive and 122d Street
New York, NY 10003
ph.: (212) 666-1640
Web site: www.nps.gov/gegr/
*mailing address:*
Superintendent, General Grant National Memorial
26 Wall Street
New York, NY 10005

It is difficult now to imagine the incredible esteem in which Ulysses S. Grant (1822-1885) was held in the Union states between the Civil War and the beginning of World War I. He and the martyred President Abraham Lincoln (1809-1865) were almost universally viewed as the two men who had personally restored national unity and honor. Despite scandals created by members of his government during his eight-year service as the eighteenth president of the United States (1869 to 1877), the American public never held Grant personally responsible for the problems in his administration. The posthumous publication of his *Personal Memoirs* (1885), which he completed just before his death on July 23, 1885, reinforced the accepted belief that he was a heroic figure who had served America well during his long military career, which extended from 1843 to 1868, and during his eight years as president. He died from throat cancer. Contemporary reports indicated that he reacted stoically to his inevitable and painful death. His inner courage further increased the public admiration for General Grant.

### Last Days

Although Ulysses S. Grant was born on April 27, 1822, in Point Pleasant, Ohio, his adopted state was New York. He had extensive connections with New York State; he attended the United States Military Academy in West Point, New York, from 1839 to 1843, and he moved permanently to New York City after his presidency ended in 1877. He entered business in Manhattan and was very well respected throughout New York City. In October, 1884, he was diagnosed with throat cancer. At that time, doctors could do very little to treat cancer (chemotherapy did not exist), and it was obvious that General Grant would not live long. In June, 1885, General and Mrs. Julia Dent Grant went to Mount McGregor in New York's Adirondack Mountains, where he died on July 23, 1885.

The public mourning was appropriate for a fallen military hero and president. His body lay in state first in the capitol in Albany and then in City Hall in New York City. The three living presidents—Grover Cleveland, Chester Arthur, and Rutherford B. Hayes—and over one million spectators viewed the funeral procession from Fourteenth Street to Riverside Park on 122d Street, where he was buried. Contemporary reports indi-

cate that this funeral procession, with sixty thousand marchers, lasted five hours. The only funeral procession comparable to it was the funeral procession twenty years earlier for Abraham Lincoln.

### Remembering a Leader

Soon after General Grant's death, a need was recognized for an impressive monument to honor the memory of such a respected military leader and president. General Grant had been buried in a temporary tomb in Riverside Park on August 8, 1885. John Duncan, a leading American architect of that era, was hired to design an appropriate mausoleum. The General Grant National Memorial was formally dedicated in the presence of President William McKinley and Grant's widow Julia on April 27, 1897, which would have been Grant's seventy-fifth birthday. At that time, his coffin was moved from its temporary tomb into a sarcophagus in Grant's Tomb. Next to General Grant's sarcophagus is an identical sarcophagus in which his wife Julia Grant was buried on December 21, 1902.

An impressive ceremony was held on April 27, 1997, to rededicate this memorial to an American hero who is still greatly respected more than one hundred years after his death. During the decades immediately after its dedication in 1897, this shrine to a war hero was visited by very large numbers of Americans, and thousands of people still visit Grant's Tomb every year. According to the National Park Service, which is responsible for maintaining this national memorial, almost 100,000 people visited Grant's Tomb in 1996. There is a visitors' center next to the mausoleum, which explains to visitors the importance of Ulysses S. Grant's role as president and military leader.

### Building the Monument

A monument as massive as Grant's Tomb was very expensive to build. This one was financed by contributions by ordinary American adults and children, who admired him so much that they recognized the need to honor this military and political leader who had done so much to preserve the republic. As designed by John Duncan, Grant's Tomb is a very impressive building whether seen by visitors to Riverside Park itself or by passengers on the tourist boats which circle the island of Manhattan. There is a large plaza in front of the mausoleum itself. To the right and the left of the front of Grant's

*Grant's Tomb.* (American Stock Photography)

monument is supported by twenty-four Ionic columns in a circle. The dome itself rises 150 feet above the level of the plaza. An interior staircase allows visitors to reach the dome. The exterior of Grant's Tomb is massive and very impressive. It is not surprising that it is still considered one of the most beautiful landmarks in New York City.

The interior of Grant's Tomb is equally magnificent. Everything inside creates an impression of solemnity and serves to remind us that General Grant's most significant accomplishment was as a military leader who won the Civil War and restored national unity and peace to the entire United States. The interior marble stairway leads to two different levels. As a visitor walks down toward the crypt, where the sarcophagi of General and Mrs. Grant are located, he or she sees rooms on whose walls are displayed maps for major Civil War battles in which General Grant participated. In each room are battle flags to honor Union soldiers from different states who fought under General Grant during the Civil War. The states honored in these trophy rooms are Illinois, Ohio, Pennsylvania, New York, Indiana, Missouri, and Wisconsin. The American flag is proudly displayed at the top of the stairway, flanked by the state flags of Ohio and Illinois. These two state flags were chosen because Ulysses S. Grant was born in Ohio, and he lived for some time in Illinois.

The crypt itself is circular. Visitors view the sarcophagi of General and Mrs. Grant from above, standing behind a circular balustrade, a railing supported by beautifully carved supports. The sarcophagi themselves are located equidistant from the floor of the crypt and the top of the balustrade and in the center of the crypt. The two gray and maroon sarcophagi rest on a base of the same

Tomb are two large flag poles. From one hangs a four-star flag to honor Ulysses S. Grant, who was a four-star general. The American flag hangs from the other pole. The exterior of the monument is made of gray granite, and the interior is made of white marble. This mausoleum is set on a square base, each side of which is ninety feet long. Three sets of steps lead to the entrance of the mausoleum. On the sides of the first level of steps are two large granite eagles, the traditional American symbol. On the second level are six massive Doric columns which support the front of this monument.

On the third level are two large bronze doors, which are open during operating hours. Each massive door is 16 feet high and 5.5 feet wide. The solemnity of the entrance definitely creates the impression that the visitor is about to enter a place of reverence. The circular dome on the top of this

color. The base and the two sarcophagi are all made from Wisconsin porphyry, which is a hard rock, usually red maroon in color. It has been estimated that each sarcophagus weighs nine thousand pounds. On the top of the left sarcophagus, the words "Ulysses S. Grant" were carved in 1897 and the words "Julia D. Grant" were added in 1902 after her death. The beauty of the sarcophagi and the simplicity of the inscriptions on them indicate to visitors that this is a solemn site for Americans because it is a visual reminder of the incredible sacrifices made by Americans during the Civil War, in which more Americans died than in all other wars combined.

In the niches in the outer walls of the crypt are busts of five Civil War Union generals and fellow West Point graduates. The generals honored along with General Grant are Generals Philip Sheridan, William Sherman, James McPherson, Edward Ord, and George Thomas. All five generals served under Grant's command during the Civil War. The visitor gradually comes to realize that this is not simply a national monument to honor the memory of Ulysses S. Grant but also a monument designed to honor all Union soldiers who fought and died during the Civil War.

On the walls in the Memorial Room are several paintings depicting major battles of the Civil War, including Lookout Mountain, Missionary Ridge, Shiloh, and Vicksburg. Other paintings depict Confederate General Robert E. Lee's surrender to General Grant at Appomattox on April 10, 1865. There are also bas-relief statues, i.e. statues which barely protrude from the wall, depicting important scenes in the military and political careers of General Grant. Inside the monument also are several allegorical statues and paintings depicting such images as the tree of life, a military helmet, which represents his service in both the Mexican and Civil Wars, an olive branch to symbolize the peace which Grant restored to the United States, and a laurel wreath, which refers to his death. Outside the mausoleum are two trees surrounded by an iron fence. A plaque by the fence indicates that the ginkgo tree and the Chinese cork tree were gifts from the Chinese government. These trees were planted just one month after the dedication of Grant's Tomb.

**Visiting the Site**
A visit to Grant's Tomb produces unexpected reactions. A naïve tourist might think that Grant's Tomb is little more than another historical landmark in a city filled with important historical buildings and landmarks, but Grant's Tomb is very different from other presidential gravesites, which simply honor the memory of the president who is buried beneath the tombstone or monument. Grant's Tomb pays homage not only to General and Mrs. Grant but also to all who sacrificed and died during the Civil War in order to restore national unity. The presence of busts honoring five Union generals serves to remind visitors that Grant would never have won decisive battles during the Civil War without the guidance of fellow generals and the heroism of soldiers who fought and died under their command. A visit to Grant's Tomb, like a visit to Arlington National Cemetery, helps people to understand the enormity of the sacrifices of those who risked their lives in the service of America.　　　　　　　　 —Edmund J. Campion

**For Further Information:**
Carpenter, John A. *Ulysses S. Grant.* New York: Twayne, 1970.

Laird, Archibald. *Monuments Marking the Graves of the Presidents.* North Quincy, Mass.: Christopher, 1971.

Lamb, Brian. *Who's Buried in Grant's Tomb: A Tour of Presidential Gravesites.* Baltimore: The Johns Hopkins University Press, 2000.

McFeely, William S. *Grant: A Biography.* New York: W. W. Norton, 1995.

Ross, Ishbel. *The General's Wife: The Life of Mrs. Ulysses S. Grant.* New York: Dodd, Mead, 1959.

Woodword, W. E. *Meet General Grant.* New York: Horace Liveright, 1928.

# Greenwich Village

**Date:** First settled by the Dutch in 1629

**Relevant issues:** Art and architecture, cultural history, literary history, political history

**Significance:** This National Historic District, the legendary site of American Bohemia, has been home to numerous important writers, artists, and political activists. It is currently a shopping, nightlife, and residential district noted for its low-rise architecture and its maze of quiet, tree-lined streets.

**Location:** Manhattan, a borough of New York City; Fourteenth Street (northern boundary) to Houston (approximate southern boundary), West Street along the Hudson River (western boundary) to First Avenue (eastern border), with the area between Fifth Avenue and First Avenue referred to as East Village

**Site Office:**
The Museum of the City of New York
1220 Fifth Avenue
New York, NY 10029
ph.: (212) 534-1672
Web site: www.mcny.org

There is no history of Greenwich Village. Rather, there are histories—each of the village's seven districts has its own unique stories to tell. If Greenwich Village, as its apologists have indicated over the years, is a "spiritual zone," then its axis mundi must be the one idea that people from many backgrounds and walks of life can come to one area and create, as John Reed put it, "something glorious," despite (or because of) the odds against them. Whether the focus has been radical politics, art, or lifestyle, individuals and groups have, with little money or with little public support, started something that would grow to infiltrate the entire American consciousness.

Taking a walk through Greenwich Village today, one sometimes finds it difficult to visit the past. The Loeb Student Center of New York University on La Guardia Place has taken over the site of the House of Genius, named for the number of famous writers who lived there, including Theodore Dreiser, Stephen Crane, Willa Cather, and O. Henry. The house owned by Henry James's grandmother, which provided the setting for his 1880 novel *Washington Square*, is long gone. Only the fronts of the Federal-style housing erected for Manhattan's elite on the square, known as the Row (between Fifth Avenue and University Place), survived development.

### Early History

The land that is now Greenwich Village was inhabited by Sapokanickan Indians before Dutch explorer Henry Hudson came upon it. The land was rich with game and fertile for cultivation. In 1629, the Dutch West India Company granted two hundred acres to Wouter Van Twiller, who immediately turned it into a tobacco plantation he named Bossen Bouwerie or "Farm in the Woods," in the area around present-day Washington Square. Van Twiller was an opportunist and his landgrabbing so alarmed the Dutch government that he was recalled in 1638.

The fortunes of the Dutch West India Company began to decline as a result of numerous wars with the indigenous people. In 1644, the company's weakness enabled African slaves who had been shipped to Manhattan to work the farms to ask for their freedom. The Dutch West India company needed the loyalty of blacks during the Indian wars and, according to historian Thelma Wills Foote in her essay for *Greenwich Village: Culture and Counterculture* (1993), granted "half-freedom," "manumitting them on the condition they labor for the company and that their offspring would be the company's property." In 1664 hardship caused the company to sell several of its slaves, and the half-freed subjects used this opportunity to petition for full emancipation, which the company granted. When the English took control of Manhattan, however, they enacted a series of oppressive racist laws that sought to debase and reverse the status of the black freedmen, many of whom owned property. (In fact, Richmond Hill, an area of the South Village now demolished, was owned by Simon Congo, a black freedman.)

Greenwich Village might have remained a sleepy farming community but for the epidemics that hit New York City, first a smallpox plague in 1739 and then in 1798 a cholera epidemic for which the city of New York established a burial site at what became Washington Square. These and other plagues drove the city's elite to escape to the hillier country of the village and purchase residences there. In 1822, a yellow fever epidemic caused a large exodus of people from the city to Greenwich Village, and many settled there permanently. The burial ground was converted to a parade ground and renamed Washington Square. The Washington Square Arch at the foot of Fifth Avenue was designed by Stanford White and erected in 1889 to commemorate the hundredth anniversary of George Washington's presidential inauguration. Statues of Washington, *Washington at War* and *Washington at Peace*, were added in 1913.

### History of Violent Activism

Collectivist, sometimes violent activism became a

*The West Village, New York City.* (NYC & Company Convention and Visitors Bureau)

as "Little Africa." There the first black Roman Catholic church had been built, and the first black theater and newspaper, *Freedom's Journal*, had been established. By 1850, the area was inhabited by French immigrants, and the black population had moved north. According to historian Terry Millar, "by the close of the 1870's, however, most of the French families had left the area for Midtown, forced away by the growing popularity of Frenchtown as a red-light district." Frenchtown became the notorious Latin Quarter, while the rest of the South Village became settled by Italian immigrants at the turn of the century.

Different accounts place the beginning of the Greenwich Village legend in different areas. One account places it in the Latin Quarter, while another puts it in the American Ward, possibly so named because it had not been settled by immigrants. American Bohemia probably originated in a dingy smoke-filled beer hall on Broadway, opened by Charles Pfaff in 1855. The patrons of Pfaff's started the first counterculture publication, the *New York Saturday Press*, among whose literary contributors was Walt Whitman.

recurring facet of Greenwich Village life. One of the first labor disputes in the area culminated in the Stonecutters' Riot of 1834. According to Daniel J. Walkowitz in his essay in *Greenwich Village Culture and Counterculture*, "Unlike many subsequent crowd activities, it was not a racial or ethnic conflict but a struggle over the use of free versus convict labor."

The University of the City of New York had purchased a parcel of land east of Washington Square for around $40,000, leaving a balance in their treasury of only $66.75. In order to save money, the university contracted with Elisha Bloomer to provide cut marble for the construction of buildings. Bloomer had first introduced the practice of using prison labor to provide goods and services. Free stonecutters attacked Bloomer's marble shop at 160 Broadway, smashing windows and doors and demolishing marble mantelpieces. The New York State National Guard was called in to disperse the crowd and remained for several days to protect the construction site.

In the 1850's, the area west of Washington Square came to be inhabited by poor immigrants who often lived in cheap, unsanitary housing conditions such as those endemic to tenement buildings erected on Bleecker Street. The South Village had long been populated by blacks and was known

## Greenwich Village in the Twentieth Century

By 1910, the village had become a congested district populated by Irish, Germans, Jews, Italians, and sailors as well as some "old New Yorkers." "Bohemians" began to flock to the village, attracted by the low rents and the quaintness of the maze of crooked streets, which had survived the city's attempt to make them conform to the grid design of 1811.

The year 1913 seems to have been pivotal in the life of the villagers, who were distinguished from the other residents of what was then called the Ninth Ward. The Liberal Club, an offshoot of another more conservative club in Manhattan, was established above Polly Holladay's restaurant, a bohemian hangout. It offered dances to which "uncorseted" ladies were admitted, lectures on birth control by Margaret Sanger, play readings, and exhibits of cubist art.

Two major events arose from the establishment of Mabel Dodge's salon 1913. The first was the International Exhibition of Modern Art, or, as it is more commonly known, the Armory Show. Although, as Rick Beard has written, the exhibition was held "considerably north of Greenwich Village, . . . it brought the Village art community to the forefront as champions of the 'new art,'" with works by such artists as Pablo Picasso, Paul Cézanne, Paul Gaugin, Jean (or Hans) Arp, and Marcel Duchamp.

## Leftist Movements

The second event was the "Paterson Pageant." Masterminded by radical journalist John Reed on a suggestion from Dodge, the pageant took place at Madison Square Garden before a crowd of seventeen thousand. The pageant dramatized the struggle of the Paterson, New Jersey, silk workers, and its cast was drawn from the ranks of the workers themselves. A critical success and financial failure, the event inspired Reed, a contributor to the left-wing journal *The Masses*, to greater levels of activism. He is renowned for heading the American Communist Party and for being deported to the Soviet Union by the U.S. government at the end of World War I. His account of the Soviet rebellion, *Ten Days That Shook the World* (1919), influenced thousands of people to join leftist causes.

*The Masses* first appeared in 1911 as a vehicle for the growing cooperative movement. After its patron withdrew funding, the journal's original editor, Piet Vlag, ceased publication. Its contributors decided to keep it going on their own, however, enlisting Max Eastman as the new editor for no pay. It became the principal organ for village intelligentsia, including Reed, Upton Sinclair, and Randolph Bourne. Later, because *The Masses* protested against World War II, several government agencies worked together to break the publication, even arresting many of its so-called conspirators.

Dodge's salon and the Liberal Club also had a hand in inspiring the formation of a small theater troupe. An affair between Dodge and Reed was the basis for a short play by Neith Boyce presented in 1915 at a Provincetown, Massachusetts, summer cottage. Buoyed by the success of their second sea-

son on Cape Cod, the Provincetown Players decided to try a winter season in the village, moving first to the parlor of a brownstone next to Polly Holladay's restaurant, and then to a better space three doors south on MacDougal Street. The Provincetown Players introduced the works of Eugene O'Neill, then known as a youthful village drunkard who frequented the worst bar in the village, called the Hellhole, but now known as one of the greatest of all American playwrights. Poet Edna St. Vincent Millay was a member of the troupe, which also gained fame producing E. E. Cummings's expressionist drama, *Him* (pb. 1927).

One of the more colorful characters in the village at this time was Guido Bruno, whose real name was Curt Josef Kisch. The publisher of *Bruno's Weekly, Bruno's Bohemia,* and *Bruno's Review of Life, Love, and Literature,* Guido Bruno is remembered as a fraud eager to exploit the tourists who came to gawk at the eccentrics of Greenwich Village. According to Terry Miller, however, "hindsight shows Bruno's roster of writers to be less trivial than legend would have us believe." He was the first to publish Hart Crane and introduced Aubrey Beardsley to an American audience. His Thimble Theatre produced the first performances of August Strindberg's *Fröken Julie* (pb. 1888; *Miss Julie,* 1912).

During the 1920's, another group of individuals came together to produce "something glorious." They were scientists and engineers, rather than bohemians, and their work flourished not in the nightlife of tearooms and "goofy" bars, but in the daylight activities of Bell Laboratories. In rather short order, they invented and advanced toll broadcasting, launching what was to become the National Broadcasting Company (NBC). They developed the methods by which sound could be synchronized with film and created the world's first soundstage. Then in 1927, reporters were called to the eleventh floor auditorium, where, on a large, odd apparatus, they saw and heard Secretary of Commerce Herbert Hoover addressing them from Washington, D.C. Bell technicians had invented television.

## Prohibition and the Literati

Prohibition brought thousands of outsiders into Greenwich Village looking for booze and easy sex, which they found in abundance. Yet some very exciting projects were also happening. In 1919, the

New School was formed in protest over New York University's ban on wartime dissent. Elizabeth Irwin, who founded the Little Red Schoolhouse, began her experiments with elementary education.

The literati of the twenties contributed to the magazine *Dial*, which published such authors as John Dos Passos, Sherwood Anderson, Virginia Woolf, Gertrude Stein, D. H. Lawrence, Archibald MacLeish, Bertrand Russell, Thomas Mann, E. M. Forster, T. S. Eliot, and H. L. Mencken, as well as the artwork of Picasso and Henri Matisse.

In 1929, the stock market crash affected Greenwich Village as much as it did the rest of America. Still, real estate developers caused rents to soar, and the Whitney Museum of Art was opened. Gertrude Vanderbilt Whitney, the wealthy granddaughter of the shipping magnate, abandoned respectable society in favor of the bohemian life, taking a studio on MacDougal Street where she collected the works of modern artists. Her collection played a significant role in the Armory Show of 1913. When the Metropolitan Museum of Art refused the generous donation of her entire collection, she decided to open her own museum. From 1931 to 1954, when the museum was moved, village residents and visitors were able to view the works of such artists as Arthur B. Davies, John Sloan, Charles Demuth, and Georgia O'Keeffe.

With six thousand dollars of borrowed funds, Barney Josephson opened Cafe Society in 1938 with the intent of creating the first racially mixed jazz club in New York. For its opening, Josephson found a then-unknown singer by the name of Billie Holiday. Among the jazz greats who subsequently performed there were Sarah Vaughan, Lena Horne, and Big Joe Turner.

### The Beat Generation

In 1943, Allen Ginsberg met his friend Lucien Carr for his first drink in the village. There Ginsberg was introduced to Jack Kerouac and William S. Burroughs. These three writers, more than any others, informed the aesthetic moment of the Beat Generation. Their respective works, *Howl* (1956), *On the Road* (1957), and *Naked Lunch* (1959), defined the mood of youth in America for generations: cynical, bored, and full of romantic idealism. They met at the San Remo, which became so famous as a Beat club that it was featured on television on the Columbia Broadcasting System (CBS). The three writers eventually parted company, while the beatniks quickly became a parody of themselves, paving the way for the appearance of the hippies.

In 1950, eighteen abstract expressionist painters, most of whom congregated at their own village facility known simply as The Club, decided to protest a juried exhibition at the Metropolitan Museum of Art. They signed a letter denouncing the conservatism of the show's jury and also critics' rejection of new art in general. It was forwarded to *The New York Times* and became front page news, leading the "Irascible Eighteen" to pose for a now-famous group portrait in *Life* magazine. Among the artists represented were Jackson Pollock, William de Kooning, Mark Rothko, and Robert Motherwell.

### The Village During the 1960's

As historians Fred W. McDarrah and Patrick S. McDarrah point out, "in the 1960's, the village became a center of social protest and change." It was in the village that the Youth International Movement, or "yippies," was begun by Abbie Hoffman and Jerry Rubin. Experimental theater flowered, such as that devised by Julian Beck's Living Theater and the underground offerings of Caffe Cino, which presented works by Lanford Wilson, Sam Shepard, and John Guare. Ellen Stuart opened her basement theater with money from an unemployment check; it is now renowned as the La Mama Experimental Theater Club. Andy Warhol created the Plastic Exploding Inevitable at the Electric Circus disco on St. Marks Place and launched the musical careers of Lou Reed and the Velvet Underground.

The village came together in the sixties for another purpose altogether. Residents helped pass the city's Landmark Preservation Law, having already organized to limit further construction in their neighborhood. As a result of continuing efforts, 2,035 structures were placed under the protection of a single landmark district comprising almost the entire West Village. One of the beneficiaries of this movement was the Jefferson Market Courthouse, built on the site of the Jefferson Market. Situated on the triangle formed by West 10th, Sixth Avenue, and Greenwich Avenue, the building has been called an excellent example of Gothic Revival and, because of its alternating bands of red brick and white granite, of the Lean Bacon Style.

## The Stonewall Rebellion

After an attempt by police in 1969 to raid the Stonewall Union, a gay bar in the village, the patrons responded by throwing rocks and bottles, surprising themselves and the police. For four nights afterward, gays rioted in the Christopher Street neighborhood to protest a history of unfair treatment. The event, now simply referred to as Stonewall, marked the beginning of the modern gay and lesbian rights movement. Today, Christopher Street and the West Village form one of America's preeminent centers of gay life.

At the end of the 1970's, with gentrification pushing its way into the rest of the village, the spirit of village enterprise moved east. Although many residents of the area dispute they live in the East Village, preferring to think of themselves as Lower East Siders, nevertheless the anarchism and experimentalism that have informed the village legend resurged in the burgeoning punk scene of such places as Manic Panic, a punk fashion and paraphernalia boutique, and CBGB's, the club that introduced Talking Heads, the Ramones, Patti Smith, and Blondie to America. Like their forerunners, these businesses were begun with little money, small support, and enormous drive and creativity.

Throughout the 1980's and 1990's, the village became a high-rent district, turning away those poor artists, writers, and thinkers who often make, out of nothing, something glorious. The spirit of Greenwich Village has been evicted from the location of Wouter Van Twiller's Bossen Bouwerie, but not from its real location; as Hippolyte Havel, village personality, anarchist, and writer once said, "Greenwich Village has no boundaries. It's a state of mind."
—*Gregory J. Ledger*

## For Further Information:

Beard, Rick, and Leslie Cohen Berlowitz, eds. *Greenwich Village: Culture and Counterculture.* New Brunswick, N.J.: Rutgers University Press for the Museum of the City of New York, 1993. A collection of essays covering many different perspectives of the area's history, people, and events. Some of the essays overlap, while others contradict.

McDarrah, Fred W., and Patrick J. McDarrah. *The Greenwich Village Guide.* Chicago: A Cappella Books, 1992. A comprehensive history-filled tourist guide.

Miller, Terry. *Greenwich Village and How It Got That Way.* New York: Crown, 1990. A tour of the seven districts of Greenwich. While its schematic organization makes it a difficult narrative, it contains a wealth of information normally left out of both histories and guide books.

Selzer, Jack. *Kenneth Burke in Greenwich Village: Conversing with the Moderns, 1915-1931.* Madison: University of Wisconsin Press, 1996. Offers a glimpse of intellectual life in Greenwich Village in the twentieth century.

# Hamilton Grange

**Date:** Established as a National Memorial on April 27, 1962

**Relevant issues:** Art and architecture, colonial America

**Significance:** Built in 1802-1803 in upper Manhattan, then scenic farmland, the Grange is the only home ever owned by Alexander Hamilton, one of the Founding Fathers. The Grange was designed by the famous American architect John McComb, Jr., and is of significance as a structural work of the Federal period. Hamilton spent nearly two years at the Grange, which he referred to as a garden refuge for a disappointed politician, before his life was cut short on July 11, 1804, by a mortal wound received in an infamous duel with Aaron Burr.

**Location:** In New York City (the Harlem section of Manhattan) at 287 Convent Avenue between West 141st and West 142d Streets

**Site Office:**
Hamilton Grange National Memorial
Superintendent, Manhattan Sites
26 Wall Street
New York, NY 10005
ph.: (212) 825-6990
Web sites: www.nps.gov/hagr/; www.national parks.org/guide/parks/hamilton-gra-1875 .htm

By the fall of 1799, Alexander Hamilton was searching for something he had always longed for—a home of his own. His life had been a series of continuous movements from rented house to rented house in the cramped quarters of lower Manhattan. Since his marriage to Elizabeth Scholar in 1780, he had moved seven times. In the process, Elizabeth had given birth to eight children. Alexander often made lengthy visits to his father-in-law's mansion in Albany. General Philip Schuyler headed one of New York's most distinguished families. He was more than happy to maintain at the mansion several of Alexander's children for extended periods of time. The situation must have proven to be a bit embarrassing for the forty-four-year-old Hamilton, a well-known lawyer and Federalist Party leader with a famous military and political career behind him. Hamilton now felt the compulsion to settle down.

A thirty-acre tract of land in Harlem, near the home of a friend, Ebeneezer Stevens, was up for sale. Hamilton had been on this land once before. Following the Battle of Long Island, he had retreated from superior British forces on the Bloomington Road. The road bisected the thirty acres. On the eastern section was farmland, and on the west was a scenic knoll overlooking the Hudson and Harlem Rivers. The western section was an ideal place to build a house.

Within a year, Hamilton contracted one of the new nation's foremost architects, John McComb, Jr., to design the Grange, named after Hamilton's ancestral home in Ayshire, Scotland. McComb was noted for designing New York City Hall, Castle Clinton on the Battery, and the Old Queens building of Rutgers University. The builder of the house was Ezra Weeks, whose brother Hamilton defended in a murder trial shortly before construction was started on the Grange. The elegant but modest house took two years to complete and ran into major construction difficulties. Expenses for building the Grange amounted to far more than Hamilton imagined, or that his modest life savings could handle. Mortgaging the Grange's farmland, and other land holdings, was necessary to complete construction.

The house was completed in February, 1803. It was a three-bay, two-story structure with elegant porches on all sides, designed in the symmetrical Federal style of architecture which was typical of the time. The upstairs area contained eight fireplaces, designed according to the new scientific principles of Count Rumford, to provide maximum heat and minimum smoke.

**Hamilton's Career**

Though he had the debt of a nation, the first secretary of the Treasury was deeply in debt in 1803. Hamilton hoped his legal practice, over time, would help reduce his indebtedness. His rise to prominence was not accompanied by a great rise to riches.

Hamilton was born out of wedlock in 1755 in the West Indies to Rachel Laviern and James Hamilton. By the time Alexander was ten, his father had abandoned the family. At the age of eleven, Alexander began work as a shipping clerk on St. Croix. His abilities and hard work gained him advancement to manager by the age of sixteen. The young Hamilton's business partners helped finance his formal education by sending him to school in New York City. After a year in preparatory school, he enrolled in Kings College (later renamed Columbia University) in 1773. Hamilton proved to be a brilliant student; however, his studies were interrupted by events leading to the American Revolution.

As a student, Hamilton publicly defended the Boston Tea Party, and he gained notice by writing three influential pamphlets attacking British mercantilist policies and upholding the boycott of British products by the Continental Congress. He cut short his education to join the Continental army in March, 1776, gaining a commission as a captain of artillery. His heroic role in the Battle of Trenton was rewarded by a promotion to colonel and a four-year position as George Washington's aide-de-camp. A close lifelong relationship was forged. Hamilton's fluid French and magnetic personality made him a good choice for a position as chief liaison officer with French forces. Hamilton rode beside Washington at the Battles of Brandywine, Germantown, and Monmouth. In the final battle of the Revolutionary War, Hamilton commanded an infantry battalion which attacked British strongholds at Yorktown.

Immediately after the war, Hamilton began a legal practice in New York City. He specialized in defending former Loyalists from discriminatory regulations. Yet national politics soon called. In 1786, Hamilton served as delegate to the Annapolis Convention, which discussed the pitiful economic plight of the new nation. At the Philadelphia Con-

*Alexander Hamilton.* (Library of Congress)

1795. By assuming both domestic and foreign debt, Hamilton's strong financial program helped restore national credit and create a national currency. Hamilton developed plans for the creation of the first National Bank of the United States. He also developed the Coast Guard and U.S. Navy to help protect national maritime trade, and he helped found the U.S. Naval Academy to train competent officers. To fill the national treasury, Hamilton instituted import duties and excise taxes. Such moves produced strong and hostile national reaction, leading to events such as the Whiskey Rebellion. Hamilton resigned from the Treasury in 1795 to return to his neglected legal practice. However, he remained close to Washington and continued to be a leader of Federalist Party politics. Above all else, Hamilton wanted to keep the new nation away from involvement in the wars following the French Revolution. To this end, Hamilton helped Washington write the "no entangling alliances" aspect of his farewell address.

In 1798, George Washington pressured a reluctant President John Adams to appoint Hamilton as Inspector General of the Army with the rank of major general. Hamilton resigned this position in June, 1800, having fallen into disfavor with Adams and a host of Federalist and Democratic-Republican politicians.

### The Grange Years
By 1800, while Hamilton was in the midst of finalizing plans for building his estate as an island of sanity, he was also working to undermine support for the reelection of Adams, a move that split the Federalists. Ultimately, the presidential election resulted in an electoral college tie between Thomas Jefferson and Aaron Burr. Although Hamilton disagreed with Jefferson's political philosophy, he intensely disliked Burr. Hamilton threw his support

vention of 1787, he became a leading advocate of dissolving the Articles of Confederation, creating in its place a strong federal government separated into legislative, executive, and judicial branches. Although New York withdrew from further discussion of a federal constitution, Hamilton, as an individual, signed the document anyway. To continue the fight for a federal government Hamilton wrote numerous newspaper articles under the nom de plume "Caesar." He also coauthored, with John Jay and James Madison, the famous eighty-five-essay collection urging states to ratify the Constitution, which became famous as *The Federalist.* For his tireless effort, Hamilton would forever be known as a Founding Father.

President Washington appointed Hamilton to be the first secretary of the Treasury, a position he held from September 11, 1789, to January 31,

to Jefferson. In a close House vote, Jefferson became the nation's third president. Hamilton's move made him even more unpopular in his already fragmented Federalist Party. Political animosity dealt him a harder blow on November 20, 1801, when Philip, his nineteen-year-old son and eldest child, died in a duel with George Eaker after a heated political exchange at a New York theater. Shortly afterward, his eldest daughter, seventeen-year-old Angelica, descended into permanent insanity due to grief. The tragedies caused Hamilton to become fixated on completing the Grange. He had the finest clay and compost brought in to transform the sandy loam soil. He designed flower garden and tree arrangements. The finest flowers, seeds, vines, and orchard trees were identified and obtained. Thirteen gum trees were planted to represent the original thirteen colonies. Numerous bird houses were constructed.

During the summer of 1802, as the Grange neared completion, Hamilton organized a large and gala open-air celebration. That he was already deeply in debt was a fact that escaped him at this joyous moment. He had lived at seven different addresses in lower Manhattan, and now he was about to have a home he loved. Visitors to the Grange after its completion late in 1802 found Hamilton content with his new life. He again practiced law, influenced opinion in a newspaper he founded called *The New York Evening Post*, and dabbled in politics. One political fact he could not ignore: Aaron Burr was running for the governorship of New York. Hamilton gave his support to Burr's Democratic-Republican rival, who won the election in a close vote. Infuriated by Hamilton's actions, Burr challenged Hamilton to a duel in June, 1804, using as a pretext a casual remark Hamilton had made at a dinner party two months before. Hamilton left his beloved Grange for the last time, heading for Weehawken, New Jersey, the same place where his son Philip had died, to meet Burr's challenge. On the morning of July 11, Hamilton received a mortal wound. By the following day, he left a family and nation in grief.

## Development of the Grange

Following Hamilton's death and until 1833, the Grange was occupied by Hamilton's widow and children. Intervention by family and friends saved the estate from almost immediate foreclosure. Between 1833 and 1879, it was used as a summer home by a series of New York families. Purchased by a real estate investor in 1879, the Grange was divided into three hundred separate rectangular building lots. Manhattan was rapidly growing northward. With the building of 143d Street, Hamilton's house was moved 350 feet in 1889 to its current site at 287 Convent Avenue. Soon it was sandwiched between St. Lukes Episcopal Church on one side and an apartment building on the other. In 1924, the Grange was purchased by a historic preservation society, which operated it as a museum until the National Park Service authorized it as a National Monument in 1962 "to commemorate the historic role played by Alexander Hamilton in the establishment of this nation." The house, containing a visitors' center and exhibits on the first floor, remained open until 1992, when concerns arose about the safety of the structure. Finally stabilized, the Grange reopened in 1998 for visitation Friday through Sunday.

Plans were soon underway to move the Grange one block away to St. Nicholas Park and place it on a nearly one-acre scenic lot. An easement demanded by the National Park Service was signed by the governor of New York in October, 1999. The Grange would be restored to its original appearance, with period furniture and a substantially improved museum depicting Hamilton's career and accomplishments, and a film and education center would be established on the ground floor. The Grange would be open seven days a week and was expected to attract a far greater number of tourists.

Nearby visitor attractions include the General Grant National Memorial, City College, Columbia University, the Morris-Jummel Mansion, the Hispanic Museum, Riverside Church, the Cathedral of St. John the Divine, and the Studio Museum in Harlem.

*—Irwin Halfond*

## For Further Information:

Broadus, Mitchell. *Alexander Hamilton: A Concise Biography*. New York: Oxford University Press, 1976. A condensed version of the classic two-volume study of Hamilton.

Brookhiser, Richard. *Alexander Hamilton, American*. New York: Free Press, 1999. A colorfully written, concise, and sympathetic treatment of Hamilton's political life and personal adventures.

Hecht, Marie B. *Odd Destiny: The Life of Alexander Hamilton*. New York: MacMillan, 1982. A well-researched and highly readable biographical treatment.

Hendrickson, Robert A. *The Rise and Fall of Alexander Hamilton*. New York: Van Nostrand, 1981. A humanistic and thorough study of Hamilton's life based on Hamilton's papers, letters, and other documents.

McDonald, Forrest. *Alexander Hamilton: A Biography*. New York: W. W. Norton, 1982. A balanced analysis of Hamilton's political career, financial policies, and historic role that is considered by many to be the standard study.

Rogow, Arnold A. *A Fatal Friendship: Alexander Hamilton and Aaron Burr*. New York: Hill & Wang, 1999. A highly readable and detailed account of the lives of the duelists, which also captures aspects of life in the early republic.

# Harlem

**Date:** Settled by the Dutch in 1636; incorporated as a village and named Nieuw Haarlem by Peter Stuyvesant in 1658; annexed to New York City in 1873

**Relevant issues:** African American history, cultural history, literary history

**Significance:** The area of central Harlem, a residential neighborhood of Manhattan, is approximately two and a half square miles. Its historic landmarks include St. Nicholas Historic District ("Striver's Row"), West 138th and 139th Streets between 7th and 8th Avenues; Hamilton Heights Historic District, Convent Avenue between West 141st and 145th; Alexander Hamilton's country home (Hamilton Grange), at 287 Convent Avenue; and Jumel Terrace Historic District, between West 160th and 162d Streets, which includes the Morris-Jumel Mansion, a colonial era estate once home to Aaron Burr. A large number of its existing structures were built in the period between 1880 and 1910. Much of Harlem is now in disrepair.

**Location:** New York City, approximately eight miles north of city hall in the borough of Manhattan. Harlem's boundaries have shifted at different times in its history. At present, its southernmost boundary at 96th street and 1st Avenue (east) runs west by northwest to 110th street above Central Park (central), due west to the eastern border of Morningside Park, and north by northwest again to 125th street and the Hudson River (west). The northernmost boundary is 165th street (central), and otherwise ends at the Harlem River on the east side and 157th street on the west side at the Hudson.

**Site Office:**
Greater Harlem Chamber of Commerce
1 West 125th Street, Suite 206
New York, NY 10027
ph.: (212) 427-7200

Harlem has been many things to many people. For a time it was an open gate to opportunity and achievement; for most who have been drawn there, it is the last stop on a hard road. In approximately 350 years of existence it has evolved from a rural village to a prosperous suburb, from an upper- and middle-income neighborhood of the city to a primary cultural center of the world. For much of the twentieth century it has been a ghetto.

The landscape of Harlem is different now, physically, from the rest of Manhattan; the buildings are generally lower than the high-rise office and apartment buildings downtown, the north-south boulevards are wider than the avenues running through midtown. It is hillier than the southern portions of the island. The neighborhood is less integrated than any other in Manhattan, the west side being populated almost entirely by African Americans, the east by Latinos. Very few whites are seen there.

Once called the "Capital of Negro America," Harlem no longer makes that claim. The title was contested even at the time it was conferred (from the 1920's to the 1940's), and now almost half of what was black Harlem is Spanish Harlem. With shifting population patterns, integration, and other changes in the United States, no community could now call itself the Capital of Black America with any real validity. Yet Harlem is, without doubt, the most storied and famous black community of America, and perhaps the world. It was, and to some extent still is, the focal point of African American culture, and as such, has been home and hothouse to much of that which is great in American culture.

## Early History

Though the Dutch had purchased Manhattan from the natives when the first European settlers arrived in Harlem in 1636, they battled the Indians for nearly a decade before establishing a colony there. In 1658 this area was incorporated as the village of New Harlem and received military protection from Peter Stuyvesant, the governor of New Amsterdam, the small city on the south end of the island.

By 1664, New Amsterdam was a British city, and in the 1670's black slaves built a wagon road connecting Harlem to what was now called New York. For the next two centuries, however, Harlem remained a mostly isolated, quiet, country village. Part of the area was good farmland; other parts were worthless marsh. Through the colonial period to about 1850, some of New York's wealthiest families kept estates there. Alexander Hamilton lived in Harlem, and his family continued to own land there a hundred years later.

By the 1830's much of the land was worn out from overuse. Farms were abandoned, and shanties sprung up on parcels of former estates. Squatters (mostly Irish immigrants) set up shacks, and land that could be sold was sold on the cheap. For lack of buyers, New York City purchased property there and sold off what it could. By 1838, the area was thought to be worthless, too remote to draw any substantial investment or interest. Though the coming of the railroad in 1837 promised easier access to the city, the New York and Harlem Railroad gained a reputation for unreliability. It did not entice many people north for years to come.

By the 1860's, wealthy New Yorkers were again in Harlem, not to work but to get away from work. Harlem was New York's first suburb. The wooded precincts were rustic and secluded, far from the noises of city life. The views of the river from its isolated promontories, the brooks and streams running thick with fish, and its very underdevelopment drew the downtown swells. Until the 1880's Harlem was a rural retreat for well-to-do gentlemen weary from their labors.

In 1880 more than a million people were living on Manhattan Island. Harlem was annexed to New York in 1873 (due to its size the village never needed any formal town government). New York's population was rising fast and prospects for its northern regions made real estate speculators feverish. By 1886, two more elevated railroads carried commuters north to Harlem. A building boom ensued, and by 1890 Harlem was one of the most desirable neighborhoods in New York. August Belmont and Oscar Hammerstein I bought property there.

## Multiethnic Communities

Black people had lived in Harlem continuously, almost from its founding. The first blacks to live in Harlem were slaves working its farms and estates in the seventeeth century. After slavery was abolished in New York, July 4, 1827, some blacks continued to live in the area as farmers, servants, and squatters. In the Civil War Draft Riots of 1863, whites in New York attacked blacks; in Harlem, black families were burned out of their homes. Most of the black population then lived in pockets of the city farther south, and when Harlem became home to the city's upper crust in the 1870's and 1880's, the number of blacks there increased as well. Mostly servants, they had churches, clubs, even a political organization. Still, only small parts of Harlem were black.

The other side of Harlem, the east side, was an Italian ghetto in the 1890's. The buildings there were built as tenements, and those that remain are still tenements. Neither Italians nor blacks, scattered though they were, were much welcomed by their more affluent neighbors. Local newspapers inveighed against them, and housing discrimination was common practice.

Jews seeking a way out of their ghetto on the Lower East Side bought land in central and east Harlem, and for a short period of time much of Harlem was Jewish. The Jews, too, were not welcomed, and they frequently bought land through fronts, a practice later used by blacks.

Mostly, however, the well-to-do did not care about the poor. New construction was everywhere and land speculation occupied residents and nonresidents alike. Fortunes were made as land values tripled. Built for the gentry, the new homes and apartment houses were grand, with large, airy rooms. By 1904 many of these were empty; they had been built for a gentry that never arrived. The population of New York soared, but not its number of wealthy. Harlem was overbuilt, at too great an expense for rents to be affordable to most people. Buildings sat vacant; mortgages were foreclosed. The gusher was shut and money was lost by the bucketful, until a black realtor, Philip A. Payton, saw the vacancies as an opportunity. Nearly thirty years later, James Weldon Johnson wrote of Payton,

> When Negro New Yorkers evaluate their own benefactors in their own race, they must find that not many have done more than Phil Payton; for much of what has made Harlem the intellectual and artistic capital of the Negro world is in good part due to this fundamental advantage: Harlem has provided New York Negroes with better, cleaner, more modern, more airy, more sunny houses than they ever lived in before.

## Harlem's African American Population

A large part of the black population of Manhattan lived in the Tenderloin, but this area was in the process of being razed to make way for Penn Station. Blacks had to go somewhere. Some white landlords, facing financial disaster, were more than willing to make dollars off blacks. Payton rented apartment houses from the owners, then rerented the apartments to blacks for a 10 percent profit. He was so successful that by the time the building boom had gone completely bust, in 1904, he founded the Afro-American Realty Company and set to buy Harlem for black people.

In one of the company's first transactions, Payton rapidly bought and then sold three houses on West 135th Street to a white-owned company. When the white-owned company evicted the black tenants, Payton bought two other houses on the street and evicted the white tenants from them. Not long after that, the white-owned company sold the first three houses back to Payton. This action made all the newspapers, and made the Afro-American Realty Company famous. As the blacks moved in, the whites, Jews, Italians, the remains of the Irish, and the gentry fled. The blacks were in Harlem to stay.

The Afro-American Realty Company was not. Payton enjoyed a brief heyday, but the resources of his company became overextended in badly timed speculative land deals. A nationwide recession in 1907 and 1908 depleted its capital, and by 1908 it had dissolved. Its properties changed hands once again.

What Payton had begun, others continued. They did so in the face of overt hostility and organized opposition, but those blacks who had tasted the better life offered in Harlem told their friends, their relatives, and their relatives' friends. They came from other parts of New York City, from all of the islands of the West Indies, and (particularly with the coming of World War I) from the American South. The North needed hands in its industries to replace those who had marched to war; it did not matter what color those hands were. Labor agents were sent south to entice the workers north. Offered better money, better living conditions, and paid transportation, they came. For many of the rural black people in the South, the move seemed like a new chance at freedom, and, for a time, it was.

## Harlem During the 1920's

With the end of World War I, America boomed, and the black people of Harlem began enjoying a prosperity they had never before known. Enough money trickled uptown from the gusher on Wall Street to fill a respectable stream through Harlem. Blacks continued to buy real estate throughout the 1920's, and by 1930 a local realtor estimated the value of black holdings as between fifty million and sixty million dollars.

Though Harlem had become black against the will of many whites, the change had taken place without violence. This was not the case in other cities around the country. Unlike other black ghettos, Harlem was centrally located, with highways and railroads running through it. The employment of blacks in New York was more diversified than in other cities. Gang labor, with its attendant segregation, was the rule in other American cities; in New York it did not exist.

So, for some, Harlem in the 1920's became paradise. Here was a safe haven in the midst of a dominant, frequently hostile white world, an opportunity at freedom. Through the 1920's Harlem made its mark on the world. In what became known as the Harlem Renaissance, black artists and thinkers formed a community preeminent on the world stage. A short list of their names reads like a Who's Who of American arts and letters. W. E. B. Du Bois, Langston Hughes, Arna Bontemps, Zora Neale Hurston, Claude McKay, and James Weldon Johnson shared the neighborhood with W. C. Handy, Duke Ellington, and Paul Robeson, to name only a few. Harlem style was envied and copied by blacks and whites. The 1920's were called the Jazz Age, and the sound of the era was mostly made in Harlem.

The creativity flowing through the little community (then only two square miles) created pride and a sense of anticipation. The "Tree of Hope," a gathering place at 7th Avenue and 131st Street, became a symbol to a generation of disenfranchised black people, and they were drawn to that hope from all over the Americas. Some black people grew wealthy and bought grand homes on what came to be known as Striver's Row, two blocks of 138th and 139th Streets between 7th and 8th Avenues. These are still thought to be some of the nicest row houses in New York. Harlem nightspots were renowned everywhere—the Cotton Club and Small's Paradise were spoken of in the same breath as the Folies Bergère, and the Apollo Theatre was as famous as any theater in New York.

For many of the new arrivals, Harlem was nowhere near the promised land. The Cotton Club was open to black performers, closed to black audiences. Blacks looking for employment still faced frequently overwhelming odds, and generally the jobs they could get were the worst paid in town. Streaming into Harlem, they were stuffed into buildings that were already overcrowded, overpriced, and underkept. Like many of the established residents, most of the newcomers were poor, but the place was bustling.

## Marcus Garvey and the Universal Negro Improvement Association

Harlemites were the first to hear the call to a new paradise, to be built in the midst of the old. The call to Africa was sounded by Marcus Garvey, whose rise and fall were equally meteoric. Born in Jamaica in 1887, Garvey made his first appearance on a Harlem stage in 1917. By 1919 he headed a large organization (the Universal Negro Improvement Association), published a newspaper (*Negro World*), and had built a theater for rallies (Liberty Hall) that held between five and six thousand people. At a rally in August of that year he announced a plan to form a republic in Africa. Poor blacks scraped donations together to buy ships for the Black Star Line, a fleet of ships that would take them home to Africa. By the end of 1921, the Black Star Line, awash in bills but not much more, sank. Not long after that, the Back to Africa movement crumbled also.

Garvey was jailed for fraud and eventually deported back to Jamaica. People had donated to the Black Star Line, but they did not book passage on it. Most blacks thought there was still a chance for opportunity in America and would not give up the struggle in the United States for a dream land that might well never exist. Yet, Garvey's ideas inspired many. A park in Harlem is named for him.

## The Depression Years

When the Great Depression hit in 1930, it hit Harlem hard. Blacks were "last hired, first fired." The black businessmen of Harlem owned small businesses such as barbershops and grocery stores, which were swept away in the destruction of the economy. By 1930 the population of central, black Harlem, was 300,000, an estimated 334 people on each acre. The "fine, airy" houses had been made over into rooming houses. The tenements of east Harlem had been built as tenements, but now in the better houses, bathrooms were sometimes being used for bedrooms. The neighborhood, part slum to begin with, began to slide.

From the beginning of the Depression to the end of World War II, Harlem declined dramatically. The magnet that once inspired hope now inspired dread. Blacks rented it, whites owned it once again. The Harlem Renaissance was long gone, its lights moved on, and Harlem itself was given over to a greater poverty than before. There were riots in 1935 and 1943, and though the area still drew whites "slumming" after dark, the tensions and crime caused Harlem to be declared off-limits to white servicemen during the war.

Harlem was not all slum, by any means, just as it is not now. Though some of its great nightclubs had moved downtown, the churches remained, as did the working people. Celebrities still called Harlem home: Cab Calloway, James Baldwin, Count Basie, Ella Fitzgerald, Billie Holiday, and long-time resident Duke Ellington. Langston Hughes remained, joined by James Baldwin, Harlem born and bred. W. E. B. Du Bois continued to live there, as did Thurgood Marshall, then a lawyer, later the first black on the United States Supreme Court. The first black heavyweight champion, Jack Johnson, lived on Sugar Hill at the same time as Joe Louis. A local spiritual leader, Father Divine, was known all over the world, and the Reverend Adam Clayton Powell, Jr., who had succeeded his father as pastor

*The Duke Ellington Memorial is unveiled in Harlem in 1997 to honor the great jazz musician and composer.* (AP/Wide World Photos)

of the Abyssinian Church, had been elected to Congress, the first black from New York to enter that body. He remained there for over twenty years.

Despite the general suffering, a spirit of community continued. Held throughout Harlem, rent parties were open to anyone and helped pay the bills. The corner of 125th Street and 7th Avenue became famous for soapbox sermons; anyone with a box and a mouth could gather a crowd. Harlem slang was imitated everywhere. Its fashions were characterized by the oversized, billowing zoot suit, available in all the primary colors.

There were drugs in Harlem, too. Cocaine was sold by the spoon, and marijuana was easy to find. Drugs did not take over the neighborhood until the appearance of heroin, sometime in the late 1940's. By the early 1950's heroin ruled its streets. Heroin addiction soon became epidemic in Harlem, destroying already fragile family ties and increasing crime in every category. The white powder blanketed the community and no one in Harlem was unaffected by it. As in other poor areas partially dependent on an underground economy and already conditioned to illicit trading in drugs and other contraband, heroin made an easy entry into Harlem life. However, heroin was different. In

his novel *Manchild in the Promised Land* (1965), Claude Brown wrote,

> Fathers were picking up guns and saying, "Now look, if you (expletive) wit that rent money, I'm gon kill you," and they meant it. Cats were taking butcher knives and going at their fathers because they had to have money to get drugs. Anybody who was standing in the way of a drug addict when his habit was down on him—from mother or father on down—was risking his life.

### Harlem in the Late Twentieth Century

By 1960, the population of Harlem was approximately 200,000, down one-third from the halcyon days of 1930. Those who could get out, did. Yet Harlem still drew people of talent and ambition. Malcolm X moved there in the mid-1950's and, based in Harlem, established himself as a leader in the Nation of Islam (the Black Muslims). He grew to national prominence as a spokesman for black frustration and pride.

The Nation of Islam had been established by Elijah Muhammad in Chicago. Malcolm X, a career criminal, was first converted to the movement in prison. Besides offering an explanation of the genesis of the races, the Black Muslims preached self-discipline, separatism, unity, and pride. Members did not drink, swear, or use drugs. After some very highly publicized confrontations with the New York City police, the Black Muslims were held in some awe by people in Harlem. As the leader and spokesman of the Harlem mosque, Malcolm X soon received more attention than Elijah Muhammad. His meteoric career saw him change his views on separatism before he was gunned down in a Harlem theater in 1964.

While most of Harlem was still black then, as it is now, Puerto Ricans had been moving into East Harlem since the 1920's. They had become predominant there and were extending west. By the late 1950's, the stream of immigrants from Puerto Rico had become torrential, and Spanish Harlem, also called El Barrio, became almost a city unto itself, coexisting uneasily with black Harlem.

Government had always been represented in Harlem by policemen and social workers, but after the nationwide riots of the 1960's and the advent of Lyndon Johnson's Great Society programs, government became ubiquitous. Some of these programs, such as Head Start, won praise. Infant mortality rates were lowered as well. However, the welfare system was much criticized by both whites and blacks for creating a permanent class of poor people, unfit to compete in society. By 1990, more than 44 percent of the population of Harlem received public assistance.

As the buildings aged, some of the worst-kept of them grew to be less than profitable. Torching these buildings for the insurance money became commonplace among the frequently absentee and mostly white landlords. Once burned, these buildings were not rebuilt. Abandoned buildings became homes to drug addicts and other squatters. As the number of consumers dwindled, so did the number of legal businesses. Much of Harlem became an urban moonscape, pocked with vacant lots and empty, forbidding, burned-out buildings. Much of it remains so. As dangerous as the neighborhood might have seemed to a visitor, it was more so to the residents.

### Signs of Rejuvenation

Due to escalating Manhattan land values in the 1980's, some forecast a new building boom in Harlem, for the same reasons that had caused the boom in the 1880's: too many people, not enough space. However, the stock market crash of 1987 stalled speculation. By the 1980's central Harlem did not even have a public high school, and New York City owned 65 percent of the land. In 1990 the population of Harlem was estimated at under 100,000, and what had once been a mecca for African Americans held only 5 percent of New York's black population. In 1930 that figure had been 72 percent. The median household income was lower than it had been in 1960.

There were some signs of life in the rubble. The Apollo Theater was renovated, and, spotlighting local acts, it broadcast a weekly show on national television. Harlem performers continued to influence popular music—rap and hip-hop were nurtured there—and black writers such as Toni Morrison were still enraptured by the neighborhood. Wealthy blacks owned homes worth half a million dollars on Striver's Row, a block away from slumbred squalor. Performers from the streets of Spanish Harlem became famous, making salsa music internationally known. Drug use among the young was down, and gentrification in the form of apartment rehabs was slowly taking place. Buildings along 125th Street had been cleaned. A ragged hotel on 116th and 8th, prominent in the heroin trade, was torn down. Some residents began to worry about whites moving into the neighborhood.

Harlem in the 1990's stands both in history and outside of it, with a checkered past sometimes glorious, and an uncertain future. It may never again be more than what it is now, no longer the Capital of Negro America, but a center of African American culture, and as such, central to all American culture.      —*Jeffrey Felshman*

### For Further Information:

Brown, Claude. *Manchild in the Promised Land.* 1965. Reprint. London: Touchstone, 2000. The autobiography of the author, who grew up in the Harlem of the 1940's. This is one of the great American autobiographies, absorbing and frequently amazing.

Johnson, James Weldon. *Black Manhattan.* 1930. Reprint. New York: Da Capo Press, 1991. An overview of black people's achievements and struggles in New York, particularly of the Harlem Renaissance, written by one who was there for many of its events. It is a sober account, dense with fact; it is well-researched history, on-the-scene reportage, and, occasionally, soul-stirring tract, all in one.

McKay, Claude. *Harlem: Negro Metropolis*. 1940. Reprint. New York: Harcourt Brace Jovanovich, 1968. A prose poem by a Harlem Renaissance writer, biased and highly readable.

Marks, Carole, and Diana Edkins. *The Power of Pride: Stylemakers and Rulebreakers of the Harlem Renaissance*. New York: Crown, 1999. An examination of African American intellectual and artistic life during the Harlem Renaissance.

Osofsky, Gilbert. *Harlem: The Making of a Ghetto: Negro New York 1890-1930*. 2d ed. Chicago: Ivan R. Dee, 1996. An exhaustive historical and sociological study. Much of its information is drawn directly from primary sources, and these are abundantly quoted, occasionally reproduced.

# Mount Lebanon Shaker Village

**Date:** Founded in 1785

**Relevant issues:** Cultural history, religion

**Significance:** Mount Lebanon was the spiritual center of the Shaker community. It was inhabited by Shakers continuously until 1947. At its peak in the mid-nineteenth century, it encompassed over one hundred thirty buildings and six thousand acres of land. In 1880, 283 Shakers lived there. Mount Lebanon Shaker Village is listed on the National Register of Historic Places.

**Location:** In the town of New Lebanon, southwest of Albany

**Site Office:**

Mount Lebanon Shaker Village
P.O. Box 628
New Lebanon, NY 12125
ph.: (518) 794-9500

For nearly two centuries the Shakers, or Shaking Quakers as they were first called, provided living proof of the viability of communistic living in America. The United Society of Believers in Christ's Second Appearing, as the Shakers officially called themselves, was founded by a working-class, illiterate woman from Manchester, England, in the late eighteenth century. The Shaker settlement in New Lebanon was the second settlement to be founded, though it soon rose to preeminence among the subsequent Shaker villages. It was the largest settlement and assumed the role of central ministry for the entire Shaker movement. From the days of the national expansion of Shakerism until the movement's decline and demise in the twentieth century, the ministry at New Lebanon—or Mount Lebanon as it was increasingly referred to after 1861—offered guidance, both practical and spiritual, to all Believers.

**Shaker Beliefs**

The Shakers called themselves Believers in Christ's Second Appearing, or Believers for short, and in the early days of the movement they considered removal and distance from the "World," the world of non-Believers, necessary for spiritual purity. The religious roots of their beliefs are obscure, but the fundamental tenets of Shakerism are celibacy, communal ownership of land and resources, and the public confession of sins. They also believed in the equality of the sexes and, drawing on the biblical texts and the sayings of their founder Ann Lee, they believed in the motherhood of God. The personality of Ann Lee assumed theological importance to them: They believed she had herself manifested the Second Coming.

The Society was organized into groups of Believers called "Families," comprising anywhere from thirty to ninety members. After the Society's initial decade in America, during which many new converts were scattered across New England, families were grouped together to form villages, and each family appointed its own representatives. Each village appointed elders and eldresses to preside over spiritual issues and deacons and deaconesses to form a governing board on temporal matters. Adjacent villages formed bisphorics. All villages came under the central control of the ministry at New Lebanon. At its height in 1839, New Lebanon itself comprised seven families consisting of 480 members.

**The Founder of Shakerism: Ann Lee**

The documentary evidence for the inception of Shakerism is scarce and little is known about its founder, Ann Lee. Partly, this scarcity can be attributed to Ann Lee's own illiteracy and consequent faith in the power of the spoken word as opposed to that of the written text. In the early days of the society, education was considered a corrosive force and was discouraged. Only in the mature phase of the movement, beginning in the mid-nineteenth century, can extensive and elaborate record keeping on the part of the Shakers be found in the form of business records, journals, letters, and Society regulations. It is also during the mature period that the Shakers began to rewrite their early history and embellish what little was known of Ann Lee.

Ann Lee was born in Manchester, one of the earliest industrial cities of England, at the height of the Industrial Revolution. She was baptized in 1742 and married to Abraham Standerin, a blacksmith, in 1762. Together they had four children, none of whom survived. In the late 1760's she became involved with a small group of religious enthusiasts who became known as Shakers due to the trembling that their worship induced. The Shakers sang and danced, screeched and succumbed to fits, generally disturbing the neighborhood and inviting antagonism. Ann Lee and her brother William both feature in the police arrest records of the time for intentionally engaging in confrontation with the public to call attention to and spread their belief.

### Other Zealous Groups

Religious zealotry and sectarianism were not confined to the Shakers. In England at the time there were several millennialist groups that derived considerable inspiration from the French Protestant Huguenot refugees in England. In 1774 Ann Lee, her husband, and a few fellow Shakers decided to leave England and head for the less repressive environment of North America. However, developments in the American colonies were hardly auspicious for a small band of English pacifists. While the colonies celebrated the Boston Tea Party and declared their independence, Ann Lee and her companions sought work as domestic help and curtailed their sectarian activities for a few years.

In 1779 the Shakers reemerged, with Ann Lee now separated from her husband, and purchased some land northwest of Albany in New York State, at a place called Ressaerwyck, or Niskeyuna by the local Indians. This first site later came to be known as Watervliet. Although this remote location allowed Ann Lee and her followers to worship freely,

they did not enjoy their isolation for long. That same summer evangelical fervor had gripped the nearby town of New Lebanon, home to the New Light settlement under Joseph Meacham. There were high expectations of an imminent millennium. News of the millennialist Shaker settlement reached New Lebanon, and Meacham decided to pay his neighbors on the other side of the Hudson River a visit. He returned to New Lebanon favorably impressed, and soon he and several others from New Lebanon had converted to the Shaker faith and given Shakerism a foothold in New Lebanon.

At the same time, the Shakers received the unwelcome attentions of authorities looking for conscripts for the Revolutionary War. The Shaker tenet of pacifism and the Believers' British heritage were seen as treacherous and as sufficient reasons for arrests and fines. During the life of the movement the Shakers were to suffer often for their refusal to fight.

### Shakerism in New England

Undeterred by official disapproval, Ann Lee and a few companions set out in 1781 on a two-year journey throughout New England to gather new converts for the movement. By the time of her death in 1784, Ann Lee's small group of Believers had swelled to many families scattered across the region. Her successor as leader of the movement, James Whittaker, recognized the need to consolidate some of these new members and gather them at a few well-chosen sites. As part of this effort he marshaled the resources with which to build the Society's first meetinghouse, at New Lebanon in October, 1785, on land owned and donated to the Society by the recent convert George Darrow.

When Whittaker died it was Joseph Meacham who assumed the leadership of the expanding Society. Meacham based himself in New Lebanon, and under his leadership the settlement there assumed its preeminence among the Shaker villages; its position as central ministry lasted until the demise of the entire Society. Partly, this shift from Niskeyuna to New Lebanon was due to its easier access to other parts of New England, making travel to the other Shaker settlements less arduous. Under Meacham the Shakers constructed their village on the mountainside above the town of New Lebanon.

## The Architecture of New Lebanon

The buildings that made up the Shaker settlement at New Lebanon were constructed to serve a practical purpose. One of the Shakers' great legacies is the emphasis on well-designed, simple, and functional buildings and furnishings. After the First Meetinghouse, with its symbolic significance for New Lebanon and for the Society as a whole, the next important project was the construction of the Great House in 1788. This building was designed specifically to accommodate the Shakers according to their communal ideal. The younger members of the Society were segregated and housed in the newly constructed Brick House and Bake House. More buildings were added in 1791 for the Second Family and for the elderly Believers. A spinning house, two shops, an office, and a kitchen were also added. The Second Meetinghouse, large enough for five hundred believers, was not built until 1824, after Meacham's death, and was given a rounded roof and distinctly different character from that of the surrounding buildings. The architecture of the settlement caused one visitor to comment that every Shaker building "has something of the air of a chapel."

Having made practical arrangements for the facilities at New Lebanon, Joseph Meacham laid down certain guidelines for the structure of the village, based on families with elders and eldresses. With this system firmly in place he released several well-regarded elders and eldresses from New Lebanon, appointing them to positions of leadership at other nascent Shaker settlements. In this way the New Lebanon template was repeated all over New England, and the central ministry retained clear control over and cohesion with the scattered Society. True to his conviction in the division of leadership between men and women in the community, Meacham appointed Lucy Wright as his counterpart at New Lebanon. Wright was to have a profound influence on the evolution and establishment of the Society.

Meacham was himself responsible for the first formal regulations governing the temporal affairs of the Society. Thus, meal and rest times were fixed, and certain standards of quality, simplicity, and beauty were set as goals for crafted goods, produce, and buildings. More importantly, a covenant for admission to the Society was drawn up. Ostensibly, this was devised to avoid legal action over the communal ownership of property and the pooling of labor in the Society. Already in the early days of the Society its elders faced issues of reimbursing disenchanted members who wanted to leave. This problem would continue to dog them, especially in the case of young male Shakers seeking to leave the Society in which they had been raised.

## Meacham Redefines Shakerism

Meacham's desire for order and for stated objectives extended to the spiritual realm too. Departing considerably from the oral tradition of Ann Lee and her companions, Meacham outlined the salient points of Shaker belief and worship in a tract entitled *Concise Statement*. A later document entitled *The Sacred and Divine Roll* also played a crucial part in establishing the Shaker creed. It was reputedly "dictated" to Philemon Stewart by an angel, who summoned him to the Holy Fountain at New Lebanon. Many Shakers reported visions and other intense spiritual experiences, and for a time Stewart was held in favor by the elders of New Lebanon; thus, his *Sacred and Divine Roll* was widely circulated in the mid-nineteenth century and was sent to heads of state all over the world. Later Stewart fell from favor, however, and his document diminished in significance.

When Joseph Meacham died, leaving behind him a young but cohesive society, his appointee Lucy Wright assumed overall leadership of the Shakers. Under her stewardship the Society saw its greatest expansion and its transition from a small, East Coast sectarian movement to a national church, with villages scattered from the far northeast in Maine to the American frontier in the Ohio Valley and Kentucky. This remarkably successful westward expansion gained many new converts for the United Society and, despite the initial trials associated with establishing settlements on frontier territory, soon added several villages to those in New England. These western villages gained a considerable local foothold and survived well into the Society's later period of decline. West Union in the Ohio Valley assumed a particular importance as the central village for the western settlers.

## Geographical Expansion

Part of the success of this westward expansion can be attributed to Wright's shrewd imitation of Meacham's earlier tactic: She placed trusted New

Lebanon elders in positions of leadership in the new villages. Despite the expansion's undoubted success, this deployment of New England Shakers in the West strained and weakened the Shaker settlements on the East Coast. From the outset the western villages assumed a distinctive character, attributable in part to the differences in climate and agricultural possibilities and in part to the external circumstances of the Shakers on the frontier. Removal from the World receded in relevance here, as issues of survival for the Shaker settlers alongside their "Worldly" neighbors became more important. There was no conscious attempt to break away from the central ministry at New Lebanon, and yet the sheer distances and consequent difficulty in communication between the central ministry and the western outposts made New Lebanon's authority over these villages tentative and remote.

This geographical expansion illustrated to the Shakers that they could not rely on regular visitors from New Lebanon to each outlying village for the transmission of information and the maintenance of central authority. By overland travel, more than one thousand miles separated New Lebanon and South Union, Kentucky; in the opposite direction, New Gloucester, Maine, was 225 miles from New Lebanon. Out of necessity, then, the more distant villages evolved a more federal relationship to New Lebanon's central authority.

The second crucial development in addressing the challenge of communication was the increased use of written correspondence between outlying villages and the central ministry at New Lebanon. These letters provide historians with a priceless source of information on the daily operations of the United Society. In addition, New Lebanon sought to cement its central supervisory role by issuing a profusion of rules. A central bureaucracy was emerging. Lucy Wright, however, resisted the compilation of these many edicts into one reference; only after her death in 1821 did the first systematic manual for the Society appear, later referred to as the Millennial Laws of 1821.

## Millennial Laws

The Millennial Laws addressed all aspects of Shaker life, from their religious beliefs to attitudes toward clothing and ornamentation, food, the care of plants and animals, business transactions, and specific "house rules." These rules gave a precise definition to Shakerism, thus distinguishing it from American life at large and lending formality to the members' separation from the World.

This desire for withdrawal from the World also underlay the Shakers' attempts at economic selfsufficiency. Many of the Shaker crafts and industries grew out of the need to provide village members with practical commodities and food. Nevertheless, as the Shakers moved into a more established phase and contended with less external hostility, they realized that for certain items it was impossible to be self-sufficient; limited trade with the World was unavoidable. Out of this necessity they drew on their extensive pool of cheap labor, and created such famous Shaker industries as seed cultivation and the manufacture of such items as chairs, brooms, baskets, and the beloved oval wooden boxes. In 1833 New Lebanon recorded sales of seeds totaling ten thousand dollars. From seed cultivation the Shakers at New Lebanon turned to the extraction of herbal essences for cooking and medicinal purposes, and in 1860 invested considerably in semi-industrial equipment for this purpose. Baskets were another source of income at New Lebanon, where up to seven hundred were made per year in the 1840's. Later sources of Shaker prosperity were the mills and weaving looms installed in the villages.

## Contacts with the Outside World

This commercial activity gave the Shakers increasing contact with the outside world, and their enthusiastic embrace of mechanization, of steam power, and of modern modes of transportation, namely the railways, have often been commented on. Mount Lebanon received its first steam heating in 1876 and its first steam laundry in 1890. In 1883 the first telephone was installed there, revolutionizing Shaker communication. Electricity came to Mount Lebanon in 1921, and the first automobile was purchased in 1918. In 1923 the radio was introduced to the village, perhaps the most symbolic bridge between the Shakers and the World. Nothing in their creed precluded the Shakers from employing the most efficient methods in their farms and in their manufacturing businesses, and their prosperity enabled them to enjoy the latest technological improvements.

In the mid-nineteenth century everything seemed to be going well for the Shakers. Several famous men visited the Shaker settlements, including Charles Dickens and Friedrich Engels. The latter was particularly interested in the successful application of the Shaker principle of communal ownership. An article by Benson John Lossing about the Shakers appeared in *Harper's New Monthly Magazine* in 1857 and substantially enhanced the general attitude toward the Shakers.

Yet they were consistently plagued by one problem. Female Shakers began to outnumber men, with the greatest discrepancy manifesting itself in the younger generation. By 1874 there were 339 female believers under twenty-one years of age but only 192 male believers under twenty-one in the entire Society. The Shakers found it increasingly hard to recruit and keep young men, and some villages had to resort to hiring outside help to complete the manual tasks on their farms. This tactic only served to increase contact with the World, and some of the behavior and attentions of the external wage laborers upset the young Shaker women.

Other events also forced more contact with the World. The Civil War, which brought so much suffering on the young American republic, could hardly leave the Shakers untouched. They once again suffered fines for refusing to send their men to fight on either side. (However, Abraham Lincoln came to be regarded as a special friend by the Shakers for his favorable intervention on the issue of conscription, and they sent him a chair as an expression of gratitude.) Naturally, the events of the Civil War had dramatically different effects on the Shaker villages in different parts of the country. Villages in the West, for example, were repeatedly ransacked for food, fuel, and lodging by passing soldiers and never really recovered from this abuse. Villages in New England were spared such direct contact.

### Shakerism in the Late Nineteenth Century

Toward the end of the century all the Shaker villages were beginning to suffer financially. Sometimes dishonest or foolish trustees of the villages borrowed or invested unwisely, and at other times natural calamities did their part. In 1875 severe fires caused immense damage to the property of one of the Mount Lebanon families, destroying the dwelling house and the herb house. Later, barn fires occurred. Each such fire had far-reaching consequences for the financial viability of the village,

and the central ministry in Mount Lebanon would regularly send out appeals to other settlements to send cash and assistance to the afflicted village. The Society as a whole was not always able to respond adequately to such calls, however, and the financial circumstances of some settlements worsened.

As membership declined—in 1883 283 Shakers lived at Mount Lebanon, but by 1900 this number had declined to 125—the Shakers' integration into the world around them seemed to increase. The North Family at Mount Lebanon in particular adopted a more progressive stance, both toward the Society and toward the Society's involvement in the social concerns of the World. Among notable progressives from the North Family were several influential women, including Antoinette Doolittle and Catherine Allen. In 1905 a Peace Convention was hosted at Mount Lebanon to which representatives of a variety of groups interested in social reform and international peace were invited. The conference was the greatest step the Shakers ever took toward integration and collaboration with the World.

Despite such attempts to rejuvenate the Society, membership continued to decline and financial problems dogged the Shakers. One after another, the villages were closed; in October, 1947, the linchpin of the United Society, the village of Mount Lebanon, was closed, and the last few elderly Shakers moved to the adjacent village of Hancock.

Some of the land and buildings at Mount Lebanon have been leased to the Darrow School, a four-year, coed preparatory school. Other buildings are now privately owned, but some have been preserved as a museum open to the public. The Shaker Museum, in nearby Old Chatham, New York, houses a collection of furniture, artifacts, documents, and photographs assembled from Shaker communities nationwide.

The history of the Shakers is not quite over, however. In 1959 one prescient eldress, Emma King, set up the Shaker Trust Fund to which the proceeds from the sale of Shaker assets should be paid. That trust still exists, though the beneficiaries are now disputed. In Sabbathday Lake, Maine, there are still some elderly Shakers, and in recent years a few much younger ones have been admitted to the village. America's most successful communal sect has captured the imagination of the public, and the

Shakers are more famous than ever as a byword for simple and beautiful design.

—*Hilary Collier Sy-Quia*

**For Further Information:**

Brewer, Priscilla J. *Shaker Communities, Shaker Lives.* Hanover, N.H.: University Press of New England, 1986. Gives a detailed view of East Coast villages up until the beginning of the twentieth century.

Desroche, Henri. *The American Shakers.* Amherst: University of Massachussetts Press, 1971. Translated from the French. Desroche focuses on details of Shaker religion and on their concept of socialism.

Gifford, Don, ed. *An Early View of the Shakers: Benson John Lossing and the Harper's Article of July, 1857, with Reproductions of the Original Sketches and Watercolors.* Hanover, N.H.: University Press of New England, 1989. Published for Hancock Shaker Village. Includes the text of "The Shakers" by Lossing and a foreword by June Sprigg.

Sprigg, June, and David Larkin. *Shaker: Life, Work, and Art.* New York: Smithmark, 2000. Discusses the social life, customs, and decorative arts of Shakers.

Stein, Stephen J. *The Shaker Experience in America.* New Haven, Conn.: Yale University Press, 1992. One of the most recent studies of the Shakers. This work gives extensive information on the entire history and development of Shakerism, from its inception until its virtual demise.

# Rockefeller Center

**Date:** Built between 1929 and 1940

**Relevant issues:** Art and architecture, business and industry, cultural history

**Significance:** New York's "city within a city," named for its founder and developer, John D. Rockefeller, Jr., eldest son and heir of John D. Rockefeller, Sr., the billionaire founder of the Standard Oil Company. The fourteen-building complex was widely criticized during its construction but quickly became the working model for urban developments around the world. Today, it is one of New York City's most-visited tourist attractions.

**Location:** Midtown Manhattan, New York City; twenty-two acres bounded by Fifth Avenue on the east, Sixth Avenue (Avenue of the Americas) on the west, 48th Street on the south, and 51st Street on the north

**Site Office:**
Rockefeller Center Management Corporation
630 Fifth Avenue
New York, NY 10111
ph.: (212) 332-3400
fax: (212) 332-3401
Web site: www.hia.com/rockctr

Although it was completed in 1940, Rockefeller Center was really the culmination of the building boom that flourished in the heady pre-Depression days of the 1920's. A monumental undertaking by any technological yardstick, the center's gargantuan proportions, totalling fifteen million square feet of rentable space, were literally unheard of during its construction. Such amenities as a private police force, the world's largest cinema, and a private street running through the complex fueled the comments of detractors and admirers alike, adding to the notoriety and allure that the center has held ever since. It is fair to say that the admirers have emerged victorious; the center has long since achieved the timeless stature its founder had desired.

**The Roaring Twenties**

In the period following World War I, the United States experienced an unprecedented industrial boom, almost overnight replacing Great Britain as the largest economy in the world and ushering in the period now fondly referred to as the Roaring Twenties.

This phenomenal increase in personal wealth in the ten years between the end of World War I and the onset of the Great Depression brought with it a gigantic building spree, the effects of which can still be seen today in older urban neighborhoods. Rockefeller Center was to become one of the final expressions of this era, even though a series of false starts did not allow the development to be built until well into the Depression.

**John D. Rockefeller**

Born in 1839, John D. Rockefeller built his first oil refinery at the age of twenty-four in order to capitalize on what he thought—correctly—would be a vast increase in the worldwide demand for petroleum products. By 1865, Rockefeller's refinery was the largest in the Cleveland area, and by 1870 Rockefeller, in conjunction with a handful of partners, incorporated the Standard Oil Company, which remains in its various forms one of the world's largest petroleum companies.

By 1872, Rockefeller had bought out most of the other refineries in the Cleveland area. Standard's control over the oil business in Cleveland allowed him to negotiate too-favorable deals with suppliers and railroads, essentially by threatening to withhold business entirely if they did not meet his price. Because he had a near-monopoly on the oil business in the Cleveland region, suppliers played along. The railroads, in particular, became unwitting allies in Rockefeller's drive to control the oil business in the United States.

Although there were no laws prohibiting monopolies at the time, public resentment of Standard's predatory practices led Rockefeller to place the stock of Standard of Ohio and its affiliates in other states in the hands of a nine-member board of trustees, thereby creating the first major United States trust company, a pattern followed by monopolies ever since.

## Standard Oil

By 1882, Standard controlled virtually all of the U.S. oil business, and industrialized states across the union began to pass antitrust laws prohibiting monopolies. In 1890, Congress responded with the Sherman Antitrust Act, and the Ohio Supreme Court declared the Standard Oil Trust illegal in 1892. Rockefeller then devolved the trust even further, spreading out the wealth to affiliated companies in other states and assembling an interlinked board of directors, leaving the same nine men in control of the entire operation. In 1899, Rockefeller reincorporated these companies into the Standard Oil Company, in New Jersey, but in 1911 the U.S. Supreme Court declared the "new" company a violation of the Sherman Act. At this time ownership was again rearranged.

Despite his business tactics, Rockefeller was a renowned philanthropist, bestowing more than half a billion dollars on various causes during his lifetime. He financed the founding of the University of Chicago in 1892, and, in conjunction with his eldest son, John Jr., created several philanthropic organizations that still bear his name, including Rockefeller University and the Rockefeller Foundation.

The wealth and power amassed by the elder Rockefeller provided the basis for everything the Rockefeller family has accomplished since. First among these benefactors was his son John Jr., who joined his father's business for a time, but devoted most of his life to philanthropy and management of the family fortune. It was he who made the Rockefeller Center a reality.

### Early History of the Center's Land

The modern history of the land upon which Rockefeller Center now sits goes back to 1801, when New York City physician and educator David Hosack bought the land and created the Elgin Botanic Garden, an important educational and scientific development in its day. In 1811 Dr. Hosack sold the land to the State of New York, which in turn bequeathed the parcel to Columbia University in 1814. The university then leased the land to private developers.

By 1929, the land was home to 229 buildings, mostly dilapidated brownstones of questionable repute, housing speakeasies and brothels and collectively forming one of the most blighted areas of the city. Columbia University received income from the property, but could easily have commanded more from proper development.

### Plans for a New Metropolitan Opera House

In 1926, during the height of the Roaring Twenties, a group of supporters of the Metropolitan Opera began a funding drive to build a new facility for their institution. In 1927, these trustees hired architect Benjamin Wistar Morris to select a site and create preliminary drawings for the new opera house. After two alternative sites proved unworkable, Morris began to prepare drawings for the Columbia property, with which the university was willing to part, for a price.

Morris envisioned a complex of buildings: the opera house at the core, fronted by a plaza and surrounded by the office buildings necessary to generate revenue for the opera company. This idea was not quite Rockefeller Center, but it was the first vision of a large, integrated, multiuse development at the site. The opera's trustees interested John D. Rockefeller, Jr., in the project in the summer of

*Rockefeller Center.* (NYC & Company Convention and Visitors Bureau)

terprise. Eventually, he took over the entire project, hiring Todd, Robertson and Todd, and Todd and Brown as management and engineering companies to oversee the planning and construction. Both companies were controlled by the same man, John R. Todd.

Eventually a lease was negotiated and signed between the Metropolitan Square Corporation and Columbia University for an initial annual rental fee of three million dollars, approximately ten times the revenues generated by the 229 buildings already on the property. With options, the lease could be extended to the year 2015, at which time the property would revert to the university.

By the autumn of 1929, the trustees of the opera company, glad to have a financial backer of Rockefeller's wealth but not entirely happy with his grandiose ideas, began to question their patron's plans. The stock market crash of that year put their fears in an entirely new light, and by December, 1929, both the trustees and architect Benjamin Wistar Morris had withdrawn from the project.

In retrospect, the withdrawal of the opera was a pivotal moment. At the time, however, the outlook was bleak. Rockefeller was left holding the lease to the university, which entailed not only the annual rent of three million dollars but also property taxes of approximately one million dollars. To back out of his deal with the university would have been unthinkable, and to simply leave the property as it was would have meant an annual loss of millions of dollars. Rockefeller had no choice but to defy the Depression and develop the property to the best of his—or anybody's—ability.

**From Opera House to a Commercial Center**

In conjunction with the Todd companies, Rockefeller dropped the idea of an opera house entirely and made the decision to go ahead with a strictly commercial development of office buildings and retail space. In the words of John R. Todd, "all plan-

1928, and the Metropolitan Square Corporation was formed to undertake the planning and construction. Originally, Rockefeller was to have donated two million dollars for construction of the plaza (which was to bear his name) and the administrative expertise necessary to acquire the property; he was then to remove himself from the proceedings, leaving the plaza and the consolidated parcel in the hands of the Metropolitan Square Corporation.

As plans for the opera house progressed, Rockefeller became ever more involved in the enning for this Square would be based upon a commercial center as beautiful as possible consistent with the maximum income that could be developed" from it.

With losses from rent and taxes mounting at the rate of $7.61 per minute, Rockefeller and Todd had to guarantee some form of future income before they could even break ground. At the time, radio was the fastest-growing industry in the country, so deals were struck with the Radio Corporation of America (RCA), the National Broadcasting Company (NBC), and the Radio-Keith-Orpheum Corporation (RKO) for a total rental income of three million dollars per year, enough to justify the commencement of construction, if only barely. (NBC and RKO were both owned by RCA, which wanted to put all its operations in the same place. This consortium was eventually broken up by the same antitrust laws that had dismantled Standard Oil a few decades earlier.)

In 1930, the enormous project of clearing and excavating the site began. The 229 buildings, comprising over 1.25 million tons of building material, were torn down and hauled away to make way for the center, the design of which had yet to be finalized.

## Architectural Plans for the Center

The consortium of architects employed to design the center came together between September, 1928, and May, 1930. Initially, Benjamin Morris had been teamed with L. Andrew Reinhard and Henry Hofmeister. On October 28, 1929, Reinhard and Hofmeister were officially appointed architects for the center, while Morris was demoted to consultant status. They were then joined by consultants Harvey Wiley Corbett and Raymond M. Hood, both of whom had experience in designing skyscrapers and were partners in leading architectural firms brought into the project the next year. The team became collectively known as Associated Architects, and, although other architects participated in the project from time to time, it was this team that created the original fourteen buildings of Rockefeller Center.

The first overall design to be presented to the center's board of directors was labeled G-3, dated January 8, 1930, and it was designed primarily by Reinhard and Hofmeister. This plan, which was temporarily shelved shortly after its introduction, featured four thirty-story buildings and several smaller buildings surrounding a central, seventy-story skyscraper that would become known as the RCA Building. A plaza and two private streets were also included in the plan, making G-3 the obvious progenitor of the eventual development. The directors returned to the abandoned G-3 concept after a design presented to the public in 1931 featuring an oval-shaped structure in place of the present-day Channel Passageway was greeted with overwhelmingly negative criticism.

In designing the center, particularly the seventy-story RCA Building and the forty-one-story International Building, the architects were both constrained and influenced by a landmark 1916 New York City zoning ordinance requiring a stepped design on all tall buildings. The purpose of the law was to prevent the city from becoming a collection of dark canyons into which neither sunlight nor fresh air could penetrate. According to a complex set of criteria, buildings could rise straight up from the pavement for a certain number of feet, dependent upon the size of frontage of the lot and its place on the block, after which the structure had to be set back a certain number of feet so that the building's profile fit within a given angle as measured from the center of the street. After these criteria had been met, a building could rise as high as its owners wished, as long as the footprint of the tower represented no more than 25 percent of the total area of the lot upon which it stood.

Unlike most zoning ordinances, the "setback law" was well-received by both architects and the general public. Setbacks not only accomplished their goal, but inspired architects to create interesting, aesthetically pleasing buildings that served their purposes well and relieved the monotony of rows of more-or-less symmetrical office buildings.

## A Design Is Finalized

Choosing a pyramidal massing scheme to stay within the limits of the law, the architects began to finalize the design of Rockefeller Center. Many short-lived ideas were brought forward, including an elaborate series of skybridges, the likes of which featured prominently in science fiction films of the day, but which were dispensed with in favor of a functional development of modern design with classical elegance. By 1932, the final design of the center had been essentially agreed upon. Individual buildings varied in terms of height, width, and setback, but there could be no doubt that they were of the same collection.

Despite the dismal economy, Rockefeller was aided in his enterprise by two important factors: The Great Depression brought building costs to an all-time low, and the accelerated research and development brought about by World War I had resulted in significant advances in technology that had not existed only a few decades earlier.

### Erection of the Center

Between 1932 and 1940, fourteen buildings were erected at the site, including the RCA Building and the International Building, the two tallest structures of the group. Other notable buildings include the bookends of the British Empire Building and La Maison Francaise, the Associated Press Building, the Palazzo D'Italia, the Time and Life Building, Holland House, and Radio City Music Hall (with six thousand seats, the world's largest cinema). The name Radio City, incorrectly applied to all of Rockefeller Center because of its preponderance of broadcasting tenants, was adopted by the planners when the time came to christen their theater.

Rockefeller Center also included a six-level, 725-car underground parking garage, the first such facility of its kind in a New York City office building. Obviously, such a facility is grossly insufficient today, but in 1939 it was a model of the Associated Architects' forward-thinking approach.

In addition to architecturally significant buildings, the center is also renowned for its attention to the open spaces between and around the buildings. Most famous of these is the lower plaza between Fifth Avenue and Rockefeller Plaza, directly west of the British Empire and La Maison Francaise buildings. Initially conceived as a fashionable shopping center, the plaza was hastily converted to an ice skating rink in the winter of 1936 after it became apparent that potential shoppers simply did not want to descend eighteen feet below street level to do their shopping. This was another fortuitous circumstance, as skating on the rink attracts thousands of people each year from October through April. The rink has been so successful that the center has invested in a complex ice management system that cools or warms the ice in order to achieve the correct level of hardness for skating. It

is in this plaza that Rockefeller Center's famous ninety-foot Christmas tree is displayed.

Even the Fifth Avenue entrance to the plaza is enticing. Six shallow pools line a two hundred-foot-long passage that leads from the avenue to the plaza. Known as the Promenade, the pools and gardens that surround them are called the Channel Gardens due to their location between the British and French buildings. The space is planted, as are all of the Rockefeller Center's open spaces, with a constantly rotating selection of seasonal plants.

Chief among the center's landscaping triumphs are the seven rooftop gardens that crown the development. Featuring American, Spanish, Japanese, Italian, English, and Dutch arrangements, the gardens are complete with streams, pools, fences, and trees. The English garden even features a sundial from England's Donnington Castle.

### The Center's Artwork

Specially commissioned artwork also figures prominently in the center. Perhaps the most famous, and most hotly debated, of these is Paul Manship's eighteen-foot statue of Prometheus that adorns the lower plaza. Rising above spouting water jets, the statue is notable mostly for its pride of place, if not for its immediately apparent artistic merit. In the 1930's detractors of the statue gave it the unflattering nickname of "Leaping Louie."

In addition to the statuary that dots the foyers, lobbies, and grounds, murals cover many of the center's walls, forming an outstanding collection of public art. Chief among these are the murals by Spanish painter José Maria Sert, located in the lobby of 30 Rockefeller Plaza. Representing humanity's intellectual mastery over the universe, the murals portray such pivotal moments in human history as the abolition of slavery, the eradication of disease, and the invention and evolution of machinery.

The Sert murals were commissioned by Nelson Rockefeller, one of John Jr.'s five sons. (Nelson became the forty-first vice president of the United States in 1974, after serving four terms as governor of New York, from 1959 to 1973.) Nelson Rockefeller had begun to take over day-to-day management of the center by the early 1930's, after the first tenants had moved in. He had long been an expert in Latin American art and had established a friendship with the famous Mexican painter Diego

Rivera. At first, Rockefeller chose Rivera to paint the murals, but the painter, whose Marxist tendencies were well known, created what amounted to a strong attack on capitalism, complete with an idealized portrait of V. I. Lenin prominently displayed in the piece. Displeased with his friend's thematic choice, especially in a building created by and devoted to capitalism, Rockefeller ordered Rivera to alter the mural. Although Rivera agreed to make the necessary changes, he did not do so.

At this point, Nelson Rockefeller ordered the mural removed, causing an immediate uproar in artistic and left-wing political circles. The painting was ingloriously chipped from the wall, priceless or not, and replaced by Sert's mural, which, for good measure, featured Abraham Lincoln and Thomas Edison, but no Lenin.

By the mid-1930's, Rockefeller Center was operating at an annual loss of approximately $4 million, and the buildings were mortgaged for $44.3 million, at the time the largest mortgage in the world. To alleviate the problem, the center's board of directors employed questionable tactics (not unlike the elder Rockefeller) to entice tenants, including offering rents below the market rate and even offering to pay off the current leases of potential tenants if they would move into the center immediately. In 1934 the owner of a competing office building, August Heckscher, sued the board, including John D. Rockefeller, Jr., and his sons Nelson and John III, but the case was dropped before it was heard in court. The center finally broke even on an operating basis in 1940 and became profitable in 1947. By the early 1950's, the center was fully occupied, at an average rate of $4.50 per square foot, and had a list of approximately fifteen hundred potential tenants waiting for the opportunity to move in. Despite the odds, the center had become an undeniable success.

## Center Statistics

Rockefeller Center officials have always been justifiably proud of the center's statistics, which are as impressive today as they were when it was built. For example, in the course of delivering 400,000 passengers per day, the center's 388 elevators travel nearly two million miles. The center's cleaning staff employs 817 people whose job is equivalent to cleaning some 10,900 six-room houses. The tallest building, renamed the G.E. Building when General Electric bought NBC, rises 850 feet into the air, while the McGraw-Hill Building's foundations descend 81 feet below the earth. The center boasts thirty-six restaurants, thirty-six travel and information bureaus, twenty-two airline offices, and nine consulates of foreign nations. The center's average daily population is approximately 240,000, a figure exceeded by only sixty cities in the United States. Tenants and visitors use 476 million gallons of water, 269 million kilowatt hours of electricity, and 1.021 billion pounds of steam for heating every year. Within the center's buildings can be found 97,500 locks and 48,758 office windows. Most revealingly, the building's owners pay more than sixty-two million dollars per year in property taxes.

In 1985, Rockefeller Center Incorporated purchased the original 11.7 acres of land owned by Columbia University for four hundred million dollars, creating Rockefeller Center Properties Incorporated (RCPI), a new corporation that allowed public investment in the center. A public offering carried out by the company's management shortly after the company's creation netted $1.3 billion for RCPI, which maintained the option to convert the loan into a 71.5 percent ownership of the property in the year 2000. In 1989, the Mitsubishi Estate Company purchased a majority interest in the Rockefeller Group, a privately held company. The move was widely criticized in the press, in both the United States and Japan, as Americans voiced their disappointment over "losing control" of one of their best-known landmarks. The Japanese press, ever mindful of Japan's growing economic power abroad, also criticized the move, noting that while buying factories abroad may make perfect economic sense, buying significant foreign landmarks was another matter altogether, and not one that was bound to be very popular in the host country. In fact, Mitsubishi does not own the center, but merely holds a controlling interest in an affiliated company.

In 1969 the center was honored with the Twenty-five Year Award by the American Institute of Architects in recognition of its timeless design. The center was finally designated a National Historic Landmark in 1988, and a New York City Landmark in 1989. The plaque installed in the Channel Gardens by the New York City Landmarks Preservation Committee fetes the Center as "one of the foremost architectural projects undertaken in America in terms of scope, urban planning and integration of architecture, art and landscaping."

—*John A. Flink*

**For Further Information:**

Jordy, William H. *American Buildings and Their Architects: The Impact of European Modernism in the Mid-Twentieth Century*. Reprint. New York: Oxford University Press, 1986. Detailed and technical, but one-fourth of the book is devoted to the Rockefeller Center and is an excellent source of information regarding its architectural development.

Morris, Joe Alex. *Those Rockefeller Brothers*. New York: Harper, 1953. A surprisingly detailed but colloquial history of the five sons of John D. Rockefeller, Jr. The chapter on the development of the Rockefeller Center concerns primarily Rockefeller and his son Nelson.

*The WPA Guide to New York City*. New York: Guilds Committee for Federal Writers, 1939. Reprint. New York: New Press, 1992. Originally published as *A Comprehensive Guide to the Five Boroughs of the Metropolis—Manhattan, Brooklyn, the Bronx, Queens, and Richmond*. A somewhat dated but intriguing description of Rockefeller Center while it was still under construction.

# Sagamore Hill

**Date:** Founded in 1963
**Relevant issues:** Cultural history, political history
**Significance:** Sagamore Hill was the permanent home of President Theodore Roosevelt from 1886 until his death in 1919. After the death of his widow, Edith Roosevelt, the home was presented to the American people as a site to commemorate President Roosevelt and his ideals. The home and nearby museum contain artifacts and displays relating to the Roosevelt family.
**Location:** Cove Neck Road near the town of Oyster Bay in Long Island, New York
**Site Office:**
Sagamore Hill National Historic Site
Sagamore Hill Road
Oyster Bay, NY 11771-1807
ph.: (516) 922-4788
Web site: www.nps.gov/sahi/

Sagamore Hill is best known as the home of the "Oyster Bay Roosevelts," the family of Theodore Roosevelt, twenty-sixth president of the United States. The home and nearby museum contain numerous artifacts from the Roosevelt family. The home itself is furnished primarily with items owned by the Roosevelts rather than only period pieces. President Roosevelt lived in the home upon its completion in 1886 and died in his sleep in his upstairs bedroom in 1919.

**Oyster Bay**

In 1873, Theodore's father, Theodore, Sr., decided Oyster Bay would be the family's summer residence as a means to escape the heat of New York City. Oyster Bay had served as home for several generations of Roosevelts, so the area was appropriate for the growing Roosevelt family. The older Roosevelt rented a large Southern plantation-style home befitting his wife's Southern roots. The home was named Tranquility. The water of nearby Oyster Bay provided an outlet for the children's energy and a means to escape the heat. Life in the country also provided a means for the younger Theodore to exercise and overcome the health problems that plagued him as a youth.

Roosevelt spent his vacations exploring the woodlands of Oyster Bay. He often spent his free time with young women in a boat on the bay reading stories and poetry. His love of the area resulted in his later plans to build a permanent home near the bay.

**Leeholm**

In 1880, Roosevelt married Alice Lee, a young woman he had met at a tea party while attending Harvard. Shortly after the wedding, the Roosevelts purchased sixty acres of land on a hilltop at Cove Neck overlooking Oyster Bay with the intention of building a manor. Named Leeholm after Mrs. Roosevelt, the home would have the massive walls and oak paneling that he admired. They also planned on including a large piazza, a large library, and a gun room which overlooked Long Island Sound. Theodore's poor health, however, probably incited by the return of severe asthma, forced postponement of their plans.

In August, 1883, Roosevelt purchased another ninety-five acres of land for twenty thousand dollars, allowing him to control the entire large estate

*Sagamore Hill, the home of Theodore Roosevelt.* (AP/Wide World Photos)

in that area. At the time of the purchase, the area was a windswept hillside with the only building being an old barn. Total cost of the purchases was approximately thirty thousand dollars; Roosevelt paid ten thousand dollars in cash and assumed a twenty-year mortgage for twenty thousand dollars.

The Roosevelts pictured Leeholm as a large, three-story mansion with twelve bedrooms and a resemblance to the state capitol building in Lansing, Michigan. The total area was approximately 155 acres, of which he kept 95 and sold the remainder to relatives.

Alice Roosevelt was not to see the home. On February 14, 1884, she died in their New York City brownstone while giving birth to their first child, Alice. Several hours earlier in the same home, Roosevelt's mother had died from typhoid fever.

On March 1, two weeks after the deaths of his wife and mother, Roosevelt signed the contract for the building of Leeholm. The New York architectural firm of Lamb and Rich had prepared the original plans prior to the death of Alice Roosevelt. Roosevelt hired John Wood and Son from Lawrence, Long Island, to be the contractors at a cost of $16,975. The total cost, including outbuildings, would be slightly more than $22,000.

Even though it was still winter, construction on the home began immediately. Roosevelt planned to have the house built by that summer, possibly to serve as a permanent home for himself and his baby daughter.

### Sagamore Hill

In December, 1886, Roosevelt married Edith Carow. Carow had been a childhood sweetheart, and following a period of mourning for his first wife, Roosevelt resumed a courtship that culminated in marriage. The Roosevelts would have five additional children.

Construction on the home at Cove Neck was completed in 1885; the family moved there permanently in the spring following their marriage. Roosevelt also changed the name of his home from Leeholm to Sagamore Hill after Mohannis, the local *sagamore* (chief) who had once signed away the rights to the land on which the estate stood. In fact, local legends suggested Mohannis Cove or Hill as the original name for the site.

The home, as it was originally built in the 1880's, was a twenty-two room Victorian structure made of frame and brick. A thirty-by-forty-foot room built from a combination of mahogany, black walnut, hazel, and swamp cypress woods was added on the north side of the building in 1905. This particular room was designed by Roosevelt's friend C. Grant La Farge, son of the artist John La Farge. The building has not been significantly altered since it was occupied by the Roosevelts.

In addition to the north room, the first floor of the home contains a large library that also served as an office for the president, a kitchen and dining room, and Edith Roosevelt's drawing room. A large center hall connects the rooms.

The second floor of the building contains the family bedrooms, the guest bedrooms, a nursery, and a room with a giant porcelain bathtub. The president's son, the future General Theodore Roosevelt, recalled watching for the "faucet lady" in the pipe of the bathtub, which he believed to be the source of the strange noises coming from the tub as the water ran out.

The third floor includes the rooms in which lived the cook and maids, a sewing room, a tutorial room for use by the children for their education, General Roosevelt's bedroom prior to his enrollment in college, and the president's gun room where he kept his collections of firearms. The gun room also served as an additional office away from the noise of the main floor where the president could write.

Most of the furnishings in the house were originally owned by the Roosevelt family, as were most of the items situated throughout the house. The large number of books attests to the wide range of interests held by the family, but particularly by the president. Roosevelt himself was the author of many of the books. The north room on the first floor, in particular, highlights the "masculine" interests of the president; it contains many of his hunting trophies and mounts, in addition to paintings, flags, and sturdy period furniture.

Roosevelt enjoyed the view of the harbor and Long Island Sound from the house, and the large piazza extending around the south and west sides of the house was built expressly for enjoying the view on warm summer nights. The grounds also contain numerous landscaped gardens.

The president's son, General Theodore Roosevelt, built his own home in 1938 on the estate near the house. Now called the Old Orchard Museum, it also contains items owned by the Roosevelt family and artifacts from the president's political career. A

daily show highlights, in film and photographs, the president and his role in shaping early twentieth century America. The show includes some of the few examples of the recorded voice of the president. Guided tours through the grounds provide examples of unusual plant life, as well as a feel for the region prior to development.

Sagamore Hill was more than just President and Mrs. Roosevelt's home. Three of their children were born there, and it was home for all of the family. By all accounts, Roosevelt was a doting father to his six children and their friends; he enjoyed romping and hiking with the children through the area. President Roosevelt advocated the "strenuous life" and could frequently be found swimming, riding horseback, or chopping wood on the estate. Except for absences due to Roosevelt's political career, the family spent most of their lives in the home.

Sagamore Hill frequently played its own part in Roosevelt's political career. The piazza was the site at which Roosevelt was formally notified of his nomination for governor in 1898, vice president in 1900, and president in 1904. In 1905, Roosevelt met in the library with the envoys from Russia and Japan, adversaries in the Russo-Japanese War. The Treaty of Portsmouth that Roosevelt brokered not only ended the war, but also resulted in his being awarded the Nobel Peace Prize.

The president's health declined precipitously in his last years. Illness acquired during his travels to remote regions of the world played a part. The death of his son Quentin in World War I also delivered a personal blow from which he never fully recovered. Roosevelt retired to the home where he would die on January 6, 1919, at the age of sixty. Edith Roosevelt lived at Sagamore Hill until her death in 1948. Both are buried in the family cemetery located down the hill from the home. In 1950, Sagamore Hill was purchased by the Theodore Roosevelt Association, a nonprofit organization that also owned the site of Roosevelt's birth in New York City. Both sites were presented as gifts "to the American people" in 1963. Since then, the sites have been supervised by the National Park Service.

**Places to Visit**
The headquarters of the Oyster Bay Historical Society is found in the Earle-Wightman House located on Summit Street in downtown Oyster Bay. Ori-

ginally built in 1720, the house subsequently underwent several expansions. A museum and research library are found within the house. Lectures, tours, and educational programs are presented throughout the year. Period costumes are worn to enhance the historical aspect of the house.

The research library within the house contains a large number of manuscripts, photographs, maps, and documents related to development of the Oyster Bay area. Nearby is an eighteenth century garden that contains a large array of ornamental plants and herbs.

Planting Fields off Mill River Road in Oyster Bay is the site of a large arboretum. An additional feature of the property is Coe Hall, an early Tudor-Revival mansion dating to the period of Queen Elizabeth I. The Hay Barn is an air-conditioned facility used for concerts, theatrical performances, and art shows.

The centerpiece of the site is the large arboretum, home of over six hundred types of azaleas, unusual varieties of trees, and five acres of over four hundred species of flowering shrubs. The greenhouses contain large collections of cacti and ferns as well as numerous exhibits.

Approximately five miles away on the edge of the sound is Cold Spring Harbor. Originally established as a whaling station, the harbor is now home to one of the major research laboratories for the study of molecular biology. Hiking trails from the laboratory can be followed to Sagamore Hill. The town, located a short walk from the laboratory facilities, also houses period homes and museums.

—*Richard Adler*

**For Further Information:**

Grant, George. *Carry a Big Stick*. Nashville: Cumberland House, 1996. This biography of Roosevelt also contains descriptions of the home.

Miller, Nathan. *Theodore Roosevelt: A Life*. New York: William Morrow, 1994. Easily readable biography that also contains vignettes of Roosevelt's family and home life.

Morris, Edmund. *The Rise of Theodore Roosevelt*. New York: Ballantine Books, 1979. Classic biography of Roosevelt. Sagamore Hill often served as a meeting place for dignitaries.

Renehan, Edward. *The Lion's Pride: Theodore and His Family in Peace and War*. London: Oxford University Press, 1999. Well-written biography of the

family and home life that draws upon previously unpublished letters and memoirs.

"Sagamore Hill." www.liglobal.com/highlights/saghill/sag1.html. Contains history and photographs.

# Saratoga

**Date:** Battles fought on September 19 and October 7, 1777

**Relevant issues:** Colonial America, military history, Revolutionary War

**Significance:** Site of two Revolutionary War battles in which the Continental forces under Major General Horatio Gates defeated the British under General John Burgoyne. The victory was crucial for the colonies, for it led to their formal alliance with France. On the centennial of Burgoyne's October 17, 1777, surrender, the cornerstone of Saratoga Monument was laid in the nearby town of Schuylerville, on the site of Burgoyne's camp the night prior to the surrender. The 155-foot granite monument was completed in 1883. In 1927 the battlefield was declared a New York State Park, and in 1938 it was declared a National Historical Park. The Saratoga Monument became part of the park in 1980.

**Location:** An area of approximately four square miles on the west bank of the Hudson River, thirty miles north of Albany and twelve miles southeast of Saratoga Springs; it can be reached via U.S. Route 4 or New York Route 32. The Schuyler House and the Saratoga Monument are located in Schuylerville, eight miles north of the main park area on U.S. Route 4.

**Site Office:**
Saratoga National Historical Park
648 Route 32
Stillwater, NY 12170-1604
ph.: (518) 664-9821
fax: (518) 664-9830
Web site: www.nps.gov/sara/

Saratoga National Historical Park commemorates two of the most decisive battles of the Revolutionary War. Although located in the community of Stillwater, it carries the name Saratoga because the battles that took place there in 1777

*John Neilson's house, which was used as headquarters for the Battle of Saratoga in 1777.* (National Park Service)

came to an end with the signing of a treaty in the town then known as Saratoga and since renamed Schuylerville, eight miles north of the battlefield.

### Historical Misconceptions

The events of the campaign of 1777 have often been portrayed inaccurately and shrouded in myths. Some reports have attempted to explain the British defeat by claiming that General William Howe's army was supposed to move north to Albany to meet General John Burgoyne's army, but this was never the plan. Other historians have exaggerated and romanticized the roles of General Philip Schuyler and General Benedict Arnold. It was, in fact, General Horatio Gates who led the Continental Army to victory over Burgoyne's army at Saratoga.

General Burgoyne, fifty-five years old, was a member of eighteenth century England's upper class. He was intelligent, handsome, and well liked by his troops, who called him "Gentleman Johnny." He also was vain and ambitious to a fault. During the winter of 1776-1777, he was at home on leave in London. This visit gave him the perfect opportunity to win favor with Lord George Germain, Britain's secretary of state for the colonies, who had grown impatient with the military leadership of Sir Guy Carleton, governor of Canada and com-

mander of British forces there. Burgoyne had served in Canada under Carleton and believed he knew what needed to be done to win the conflict there.

### British Campaign Plans

On February 28, 1777, Burgoyne presented to Germain his "Thoughts for Conducting the War from the Side of Canada." In it he discussed alternatives for the campaign, but he did not define his objectives. He left the overall strategic planning to the king and his ministers. Burgoyne felt that with a force of eight thousand soldiers, two thousand Canadians, one thousand Indians, and some artillery, he would be able to take Fort Ticonderoga by early summer. He could then push onward to Albany, opening up communications along the Hudson River with General William Howe's army in New York City. A second offensive line could be launched eastward through the Mohawk Valley at the same time as a diversionary tactic. It was an ambitious plan for a man who had never commanded Indians and who knew little about the difficulties of traveling across the mountainous American terrain. He was quite sure of himself, however, and he reportedly made a bet with a friend for the amount of fifty guineas that he would return victorious to London by the following Christmas.

On March 26 Burgoyne's plan was approved in the form of orders to Carleton to provide Burgoyne with the men and matériel he needed to carry out his advance to Albany. Lieutenant Colonel Barry St. Leger would move eastward down the Mohawk Valley simultaneously in the diversionary offensive. Both were then to put themselves under General Howe's command once they reached Albany. Until then they were to make their own decisions as to what would be necessary to suppress the rebellion.

At the same time, General Howe was formulating his own plans for a campaign. Howe repeatedly

changed his plans to reflect the changes in the Continental defense. His initial plan for 1777 included an advance up the Hudson to Canada and the capture of Boston. A month later he changed the strategy to defer the attack on Boston in favor of a push on Philadelphia, considered a colonial stronghold.

Howe changed his plan again following the successful offensives by George Washington's army in New Jersey in January, 1777. He still would advance toward Philadelphia, but by sea. He would leave some troops stationed at the lower Hudson to retain control of New York City and to open connections with the northern army once they had pushed through to the Highlands. Germain approved the plan, adding that he hoped the Philadelphia campaign would be over by the time the northern army reached Albany, so that Burgoyne and St. Leger could put their armies under Howe's command. Given the obstacles of the rugged country and the unpredictable weather, this was an unrealistic goal. Germain had authorized two separate campaigns hundreds of miles apart with little coordination between the two.

Howe's change of plan, to advance by sea, was to have important repercussions on the results of the war. By removing most of his army from New York, he allowed Washington to send troops northward to stop the advance from Canada. The seven thousand British troops left behind under Sir Henry Clinton would not in the end prove to be of any use to Burgoyne.

### The Lake Champlain-Hudson River Waterway

Long before the American Revolution, the Lake Champlain-Hudson River waterway was an important link between Canada and Manhattan for traders, missionaries, Indians, and soldiers. General Burgoyne chose this route for his advance toward Albany. On June 17, 1777, he set out from St. Johns, Canada, with nine thousand troops, including British regulars, German mercenaries, Canadians, and Indians.

In early July the Continentals defending Fort Ticonderoga were caught off guard by the British led by Lieutenant Colonel John Hill and decided to retreat south to Fort Anne. General Arthur St. Clair, who was in command of the Americans, made the decision to evacuate Fort Ticonderoga when it became apparent that the fort could not be defended against British artillery that had been carried up to the summit of a nearby mountain. The reaction to the retreat was one of surprise and dismay by the leaders of the Continental Army and jubilation by the British, who felt that victory could not be far away. Both armies shifted their focus from New York City and New Jersey to northern New York.

On July 8, the Continentals, camped at Fort Anne, took the offensive and attacked the British camp, forcing Colonel Hill to send for more reinforcements. Both sides stood their ground for nearly three hours until the Continentals, who were running out of ammunition, burned what was left of Fort Anne and retreated to Fort Edward. General Burgoyne sent orders for Hill to pull back until all of the artillery and provisions could be moved closer to Fort Edward. This delay gave the Continentals time to thwart Burgoyne's advance by felling trees across the roadways, making the transport of matériel difficult.

One of the major weaknesses in Burgoyne's army was that it did not have an effective transport system. Lacking the necessary vehicles and animals, his army had to depend on civilians to transport its artillery and provisions on overland routes. By July 30, Burgoyne reached Fort Edward, but with only a fraction of his artillery. The Continentals under General Philip Schuyler had done an excellent job of slowing their passage from Lake George. Meanwhile the Continentals, about 4,500 strong, having decided that Fort Edward was not in good condition, moved south to a location north of Albany and began to build fortifications there.

Burgoyne, knowing that he was going to need more horses and provisions, sent some of his men to a site near Bennington, Vermont, with the intention of capturing animals and supplies from the New England militia. This attempt failed when the British were beaten back to their camp by the troops under General John Stark. The British lost more than five hundred soldiers in the skirmish. This was bad news for Burgoyne, who by this time had received word that Howe was moving toward Philadelphia. His next setback was the news that St. Leger had abandoned the advance down the Mohawk and had retreated to Canada. Now there would be no diversion from the west to occupy the enemy while he carried out his plan. Determined not to retreat, Burgoyne's army braved heavy rains and crossed to the west bank of the Hudson near Saratoga on September 13.

By this time, the Continental Congress had removed Schuyler from command of the army's Northern Department and replaced him with General Horatio Gates. For some time the Americans had wanted a more aggressive commander than Schuyler, whom they held responsible for the loss of Fort Ticonderoga.

**General Horatio Gates**

Gates came from humble beginnings as the son of the housekeeper to the duke of Leeds. He worked his way up in the British Army, which was highly unusual, since most officers' commissions were purchased by wealthy gentlemen. Gates earned a recommendation during the War of the Austrian Succession and was quickly promoted to serve in Nova Scotia in 1752. He was then promoted again during the French and Indian War. Convinced that he would be unable to find a profitable position in peacetime, Gates sold his commission in 1769 and settled in Virginia, where he met George Washington's brother. Ambitious and reliable, Gates was first appointed as the adjutant general of the Continental Army, then promoted to major general in 1776. His appointment on August 3, 1977, to command the Northern Department revitalized the Continental Army.

General Gates had on his staff a talented Polish engineer, Thaddeus Kosciuszko, who selected an excellent site north of Stillwater where Gates's army would be able to make a stand. It was called Bemis Heights, after Jotham Bemis, the owner of a tavern at the foot of the hill. At this point on the river, the bluffs rising up on the west bank left only a narrow passage between them and the Hudson. To the west the terrain was difficult to pass through. They would be able to guard the river by cannon placed on the bluffs. To fortify the site, the Continentals built log walls at strategic points to defend their line, which ran north along the river and then southwest to Neilson's Farm.

By September 17, Burgoyne had moved south to within four miles of the American camp. He prepared to attack. On September 19, the British sent out three columns. One, under General Simon Fraser, was to move west and southwest along the wagon road; the center column, under General James Hamilton, moved south on a road two miles inland; the left column, consisting of German mercenaries, marched along the river road.

A Continental light infantry unit was formed by joining together Colonel Daniel Morgan's corps of 350 riflemen and an equal number of Major Henry Dearborn's musketmen. The accuracy of the rifles and the rapid firepower of the muskets were an effective combination. The unit caught the British advance guard by surprise at Freeman's Farm. While the British sent for more reinforcements, Colonel Morgan used a turkey call to call in other Continental units. They were able to hold off the British advance for the entire afternoon. The British had the advantage of cannon, but Morgan's riflemen were able to shoot the gunners with remarkable accuracy. By the time General Friedrich von Riedesel arrived with his German troops from the river road, the day had begun to grow dark and the firing stopped.

For the next seventeen days, both sides fortified their positions. The British strengthened their line from the Great Redoubt on the bluffs to Freeman's Farm. They built the Balcarres Redoubt and the Breymann Redoubt. The Continentals sent for more men and supplies.

During this time a quarrel arose between General Gates and General Benedict Arnold, who felt slighted by Gates's omission of his name from the report of the battle to the Continental Congress. Gates relieved him of his command and took over Arnold's division himself. The situation could have divided the colonists along regional and personal lines, but they remained unified and resolved.

Burgoyne postponed his next offensive awaiting word that General Clinton would be able to attack the Highlands to the south. The delay that this caused was critical, given the low supply of British provisions. By the end of September, there was still no help from Clinton, and the Continentals had cut off Burgoyne's communication with Canada by attacking Fort Ticonderoga. The British were isolated.

**The British Attack**

Realizing that his provisions would not last beyond October 20, Burgoyne decided to risk everything and launch an attack on October 7. He proposed a compromise to Fraser and von Riedesel, who wanted to retreat: he would attack the left wing

with a third of his troops on October 7. If necessary, the rest of the troops could back them up on October 8. Only if the situation proved to be impossible would they retreat on October 11.

By this time the Continentals had built up their force to about 13,000. The British had only about 4,400 regulars remaining; they marched southward steadily to a clearing on the Barber's Farm, the left and right flanks advancing through the woods. General Enoch Poor's New Hampshire brigade forced the grenadiers of the left flank back to the ridge where the original line had formed. Morgan's men attacked the right flank. Burgoyne sent word to the troops to pull back to camp. The German line held their own for a while at the center against General Ebenezer Learned's men, but once they were exposed on either side by the retreat of both flanks, they, too, had to retreat. In the course of the battle, General Fraser was killed by a rifleman. By late afternoon General Abraham Ten Broeck's New York militia arrived to join in the battle. The British had no choice but to retreat to their camp.

Inspired by their victory on the battlefield, the Continentals decided to attack the Balcarres Redoubt. They charged across the open field, but they were successfully repelled by the British firing from behind the log walls. General Learned, joined by Benedict Arnold, began an attack on the stockades beyond the Freeman farmhouse, which were only lightly manned. This opened the way to attack the Breymann Redoubt, where only two hundred Germans were left defending the fortification. Far outnumbered by the Continentals, most of the Germans fled when their commander fell. During the attack, Arnold's horse was shot, causing him to fall and break his leg.

At dusk the fighting stopped, and Burgoyne and his troops retreated to the Great Redoubt. At sunset the following day, a group of officers carried the body of General Fraser up the hill of the Great Redoubt to be buried. The Americans continued to shoot cannon even during the service. Burgoyne knew he had either to surrender or to retreat.

Slowed by rain and by fighting the current upstream, weakened by a lack of provisions for their animals, the British army suffered an increasing number of deserters with each day of their retreat. On October 9 they reached Saratoga and set up camp. They burned the Schuyler estate so that the

Continentals, who were following them from behind, could not use the buildings as shelter.

While Gates's men followed the British northward, General John Stark's men moved southward from Fort Edward. By October 12, Burgoyne realized that he was surrounded. His food rations were running out, and his men were constantly under siege. The next day his council of war voted to open negotiations to surrender honorably. An advance guard moved forward under a white flag. Negotiations continued for two days. Burgoyne, still hopeful that Clinton's men would be able to reach them from the south, tried to forestall the inevitable. The terms were finally set on the evening of October 15.

### The British Surrender

The surrender ceremony took place at Saratoga on October 17. The British laid down their arms and ammunition and prepared for their march to Boston, from where they were to sail to England. The Continental Congress did not like the terms of the Saratoga Convention, however, and managed to find reasons to delay the British troops in America until the end of the war.

The victory did much to raise the morale of the Americans, who had begun to lose heart after General Howe took Philadelphia. More important, it helped to enlist the support of France, who had maintained a neutral position, at least publicly. The French had been waiting for a decisive victory such as the one at Saratoga to join in the effort to inflict defeat on the British Empire. On January 8, 1778, France agreed to enter an official alliance with the United States, giving assistance to the Americans in the form of men, materiel, and sea power.

### Modern Preservation Efforts

Today's visitor to the Saratoga National Historical Park will find a site that looks remarkably the same as it did in the fall of 1777. The visitors' center provides guides and maps which, together with the exhibits inside the center and the historical plaques marking each stopping point, will help the visitor to visualize the two battles that took place there.

The Schuyler House is located in Schuylerville, formerly called Saratoga, eight miles north of the park on U.S. Route 4. Built by Philip Schuyler in 1777 to replace the original house that was burned by the British, it has since been restored. Before the

American Revolution, Schuyler's 1,900-acre estate was a center of farming and trade. Today the house and twenty-five acres of land surrounding it are owned by the National Park Service. The interior furnishings were secured by the Old Saratoga Historical Association.

The Saratoga Monument, also in Schuylerville, commemorates the surrender of Burgoyne's army on October 17, 1777. The cornerstone was laid on the occasion of the centennial of the surrender in 1877, and the monument was erected with funds donated by individuals and by the state and federal governments. The 155-foot tower was completed in 1883 on the site of Burgoyne's camp on the eve of the surrender. Overlooking the Hudson, the monument combines Gothic and Egyptian architectural styles. There are three bronze statues commemorating Generals Schuyler and Gates and Colonel Morgan. The fourth niche is empty, symbolizing the role played by Benedict Arnold at Saratoga. In 1980 New York State relinquished control of the monument to the National Park Service as part of the Saratoga National Historical Park.

—*Sherry Crane LaRue*

**For Further Information:**

Cuneo, John R. *The Battles of Saratoga: The Turning of the Tide.* New York: Macmillan, 1967. A concise and scholarly account of the two battles. It includes a chronology of important events from November 30, 1776, to January 9, 1778. In his epilogue Cuneo addresses some of the problems with other historians' accounts and invites the reader to read all written history with a healthy degree of skepticism.

Elting, John R. *The Battles of Saratoga.* Monmouth Beach, N.J.: Philip Freneau Press, 1977. A detailed analysis of the campaign of 1777 written by a military historian with a special emphasis on weaponry and tactics. Colonel Elting's scholarly research of primary source material helps to debunk some of the myths that have plagued the history of Saratoga for over two hundred years. The book includes appendices explaining the weapons and nomenclature of the period, as well as a list of officers serving in each of the armies.

Luzader, John. *Decision on the Hudson: The Saratoga Campaign of 1777.* Washington, D.C.: National Park Service, 1975. Offers the reader a detailed account of the two battles and other related battles, such as Bennington, Fort Ticonderoga, and Fort Stanwix. There are many quotes from journals written by men in both armies. A detailed appendix gives information on weapons, tactics, and military organization.

Murray, Stuart. *The Honor of Command: General Burgoyne's Saratoga Campaign.* Bennington, Vt.: Images from the Past, 1998. Discusses the role of Saratoga in the Revolutionary War. Includes bibliographical references.

# Seneca Falls

**Date:** Women's Rights Convention held in 1848
**Relevant issues:** Business and industry, political history, social reform, women's history
**Significance:** Seneca Falls is the home of the Women's Rights National Historical Park, established in 1980 as a tribute to the women's rights movement. The park includes the home of activist Elizabeth Cady Stanton; the Wesleyan Chapel, where the Women's Rights Convention of 1848 was held; Declaration Park, honoring women's rights and the convention with a 140-foot waterfall cascading over the Declaration of Rights and Sentiments of Women etched in stone; and the McClintock house in the neighboring town of Waterloo. Also in Seneca Falls is the Urban Cultural Park, which examines the town's contribution to the Industrial Revolution.
**Location:** Western New York State, midway between Rochester and Syracuse
**Site Office:**
Women's Rights National Historical Park
136 Fall Street
Seneca Falls, NY 13148
ph.: (315) 568-2991, (315) 568-0024
Web site: www.nps.gov/wori/

Many of the nineteenth century reform movements have roots in Seneca Falls, New York. These movements, such as abolitionism, temperance, the Free-Soil Party, and women's rights, have shaped the social fabric of the United States. Today, the town of approximately 7,370 is the site of several restored buildings relating to the women's movement and the Industrial Revolution. In-

cluded in the historic region are the National Women's Hall of Fame, Elizabeth Cady Stanton's home, the Wesleyan Chapel, and the Urban Cultural Park.

## Early History

Seneca Falls is a prime example of the transformation from rural agrarianism to twentieth century technology, from a paternalistic society to a more equally representative society. The town is located on the Seneca River along a series of waterfalls, which made it ideal for industrial development and as a commercial and transportation center. In 1782 New York State appropriated 1.6 million acres in the western part of the state for veterans of the Revolutionary War. The first white settler, Job Smith, portaged (transported around the falls on land) goods and settlers moving westward.

By 1794 the state had laid out the Great Western Road, which facilitated westward migration and established Seneca Falls as a terminus for moving individuals and goods around the falls. Western land speculation enticed individuals such as Stephen N. Bayard to purchase large tracts of land. The Bayard Company purchased much of the potentially commercial land in Seneca Falls in 1791. From 1794 to 1816, the company not only controlled the commercial navigation and production along the river but also constricted the town's growth. By refusing to lease land or water rights, the company restricted competition and the variety of goods produced. The company operated mills to process raw materials and distribute them locally.

When the Seneca-Cayuga Canal opened in 1817, other industries began moving in, and in 1826 the Bayard Company divided its property among three stockholders who promptly sold the land to the townspeople. The town boomed. Within seven years the population increased from two hundred to two thousand, and diversified its industry to include flour milling, textiles, paper, and other small manufacturing enterprises. The Industrial Revolution had taken the village by storm, displacing the frontier and agricultural economy and making the town a regional trade and manufacturing center.

## The Importance of Water

Water dictated the growth of Seneca Falls. While the falls presented some navigational problems, they were controlled by the Seneca Lock Company, founded in 1813. In 1827, the state took charge of the decrepit lock system and followed that move by purchasing the Seneca-Cayuga Canal and connecting it to the Erie Canal in 1828. The Erie Canal connection opened western markets, which greatly needed the manufactured goods the town produced. By the 1840's most of the grain producers had migrated westward to the better soils of Ohio and Michigan, leaving Seneca Falls as a major producer of pumps, fire engines, and stoves.

The Seneca Falls that Elizabeth Cady Stanton moved to in 1847 was not only in the process of economic changes but also in the midst of a social transformation. The workforce was absorbing increasing numbers of foreign-born people, primarily refugees from the Irish potato famine. These Irish immigrants initially had been hired to build New York State's extensive canal system.

The community also was physically different from most manufacturing towns. An overwhelming number of residents either owned their own dwellings or rented a single-family house; the town had a ratio of one house for every five persons. The unique development of the town is partly due to one of the town's major developers, Gary V. Sackett. Sackett provided many of the Irish immigrants with low-interest loans allowing them to build modest houses in a developed, working-class neighborhood. Despite the manufacturing economy in Seneca Falls, the traditional company-owned housing never developed, nor did the habit of paying workers in company scrip.

## A Mix Ripe for Reform Movements

This new social mix and rapid economic growth created an atmosphere ripe for numerous reform movements such as abolitionism, temperance, revivalism, women's rights, and spiritualism. There were many social influences at work in Seneca Falls. Single women worked in the mills, and married women did piecework at home. Married women were often isolated from their husbands, who worked long hours and then frequented bars. The town's religious mix included Methodists, Baptists, Presbyterians, and Quakers. The reformist atmosphere led revivalist Charles Grandison Finney to call this area the "burned-over district."

To examine the development of the women's movement in Seneca Falls without considering these other reform influences ignores the origins of the movement. Many of the women who became leaders in Elizabeth Cady Stanton's crusade for women's rights were first activists in either the temperance or antislavery movement. Women approached the antislavery effort with enthusiasm and vigor equal to that of men, but were denied equal voice. In 1843 Presbyterian church member Rhoda Bement challenged her pastor, the Reverend Horace P. Bogue, when he refused to advertise an upcoming lecture by female abolitionist Abby Kelley. Bement vehemently and publicly protested Bogue's decision, claiming he was in favor of slavery and was not acting on his professed antislavery convictions. Bement, like many other ardent reformers, believed that the immediate correction of society's ills was the purpose of the revivalism prevalent in the churches. Bogue advocated a more moderate approach and objected to women speaking in public. Bement was excommunicated. In 1840 Elizabeth Cady Stanton and Lucretia Mott had experienced similar rejection when they were excluded from participating in the floor discussion at the World Anti-Slavery Convention in England.

The temperance movement also prepared women for activism in the women's rights movement, especially in Seneca Falls. Much of women's interest in the temperance movement stemmed from their lack of legal rights and fears of beatings from drunken husbands. Temperance meetings often resembled religious revivals, with persons in attendance pledging abstinence from strong drink. In the Seneca Falls region the most notable activism came from the nearby town of Waterloo and its large population of Hicksite Quakers. Mott, one of the original organizers of the women's rights convention, was a Quaker and active in the temperance movement. Waterloo resident and temperance crusader Amelia Bloomer published a journal called *The Lily*, which preached the temperance doctrine. When her participation in temperance activities was restricted because she was female, her journal became a major forum for Stanton and women's issues.

### The Women's Movement
Women's involvement, or rather the denial of their full, public involvement in various reform movements, logically led to their participation in the women's rights movement. Prior to the mid-1830's,

women had very few legal and social rights. Legally, they could not hold, inherit, or control property. Women could not vote, could hold few professional positions, could not attend college or university. They were not permitted to speak or express their opinions in public. Working women usually gave their wages to a father or husband. Inherited property always went to the male head of the household, or in some cases a male guardian, no matter what the age of the woman, even if the property had belonged to the woman's family. Arguments against women holding property centered around the belief that if a woman had control of property, she could and would destroy her marriage.

In 1836, the New York legislature began consideration of the Married Woman's Property Act, which would allow married women to retain rights to and control of property brought to or inherited after the marriage. Debate became an annual affair, with the proposal succeeding in 1848 only after wealthy landowners realized this law protected their property from greedy sons-in-law. Further, husbands could protect their families in the event their businesses were sued; their possessions could not be seized to cover business losses if they were registered in the wives' names. Passing of the act planted the idea that women could control their personal property and have individual rights. As property entitled holders to rights in the United States, the next logical step was women's rights.

### Elizabeth Cady Stanton
The year 1848 was fortuitous for Elizabeth Cady Stanton, who had moved to Seneca Falls with her husband Henry, a lawyer and reformer, the previous year. Elizabeth had led an intellectually stimulating and rather domestically free life in Chelsea, Massachusetts, near Boston. In her childhood, she witnessed many women who had no legal rights seeking help from her father, a lawyer. She also recalled being teased over her lack of legal rights. As a young woman, she studied at Troy Female Seminary, an experience that encouraged her to believe in the right and necessity of women's education. At twenty-five, she met and married Henry Stanton, a law student who was active in the abolitionist movement and would become supportive of his wife's quest for rights. Their marriage further provided contacts with other reformers of the day. In Boston,

*Elizabeth Cady Stanton, the main organizer of the 1848 Women's Rights Convention in Seneca Falls.* (Library of Congress)

where Henry set up a law practice, she met such individuals as Ralph Waldo Emerson, William Lloyd Garrison, Nathaniel Hawthorne, John Greenleaf Whittier, and Frederick Douglass. She even spent time at Brook Farm, an experimental utopian community in West Roxbury, Massachusetts.

Because the Boston winters proved hazardous to Henry's health, the Stantons and their three children moved to Seneca Falls in 1847. The change was drastic for Elizabeth. She became consumed with management of the household and land her father had provided. The house was located on the corner of Washington and Seneca Streets, near Locust Hill, an area newly developing. Despite ready access to the Irish working-class neighborhood, Stanton was isolated on the outskirts of town. The house was fairly large with many wings, two of which remain today. Henry was fond of growing fruit trees and Elizabeth flowers.

Servants were hard to keep because of the town's need for industrial labor. With few servants, a large house, and small children, Elizabeth Cady Stanton had very little time for the intellectual affairs of her former Boston existence. She did become involved in the community, performing the roles of homeopathic doctor, mother confessor,

and midwife to many of the Irish immigrants. These encounters with women poorer than herself sharpened her sense of the need of rights for women. These women were powerless to change their poverty and their alcoholic husbands.

An afternoon tea and impromptu discussion session held at the home of Jane Hunt in Waterloo early in July, 1848, evolved into the Women's Rights Convention, held later that month. Hunt, Stanton, Lucretia Mott, Mott's sister Martha C. Wright, and Mary Ann McClintock discussed injustices inflicted upon women in many of the reform movements with which they were involved and in the poorer Seneca Falls communities. All but Stanton were members of the Hicksite Quakers, a very liberal and egalitarian division of the Quaker church. The women were advocates of a very active and immediate role in the abolitionist and temperance movements. What arose from their discussions was the first draft of the Declaration of the Rights and Sentiments of Women and a call for a women's convention, which began July 19.

### Declaration of the Rights and Sentiments of Women

The Declaration of the Rights and Sentiments of Women was patterned after the Declaration of Independence and included a list of grievances and injuries. The women wanted to prevent male relatives from taking women's wages. They believed women should have equal pay for equal work and equal access to some positions. They objected to the application of different moral standards to women and desired egalitarian divorce laws. They asked for full property rights, right to education, and the right to vote. The document proclaimed that man had endeavored "to destroy (woman's) confidence in her own powers, to lessen her self-respect, and to make her willing to lead a dependent and abject life." Because of Stanton's previous life experiences, because of the women's location in the "burned-over district" and their involvement in reforms, because of the state of New York's debate over women's property rights, and because of the Quaker influence, the time for a women's rights convention was right.

Stanton and her associates never dreamed that the convention would draw three hundred women and men. They gathered in Seneca Falls for two days of rousing speeches and discussion of the Declaration in Wesleyan Chapel. Before the convention could begin, Stanton's nephew had to be hoisted over the crowd and sent through a window to open the chapel's door. Originally, the organizers had intended the first of the two days to be exclusively a forum for women; however, the number of men who attended convinced the female participants to allow everyone to participate fully. Heated discussion evolved around the franchise issue, with many women voicing concern that such a radical idea would detract from their cause. Henry Stanton, who supported many of his wife's views, refused to attend the convention because of it.

Many doubters, including women, questioned whether women had the intelligence to vote. Supported by Stanton and Frederick Douglass, the franchise issue passed by a narrow margin. At the close of the second day, anyone who wished signed the Declaration. It is unknown how many individuals originally signed that document: No original copy remains, and many of its signers withdrew their names because of the adverse publicity afterward. Finally, sixty-eight women and thirty-two men left their signatures on the document.

The success of the convention was due in part to the composition and relationships of those who attended. Most of the signers were from New York State and of European descent, and 69 percent of the signers lived either in Seneca Falls or in Waterloo. Only three individuals came from more than forty miles away, and all of them were visiting relatives. Most people attended with a relative—a sibling, parents, or husband. Economically, a plurality of the attendees came from manufacturing backgrounds, with farmers and tradespeople also well represented.

Outside reaction to the Declaration and convention was a mixture of ridicule, curiosity, and, occasionally, support. Horace Greeley in his *New York Tribune* objectively discussed the issues raised at the convention. While he believed in natural rights, he also thought women preferred domestic duties. He did provide Elizabeth Cady Stanton a forum to discuss and spread her ideas. However, most newspapers viewed this reform movement with much disdain.

After the convention, Elizabeth Cady Stanton remained involved in the women's rights movement, continuing to write, occasionally lecture, and care for her burgeoning family. Because of her children, who eventually numbered seven, Stanton was often unable to travel, but did attract intellectuals to her Seneca Falls home. Henry was occasionally driven to a local hotel when the house became crowded with guests. Elizabeth was very progressive in other areas of her life. She believed that children had rights and were able to formulate their own opinions, much to the neighbors' chagrin. Believing in the benefits of physical activity, she had a billiard table and gymnasium set up for her children. Contrary to the stereotype of reform-minded women, she enjoyed traditional domestic duties, including cooking and playing games with the children.

## Susan B. Anthony

Among the visitors to Stanton's home in this period was Susan B. Anthony. Anthony met Stanton on a trip to Seneca Falls in 1851 and often returned to care for the children while Stanton wrote speeches that Anthony then delivered around the nation. Their bond carried the women's movement toward the twentieth century. The Stantons left Seneca Falls in 1862 for Brooklyn, New York. Elizabeth Cady Stanton continued to be a women's rights activist until her death in 1902.

Slowly Seneca Falls's leading role in reform movements declined. Many of the landmarks from the women's rights convention were transformed for other uses, the Wesleyan Chapel becoming at various times a laundromat, an opera house, a theater, a hall, and a garage. Numerous commemorations and anniversaries were celebrated in Seneca Falls throughout the twentieth century. However, not until the late 1970's and early 1980's did the reform and feminist spirit return.

In the summer of 1983, the Women's Encampment for a Future of Peace and Justice was held on purchased lands surrounding the Seneca Army Depot. The gathering was inspired by a similar peace camp at Greenham Common, England, in 1981. The purpose of the Seneca Falls camp was two-fold—to protest the first-strike nuclear weapons supposedly housed at the depot and to engage in an all-female communal gathering. Members of the encampment were to share duties equally. Governance was supposed to be through consensus building, not through hierarchical leadership. The communal effort failed because chores were not equally shared. However, on August 1, 1983, at noon, approximately three thousand women peacefully marched in protest, amid counter-demonstrations, to the army depot. For a while after 1983, a small encampment remained, but it engaged in no further mass protests.

### Modern Preservation Efforts

Today Seneca Falls has rediscovered its past. In 1977 the town, with money from the state of New York, created the Urban Cultural Park to celebrate the town's role in the industrial development of the region and in U.S. commerce. Numerous nineteenth century buildings have been preserved and restored. The Women's Rights National Historical Park was officially founded December 28, 1980, when President Jimmy Carter signed a bill to establish it. The Elizabeth Cady Stanton Home has been restored and the McClintock Home in Waterloo is undergoing restoration.

The Hunt House is privately owned. As the Wesleyan Chapel's original design could not be found, its restoration consisted of gutting the current structure, leaving the original walls to encourage visitors to focus on the events and not the building. Between the chapel and visitors' center is Declaration Park, a grassy area that includes a 140-foot waterfall with the stone behind inscribed with the Declaration of the Rights and Sentiments of Women. The visitors' center displays seventeen bronze statues of individuals active in the women's rights movement. Most exhibits are interactive and focus on the convention. —*Jenny Presnell*

### For Further Information:

Gurko, Miriam. *The Ladies of Seneca Falls: The Birth of the Woman's Rights Movement.* New York: Macmillan, 1974. An excellent overview of the movement and the principal players. It discusses activists beyond Seneca Falls as well.

Stanton, Elizabeth Cady. *Eighty Years and More: Reminiscences 1815-1897.* London: T. Fisher Unwin, 1898. Reprint. Boston: Northeastern University Press, 1993. Stanton's autobiography. Dates and some remembrances are not always exact but very interesting.

Swain, Gwenyth. *The Road to Seneca Falls: A Story About Elizabeth Cady Stanton.* Minneapolis: Carolrhode Books, 1996. A biography of Stanton for juvenile readers. Illustrated by Mary O'Keefe Young.

Weber, Sandra S. *Women's Rights National Historical Park: Seneca Falls, New York.* Washington, D.C.: Government Printing Office, 1985. A study prepared by for the National Park Service. Provides a wealth of information regarding Seneca Falls's history and prominent activists in the women's movement.

# Statue of Liberty and Ellis Island

**Date:** Statue of Liberty was presented to the United States in 1886; Ellis Island was the gateway to millions of immigrants between 1892 and 1954

**Relevant issues:** Art and architecture, cultural history, political history

**Significance:** Presented to the people of the United States by the people of France, the Statue of Liberty recognizes the friendship between the two nations. The statue, on Liberty Island, rises more than three hundred feet from its tip to the bottom of its pedestal. It was established as a national monument in 1924, placed under the management of the National Park Service in 1933, and underwent an extensive $69.8 million renovation just prior to the statue's centennial in 1986. Ellis Island was the gateway to more than twelve million immigrants between 1892 and 1954. Because of its historic importance in the settling of the United States, Ellis Island was declared a part of the Statue of Liberty National Monument in 1965 by President Lyndon B. Johnson. After undergoing an eight-year, $156 million renovation through the efforts of the Statue of Liberty-Ellis Island Foundation, it was opened to the public as a museum in 1990.

**Location:** Islands in Upper New York Harbor, off Liberty State Park; New Jersey is to the west, Governor's Island is to the east, and Manhattan is to the northeast

**Site Office:**
Statue of Liberty National Monument and Ellis Island
Liberty Island
New York, NY 10004
ph.: (212) 363-3200
fax: (212) 363-6304

*The Statue of Liberty.* (New York Convention and Visitors Bureau)

The Statue of Liberty and Ellis Island have existed side by side in upper New York Harbor for more than a century. The Statue of Liberty was the first object that greeted millions of immigrants as they arrived in New York Harbor. It represented their hopes and cherished aspirations. Nearly all of these immigrants were fleeing political or religious oppression and grinding economic depression. Ellis Island, which opened in 1892, was the gateway to freedom through which the immigrants had to pass in order to gain entry to the United States. It was often a painful and fearful passage as the new arrivals struggled through the labyrinth of regulations, physical and mental examinations, and other barriers that separated them from freedom.

### Origins of the Statue

The Statue of Liberty owes its origin to a dinner party hosted by Edouard René Lefebvre de Laboulaye in France in 1865. Laboulaye, a scholar and jurist opposed to the autocratic regime of Napoleon III, commented during the course of the evening on the close sympathy between the ideals of the United States and those he wished to rekindle in France. "Wouldn't it be wonderful," he proclaimed, "if the people in France gave the United States a great monument as a lasting memorial to independence and thereby showed that the French government was also dedicated to the idea of human liberty?" Laboulaye's words stuck in the memory of one of the guests, Frédéric-Auguste Bartholdi, a thirty-one-year-old sculptor.

Bartholdi started as a painter but soon switched to sculpture, a medium that lent itself to his passion for large, patriotic works. A trip to Egypt, where he toured the pyramids and the Sphinx, only reinforced this love of the monumental. In Egypt he also formed a friendship with the builder of the Suez Canal, Count Ferdinand-Marie de Lesseps. In 1867, Bartholdi created plans for a massive sculpture to be placed at the entrance of the canal. The sculpture, based on the Colossus of Rhodes, was to be twice the size of the Sphinx. Bartholdi envisioned a robed Egyptian peasant woman with light shining from her headband and from a torch in her raised hand. Despite repeated revisions made to please Isma'il Pasha, the ruler of Egypt, the plans were ultimately rejected. In later years Bartholdi denied that the plans for this work influenced his design of the Statue of Liberty, but the resemblance is unmistakable.

Following the Franco-Prussian War, Bartholdi was again urged by Laboulaye to create a monument linking the shared ideals of France and the United States. This time, Laboulaye made his appeal more directly. According to Bartholdi's later accounts of their conversation, Laboulaye told him to go to America and "propose to our friends over there to make with us a monument, a common work, in remembrance of the ancient friendship of France and the United States. . . . " Laboulaye gave the sculptor letters of introduction to prominent Americans and on June 8, 1871, sent him to the United States.

### Bartholdi Chooses a Site

Bartholdi arrived in New York Harbor, which he immediately recognized as the perfect place for the monument, "where people get their first view of the New World." More particularly, he chose

Bedloe's Island, "an admirable spot" in the middle of the bay. (The site would be renamed Liberty Island in 1956.)

Once in America, Bartholdi pressed his case for the monument to men such as President Ulysses S. Grant, Henry Wadsworth Longfellow, and Horace Greeley. Bartholdi crossed the nation by train, stopping at Detroit, Chicago, Omaha, and San Francisco. At every stop he found great enthusiasm for his project, but scant willingness to raise funds for its construction. Bartholdi returned to France and bided his time, all the while refining his plans for the Statue of Liberty.

In 1874 France's Third Republic was established, and Laboulaye and Bartholdi revived their plans for the statue. They decided that the costs of the monument should be divided between the two countries: France would pay for the construction of the statue; America, for the foundation and pedestal. The statue was to be completed by July 4, 1876, the centennial anniversary of the signing of the Declaration of Independence.

### Planning the Construction

Bartholdi decided to construct the statue using a procedure known as repoussé, in which sheet metal is hammered inside a mold and applied as an outer skin to a skeletal support. This method cost less than carved stone or cast bronze, and the resulting statue would weight significantly less, a paramount concern when shipping a work of this monumental scale across the Atlantic. To create the statue's copper skin, Bartholdi chose the firm of Caget, Gauthier and Company, whose craftsmen were skilled in repoussé. For the intricate wooden skeleton, he turned to engineer Alexandre-Gustave Eiffel, then known primarily for his iron railroad bridges, and soon to be made famous by the Eiffel Tower of the 1889 Paris World's Fair.

When it became apparent that the statue could not possibly be finished in time for the U.S. centennial, Bartholdi reasoned that he could at least have the raised arm and torch ready for the opening of the International Centennial Exhibition in Philadelphia. Even this fragment of the work was not completed in time for the opening of the exhibition, however; it was unveiled in Philadelphia that August. Two other pieces by Bartholdi were also shown at the exhibition, and the sculptor was desig-nated as the official French representative there. This high visibility allowed him to create great enthusiasm for his Liberty monument.

Bartholdi next set his sights on creating equal enthusiasm for Liberty on the other side of the Atlantic. He worked furiously to complete the head of his statue for the opening of the Paris World's Fair in May, 1878. Once again, he was late; the head was unveiled in Paris in June.

### Funding the Statue

As had been the case with Bartholdi's 1871 trek across the United States, however, the enthusiasm generated by the two exhibitions did not translate into funds for the monument. In France, Bartholdi solved the problem through a series of ingenious fund-raising schemes, such as a lottery and the sale of miniature signed and numbered clay replicas of the statue. By the end of 1879, 250,000 francs had been raised. In America, almost no money had been raised. In 1884, with the statue nearing completion, only $182,491 had been raised for the pedestal and the foundation.

To the rescue came Joseph Pulitzer, the publisher of the *St. Louis Dispatch* and *The World*, who saw the opportunity not only to raise funds for the project, but to increase his paper's circulation as well. He accomplished his goals by running editorials every day in *The World*, attacking the nation's wealthy for ignoring the project and calling on the masses to contribute directly: "*The World* is the people's paper and it now appeals to the people to come forward. . . . Let us not wait for the millionaires to give this money. It is not a gift from the millionaires of France to the millionaires of America, but a gift of the whole people of France to the whole people of America." In return for their donations, Pulitzer promised to print the name of every single contributor. The campaign achieved both of Pulitzer's goals: By August, 1885, the paper's circulation had increased by half a million, and $100,000 had been raised for the completion of the pedestal.

Meanwhile, a design by renowned New York architect Richard M. Hunter was selected for the base. His plan called for an eighty-nine-foot-high pedestal resting on a concrete base that rose from the eleven-pointed star-shaped walls of Fort Wood. Overseeing the construction was Charles P. Stone.

## The Statue Is Assembled and Dedicated

The statue itself had been completed since June, 1884. A year later it was dismantled and shipped to the United States in 214 wooden crates. It took six months to reassemble the statue and mount it on its base. When completed, the monument reached a total height of 305 feet. It would be the tallest structure in New York until the construction in 1899 of the 310-foot St. Paul's Building.

The Statue of Liberty was unveiled on October 25, 1886. On hand at the ceremony were President Grover Cleveland and the French ambassador. Given the honor of pulling the cord that would drop the French tricolor veil covering the statue's face was the monument's creator, Frédéric-Auguste Bartholdi. (Bartholdi was to pull the cord when Senator William M. Evarts finished his speech, but he mistakenly let the veil drop after Evarts momentarily paused to take a breath.) In his speech, President Cleveland said, "We will not forget that liberty has made here her home, nor shall her chosen altar be neglected."

## "The New Colossus"

Although Emma Lazarus's poem "The New Colossus" is now inextricably associated with the Statue of Liberty, a plaque inscribed with her words was not affixed to the interior of the pedestal until 1903. Lazarus, a New York resident, had written the poem in 1883 as part of the American fund-raising efforts for the monument. It concludes,

> . . . "Give me your tired, your poor,
> Your huddled masses yearning to be free,
> The wretched refuse of your teeming shore.
> Send these, the homeless, tempest-tost to me,
> I lift my lamp beside the golden door!"

It was these sentiments that attracted millions of immigrants to the United States in the late nineteenth and early twentieth centuries. If the newly arrived immigrants looked with hope and wonder at the Statue of Liberty, "the Mother of Exiles," it was with trepidation that they approached the monument's neighbor in New York Harbor: Ellis Island, the "Isle of Tears."

## Early History of Ellis Island

The local Native Americans had called the island Kioshk, or Gull Island, for the birds that inhabited it. In July, 1683, it was purchased by the Dutch, who named it Little Oyster Island. The island changed owners several times over the next hundred years, finally passing into the hands of Samuel Ellis.

In the 1780's, with the possibility of renewed hostilities with the British looming ever closer, the island was leased from Ellis's heirs by the state of New York, which planned to build a fort there. In 1808 the state transferred its lease to the federal government, which recommended that the state buy the island outright and sell it, in turn, to the federal government. On the eve of the War of 1812, the government completed the construction of Fort Gibson there. The fort never saw hostilities, however, and eventually came to be used as an ammunition storage depot.

It was not until 1890 that the Congressional Committee on Immigration selected Ellis Island as the location of the new immigration station for the Port of New York. Before construction could begin on the station's facilities, the island itself had to be prepared. A two hundred-foot-wide channel was dredged, a dock constructed, and the soft clay ground was solidified with landfill taken from the excavation for the New York subway and Grand Central Station. Once the foundations were stabilized, work began on the immigration facilities themselves. The two-story main building was approximately four hundred feet long and one hundred fifty feet wide, with baggage rooms on the first floor and the inspection hall above. Also constructed were a dormitory, a hospital, kitchens, and an electrical plant.

## Opening of the Immigration Center

By the time the station was opened on New Year's Day, 1892, it had cost $500,000, considerably more than Congress's initial $150,000 appropriation. In these early years the station was busy, but the activity was not nearly as hectic as it would become later. This slower pace was in part the result of stricter contract labor and immigration legislation passed in 1885 and 1891. The station's staff averaged between 500 and 850 personnel, including interpreters, clerks, guards, matrons, cooks, doctors, nurses, and engineers. Early on, this staff was known to be open to corruption. Inspectors demanded bribes or sexual favors; false citizenship certificates were issued; railroad tickets were sold at inflated prices;

clerks lied about monetary exchange rates and pocketed the difference.

A fire on June 14, 1897, destroyed the original pine buildings (amazingly, with no loss of life), and an additional $1.5 million was required to rebuild facilities. The new main building—338 feet long and 168 feet wide—still stands and is considered one of the finest large-scale brick structures in New York. In addition to the construction of other buildings on the main island, the three-acre Island Number Two was also added. (A third island would be added in 1913.) The facilities reopened on December 17, 1900. In April, 1902, a new commissioner was appointed, William Williams, who rooted out the corruption among the station's personnel.

Soon, immigrants were streaming into Ellis Island in record numbers for which the station was totally unprepared. The new facilities had been constructed to accommodate only half a million people a year. In fact, the station would process roughly three times that number of immigrants per year—five thousand per day—between 1903 and 1914, the peak years at the island.

Not all immigrants entering New York Harbor passed through Ellis Island. Those passengers traveling in first or second class were inspected aboard ship; few were sent on for full inspection at the island. Mostly, it was the poorer immigrants traveling in steerage who were inspected at the station's facilities. Steerage itself was a nightmare. In a 1911 report to the president, the U.S. Immigration Commission reported that

> ventilation is always inadequate and the air soon becomes foul. The unattended vomit of the seasick, the odors of the not too clean bodies and the awful stench of the nearby toilet rooms make the atmosphere such that it is a marvel that human flesh can endure it.

**Processing Immigrants**

After a brief period of quarantine aboard ship, immigrants—now emotionally and physically exhausted—faced the rigors of the inspection at Ellis Island. As each passenger passed with an interpreter at his or her side, a doctor would examine the immigrant's face, hair, and hands. Often, entire groups would be made to bathe with disinfectants. About 10 percent of those examined would be marked by the doctor with a white chalk letter, indicating that the immigrant was to be kept for further medical testing. Particular letters indicated different diseases. All immigrants were examined by the feared "eye men" testing for trachoma, a disease that could cause blindness or death, and which accounted for more than half of all detentions. In addition to these medical examinations, immigrants could also be given psychological tests meant to weed out the "feeble-minded." Finally, immigrants were asked a series of questions designed to verify the information on their ships' manifests.

Only about 2 percent failed the various tests. The rest proceeded to the Money Exchange, the railroad ticket office, and, finally, the baggage room. With their official landing cards in hand, they could then leave the island and enter their adopted nation. It is estimated that more than twelve million people, or more than 70 percent of all the nation's immigrants, passed though Ellis Island during its years of operation, 1892 to 1954.

*The interior of the museum on Ellis Island.* (PhotoDisc)

882 • New York

Immigration slowed to a virtual stop with the start of World War I. On July 30, 1916, a saboteur exploded fourteen barges loaded with dynamite in New York Harbor. Once again, the facilities at Ellis Island needed to be repaired, this time at a cost of $300,000. Once restored, the facilities were used to house citizens of enemy countries; the medical facilities were used by the army and navy. A magnificent vaulted ceiling was added to the main building in 1918.

### Attempts to Reduce Immigration

After the war, attempts were made to reduce the number of immigrants entering the country. A 1917 law requiring immigrants to read at least forty words in their native language hardly put a dent in the flood of people passing through Ellis Island. In the 1920's, however, Congress passed strict new immigration laws, culminating with the quota system that went into effect in 1929. As part of these changes, immigrants were to be inspected before their departure from their country of origin, not upon their arrival in the United States. Immigration dropped drastically. World War II saw a temporary burst of activity at Ellis Island, which was again used as a detention center for enemy aliens. The facilities were finally closed in 1954, in which year only 21,500 immigrants were processed there.

Ellis Island sat abandoned for more than twenty years. In 1965 it was made part of the Statue of Liberty National Monument (which had been established in 1924). Guided tours of the island were given from 1976 to 1984, but much renovation was needed.

### Modern Preservation Efforts

In 1982, the Statue of Liberty-Ellis Island Foundation was created to restore both sites. Similar to Joseph Pulitzer's fund-raising drive for the Statue of Liberty a century earlier, this foundation, headed by businessman Lee Iacocca, sought private contributions. It was hugely successful, raising more than $295 million.

Restoration of the Statue of Liberty, which included cleaning its copper skin and replacing its torch, was completed by July 4, 1986. An elevator takes visitors to the foot of the statue, but those wishing to look out from the observation deck in the crown must climb the 354-step staircase. A permanent exhibition in the museum at the base of

the statue tells the monument's history. Ellis Island was reopened in 1990. While most of the restored buildings are off-limits to visitors, the 100,000-square-foot main building is open to the public and houses the Immigration Museum. An estimated two million people visit the Statue of Liberty every year; approximately a million and a half people visit Ellis Island annually.      —*Terence J. Sacks*

**For Further Information:**

*Ellis Island and Statue of Liberty: The Immigrant Journey.* 8th ed. San Francisco: American Park Network, 1998. A succinct but still comprehensive account of both landmarks.

Shapiro, Mary. *Gateway to Liberty: The Story of the Statue of Liberty and Ellis Island.* New York: Random House, 1986. A detailed, vivid account of the history and development of both Ellis Island and the Statue of Liberty.

Shapiro, William E. *The Statue of Liberty.* New York: Franklin Watts, 1985. Written on a somewhat simpler level but contains many interesting and amusing anecdotes about the statue and its creator.

# United Nations

**Date:** United Nations founded on October 24, 1945; headquarters completed in 1950

**Relevant issues:** Political history, social reform

**Significance:** The United Nations is a voluntary organization of nations that have joined forces to work for world peace. The chief architect for its headquarters was Wallace K. Harrison. The Secretariat Building, General Assembly Building, and Conference Building were completed in August, 1950, and the Dag Hammarskjöld Library was added in 1961.

**Location:** An eighteen-acre site on Manhattan, bordered by 48th Street to the north, 42d Street to the South, United Nations Plaza (part of First Avenue) to the west, and the East River to the east

**Site Office:**
Public Inquiries Unit
Department of Public Information
United Nations, GA-57
New York, NY 10017
ph.: (212) 963-4475, 963-9246

fax: (212) 963-0071
Web site: www.un.org
e-mail: inquiries@un.org

After World War II, the biggest war in history, there was a widespread desire to create an organization of like-minded nations to seek peaceful solutions to the world's conflicts and thereby avoid a repetition of global war. A precedent had been set in 1919 after World War I with the establishment of the League of Nations. During the Versailles Peace Conference President Woodrow Wilson of the United States put forward the deep-rooted American political conviction of self-determination for all peoples.

### Early Expressions of the Principle of Self-Determination

The idea of self-determination went back to the Monroe Doctrine (promulgated by President James Monroe in 1823) and has remained a cornerstone of U.S. foreign policy. However, the idea of self-determination ran contrary to the views of the European allies who in 1919 were not prepared to relinquish their empires and who forced a punitive peace treaty on the defeated Germany. The League of Nations was not given sufficient autonomy or resources and did not survive the aggressions of World War II. Nevertheless, the idea of a supranational organization had been born.

The political landscape after World War II was very different from the atmosphere at Versailles in 1919. Political self-determination for former colonies and non-self-governing people was an accepted concept, and the need for a neutral forum for peaceful arbitration was readily recognized. Many nations also were more prepared to commit significant resources to the United Nations than they had been to the League, and the strong desire for peace encouraged the participating nations to vest considerable political power in the United Nations.

### The World in 1945

The former Allies who together had won World War II, however, soon found that fundamental differences in ideology were dividing the world once more. For forty years after the United Nations was called into existence its efforts at peaceful mediation and at the promotion of self-determination were frustrated by the allegiances of the Cold War. The world continued to witness terrible hardship and violent conflicts, which the United Nations seemed helpless in avoiding. While its political mediating power was frequently frustrated, the United Nations made great progress in alleviating human suffering through the work of its educational and health agencies. The World Health Organization (WHO), the United Nations Children's Fund (UNICEF), and others have to many become household terms since World War II. This continuing work of the United Nations at improving conditions around the world has secured its existence and has earned it global respect. Furthermore, since 1989 and the end of the Cold War, the world has looked to the United Nations with new hopes for its effectiveness in keeping peace and serving as a mediator in the still-changing global political landscape. In the early 1990's, the United Nations accepted twenty-six new members.

### Official Birth of the United Nations

The United Nations was officially born on October 24, 1945, when the United Nations Charter was signed by the last of the delegates who had unanimously adopted the charter at the United Nations Conference on International Organization in San Francisco on June 26, 1945. Germany's unconditional surrender had come just a month before on May 7-8 and the Japanese were yet to surrender on August 14, after two atomic bombs were dropped on Hiroshima and Nagasaki on August 8 and 9. The charter begins:

> We the peoples of the United Nations determined to save succeeding generations from the scourge of war, which twice in our lifetime has brought untold sorrow to mankind, and to reaffirm faith in fundamental human rights, in the dignity and worth of the human person, in the equal rights of men and women and of nations large and small, and to establish conditions under which justice and respect for the obligations arising from treaties and other sources of international law can be maintained, and to promote social progress and better standards of life in larger freedom . . .

The twofold approach to keeping global peace is clear in this opening statement: Peace will be promoted through the mediation and arbitration powers of the United Nations and the recognition of

*The United Nations headquarters in New York City.* (NYC & Company Convention and Visitors Bureau)

United Nations peacekeeping forces. Yet long-term measures to ensure world peace include the advancement of education, health, and respect for personal dignity.

This charter was drafted by the representatives of the fifty countries who attended the San Francisco conference from April 25 until June 26, 1945. The unanimous adoption of the charter was the culmination of a process that began at the height of World War II. In 1941 President Franklin D. Roosevelt of the United States and Prime Minister Winston Churchill of the United Kingdom held a secret meeting on a battleship in the Atlantic Ocean. The result of their discussions on resolving world disputes without resorting to war was called the Atlantic Charter when it was made public in August of that year. Representatives from twenty-six countries met in Washington, D.C., in January, 1942, to accept the Atlantic Charter and to sign the United Nations Declaration. This declaration announced an intention to win the war and then to es-

tablish ways to ensure lasting peace through a United Nations organization.

The Moscow Declaration, signed by China, the Soviet Union, the United Kingdom, and the United States in Moscow in October, 1943, reiterated this intention. With the addition of France, these nations were to play the most decisive part in the Constitution of the United Nations. In 1944 a conference was held at an estate called Dumbarton Oaks in Washington, D.C., to discuss definite plans for the structure of the United Nations. Finally, in February, 1945, President Roosevelt, Prime Minister Churchill and Soviet Premier Joseph Stalin met in Yalta in the Soviet Union. There they determined the voting system to be used in the United Nations Security Council and set the date for the San Francisco conference later that year.

**Organization of the United Nations**

The United Nations that was thereby called into existence consisted of six parts: the General Assembly, the Security Council, the International Court of Justice, the Trusteeship Council, the Economic and Social Council, and the Secretariat. The General Assembly is the central organ of the United Nations, in which each member has one vote and to which each member can bring a dispute or a matter for discussion. The General Assembly has a president elected annually by the member nations and meets regularly once a year for three months, starting in September. The General Assembly receives reports from other United Nations organs and can discuss any issue brought to its attention either by a member or by the Secretary-General, whom it appoints. On these issues, it can make recommendations but does not have legal power to enforce them. The weight of the General Assembly's recommendations depends on their concurrence with the views and public opinion of almost every country in the world.

The Security Council was designed to have means of enforcing its resolutions. Its mandate is purely to discuss and decide upon matters of world peace. All United Nations members have agreed to accept its decisions and to enforce them. Not only does the Security Council wield more executive power than the General Assembly, it is much smaller, consisting of only fifteen members. Five of these are permanent members, and each permanent member holds the power of veto in Security

Council decisions. The five permanent members are China, France, the United States, the United Kingdom, and the Russian Federation (formerly the Soviet Union). The remaining ten members are elected by the General Assembly for two-year terms. To pass a Security Council resolution nine members must agree, including all five permanent members. The Security Council can be called together at any time and at short notice. Any country, even if it is not a member of the United Nations, can bring a matter to the attention of the Security Council. The Security Council makes decisions on whether to send United Nations peacekeeping forces to an area of conflict. These peacekeeping forces were first employed in 1948 to monitor the relations of the newly founded Israel with its Arab neighbors. In 1988 the United Nations peacekeeping forces were awarded the Nobel Prize for Peace.

The International Court of Justice is a law court in which to settle disputes between countries. No individual can bring a case before this court. The court's authority rests on the fact that once a country agrees to let the court act on a case, it is bound to honor the court's decision. The court, consisting of fifteen judges elected by the General Assembly and the Security Council, with no two from the same country, sits in permanent session in The Hague, in the Netherlands. All judgments depend on the approval of at least nine judges.

The Trusteeship Council was established to supervise the advancement of trust territories—territories in which people could not choose their governments. Now most of the old empires' colonies have been granted independence, and there is only one of the original eleven trust territories left for the Trusteeship Council, which consists of the five permanent members of the Security Council, to oversee.

The Economic and Social Council (ECOSOC) encompasses some of the best-known United Nations agencies and commissions. Uniting all these agencies and commissions is a concern for problems of economic development and social issues such as human rights and health. The fifty-four members of ECOSOC are elected by the General Assembly for three-year terms. They meet annually and make decisions by majority vote.

**U.N. Commissions**
Some of ECOSOC's commissions handle specific issues, such as the Commission on Human Rights. Others are concerned with a specific area, such as Africa, Europe, Asia, or Latin America. Then there are sixteen specialized agencies, including the United Nations Educational, Scientific and Cultural Organization (UNESCO), WHO, the World Bank and the International Bank for Reconstruction and Development (IBRD), and the International Monetary Fund (IMF). GATT, the General Agreement on Tariffs and Trade, is also an ECOSOC agency. There also are fourteen United Nations programs working closely with ECOSOC, of which UNICEF is the most famous. It works to improve child welfare around the world, through better health and education as well as through improved living conditions and safer environments.

Finally, there is the Secretariat, which together with the United Nations Secretary General, forms the staff of the United Nations, carrying out the work of all the United Nations organs. Approximately twenty-nine thousand people work for the United Nations Secretariat, only seven thousand of whom are based in New York. The rest are spread throughout branch offices and the United Nations missions all over the world. The United Nations works with six official languages: Arabic, Chinese, English, French, Russian, and Spanish. This means that a delegate speaking any of these during a General Assembly or other meeting will have his comments translated by the simultaneous interpreters. The two working languages are English and French, meaning that all documents are written in these two languages.

The Secretary-General is the chief officer of the United Nations. The Security Council recommends a candidate to the General Assembly, which then appoints the Secretary-General for a period of five years. This person is responsible for the smooth operation of the United Nations and is also given the same political power as a member of the General Assembly. The Secretary-General can propose matters for discussion to the Security Council and often is called upon to act as mediator in international disputes before they are brought to the official attention of the Security Council.

There have been several Secretaries-General since the inauguration of the United Nations: Trygve Lie, from Norway (1946-1952); Dag Hammarskjöld, from Sweden (1953-1961); U Thant, from Myanmar (1961-1971); Kurt Waldheim, from

Austria (1972-1981); Javier Pérez de Cuéllar, from Peru (1982-1991); Boutros Boutros-Ghali, from Egypt (1992-1996); and Kofi Annan, from Ghana (1997-    ). Hammarskjöld died in 1961 in an unexplained plane crash in northern Rhodesia while on a United Nations mission in Africa.

### The United Nations Begins Its Work

The General Assembly held its first-ever meeting in London in 1946 and there decided that the United Nations should have its headquarters in the United States. In 1946, John D. Rockefeller, Jr., donated eight million dollars with which to buy a portion of the land along the East River in Manhattan. The rest of the land was given by the city of New York, making up a site totaling eighteen acres. Despite its location in New York, the United Nations Headquarters stands on international territory, governed by the United Nation's own laws, policed by its own security officers, flying its own blue-and-white flag, and issuing its own postage stamps. The New York headquarters consists of several separate buildings, and in recent years further adjacent office space has been taken in addition to the original buildings.

Once the site, then a run-down area of light industry and slaughterhouses, had been decided upon, the U.S. architect Wallace K. Harrison was appointed to lead a ten-member board of internationally renowned architects and design consultants who had all been nominated by their governments. The members of the board were N. D. Bassov (Soviet Union), Gaston Brunfaut (Belgium), Ernest Cormier (Canada), Charles E. Le Corbusier (France), Liang Ssu-cheng (China), Sven Markelius (Sweden), Oscar Niemeyer (Brazil), Howard Robertson (United Kingdom), G. A. Soilleux (Australia), and Julio Villamajo (Uruguay). Together they decided that the administrative offices of the United Nations would have to be housed in a tall building due to the restricted space on the site.

### The Site of the U.N. Building

The firm bedrock of the Manhattan schist, on which most of the city's skyscrapers are built, runs through part of the site, making the erection of the thirty-nine-story Secretariat Building possible. Elsewhere on the site, between 46th and 47th Streets, the bedrock dips sixty feet below sea level, and formed Turtle Bay in the nineteenth century. Today this area is filled in and lies beneath the large lawn in front of the General Assembly building. The Secretariat was built on the southern portion of the site in order to provide easy access to 42d Street, one of Manhattan's main arteries for public transportation. It was positioned on a north/south axis to prevent it from casting a long shadow over the rest of the site.

The designers decided that the tall aluminum, Vermont marble, and green-tinted glass facade of the 550-foot-high Secretariat Building and the sloping structure of the General Assembly Building, with its concave walls and shallow dome, should rise out of a landscaped, park-like, plateau. The site stretches from United Nations Plaza on First Avenue right up to the river's edge, where the landscaping and the Conference Building are cantilevered over Franklin D. Roosevelt Drive along the East River. The first plans were deemed by Secretary-General Lie to be too lavish and expensive and were accordingly scaled down. Mainly this meant reducing the height of the Secretariat Building to its present thirty-nine stories—from the proposed forty-five—and omitting plans for a library. The amended sixty-five million dollar plan—down from eighty-five million dollars—was approved by the General Assembly in November, 1947.

### Construction Begins

In January, 1949, four large New York construction firms began work; they completed the headquarters in August, 1950. In 1961, there was a major addition to the headquarters with the completion of the Dag Hammarskjöld Library as a result of a donation from the Ford Foundation. Additions since then have included a staff cafeteria and a document processing plant, as well as expanded office space for UNICEF and other United Nations agencies.

When the United Nations Headquarters was inaugurated, many gifts arrived from the governments of the member nations. Some countries contributed materials used in the construction of the buildings and others provided furnishings. Many countries sent works of art, which are displayed throughout the buildings and can be viewed by visitors to the United Nations. Among the many gifts to the United Nations headquarters there are two rugs, woven by the indigenous people of the Andes and given by Ecuador; a tapestry, *Le Ciel* by Matisse, given by France; black pebbles from Rhodes in the fountain pool in the Secretariat plaza given by Greece; a replica of an original stele (dated 1750 B.C.E.) listing the laws of Hammurabi, the oldest written legal codes, given by Iraq; a four-ounce moon rock and a United Nations flag carried on Apollo 11 during its moon landing in 1969 given by the United States; and the Foucault pendulum, given by the Netherlands, which provides a visual proof of the earth's rotation. Individuals have bequeathed gifts also: Both Salvador Dalí and Marc Chagall have donated pieces of their own work to the United Nations headquarters.

These gifts, ranging from the practical—furnishings provided by Austria, Germany, Norway, and Sweden—to the symbolic, such as the bronze Japanese peace bell cast from coins from more than sixty nations, are a measure of the inspiration the United Nations has provided in the nearly fifty years of its existence, as well as of the hopes and aspirations that are placed in it. Together, the gifts make up a cornucopia of artistic achievement and present a fitting testimony to the diversity of the earth's five billion people represented at the United Nations. Now, as in 1945, the United Nations believes that "recognition of the inherent dignity and of the equal and inalienable rights of all members of the human family is the foundation of freedom, justice and peace in the world" and that "the advent of a world in which human beings shall enjoy freedom from fear and want" is "the highest aspiration of the common people" (extracted from the preamble to the Universal Declaration of Human Rights, adopted and proclaimed by the General Assembly on October 10, 1948).

—*Hilary Collier Sy-Quia*

**For Further Information:**

Altschiller, Donald, ed. *The United Nations' Role in World Affairs.* New York: H. W. Wilson, 1993. For more detailed information and analysis, as well as for current interpretations, see this excellent collection of articles and essays.

Coyle, David Cushman. *The United Nations and How It Works.* New York: Columbia University Press, 1966. A good historic overview of the structure of the United Nations, the functions and activities of its agencies and special programs, and its achievements.

Macqueen, Norrie. *The United Nations Since 1945: Peacekeeping and the Cold War.* New York: Addison Wesley Longman, 1999. A history of the United Nations and its role in the Cold War.

Moore, John Allphin, Jr., and Jerry Pubantz. *To Create a New World? American Presidents and the United Nations.* New York: Peter Lang, 1999. Examines the relationship between U.S. presidents and foreign policy decisions and the United Nations.

# Vanderbilt Mansion

**Date:** Construction begun in 1897
**Relevant issues:** Art and architecture, business and industry, cultural history
**Significance:** The Vanderbilt Mansion was designed by Stanford White, one of America's premier Gilded Age architects, and provides an outstanding example of the Beaux Arts style of building popular in the late nineteenth century. In addition, it was owned by Frederick William Vanderbilt, a grandson of Cornelius "Commodore" Vanderbilt, and a successful businessman in his own right. With its antique-filled rooms and beautifully landscaped grounds, the Vanderbilt Mansion National Historic Site serves as an exemplar of the Gilded Age lifestyle, a time when millionaires enjoyed flaunting their wealth through the construction of lavish country houses and through entertainment on a grand scale.
**Location:** 10 miles north of Poughkeepsie, New York, just south of the village of Hyde Park, on the east bank of the Hudson River
**Site Office:**
Vanderbilt Mansion National Historic Site
4097 Albany Post Road
Hyde Park, NY 12538
ph.: (914) 229-9115
Web site: www.nps.gov/vama/

The Vanderbilt Mansion, located on the outskirts of the village of Hyde Park, New York, is visited by thousands of tourists every year. Visitors come to admire one of the finest examples of a Beaux Arts private residence in the United States. Designed by the famous architectural firm of McKim, Mead, and White, the three-story, masonry house is reminiscent of a sixteenth century Venetian palace. Surrounded by magnificent gardens, the house and the landscaping would seem to have been designed as a coherent whole. The truth is that the gardens came first.

The bluff top overlooking the Hudson River was actually the site of a substantial private residence before the estate was purchased by Frederick William Vanderbilt in 1895. The lower Hudson River valley became a favorite seasonal residential area for New York City's wealthy businessmen comparatively early in the nineteenth century. Millionaires often owned multiple residences: one in the city, where they might spend the winter months; one at the seashore; one in the country; and sometimes a hunting lodge in the mountains. The area along the lower Hudson River quickly became the place to live during the late spring and early fall months. Wealthy property owners generally stayed away in the summer, when it became too hot and humid, and in the winter, when they would stay in the city or head to southern climates.

In any case, the gardens at the Vanderbilt Mansion Historical Site date from the 1840's, when Walter Langdon, Jr., a grandson of millionaire John Jacob Astor, began laying out new gardens and constructing walls and conservatories. Langdon hired the architectural firm of Sturgis and Brigham of Boston to design a gardener's cottage and tool house. Those buildings are still standing, although the greenhouses Langdon constructed no longer survive. Langdon established the general location and layout of the gardens, although the plantings today are based on garden designs used by the Vanderbilts.

It was, in fact, the gardens established by Langdon that attracted Frederick William Vanderbilt to the property. Vanderbilt had a passionate interest in horticulture. While it was fashionable for Gilded Age millionaires to purchase country estates that included working farms and gardens, for most, gardening was a casual interest. Livestock, produce, and flowers might be entered in local fairs, with the property owner playing the role of landed gentry, but the real work was done by hired help. The millionaires themselves generally took little actual interest in the gardens as long as there were sufficient cut flowers for decorating rooms when they entertained. Vanderbilt, in contrast, has been described as being at his happiest when clos-

eted with his gardeners discussing seed purchases, garden designs, the progress of certain varieties as opposed to others, and so on. From the time the house was completed in 1898 until he died in 1938, Vanderbilt remained in constant touch with the garden and farm staff. When he was in residence, his day would begin with a meeting with the head gardeners, and when he was away he maintained a steady correspondence, providing direction and receiving daily reports.

**Lavish Construction a Vanderbilt Tradition**
Initially, however, the Vanderbilts' attention was on the house they planned to build. Frederick William Vanderbilt was a member of one of America's wealthiest families. A grandson of Cornelius "Commodore" Vanderbilt (1794-1877) and the son of William Henry Vanderbilt (1821-1885), Frederick William Vanderbilt inherited a substantial fortune built on investments in railroads and other industries. His father had been that rare individual, the son of a millionaire who inherited a huge fortune and built it into a larger one.

Along with the wealth came the expectation of a lavish lifestyle. William Henry Vanderbilt began the family tradition of constructing mansions on the grand scale. His father, Commodore Vanderbilt, had been a self-made man, a millionaire who had created his wealth through hard work and shrewd investing. The family had no social standing other than what it could claim through new wealth. The Vanderbilts' palatial houses filled with antiques and artwork purchased in Europe helped provide an appropriately impressive setting as well as implying an ancestral heritage they did not actually possess. Commodore Vanderbilt had been snubbed by the upper classes in New York City. His children and grandchildren used his money to gain entree, and, once there, pursued a lifestyle worthy of European royalty. Thus, William Henry began the Vanderbilts' construction spree by constructing a lavish house on Fifth Avenue, designed by Richard Morris Hunt, a Paris-trained architect.

Each of William Henry's eight children would eventually build an opulent mansion on New York's Fifth Avenue. They also constructed huge summer houses in Newport, Rhode Island, and other fashionable resort areas, which they referred to as "cottages," and country estates. These estates

*The living room at the Vanderbilt Mansion in Hyde Park.* (Courtesy NPS, Roosevelt-Vanderbilt National Historic Sites, Hyde Park, New York)

were often thousands of acres in size and might employ hundreds of workers. George Washington Vanderbilt surprised family members by choosing the unfashionable hills of North Carolina as the location of Biltmore, a Hunt-designed building inspired by French chateaux. Frederick William stayed closer to the traditional haunts of New York millionaires when he selected his estate on the Hudson.

At the time of its purchase by Vanderbilt the mansion was known as Hyde Park, and the village of Hyde Park itself at one time was inhabited primarily by workers on the estate. Today most people associate the name Hyde Park with President Franklin Delano Roosevelt. The Roosevelt family home (now also a National Historic Site and home of the Roosevelt presidential library and archives) is located close to the Vanderbilt estate, and FDR himself no doubt took a twelve-year-old boy's lively interest in observing the 1896 to 1898 construction of the Vanderbilt house.

In addition to the property at Hyde Park, Frederick Vanderbilt owned residences in New York City; Palm Beach, Florida; and the Adirondack Mountains of upstate New York. Once the house at Hyde Park was completed, Vanderbilt would be in residence only a few months out of the year, in late spring and in early fall, even though by Vanderbilt standards he was a virtual recluse. He shunned the limelight, preferring gardening over socializing, and spoke of the mansion as a place he could go to escape from the headaches of both city life and the notoriety that went with the family name.

### Designed to House Objets d'Art

Construction of the mansion began in 1896. While Charles McKim had designed an exterior that would remind visitors of an Italian ducal palace, his partner Stanford White's hand is clearly visible in the interior floor plan. White made a practice of scouring the markets of Europe for antiquities and architectural artifacts that could be incorporated into his clients' buildings in the United States. These purchases ranged from antique Oriental rugs to entire buildings. He would purchase literally entire rooms, complete with wooden panelled walls and ceilings, mantels, and other fixtures, and have them dismantled and shipped to the United States. He then would design houses to provide the proper setting for the antiques he had obtained for his clients.

In the case of the Vanderbilt Mansion, White found a magnificent carved wooden dining room ceiling. This room is one of the first that visitors are shown on their tours of the mansion. It is at the right end of the main entrance hall. The already finished ceiling probably dictated the size and proportions of the room, and, to maintain balance in the overall floor plan, the proportions of the drawing room at the other end of the first floor of the house as well. The dining room also contains an Isphahan rug, quite possibly purchased at the same time as the ceiling, and antique stone chimney breasts. The Renaissance-era chairs in the main entry hall, antique tapestries in both the dining room and the drawing room, and the marble columns in the drawing room were also purchased by White on one of his frequent trips to Europe. The first floor ceilings are fourteen feet high.

A magnificent curved marble staircase leads to the second floor. It is while ascending the stairs to the second floor that visitors are likely to notice the plaster detailing on the first floor ceiling. Although many of the construction workers for the house were from the local area, European craftsmen were hired for the ornate plaster work. The second floor of the mansion houses Mr. Vanderbilt's bedroom, Mrs. Vanderbilt's bedroom, guest rooms, and a room for Mrs. Vanderbilt's personal maid. In keeping with the general tone of opulence, Louise Vanderbilt's room is modeled on a queen's bedroom from a French palace. The canopied bed stands on a raised dais and is separated from the rest of the room by a curved railing. The room, which was decorated by Ogden Codman, a well-known interior designer of the time, is intensely feminine. Although the furnishings appear to be antiques from the French rococo period, they are actually reproductions built by Paul Sormani, a noted French cabinetmaker of the 1890's. The Savonnerie rug on the floor was custom made to fit the room.

Frederick Vanderbilt's bedroom, with its dark woods and red draperies, is stereotypically late nineteenth century masculine. In addition, where Mrs. Vanderbilt's room can be seen as an example of the new style of decorating championed by Edith Wharton and Codman, a rejection of Victorian eclecticism and clutter, Frederick Vanderbilt's bedroom is a mix of styles and periods. Antiques and contemporary pieces were used together with no attempt being made to imitate any particular historical period.

### Owners' Lives Affect Design

The fact that Frederick and Louise Vanderbilt had separate bedrooms does not imply any problems within their marriage. It was the custom of the wealthy, and even the middle class, during the nineteenth century for husbands and wives to have separate bedrooms. Vanderbilt was reportedly devoted to his wife, whom he had married over the strong objections of his father. Louise Vanderbilt was twelve years older than her husband and divorced from his cousin. Following her death, Frederick Vanderbilt moved to a bedroom on the third floor of the house and made the gardens the focus of his passion. The couple had no children.

The third floor of the house contained guest rooms occupied by single women who visited the Vanderbilts. Single men stayed in a separate guest house on the estate. Louise Vanderbilt, perhaps because she had experienced the personal scandal of being a divorcee at a time when divorce was uncommon, insisted that guests always behave with proper decorum.

### Modern Conveniences Complement Antiques and Reproduction Pieces

Despite the lavish use of both genuine antiques and reproduction pieces, which gives the house a period feel, the Vanderbilt Mansion was an extremely modern building. The architects and builders incorporated all the latest conveniences into its construction, including electrical lighting and thoroughly modern plumbing. Electricity was provided by a hydroelectric plant on the estate. The building itself has a steel and concrete frame hidden beneath its façade of Indiana limestone, and is virtually fireproof. Still, even the most mundane aspects of the house reflect the wealth of its builders. The plumbing fixtures—the exposed pipes, faucet taps, and so on—in the bathrooms used by the Vanderbilts and their guests are silver-plated and were kept polished by the cleaning staff.

### Rescued from Decay by Volunteers

Following Frederick Vanderbilt's death in 1938, the house passed to a niece. Unable to maintain the property, she persuaded President Roosevelt to accept the house as a national monument. The federal government did maintain the mansion itself in good condition, operating it as a historic site and opening it to the public for tours, but could not afford to keep up the gardens. They fell into disarray and were eventually fenced off as a hazardous area. In 1984 local residents formed a volunteer association, the Frederick William Vanderbilt Garden Association and, in cooperation with the National Park Service, have now restored the gardens to close to the original condition. The Vanderbilt Mansion National Historic Site is open to the public seven days a week from 9:00 A.M. to 5:00 P.M. except for Thanksgiving, Christmas, and New Year's Day. The grounds are open year-round from 7:00 A.M. until sunset.      —*Nancy Farm Männikkö*

### For Further Information:

Croffut, W. A. *The Vanderbilts and the Story of Their Fortune.* New York: Ayer, 1989. A general history of the Vanderbilt family.

Lessard, Suzannah. *The Architect of Desire: Beauty and Danger in the Stanford White Family.* New York: Bantam Doubleday Dell, 1996. Stanford White was one of the most talented architects of the Gilded Age. He was also one of the most colorful. This book provides an intriguing glimpse into his legacy.

Patterson, Jerry E. *The Vanderbilts.* New York: Harry N. Abrams, 1989.

Vanderbilt, Arthur T. *Fortune's Children: The Fall of the House of Vanderbilt.* New York: William Morrow, 1991. An intriguing family history written by a Vanderbilt.

White, Samuel G., and Jonathan Wallen. *The Houses of McKim, Mead, and White.* New York: Rizzoli International, 1998. Beautiful photos of McKim, Mead, and White structures.

Wilson, Richard Guy, et al. *Architecture of McKim, Mead, and White in Photographs, Plans, and Elevations.* New York: Dover, 1990.

# Wall Street

**Date:** Original wall erected across the northern end of New Amsterdam in 1644

**Relevant issues:** Business and industry, colonial America

**Significance:** Wall Street and its immediate area form one of the world's great financial centers. The New York Stock Exchange, the American Stock Exchange, major banks and insurance companies are to be found there, and the World Trade Center is a few blocks away. New York City was the capital of the United States from 1789 to 1790, and George Washington was inaugurated in 1789 in Federal Hall on Wall Street. Many Wall Street buildings are historic landmarks, and the rebuilt Federal Hall is a National Memorial.

**Location:** New York City; slightly less than a mile long, running generally east-west across the southern tip of Manhattan from Broadway at its west end, intersecting in turn Broad Street (running south) and Nassau Street (running north), William Street, Pearl Street, Water Street and, at its east end, South Street and the East River docks

**Site Office:**
New York Convention and Visitors Bureau

Visitors Information Center
810 Seventh Avenue
New York, NY 10019
ph.: (212) 484-1222
Web site: www.nycvisit.com

Wall Street had its roots in the colonization of Manhattan's southern end by the Dutch in 1626. As the settlement, called New Amsterdam, grew, a crude wall was erected across its northern end in 1644 to discourage attacks by Indians and English settlers living to the north. The path along this wall evolved into Wall Street. The English took over the colony peacefully in 1664. Renamed New York, it became a center for trade, with much of the commercial activity centered on Wall Street. The Dutch had improved the wall in 1653, constructing a wooden barrier, actually little more than a glorified fence the wooden planks of which were frequently stolen for use in settlers' houses. The wall was dismantled in 1699.

### Early History

Wall Street's taverns, coffeehouses, and auction marts were gathering places for traders in shipping, insurance, commodities, and slaves almost from the beginning of English rule. Financial assets such as stocks and bonds, however, were seldom bought or offered for sale there in colonial days. Bonds and the shares of joint-stock companies—that is, companies with shares individually owned and freely transferable—were actively traded in London during the 1700's, but few of these instruments were to be found in the American colonies. The American Revolution led indirectly to Wall Street's coming financial prominence.

New York became the temporary national capital, and Congress met there, convening at the former city hall building, renamed Federal Hall, at what is now 26 Wall Street, near Nassau Street. In April, 1789, George Washington was inaugurated as the first U.S. president on a second-floor balcony of Federal Hall, wearing a simple brown suit to avoid any suggestion of royalty. Meanwhile the end of the Revolutionary War had seen veterans and creditors paid off with promissory notes called scrip since the money of the time was nearly worthless. Secretary of the Treasury Alexander Hamilton concocted a scheme to convert the equally worth-

*The New York Stock Exchange on Wall Street.* (Digital Stock)

dealt largely in commodities promptly turned to trading U.S. government bonds, and shares in the early joint-stock companies which were mostly banks founded by, among others, Alexander Hamilton and Aaron Burr, who would kill Hamilton in a duel in 1804. At first trading in stocks and bonds took place informally, much of it under a buttonwood tree in front of what is now 68 Wall Street or, during bad weather, in Wall Street coffeehouses. Twenty-four of the most active brokers signed an agreement on May 17, 1792, to cooperate with each other (at the expense of other traders) and to set fixed commission rates in their dealings. Known as the Buttonwood Agreement, this document can be considered the beginning of the New York Stock Exchange.

In 1793, the group moved into the newly built Tontine Coffee House. In 1817, a formal constitution was adopted and the traders took the name of New York Stock & Exchange Board. The name was changed to New York Stock Exchange in 1863, and in 1865 exchange memberships were made saleable; before that, each trader held his membership for life. Also in 1865, the exchange moved into its first permanent home on Broad Street just south of Wall. To accommodate increased business, a larger building, at the corner of Broad and Wall, was completed in 1903. That building continues in use today, having received various additions and improvements over the years. By the early 1990's, more than two thousand companies had their stock traded on the New York Stock Exchange, and the exchange had more than five hundred member firms. The exchange allows visitors to view its operations from a gallery above the trading floor. Several other exchanges, including the nearby American Stock Exchange, have been established in New York and elsewhere; however, the New York Stock Exchange remains particularly large and influential.

### Cornelius Vanderbilt

The history of Wall Street is crowded with the names of prominent, some would say notorious, business people, traders and speculators. Cornelius Vanderbilt (1794-1877) earned his title of "Commodore" by investing in steamboat transportation on the Hudson River and becoming the leading steamboat owner in the United States. He built a railroad, the Accessory Transit Company,

less scrip into U.S. bonds at the face value of the scrip. Political insiders such as Hamilton and the U.S. Congress could accumulate scrip at less than face value and convert it into the more valuable bonds when the conversion was authorized by Congress. Some in Congress resisted this idea but Thomas Jefferson used his influence to help the bond legislation pass in return for guarantees that the capital would be relocated farther south, on the Potomac River. In 1790 the capital was relocated to Philadelphia and eventually to the new city of Washington, D.C. The bonds proved to be a bonanza for insiders and quickly became the first actively traded financial assets in the coffeehouses and along the curbs of Wall Street.

### Trade in Stocks and Bonds Begins

Wall Street merchants and auctioneers who had

across Nicaragua, and when local politicians interfered with the railroad, he hired a private army to seize the country and run it for him. Trading and manipulating railroad shares on Wall Street, he put together smaller lines to create the New York Central Railroad system. His career included the use of numerous speculative practices that later become illegal: the "corner," by which a majority of a company's stock was purchased and the short sellers (who had sold borrowed stock) were forced to pay exorbitant prices for shares; "watering" a company's stock, whereby shares were printed and issued without the company's authorization; and the dissemination of false information about a company's prospects in order to manipulate the price of the company's stock.

### J. P. Morgan

The title of Wall Street's most famous and influential financier belongs to John Pierpont Morgan (1837-1913). Taking over his millionaire father's banking firm, J. P. Morgan quickly became a leader in financing American business. He attracted Wall Street's attention by defeating Jay Gould and Jim Fisk in a battle for control of the Albany and Susquehanna Railroad in 1869. In 1879 he organized a syndicate to purchase the controlling stock in the New York Central Railroad from Commodore Vanderbilt's son, William K. Vanderbilt. An attempt by Morgan to take over the Northern Pacific Railroad in 1901 led to an antitrust battle with President Theodore Roosevelt which Roosevelt won after a controversial 1904 U.S. Supreme Court decision against Morgan's interests.

In 1901 Morgan staged his greatest coup when he organized the United States Steel Corporation, then the largest corporation in the world, from the steel holdings of Andrew Carnegie and other steel, shipping, and mining interests. His firm played a major role in financing International Harvester, American Telephone and Telegraph, General Electric, and many other major industrial companies and railroads. Morgan did attract enemies. On September 16, 1920, a bomb concealed in a horse-drawn wagon exploded in front of the Morgan bank at the southeast corner of Broad and Wall Streets. Thirty-three people were killed and many injured. The attack was subsequently blamed on anarchists but the perpetrators were never found. (The event was strangely echoed by the 1993 bombing of the World Trade Center building only a few blocks from Wall Street.) Scars from the 1920 explosion could be seen for a long time on the austere marble building at 23 Wall Street. A modern forty-seven-story building completed in 1989 at 60 Wall Street is the current headquarters of J. P. Morgan & Company.

The list of prominent Wall Street operators is long: Daniel Drew, who controlled and looted the Erie Railroad; Jay Gould, speculator and railroad builder best known for the Union Pacific Railroad; Russell Sage, who used his speculative gains to found a college in Troy, New York, named for himself; Hetty Green, a ruthless speculator and a rare example of a woman operating successfully on her own on nineteeth century Wall Street (the stockbroking sisters Tennie C. Claflin and Victoria Woodhull were protégées of Commodore Vanderbilt); and Jesse Livermore, who made millions on Wall Street, much of it while lounging on his yacht, and committed suicide in 1940 after the Great Depression of the 1930's ended his speculative career.

### The Great Crash of 1929

For Wall Street the great historic event of the twentieth century was the crash of October 29, 1929, when heavy, uncontrollable selling wiped out years of price increases in one day. This is considered, in the United States at any rate, the beginning of the Great Depression of the 1930's. During the decade massive unemployment, business failures, and widespread poverty caused economic trauma for U.S. residents, not really relieved until the start of World War II. Many citizens blamed the Wall Street financial community, and called for reform. The election of Franklin D. Roosevelt as president in 1932 led to prompt legislative action.

The Banking Act of 1933 separated investment banking from commercial banking. For example, J. P. Morgan & Company was split into two companies, the new firm of Morgan, Stanley and Company taking over the investment operations. "Truth in securities" was mandated by the Securities Act of 1933, which required complete disclosure of all significant facts about a company in which stock was sold. The Securities Exchange Act of 1934 established the Securities and Exchange Commission (SEC) with powers to regulate all U.S. stock exchanges.

## Wall Street as a Symbol

To a large extent Wall Street has become more than a place but also a symbol, dominating the nation's concept of big business, financial power, and national prestige. The very words "Wall Street" have been personified so that observers say that "Wall Street thinks . . . " or "Wall Street believes . . . ," as though the street was not just a collection of large financial institutions but an actual thinking being. Thanks to the powerful linkages created by modern computers and telecommunications, this is not an entirely fanciful idea. Nevertheless, Wall Street is not just a process whereby hundreds of millions of shares and billions of dollars of value are exchanged every working day. It is also a place, a physical street lined with large buildings of diverse architectural styles from Ancient Greek to the most modern office towers, and many of these are historically significant.

## Trinity Church

One of the most famous buildings related to Wall Street is not a business place at all but a church. Trinity Church's location on the west side of Broadway facing the intersection of Broadway and Wall Street has made it one of the best known and most photographed landmark churches in New York City. The present church in the Gothic Revival style is the third church building on the site, the first one dating from 1697 and the second from about 1780. The present structure dates from 1846 and includes a small museum of New York history, which is open to the public. Alexander Hamilton, Robert Fulton, and other dignitaries are interred in the burial ground surrounding the church.

Another notable and historic building is Federal Hall at the northeast corner of Broad and Wall Streets near Nassau Street. The first Federal Hall, originally a city hall building, was the nation's capitol building until 1790 and the site of George Washington's first inauguration and the first meetings of the Congress. The original building was scrapped in 1812 and rebuilt in its present Greek-revival form in 1842. It served as a U.S. Custom House until 1862, when it became a subtreasury building. The building was designated a National Historic Site in 1939 and a National Memorial in 1955. It contains a museum of democratic government. In addition to the stock exchanges and headquarters of various financial firms, another business-related site is the Museum of American Financial History at 24 Broadway. It contains many examples of Wall Street memorabilia such as obsolete stock tickertape machines and antique stock and bond certificates.                  —*Bernard A. Block*

## For Further Information:

Clews, Henry. *Fifty Years in Wall Street*. New York: Irving Press, 1908. Clews was one of the best known brokers on Wall Street in the late nineteenth to early twentieth centuries. His Henry Clews and Company was a prestigious brokerage house. Clews was also one of the first financial journalists, pioneering the stock market letter and writing financial columns for the newspapers. His memoir is an entertaining and shrewd portrayal of the characters and events of Wall Street from the 1850's to the early 1900's.

Dolkart, Henry. *Guide to New York City Landmarks*. 2d ed. Washington, D.C.: Preservation Press, 1998. Offers architectural and historical details for many New York City buildings and locations.

Sharp, Robert M. *The Lore and Legends of Wall Street*. Homewood, Ill.: Dow Jones-Irwin, 1989. A popular retelling of many picturesque events in American financial history.

Thomas, Dana L. *The Plungers and the Peacocks*. 2d ed. New York: William Morrow, 1989. Retells Wall Street history in anecdotal style. A popular book.

Warshow, Robert I. *The Story of Wall Street*. New York: Greenberg, 1929. An older but knowledgeable and well-illustrated stock market history published just before the onset of the Great Depression.

Wolfe, Gerard R. *New York: A Guide to the Metropolis*. New York: McGraw-Hill, 1994. An excellent source for architectural and historical information.

# West Point

**Date:** Founded as a military outpost in 1778
**Relevant issues:** Education, military history, political history, Revolutionary War
**Significance:** West Point was the site of an important fort controlling passage on the Hudson River. It was this fort that General Benedict Arnold (1741-1801) attempted to betray to En-

*Officers review the West Point bicentennial class of 2002.* (AP/Wide World Photos)

and steep cliffs called "the Hudson Highlands." The river narrows and makes an S-curve, which is commanded by the present site of West Point. The navigable width of the Hudson at this point is approximately one-quarter mile.

At the beginning of the Revolutionary War both sides recognized the importance of the Hudson River Valley system. For the British, military success hinged on control of the Hudson Valley. If they could seize and hold the waterway, by taking or destroying the forts which guarded it, New England would be cut off from the middle and southern colonies, which contained two-thirds of the population and most of the food and wealth. The British would be able to move troops down from Canada to dominate New York and New England, and could then use their fleet to control southern towns and cities, most of which lay on navigable rivers. If the colonists could control the Hudson, they might be able to defeat this British strategy.

In May of 1775, at the urging of General George Washington and Colonel Benedict Arnold, the Continental Congress deputed two New Yorkers—Christopher Tappen and Colonel James Clinton—to "go to the Highlands and view the banks of Hudson River there, and report to this Congress the most proper place for erecting one or more fortifications...." Tappen and Clinton determined that West Point was the best site for the major fort. Here the river was narrow and its currents and tides difficult to navigate. Guns placed at the Point and on Marter's Rock (now known as Constitution Island) on the east bank of the river would command the entire navigable channel. Moreover, Tappen conceived a scheme to place a chain or boom across the river at this point to impede vessels attempting to pass. Construction began in the fall of 1775; by 1778 the fort was garrisoned and essentially in full operation. Guns were sited on both sides of the river, and the boom suggested by Tappen closed the river to shipping except when opened by the garrison. Although under continuous occupation

gland during the Revolutionary War. Since 1802, it has been the site of the United States Military Academy, the professional school for prospective Army officers. West Point is the oldest continuously occupied military post in America.

**Location:** On the west bank of the Hudson River, 50 miles north of New York City

**Site Office:**
United States Military Academy
Visitors Center
West Point, NY
ph.: (914) 938-2638
Web site: www.usma.edu

West Point's importance in American history lies in its role in the American Revolution; its continuing importance is rooted in its identity as the site of the United States Military Academy, whose function is to train the professional officer corps which has led the Army during U.S. wars. Most of the great military leaders of the country have been West Point graduates. Some of the most notable are Ulysses S. Grant, Robert E. Lee, John J. Pershing, Douglas MacArthur, Dwight D. Eisenhower, and Norman J. Schwarzkopf.

### Revolutionary Heritage
About fifty miles north of New York City the Hudson River runs through a region of high mountains

by troops, West Point did not formally become U.S. government property until 1790, when Congress appropriated money for its purchase.

## Benedict Arnold's Treachery

Benedict Arnold was born in Norwich, Connecticut, in 1741, the son of a merchant. At the outbreak of the Revolutionary War he volunteered for service. He was with Ethan Allen in the successful attack on British-held Fort Ticonderoga. He went on to serve the Patriot cause as a commander of distinction and brilliance in the attack on Quebec, in the defeat of a superior British flotilla near Valcour Island, New York, and in the great American victory at Saratoga, where he was in command of the advance guard. He was twice seriously wounded. However, Arnold became disaffected. He believed that his accomplishments had been inadequately rewarded and that he had been unfairly denied promotion. Moreover, he was accused of misappropriating government property and had to face a court-martial. Although acquitted, he felt that his exoneration was grudging and incomplete.

In May of 1779, a month after his marriage to Peggy Shippen, the daughter of a Loyalist family, Arnold surreptitiously offered his services to the British. His contact, through an intermediary, was Major John André, an English officer on General Sir Henry Clinton's staff. During the following fifteen months he passed intelligence on Patriot movements to the British. On at least two occasions he gave them details of George Washington's personal movements, in the hope that British troops might kill or capture him. After being appointed to command at West Point, Arnold devised a plan to betray the fort to the enemy. To that end, in September, 1780, Arnold met with André in a house just below the fort. At this meeting the details of the fort's surrender were established. Arnold was to receive £20,000 (about $100,000) for his treason.

After the meeting, André, who had come upriver on the British sloop *Vulture*, was prevented from returning aboard her because she had been seriously damaged by heavy cannon fire from Constitution Island. He tried to return to the British lines by an overland route, but was intercepted by Patriot militiamen and searched. Plans of the fort in Arnold's handwriting were discovered in his boot, and he was arrested as a spy. As soon as Arnold learned of André's capture he fled by boat,

and was able to reach the *Vulture* safely. The plot to hand West Point over to the British had failed. So close had it come to fruition, however, that the British garrison in New York had already cancelled leaves in preparation for the attack. Many military historians believe that the Revolutionary War would have been lost had Arnold's plot succeeded and West Point fallen.

Arnold later served in the British army. After a short court-martial, André was hanged as a spy.

## Establishment of the Military Academy

After the Revolution, the land on which West Point had been built was purchased by the government. In 1802 Congress passed an act establishing the United States Military Academy at West Point. In its earliest years the academy was primarily an engineering school whose main purpose was to train army officers to help with civil engineering projects—bridges, dams, forts, arsenals, and the like. In 1812 the academy was reorganized and expanded. It began to acquire its distinctive traditions and role in training combat officers with the superintendency of Colonel Sylvanus Thayer (1817-1833), whose mark on the physical plant and curricular development of the institution cannot be overestimated.

Nearly all of the most senior and successful commanders on both sides of the American Civil War were West Point graduates. Their successes helped to solidify the school's reputation. From 1866 on, Congress allowed the appointment of superintendents from branches of the Army other than the Corps of Engineers. This change resulted in a broader curriculum for cadets. Further important modernizations, both curricular and organizational, took place during the superintendency of General Douglas MacArthur in the 1920's, many of them against the wishes of the academy staff of the time. Diversification of the curriculum and greater promotion of physical fitness through the athletic program were among MacArthur's reforms. New rules regarding "hazing," which had actually resulted in the deaths of several cadets, were also instituted. Indeed, MacArthur himself had been seriously hazed in his first year at the academy. Although "plebes"—the United States Military Academy equivalent of freshmen—are still harassed, the sometimes extreme physical violence which once characterized hazing no longer exists.

Additional curricular changes took place after World War II when it had become clear that officers must possess scientific and technological knowledge in addition to military and leadership skills. In 1964, President Lyndon B. Johnson signed legislation increasing the strength of the Corps of Cadets from 2,529 to 4,417. To keep up with the growth of the Corps, a major expansion of facilities at the academy began shortly thereafter. Women were admitted to the academy for the first time in 1976 and now make up 15 percent of the student body. At the turn of the century, the Corps of Cadets numbered about four thousand.

### Administration and Curriculum

The academy is under the jurisdiction of the Department of the Army, which appoints a superintendent, who exercises military command of the academy and the military post. The other senior leaders are the Commandant of Cadets and a Dean, who is primarily responsible for the academic program.

Admission is limited to unmarried United States citizens between the ages of seventeen and twenty-three. To be admitted to the academy candidates must first be nominated by a United States senator or representative. A limited number of service-connected nominations are also available through the president or Secretary of the Army for people already enlisted in the military and children of deceased veterans or Medal of Honor winners. After nomination, applicants are judged according to competitive examinations and academic records, as well as extracurricular activities and character recommendations.

In addition to a core of professional courses, cadets may take optional majors in many of the traditional disciplines of science, engineering, humanities, and social science. The four-year course of study leads to the degree of bachelor of science and a commission as second lieutenant in the United States Army. Graduates are expected to serve a term of at least five years in the Army.

### Places to Visit

West Point is an extraordinarily beautiful place. The Hudson River and the surrounding Hudson Highlands offer wonderful scenic vistas. At West Point itself is a large visitors' center, which should be the tourist's first stop. There is also a mu-seum (pieces of Christopher Tappen's boom chain from 1778 are among the exhibits), the West Point military cemetery, which was established in 1817, and side trips across the river to Constitution Island, where some of the original artillery sites may be seen. The campus itself and the academy's buildings are themselves worth seeing. Guided tours are available at nominal fees.

*—Robert Jacobs*

### For Further Information:

Chamber of Commerce of Orange County. www.orangeny.org. This Web site is for Orange County, New York, the site of West Point.

Heise, J. Arthur. *The Brass Factories: A Frank Appraisal of West Point, Annapolis, and the Air Force Academy.* Washington, D.C.: Public Affairs Press, 1969. Critical appraisal of the curricula and honor systems at the service academies.

Manchester, William. *American Caesar: Douglas MacArthur, 1880-1964.* Boston: Little, Brown, 1978. Chapters 1 and 3 of this full-length biography of MacArthur give details of his years as a cadet and as superintendent, respectively.

Morpurgo, J. E. *Treason at West Point: The Arnold-André Conspiracy.* New York: Mason/Charter, 1975. Focuses on the details of the conspiracy to surrender the fort. Presents John André's role very sympathetically.

Palmer, Dave Richard. *The River and the Rock: The History of Fortress West Point, 1775-1783.* New York: Greenwood, 1969. Detailed history of the establishment of West Point, its role in the Revolution, and Arnold's treason.

Randall, Willard Sterne. *Benedict Arnold: Patriot and Traitor.* New York: William Morrow, 1990. The best and most informative biography of Benedict Arnold.

Simpson, Jeffrey. *Officers and Gentlemen: Historic West Point in Photographs.* Tarrytown, N.Y.: Sleepy Hollow Press, 1982. Perspective on the changes and growth at West Point—on campus and in the surrounding countryside.

Smith, Dale O. *Cradle of Valor: The Intimate Letters of a Plebe at West Point Between the Two World Wars.* Chapel Hill, N.C.: Algonquin Books of Chapel Hill, 1988. Smith's letters to and from his family during his Plebe year, interspersed with interesting discussion of the changes at West Point since Smith's cadet years.

# Woodstock Festival Site

**Date:** August 15-17, 1969

**Relevant issues:** Cultural history, political history, social reform, Vietnam War

**Significance:** In the summer of 1969, the town of Bethel was the site of Woodstock, the largest outdoor rock-and-roll concert in American history.

**Location:** Max Yasgur's farm, at the junction of Yasgur Road and 17B in Bethel, Sullivan County, approximately one hundred miles northeast of New York City

**Site Office:**

Woodstock Nation Foundation
ph.: (914) 557-0086
Web site: woodstocknation.org
e-mail: liberty@woodstocknation.org

The 1969 gathering called Woodstock represented one of the final events for the counterculture during the contentious 1960's. In an attempt to raise money to protest the Vietnam War and to celebrate the new social freedoms associated with sex, drugs, and rock and roll, half a million people assembled to participate in a weekend full of concerts, art shows, and political statements. The original site was eventually purchased after Max Yasgur's death, and developers built a natural amphitheater on the land. Over the years, Bethel officials have attempted to block any attempts to reconvene another festival, but thousands still return or conduct annual pilgrimages to the farm to commemorate the importance of the original event.

## Organizing the Festival

The producers of the outdoor concert at Woodstock shared the same disdain for mainstream America that the counterculture displayed throughout the 1960's. The idea was hatched by two affluent young men who were searching for investments that differed from traditional Wall Street enterprises. John Roberts, a graduate student at the University of Pennsylvania, whose family had developed a major pharmaceutical company, and Joel Rosenman, a recent Yale Law School graduate, decided to forsake education and the law in order to invest in rock and roll. In February, 1969, they met with two other young entrepreneurs, Artie Kornfield and Michael Lang, and hatched a scheme to produce the music festival. Kornfield and Lang

hoped to build a new, state-of-the-art recording studio outside New York, and Roberts and Rosenman agreed to finance its construction from the profits obtained through a promotional concert at Woodstock. They paid a local farmer, Max Yasgur, fifty thousand dollars for the use of his one-thousand-acre farm and decided to charge eighteen dollars per ticket for an anticipated crowd of fifty thousand.

The planning proved to be extremely difficult. The stage was seventy-six feet long and accommodated a sixty-foot revolving turntable that would allow performers quick access to and egress from the stage. The developers had to build elevator access and also arrange for the preparation and installation of telephone poles and electrical towers. Other concerns centered around toilet facilities, food, and medicine. Unaware that approximately half a million people would attend, the promoters were grossly underprepared and lacked the basic amenities required for an orderly event.

Members of the notorious Hog Farm Commune in New Mexico were recruited to furnish food, and they agreed to cook, provide cleanup service, and coordinate security. They shipped in tons of oats, wheat germ, honey, and onions, and fifteen hundred pounds of bulgur wheat. Organizers also erected a five-acre shopping center by the Hog Farm Commune, where hippies sold leather goods, incense, tie-dyed shirts, and other crafts. They set up a small petting zoo for the children and lined the campgrounds with pay phones, portable toilets, and medical tents. Although these supplies proved to be inadequate, hardly any disturbances occurred, as the crowd handled all the inconveniences with a commitment to peace, harmony, sharing, and togetherness.

## The Woodstock Music and Art Fair: An Aquarian Exposition

Woodstock quickly surpassed everyone's expectations. While the promoters expected anywhere from 50,000 to 200,000 fans at the concert, approximately 500,000 attended the festivities, and some experts estimated that almost 2 million attempted to come, but traffic problems prevented them from entering Max Yasgur's farm. The crowds became so exhaustive that the New York State Police were forced to close the interstate to the site. New York Route 17B into Bethel was backed up for over thir-

*A plaque now stands on the original Woodstock site in Bethel. Musical veterans of that concert, including David Crosby and Richie Havens, played there again in 1999.* (AP/Wide World Photos)

the summer, interest continued to swell. Local radio stations and music stores added to the hype, and newspaper ads promised concert goers that this event would celebrate and champion the causes of the counterculture and student movement. Organizers arranged performances by such leading bands as the Jefferson Airplane, the Who, the Grateful Dead, Credence Clearwater Revival, Sly and the Family Stone, Santana, Arlo Guthrie, Joan Baez, Janis Joplin, Richie Havens, the Band, and Crosby, Stills, and Nash. Advertised as the greatest mass entertainment event in history, Woodstock did not disappoint its audience.

Yet the concert began more with a whimper than a bang. When people began to arrive on Friday, they became increasingly annoyed by the lack of facilities, and some of the performances were better suited for a smaller and quieter environment. The music started on Friday night at 6:00 P.M. as Country Joe McDonald and the Fish performed their renowned "Fixin' to Die Rag." Country Joe ignited the crowd when he broke into his spirited attack on United States foreign policy, Wall Street, and the Vietnam War. After this song, conditions rapidly deteriorated. The promoters had scheduled several folksingers and classical musicians such as Baez and Indian sitarist Ravi Shankar for the opening night, and much of the audience appeared bored. A torrential downpour of rain, moreover, turned Yasgur's farm into a mud pit.

When the event continued on Saturday many people suddenly became aware of the enormity of the crowd. Some described it as a war zone, but for most, the festival quickly became a place where people conducted themselves freely and openly flouted restrictions that had previously been placed upon them by school administrators, police, parents, and government officials. A stream of announcements from the stage calmed the crowd's nerves and anxieties concerning the lack of toilets, medicine, and food. One individual, Chip Monck, pacified many fears by calmly reminding the audi-

teen miles as people abandoned their vehicles and walked to the show. Route 17, an alternative road through the Catskill Mountains, failed to provide any relief either. By Saturday, local police considered the situation hopeless as more young people were still attempting to make it to the event. Yet despite the largest traffic jam in New York history, there were virtually no disturbances. Instead of wildly honking horns and shouting at their fellow travelers, young people camped out by the side of the road. They brought out guitars and harmonicas and held impromptu gatherings; people shared food and drink, and many openly used and shared marijuana and psychedelic drugs.

The event's main attraction, however, was the music. Promoters managed to secure the participation of many leading rock performers, and during

ence that half a million people would need to cooperate if the festival was to succeed. Others read press reports from the stage that predicted that the gathering would inevitably succumb to violence, anarchy, and death. Promoters challenged the audience and asked them to demonstrate to all of the world how, if left to their own devices, the counterculture was capable of generating only peace, love, and understanding. By the time the music started, people were helping others who were freaking out on bad acid trips and sharing meager food supplies. Others frolicked in the mud, skinny dipped in the ponds, and made love in the open fields. Woodstock had spontaneously evolved into a tightly knit community overnight.

The music presented on Saturday also helped. Hard-hitting performers such as Credence Clearwater Revival and Janis Joplin brought the audience to its feet. Santana enchanted the crowd with its mixture of Latin rhythms and rock beat. The classic San Francisco sound of the Jefferson Airplane and the Grateful Dead also cast a captivating spell over the crowd. By the time Sly Stone performed his song "Higher," the concert appeared to be a rousing success.

Yet behind the scenes, promoters were forced to solve numerous logistical problems. Performers had to be helicoptered to the stage, emergency supplies had to be obtained, some bands refused to perform until paid and organizers were forced to convince a local bank manager to fly in with cashier checks. Citizens in Bethel asked for the National Guard, but the organizers assured city officials that the appearance of troops would fuel, rather than erase, any potential catastrophes. Music was continually played to keep the audience busy, and by the third day, many wondered whether the festival would degenerate into a sea of violence.

The rain returned on Sunday. The staff was worried that electrical towers would eventually topple over in the mud and kill thousands, but once the storm subsided, the bands treated the audience to some of the most memorable performances in the history of rock and roll. Joe Cocker's rendition of the Beatles' song "With a Little Help from My Friends" transformed the English singer into an international star. Crosby, Stills, and Nash played for the first time before a live audience. Finally, as the concert moved into early Monday morning, Jimi

Hendrix delivered his rousing version of "The Star-Spangled Banner" on the electric guitar. When the final curtain dropped on Woodstock, many agreed that it was the simply the most significant musical event of the decade.

The event, however, exposed some of the contradictions in the counterculture. Many young people believed that all of their efforts should be devoted to stopping the Vietnam War. Some, on the other hand, maintained that the only way that one could live freely was by dropping out of the political mainstream in order to seek personal enlightenment through drugs and communal living. One particular act underscored this dilemma. Yippie leader and activist, Abbie Hoffman, traveled to Woodstock and attempted to use the stage to champion various causes. He became increasingly frustrated by the lack of political content in the show and tried to rally support for a jailed activist while the Who was playing; Pete Townshend hit Hoffman with his guitar and drove him off the stage. The audience's response seemed to indicate that Woodstock should remain a cultural celebration rather than a political affair.

**Aftermath**

The Woodstock staff completed the cleanup of Yasgur's farm in an orderly fashion in less than five days, leaving only a muddy field behind. While most people in Bethel feared the worst, the festival was free of violence. Two people died from drug overdoses, but two babies were also delivered. Disturbances did not break out into the outlying areas, and little property damage was done in the community.

The town of Bethel, however, has resisted all efforts to turn this site into a historic place. They have used snow plows, dug trenches, and dumped manure in an unsuccessful attempt to keep people from flocking to the town. Yet both old hippies and curious onlookers continue to visit the festival site, and annual reunions are arranged. Nevertheless there is very little to see. A small monument, decorated with the festival's symbol—a dove perched upon a guitar—overlooks an empty field where half a million people participated in the largest mass entertainment event in history.

There is no admission fee, nor are there tour guides. In fact, Bethel has become a piece of counterculture trivia. Most people assume that the festival took place in Woodstock, New York, located an hour north of the town. Woodstock houses a thriving industry in counterculture memorabilia with small shops hawking tie-dyed shirts, peace posters, and other miscellaneous items. There are not even road signs directing visitors to the farm, but if they travel along Route 17B to where it intersects Yasgur Road, they can look out across the open field that once held an audience that overcame almost insurmountable obstacles to participate in a festival celebrating peace, love, and understanding.

—*Robert D. Ubriaco, Jr.*

**For Further Information:**
Anderson, Terry H. *The Movement and the Sixties.* New York: Oxford University Press, 1995. Details the entire history of the counterculture and places the 1969 Woodstock festival in its proper historical context.

Curry, Jack. *Woodstock: The Summer of Our Lives.* New York: Weidenfeld & Nicolson, 1989. A comprehensive history of the event, containing numerous interviews with individuals who attended the concert.

Curtis, Jim. *Rock Eras: Interpretations of Music and Society, 1954-1984.* Bowling Green, Ohio: Bowling Green State University Popular Press, 1987. Explores the sociological and political messages in rock music and contains an insightful chapter on the 1969 event.

Hoffman, Abbie. *Woodstock Nation: A Talk-Rock Album.* New York: Vintage Books, 1969. Both a political memoir and a political manifesto, this text sheds light on one of the most controversial participants at the event.

Makower, Joel. *Woodstock: The Oral History.* New York: Doubleday, 1989. An extensive collection of personal histories that also provides essential information and recollections from the festival's promoters.

# Other Historic Sites

## African Burial Ground

*Location:* New York City, New York County
*Relevant issues:* African American history
*Statement of significance:* The area of the African Burial Ground was known and used as part of New York's common land until the late eighteenth century; the site is currently characterized by an environment built in the nineteenth and twentieth centuries, under which a large portion of the burying ground is preserved. Throughout the eighteenth century, the city's free and enslaved Africans buried their dead here. The more than four hundred individuals whose remains have been recovered from this site represent a much larger population whose role in the formation and development of this city and, by extension, the nation, is critical.

## Anthony House

*Location:* 17 Madison Street, Rochester, Monroe County
*Relevant issues:* Social reform, women's history
*Web site:* www.susanbanthonyhouse.org
*Statement of significance:* Active in numerous reform movements, Susan B. Anthony (1820-1906) was a leader in the women's rights movement of the nineteenth century. Her Rochester residence (1866-1906) is now a museum.

## Armstrong House

*Location:* New York City, Queens County
*Relevant issues:* African American history, cultural history
*Statement of significance:* From 1940 to 1971, this two-and-a-half-story brick structure was the home of the world-famous musician Louis Armstrong (1901-1971).

## Arthur House

*Location:* New York City, New York County
*Relevant issues:* Political history
*Statement of significance:* Chester A. Arthur (1829-1886) returned to this five-story brownstone townhouse, his home before his presidency, after his term as president ended in 1885. He is best remembered for his support of civil service reform.

## Austen House

*Location:* New York City, Richmond County

*Relevant issues:* Art and architecture

*Statement of significance:* For seventy-eight years, this was the home Alice Austen (1866-1952), a remarkable photographer whose work predates in subject matter and technique the photographs of other giants in the field. Austen began her career in the 1870's, and, although she used subjects as other women photographers of her time, her pictures have a realistic and natural edge rather than the blurry romantic view advocated by magazines of the time. Austen also veered away from the conventional studio poses; instead she took pictures of people during the course of their normal activities.

## Bell Telephone Laboratories

*Location:* New York City, New York County

*Relevant issues:* Science and technology

*Statement of significance:* This was the home (1898-1966) of America's largest industrial research laboratory, responsible for numerous contributions to pure science as well as pioneering work in telecommunications technology.

## Brown Farm and Gravesite

*Location:* John Brown Rd., Lake Placid, Essex County

*Relevant issues:* Civil War, political history

*Statement of significance:* Few of those who have sung "John Brown's body lies a-mouldering in his grave," know that his grave is here in upstate New York. It was from his small, plain, unpainted frame farmhouse that the famous and controversial abolitionist John Brown (1800-1859) set forth, first to Kansas, then to Harpers Ferry, with his plan to exorcise slavery from America by armed confrontation. At his request, his body was returned here for burial after he was tried for treason and executed in 1859. From the moment he was interred, the farmhouse and gravesite were regarded as a shrine, and from them "his truth goes marching on." The property was deeded to the state of New York in 1896 and is open to the public as a State Historic Site.

## Buffalo State Hospital

*Location:* Buffalo, Erie County

*Relevant issues:* Art and architecture, health and medicine

*Statement of significance:* Begun in 1872, this is an important transitional building in the developing style of H. H. Richardson. It is the first major work on which he collaborated with Frederick Law Olmsted and his partner, Calvert Vaux, who sited and landscaped the property. Also significant in the history of treatment for the mentally ill as its plan followed the system developed by Dr. Thomas Kirkbride, one of the first physicians to treat insanity as an illness.

## Bunche House

*Location:* New York City, Queens County

*Relevant issues:* African American history, political history

*Statement of significance:* Home of Ralph Bunche (1904-1971), the distinguished African American diplomat and scholar who served as undersecretary-general of the United Nations and who received the Nobel Peace Prize for his 1949 contributions to peace in the Middle East.

## Canfield Casino and Congress Park

*Location:* Saratoga Springs, Saratoga County

*Relevant issues:* Cultural history, health and medicine

*Statement of significance:* These two important sites, at the center of the community, established the international fame of Saratoga Springs—"the Queen of the Spas"—as a health resort and gambling center for much of the nineteenth century. Congress Park was intimately associated with Dr. John Clarke, the popularizer of Saratoga water. The Casino recalls the careers of John Morrissey and Richard Canfield, the two gambling impresarios who turned Saratoga Springs into America's Monte Carlo.

## Carnegie Hall

*Location:* New York City, New York County

*Relevant issues:* Cultural history

*Web site:* www.carnegiehall.org

*Statement of significance:* Constructed in 1891 and named for principal benefactor Andrew Carnegie (1835-1919), the hall has been the scene of performances by major musical artists. It also was the home of the New York Philharmonic from 1926 to 1936.

## Chrysler Building

*Location:* 405 Lexington Avenue, New York City, New York County

*Relevant issues:* Art and architecture

*Statement of significance:* Built for Walter P. Chrysler in "Style Moderne," the building exemplifies the machine age in architecture and is symbolic of 1920's New York.

## Conference House

*Location:* New York City, Richmond County

*Relevant issues:* Colonial America, political history, Revolutionary War

*Statement of significance:* On September 11, 1776, this was the scene of a meeting between Lord Richard Howe and a committee of the Continental Congress. The British admiral offered amnesty in exchange for withdrawal of the Declaration of Independence.

## Conkling House

*Location:* Utica, Oneida County

*Relevant issues:* Political history

*Statement of significance:* This was the New York home (1863-1888) of Roscoe Conkling, the senator and political boss who gained control of New York's Republican party organization in 1870 and created a bitter rift in the party that persisted for two decades.

## Cooper Union

*Location:* New York City, New York County

*Relevant issues:* Political history

*Statement of significance:* This educational center was the scene of a speech by Abraham Lincoln in 1860 concerning the slavery issue that brought him national prominence.

## Draper House

*Location:* Hastings-on-Hudson, Westchester County

*Relevant issues:* Science and technology

*Statement of significance:* This was the home (1840-1882) of John W. Draper, the well-known mid-nineteenth century scientist who, in addition to significant contributions to physics and chemistry, also wrote important works in intellectual history.

## Eastman House

*Location:* Rochester, Monroe County

*Relevant issues:* Business and industry, cultural history, science and technology

*Statement of significance:* Home (1905-1932) of George Eastman, who made photography a popular pastime. He developed a simple camera in 1888 and marketed the first roll film.

## Eldridge Street Synagogue

*Location:* New York City, New York County

*Relevant issues:* Religion

*Statement of significance:* The Eldridge Street Synagogue (1887) is the most important artifact of Eastern European Orthodox Judaism in America. It is the first great house of worship built by Eastern European Jews in the United States, located in the neighborhood through which more Jewish immigrants have passed than any other.

## Ellington Residence

*Location:* New York City, New York County

*Relevant issues:* African American history, cultural history

*Statement of significance:* Long-term residence (1939-1961) of Duke Ellington (1899-1974), regarded by many critics as one of the most creative American composers of the twentieth century and one of the leaders in developing and expanding jazz forms.

## Fillmore House

*Location:* East Aurora, Erie County

*Relevant issues:* Political history

*Statement of significance:* This is the only remaining residence of Millard Fillmore (1800-1874), the thirteenth president of the United States, who built this house and resided here from 1826 to 1830.

## Fish House

*Location:* New York City, New York County

*Relevant issues:* Political history

*Statement of significance:* This was the residence (1808-c. 1838) of Hamilton Fish (1808-1893), President Ulysses S. Grant's secretary of state (1869-1877). During his tenure, he proved to be an exceptional manager and added stability to a demoralized administration.

## General Electric Research Laboratory

*Location:* Schenectady, Schenectady County

*Relevant issues:* Science and technology

*Statement of significance:* Established in 1900, this is recognized as the first industrial research facility in the United States. The General Electric Research Laboratory has made major contributions to scientific knowledge, especially in the areas of physics and chemistry.

## Haynes House

*Location:* South Granville, Washington County

*Relevant issues:* African American history, religion

*Statement of significance:* This was the latter-day (1822-1833) home of Lemuel Haynes, the first ordained African American minister in the United States, who was also the first black minister to a white congregation.

## Henry Street Settlement and Neighborhood Playhouse

*Location:* New York City, New York County

*Relevant issues:* Social reform

*Statement of significance:* Founded in 1895, this was one of the leading institutions in the settlement house movement in the United States. Lillian Wald (1867-1940), suffragist and pacifist, lived and worked here for nearly forty years. She founded both this famous settlement house and a citywide visiting nurse service.

## Henson Residence

*Location:* New York City, New York County

*Relevant issues:* African American history

*Statement of significance:* This was the latter-day home (1929-1955) of Matthew Henson (1866-1955), the African American explorer who served as an assistant to Robert E. Peary. His best-known achievement came in 1909 when he became the first man to reach the North Pole.

## Holland Tunnel

*Location:* New York City, New York County

*Relevant issues:* Art and architecture, science and technology

*Statement of significance:* Until the late 1920's, there were no tunnels or bridges to carry the ever-increasing vehicular traffic between the nation's largest city and the mainland; all automobiles, trucks, and horse-drawn vehicles were carried across the Hudson River by ferry. The Holland Tunnel, opened in 1927, was the first subaqueous tunnel in the world specifically designed for the requirements of automobile traffic. Its design was based on an extensive research program conducted to determine the effects of auto emissions on tunnel motorists, and the most efficient method of ventilation to eliminate the associated health and safety risks. Virtually all subaqueous automobile tunnels base their ventilation systems on these findings.

## Hudson River Historic District

*Location:* Staatsburg, Dutchess County

*Relevant issues:* Colonial America, cultural history, European settlement

*Statement of significance:* This thirty-square-mile cultural landscape on the eastern shore of the Hudson River is composed of several villages that are traditional rural communities. With its singular origins as a Dutch colony, its peculiar semifeudal system of colonial government, its remarkable diverse ethnic populations, and its rigid class structure, the region holds a unique position in the settlement and social history of the nation. The origins of permanent settlement begin about 1688 and continue to the present time. The district is also notable for the preservation of its aristocratic estates and Gilded Age mansions. These remarkable county seats, together with the sedate Dutch homesteads, rustic German tenant farms, and industrious Yankee towns, create a rich landscape.

## Jay Homestead

*Location:* Katonah, Westchester County

*Relevant issues:* Political history

*Statement of significance:* This was the country seat and farm of John Jay (1745-1829), the distinguished statesman, jurist, and diplomat. He inherited it at the peak of his political career and personally developed it, spending his retirement years (1801-1829) here.

## Johnson Residence

*Location:* New York City, New York County

*Relevant issues:* African American history, cultural history, literary history, social reform

*Statement of significance:* From 1925 to 1938, this was the home of James Weldon Johnson (1871-1938), the versatile African American composer of popular songs, poet, writer, general secretary of the National Association for the Advancement of Colored People (NAACP), and civil rights activist.

## Kate Mullany House

*Location:* Troy, Rensselaer County
*Relevant issues:* Business and industry, political history, social reform
*Statement of significance:* Kate Mullany, who organized and led Troy's all-female Collar Laundry Union in the 1860's, was America's most prominent female labor leader. Male unionists recognized her group as the only bona fide female union in the country and applauded her success in bargaining with laundry owners for her objectives. Mullany and her cohorts also supported other working unions and labor activity. She lived in this typical working-class brick rowhouse from 1869 until her death in 1906.

## King Manor

*Location:* New York City, Queens County
*Relevant issues:* Political history
*Statement of significance:* Rufus King (1755-1827), who lived in this Colonial mansion intermittently from 1806 until his death in 1827, enjoyed a distinguished career in public service. He sat in the Continental Congress (1784-1786), signed the U.S. Constitution (1787), and served as U.S. senator (1789-1795) and minister to Great Britain (1796-1803). He was also the Federalist Party's vice presidential nominee (1804, 1808) and presidential candidate (1816).

## Langmuir House

*Location:* Schenectady, Schenectady County
*Relevant issues:* Science and technology
*Statement of significance:* From 1919 to 1957, this was the home of Irving Langmuir (1881-1957), the distinguished General Electric chemist and inventor, and winner of the 1934 Nobel Prize in Chemistry for his work in surface kinetics.

## Lightship No. 87 "Ambrose"

*Location:* New York City, New York County
*Relevant issues:* Naval history, science and technology
*Statement of significance:* Now known by its last official designation, *Ambrose*, No. 87 was built (1907) to serve as the first lightship on the newly established Nantucket station, where it served to guide mariners into the nation's busiest port, New York. No. 87 is also important in the history of radio, being the first successful shipboard radio beacon used to guide ships at long distances in poor weather.

## Lindenwald

*Location:* Kinderhook, Columbia County
*Relevant issues:* Political history
*Statement of significance:* This was the home for twenty-one years, until his death in 1862, of Martin Van Buren (1782-1862), the eighth president of the United States.

## McKay Residence

*Location:* New York City, New York County
*Relevant issues:* African American history, literary history
*Statement of significance:* This was the residence, from 1941 to 1946, of Claude McKay, the African American poet and writer often called the "Father of the Harlem Renaissance."

## Macy and Company Store

*Location:* New York City, New York County
*Relevant issues:* Business and industry
*Statement of significance:* Built in 1901-1902, this was long the world's largest department store under one roof. The story of Macy's is a major chapter in American retail history.

## Metropolitan Life Insurance Company Building

*Location:* New York City, New York County
*Relevant issues:* Art and architecture, business and industry
*Statement of significance:* Completed in 1909, this building became symbolic of a company representing the growth and development of the American life insurance industry in the late nineteenth and early twentieth centuries. It was the world's tallest masonry and steel structure until 1913, and it remains a prominent feature of the New York skyline.

## Metropolitan Museum of Art

*Location:* New York City, New York County
*Relevant issues:* Art and architecture
*Web site:* www.metmuseum.org

*Statement of significance:* Built in several stages beginning in 1874 and extending over four city blocks on the east side of Central Park, this is one of the most prestigious museums in the world for its imposing building and the quality of its collections. Although its component parts were designed by eminent architects in diverse architectural styles, they are well related in scale to one another. Most significant architecturally are the dramatic Fifth Avenue facade and Great Hall designed by Richard M. Hunt. The other architects responsible for the building are Calvert Vaux and Jacob Wrey Mould; McKim, Mead and White; and Kevin Roche, John Dinkeloo and Associates.

## Mohawk Upper Castle Historic District

*Location:* Danube, Herkimer County
*Relevant issues:* American Indian history
*Statement of significance:* Archaeological and architectural resources located in this district are associated with Nowadaga, the most westerly part of the major eighteenth century Mohawk Indian community of Canajoharie. During the eighteenth century, Mohawk people regarded Canajoharie as the most important community in the western half of Kanienke, their name for the Mohawk River Valley heartland. Included in the district is the still-standing Indian Castle Church, a wooden-framed Anglican chapel built in 1769.

## Morgan Library

*Location:* New York City, New York County
*Relevant issues:* Cultural history, literary history
*Statement of significance:* J. Pierpont Morgan (1837-1913), an important financier, organized U.S. Steel and was influential in the railroad industry. This Renaissance-style library (1902-1907) contains literary and artistic collections.

## Morrill Hall, Cornell University

*Location:* Ithaca, Tompkins County
*Relevant issues:* Education
*Web site:* www.cornell.edu/campus/infobase/ morrill.hall.html
*Statement of significance:* Constructed in 1866-1868, this was the original building of Cornell University. Cornell's founding marked a revolution in American higher education, for it offered training on the basis of equality among the disciplines to prepare students for useful careers in the post-Civil War era. It is named for the author of the Morrill Land Grant Act of 1862.

## Morse House

*Location:* 370 South Street, Poughkeepsie, Dutchess County
*Relevant issues:* Science and technology
*Statement of significance:* Samuel F. B. Morse (1791-1872) purchased this house in 1847, three years after his successful telegraphic transmission of a message from Washington, D.C., to Baltimore. He used it as his summer residence and enlarged it into the present octagon-shaped structure.

## Mount House

*Location:* Stony Brook, Suffolk County
*Relevant issues:* Art and architecture
*Statement of significance:* William Sydney Mount (1807-1868) produced most of his genre paintings in this large farmhouse. His genre scenes reflect his individualism, insistence on realistic portrayals, and reliance on his own region and its people for subject matter.

## New York Public Library

*Location:* New York City, New York County
*Relevant issues:* Cultural history, literary history
*Statement of significance:* Completed in 1911, this is a major U.S. research center and cultural institution, with extensive and invaluable manuscript and rare book collections.

## New York Studio School of Drawing, Painting, and Sculpture

*Location:* New York City, New York County
*Relevant issues:* Art and architecture
*Statement of significance:* This was the original site of the Whitney Museum of American Art, the first museum to be exclusively devoted to American art of the twentieth century and the greatest single sponsor of nonacademic artists in the country. The result of a partnership between two extraordinary women—Gertrude Vanderbilt Whitney and Juliana Rieser Force—the property functioned as a hive of working and living spaces for a number of esteemed American painters, sculptors, and composers and was the

locus of an unrivaled program of exhibitions and philanthropy that shaped the fortune of two generations of American artists.

## New York Yacht Club Building
*Location:* New York City, New York County
*Relevant issues:* Cultural history, sports
*Statement of significance:* This is the home of America's oldest and foremost yachting organization (1844). Established as a private men's club and renowned as the longtime home of the America's Cup, the structure (1900) is a brilliant example of the Neo-Baroque style and today is still highly evocative of the Gilded Age in America and of the Beaux-Arts architecture of that era.

## Newtown Battlefield
*Location:* Elmira, Chemung County
*Relevant issues:* Military history, Revolutionary War
*Statement of significance:* Site of a battle (August 29, 1779) that was a result of an expedition led by Major General John Sullivan and was the major American military effort of 1779. General George Washington ordered the Sullivan expedition as a counteroffensive against the Iroquois, who, as allies of the British, in 1778 had raided settlements in the Mohawk Valley of New York and in western Pennsylvania.

## Niagara Reservation
*Location:* Niagara Falls, Niagara County
*Relevant issues:* Cultural history
*Statement of significance:* Established in 1885, this area provides a view of Niagara Falls from a non-commercial area. In creating this reservation and eliminating commercial eyesores that had sprung up along the shoreline near the falls, New York became the first state to use its power of eminent domain to acquire land for aesthetic purposes. This stands as a tremendous victory in the struggle to save grand aspects of America's natural scenery.

## Old Main, Vassar College
*Location:* Poughkeepsie, Dutchess County
*Relevant issues:* Education, women's history
*Statement of significance:* Constructed between 1861 and 1865, this is one of the earliest and most successful expressions of the Second Empire style in the United States and one of the few remaining grand-scale examples of the style. It was the original building for Vassar College, one of the first colleges for the education of women in the United States offering an education similar to that available to men at Yale and Harvard.

## Old New York County Courthouse
*Location:* New York City, New York County
*Relevant issues:* Legal history, political history
*Statement of significance:* The Old New York County Courthouse symbolizes a classic episode in the annals of American graft and corruption. It is a monument to the machinations of William Marcy ("Boss") Tweed (1823-1878), who ran the most infamous political machine in American history. This building embodies the Tweed Ring, its power, and the paradox whereby it provided services for the city and gained corrupt profits for itself.

## Oneida Community Mansion House
*Location:* Oneida, Madison County
*Relevant issues:* Social reform
*Web site:* www.oneidacommunity.org
*Statement of significance:* Oneida (founded 1848) was a nineteenth century communitarian experiment which flourished until 1879. This large brick mansion is essentially unchanged.

## Paine Cottage
*Location:* New Rochelle, Westchester County
*Relevant issues:* Literary history, political history, Revolutionary War
*Statement of significance:* Thomas Paine (1737-1809), propagandist for the American and French Revolutions and author of *Common Sense* (1776) and *The Age of Reason* (1794-1795), occupied this saltbox cottage from 1802 until 1806. He was buried here in 1809.

## Plattsburgh Bay
*Location:* Plattsburgh, Clinton County
*Relevant issues:* Military history, naval history
*Statement of significance:* An American naval victory here on September 11, 1814, in the War of 1812, resulted in the destruction of the British fleet on Lake Champlain and compelled British invading troops to withdraw to Canada.

## The Players Club

*Location:* New York City, New York County

*Relevant issues:* Cultural history

*Statement of significance:* This building was donated in 1888 by Edwin Booth (1833-1893), founder and first president of the Players Club, to be the clubhouse of that famous theatrical organization. It houses a fine and rare collection of theatrical literature and memorabilia.

## Playland Amusement Park

*Location:* Rye, Westchester County

*Relevant issues:* Cultural history

*Statement of significance:* Opened in 1928, this is the first totally planned amusement park in America and was designed specifically to accommodate automobile travelers. After more than fifty years, its Art Deco design and architecture remain essentially unaltered, and it has served as a prototype for contemporary theme parks. Several of the park's rides are of major individual significance because of their rarity.

## Plymouth Church of the Pilgrims

*Location:* New York City, Kings County

*Relevant issues:* Religion, social reform

*Statement of significance:* Henry Ward Beecher (1813-1887), noted abolitionist and minister of Plymouth Church, made the church (1849) a center of antislavery sentiment.

## Pollock House and Studio

*Location:* East Hampton, Suffolk County

*Relevant issues:* Art and architecture

*Web site:* www.pkhouse.org

*Statement of significance:* From 1945 until his death, this was the home and workplace of Jackson Pollock (1912-1956), considered one of the most revolutionary figures in the history of twentieth century art and a key ingredient in what has been called "the triumph of American painting." With Pollock taking his art to a transcendent level and other artists of talent seizing courage from his bold example, the locus of the art world shifted from Paris to New York. It was while living here with his wife Lee Krasner that Pollock, in 1947, invented the technique of pouring and propelling paint through the air and initiated his use of metallic paint. Pollock created the most forceful oeuvre of his time.

Krasner worked in his shadow, devoting much of her time and energy to saving Pollock from destruction; nevertheless, she found time to work at her own Abstract Expressionist painting and is now recognized as an important artist.

## Pupin Physics Laboratory, Columbia University

*Location:* New York City, New York County

*Relevant issues:* Science and technology

*Statement of significance:* Initial experiments on the nuclear fission of uranium were conducted here by Enrico Fermi (1901-1954). The uranium atom was split here on January 25, 1939, ten days after the world's first atom-splitting in Copenhagen, Denmark.

## Radeau "Land Tortoise"

*Location:* Lake George, Warren County

*Relevant issues:* Naval history

*Statement of significance:* Radeau, French for "raft," refers to a craft whose flat-bottomed, platform-like construction and simple planking are suggestive of this most elementary, utilitarian type of vessel. As the only known survivor of its type, *Land Tortoise* is unique, and although it now lies at a depth of more than one hundred feet, the radeau is remarkably well preserved. Built in 1758 by British and provincial forces to be used during the French and Indian War, it was deliberately scuttled within two days of its launching on Lake George, to be recovered the following year. That never happened, and in spite of its name, *Land Tortoise* has remained on the bottom of the lake ever since. It is accessible to the diving public as a New York State Submerged Heritage Preserve.

## Robeson Residence

*Location:* New York City, New York County

*Relevant issues:* African American history, cultural history

*Statement of significance:* This was the residence (1939-1941) of Paul Robeson (1898-1976), the famous African American actor, singer, scholar, and athlete who in the 1940's and 1950's suffered public condemnation for his political sympathies but was widely acclaimed for his artistic talent.

## Robinson House

*Location:* New York City, Kings County

*Relevant issues:* African American history, sports

*Statement of significance:* This was the home (1947-1950) of Jackie Robinson (1919-1972), the baseball player who in 1947 became the first African American to play in the major leagues, thus breaking the color barrier to full integration in professional team sports.

## Rockefeller Estate

*Location:* Mt. Pleasant, Westchester County

*Relevant issues:* Business and industry

*Statement of significance:* This was the estate (1893-1937) of John D. Rockefeller (1839-1937), one of America's most famous and controversial magnates, who is best remembered for his organizational genius in industry and for the scale and organization of his philanthropic activities.

## Root House

*Location:* Clinton, Oneida County

*Relevant issues:* Political history

*Statement of significance:* Secretary of war (1899-1903) under Presidents William McKinley and Theodore Roosevelt, and secretary of state (1905-1909) under Roosevelt, Elihu Root (1845-1937) bought this Federal-style house in 1893. He considered it his permanent home throughout his government service, and he died here in 1937.

## Roycroft Campus

*Location:* East Aurora, Erie County

*Relevant issues:* Art and architecture

*Statement of significance:* This Arts and Crafts movement community was founded by Elbert Hubbard (1856-1915) in 1895 as an artistic revolt against the mass production of applied arts. The theory was that in its medieval craft guild setting, craftsmen could live and work, making beautiful objects by hand. They produced fine hand-painted and -bound books, paintings, carvings, metalwork, and ceramics.

## Saint George's Episcopal Church

*Location:* New York City, New York County

*Relevant issues:* African American history, cultural history, religion

*Statement of significance:* Home church (1908-1948) of Harry Thacker Burleigh (1866-1949), the African American composer, arranger, and singer who helped establish the Spiritual in the attention and acceptance of all Americans, including classically trained musicians.

## Saint Patrick's Cathedral

*Location:* New York City, New York County

*Relevant issues:* Art and architecture, religion

*Statement of significance:* Climaxing James Renwick's career, this cathedral is the first large-scale Medieval-style church in America. Begun in 1858, its spires were completed in 1888.

## Saint Paul's Chapel

*Location:* New York City, New York County

*Relevant issues:* Colonial America, religion, political history, Revolutionary War

*Statement of significance:* One of the only surviving churches of New York City's colonial era, this structure was built from 1764 to 1766. It was a place of worship for both American and British military officers during the American Revolution; George Washington came here for a special service after his inauguration in 1789.

## Sanger Clinic

*Location:* New York City, New York County

*Relevant issues:* Education, health and medicine, social reform, women's history

*Statement of significance:* From 1930 to 1973, this house served as the clinic established by Margaret Sanger (1879-1966), a pioneer in birth control. According to Sanger, her career as an advocate and educator in this field began with the death of a woman who had been told by her doctor that another child could kill her and yet received no contraceptive information from this doctor save abstinence; the woman died trying to end an unwanted pregnancy. Sanger, who coined the term "birth control," dedicated her life to winning reproductive autonomy for women by administering safe, harmless information in order to give women a choice about parenthood. She established herself as a speaker and writer on sexual reforms, educating women on sex, venereal disease, and birth control.

## Saratoga Spa State Park

*Location:* Saratoga Springs, Saratoga County

*Relevant issues:* Health and medicine

*Statement of significance:* This spa was established in 1909 to conserve and develop Saratoga's springs for public benefit. A leading exponent of hydrotherapy, Dr. Simon Baruch, guided the spa's development in its early years. The major complex was constructed in the 1930's and includes a hotel, two bathhouses, a swimming pool, a bottling plant, an administration and research center, and a grand Hall of Springs in the European style.

## Scott House

*Location:* New York City, New York County

*Relevant issues:* Military history, political history

*Statement of significance:* Winfield Scott (1786-1866), victorious general in the Mexican War and Whig presidential candidate in 1852, lived in this brownstone from 1854 to 1855.

## Seward House

*Location:* Auburn, Cayuga County

*Relevant issues:* Political history

*Statement of significance:* William H. Seward (1801-1872) served as governor (1839-1843) and U.S. senator from New York (1848-1861), emerging as a leading antislavery figure in the Whig, and later, Republican Parties. As secretary of state (1861-1869), he negotiated the purchase of Alaska from Russia (1867). This house was his permanent residence from 1824 until his death.

## Sixty-ninth Regiment Armory

*Location:* New York City, New York County

*Relevant issues:* Art and architecture, military history

*Statement of significance:* The Sixty-ninth Regiment Armory is nationally significant for its association with the "Fighting 69th," the renowned local unit of the New York National Guard. The unit served with distinction during World War I and World War II. It is also nationally significant as the site of the 1913 Sculpture and Painting Exhibition of contemporary art, the first such major exhibition in America and one of the most significant events in the history of modern art.

## Slabsides

*Location:* West Park, Ulster County

*Relevant issues:* Literary history

*Statement of significance:* From 1895 to 1921, this was the summer residence and retreat of the noted scientist and nature writer John Burroughs (1837-1921). The cabin is called "Slabsides" because of its bark-covered siding.

## Smith House

*Location:* New York City, New York County

*Relevant issues:* Political history

*Statement of significance:* This three-story Victorian brick rowhouse was the home of Alfred E. Smith (1873-1944) from 1907 to 1923. Smith was governor of New York and the Democratic candidate for president in 1928, the first Roman Catholic nominee by a major party.

## Sousa House

*Location:* Port Washington, Nassau County

*Relevant issues:* Cultural history

*Statement of significance:* John Philip Sousa (1854-1932), a band director and composer, was best known for his marches, including "The Stars and Stripes Forever." He lived here from 1915 until his death.

## Steepletop

*Location:* Austerlitz, Columbia County

*Relevant issues:* Literary history

*Statement of significance:* Edna St. Vincent Millay (1892-1950) was a leader in the bohemian culture movement of the 1920's and an important literary figure. She purchased this two-story clapboard house in 1925.

## Stony Point Battlefield

*Location:* Stony Point, Rockland County

*Relevant issues:* Military history, Revolutionary War

*Statement of significance:* On July 15, 1779, the Patriot victory at Stony Point, under General "Mad Anthony" Wayne, ensured General George Washington's control of the Hudson River and West Point.

## The Sullivans

*Location:* Buffalo, Erie County

*Relevant issues:* Naval history, World War II

*Statement of significance:* Named for the five Sullivan brothers who lost their lives in the Battle of the Solomon Islands, USS *The Sullivans* (1943) is an excellent example of the Fletcher Class, the largest and most important class of U.S. destroyers in World War II, forming the backbone of destroyer forces throughout the war. It took part in intense combat, rescuing downed aviators and earning nine battle stars for its service.

## Sunnyside

*Location:* Tarrytown, Westchester County
*Relevant issues:* Literary history
*Statement of significance:* This stone house, purchased by writer Washington Irving (1783-1859) in 1835, was his home until his death. He is best remembered for his tales of the Hudson River Dutch settlements.

## Tenement Building at 97 Orchard Street

*Location:* New York City, New York County
*Relevant issues:* Social reform
*Statement of significance:* This six-story brick tenement is an outstanding survivor of the vast number of humble buildings that housed immigrants to New York during the greatest wave of immigration in American history. Erected in 1863-1864, it represents the first rush of tenement building in New York City. The top two floors of 97 Orchard Street contain rooms, wallpaper, plumbing, and lighting preserved as they were left in the 1930's, when they were boarded up and sealed until their discovery in 1988. Something of an urban time machine, the building is able to convey a vivid sense of the deplorable living conditions experienced by its tenants, who, during its seventy-two-year tenure as housing, may have numbered as many as ten thousand.

## Tilden House

*Location:* New York City, New York County
*Relevant issues:* Political history
*Statement of significance:* Occupied today by the National Arts Club, this building was the residence (c. 1860-c. 1885) of Samuel J. Tilden (1814-1886), one of the central figures in the disputed Tilden-Hayes presidential election (1876) and resultant compromise of 1877, events which for all practical purposes ended Reconstruction. Tilden exposed the infamous Tweed and Canal Rings and is an outstanding representative of the conservative political reformers of the 1870's.

## Triangle Shirtwaist Factory Building

*Location:* New York City, New York County
*Relevant issues:* Disasters and tragedies, social reform
*Statement of significance:* On the afternoon of March 25, 1911, one of the worst industrial disasters in American history took place: Fire swept through the Triangle Shirtwaist Factory, resulting in the deaths of 146 workers, most of them young women. Many suffocated or were burned to death, trapped behind crowds or locked doors; over a third of them leaped to their deaths from the windows of the factory, which occupied the eighth, ninth, and tenth floors of this building, out of the reach of the fire department's ladders. The tragedy shocked the nation and galvanized the labor movement to press for progressive factory legislation; by 1914, thirty-six new labor laws were on the books in the State of New York. The fire is credited with changing both factory and fire prevention laws throughout the country.

## Tubman Home for the Aged

*Location:* Auburn, Cayuga County
*Relevant issues:* African American history, social reform
*Statement of significance:* Harriet Tubman (1821-1913), the most famous "conductor" on the Underground Railroad, personally led more than three hundred slaves to freedom. She established this home for aged and indigent African Americans in 1908.

## Union Square

*Location:* Between E. 14th and E. 17th Streets and Union Square West and Union Square East, New York City, New York County
*Relevant issues:* Business and industry, political history, social reform
*Statement of significance:* Located in lower midtown Manhattan, Union Square is nationally significant for the role it has played in American labor history. While the park has been the focal point for well over a century for parades, mass gatherings, soap-box orations, and demonstrations, its particular moment in history occurred on September 5, 1882, when the first Labor Day Parade took place. This marked the beginning of organized labor's twelve-year effort to secure passage

of national legislation that would set aside one day each year to recognize the contributions and achievements of American laborers.

## United Charities Building

*Location:* New York City, New York County

*Relevant issues:* Social reform

*Statement of significance:* Completed in 1893 and built entirely at the expense of a wealthy businessman, this building was intended to provide charitable groups with a central building and lower rent than they would have elsewhere. The original tenants were the Charities Organizations Society, the Association for the Improvement of the Condition of the Poor, the Children's Aid Society, and the New York City Mission and Tract Society; a later and perhaps most important tenant was the National Consumer's League, an influential reform organization which fought for legislation regulating child labor, women's labor, and wages and hours in general.

## Vassar College Observatory

*Location:* Poughkeepsie, Dutchess County

*Relevant issues:* Science and technology, women's history

*Statement of significance:* This observatory was built in 1865 on the campus of Vassar College for Maria Mitchell (1818-1889), astronomer, professor, crusader for women's higher education and professional advancement, and the first woman elected to both the American Academy of Arts and Sciences and the American Philosophical Society. The custom-designed building was Mitchell's home, laboratory, and classroom for the last twenty years of her life. Her emphasis on high scientific standards and feminist ideals made Mitchell a role model for both the women she taught and those who followed her in the struggle for equality.

## The Voorlezer's House

*Location:* New York City, Richmond County

*Relevant issues:* Colonial America, European settlement, religion

*Statement of significance:* This house was constructed by the early Dutch settlers before 1696 to serve as a church, a school, and the residence of the *voorlezer,* the layman chosen to assist the pastor in the church services and keep the church records. In addition to his religious duties, he often conducted school, in which elementary reading, writing, arithmetic, and religious catechism were taught.

## Woolworth Building

*Location:* 233 Broadway, New York City, New York County

*Relevant issues:* Art and architecture, business and industry

*Statement of significance:* From its completion in 1913 until 1930, this building was the world's tallest. It stands today as a monument not only to F. W. Woolworth (1852-1919), originator of the variety chain store, but also to its architect, Cass Gilbert (1859-1934). Gilbert won acclaim for his use of Gothic forms and detail, well adapted to the soaring verticality of the skyscraper.

## Wyckoff House

*Location:* New York City, Kings County

*Relevant issues:* Colonial America, European settlement

*Statement of significance:* This house is a major and little-altered example of a type of frame house much used by Dutch settlers on western Long Island. The original section was constructed about 1652, with later enlargements. It is the earliest known example of a Dutch saltbox frame house developed in America, and was probably the first house built on Long Island by white men.